WRIGLEY FIELD

THE FRIENDLY CONFINES AT CLARK AND ADDISON

EDITED BY GREGORY H. WOLF

ASSOCIATE EDITORS

LEN LEVIN, BILL NOWLIN, AND CARL RIECHERS

Society for American Baseball Research, Inc.
Phoenix, AZ

Wrigley Field – The Friendly Confines at Clark and Addison

Edited by Gregory H. Wolf
Associate Editors: Len Levin, Bill Nowlin, and Carl Riechers

Cover Photo:
National Baseball Hall of Fame, Cooperstown, New York

All photos are credited in book; otherwise public domain.

ISBN 978-1-970159-01-1
(Ebook ISBN 978-1-970159-01-1)

Book design: David Peng

Society for American Baseball Research
Cronkite School at ASU
555 N. Central Ave. #416
Phoenix, AZ 85004
Phone: (602) 496-1460
Web: www.sabr.org
Facebook: Society for American Baseball Research
Twitter: @SABR

TABLE OF CONTENTS

FOREWORD

By Gregory H. Wolf

WRIGLEY FIELD EVOKES A FEELING OF perpetual summer, youth, and dreams. The name of the jewel at the intersection of Clark and Addison in the Windy City conjures up myriad images, from the ivy on the outfield walls and the hand-operated scoreboard to Cubbie blue and the vibrant neighborhood in which the ballpark is located. Wrigley Field transcends time and transports its guests to a different epoch, to a green oasis in the middle of bustling city. Built less than 50 years after the Civil War, it was inaugurated before the First World War when Woodrow Wilson was the president of the United States. More than a century later, it remains a testimony to the enduring power of our national pastime.

Wrigley Field: The Friendly Confines at Clark and Addison is a baseball ode to a storied ballpark, whose history is evoked through detailed summaries of 100 games played there and several feature essays. Be it Weeghman Field, Cubs Park, or Wrigley Field, baseball has been played at the steel and concrete baseball cathedral since 1914, more than a century. That made our task of choosing just 100 games to include a difficult one. Some of the games have historical significance, like the first regular-season contests at the ballpark by the Chi-Feds in 1914 and the Cubs two years later; or the first official major-league night game played in the park, in 1988, including the rained-out first attempt. Other games recall great, historically significant, or milestone feats, such as Hack Wilson's big-league-record 191st RBI in 1930, Gabby Hartnett's transcendent "Homer in the Gloamin'" in 1938, the "Ryne-Sandberg-Game" in 1984, Kerry Woods' 20-punchout masterpiece in 1998, or the nightmarish (for Cubs fans) "Bartman Game" from 2003.

For all the talk about "Lovable Losers," Wrigley Field has a rich postseason history, and this volume contains every World Series game played on the North Side. Cubs losses in the fall classic in 1929, 1932, 1935, 1938, and 1945 were erased by the monumental victory in the 2016 World Series over another long-suffering club, the Cleveland Indians. Included, too, are other postseason games, such as the first two contests of the 1984 NLCS when the Cubs beat the San Diego Padres twice to be oh-so-close to the World Series, the dreaded collapse in Games Six and Seven of the 2003 NLCS against the Florida Marlins, the clinching game against the Los Angeles Dodges in the 2016 NLCS, and five games at Wrigley Field from the 2017 NLDS and NLCS.

It would have been easy to create a volume consisting solely of great games by Hall of Famers or All-Stars who played for the Cubs, like Pete Alexander, Rogers Hornsby, Ernie Banks, Ron Santo, and Billy Williams; however, we were guided by an overarching principle: to present the history of the Cubs and Wrigley Field through the baseball games played at the ballpark. For us that meant also including games focusing on and showcasing as many different players as possible, some well-known, others less so, from Hank Sauer, Milt Pappas, Dave Kingman, and Andre Dawson to Lefty Tyler, Hank Leiber, Walt Moryn, and Roosevelt Brown. If you're looking for the youngsters and emerging stars from the recent successful Cubs teams, we got 'em: Javier Baez, Kris Bryant, Anthony Rizzo, Kyle Schwarber, and the crew.

Wrigley Field was not only a site for major-league baseball. This volume introduces readers to games played in the All-American Girls Professional Baseball League (AAGPBL) in 1943 and 1944, which

Joe Maddon took over the reins as Cubs skipper for the 2015 and the following year led the North Siders to their first World Series championship since 1908. (Photo by Norm Hall/Getty Images)

was founded by Cubs owner Philip K. Wrigley; as well as amateur contests, including a game between high schools from New York City and Chicago, an Esquire All-American Boys game, and a Hearst Sandlot Classic.

The feature essays contextualize the ballpark's history. Included are an in-depth historical sketch of Wrigley Field itself and shorter pieces focusing on the pulsating Wrigleyville neighborhood, the Curse of the Billy Goat, and the evolution of the Cubs nickname over the course of franchise history beginning in 1876. The Chicago Orphans? The Chicago Colts? Those one-time names just don't seem right! Chicago's other major-league ballpark, Comiskey Park, located on the city's south side, was known for hosting Negro League ballgames, especially the East-West All-Star Games; Wrigley Field's much less rich history with Negro baseball is presented in a compelling essay. For all the trivia

buffs, we end with a stat- and factoid piece. You can take this volume with you to a sports bar and win a round of drinks.

Members of the Society for American Baseball Research (SABR) made this book possible. These volunteers are united by a passion for researching and writing about baseball history. I thank all of the authors for their contributions, meticulous research, cooperation through the revising and editing process, and finally their patience. I am impressed with your dedication to preserve baseball history by combing archives, interviewing players, and telling the story of so many exciting games played in, and the history of, Wrigley Field.

We had an All-Star editorial team. The second reader, Bill Nowlin, read every submission and always provided prodding questions about content. This is the eighth book we've worked on together, and I think he anticipates my questions before

I ask them. Carl Riechers was the fact-checker. He verified every statistic and fact in every essay, and offered addition insights, suggestions, and information for authors to consider. The copy editor was Len Levin, who has served in this capacity for all of the SABR books. I am not sure what we would do without his deft touch – he made us all look good. It has been a pleasure to once again work on a book project with such professionals, with whom I corresponded practically every day, and typically more than once.

This book would not have been possible without the generous support of the staff and Board of Directors of SABR, SABR Publications Director Cecilia Tan, and designer David Peng.

We express our thanks and gratitude to Matthew J. Richards, vice president and general manager sales at Getty Images, for arranging the overwhelming majority of photos included in this volume, as well as to Andy Krause, sport product manager at Getty Images, for assisting us with individual images. Special thanks also to John Horne of the National Baseball Hall of Fame for supplying the cover photo.

And finally, I wish to thank my wife, Margaret, and daughter, Gabriela, for their support of and endless patience with my baseball pursuits. They're accustomed to me working on my "SABR-stuff." Thankfully, they are also baseball fans who love attending games at Wrigley Field, or wherever else all baseball travels take us.

This book is ideal for a 10-minute break or a few hours on a lazy afternoon. Sit down, open it up, and read about some great games and the history of Wrigley Field.

Gregory H. Wolf
June 1, 2019

THE FRIENDLY CONFINES
OF WRIGLEY FIELD

By Scott Ferkovich

IT WAS BUILT ON THE SITE OF A FORMER theological seminary (of all places). It is one of the most renowned addresses in baseball history, nestled in a vibrant urban neighborhood that takes on the atmosphere of a block party on game days. It has seen the Babe's called shot, Gabby's Homer in the Gloamin', and the curse of the billygoat. It was the stamping grounds of High Pockets and Kiki, of Jolly Cholly and Hack, of the Mad Russian and Mad Dog, of Mr. Cub, Ryno, and the Hawk. It is as well-known for its famous foliage and its Bleacher Bums as it is for some of the heartbreak and incompetency that it has seen on the field. For decades, it stubbornly refused to evolve, becoming a symbol of "baseball as it was meant to be played." To many, it is a kind of pastoral palace, a living fossil where folks can cling to their own rose-colored versions of the past. It has been a lovable dinosaur where progress died faster than the fleeting hopes of April and May. It is the unexpected answer to one of the more intriguing trivia questions you are likely to hear: What sporting venue has hosted the most NFL games ever? It has been immortalized in songs, in movies, in television commercials, and in its own cottage industry of coffee-table books and tributary tomes. It remains a must-see tourist attraction in a city full of them. It is the Friendly Confines of Wrigley Field.

Rewind way, way back, to a time when the Woodrow Wilson family resided at 1600 Pennsylvania Avenue, when Charlie Chaplin starred in his first film, and when the Ford Motor Company announced an eight-hour workday and a minimum wage of $5 a day. Back to 1914. The ballpark that sprouted up at 1060 West Addison Street in Chicago's Lake View neighborhood was initially the home of the Chicago entry in the Federal League. The team was known as the Federals (Chi-Feds for short) and was owned by Charles Weeghman, who named the park after himself. The Federal League, then in its first year of existence, was an upstart circuit in direct competition with the established National and American Leagues. The Chi-Feds were able to lure such established stars as the Cincinnati Reds' shortstop Joe Tinker (of Tinker-to-Evers-to-Chance fame), and pitcher Mordecai "Three Finger" Brown of the Chicago Cubs. The Chi-Feds finished second in 1914, then changed their name to the Whales for 1915, a season in which they finished tied with the St. Louis Terriers for first place. The Federal League was gone by 1916. Weeghman, however, bought the National League's crosstown Chicago Cubs, who played at old West Side Park, and immediately moved them into Weeghman Park. The Cubs played their first game in their new home on April 20, 1916. The home team beat the Cincinnati Reds in 11 innings.

At this time, the park at Clark and Addison was a single-decked structure of steel and concrete. Weeghman had hired Zachary Taylor Davis (the architect of Comiskey Park, on the South Side of Chicago) to design the ballpark. The grandstand on the Clark Street (third base) side extended halfway to left field. The grandstand on the Addison Street (first base) side extended all the way to the right-field corner. One of the old seminary buildings loomed beyond the left-field fence, until it was demolished after the 1914 season, to be replaced by a bleacher section. The houses on Waveland Avenue (beyond the left-field wall) and Sheffield Avenue (beyond the right-field wall) have for the most part remained

A beautiful weekday afternoon game at Wrigley Field in May 2018. (Photo courtesy of Gregory H. Wolf)

strikingly unchanged. In 1915 the scoreboard, which had originally been in left field, next to the seminary building, was moved to center. During these early years, only a brick wall extended from the right-field corner to center field. In 1916, while the Cubs cavorted on the field inside the park, a genuine cub bear frolicked in a cage stationed directly outside the park on Addison Street.

Weeghman earned the favor of the fans during this period, as he made it a policy to allow spectators to keep any ball hit into the stands. This was an especially novel idea for a time when fans were required to return any balls hit their way.

One of the more remarkable games in baseball history took place at the park on May 2, 1917. Hippo Vaughn of the Cubs and Fred Toney of the Cincinnati Reds both threw no-hit ball for nine innings. Vaughn retired the first Red in the top of the tenth, then gave up two consecutive hits, resulting in a run. Toney set the Cubs down in order in their half of the inning, getting the win and the no-hitter. At the time the game was considered a "double no-hitter," but under current rules only Toney is credited with a no-no. It

remains the only game in which neither team got a hit in regulation.

A new era was ushered in at the corner of Addison and Clark in 1918. That was when Weeghman sold his interest in the Cubs to minority shareholder William Wrigley, Jr., the magnate who had made his money in the production of chewing gum. By 1921, Wrigley had bought out the other shareholders and taken complete control of the club. The ballpark, which had been known at various times (in addition to Weeghman Park) as the North Side Ball Park, the Federal League Ball Park, and Whales Park, was by now going by the name of Cubs Park.

Baseball wasn't the only game in town on the North Side. In 1921, George Halas's Chicago Staleys, a team in the fledgling American Professional Football Association (which became the National Football League in 1922), played their first game at 1060 West Addison. By the next season, they would change their nickname to the Bears. The blue and orange, "the pride and joy of Illinois," would be a gridiron fixture in Lake View for the next half-century. The first NFL Championship game ever was held on December 17, 1933, at Wrigley Field. The Bears defeated the New York Giants, 23-21. That team, coached by Halas, featured NFL greats halfback Red Grange and fullback Bronko Nagurski.

To William Wrigley's credit, he was never hesitant to spend money on expansion and upkeep of his ballpark. The grandstand was double-decked in time for the 1928 season, and new bleachers were added from the right-field corner to center field, increasing the capacity from 18,000 to 32,000. However, a perennial problem during Wrigley's early tenure as owner was the disorganized appearance and surly attitude of ushers at the ballpark. Incredibly (to modern practice), ushers were simply recruited the day of the game from random men (or kids) off the street. They often were derelict in their duties, keeping the best seats for themselves and their friends, and taking bribes from folks looking for better seats. Then one afternoon, Andy Frain approached Wrigley's box seat and told him that he could do a better job of organizing men to work the aisles. Frain had some success doing the same thing at Chicago Stadium, for Blackhawks hockey games. Wrigley agreed to Frain's proposal, and he was immediately put in charge of hiring and organizing the Wrigley Field ushers. Through Wrigley's capital investment, Frain outfitted his employees with their traditional blue and gold uniforms, and instructed them in how to act politely and professionally. Andy Frain later expanded his business to ballparks and stadiums around the country. The company that bears his name still flourishes.

The Cubs had gone to the World Series in 1918 (losing to the Red Sox in six games), but the team finished in the second division for half of their seasons during the 1920s. Despite lackluster play on the field, the Cubs were developing a growing legion of fans, thanks to William Wrigley's marketing savvy. The Cubs became one of the first teams in baseball history to fully take advantage of the new phenomenon called radio. Most team owners feared that game broadcasts would reduce attendance, as fans would stay at home and listen for free. But Wrigley had the foresight to see that games on radio

were the ideal marketing tool. Also, since all games were played in the daytime, many of the fans listening to Cubs broadcasts were housewives. Wrigley took advantage of this emerging demographic through the promotion of Ladies Day games, which frequently drew packed houses to the ballpark and became a staple for years. By the summer of 1927, Cubs Park had been renamed Wrigley Field. That year, the Cubs drew over one million paying customers, becoming the first National League team to top the million mark. They continued to do so through 1931. The crowds that came out to Wrigley Field during these years got a firsthand look at some of the best Cubs teams ever assembled.

The team that Wrigley and team president William Veeck put together was a colorful, talented group of players who were a perfect fit for the Roaring Twenties. In 1929 manager Joe McCarthy's club won 98 games to take the National League pennant. The team's outfield that year was exceptional, with Kiki Cuyler, Riggs Stephenson, and Lewis "Hack" Wilson hitting a combined .355 and each driving in over 100 runs. Thirty-three-year-old Rogers Hornsby, in his last great year as a player, hit 39 home runs with 149 RBIs, while hitting .380. First baseman Charlie Grimm knocked in 91 runs to complement a .298 average. The pitching staff featured 19-game-winner Charlie Root, 18-game-winner Guy Bush, and Pat Malone, who topped the National League with 22 wins.

The 1929 World Series was the first one played at Wrigley Field. (Their home games for the 1918 Series had been moved to Comiskey Park, which had a higher seating capacity.) Their 1929 opponents were Connie Mack's Philadelphia Athletics, a team featuring future Hall of Famers Mickey Cochrane, Jimmie Foxx, Al Simmons, and Lefty Grove. The Mack Men trounced the Cubs, winning in five games.

The team finished a close second in 1930. In a year when offense exploded around professional baseball, Hack Wilson put on one of the most stunning displays of hitting ever seen. He slugged 56 homers, setting what was the National League record at the time, while batting .356. He batted in 191 runs, a record that stands as of 2014. But his career sank like a stone after that. In 1931 he managed only 13 homers, 61 RBIs, and a .261 average. Before the next season, Wilson was sent packing, initially to the St. Louis Cardinals and then to the Brooklyn Dodgers. He was out of baseball by 1934.

With the passing of William Wrigley, Jr. in January of 1932, his son, Philip K. Wrigley, took over the ownership reins of the team. "P.K.," as he was affectionately called, would always consider the Cubs, and Wrigley Field especially, among his most cherished possessions. One of the reasons Wrigley Field has lasted so long is that both Wrigleys, father and son (as well as Charles Weeghman before them), always took such good care of the park. Whatever Philip Wrigley's shortcomings as a baseball owner, it cannot be denied that he was a clever marketer. He clearly understood that by beautifying Wrigley Field, and keeping it clean and well-manicured, he could draw paying crowds to an afternoon of baseball in the sunshine, even if the team on the field was only ordinary. Every year, the ballpark got a fresh coat of paint. During the season, the place was kept in immaculate condition.

The Cubs made it back to the fall classic in 1932, taking on the New York Yankees. This was the Series that featured the most debated and dissected event in Wrigley Field history. It was Babe Ruth's "Called Shot." The seemingly endless dispute about whether Ruth did or did not point to the center-field bleachers before slamming his second home run off Charlie Root in Game Three is one of those questions that keep baseball historians up at night. According to the story, the Cubs bench jockeys had been riding The Babe during the first two games of the Series. When he stepped up to the plate, he supposedly made a gesture in the general direction of center field. Some witnesses claim he was merely pointing toward the Cubs dugout. Whatever the case, Ruth hit a shot that carried to the right of the center-field scoreboard, sailing past the temporary bleachers that had been built just beyond the park's outer wall. Estimates had the ball traveling 490 feet. It was Ruth's last

World Series home run. New York, led by former Cubs manager Joe McCarthy, swept the Cubs in four games.

Today, the prevailing sentiment among most Wrigley Field patrons is that baseball (and the Cubs in particular) goes better with a cold beer or two. Or three. It wasn't until the 1933 season, however, that beer was first sold at Wrigley Field. Even then, it was only on tap, and it was only 3.2 percent alcohol. When Prohibition was finally repealed in December of that year, a bevy of bars and restaurants opened up around the ballpark.

The main entrance at the corner of Addison and Clark is noted for its neon Art Deco marquee with the words "Wrigley Field Home of Chicago Cubs." It was designed by the Federated Sign Company. For decades, it was blue with white lettering, but in 1965 it was repainted the red and white color scheme that still existed in 2014.

In 1937 a significant remodeling of Wrigley's outfield bleachers took place. A new brick wall now ringed the entire outfield. The bleachers were expanded, and, most importantly, raised. They had been at field level, but would now be elevated to their present height of just above the brick fence. While Wrigley claimed this was done in order to give fans in that section a better view, in truth the change was as much a product of necessity as anything else: the grounds crew needed the space created beneath the new bleachers to store their mowers, rollers, and chalkers. Hence the metal doors in the brick wall (which for years were maroon-colored, unlike the green of later years).

As part of the refurbishment, the hand-operated scoreboard was built above the center-field bleachers. Fluttering atop the scoreboard are colorful flags, one for each National League team, showing the order of that day's standings from top to bottom. Another enduring scoreboard tradition at Wrigley was the raising of a white flag sporting a blue "W" for a Cubs win or a blue flag with a white "L" for a loss. The flags were made easily visible to neighborhood residents strolling along Sheffield or Waveland Avenue, or commuters passing by on the nearby elevated train.

A crossbar was attached to the top of the scoreboard, with a green light on one end, for a victory, and a red light on the other end, for a loss. This was for the benefit of train riders passing by late at night. The rear of the scoreboard, as seen from outside above the bleacher entrance, also became iconic, with the words "Chicago Cubs" in white block lettering on the image of a waving blue flag. At night, the letters light up in bright neon red.

Not only do the scoreboard team flags indicate the order of the NL standings, they also reveal which way the wind is blowing. This is of vital importance at Wrigley Field, which can be either a hitter's haven or a pitcher's paradise on any given day, depending on whether the Lake Michigan breezes are blowing out or in.

By the end of 1937, the world's best-known example of *parthenocissus tricuspidata*, or Boston Ivy, had been planted around the entire base of the brick wall. Bill Veeck (son of William Veeck, who died in 1933), claimed in his autobiography that he, along with a couple of groundskeepers, planted the mix of bittersweet and Boston Ivy one night by the light of incandescent bulbs strung along the outfield wall for that very purpose. The veracity of Veeck's version of events is open to question. Whoever planted it and when, the Boston Ivy soon overtook the bittersweet, and the rest is horticultural history. Outfielders patrolling Wrigley Field are duly instructed to throw both arms up as a signal to the umpires when a struck baseball is hidden within the ivy, rather than search for the sphere; thus keeping the play alive.

Everybody loves a good walk-off home run, and Gabby Hartnett's Homer in the Gloamin' at Wrigley Field remains one of the most legendary. To set the scene: The Cubs and Pirates went into their game of September 28, 1938, with Chicago trailing Pittsburgh by a half-game in the standings. The contest entered the ninth inning tied at five runs apiece. As the late-afternoon gloom descended at the corner of Addison and Clark, the umpires made the announcement that if the game remained tied after regulation, it would be called on account of darkness. According to the rule in place at the time, the game would have to be

replayed in its entirety the next day, necessitating a doubleheader. The Cubs came to bat in the bottom of the ninth. On the hill for the Pirates was hard-throwing reliever Mace Brown. After Brown got the first two batters out, Gabby Hartnett stepped up to the dish. He quickly found himself in an 0-and-2 hole. Then, in a classic example of fact trumping fiction, Hartnett stroked a home run that landed in the left-center-field bleachers. The darkening ballpark exploded in bedlam, with players and fans running onto the field. The Cubs won the game, 6-5, and took over first place by a half-game. They beat the Pirates the next day as well, to sweep the three-game series. They eventually took the National League pennant by two lengths over Pittsburgh.

Baseball history is full of what-ifs. What if Ted Williams had played in Yankee Stadium with its short right-field porch? What if Joe DiMaggio had played in Fenway Park with its Green Monster? What if the Mets had drafted Reggie Jackson instead of Steve Chilcott? Then there is the question, "What would have happened if the Japanese hadn't bombed Pearl Harbor?" The answer to that one is easy. Wrigley Field would have had lights installed for the 1942 season. Philip Wrigley was never a fan of baseball under the stars, but in order to boost attendance he reluctantly decided to give it a try. The club had even obtained light towers, which were sitting under the stands at Wrigley Field, waiting to be erected. With the tragic events of December 7, 1941, however, America was thrust into World War II. Wrigley chose to donate the lights and the metal towers to the war effort. Soon after, Wrigley proclaimed that as long as he was alive, night baseball would never happen at the park that bore his name. He turned out to be a prophet.

Wrigley Field's other tenant, the Chicago Bears, had one of their most successful decades in the 1940s. Known as the Monsters of the Midway and led by quarterback Sid Luckman, they appeared in five NFL Championship games from 1940 to 1946, winning four of them.

One of the more legendary subtexts in Wrigley Field history is the Curse of the Billygoat. In 1945 the Cubs faced off against the Detroit Tigers in the World Series. A Chicago tavern owner, Billy Sianis, tried to enter the park with his pet goat. After all, he had a ticket for the goat, so why not? Sianis and the billygoat were let in, and made their way down to their box seats. As the story goes, some of their immediate neighbors were put off by the odor emanating from the goat. The goat and his escort were swiftly shown the exit doors. Later, Sianis supposedly put a curse on the Cubs for insulting his goat. They lost that Series to the Tigers in seven games. Of course, curses don't mean a thing. And of course, the Cubs haven't made it back to the fall classic since. (Sianis's nephew, Sam Sianis, ventured down to Wrigley Field in 1973, again with a goat, and was again asked to make tracks. Sam was invited onto the field in 1994, along with a goat, in order to remove the curse.)

Looking back on the years 1929 to 1945, one can easily make the argument that they were a kind of Golden Age for the Cubs at Wrigley Field. During that 17-year period, the team went to the World Series five times (1929, '32, '35, '38, and '45), although they didn't win any of them. From 1926 to 1938 they led the National League in attendance eight times, while five times they drew the second-most at the gate. The 1938 season was the last in which the Cubs led the league in attendance. After their final World Series appearance, in 1945, the club finished third in 1946 with a record of 82-71, 14½ games off the pace. They would not have a season over .500 for the next 16 years.

If 1929 to 1945 was indeed a Golden Age, then the decades of the 1950s and 1960s were a nadir at Wrigley Field. Attendance was annually near the bottom of the league, and an aging Philip Wrigley was no longer as vigilant about keeping his ballpark in pristine condition. The surrounding neighborhood, while not exactly deteriorating, was getting a bit rough around the edges. Most importantly, the Cubs were becoming irrelevant in Chicago, as team owner Bill Veeck and his White Sox were growing in popularity, buoyed by their 1959 "Go-Go Sox" team that went to the World Series. From 1951 to 1965,

Comiskey Park drew over one million fans every year but one, while the Cubs topped the million mark only once (1952). In 1962 the Cubs lost 103 games to finish ninth behind the expansion Houston Colt .45s, and were led by Philip Wrigley's "College of Coaches," an eight-man committee in lieu of a full-time manager.

Perhaps the low point of the organization was the 1966 season, when the team again lost 103 and finished tenth, which allowed the New York Mets to escape last place for the first time as a franchise. Only 635,891 fans passed through the turnstiles that year. (On September 21 a small get-together of only 530 fans bothered to show up.) But in the midst of these quiet days at Wrigley, a small group of young fans, who regularly sat in the sparsely populated bleachers, decided to form a loose club. They were extremely vocal in their encouragement of their favorite Cubs (and equally strident in their discouragement of the opposition). They showed up to games wearing yellow hard hats, ready to yell, sing, and drink beer (they were even known to drink with the players at local watering holes after the games.). As their numbers grew, so did their legend, and the Bleacher Bums were born. By the early 1970s, many of the original members had drifted away, to be replaced by new blood. The nickname endured, however, and over time the Wrigley Field bleachers took on more and more of a party atmosphere, which carries on.

After nearly two decades of mediocre baseball, 1969 saw the first pennant race on the North Side since 1945. Suddenly the fans began to pack Wrigley Field, to the tune of 1,674,993, at the time a club attendance record. What they witnessed was a talented team managed by Leo Durocher, with four future Hall of Famers (Billy Williams, Ron Santo, Ferguson Jenkins, and Ernie Banks). Banks was the feel-good story of the year. Having forged a brilliant career at the Friendly Confines since joining the Cubs in 1953, and seemingly doomed to endure one dismal season after another, it looked as though Mr. Cub, at age 38, would have his best chance to reach the postseason.

Wrigley Field's iconic marquee at the ballpark's main gate at Clark and Addison was installed in 1934. (Photo courtesy of Gregory H. Wolf)

The 1969 Cubs never spent a day in second place the first five months of the season. On August 16 they had a nine-game lead over the surprising second-place New York Mets. From that point, it was a disaster of epic proportions. The Mets seemingly refused to lose, carving out two big winning streaks of nine and ten games while the Cubs won just eight of 25 games in September. When the dust settled, a season that had begun with so much promise for Chicago ended up in bitter defeat. And it wasn't even close. The Mets took the NL East division by eight games over the Cubs.

For Banks, it proved to be his last productive season. His final moment of glory at Wrigley came on May 12, 1970, when he hit his 500th career home run. He retired as a player in 1971. His infectious love for the game, and for Wrigley Field, made him a favorite of Cub fans, and his familiar "Let's play two!" has become one of the game's enduring catch-phrases.

After an infamous 1970 Opening Day in which several rowdy bleacher fans leaped over the ivy-covered brick wall, the Cubs decided to make a change. They installed a wire screen along the top of the wall, which angled 42 inches out over the playing surface. To modern bleacher patrons, it is a well-known feature, also serving to help prevent littering onto the field.

Ever since the late 1950s, professional football was becoming increasingly popular. But it was also becoming increasingly clear that Wrigley Field was inadequate as a football facility. The beginning of the end came with the merger of the National Football League and American Football League in 1966. In order to accommodate more paying customers, the new NFL dictated that all stadiums were to have a minimum capacity of 50,000. Cozy Wrigley Field obviously did not. The Bears played their final game at Addison and Clark on December 13, 1970, a victory over their arch rival Green Bay Packers.

To generations of Wrigley Field patrons, the voice of public address announcer Pat Pieper was a familiar part of the game-day experience. Pieper, a former popcorn and peanut vendor at old West Side Park, served as the announcer at Clark and Addison from 1916 until his death in 1974. His signature call at the beginning of every contest was "Attention! ... Attention please! ... Have your pencil ... and scorecards ready ... and I'll give you ... the correct lineup ... for today's ballgame!"

The decades of the 1960s and 1970s saw baseball undergo seismic shifts, and the ballpark landscape was not immune to this change. Teams were abandoning their classic old ballparks and moving into modern stadiums. The vast majority were multipurpose facilities surrounded by parking lots rather than neighborhoods. Many of them featured that bane of '70s baseball, artificial turf. They were better suited to football than baseball, and were totally lacking in charm or distinctiveness. They were derisively called "cookie cutters," or "concrete doughnuts" because of their circular sameness. Richie Hebner once said of them, "I stand at the plate in the Vet (Veterans Stadium in Philadelphia) and I don't honestly know whether I'm in Pittsburgh, Cincinnati, St. Louis, or Philly. They all look alike."[1]

In the midst of this progress, Wrigley Field remained as familiar as always. (Incredibly, however, Philip Wrigley had seriously considered installing artificial turf at the park in the late '60s.) On the field, the Cubs endured some lean years in the '70s. Nevertheless, the fans continued to come out to the old ballpark, as the club annually topped the million mark in attendance. That the Cubs were able to draw this well despite the mediocre team on the field, is amazing when one considers the team's philosophy regarding ticket sales. According to Stuart Shea in his book, *Wrigley Field: The Unauthorized Biography,* "The Cubs had a long-standing practice of selling all 3,250 bleacher seats, as well as all lower- and upper-deck grandstand tickets, only on the day of the game."[2] Shea added, "P.K. Wrigley believed that fans should have the walk-up option, and all grandstand and bleacher seats were day-of-game sales only while

he continued to own the club."[3] Philip Wrigley died in 1977, and four years later the Wrigley family sold the team to the Chicago Tribune Co. By the late '80s, no more "day-of-game" tickets were sold at Wrigley.

WGN was the local Chicago television station (Channel 9) which aired every Cubs game. In 1978 it began broadcasting nationally via the emerging medium of cable TV. Not many American TV sets were cable-ready at this time, but within a few years the number of subscribers had grown astronomically. WGN, along with Atlanta's WTBS, which (at the time) broadcast all Atlanta Braves games, became what were known as "superstations." Fans from all over the country could tune in to WGN in the summertime and catch a Cubs game. The Cubs, and Wrigley Field, were getting more national television exposure than they ever had before.

Harry Christopher Carabina, born in 1914, and better known as Harry Caray, was the longtime radio and TV broadcaster, at various times, for the St. Louis Cardinals, St. Louis Browns, Oakland Athletics, and crosstown White Sox. He joined WGN in 1981, eventually pairing with former Cub and White Sox pitcher Steve Stone in 1983. The dry-witted, tell-it-like-it-is Stone was the perfect foil for Caray in the broadcast booth. As an announcer, Caray was an unrepentant homer. From his over-the-top glee at every Chicago victory ("Cubs win!! Cubs win!! Cubs win!!), to his frustration at their frequent failures ("Heee popppped it upp!"), he made it sound as if you were listening to your lovable old uncle broadcast the game. Still, Caray was an astute observer of the game who knew when the Cubs deserved criticism. He was notorious for butchering player names; Bret Barberie, Heathcliff Slocumb, and Mark Grudzielanek were always an adventure. But Caray was most famous for his ritual of belting out "Take Me Out to the Ballgame" on the Wrigley Field public address system during the seventh-inning stretch, and getting the crowd to sing along with him. It was a tradition he had actually started back in his Comiskey Park days after a suggestion from Bill Veeck during his second tenure as the White Sox owner. (After Caray's death in 1998, the team began a new Wrigley Field tradition of having a different celebrity sing the song at every game.)

In 1984 the Cubs, led by MVP second baseman Ryne Sandberg, came out of nowhere and won the NL East Division with a record of 96-65. That season also marked the first year of the Cubs drawing over two million fans to Wrigley Field. In the best-of-five National League Championship Series, against the San Diego Padres, Chicago won the first two games at Wrigley Field. The television networks salivated at the prospect of a Cubs-Tigers World Series, but it wasn't to be. The Cubs lost the next three in San Diego, and it was the Padres who would advance to the World Series against Detroit (and lose). A glorious season for Chicago had ended in heartbreak.

To many baseball purists during these years, Wrigley Field had become the perfect antidote to the modern cookie-cutter stadium. In a baseball world that had grown weary of artificial turf, sterile domes, and concrete doughnuts surrounded by parking lots, Wrigley (along with Boston's Fenway Park) came to symbolize baseball played on grass, in an intimate setting, where you were closer to the players. A game at Wrigley had a neighborhood feel, where people on rooftops across the street could set up a few lawn chairs and a grill, and make an afternoon of it. And the most wonderful thing of all, for Cubs fans, was that Wrigley Field remained the last major-league ballpark without lights. Games were played in glorious sunshine. You could take the afternoon off from work, hop on the El train, buy a cheap bleacher ticket, take your shirt off, and enjoy the festive atmosphere. As Bill Veeck once said, "An afternoon in the bleachers is the greatest buy in the country. Drinking a few beers and telling a few lies, you can't beat the entertainment."[4]

After the 1984 season, mounting pressure had been put on the Cubs, from both the National League and the major television networks, to install light towers. A heated debate grew among Wrigleyville residents. Many felt that the introduction of night games would result in an increase in noise and rowdiness, while others, particularly bar and restaurant owners, welcomed the change, feeling it would bring in more

business. A compromise was reached. Lights would be installed, but there would be a limit of 18 night games per season, an average of less than one per week. The first night game was scheduled for August 8, 1988, versus the Philadelphia Phillies. However, by the fourth inning, rain began to fall hard, and after a two-hour delay, the contest was finally called. The first official night game, therefore, was August 9. The Cubs beat the Mets, 6-4, in front of 36,399 fans. Wrigley Field had been the last major-league ballpark without lights, a distinction it held for 40 years, ever since Briggs Stadium (later renamed Tiger Stadium) installed lights in 1948.

Another economically necessary upgrade, but one that received less sentimental fanfare, was the construction in 1989 of 67 luxury suites directly below the upper-deck stands, from foul line to foul line. A new press box was also built.

In 1990 Wrigley Field hosted its first All-Star Game in nearly 30 years, a 2-0 American League victory. It was only the third All-Star Game ever played in the Friendly Confines. The first was in 1947, when the American League bested the National League, 2-1. In 1962 the AL trounced the NL, 9-4, during the second All-Star contest played that season.

As the final decade of the 20th century approached, the cookie-cutter stadiums, which had been universally panned almost from the beginning, were now increasingly obsolete. Fans in Pittsburgh, Cincinnati, St. Louis, Philadelphia, and other baseball towns waxed nostalgic about their long-lost fields of dreams. After the 1990 season, Comiskey Park on Chicago's South Side would succumb to the wrecking ball. Of the classic ballparks, only three remained: Wrigley, along with Fenway Park in Boston and Tiger Stadium in Detroit. (Four, if one were to include a rebuilt Yankee Stadium in the list.) But a new era of ballpark design was about to emerge. In 1992 Oriole Park at Camden Yards in downtown Baltimore opened its doors. Groundbreaking in design, it hearkened back architecturally and esthetically to the grand old ballparks, while giving fans all the modern amenities. The Retro Park movement had begun in earnest. Planners and designers of these new ballparks would look to the Friendly Confines and the other classic yards for inspiration.

The Cubs, meanwhile, continued to come up short in their quest for a world championship, losing in the NLCS in 1984, 1989, 2003, and 2015. Not since 1908 had the Cubs won a World Series, long before they even played at Wrigley.

Then came the summer of 2016.

Led by manager Joe Maddon, the Cubs dominated all season long, winning 103 games. The offense was powered by young stars Kris Bryant, Anthony Rizzo, and Addison Russell, while the pitching staff was anchored by John Lester, Kyle Hendricks, Jake Arrieta, and John Lackey. Never had the team's fans had such high hopes going into the postseason, and the heavily-favored Cubs delivered the goods, rolling over the Giants and the Dodgers in the first two rounds. In the World Series, they squared off against the Cleveland Indians, another Cinderella team that hadn't won it all since 1948. The Cubs finally exorcised their ghosts (and goats), taking the Game Seven, extra-inning thriller in Cleveland. The next season, they made it three straight appearances in the NLCS, before bowing to Los Angeles.

And so Wrigley Field endures. In the 2004 season, the Cubs drew over three million fans to Wrigley Field for the first time, and have topped the figure nine times since (through 2018). Its place in the American sporting consciousness is secure, even as the ballpark has undergone major renovations in the past several years. Current Cubs owner Tom Ricketts understandably wanted to tap new revenue sources from the aging park, and one of those ways was with more and more advertising signage. Newer luxury suites were also added, along with renovated concourses, able to accommodate fancier concession stands and souvenir shops. The streets immediately surrounding the park witnessed a flurry of new construction to enhance fans' gametime experience. Perhaps the most controversial improvement to Wrigley Field, however, was a pair of high-definition video boards above the left- and rightcenter-field bleachers. Purists may howl, but the metamorphosis of Wrigley Field is nearly complete. Once a haven for daytime baseball, the 2017 Cubs schedule included more than 36 home night games. Ricketts insisted that in order for the Cubs to win a World Series, Wrigley Field would have to be transformed into a thoroughly modern venue, and he has proven to be correct. Now over a century old, Wrigley Field remains the Friendly Confines to legions of baseball fans.

SOURCES

Benson, Michael, *Ballparks of North America: A Comprehensive Historical Reference to Baseball Grounds, Yards and Stadiums, 1845 to Present* (Jefferson, North Carolina: McFarland & Company, 2009).

Dickson, Paul, *Bill Veeck: Baseball's Greatest Maverick* (London: Bloomsbury Publishing, 2012).

Ehrgott, Roberts, *Mr. Wrigley's Ball Club: Chicago and the Cubs During the Jazz Age* (Jefferson, North Carolina: McFarland & Company, 2013).

Gillette, Gary, and Eric Enders, *Big League Ballparks: The Complete Illustrated History* (New York: Metro Books, 2009).

Jacob, Mark, and Stephen Green, *Wrigley Field: A Celebration of the Friendly Confines* (New York: McGraw Hill, 2003).

McNeil, William, *Gabby Hartnett: The Life and Times of the Cubs' Greatest Catcher* (Jefferson, North Carolina: McFarland & Company, 2004).

Shea, Stuart, *Wrigley Field: The Unauthorized Biography* (Dulles, Virginia: Potomac Books, 2004).

Smith, Ron, *The Ballpark Book: A Journey Through the Fields of Baseball Magic* (St. Louis: The Sporting News, 2000).

Stout, Glenn, *The Cubs: The Complete Story of Chicago Cubs Baseball* (New York: Houghton Mifflin, 2007).

Baseball-Reference.com

NOTES

1   Charles A. Santo, *Sport and Public Policy: Social, Political, and Economic Perspectives* (Champaign, Illinois: Human Kinetics), 73.

2   Stuart Shea, *Wrigley Field: The Unauthorized Biography* (Dulles, Virginia: Potomac Books, Inc., 2004), 266.

3   Ibid.

4   Paul Dickson, *Bill Veeck: Baseball's Greatest Maverick* (London: Bloomsbury Publishing, 2012), 329.

WRIGLEYVILLE NEIGHBORHOOD

By Alan Reifman

... [T]oo many parks aren't situated where they should be – and that is, preferably, not just in a city but in a neighborhood.

—Travis Sawchik[1]

SAWCHIK IS NOT ALONE IN PRAISING

Wrigleyville. Kevin Kaduk titled his diary of attending the full 2005 Cubs home slate, *Wrigleyworld: A Season in Baseball's Best Neighborhood.*[2] Brad Null and Dave Kaval, who toured all major-league parks in 1998, wrote about seeking the nightlife wherever they went, but only in Wrigleyville finding "daylife."[3]

Part of Wrigleyville's appeal is the ballpark's longevity and sense of history. Except for Wrigley and Boston's Fenway Park,[4] all neighborhood ballparks from the early and mid-twentieth century are gone (e.g., Brooklyn's Ebbets Field, DC's Griffith Stadium, and Philadelphia's Shibe Park), and most current ballparks are either downtown or someplace with vast parking lots. Wrigleyville is such a bona fide *residential* neighborhood that Cubs President Theo Epstein and several players live there. Epstein described its advantages: "For a night game after batting practice, it's like a dead time usually for an hour or an hour and a half. ... I like to walk home and have dinner with my kids, do the bedtime thing and make it back for first pitch. ... I don't know where else you could do that."[5]

With its nightlife, daylife, and convenient living, Wrigleyville is a popular area to many, but it also has its detractors. Through examination of the area and its inhabitants, social atmosphere, and historical evolution, readers not already intimately familiar with Wrigleyville may get a better idea of its attractions and less pleasant aspects.

BASIC INFORMATION
LOCATION

As depicted below, Wrigley Field is surrounded by Clark Street, Addison Street, Sheffield Avenue, and Waveland Avenue, on Chicago's north side. It sits roughly four miles north of the downtown Loop and a mile west of the Lake Michigan shoreline.

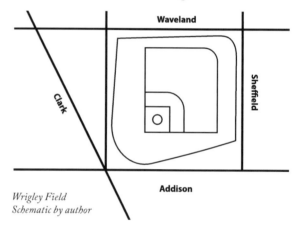

Wrigley Field
Schematic by author

Wrigleyville is not one of Chicago's 77 official "community areas," but falls instead within the Lake View jurisdiction. Sources differ on Wrigleyville's precise boundaries, but most define them as extending three to five blocks beyond the ballpark on all sides. Expanding the perimeter, Kaduk richly describes Wrigleyville's location: "gritty Irving Park to the north, artsy Belmont to the south, yuppie Southport to the west, and gay Halsted to the east."[6]

DEMOGRAPHICS

Trendy and close to entertainment, the lake, and public transportation, Wrigleyville living is naturally expensive. The real-estate website Trulia found Wrigleyville housing to cost 2.2 times as much as the Chicago average, tying for the major leagues' fourth highest ratio.[7] My informal survey of Wrigley-area apartment ads discovered rental prices approaching $2,000 a month and costs of $400,000 to $500,000 to own.

Looking at Census tracts near Wrigley, the area's racial-ethnic composition is roughly 90 percent white; among other groups, Hispanic residents are slightly more numerous than Asian and African-American residents.[8] Scott Simon describes neighborhoods near Wrigley as "some of the most truly diverse in America."[9] This characterization is especially true of neighborhoods extending from Wrigley to Chicago's northern boundary.[10]

Nearly one-third of Wrigleyville residents are in their 20s.[11] Its sports, music, and drinking venues attract young people – Chris Erskine deems the area a "post-collegiate playground"[12] – but high rents would seem unaffordable for young workers. Perhaps some double- or triple-up with roommates, but many young adults in Wrigleyville are college-educated, with reasonably high incomes for their age.[13] Urban-planning expert Richard Florida highlights the growing economic role of artists, architects, technology workers, writers, and the like, and how they are attracted to places known for tolerance and amenities.[14] These workers, known as the "creative class," are indeed highly common in Wrigleyville.[15]

SOCIAL ATMOSPHERE

Pregame excitement builds as fans converge on Wrigley from all directions. Elevated train lines (the "El") deliver fans a block from the ballpark (see photo). Parking is very limited, so drivers have to explore residential areas (sometimes several blocks

Photo courtesy of Alan Reifman

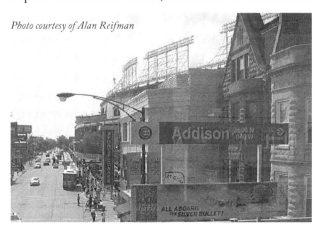

from Wrigley) and pay to park in someone's garage. Souvenir stands, bars, restaurants, and apartment buildings with rooftop bleachers create a buzz of activity.

DRINKING AND REVELRY

One stadium-discussion site claims, "No other ballpark in the country can compete with the sports bars that you will find outside of Wrigley Field."[16] Kaduk notes that a quarter-mile stretch of Clark Street by Wrigley contains 21 bars.[17] The bar Murphy's Bleachers (shown below) is behind center field. Kaduk coined the term "Disneyland bars" for six establishments – Sluggers, the Cubby Bear, Hi-Tops,[18] Murphy's, Sports Corner (visible in the El-station photo), and Casey Moran's – whose popularity has made them tourist attractions.

Photo courtesy of Alan Reifman

Not surprisingly, Wrigleyville (Lakeview, technically) has the highest rate of binge-drinking in Chicago and one of the highest levels nationally.[19] Statistics on public-urination infractions show the area near the Wrigley El station to lead the city in this behavior.[20] Even on an El ride to the game, some passengers can be loud and obnoxious, having apparently engaged in pregame drinking.

Ballpark-area bars have also been criticized from a beverage-connoisseur perspective. One Wicker Park barkeep, specializing in craft and international beers, announced, "We wanted to do something with integrity, and not just open a place with a bunch of beer and TVs. ... We're digging in our heels and saying we're not allowing our neighborhood to become another Wrigleyville."[21]

ROOFTOPS

Bleacher seating atop apartment buildings, looking into the ballpark, is a phenomenon closely associated with Wrigley Field. However, similar viewing is, or has been, available in other cities.[22] Whereas yesterday's apartment-dwellers could go upstairs during a game at their leisure, today's Wrigley rooftops involve tickets, food and beverage service, and other stadium-type amenities. In recent decades "many of the apartments were cleared out, renovated, and turned into full-blown business ventures."[23] Nearly all the buildings have an inside floor like a major-league club level,[24] whereas some are total shells with no apartments at all.[25] One might pay around $100 to sit on a rooftop with an all-you-can-eat (and drink) buffet of ballpark-type fare.[26] The Cubs and rooftop owners have disputed whether the latter is stealing the former's product. Rooftop owners have paid the team a share of rooftop profits in settlements,[27] but the issue seems increasingly moot, as the Cubs' owners, the Ricketts family, have been purchasing the buildings.[28]

Photo courtesy of Alan Reifman

MUSIC SCENE

Wrigleyville is also a live-music hub. The Cubby Bear does double duty as a music venue at night. Outside of sports bars, fans of pop-rock, heavy-metal, and the like can also go to small (roughly 1,000-seat) concert halls, including the Vic Theatre and Metro.[29] Most bands are local, with occasional appearances by nationally and internationally known acts. Wrigley Field itself has also become quite a concert venue, hosting such major acts as Bruce Springsteen, Pearl Jam, and Paul McCartney in recent years.[30]

BALLPARK NOISE

Some sounds – such as the park's organ music as one walks toward Wrigley – can enhance anticipation for the game. However, installation of a new Wrigley videoboard and sound system in 2015 took the volume to a new level. One resident, 12 blocks away, heard the national anthem so loudly he mistakenly blamed his neighbor's television.[31] There's also a YouTube video claiming to pick up the crowd singing "Go Cubs Go" from a mile away![32]

PAST AND FUTURE

Wrigleyville has evolved over the past half-century from industrial – with the triangle between Clark Street and the ballpark containing large coal silos until 1961[33] – to eclectic and quirky.[34] The latest construction projects suggest Wrigleyville's next phase may be as a playground for the rich, which has alarmed many longtime observers.[35]

Simon sees Wrigleyville's post-industrial transformation as presaging the 1988 debut of night games. In the 1970s, "A neighborhood of families who worked long hours in factories and warehouses began to become prime territory for youngish urban professionals ... [who] liked the brio and dash of living near Wrigley, and cared less about quiet streets by 10:00 p.m." (p. 53).[36]

The 1970s and '80s were also a heyday for eclectic and quirky tastes in Wrigleyville. *Rolling Stone* magazine recalls nostalgically the establishments offering "all things counter culture, from punk and metal to goth," to comic books, to items "from bullet belts to bongs."[37] Many of these establishments, sustained by inexpensive rents at the time, are now gone.

As Wrigleyville continued in its trendiness and, some argue, Cubs management sought to monetize more activities from fans' ballpark visits to fund a more competitive team in the new century,[38] a shift toward more upscale clients seemed to accelerate. Construction has occupied large chunks of Addison and Clark (as of mid-2017), with new establishments to include a Cubs office building, team store, "boutique" hotel,[39] apartments, restaurants, and other commercial space.[40] Fans of the displaced McDonald's[41] on Clark need not worry, however. The hotel being erected in its place will include a McDonald's inside.[42]

What does the future hold for Wrigleyville? In this author's view, the neighborhood's eclectic aspects – the music, the arts, the counter-culture – probably won't disappear anytime soon. However, as the immediate ballpark area becomes more upscale, many wild, weird, and wonderful aspects may be driven to the outskirts of Wrigleyville or even to other neighborhoods.

NOTES

1   Sawchik covered the Pirates for the *Pittsburgh Tribune-Review* from 2013-2016 and also wrote the book *Big Data Baseball* (Flatiron Books, 2015). This quote is from FanGraphs, Sawchik's new home. fangraphs.com/blogs/the-new-generation-of-ballparks-is-pushing-us-away/.

2   Kevin Kaduk, *Wrigleyworld: A Season in Baseball's Best Neighborhood* (New York: Penguin Books, 2006).

3   Brad Null and Dave Kaval, *The Summer That Saved Baseball* (Nashville: Cumberland House, 2001), 262-270.

4   The Kenmore Square area near Fenway Park draws some comparisons to Wrigleyville. Cubs manager Joe Maddon offered this view on the two communities: "[Fenway] is wonderful inside, just like Wrigley is. The difference is the location itself. We're in a neighborhood. When you drive up to the ballpark, there is no freeway [akin to the Massachusetts Turnpike] along the outfield there. There are some restaurants and bars, etc., around [Fenway], which is kind of cool. But Wrigley is just a big neighborhood ballpark, and I love it for all of that." Paul Sullivan, "Tale of two (baseball-mad) cities – and of two ballparks," *Chicago Tribune*, April 28, 2017. chicagotribune.com/sports/columnists/ct-cubs-red-sox-comparisons-sullivan-spt-0429-20170428-column.html.

5   Paul Sullivan, "A Cub next door? Players embrace Wrigleyville living," *Chicago Tribune*, August 15, 2016. http://www.chicagotribune.com/sports/baseball/cubs/ct-cubs-living-in-wrigleyville-spt-0816-20160815-story.html

6   Kaduk, 35.

7   "America's Most Expensive Baseball Stadium Neighborhoods," *Forbes*, March 28, 2013. By cost per square foot, the area by San Francisco's AT&T Park is the most expensive ballpark neighborhood ($653), but because housing is very expensive in the Bay Area generally, living near the Giants' home was only 1.3 times as pricey as in San Francisco overall. forbes.com/sites/trulia/2013/03/28/americas-most-expensive-baseball-stadium-neighborhoods/#4b9838a44f50.

8   Census tracts near Wrigley Field and their racial-ethnic breakdowns are as follows: Census Tract 061200 (Whites 90.4%, Hispanics 6.2%, Blacks 1.5%, Asians 3.6%, others 4.4%); Census Tract 83200 (Whites 88.8%, Hispanics 7.5%, Blacks 2.2%, Asians 5.3%, others 3.6%); Census Tract 061000 (Whites 89.9%, Hispanics 6.4%, Blacks 1.8%, Asians 3.4%, others 4.9%); Census Tract 061100 (Whites 92.5%, Hispanics 4.8%, Blacks 1.3%, Asians 3.3%, others 2.8%). Obtained via usa.com/.

9   Scott Simon, *My Cubs: A Love Story* (New York: Blue Rider Press, 2017), 132.

10 Emily Chow, Christopher Groskopf, Joe Germuska, Hal Dardick, and Brian Boyer, "Reshaping Chicago's Political Map: Race, Ward-by-Ward," *Chicago Tribune*, July 14, 2011. As of 2010, in all or parts of City Council Wards 40, 46, 48, 49, and 50 (north of Wrigley and near the Lake Michigan coast) no racial-ethnic group comprised more than 50% of the area population. This pattern reflects less numerical domination by any one group in a ward and, therefore, greater diversity. For example in Ward 49 (Rogers Park and West Ridge), Whites comprised 37% of residents, African-Americans 28%, and Hispanics 24%. media.apps.chicagotribune.com/ward-redistricting/index.html.

11 According to Town Charts, Wrigley's "ZIP code 60613 has one of the largest proportions of people 20 to 29 year olds at 31.5% of the total and is ranked #3" among Chicago ZIP codes. towncharts.com/Illinois/Demographics/60613-Zipcode-IL-Demographics-data.html.

12 Chris Erskine, "My Guitar Gently Weeps for Chicago, John Prine, Sinful Sandwiches and the Old 'Hood Near Wrigley," *Los Angeles Times*, August 19, 2017. latimes.com/home/la-hm-erskine-column-20170819-story.html

13 Kaduk.

14 Richard Florida and Charlotta Mellander, "'There Goes the Neighbourhood.' How and Why Bohemians, Artists and Gays Affect Regional Housing Values," Martin Prosperity Institute, Rotman School of Management, University of Toronto, 2007. creativeclass.com/rfcgdb/articles/there%20goes%20the%20neighborhood.pdf.

15 Richard Florida, "Class-Divided Cities: Chicago Edition," City Lab/*Atlantic Monthly* Group, February 4, 2013. The Census tract including Wrigley Field contains 45% creative-class, 50% service-industry, and 5% working-class employees; in Wrigleyville areas just beyond the ballpark, the creative class rises to 60% of workers. For comparison, Guaranteed Rate Field, home of the White Sox on Chicago's South Side, has far more of its surrounding tracts dominated by service workers. citylab.com/equity/2013/02/class-divided-cities-chicago-edition/4306/.

16 Ballpark Chasers, "Wrigley Field." ballparkchasers.com/notes/Wrigley_Field.

17 Kaduk.

18 Hi-Tops is no longer in operation. See: Sean Parnell, "Hi-Tops," Chicago Bar Project. chibarproject.com/Memoriam/HiTops/Hi-Tops.htm.

19 Matt Lindner, "Lakeview Has the Highest Rate of Binge Drinking in Chicago," *Chicago Tribune*, December 22, 2016. chicagotribune.com/lifestyles/ct-lake-view-binge-drinking-1221-20161221-story.html.

20 Mark Konkol and Tanveer Ali, "Wrigleyville Is Chicago's Public Urination Capital, Data Shows," *The Block Club*, August 24, 2015. dnainfo.com/chicago/20150824/wrigleyville/wrigleyville-is-chicagos-public-urination-capital-data-shows.

21 Peter Frost, "Restaurateurs: We Won't Let Wicker Park Become Wrigleyville," *Crain's Chicago Business*, January 28, 2015. chicagobusiness.com/article/20150128/BLOGS09/150129797/restaurateurs-we-wont-let-wicker-park-become-wrigleyville.

22 Former ballparks with rooftop viewing included Shibe Park and Griffith Stadium. See: Ryan Swanson, "Ballparks We Miss: Shibe Park (1909–1970)," *The National Pastime Museum*. August 16, 2017. thenationalpastimemuseum.com/article/ballparks-we-miss-shibe-park-1909-1970; and "Parks of the Past: Griffith Stadium, Washington D.C." (Reddit discussion topic). reddit.com/r/baseball/comments/1rhtfd/parks_of_the_past_griffith_stadium_washington_dc/. Regarding current ballparks, high-rise apartments and condominiums have been advertised in recent years with views into D.C.'s Nationals Park and San Diego's Petco Park. See Benjamin Freed, "Residents of New Navy Yard Building Will Be Able to Watch Nationals Games From the Roof," *Washingtonian*, April 7, 2016. washingtonian.com/2016/04/07/new-navy-yard-apartment-building-will-come-with-ultimate-perk-free-baseball/ ; JD Land, Preview of "Flrst" apartment building in Washington, DC. jdland.com/dc/flrst.cfm ; and "Icon San Diego Condos with awesome views into the Padre's *(sic)* Petco Park!" youtube.com/watch?v=gcshxwzxrCc.

23 Ryan Davis, "How I Learned That the Wrigley Rooftops Aren't Evil," *Chicago Now/Cubs Insider*, August 13, 2014. chicagonow.com/cubs-insider/2014/08/how-i-learned-that-the-wrigley-rooftops-arent-evil/.

24 See the slickly produced marketing website wrigleyrooftopsllc.com/ for extensive photographs of each building's baseball-viewing amenities.

25 Barry Bearak, "Cubs' Owners Are Rebuilding While Root, Root, Rooting," *New York Times*, September 19, 2014. nytimes.com/2014/09/21/sports/baseball/as-cubs-slowly-rebuild-theres-shouting-from-the-rooftops.html.

26 Ibid.

27 Becky Yerak, "Wrigley Rooftops' Quirky Past Preceded Big Business, Sour Relationship With Cubs," *Chicago Tribune*, October 28, 2016. chicagotribune.com/business/ct-wrigley-rooftops-history-1028-biz-20161027-story.html.

28 Jay Koziarz, "Ricketts Family Now Controls Majority of Wrigley Field Rooftops," *Curbed Chicago*, January 13, 2016. chicago.curbed.com/2016/1/13/10847008/ricketts-purchase-three-rooftops-for-majority-controll.

29 "The 15 Best Places With Live Music In Lakeview, Chicago," *Four Square*, August 21, 2017. foursquare.com/top-places/lakeview-chicago/best-places-live-music.

30 Greg Kot, "Shows That Shook Wrigley All Night Long," *Chicago Tribune*, April 1, 2014. chicagotribune.com/ct-ent-0402-wrigley-concerts-20140401-column.html.

31 Patrick M. O'Connell, "Residents Complain Wrigley Field Is Louder Than Previous Years," *Chicago Tribune*, April 6, 2015. chicagotribune.com/news/local/breaking/ct-wrigley-field-noise-met-20150406-story.html.

32 "'Go Cubs Go' From a Mile Away" youtube.com/watch?v=3U8WaNbZoPU.

33 Digital Research Library of Illinois History Journal, "Silos at Wrigley Field?" December 1, 2016. drloihjournal.blogspot.com/2016/12/wrigley-field-silos-at-wrigley-field.html.

34 For a highly detailed history of both Wrigley Field and its surrounding neighborhood, especially the first three decades, see Stuart Shea, *Wrigley Field: The Long Life and Contentious Times of the Friendly Confines* (Chicago: University of Chicago Press, 2014). Another book seemingly in this genre is *Wrigleyville*, by Peter Golenbock (New York: St. Martin's/Griffin, 1999), but it concentrates primarily on the Cubs' on-the-field history.

35 In his book *A Nice Little Place on the North Side* (New York: Crown Archetype, 2014), 175, George Will writes, "As [Wrigley Field] enters its second century, however, the residential neighborhood is, if not unhappy, certainly uneasy, and those who love the ballpark worry that its unassuming character might perish."

36 towncharts.com/Illinois/Demographics/60613-Zipcode-IL-Demographics-data.html.

37   Jason Diamond, "Chicago Cubs and the Last Days of Old, Weird Wrigleyville," *Rolling Stone,* September 27, 2016. Embedded in the online *Rolling Stone* article is a great YouTube video from 1984 of the Cubby Bear's dual existence: sports bar by day to punk-rock mosh-pit by night. rollingstone.com/sports/chicago-cubs-wrigleyville-neighborhood-experiences-change-w441949.

38   Stuart Shea (Ibid. Note 36) discussed the Cubs' recent strategies to increase revenues and fund a better team at the SABR 45 conference's Ballparks Committee meeting, in Chicago (2015).

39   The phrase "boutique hotel" appears on the hotel's website (hotelzachary.com/), as part of its effort to attract customers.

40   The *Chicago Sun-Times* published an excellent overview of all the construction projects surrounding Wrigley Field, including maps, photographs, and artist renderings. Eric White, "The New Wrigleyville: 4 Big Projects Going Up Around Cubs' Home," *Chicago Sun-Times,* April 12, 2017. chicago.suntimes.com/sports/the-new-wrigleyville-4-big-projects-going-up-around-cubs-home/.

41   Patrick M. O'Connell, "Cubs Fans Already Missing Torn-Down McDonald's Near Wrigley," *Chicago Tribune,* April 5, 2016. chicagotribune.com/news/ct-wrigley-field-mcdonalds-met-20160405-story.html.

42   "As the Cubs Enter the Playoffs, Hotel Zachary Preps for Its Inaugural Season," *Building Up Chicago,* September 27, 2016. buildingupchicago.com/2016/09/27/as-the-cubs-enter-the-playoffs-hotel-zachary-preps-for-its-inaugural-season/.

THE EVOLUTION OF NICKNAMES
FOR THE NORTH SIDERS

By Glen Sparks

FIRST, THEY WERE THE "CHICAGO BASE Ball Club."[1] They would not be the Cubs until much later. Some sportswriters and baseball fans – at various times and for different reasons – also knew Chicago's National League team as the Orphans, Colts, Panamas, Remnants, and by many other aliases. Yes, they were even the Microbes for a while.

Local businessmen founded the franchise on October 1, 1869, as a member of the National Association of Base Ball Players. The new squad won its first game, 7-1, on April 29, 1870, against the St. Louis Unions. Team uniforms featured white hose, white flannel caps, and white shirts with blue trousers. Not surprisingly, many fans began calling their base ball club the "White Stockings."[2] Some preferred "the Chicagos" or the Chicago Nine. In 1876, Chicago joined the fledgling National League.

William Hulbert, a longtime Chicago resident and grocery-store owner, invested in the White Stockings. He quickly became one of the team officers and, later, its president. Hulbert disapproved of gambling, drinking, and most other vices. So did Albert Goodwill Spalding, an Illinois native and one of baseball's top pitchers. Hulbert lured Spalding away from the Boston Red Stockings (the forerunner of the Boston Braves). Spalding, a right-handed thrower and future sporting-goods mogul, won 47 games in 1876. Infielder Ross Barnes hit .429, and catcher James "Deacon" White led the league with 60 RBIs.

Hulbert also had purchased Adrian "Cap" Anson's contract from the Philadelphia A's before the 1876 campaign. The hard-hitting first basemanbatted .356 in his debut season as a White Stocking. A player-manager with Philadelphia in 1875, Anson eventually took over those twin duties in Chicago. The White Stockings roster boasted several talented young players in addition to Barnes and White They included infielder Tom Burns and outfielders George Gore and Abner Dalrymple.. Many sportswriters began calling the team "Anson's Colts,"[3] or, simply, "the Colts," who won their first pennant in 1876. (Spalding retired as a pitcher after his first season with Chicago. He played one year in the infield and joined the team's front office. Hard-throwing Larry Corcoran and curveball artist Fred Goldsmith took over as the team's main pitchers a few years later.)

The White Stockings signed Mike "King" Kelly in 1880. Just 22 years old, the Troy, New York, native already had gained a reputation as one of the game's smartest and best players. Yes, he drank. He also sprayed line drives around the field. Supposedly, he invented the hook slide. Every spring, he swore to give up his carousing.

The Colts won more pennants, in 1880-82 and 1885-86. However, Anson and Spalding (promoted to White Stockings president after Hulbert died in 1882) grew tired of babysitting whiskey-soaked ballplayers. They shipped Kelly to the Boston Beaneaters after the 1886 campaign. The team's slide soon began. Anson's later clubs struggled to reach .500 even as the player-manager kept hitting and driving in runs. Following a disappointing 59-73 season in 1897, Anson was let go by Chicago after spending 27 seasons in the big leagues. The players had lost their leader, their "Pop." They were now, and hit above .300 almost every season. Baseball writers voted him into the Hall of Fame in 1939, 17 years after his death at the age of 69. His legacy as a baseball player is tainted by his racial insensitivity. Anson refused to play games with African-American ballplayers.)

The upstart American League began play in 1901. Eight teams were formed, the same number as in the National League. The Chicago club opted to be the White Sox, not a far stretch from the old White Stockings. Several American League teams raided National League squads. The Orphans were no exception. The 1901 squad finished a woeful 53-86 and in sixth place. Club officials began a large-scale rebuilding project. This time, many newspapers decided that the team should be known as the Remnants.

The Cubs nickname appeared in print for the first time on March 27, 1902, in the *Chicago Daily News*. Chicago had hired Frank Selee, a quiet New Englander, to run the club, which was once again made up of young, enthusiastic ballplayers. The headline, written when every team is filled with optimism, read "Selee Places His Men."[4] Below that, the subhead read "Manager of the Cubs Is in Doubt Only on Top Positions." It was as simple as that.

No byline accompanied the article, which was not unusual in that era. Charles Sensabaugh may have written the headline, though. He was the *Chicago Daily News* sports editor at the time. But why did he pick "Cubs"? Glenn Stout and Richard A. Johnson reported in their 2007 book *The Cubs: A Complete History*: "The term 'cub' was common slang for a young ballplayer."[5] The writers also give some credit to an unknown typesetter. "Had the word not appeared with the capitalized 'C,' it might not have stood out," Stout and Johnson wrote.[6]

Baseball historian John Snyder wrote: "The (Cubs) name caught the imagination of the public and began to be used in everyday speech until it became part of the team's identity."[7] Even so, some sportswriters still preferred the Colts moniker. (Writers and fans quickly retired the Orphans.)

Cartoonists loved the "Cubs." In 1906, Chicago's two ballclubs met in a crosstown World Series. One newspaper printed an editorial cartoon after the Series showing a figure clad only in white stockings, along with a bearskin nailed to the wall and six white

socks hanging on a clothesline. The White Sox had won the fall classic in six games.[8]

By 1907, the team was "universally called the Cubs by all the newspapers. That year, the name 'Cubs' first appeared on the club's scorecards."[9] Credit for that might go to Frank Chance of Tinker to Evers to Chance fame. The first baseman from Salida, California, served as the Chicago player-manager from 1905 to 1912 after breaking in with the team in 1898. Chance "insisted in 1907 that the club be called the 'Cubs' exclusively. The Chicago newspapers fell in line. The Cubs nickname was "officially recognized during the 1907 World Series, when new coats were issued to the players sporting a large bear figure on each sleeve."[10]

This time, the Cubs swept the Detroit Tigers to earn their first Series title. Harry Steinfeldt hit .471 (8-for-17), Johnny Evers batted .350 (7-for-20), and the Chicago pitching staff posted a combined 0.75 ERA. Every player received a World Series medal. Not surprisingly, the medals bore the mark of a bruin. The *Chicago Tribune* explained: "Its center represents in rose gold the 'world,' on which is mounted in relief the profile of a bear cub holding a large diamond in his teeth, which are to be of aluminum. A ruby represents the cub's eye. The figures '1907' will be raised slightly. Circling this field is a band of Roman gold bearing the inscription 'World's Champions.'"[11]

Of note, the Cubs' 1908 uniform "featured an emblem of a rather lackadaisical bear holding a bat."[12] Also in 1908, a teenager wearing a bear suit during a summer heat wave entertained the crowd at Wrigley Field. This early team mascot "had to fan himself by pulling a string that opens and closes a space in front of his mouth."[13] After a big win, the mascot cheered the Cubs. The fans, though, "threw cushions at it."[14]

It may seem surprising that the Chicago franchise ever finally settled on a long-lasting nickname. They went through so many short-term ones. Chicago trained one spring in New Mexico. Thus, some writers labeled its players the Desert Rangers. At least one writer noticed that many players were sporting Panama-style hats one year. So ... the Panamas.[15] Another year, several team members looked a bit short in stature, such as 125-pound Johnny Evers. They would be the Microbes. In fact, the *Chicago American* edition of September 26, 1903, ran a banner headline across the front page: "Microbes Make Stand for Second Place."[16] Maybe the funniest short-term nickname, though, was the Spuds, a reference to Irish-American Charles Murphy, who owned the Chicago club from 1906 to 1913.[17] That one didn't gain much traction.

The Cubs stood out as one of baseball's early dynasties in the World Series era. They earned three straight pennants (1906-1908) and back-to-back World Series championships. From 1906 through 1945, the Cubs won 10 National League pennants. Quickly, though, the team's fortunes changed. Chicago did not finish above .500 throughout the 1950s and did not win a pennant from 1946 through 2015. At long last, in 2016, they beat the Los Angeles Dodgers to win the National League Championship Series and knocked off the Cleveland Indians in seven games to celebrate a World Series title.

The Cubs remain one of baseball's most beloved franchises. They are valued at $2.675 billion, according to an estimate in forbes.com, the fourth most valuable team in major-league baseball.[18] They certainly have used some colorful names through the years. Some people still call them the Baby Bears, the Cubbies, the North Siders, and, unfortunately, due to that championship drought, the Lovable Losers. More than anything else, though, they are now and probably forever, the Cubs.

NOTES

1 Glenn Stout, Glenn and Richard A. Johnson, *The Cubs* (Boston, New York: Houghton Mifflin: 2007).

2 "Base Ball, Chicagos vs. Atlantics," *Chicago Tribune*, July 26, 1874.

3 "Anson's Colts Defeated in the Opening Game at the Hub," *Chicago Tribune*, July 11, 1890.

4 "Selee Places His Men," *Chicago Daily News*, March 27, 1902.

5 Stout and Johnson, *The Cubs*.

6 Ibid.

7 John Snyder, *Cubs Journal: Year by Year and Day by Day With the Chicago Cubs Since 1876* (Covington, Kentucky: Clerisy, 2005).

8 John Devaney, *The World Series: A Complete Pictorial History* (Skokie, Illinois: Rand-McNally, 1972).

9 Art Ahrens, *Chicago Cubs: Tinker to Evers to Chance (Images of Baseball)* (Charleston, South Carolina: Arcadia Publishing, 2007).

10 Snyder, *Cubs Journal*.

11 "Origin of the Cubs." Wrigleyivy.com.

12 Cait Murphy, *Crazy '08: How a Cast of Cranks, Rogues, Boneheads, and Magnates Created the Greatest Year in Baseball History* (New York: HarperCollins, 2007).

13 Ibid.

14 Ibid.

15 Ibid.

16 "We solve the mystery of the Cubs' early name: The Microbes." Timeout.com

17 "Spud Slump Not Serious," *Chicago Tribune*, July 29, 1906.

18 "The Business of Baseball," Forbes.com forbes.com/teams/chicago-cubs/.

NEGRO BASEBALL AT WRIGLEY FIELD

By Alan Cohen

WELL INTO THE TWENTIETH CENTURY, blacks were barred from participating in baseball games at Wrigley Field, even though there had been Negro League baseball in the area for many years.

The first evidence of a change in this practice did not come until 1942. Wrigley Field opened its door to Negro baseball during the years of World War II and there were several meaningful encounters.

With America's entrance into the war, Dizzy Dean formed a team consisting almost entirely of recently drafted and enlisted major-league and minor-league players, and barnstormed around the United States. On May 24, 1942, Dean's "all-star" team faced Satchel Paige and the Kansas City Monarchs of the Negro American League in a game at Wrigley Field, the first time a black team ever played there. R.S. Simmons wrote in the *Pittsburgh Courier*, "this was the first time, sepia ball players ever played at the Cubs Park."[1]

As noted by Timothy Gay in *Satch, Dizzy, and Rapid Robert*, "Most fans that afternoon were dark-skinned, an unheard of happenstance at Wrigley, which had always been off-limits to Black baseball. The Negro Leagues' annual East-West Classic (all-star game) and other big blackball matchups were traditionally played at Comiskey Park on the city's South side, home to a teeming Ghetto known as the Black Belt.[2]

Among the players on Dean's squad was Zeke Bonura, then in the Army, who had played for both the White Sox and Cubs during his major-league career. It was "Zeke Bonura Day," and the fan favorite, known affectionately as Banana Nose, was given a floral offering with banana trimmings before the game.[3] He averaged .317 in his four seasons with the White Sox, and twice finished in the top 20 in

the MVP balloting. In 1937, he led the White Sox in batting (.345) home runs (19), and RBIs (100).

The Monarchs defeated Dean's All-Stars 3-1 in front of a crowd of 29,775. It had been expected that Bob Feller would pitch for Dean's team. He was in the Navy, but naval authorities would not let him participate. Nevertheless, the game's organizer, Abe Saperstein, sent $1,000 to Feller. That money was donated to Navy relief.[4]

The best player in Dean's lineup was Cecil Travis, who came to the game from Camp Wheeler in Georgia. He had been runner-up in the American League batting race in 1941. He went 0-for-3 in the game.

Dean pitched one inning for his team, retiring the Monarchs in order as Bill Simms lined to center field, Herb Cyrus grounded to shortstop, and Ted Strong popped to second base. Hilton Smith later told author John Holway that Dean "wasn't too good; we kind of carried him along."[5] Dean gave way to Johnny Grodzicki, who hurled for the Cardinals at the end of the 1941 season before going into the Army. He pitched through the sixth inning. He later was assigned to the 17th Airborne Division and fought in Europe in 1944 and '45. He was wounded on March 30, 1945. He and his unit had been dropped behind enemy lines five days earlier. A shell exploded near his position and shrapnel became lodged in his leg. Grodzicki's wounds never fully healed,[6] but he did come back to appear in 19 games with the Cardinals in 1946 and 1947.

Paige pitched six innings and gave up only one third-inning run and two hits. He struck out two batters (Grodzicki and catcher Ken Silvestri). Silvestri came to the game from Camp Custer, Michigan, where he was managing the base's baseball team. It was a strange set of circumstances that allowed the Dean All-Stars to break the ice in the third inning. Joe Gallagher, the left fielder, singled to lead off, beating out a slow roller to third base. Gallagher was serving at Jefferson Barracks in Missouri. With Grodzicki batting, catcher James "Joe" Greene of the Monarchs called for a pitchout. As expected, Gallagher was running on the play. Grodzicki reached out and bunted the ball. With second baseman William "Barney" Serrell moving over to cover second and first baseman Buck O'Neil charging to field the bunt, there was nobody covering first, and Grodzicki was safe. Paige picked up the bunt and was charged with a throwing error when his throw the unoccupied base hit Grodzicki and allowed Gallagher to advance to third.

With runners at the corners, Emmett "Heinie" Mueller, who had played for the Phillies before the war, and, like Gallagher, was at Jefferson Barracks, forced Grodzicki at second, Gallagher scoring on the play.[7] There was no further scoring as Paige got Claude Corbitt to ground back to him. Paige grabbed the comebacker, forced Mueller at second, and Serrell threw to first baseman O'Neil for the double play to complete the inning.

The 1-0 lead did not last long. The Monarchs tied the score in the top of the fourth inning. Cyrus led off with a single and moved to second when Ted Strong executed a sacrifice bunt. Cyrus scored on a single by Willard Brown, Brown's second hit of the game. Grodzicki struck out Greene and O'Neil, and the score was tied at 1-1 after four innings. It would remain that way until the eighth inning.

Hilton Smith relieved Paige in the seventh inning, and was the beneficiary when the Monarchs scored two eighth-inning runs. By then Al Piechota, who had replaced Grodzicki, was in his second inning of work. He had pitched for the Braves in 1940 and 1941, and was in the Navy at the time of the game. Bill Simms singled to lead off the inning and advanced to second on a bunt by Cyrus. He moved to third when Strong flied out to right. Piechota issued an intentional pass to Brown, who stole second base. Joe Greene, the Monarchs catcher, was at the plate. On

a 3-and-2 pitch, he cleared the bases with a looping line drive to center field that that fell in front of the charging center fielder, Thomas "Red" Johnson. The ball skipped past Johnson and Greene wound up at second base with a double. O'Neil's single advanced Greene to third, but he was stranded there when Serrell grounded out.

That completed the scoring. Smith struck out three batters (Bonura, Johnson, Piechota) in his three innings on the mound and was credited with the 3-1 win.[8] Mueller lined a single off Smith in the ninth inning, but Dean's squad came up empty. Corbitt grounded to short, forcing Mueller at second base. The final play of the game was described by Fay Young in the *Chicago Defender*: "Dangerous Cecil Travis, late of the Washington Senators, slammed one at (Jesse) Williams who came up with it, tossed to Serrell to kill Corbitt going into second and then Serrell's rifle peg to Joe (sic) O'Neil at first completed a lightning double play when Joe scooped the ball up with one hand."[9] Piechota was charged with the loss.

Gallagher, one of the first ballplayers drafted into the Army (he was inducted on May 12, 1941), did not play in the majors after the war, and went on to coach at the collegiate level. Mueller, who had homered in his first big-league at-bat, did not play in the majors after returning from the Army in 1946. He went on to manage in the minor leagues.

Corbitt had yet to appear in a big-league game when he played for the Dean All-Stars. He started off in the Yankees farm system in 1937 and batted over .300 in each of his first four minor-league seasons. During the 1941 season he was in the Dodgers organization at Montreal, where he batted .282. After the war, he made his major-league debut with the Dodgers. Prior to the 1946 season, he was sold to Cincinnati, and he played parts of three seasons with the Reds.

Playing right field for Dean's team was George Archie. Archie had batted .269 in 105 games with Washington in 1941 before being sent to the St. Louis Browns toward the end of the season. He joined the Army two days after Pearl Harbor and after the war played briefly in 1946 with the Browns. He got into four games at the beginning of the season, but was sent to the minors and played in the minors through 1950.

Many of the Monarchs players were forgotten as the years passed. Satchel Paige and Willard Brown witnessed the end of segregation and played in the major leagues. Each was enshrined at the National Baseball Hall of Fame and Museum at Cooperstown. Paige was inducted in 1971 and Brown in 2006. Brown, at age 32, played 21 games with the 1947 St. Louis Browns. He was the fourth player of color to play in the majors, and the highlight of his short major-league career was a two-run game-tying inside-the-park homer off Hal Newhouser of Detroit on August 13, 1947. The homer was the first by a player of color in the American League. Brown served in Europe during World War II and was one of two black players (the other being Leon Day) on the OISE (Overseas Invasion Service Expedition) All-Stars in the 1945 ETO (European Theater of Operations) Championship.[10]

Paige, at age forty-something, joined the Indians in 1948 and went 6-1 as Cleveland advanced to the World Series. He made one appearance in the Series, retiring both Boston Braves he faced in a lopsided Indians loss in Game Five. The Tribe clinched the Series the following day.

But the pace of integration was all too slow. The other eight Monarchs who played that day would not have the opportunity to exhibit their skills at the major-league level. Smith, at age 41, finished his career with the Monarchs in 1948, and was inducted into the Hall of Fame at Cooperstown in 2001. Catcher Joe Greene served in World War II and finished with the Cleveland Buckeyes in 1948. Serrell drifted from the Monarchs to the Mexican League and played briefly, in 1951, with San Francisco in the Pacific Coast League. Herb Cyrus, after his first three years with the Monarchs, played under his given name of Herb Souell. By the time he received an invite to play in the minor leagues, it was 1952, he was 39, and his talents had eroded. The shortstop Jesse "Bill" Williams was also 39 in 1952 when he first played on an integrated team. He was in 126 games

with Vancouver in the Class-A Western International League and batted .251. Bill Simms, who played left field and was the first batter in the game, last played, at age 35, for the independent Black Crackers in 1944. Ted Strong, the right fielder, like Greene served in the military during World War II. At 34, he last played for the Indianapolis Clowns in 1948. He was also an accomplished basketball player and played with the Harlem Globetrotters beginning in the 1930s.

But Buck O'Neil left an unmatched legacy. By the time baseball integrated in 1947, he was past his prime. He lost three seasons serving in the Navy during World War II. After his playing days he joined the Chicago Cubs as a scout (Lou Brock was his most famous find), and in 1962 became one of the team's coaches. In later life, the affable O'Neil was instrumental in founding and promoting the Negro Leagues Baseball Museum in Kansas City, and his appearance on the Ken Burns production of Baseball earned him a new fan following. His statue at the Hall of Fame in Cooperstown is one of the first things visitors see, and an annual award is given in his honor.

On July 26, 1942, Paige was honored at Wrigley Field as the Monarchs played a doubleheader against the Memphis Red Sox. The two teams were contending for the championship of the Negro American League and Paige was scheduled to oppose lefty Verdel Mathis of Memphis. Paige received a gold watch from the Chicago Defender that was inscribed, "From the World's Greatest Weekly to the World's Greatest Pitcher."[11] He also received a radio, a suit of clothes, a traveling bag, and other gifts from participating Chicago merchants.[12] Memphis won the opener, 10-4, and Kansas City won the second game, 4-2.

Promotions were not uncommon when Negro baseball was on the bill and on June 4, 1944, more than 18,000 were on hand to see a doubleheader. When the ballplayers were not on the field, there was a track and field exhibition featuring Jesse Owens, winner of four gold medals at the 1936 Berlin Olympics, and Helen Stephens, a white track and field athlete who won two gold medals in Berlin. In the 100-yard dash, Owens gave Stephens a 10-yard lead at the start and Stephens held the lead until the 75-yard mark. She looked back, and Owens ran past her, winning the race by a yard. "Don't look back," of course, was a favorite saying of Satchel Paige. His Kansas City Monarchs were there and played two games, defeating the Chicago Brown Bombers 9-1, in the opener, and defeating a team of Chicago firemen 4-3 in the second game.[13] Pitching for the firemen was Leroy Parmelee, who had pitched for the New York Giants and three other teams during a 10-year major-league career.

Negro baseball at Wrigley Field came to an abrupt halt in 1945. In the aftermath of an incident on June 17, 1945, the fee for Negro teams using Wrigley Field was increased to a $5,000 guarantee, which was prohibitively expensive.[14] In a game between the Clowns and the Memphis Red Sox, Jim Ford, playing for Memphis, struck an umpire, Mr. Armstrong. The behavior of the Memphis manager, Larry Brown, especially drew the ire of Cubs officials. Brown joined the melee and threatened the other umpire, Mr. Young. Negro American League President J.B. Martin did not take the matter seriously, imposing a small fine of $50 on Ford. Cubs management effectively said, "No Negro teams in Wrigley Field."[15] The umpires did not want to continue the game and did so only after being warned by Brown that "such actions (stoppage of play) would cause park owners to bar his club from use of the park." Pursuant to the increase in fees, a game between Kansas City and Birmingham that had been scheduled at Wrigley for July 8 was moved to Kansas City.[16]

After Jackie Robinson made his debut with the Brooklyn Dodgers in 1947, there was pressure in Chicago to sign a black player. Two players from the Chicago American Giants were at a tryout, Harold Mason and John F. Ritchey. Among the voices for change was Fay Young, a Negro sportswriter, who accompanied Ritchey to the tryout. But it wouldn't be until September 17, 1953, and the arrival of Ernie Banks, that a black ballplayer would wear the flannels of the Chicago Cubs at Wrigley Field.

SOURCES

In addition to the sources shown in the Notes, the author used Baseball-Reference.com.

NOTES

1   R.S. Simmons, "Satchel Paige Baffles Dizzy Dean's All-Stars Before 29,000: Hilton Smith Stars in Relief Role as Monarchs Win, 3-1," *Pittsburgh Courier*, May 30, 1942: 16. Simmons's play-by-play accounts of the game were a major source for this article.

2   Timothy M. Gay, *Satch, Dizzy, and Rapid Robert: The Wild Saga of Interracial Baseball Before Jackie Robinson* (New York: Simon and Schuster, 2010), 2.

3   "Dean's Service Team Loses," *The Sporting News*, May 28, 1942: 15.

4   Associated Press, "Cracks Down on Promotional Tilts," *Daily Illinois State Journal* (Springfield), June 5, 1942: 22.

5   Gay, 12.

6   Gary Bedingfield, *Baseball in Wartime* (online), March 24, 2007.

7   Howard Martin, "Monarchs, Plus Paige, Beat Stars, Minus Feller, 3 to 1," *Chicago Tribune*, May 25, 1942: 19.

8   United Press, "Navy Flags Bob Feller's Barnstorming, so 29,775 See Satchel Paige's Nine Win," *Philadelphia Inquirer*, May 25, 1942: 21.

9   Fay Young, "Through the Years: Past Present Future," *Chicago Defender*, May 30, 1942: 19.

10 Tim Wendel, "The GI World Series," *The National Pastime Museum*, December 10, 2015.

11 "Chicago to Honor Satchel Paige Sunday: Paige Will Face Lefty Mathis and Memphis at Wrigley Field July 26 – Defender to Give Gold Watch," *Chicago Defender*, July 25, 1942: 19.

12 "Paige Will Pitch and Catch Gifts at Game Today," *Chicago Tribune*, July 26, 1942: 2, 4.

13 Associated Press, "Owens Beats Helen Stephens by Less Than Yard in Century Dash," *St. Louis Post-Dispatch*, June 5, 1944: 6A.

14 Albert Anderson, "Chicago Cubs See Promise in Ritchey, Race Catcher," *New Journal and Guide* (Norfolk, Virginia), September 27, 1947: 22.

15   "Rental Fee Hiked to $5,000; Fans, Players Responsible: Poor
      Public Conduct. Violence on Field Forces Cubs' Management
      to Demand Bigger Guarantee in Chicago," *Pittsburgh Courier*,
      July 7, 1945: 16.

16   "No More Negro Baseball Games at Wrigley Field," *Chicago
      Defender*, July 7, 1945: 7.

FEDS OPEN WEEGHMAN PARK, PITCHER JOHNSON ENJOINED

APRIL 23, 1914
CHICAGO CHI-FEDS 9, KANSAS CITY PACKERS 1

By Mike Lynch

THE FEDERAL LEAGUE KANSAS CITY Packers and Chicago Chi-Feds played the first game ever at Weeghman Park on April 23, 1914, to an overflow crowd of 21,000, much fanfare, and chilly weather. "Chicago took the Federal League to its bosom yesterday," wrote Sam Weller in the *Chicago Tribune*, "and claimed it as a mother would claim a long lost child."[1] The ballpark's capacity was 18,000, but Weller estimated that 3,000 more fans were standing in the back of the grandstand or on the field. Thousands more had to be turned away, but many took residence in windows and on roofs of nearby buildings.[2]

"Owners [Charles] Weeghman and [William] Walker of the north side club and President [James] Gilmore of the new league were so overjoyed with the spectacle that they almost wept," Weller wrote, "and there is little doubt that it was an epochal day in the history of the national game."[3] Weeghman realized early on that his venue wouldn't be big enough to accommodate the massive crowd, but longtime business manager Charles Williams, who spent 25 years in the Cubs front office, had everything working beautifully, "just as if the whole thing had been rehearsed."[4]

All were met by a cold wind blowing in off Lake Michigan, but that didn't temper the enthusiasm or pomp that followed. More than a thousand members of the North Side Boosters' Club held a parade; the Bravo El Toro Club attempted to stage a bullfight on the field, but the bull refused to cooperate; members

of the Ladies of the Grand Army of the Republic marched around the field with an American flag led by a band while players from both teams followed behind.[5]

Chi-Feds manager Joe Tinker, who served as the Cubs' shortstop from 1902 to 1913 and would again briefly in 1916; his wife; and Weeghman were all presented flowers, and the latter was also given a silver loving cup. Corporation Counsel William H. Sexton threw out the first pitch in Mayor Carter H. Harrison's absence and the game began.[6]

Taking the mound for the visitors was George Howard "Chief" Johnson, a Native American born on the Winnebago Reservation in Nebraska who attended the Carlisle Indian School in Pennsylvania with Jim Thorpe, arguably the world's greatest athlete at the time and a future major leaguer himself. Johnson began his career in the Class-A Western League in 1909 and pitched there until 1912, mostly with the St. Joseph Drummers, for whom he went 56-39 from 1910 to 1912.

Johnson's 23-10 showing in 1912 caught the attention of the Chicago White Sox, who purchased his contract only to release him before Opening Day 1913, allegedly because White Sox skipper Nixey Callahan learned that Johnson was a Winnebago and members of that tribe were blacklisted because of their supposed affinity for alcohol.[7]

The Cincinnati Reds cared nothing for that rumor and signed Johnson. He made his major-league debut on April 16, 1913, against the St. Louis Cardinals and tossed seven shutout innings to earn his first win. Johnson went on to pace the Reds in almost every pitching category, including wins with 14. The *New York Times* described him as "fat" and "wooden," but one who could "deal out ciphers with as much success as the more illustrious [Walter] Johnson of Washington."[8]

The following season, 1914, Johnson made a start for Cincinnati on April 18 and lasted only four innings in an 8-5 loss to Pittsburgh. Then he jumped to the Kansas City Packers of the Federal League for a reported $3,000 bonus and $5,000 salary.[9] When Johnson took the mound against the Chi-Feds on April 23, 1914, he did so despite an injunction issued by Judge Charles M. Foell that barred him from pitching for Kansas City.[10]

The Packers would have been better off had they obeyed the injunction as Johnson proved ineffective through two innings of work before he was served with papers and removed from the game. After setting Chicago down in the first, Johnson ran into trouble in the second. Center fielder Dutch Zwilling hit a double into the crowd, right fielder Al Wickland advanced Zwilling to third on a bounder in front of the plate, and second baseman Jack Farrell plated the first run of the game with a single to left. Catcher Art Wilson knocked in two more runs with a home run over the left-field wall and Chicago was out to a 3-0 lead.

In two innings of work Johnson allowed three runs on five hits and a walk while fanning one.[11] Fellow Nebraska native Dwight Stone took the hill for the Packers in the third and issued a walk to Tinker and a single to first baseman Fred Beck. Zwilling poled another double to score the fourth run of the game and send Beck to third, but Stone escaped without further damage when Beck and Zwilling were both thrown out at the plate on subsequent plays.

The Chi-Feds struck again in the fourth when Wilson belted his second homer of the game, this one clearing the scoreboard in left and landing on Waveland Avenue. Max Flack slapped a one-out double into the crowd and Tinker followed a free

In the first regular-season game ever played in Wrigley Field, which at the time was called Weeghman Park and was home to the Chi-Feds of the Federal League, and not the Cubs, Claude Hendrix tossed a five-hitter to beat the Kansas City Packers.

pass to Rollie Zeider with a base hit that plated Flack to push the score to 6-0.

Then they added two more tallies in the sixth when Wilson drew a one-out walk, moved to second on pitcher Claude Hendrix's single, and advanced to third on second baseman Duke Kenworthy's error on a Flack grounder that filled the bases. Zeider drove in Wilson and Hendrix with a single to increase Chicago's lead to 8-0, but Flack was caught in a rundown and Tinker grounded out to end the inning.

Meanwhile Hendrix, a 6-foot-tall spitball artist from Kansas, who made his major-league debut with the Pirates in 1911, then won 24 games for them in his sophomore season, was mowing down Kansas City batters with relative ease. Weller wrote that Hendrix "simply breezed through the combat without being in danger at any time."[12] Indeed, Hendrix surrendered only two hits through seven innings before allowing his only run in the eighth.

With an eight-run lead in the eighth Hendrix either got careless or started grooving pitches to try to put a quick end to the game. Catcher Ted Easterly led off the frame with a home run to left, and pinch-hitter Grover Gilmore and right fielder John Potts both singled. But a double play erased the threat and Hendrix was off the hook with only one run on his ledger.

Not to be outdone, the Chi-Feds added one more run to their total in the bottom of the eighth on a potentially dangerous play. Farrell singled, advanced to second on an out, and went to third on a passed ball. With Hendrix, a solid hitter, at the plate, Farrell broke for home in an attempted steal. Hendrix didn't know it was coming and swung at the pitch. "Johnny tried to steal home, but just when he was about to hit the dirt Hendrix singled to center, so Johnny came in straight up," wrote Weller.[13]

Hendrix was forced at second and Zeider tapped back to pitcher George Hogan to end the inning, then Hendrix shut the Packers down in the ninth to seal an easy 9-1 victory.

POSTSCRIPT

Because of numerous injunctions in 1914, Chief Johnson didn't start pitching regularly for Kansas City until late July. He went 9-10 with a 3.26 ERA and followed that up with a 17-17 showing in 1915 and a 2.75 ERA. He spent another three years in the Pacific Coast League before calling it a career. Concerns about alcoholism proved to be founded as he had several run-ins with the law and abandoned his wife. On June 12, a "drunk and belligerent" Johnson was shot to death in Des Moines, Iowa, over a gambling dispute.[14] He was 36.

SOURCES

In addition to the sources cited in the Notes, the author also accessed Retrosheet.org, Baseball-Reference.com, and SABR.org.

NOTES

1   Sam Weller, "Chicago Welcomes Feds, Who Triumph Over Packers, 9-1," *Chicago Tribune*, April 24, 1914: 15.

2   Ibid.

3   Ibid.

4   Ibid.

5   Ibid.

6   Ibid.

7   Thom Karmik, "'Chief' Johnson and the 'Winnebago Ban,'" baseballhistorydaily.com/2012/08/23/chief-johnson-and-the-winnebago-ban/, accessed June 11, 2017.

8   "Giants Picked Off Bases in Fast Plays," *New York Times*, May 9, 1913: 9.

9   Thom Karmik, "More 'Chief' Johnson," baseballhistorydaily.com/tag/george-johnson/, accessed June 11, 2017.

10 "Packers Lose Johnson," *Ottawa* (Kansas) *Daily Republic*, April 24, 1914: 6.

11 Baseball-Reference.com and Retrosheet.org have Johnson allowing four runs, but based on newspaper reports, that's impossible. Every report found had him being served papers and removed from the game before the third inning, at which time the Chi-Feds had three runs. They scored their fourth run in the third, but Sam Weller of the *Chicago Tribune* has Dwight Stone starting the third inning and allowing the fourth run, not Johnson. His account includes a play-by-play of every run scored and I have every reason to believe it's accurate.

12 Weller, "Chicago Welcomes Feds, Who Triumph Over Packers, 9-1," *Chicago Tribune*, April 24, 1914: 16.

13 Ibid.

14 "Grand Jury to Probe Death of Chief Johnson," *Des Moines Register*, June 16, 1922: 3.

WHALES CLINCH FEDERAL LEAGUE TITLE

OCTOBER 3, 1915
CHICAGO WHALES 3, PITTSBURGH REBELS 0
(7 INNINGS, GAME TWO OF DOUBLEHEADER)

By Mark S. Sternman

A REBEL WITHOUT A GLOVE OF GLUE allowed the Chicago Whales to eke out the second and final title in the truncated two-year history of the Federal League. By rebuffing the Pittsburgh Rebels 3-0 in the second game of a doubleheader halted by darkness after 6½ innings on the last day of the season, the Whales won the crown by one one-thousandth of a percentage point.

With the triumph, Joe Tinker became the last of the "trio of bear cubs … fleeter than birds" to lead his team to a title. Frank Chance had managed the Cubs to NL pennants in 1906, 1907, 1908, and 1910. Johnny Evers had captained the Braves to a 1914 World Series win. Going into the 1915 season, Tinker had a record of five games under .500 as a manager after heading the Reds in 1913 (64-89) and the Chi-Feds (the first nickname of the Chicago Federal League entry) in 1914 (87-67).

The Whales and the Rebels closed the 1915 season by playing six games against each other in two cities in five days. The first four games would take place in Pittsburgh. When the series began, three teams remained in contention:

Pittsburgh	84	63	.571	--
St. Louis	85	65	.567	0.5
Chicago	82	64	.562	1.5

Chicago beat Pittsburgh 6-3 on September 29 to slip into second place. The Rebels rebounded to tip the Whales 8-4 and send Chicago back to third place on September 30. As a result of rain on October 1, the season would come down to a pair of doubleheaders,

the first in Pittsburgh on October 2 and the second in Chicago on October 3.

With a sweep in Pittsburgh, the Whales went from third to first with one day to go. The events in Pittsburgh generated considerable excitement in Chicago: "Even before the report of the Whales' double victory ticked over the wires … [Chicago] President Charles H. Weeghman sent out letters to … friends inviting them to be present at Whales park today to see Tinker's boys win the pennant. Secretary Williams … was making preparations to handle the largest crowd in the history of the north side park."[1]

The preparations proved necessary. In a "spectacular battle"[2] in front of a sold-out crowd that filled the elevated trains, the streets, and even parts of the playing field, Chicago took the title thanks to a two-hitter by Bill Bailey, a Whale-come-lately, acquired from the Baltimore Terrapins on September 14. Having staggered to a 3-18 record for the 1910 St. Louis Browns, Bailey did little better for Baltimore five years later with a 6-19 record. But wearing the duds of the Whales, he surged to a 3-1 mark, with all three wins coming by shutout. A "fortunate addition to the Whale forces,"[3] Bailey had three whitewashings in five games started for Chicago; over the rest of his career, he had just five shutouts in 112 games started.

Elmer Knetzer had received credit for the victory in the opener of the doubleheader thanks to three innings of one-hit relief. Knetzer improved to 18-14 as the Rebels rallied to sink the Whales 5-4 in 11 innings. Center fielder-manager Rebel Oakes, from whom Pittsburgh took its name, tapped the right-handed Knetzer to start the nightcap although a newspaper brief from the prior day had indicated that the southpaw Frank Allen would start instead.[4] Going into the final game, Allen had a 2-2 record against Chicago in 1915, while Knetzer was 1-3 following his relief effort earlier in the day.

Through five innings, the teams combined to place just one man in scoring position. In the third, Chicago shortstop Mickey Doolin, also picked up by the Whales from the Terps in September, singled and stole second base but did not advance beyond that bag.

Doolin started the triumphant rally in the sixth with a second single. Eschewing a steal attempt this time, Doolin went to second on Bailey's sacrifice. Leadoff man Rollie Zeider grounded out, pushing Doolin to third.

At this point in the contest, Knetzer had held Chicago scoreless for 8⅔ innings that, yielding just four hits in the process, but to end the inning he had a big obstacle to overcome in Max Flack, the right fielder for the Whales who would finish the 1915 season with a .314 batting average, tied for the third-highest mark in the Federal League.

"Knetzer worked the count to two and two … then Max caught one on the nose and drove a terrific loft to right center," the *Chicago Tribune* reported. "Oakes and [Cy] Rheam dashed madly after the ball and the Rebel did manage to get his hands on it, but the sphere hopped out and into the crowd for two bases, driving in … the one run necessary."[5]

Dutch Zwilling followed Flack's 20th double of the season with a two-bagger of his own. The hit drove in Flack and gave Zwilling his 94th RBI of the campaign, which would allow him to edge out Ed Konetchy of the Rebels (93) for the Federal League's final RBI crown.

Art Wilson's bloop scored Zwilling to push the Chicago lead to 3-0. Charlie Pechous followed with a single, meaning that the Whales had four consecutive hits off Knetzer after getting only four

off him over his prior 8⅔ innings. Baseball is indeed a funny game.

Too late, Oakes opted to replace Knetzer with Allen, who retired Les Mann on a popout to Konetchy.

Bailey set down Pittsburgh in the seventh before play ceased. "Before the second game started, Umpire Bill Brennan asked the press box the exact minute of sundown" according to the *Tribune*. "It was 5:24, and apparently Brennan warned both clubs he would call the game at that precise moment, for all the athletes understood the battle was over after Pittsburgh's seventh. The watches showed 5:25 when the last putout was made."[6]

Had Oakes held on to the ball, the game likely could have ended in a scoreless tie. In that case, Pittsburgh would have won the crown with the final standings looking like this:

Pittsburgh	86	66	.566	--
St. Louis	87	67	.565	--
Chicago	85	66	.563	0.5

The Flack swat in the nick of time saved the Chicago nine as the Whales won the 1915 FL title[7] by the slimmest of margins:

Chicago	86	66	.566	--
St. Louis	87	67	.565	--
Pittsburgh	86	67	.562	0.5

SOURCES

In addition to the sources cited in the Notes, the author also accessed Retrosheet.org, Baseball-Reference.com, and SABR.org.

NOTES

1 This quotation comes from an article in a box with neither author nor headline on the front page of the sports section of the *Chicago Sunday Tribune*, October 3, 1915. Tinker "enjoyed great success as player-manager of the Chicago Whales. Playing in their brand-new ballpark, Weeghman Field, the Whales finished a close second in 1914 and won the Federal

James A. Gilmore (left), president of the Federal League, and Charles Weeghman, founder of the Chicago Whales. Weeghman built Wrigley Field, which was originally called Weeghman Park, and bought the Cubs in 1916 when the Federal League disbanded after two seasons.

League pennant the following year, *outdrawing the Cubs in both seasons.*" Lenny Jacobsen, "Joe Tinker," sabr.org/bioproj/person/bc0df648 (emphasis added).

2   J.J. Alcock, "Whales Win Pennant as 34,000 Fans Cheer," *Chicago Tribune*, October 4, 1915: 13.

3   Ibid.

4   "Notes of the Whales," *Chicago Sunday Tribune*, October 3, 1915.

5   Alcock. Presumably the reference to the crowd was to spectators on the field rather than on the other side of the fence, which would have given Flack a homer rather than a ground-rule double. Perhaps the proximity of the large crowd affected Oakes's ability to catch the ball. "Oakes took after the drive, tracking the ball in the dusk, and headed towards the roped-in standing crowd along the perimeter of the outfield. For a costly moment, just short of the standees, he took his eye off the ball's flight, and it 'struck his glove and bounded out.'" Phil Williams, "Rebel Oakes," sabr.org/bioproj/person/37539897.

6   "Notes of the Whales," *Chicago Tribune*, October 4, 1915: 13.

7   For a closer look at the 1915 Chicago Whales, see Mark S. Sternman, "The Last Best Day: When Chicago Had Three First-Place Teams," available at sabr.org/research/last-best-day-when-chicago-had-three-first-place-teams.

FIRST CUBS GAME AT WRIGLEY FIELD

APRIL 20, 1916
CHICAGO CUBS 7, CINCINNATI REDS 6
(11 INNINGS)

By Bob LeMoine

During the 2017 baseball season, the Chicago Cubs surpassed 8,000 regular-season games played at Wrigley Field. The season included the raising of the team's first World Series championship gained while calling Wrigley Field home. A century earlier, the Cubs played their first game at Wrigley (then called Weeghman Park), to a packed Chicago crowd that couldn't wait to see their new Cubs. The fans have flocked to that "nice little place on the north side"[1] ever since. This is the story of that very first game, on April 20, 1916, when James Crusinberry of the *Chicago Tribune* observed that it was "quite convincing that the Cubs have found a welcome to the north side."[2]

Crusinberry described the "newness and a curiosity of things" that characterized the day. "It was the first time many of the players and doubtless many of the fans had ever seen the north side ball park." Weeghman Park had been around since 1914, when it was home to the Chicago Federals, later named the Whales, of the short-lived Federal League. When the Federal League disbanded, owner Charles Weeghman coaxed the National League Cubs to his steel and concrete park at 1060 West Addison Street. "They seemed to have no trouble finding it," Crusinberry wrote,[3] and fans have found their way ever since. The estimated 20,000 spectators started flooding in from noon until game time at 3 P.M. A "gang of carpenters"[4] had constructed a row of seats on the field in front of the grandstand, and "a double row of benches circled the outfield."[5]

A mile-long parade stretched from downtown to the ballpark with every car bearing a banner. More than 200 Cincinnati fans made the journey north, with Reds President Garry Herrmann part of the caravan, and they participated in the parade as well.[6] A half-dozen bands performed, some playing even when Judge Scully was giving opening remarks (which few could hear). Explosions were heard in center field when the American flag was raised. A black bear was led to home plate by "expert" Cy De Vry of the Lincoln Park Zoo and performed tricks for the crowd.[7] Fans were, as they would for decades to come, watching the game from the rooftops across the street.[8]

The world was at war, and the United States teetered on the brink of joining it. President Woodrow Wilson had just given an ultimatum to Germany's Kaiser Wilhelm II to stop its submarine warfare or suffer "a severance of diplomatic relations," wrote the *Tribune*, its headline reading "Final Word to Kaiser. Nation Awaits Berlin's Reply."[9] But the world was on hold for at least a day in Chicago. "Whatever the Kaiser has to say to Woodrow Wilson today," wrote Crusinberry on the eve of Opening Day, "doesn't go on the north side in Chicago, because this is the day when the new Cubs have their grand opening at Weeghman Park."[10]

Claude Hendrix, a six-year veteran, was taking the hill for Chicago. Hendrix had dropped a 4-3 decision in Cincinnati on Opening Day, six days earlier. Hendrix was 87-56 lifetime. He was opposed by Pete

Schneider in a return matchup from Opening Day. Schneider, in his third season, had lasted only three innings on Opening Day and took a no-decision. Hank O'Day and Mal Eason were the umpires.

The Reds wasted no time as Red Killefer laced a single to left on the first pitch of the game. Buck Herzog sacrificed him to second. After a fly out by Hal Chase, Hendrix walked and back-to-back Texas Leaguers over second scored the two runners. Cincinnati led 2-0.

Chicago tied the score in its half of the first. Cy Williams singled to right, sending Max Flack to third with Williams taking second on the throw. Schneider caught the relay to third and in his haste to nab Williams, threw the ball into right field. Flack scored and Williams went to third. Vic Saier's infield single scored Williams.

Chicago took the lead in the fourth when William Fischer doubled with two out and scored on Steve Yerkes's single. The Reds rallied to take the lead back in the fifth when Cubs shortstop Eddie Mulligan booted a couple of grounders and two runners scored on Herzog's single. Cincinnati led 4-3. They extended the lead to 5-3 in the sixth on a home run by Johnny Beall "over the right wall and clear across Sheffield Avenue on the front porch of a flat building."[11] Fischer of the Cubs was robbed of a hit in the bottom of the sixth when Tommy Griffith "raced to the foul line and stabbed a line drive with one hand just before the ball hit the earth."[12]

Hendrix lasted until he got into a bases-loaded jam in the seventh. Manager Joe Tinker removed him for Tom Seaton, who struck out Baldy Louden to end the threat. In the top of the eighth, Jimmy Lavender allowed a walk and singles by Killefer, Herzog, and Chase to add an insurance run for the Reds, who now led 6-3.

Chicago fans often learned over the next 100 years that the Cubs were never out of a game, so it is appropriate that they would play come-from-behind baseball in their inaugural game at their new home. In the eighth, Saier doubled, and a single by Mickey Doolan (who had replaced Mulligan at shortstop) drove Schneider from the game. Fred Toney came in

from the bullpen and yielded run-scoring singles to Fischer and pinch-hitter Jimmy Archer as the Cubs cut the lead to 6-5.

Limb McKenry came in to pitch for the Reds in the ninth. Flack led off with a double. Williams sacrificed him to third and Heinie Zimmerman tied the game with a double. In the *Cincinnati Enquirer* version by Jack Ryder, Reds outfielders would have caught these doubles "if the seats had been out of the way."[13] The ground rules, "which allowed only two bases on a hit into the slim crowd that surrounded the outfield," were to blame, Ryder wrote. "Two or three of the Cub doubles would have been caught on an open field, while a couple of Red long boys would have gone for three bases under normal conditions."[14] Left-hander Al Schulz was summoned from the bullpen to prevent further damage. The game remained tied through the 10th.

With one out in the Cubs' 11th, Williams "poled one into the right field crowd"[15] for a double, and Zimmerman was walked intentionally. Williams scored the winning run on Saier's line-drive single over second base just after 6 P.M.

The Cubs had a memorable win on Opening Day, their first in the history of Weeghman Park/ Wrigley Field. It was probably accurate reporting by Crusinberry that it was the "biggest and noisiest" Opening Day in Cubs history to that point.[16] Gene Packard picked up the victory with three scoreless innings in relief, while Schulz took the loss.

The extra seats were not actually needed but "a straggling hundred or two of rooters were allowed to file out there and sit down, though there was plenty of room in the stands," the *Cincinnati Enquirer* griped. "But for these obstructions, which were quite unnecessary, the Reds would have won the game handily."[17]

The memorable first game was also witnessed by a man who would see thousands of others over the next 59 years. Pat Pieper became the Cubs' public-address announcer, a position he held until his death in 1974. Before the days of a microphone, Pieper called out the starting lineups with a megaphone. "Carrying that megaphone (it weighed 14 pounds) and walking

Fresh off two seasons with 20 victories for the Kansas City Packers in the Federal League, Gene Packard earned the victory in the Cubs' first game at Weeghman Park. In eight major-league seasons, he went 85-69, including 10-6 as a swingman for the North Siders in 1916.

up and down in front of the stands could really take something out of you," Pieper said decades later. "A lot of times I lost five or six pounds during a game."[18]

On that day he welcomed Cubs fans to their new home on the north side, and was part of a tradition that continues to this day.

SOURCES

In addition to the sources cited in the Notes, the author also accessed Retrosheet.org, Baseball-Reference.com, SABR.org, and *The Sporting News* archive via Paper of Record.

NOTES

1   George F. Will, *A Nice Little Place on the North Side: Wrigley Field at One Hundred* (New York: Crown Archetype, 2014).

2   James Crusinberry, "Cubs Beat Reds, 7-6, in 11th, Before 20,000 Fans," *Chicago Tribune*, April 21, 1916: 19.

3   Ibid.

4   Crusinberry, "Army of Fans Awaits Call to Greet Cubs," *Chicago Tribune*, April 20, 1916: 15.

5   Crusinberry, "Cubs Beat Reds."

6   "Cincinnati Fans at Opener Today," *Chicago Tribune*, April 20, 1916: 15; "Notes of Cubs' Opener," *Chicago Tribune*, April 21, 1916: 19.

7   "Notes of Cubs' Opener."

8   Thomas F. Scully (1870-1919) was a Cook County (Illinois) judge. See "Two Chicago Judges Taken by Death," *Chicago Tribune*, September 12, 1919: 1. The *Chicago Tribune* reported that "several hundred snipers saw the game from the roofs and windows of the flat buildings across the street. See Cruisenberry, "Cubs Beat Reds."

9   Page One of the *Chicago Tribune*, April 20, 1916.

10 Crusinberry, "Army of Fans."

11 Crusinberry, "Cubs Beat Reds."

12 "Notes of Cubs' Opener."

13 "Notes of the Game," *Cincinnati Enquirer*, April 21, 1916: 6.

14 Jack Ryder, "Sad Day," *Cincinnati Enquirer*, April 21, 1916: 6.

15 "Cubs Beat Reds."

16 Ibid.

17 "Notes of the Game.," *Cincinnati Enquirer*.

18 "Frank (Pat) Pieper," *The Sporting News*, November 9, 1974: 54.

FRED TONEY DEFEATS HIPPO VAUGHN IN EPIC DUEL

MAY 2, 1917
CINCINNATI REDS 1, CHICAGO CUBS 0

By Mike Lynch

ON MAY 2, 1917 THE CINCINNATI REDS and Chicago Cubs squared off at Chicago's Weeghman Park for the first game of a four-game series. At 10-7 the Cubs sat in second place, only a half-game back of the eventual National League champion New York Giants. The Reds were in sixth place with a mark of 9-10, but were only 2½ games off the pace in the still young season.

On the mound for the Reds was Fred Toney, a big, powerful right-hander known for his strength and arsenal of pitches.[1] The Tennessee native began his pro career with Winchester of the Blue Grass League in 1908 and quickly established himself as a top hurler, winning 45 games in 1909-1910, including a 17-inning no-hitter against Lexington on May 10, 1909, in which he fanned 19 batters.

Toney made his major-league debut with the Cubs on April 15, 1911, but it wasn't until he was claimed off waivers by the Reds in 1915 that he finally blossomed, going 17-6 with a 1.58 ERA that was second best in the NL. Only Grover Cleveland Alexander had a better ERA than Toney's 1.98 in 1915-1916, and he was one of the circuit's best pitchers again in 1917, going 4-1 with a 2.30 ERA prior to the May 2 tilt.

His mound opponent was Jim "Hippo" Vaughn, a 6-foot-4 left-handed behemoth known for his hard fastball and competitiveness.[2] Vaughn's pro career began a year before Toney's, in 1907 with Corsicana of the North Texas League, and he made his major-league debut with the New York Yankees on June 19, 1908.

But, like Toney, it took a change of scenery before Vaughn became a consistent winner; from 1913, his first season with the Cubs, until 1920, his last winning season, Vaughn won 148 games and posted a 2.14 ERA, second in the NL to Alexander over that period. On May 2 Vaughn was 3-1 with a 2.25 ERA and had just beaten the Reds on April 25, striking out a season-high 11 batters in a 4-2 complete-game victory.

Conditions were less than favorable for a ballgame. It was cold and blustery as a stiff breeze blew off Lake Michigan, and the field was "soggy and slow" from recent rains.[3] Jack Ryder of the *Cincinnati Enquirer* reported that only 2,500 brave souls were there to witness baseball history, over 2,000 less than average for Weeghman Park that year.[4]

Third baseman Heinie Groh led off the game for the Reds and fanned, then shortstop Larry Kopf grounded out. Greasy Neale, Cincinnati's regular left fielder who was in center to fill in for an injured Edd Roush, belted a long drive to center field, but Cy Williams corralled it for the third out of the inning. It would be the only Cincinnati ball to leave the infield for the next nine innings. Toney retired Rolly Zeider, Harry Wolter, and Larry Doyle in order to send the game to the second.

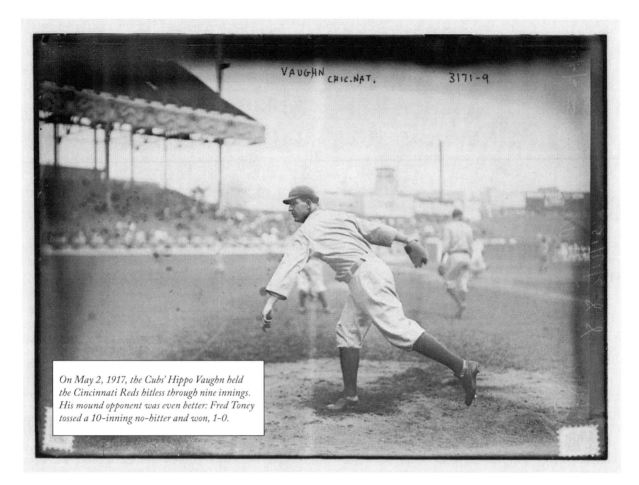

VAUGHN CHIC.NAT, 3171-9

On May 2, 1917, the Cubs' Hippo Vaughn held the Cincinnati Reds hitless through nine innings. His mound opponent was even better: Fred Toney tossed a 10-inning no-hitter and won, 1-0.

Toney said later that he didn't like the conditions and didn't have his usual stuff, but he continued to baffle Cubs batters with his assortment of pitches.[5] Vaughn set down Hal Chase, Jim Thorpe, and second baseman Dave Shean in order in the second. Toney ran into a spot of trouble in his half, but worked out of a jam. Fred Merkle led off with a hot liner that was speared by Groh, Williams walked with one out and advanced to second on a grounder to third, but Art Wilson, the Cubs backstop, popped out to Kopf to end the threat. It would be the only time a Cub reached second.

Both pitchers easily retired the side in the third, then Vaughn had to escape a jam of his own when he walked Groh to lead off the fourth. Kopf bounded into a double play to clear the bases, but Zeider muffed Neale's grounder to give the Reds a runner on first with two outs. Neale attempted to steal second, but was gunned down by Wilson to end the frame.

Toney had no issues in the bottom of the fourth, and Vaughn narrowly escaped with his no-hitter intact when Thorpe clubbed a long liner down the left-field line that landed just foul. But the big southpaw set the Reds down again without allowing a hit. Williams drew another free pass in the bottom of the fifth, Les Mann lined out to left fielder Manuel Cueto, then Wilson hit a pop fly to Shean, who purposely dropped the ball in hopes of turning a double play. He retired Williams at second but Wilson was safe at first. Cubs third sacker Charlie Deal smacked a long fly to center, but Neale made a nifty running catch to retire the side.

Through six innings neither team had sniffed a hit or gotten past second base. The fans sensed what was happening and began rooting for both pitchers.[6]

Vaughn took the hill for the seventh and ran the count on Groh to 1-and-2 before Groh snapped and gave home-plate umpire Al Orth his unsolicited opinion about Orth's strike zone. Groh was ejected and replaced by Gus Getz, who walked in Groh's stead. But Kopf grounded into his second double play of the game, and Vaughn easily retired Neale. Toney dispatched the Cubs again in the bottom of the seventh, and Vaughn did the same to the Reds in the top of the eighth.

It was during the bottom of the eighth that Vaughn realized he was throwing a no-hitter.[7] The Cubs lefty was so focused on keeping the game "well in hand" that he hadn't realized he was only one inning away from tossing his first no-hitter. Toney was of the same mindset, just trying to keep the Cubs off the scoreboard until his boys finally broke through against Vaughn.[8]

Vaughn dispatched the Reds in the ninth, then Toney set down the Cubs in order and the game went into extra frames with both sides still without a hit. Getz led off the top of the 10th and skied a foul pop to Wilson for the first out. That brought up Larry Kopf, who had grounded out three times, including twice into rally-killing double plays. By his own admission Vaughn "grew careless" and took one chance too many.[9]

Kopf shot a drive between Doyle and Merkle, the latter making a diving effort to no avail. It was a clean hit and the double no-hitter was over. Though the hometown throng was disappointed, the fans gave Kopf a nice ovation for ending Vaughn's masterpiece. Neale poked a fly ball to Williams for out number two and it looked as if Vaughn would escape with his shutout intact, but Williams misplayed Chase's line drive and suddenly there were Reds at first and third with two outs.[10] Chase stole second while Wilson wisely held the ball rather than risk Kopf scoring on a throw.

With two on and two out, Jim Thorpe topped a short grounder in front of the plate that rolled up the third-base line. Vaughn went after it, figuring Deal wouldn't be able to race in from third in time to record the out. He also knew he wouldn't get

Thorpe, a former Olympic gold medalist, at first base, so he tried to scoop the ball to Art Wilson in an effort to nab Kopf at the plate.

Kopf slid safely past Wilson, who then dropped the ball. Chase attempted to score as well, but Wilson recovered in time to tag him out and end the inning.[11] The Reds went up 1-0 and Toney needed only three outs to complete his no-hitter. He began the bottom of the 10th by fanning Larry Doyle. Up stepped Fred Merkle, the Cubs' cleanup hitter, and he delivered a blow to left that looked as though it would not only end Toney's no-hit bid, but also tie the score. "It looked like a home run into the left bleachers," wrote the *Commercial Tribune*, "but little Mr. Cueto of Cuba dashed back until he hit the wall and then speared the ball over his head."[12]

With two outs and a near miss it was up to Cy Williams to keep the Cubs alive. Williams wasn't the hitter he'd been in 1916 when he led the National League in home runs, but he was still dangerous. In fact, he showed how dangerous he was when he fouled off two two-strike pitches, including a long line drive down the right-field line that landed a foot foul. Toney threw another ball to run the count full and some speculated he was going to walk Williams again to face the less threatening Leslie Mann, but he came back with a side-arm curve and Williams swung and missed to complete Toney's historic no-hitter.

Never before or since have two pitchers thrown nine no-hit innings in the same contest.

NOTES

1   ourgame.mlblogs.com/2012/02/04/. "He threw a variety of stuff," wrote John Thorn, Major League Baseball's official historian, "spitballs, fastballs, curves, and an overhand sinker that faded away from left-handed batters just as [Christy Mathewson's] 'fadeaway,' or screwball, once had."

2   Bill James and Rob Neyer, *The Neyer/James Guide to Pitchers: An Historical Compendium of Pitching, Pitchers, and Pitches* (New York: Fireside, 2004), 411-412. "Big Jim Vaughn used to pitch the particular kind of ball a batter liked best just to show him that he couldn't hit it," Pete Alexander told *Baseball Magazine* in 1925, as reported by Neyer/James.

3   "The weather was bitterly cold," wrote Jack Ryder of the *Cincinnati Enquirer*, "and it was a wonder that even so many fans turned out to shiver in the arctic breezes off the lake," May 3, 1917.

4   Baseball-Reference.com and Retrosheet.org list that day's attendance at 3,500; the Cubs averaged 4,678 fans per game at Weeghman Park in 1917.

5   "It was rather a cold day and I was not feeling in my best form when the game started," Toney said. "I didn't have so much stuff as I sometimes do for the first six innings." Vaughn concurred. "The boys said [Toney] didn't seem to have as much on the ball as usual," *Baseball Magazine*, July 1917.

6   "Toney and Vaughn were both in magnificent form," wrote Ryder, "working with the precision of a machine. As round after round went by without either side getting the suspicion of a safety the crowd became wildly excited, urging on both the great pitchers to continue their wonderful work," Jack Ryder, *Cincinnati Enquirer*, May 3, 1917.

7   "I was sitting on the bench and happened to make a remark that we weren't hitting Toney very much," Vaughn told *Baseball Magazine*. "One of the fellows assented to this and then added that [the Reds] weren't hitting me very much either. Then I recalled that they hadn't made a safe hit off my delivery," *Baseball Magazine*, July 1917.

8   "I didn't fully realize it was a no-hit game until the ninth inning," Toney explained later. "Then I took time to get my breath and my bearings and made up my mind to put all I had on whatever other balls I pitched." Ibid.

9   "I had been putting a fastball over the plate for my first strike right along and put over one too many," Vaughn explained. Ibid.

10   Rich Coberly, *The No-Hit Hall of Fame: No-Hitters of the 20th Century* (Newport Beach, California: Triple Play Publications, 1985), 48. "Cy scarcely had to move," reported the *Cincinnati Commercial Tribune*, per Coberly's book, "but if he had advanced two steps he could have taken it in front of his belt buckle. Instead, he had to catch it at his ankles, and he muffed the ball."

11   *Cincinnati Enquirer*, May 3, 1917. The *Commercial Tribune* reported that Vaughn's toss hit Wilson in the shoulder and that Kopf crashed into the catcher before he scored. Kopf himself told John Thorn that (in Thorn's words) he "stopped dead in his tracks" when he saw Vaughn shovel the ball to Wilson and it was only after he realized that Wilson was frozen with confusion that he continued home to score. "Kopf, seeing Wilson standing there like a zombie as the ball rolled a few steps away, dashed home with the run," wrote Thorn. See Coberly, 48, and ourgame.mlblogs.com/2012/02/04/.

12   Coberly.

TYLER OUTDUELS WATSON IN 21-INNING MARATHON

JULY 17, 1918
CHICAGO CUBS 2, PHILADELPHIA PHILLIES 1

By Gregory H. Wolf

WHEN CHICAGO CUBS HURLER GEORGE "Lefty" Tyler arrived at Weeghman Park for the final game of a four-game series against the Philadelphia Phillies, the 28-year-old New Hampshirite probably expected a day off – and for good reason. Acquired in the offseason from the Boston Braves, where he had amassed a 92-92 record in parts of eight seasons, Tyler was only three days removed from the busiest stretch in his career. Over 15 days (June 30-July 14), he had started five times and logged 41⅔ innings, winning thrice to improve his record to 12-5. Ordered by skipper Fred Mitchell to warm up with all of the pitchers, except ace Hippo Vaughn, scheduled to start the following day, Tyler could not have imagined that he was on the precipice of a test of endurance that few pitchers had ever experienced.

In the midst of an 18-game homestand, the Cubs (55-25) were cruising to their first pennant since 1910. Leading the New York Giants by six games, the Cubs had won five straight before manager Pat Moran's Phillies swept them in a doubleheader a day earlier. Three years removed from their last pennant, the fourth-place Phillies (37-40) were struggling and looking forward to ending their season-long 25-game road swing and returning the City of Brotherly Love.

The weather in Chicago evoked late spring more than midsummer, resulting in a small crowd on the North Side.[1] Temperatures hovered in the low 60s and the *Philadelphia Inquirer* noted that the "wind [was] blowing straight off the lake," portending a

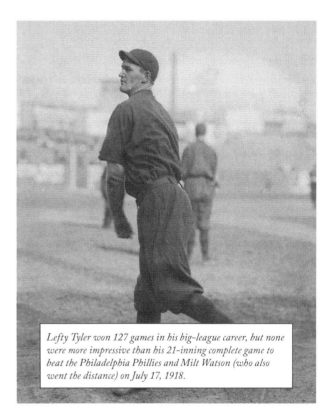

Lefty Tyler won 127 games in his big-league career, but none were more impressive than his 21-inning complete game to beat the Philadelphia Phillies and Milt Watson (who also went the distance) on July 17, 1918.

pitchers' duel in the four-year-old park located less than a mile west of Lake Michigan.[2]

After Tyler set down the Phillies 1-2-3 in the first, the Cubs took their swings at 28-year-old right-handed swingman Milt "Mule" Watson, whom Philadelphia had acquired during spring training from the St. Louis Cardinals. His 4-2 record thus far in 1918 improved his slate to 18-21 in parts of three campaigns. Max Flack led off with a walk, and then scampered to third on Charlie Hollocher's grounder just beyond the reach of first baseman Fred Luderus.

Les Mann's grounder plated Flack for the game's first run. It would be the equivalent of more than two complete regulation games before the Cubs scored again.

Mowing down the Phils, Tyler allowed his first hit, in the third, when Bert Adams singled with one out, and then encountered trouble the next frame. Cy Williams reached safely when shortstop Hollocher fumbled his grounder and moved up a station on Luderus's one-out single. The Phils caught a break when catcher Bill Killefer dropped a third "foul-strike" with Gavvy Cravath at the plate.[3] Given another chance, the NL's most fearsome home-run hitter, en route to pacing the circuit in round-trippers for the fifth time in the last six seasons, lined a two-out single, driving in Williams while Luderus reached third. After Cravath stole second, Tyler fanned Ed Hemingway to end the threat.

The Cubs threatened in the fifth when Killefer led off with a bunt and moved to third on Flack's one-out single, but was left stranded when "hard fate" intervened, wrote the *Inquirer*, and the next two batters were retired.[4]

The contest was unraveled as a classic Dead Ball Era pitchers' duel. Watson held the Cubs hitless from the seventh inning to the 12th;[5] Tyler yielded only five hits through the first 13 frames.[6] As the game wore on, both hurlers faced pressured-packed situations with runners in scoring position. In the 12th, Cravath reached on a two-out walk, Tyler's only free pass of the game, and stole second. Hemingway's hard grounder looked as though it would get by second baseman Zeider, but "Bunions" made what Chicago and Philadelphia papers described as a game-saving barehanded catch and throw to first to end the frame.

The Phillies "played an uphill game all the way," opined the *Philadelphia Public Ledger*, as the Cubs relentlessly attacked Watson.[7] In the 13th, Fred Merkle and Dode Paskert led off with singles, putting Watson on the ropes. Merkle committed a costly boner when he was picked off second by catcher Adams after Charlie Deal missed a bunt. Deal eventually singled, but the Cubs had failed to advance a runner to third with one out. Zeider grounded into the game's only double play to end the frame.

"Tyler's hardest innings," noted sportswriter I.E. Sanborn of the *Chicago Tribune*, were the 15th and 16th when great defense saved the game.[8] Left-fielder Les Mann made a running catch of Cravath's deep fly, robbing the slugger of extra bases, for the first out of the 15th. After Hemingway singled and moved to third on Adams's single, Tyler retired the next two batters. In the 16th, Irish Meusel's two-out smash with Milt Stock on second "threatened to hit the wall in deep right," wrote Sanborn, but Flack made a running stab with his shoulder against wall.[9]

Sandwiched between those scoring chances was the Cubs' best opportunity to end the game. Mann and Merkle reached with one-out singles in the 15th and moved up a station on Watson's balk. Watson intentionally passed Paskert to load the bases. With the infield drawn in, Deal hit a grounder and Adams tagged out Mann at the plate. Watson retired Zeider for the third out.

In the 16th, umpires alerted both teams that the game would be called at 7 P.M. so that the Phillies could catch their 8 P.M. train to Pittsburgh.[10] Neither Watson nor Tyler paid attention to that pronouncement and seemed to catch a second wind. Chicago squandered a chance to end the game in the 19th when Luderus snared Mann's two-out hot liner with Flack and Hollocher on base via singles.

The game was in rarefied territory as the 21st inning got underway with Tyler and Watson still battling. In only one other game in NL history had both starters logged at least 20 innings. That occurred precisely four years earlier when the Giants' Rube Marquard outlasted the Pittsburgh Pirates' Babe Adams in 21 innings, 3-1, at Forbes Field. It had happened once in the AL when Philadelphia rookie Jack Coombs and Boston's Joe Harris each went the distance in the Athletics' 4-1 victory in 24 innings over the Americans on September 1, 1906.[11]

Future Hall of Famer Dave Bancroft led off the 21st with a single, after which the Phils caught a break. According to the *Tribune*, Williams hit a high chopper toward Merkle, who "knocked it down"; however, Tyler failed to cover first, wasting a double-play opportunity.[12] Stock's deep fly to right field enabled Bancroft to reach third, where he was stranded.

As the 7 P.M. deadline rapidly approached, the Cubs were the recipients of Dame Fortune's blessings. Mitchell called on Turner Barber, mired in an 8-for-52 season-long slump, to pinch-hit for Zeider, hitless in eight at-bats in the game. Barber reached on a swinging bunt, when according to the *Public Ledger*, Watson slipped and fell and was unable to reach the ball.[13] The Cubs' luck, however, was just starting. Killefer attempted to bunt, but was struck on his trousers by a ball. Pinch-hitting for Tyler, rookie Bill McCabe, who had hit safely in only four of 27 at-bats, attempted to sacrifice. The unintentional result was a perfect bunt to the third-base side to load the bases. The ball "started foul, hit a lump of dirt, and rolled back into the diamond," wrote Sanborn.[14] Flack's fifth hit drove in Barber for the game-winner, ending the contest in approximately four hours.[15]

Chicago and Philadelphia newspapers were quick to praise both teams' excellent fielding, especially that of shortstops Bancroft and Zeider, who handled flawlessly 19 and 12 chances respectively, and keystone sacker Hemingway (15 chances). "Time and time again they chipped in with startling bits of fielding," gushed the *Inquirer*.[16]

The story of the game, however, was the pitchers. "Tyler's exhibition was remarkable," opined the *Public Ledger*. "He pitched beautifully all day and time and time again pitched himself out of the hole by sheer nerve."[17] He faced 77 batters, yielding 13 hits and walking one while fanning eight. His only run was unearned. Tyler's heroic effort also marked the last of 16 times that he hurled at least 10 innings in a game. Watson, who was "in more dangerous positions" throughout the afternoon, continued the *Ledger*, was the hard-luck loser. He gave up 19 hits, walked four (two intentionally), whiffed five, and faced 82 batters. Only two of the game's 32 hits went for extra bases; Hemingway and Hollocher doubled for their respective clubs. The Cubs-Phillies 21-inning

game was one shy of the then NL record, set on August 22, 1917, when the Brooklyn Robins beat the Pirates, 6-5;[18] the aforementioned Boston-Philadelphia game was, at the time, the longest game in big-league history.

SOURCES

In addition to the sources cited in the Notes, the author also accessed Retrosheet.org, Baseball-Reference.com, SABR.org, and *The Sporting News* archive via Paper of Record.

NOTES

1   No attendance figure for the game is available. The "size of the crowd was down, but it was an enthusiastic one," was noted in "Cubs Defeat Phils in 21 Inning Game," *Philadelphia Inquirer*, July 18, 1918: 12. The Cubs average of 4,558 spectators per game in 1919 led the NL.

2   "Cubs Defeat Phils in 21 Inning Game."

3   "Phillies Open at Pittsburg[h]," *Evening Public Ledger*, July 18, 1918: 13.

4   "Cubs Defeat Phils in 21 Inning Game."

5   "Phillies Open at Pittsburg[h]."

6   I.E. Sanborn, "Cubs Emerge Winners After Battle of 21 Innings, 2-1," *Chicago Tribune*, July 18, 1918: 9.

7   "Phillies Open at Pittsburg[h]."

8   Sanborn.

9   Ibid.

10 "Cubs Defeat Phils in 21 Inning Game."

11 "Athletics Win 24-Inning Game From Bostonians," *Philadelphia Inquirer*, September 2, 1906: 1, 15.

12 Sanborn.

13 "Phillies Open at Pittsburg[h]."

14 Sanborn.

15 Box scores did not provide the length of the game. The *Public Ledger* noted that the game was "[O]ne of the fastest. Twenty-One full innings were squeezed into four hours. ..."

16 "Cubs Defeat Phils in 21 Inning Game."

17 "Phillies Open at Pittsburg[h]."

18 The Dodgers victory is noteworthy. It was their fourth consecutive extra-inning game (in five days). The others lasted 14, 10, and 13 innings for a total of 59 innings. Brooklyn went 1-2-1 in those contests.

CUBS CLINCH FIFTH PENNANT IN 13 YEARS WITH DOUBLEHEADER SWEEP

AUGUST 24, 1918
CHICAGO CUBS 3, BROOKLYN ROBINS 1
(GAME TWO OF DOUBLEHEADER)

By Mike Lynch

ON AUGUST 24, 1918, THE CHICAGO CUBS hosted the fifth-place Brooklyn Robins, who were 24½ games back of first place but had won nine of 15 games against the front-running Cubs. The second-place New York Giants were 10½ games out of first with a little more than a week left in the season and the Cubs were on the verge of clinching their fifth pennant since 1906. The 1918 season was scheduled as usual and teams were expecting to play the same 154-game set they'd been playing since 1904, but that would be interrupted by the United States' entry into World War I.

On April 4, 1917, the US Senate voted in favor of President Woodrow Wilson's request for a declaration of war against Germany. The House agreed two days later and the nation was effectively an entrant into World War I, triggered on June 28, 1914, with the assassination of Austrian Archduke Franz Ferdinand. Two major factors finally helped Wilson convince Americans it was time to aid the Allies against the Central Powers. Germany reneged on an agreement to stop targeting US ships with their submarines, and its foreign minister sent a telegram asking Mexico to join it in the war in return for help regaining territory it lost to the United States in the Mexican-American War.[1]

Thanks to the Selective Service Act, which required men from 21 to 30 to register for military service, and 2 million volunteers, approximately 4.8 million soldiers were sent to Europe to fight the Central Powers. But General Enoch H. Crowder, the judge advocate general of the United States Army, wanted to ensure that every able-bodied man assisted in the war effort, so he issued a "work or fight" order on May 23, 1918, declaring that baseball was a "non-essential occupation," and that baseball players had until July 1 to enlist in the military or get a job in a shipyard or defense plant. If they declined to do either, they would be inducted into the service.[2]

At the time of the announcement, the 1918 season was still young. The Giants had played 30 games, won 23 of them and held a four-game lead over the Cubs; the American League's Boston Red Sox had played 31, won 19 and boasted a two-game edge over the New York Yankees and Cleveland Indians.

In July, Secretary of War Newton D. Baker officially enacted the work-or-fight order and baseball had a problem on its hands. Washington Senators catcher Eddie Ainsmith lost an appeal of his draft eligibility on July 19 and was expected to join the military. Two days later AL President Ban Johnson ordered the league to cease its operations.[3] But two coalitions that included Red Sox owner Harry Frazee, Washington Senators owner Clark Griffith, and all eight National League magnates persuaded Crowder and Baker to allow the season to continue until September 1 with the World Series to be completed by September 15.[4]

By the end of July, the Cubs had taken over first place in the NL, holding a 3½-half-game lead over the Giants, who had the only chance of catching them. The next closest team, the Pittsburgh Pirates, was already 11½ games off the pace and the rest were at least 16½ games back.

By mid-August the Cubs had stretched their lead to six games over the Giants and they extended it to eight with a doubleheader sweep over the Phillies on August 17 and a Giants loss to the Cincinnati Reds. Time was running out on John McGraw's men and the hole was even deeper at the end of play on August 23, when the Giants sat 10½ games off the pace with a little more than a week left in the season.

All the Cubs needed to do to clinch the pennant was take both games of a doubleheader against Brooklyn at Chicago's Weeghman Park on August 24. The first step was easier than it should have been against pitcher Burleigh Grimes, who had won 10 consecutive decisions, including nine starts. But Chicago rolled to a convincing 8-3 win in the first tilt behind a 15-hit attack led by Charlie Picks' three safeties, and a nifty outing by Claude Hendrix, who earned his 19th win against only six losses. The second affair pitted Cubs rookie hurler Speed Martin against veteran right-hander Larry Cheney.

Martin had made his season debut on August 3 and was making only his third start of the season and fifth of his young career. In his first six appearances, three as a reliever, the six-foot righty was brilliant, going 3-1 with a 0.68 ERA, and had just tossed a three-hit shutout against the Boston Braves five days earlier. He also helped secure a 3-2 win over the Giants with an inning of scoreless relief just a day before.

Cheney, on the other hand, was in his seventh full big-league season. Having debuted on September 9, 1911, the spitball artist threw 10 scoreless innings for the Cubs in a cup of coffee before taking the NL by storm in 1912 with a league-leading 26 wins. He won at least 20 games in his first three seasons, going 67-42 from 1912 to 1914, but his days of dominance were all but over by 1918, and he was 11-11 with a slightly-worse-than-league-average 2.83 ERA going into the August 24 contest.

Just as it had in game one, Brooklyn struck first, this time with a run in the top of the third. Catcher Otto Miller doubled, Cheney moved him to third with a sacrifice bunt, and Miller came home on a wild pitch. It could have been worse had Pick not made a "spectacular stab" of Jimmy Johnston's line drive that saved Martin from another base hit.[5] Johnston had also been robbed of a hit in the first game when center fielder Dode Paskert made a nice running grab on a shot destined for extra bases.

Losing a second hit in as many games was too much for Johnston and he lost his composure. "This peeved Jimmy so much," wrote the Chicago Tribune's I.E. Sanborn, "that he threw the ice water pail out of the Robins' dugout and made them all go dry the rest of the day."[6] Unfortunately Brooklyn's bats also went dry and they didn't score the rest of the day, either. Meanwhile, the 32-year-old Cheney was channeling his younger self and had a shutout going until the bottom of the seventh, when the Cubs plated two to take the lead.

Fred Merkle, the former Giant who helped the Cubs win the 1908 NL pennant with a baserunning blunder that earned him the nickname "Bonehead," followed a Paskert out with a free pass, then tied the score at 1-1 on a Pick two-bagger to left. Pick scampered to third on a wild pitch and, after Cheney retired Charlie Deal for the second out, Brooklyn manager Wilbert Robinson ordered an intentional walk to catcher Bill Killefer.

Killefer was a weak-hitting catcher with a .229 career average going into the 1918 season, who was hitting .220 on August 18 before he left the team for a fishing trip near his boyhood home in Paw, Michigan. But he was an outstanding defensive catcher, prompting Sanborn to quip, "If [Killefer] is as good at catching fish as baseballs there are some vacant 'homes' in the depths of Paw Lake."[7]

The Cubs backstop was 1-for-2 with a strikeout against Cheney in his two previous at-bats and the even more anemic Martin was on deck, making Robinson's decision easy. But Killefer spoiled the strategy when he offered at ball four and "pickled"

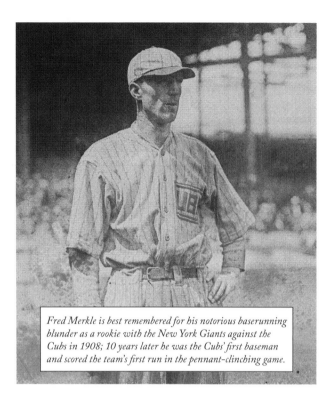

Fred Merkle is best remembered for his notorious baserunning blunder as a rookie with the New York Giants against the Cubs in 1908; 10 years later he was the Cubs' first baseman and scored the team's first run in the pennant-clinching game.

it for a single over second, "driving in the run that would have been enough to win."[8]

Chicago added a run in the bottom of the eighth for good measure and the 3-1 victory earned the Cubs their first pennant since 1910. "As nearly as can be doped out of the tangle produced by the curtailed schedule," waxed Sanborn, "the Cubs drove the ultimate spike into the 1918 National league pennant yesterday. ... The McGrawites cannot play enough games to catch up even if the Cubs lose the rest of their own battles."[9]

Indeed. The Cubs went 84-45 in the abbreviated season and finished 10½ games ahead of the Giants before losing the World Series in six games to the Boston Red Sox.

SOURCES

In addition to the sources listed below, the author also consulted Baseball-Reference.com, Retrosheet.org, and *The Sporting News*.

NOTES

1   US State Department's "Office of the Historian" web page (history.state.gov/milestones/1914-1920/wwi); The 1914 Allies, Russia, France, and Great Britain, were joined by Italy in 1915, Romania in 1916, and the United States in 1917. The Central Powers were originally Germany and Austria-Hungary before they were joined by the Ottoman Empire in 1914 and Bulgaria in 1915.

2   Eugene C. Murdock, *Ban Johnson: Czar of Baseball* (Westport, Conn.: Greenwood Press, 1982), 124; "Baseball May Stop if New Order Stands," *New York Times*, May 24, 1918.

3   J.V. Fitz Gerald, "Baseball's Fate Up to Majors' Meetings," *Washington Post*, July 21, 1918.

4   Michael Lynch, *Harry Frazee, Ban Johnson and the Feud That Nearly Destroyed the American League,* (Jefferson, North Carolina: McFarland, 2008), 51. If the sporting world thought it was immune to the war it was served a heaping dose of reality in mid-July when Lieutenant John W. Overton, a former Yale track star who held the world record in the indoor mile at 4:16, was killed in action in France during the Second Battle of the Marne.

5   I.E. Sanborn, "It's All Over! Flag for Cubs; Land 2 Games," *Chicago Tribune*, August 25, 1918.

6   Ibid.

7   Ibid.

8   Ibid. Recording a hit during an intentional walk was much more common in the Deadball Era than it is today, especially now that pitches aren't even thrown per 2017 rules. But if you're wondering how the fourth ball was close enough to hit, consider that Cheney led the National League in wild pitches six times in nine seasons and walked over 100 men in a season three times, including a league-leading 140 in 1914.

9   Ibid.

OLD PETE NEEDS ONLY 58 MINUTES FOR SHUTOUT

SEPTEMBER 21, 1919
CHICAGO CUBS 3, BOSTON BRAVES 0

By Gregory H. Wolf

IN 2017 A MAJOR-LEAGUE GAME typically lasted more than three hours. Imagine completing one in less than one hour? That's what the Chicago Cubs' Pete Alexander did when he needed just 58 minutes to shut out the Boston Braves on the north side of the Windy City. [Alexander] "figured the game was not worth wasting any time on," sardonically quipped sportswriter James Crusinberry in the *Chicago Tribune*.[1]

When players arrived at Weeghman Park for a Sunday afternoon game to conclude a three-game series, there was little incentive to play other than pride (and the offseason contract) as the season wound down. Skipper Fred Mitchell's Cubs (72-60), in third place, 19½ games behind the front-running Cincinnati Reds, were making their season finale in the six-year-old steel and concrete ballpark, originally built for the Whales of the Federal League, to finish a 14-game homestand. The sixth-place Braves (54-78), whom manager George Stallings had guided to an unlikely World Series title five years earlier, had reached the end of a grueling 18-game road swing, and were playing on an opponent's diamond for the 25th time in their last 28 contests. The Braves could be forgiven for looking forward to their Pullman sleeper coaches on their evening train ride back to the Hub, while the Cubs undoubtedly regretted leaving their homes and the friendly confines to travel to St. Louis and kick off a season-ending road trip.

The Cubs had been widely predicted to capture their second consecutive pennant in 1919, but their season had not unfolded as anticipated. One of the reasons for the disappointments was starting pitcher Grover Cleveland Alexander. Once considered the best hurler in the NL, "Old Pete" had won 190 games in seven campaigns with the Philadelphia Phillies (1911-1917), but had made only three appearances for the Cubs in 1918 before he was called to duty and served on the front lines in the World War. His harrowing experiences in a field artillery unit had left him shellshocked, deaf in one ear from a shrapnel injury, and with a damaged right arm from firing howitzers. He also developed alcoholism and epilepsy. Not in baseball shape as the season started, Alexander struggled and missed four weeks with arm pain. Since his return on July 15, he had looked like the hurler who had won 30 or more in three straight seasons and was victorious in 10 of his last 16 decisions with a 1.49 ERA to improve his slate to 14-11 (1.87). Toeing the rubber for the Beantown nine was right-hander Red Causey (13-6, 3.87 ERA), acquired along with three others on August 1 in a blockbuster trade with the New York Giants for southpaw Art Nehf.

A crowd of 5,000 braved the threatening, dark skies to take in the last Cubs game of the decade. The game emerged as a typical pitchers' duel of the Deadball Era. The Braves squandered a scoring chance in the first when Charlie Pick reached on first baseman Fred Merkle's error with one out and moved to third on Ray Powell's single before Alexander retired the next two batters. The Cubs

In his first full season with the Cubs, Hall of Famer Pete Alexander needed just 58 minutes to throw a complete-game shutout against the Boston Braves. In nine campaigns with the Cubs, Old Pete recorded 128 of his 373 career victories.

also threatened in the first when Charlie Hollocher belted a doubled against the wall in right with one out, followed by Buck Herzog's walk, but could not push a run across.

Both the *Tribune* and *Boston Herald* noted that the players went about their business with alacrity, hurrying to and from their positions between innings, almost as if they were attempting to complete the game in record time.[2] They also declared that it was Alexander's goal to complete in a game in less than an hour. Cubs backstop Bill Killefer, opined Crusinberry, "gave the sign unusually fast and Alex tossed the ball up almost before the sign were given."[3]

While Alexander escaped a triple by Walter Holke in the fourth, Causey had yielded only one hit until Old Pete came within "four feet" of blasting a home run, in the fifth.[4] Powell fielded the carom off the wall in right field and held Alexander to a long single.

After the Braves squandered Tony Boeckel's leadoff single in the sixth, the Cubs got on the board when Merkle reached on a surprise bunt and advanced to third on Turner Barber's double. Up stepped Charlie Deal, whose two-run home run in the first game of the doubleheader the day before accounted for all of the runs in the Cubs' victory. He lined a double to left-center field, driving in both runners.

Employing a bit of "trickery," according to Crusinberry, the Cubs tacked on another run in the eighth.[5] Facing Al Demaree, who had replaced Causey to start the frame, the Cubs loaded the bases on a walk by Hollocher and singles by Herzog and Merkle with no outs. After Barber fanned, Deal hit a short popup to the grass behind second base. Hollocher bluffed a dash home; when keystone sacker Charlie Pick took the bait and hesitated, Hollocher sprinted home, sliding across the plate as Pick's throw sailed high.

Alexander continued heaving the ball over the plate in the ninth, daring the Braves to hit the orb. Powell led off with a double, but was stranded at third when Alexander retired Dixie Carroll to complete the shutout in 58 minutes.

The contest was remarkably swift even in an era when games averaged approximately 1 hour and 58 minutes to complete.[6] Alexander finished with a six-hitter, fanned four and walked none while facing 33 batters. The Cubs collected nine hits. All told, 67 batters came to the plate; stated differently, a player stepped into the batter's box every 52 seconds. On this same day, Sherry Smith of the Brooklyn Robins defeated the Cincinnati Reds, 3-1, in the Queen City in 55 minutes. One week later, on September 28, the New York Giants' Jesse Barnes tossed a complete game against the Philadelphia Phillies in the Polo Grounds in just 51 minutes, in the fastest nine-inning game in major-league history, a record that will presumably never be broken. Remarkably, 70 batters came to the plate in that game; or once every 43.1 seconds, which is about the time between pitches in the contemporary game.

A week later, the 32-year-old Pete Alexander tossed his second consecutive shutout, 2-0, against the Reds to conclude his first full season with the Cubs since his blockbuster trade with a disappointing 16-11 record. However, he led the NL in ERA (1.72) for the fourth time and shutouts (9) for the sixth time. Alexander rebounded in 1920 to win an NL-best 27 games and once again paced the circuit in ERA (1.91), but struggled the rest of his career with alcoholism and the psychological effects of the war. He retired after the 1930 season with a career record of 373-208, including 90 shutouts.

SOURCES

In addition to the sources cited in the Notes, the author also accessed Retrosheet.org, Baseball-Reference.com, and SABR.org.

NOTES

1   James Crusinberry, "Cubs Close the Season with Victory Over Braves, *Chicago Tribune*, September 22, 1919: 15.

2   "Alexander Wastes No Time by Trimming Tribe," *Boston Herald*, September 22, 1919: 10.

3   Crusinberry.

4   "Alexander Wastes No Time by Trimming Tribe."

5   Crusinberry.

6   Data about length of games for the 1919 season is not complete. The average for 1917 was 1:51; for 1920 1:51; between 1910 and 1933, the average length of games fluctuated between 1:51 and 1:59. See baseball-reference.com/leagues/MLB/misc.shtml.

NATIONAL HIGH SCHOOL POWERHOUSES MEET IN THE FRIENDLY CONFINES

JUNE 26, 1920
HIGH SCHOOL OF COMMERCE (NEW YORK CITY) 12
LANE TECHNICAL SCHOOL (CHICAGO) 6

By Alan Cohen

The New York Boys have a 17-year-old boy of 190 pounds on first base who is a regular Babe Ruth. If he gets a high fast one, he'll slam it over the right field wall at the Cubs' Park.

—James Crusinberry, *Chicago Tribune*,
June 19, 1920.[1]

MORE THAN 6,600 FANS ASSEMBLED AT Cubs Park for a contest between the top high-school teams of Chicago and New York and a championship aura prevailed. New York's High School of Commerce had advanced to the New York City championship by defeating Flushing (Queens) High School 7-2 in the semifinals and Commercial (Brooklyn) High School in the finals, 6-5. Lane High School had taken the Chicago championship by defeating rival Englewood High School.

Prior to departing for Chicago from New York's Grand Central Station, the 16 New York players had practiced under the watchful eye of Coach Harry Kane at Brooklyn's Ebbets Field. The entourage going to Chicago included Kane, the players, and the school's director of athletics, A.K. Aldinger.

When they arrived in Chicago, the host team, led by the school band, accompanied them on a parade through the city to their hotel. While in Chicago the boys from Commerce stayed at the Hotel Sherman. Sponsors of the event included the *Chicago Tribune*,

the *New York Daily News* and William Veeck Sr., president of the Chicago Cubs.

At Wrigley, the Lane team was led on to the field by their school's marching band and throughout the game music was provided by Jack Bramhall's jazz band. The partisan locals were urged on in the cheering by three of Lane's top cheerleaders, and taking the field to perform was the famous vaudevillian jazz dancer Joe Frisco, known for, among other things, telling his audiences, "Don't applaud, folks, just throw money."

Commerce scored three first-inning runs off Tom Walsh to take the early lead but Lane tied things up in the third inning. Commerce regained the lead with a run in the fourth inning, and a pair of fifth-inning runs made the score 6-3. But Lane pulled to within one run with a pair of fifth-inning runs. Walsh, Lane's star pitcher, left the game with a sore arm after five innings, and the Windy City boys were somewhat hampered as his replacement, Norris Ryrholm, generally toiled at shortstop or behind the plate. On this day, he had caught the first five innings.

Most of the game's players were not heard of again, including New York's battery of Jacobs and McLaughlin. Jacobs scattered 12 hits, and catcher McLaughlin, who was hurt in a collision in the sixth inning, momentarily left for a courtesy runner but returned to catch the final four innings. And then there was the Chicago shortstop with the melodic name of Salvatore Pasquinelli. Long-term baseball fame would elude him as well.

The star of the game was "Lou Gherig"[2], that 17-year-old who played first base for the Easterners. He had contributed extra-base hits in each of his squad's final two games in New York and was highly heralded. As the ninth inning began, Commerce led 8-6, although the Midwesterners were outhitting them. Gehrig, hitless to that point with two walks in four plate appearances, drove the ball over the fence atop the right-field wall with the bases full. The ball landed on Sheffield Avenue and came to rest on a porch across the street. The grand slam ended the scoring. The article in the *New York Times* indicated that Gehrig had been "touted as the Babe Ruth of the high schools in New York."[3]

After the game, the players from both teams were escorted to the Olympic Theater, where they saw the play *Poker Ranch.*

Twelve years later, the player whose grand slam broke the game open returned to Chicago for the World Series. By that point Lou Gehrig was in his ninth season with the New York Yankees and was tbatting behind Babe Ruth. On October 1, 1932, Gehrig hit two homers at Wrigley Field, as did Ruth as the Yankees won 7-5 to take a commanding 3-0 lead in the World Series. They completed the sweep the next day. It was the last time that Ruth and Gehrig would be together on a championship team.

SOURCES

In addition to the sources cited in the Notes, the author also consulted:

Crusinberry, James. "New York Preps Down Lane Tech in Hitfest, 12-6, Gherig Swats Homer with the Bases Loaded," *Chicago Tribune*, June 27, 1920: 2-1.

Crusinberry. "Lane Plans Noisy Welcome for New York Prep Champs," *Chicago Tribune*, June 24, 1920: 15.

NOTES

1   James Crusinberry. "Englewood and Lane Meet Tuesday for Championship," *Chicago Tribune*, June 19, 1920: 13.

2   Gehrig's name was often misspelled in newspaper articles during his high school years. The proper spelling was always Gehrig.

3   "Commerce Team Wins," *New York Times*, June 27, 1920: Sports 2.

OLD PETE OUTDUELS ROOKIE HAINES IN 17 INNINGS

OCTOBER 1, 1920
CHICAGO CUBS 3, ST. LOUIS CARDINALS 2
(17 INNINGS)

By Gregory H. Wolf

THE BIGGEST STORY IN BASEBALL HISTORY was breaking in Chicago as the Cubs and St. Louis Cardinals took the field in the Windy City to kick off a three-game set to end the regular season. Three days earlier, star pitcher Eddie Cicotte of the Chicago White Sox had testified in a Cook County courthouse before a grand jury charged with investigating rumors of fixing the previous year's World Series. His confession to participating in the gambling scandal sent shock waves throughout baseball and indeed the country. Charles Comiskey, owner of the White Sox, subsequently suspended seven players implicated in the scheme for their season-ending series in St. Louis against the Browns, all but ensuring that his club would not capture its second consecutive pennant. Headlines in papers across the county called for a tribunal to establish order in baseball. Sam Breadon, owner of the Cardinals, got more exposure in the Gateway City than his team when he, and Browns owner Phil Ball, voiced approval of a plan of "'prominent men' to assume control of baseball and regulate affairs."[1]

Given the gravity of the sandal encompassing baseball, it's no surprise that a late-season contest between two second-division clubs received scant copy, even in local newspapers. The fifth-place Cubs (74-77), whom manager Fred Mitchell had guided to a pennant two years earlier, were 16½ games behind the Brooklyn Robins, and had lost five of their last seven games. Skipper Branch Rickey's Redbirds (73-78), one game behind the Cubs in sixth place, were playing their 23rd consecutive game on the road.

The pitching matchup was a classic case of youth versus experience. Toeing the rubber for the North Siders was 33-year-old Pete Alexander, whose 26-14 slate thus far in '20 had pushed his career record to 234-114. Suffering from a sore right arm and loss of hearing, the results of his service in a field artillery unit in World War I, Old Pete was battling alcoholism and epilepsy as he laid claim to be the league's best pitcher, who had once won 30 or more games in three consecutive seasons as a Philadelphia Phillie (1915-1917). His opponent was hard-throwing Jesse Haines, a 26-year-old rookie, who had developed into a dependable workhorse despite a lackluster 13-19 record. (Haines was not yet the knuckleballer for which he is best known as being.)

On a cool, autumnal day with temperatures in the 50s, a paltry crowd about 600 was on hand for a Friday afternoon of baseball at the intersection of Clark and Addison, where spectators were treated to one of the best-pitched games of the season.[2] "[The] players on each side hustled and battled as if they grand jury was watching them," remarked sportswriter James Crusinberry in the *Chicago Tribune*, invoking the legal turmoil encompassing baseball.[3]

Defensive miscues resulted in each team's initial run.[4] Rogers Hornsby, en route to leading the circuit in batting (.370) for the first of six consecutive seasons and seven times in his storied career, laced a two-out single that center fielder Dode Paskert bobbled, enabling Milt Stock to race home from second in the opening frame. In the second, the Cubs' Fred Merkle led off by getting hit by a pitch, stole second with two outs, and then scored on Stock's errant throw to first from the hot corner on Charlie Deal's grounder.

Alexander, a capable hitter, helped his own cause in the fifth. After William Marriott lined a two-out double down the left-field foul line, Old Pete slapped a single over second base to drive in his career-best 14th run and give the Redbirds the lead. In the next inning, the Cubs wasted a leadoff single by Zeb Terry, who was caught stealing following Turner Barber's foul out on a bunt. Merkle followed with a double in the left-center gap, but was left stranded.

The Cardinals tied the game, 2-2, in the eighth on Stock's one-out single driving in Hal Janvrin, who had reached on a fielder's choice and stole second. On the play Stock advanced to second on the throw home, but Hornsby and Germany Schultz came up empty against Old Pete.

Haines, who had yielded six hits through six innings, commenced one of the best stretches of his eventual 19-year Hall of Fame career. He held the Cubs hitless for 9⅔ innings (and walked three) until Marriott singled with one out in the 16th. The only problem for the Cardinals was Alexander, who bent, but did not break.

The Cardinals squandered excellent chances to take the lead in the ninth, 10th, 12th, and 16th innings, but could not find a clutch hit. Doc Lavan led off the ninth with a laser that bounced off Alexander's chest, reported the *St. Louis Star and Times*.[5] Old Pete recovered to field the ball but his throw was late to first. Lavan moved up a station on a sacrifice bunt, but was left stranded. Heinie Mueller walked to lead off the next inning and then advanced to second on Stock's single, bringing Hornsby to the plate. After Alexander punched out Hornsby, he walked Schultz to load the bases, but retired Lavan

to end the threat. The 12th inning might have been the most exciting. The Redbird loaded the bases on singles by Mueller and Stock sandwiched around Alexander's throwing error on Janvrin's sacrifice bunt. Alexander dispatched the next three hitters on routine popups, including Hornsby's fly to shallow right with no outs. After squandering Hornsby's leadoff single in the 15th, Haines and Mueller lined consecutive one-out singles in the 16th, only to come up empty yet again. Thankfully Rickey was a well-known religious man; other skippers would have probably let loose profanity-laced invective by this point.

After Alexander worked around a two-out single by Lavan in the 17th, Babe Twombly singled to center, the first Cubs leadoff hitter to reach base since the eighth inning. Haines, who had pitched into extra innings three other times this season, including tossing 13 innings in a heartbreaking 3-0 loss to the Pittsburgh Pirates in his second start of the season, could be forgiven for tiring. After he fanned Terry, Barber rapped a single to push Twombly to third. Haines intentionally walked Merkle to load the bases and set up a play at any base. To the plate stepped Paskert, hitless in his previous six trips to the plate. With the outfield playing in, Paskert singled to left to drive in the winning run, ending the game in 2 hours and 45 minutes.

Paskert's hit secured Alexander's league-leading 27th victory. The 17-inning outing was the longest in Old Pete's career, though he was far from at his best. He yielded 16 hits and walked three while facing 69 batters, yet surrendered only one earned run. In the last dominant season in his Hall of Fame career, Alexander also paced the senior circuit in ERA (1.91), innings (363⅓), complete games (33), and strikeouts (173). Haines's career-longest 16⅓-inning outing ended in a bitter loss, his 20th, in a game he probably should have won had his teammates connected off Alexander when it most counted. He faced 59 batters, fanned eight, walked four, and surrendered 10 hits; two of the three runs off him were earned. Haines, who ultimately played for the Cardinals for 18 seasons, leading them to five pennants and three

World Series titles, concluded the season with an NL-most 47 appearances and a career-best 301⅔ innings. Given the moniker "Old Jess" in his later years, Haines retired as the franchise leader in wins (210), complete games (209), appearances as a pitcher (554), and innings pitched (3,203⅔).

The pitching adversaries in this game teamed up in one of the most famous games in Cardinals and World Series history on October 10, 1926. Facing the New York Yankees in Game Seven at Yankee Stadium, Haines departed with a 3-2 lead, with the bases loaded and two outs in the seventh, the knuckles on his right hand bleeding from his mesmerizing hard floater. Alexander, whom the Cardinals had acquired on June 22 that season, entered in what is regarded as one of the best relief appearances in the history of the Fall Classic. He fanned Tony Lazzeri to end the threat, then set down six of the next seven batters, issuing only a walk to Babe Ruth in the ninth to secure the Cardinals' first world championship.

SOURCES

In addition to the sources cited in the Notes, the author also accessed Retrosheet.org, Baseball-Reference.com, and SABR.org.

NOTES

1 "High Baseball Court Favored by St. Louis Men," *St. Louis Star and Times*, October 2, 1920: 4.

2 James Crusinberry, "Cubs Go 17 Innings to Beat Cards, 3-3; Aleck Mound Hero," *Chicago Tribune*, October 2, 1920: 15.

3 Ibid.

4 Neither BaseballReference.com or Retrosheet.org has the play-by-play for this game; however, a detailed play-by-play is available at "Haines Battles With Alexander in Chicago Park," *St. Louis Star and Times*, October 1, 1920: 20.

5 Ibid.

Future Hall of Famer Jesse Haines completed the first of his 18 seasons with the St. Louis Cardinals by tossing 16⅓ innings, including 9⅔ hitless frames, against the Cubs on October 1, 1920, but lost 3-2, to another Hall of Famer, Pete Alexander, who also went the distance.

49 RUNS ON 51 HITS

AUGUST 25, 1922
CHICAGO CUBS 26, PHILADELPHIA PHILLIES 23

By Mike Huber

FROM 1901 THROUGH THE END OF THE 2015 major-league season, one of the two teams has scored 20 or more runs in at least 236 games.[1] Only twice has each team scored at least 20 runs. Both games involved the Philadelphia Phillies and the Chicago Cubs, and both games were played in Chicago. The first, on August 25, 1922, was played before approximately 7,000 fans in Cubs Park, and the Phillies prevailed, 26-23.[2] This set a record for the most runs scored in a major-league game.[3]

Philadelphia batters had 26 hits, while the Cubs hitters mustered 25. (The 51 hits in the game also smashed the existing record, set on June 9, 1901, when the New York Giants and Cincinnati Reds collected 49 hits as the New Yorkers beat the Reds, 25-13.[4]) The Phillies and Cubs pitchers faced a total of 125 batters and walked 21 of them. Jimmy Ring started the game for the Phillies, and Tony Kaufmann took the mound for Chicago.

The game began normally enough. With one out in the top of the first, Philadelphia's Frank Parkinson singled and was forced at second on a Cy Williams grounder to first. Williams was then caught stealing. Three up, three down. Chicago's Cliff Heathcote led off the bottom of the first with a single to center. He moved up two bases on two groundballs and scored on Ray Grimes's single to center. Philadelphia sent nine batters to the plate in the top of the second, and with four singles, two Cubs errors, and a walk, the Phillies scored three unearned runs.

Chicago then erupted for 10 runs in the bottom of the second. With two outs and men on first and second, Phillies third baseman Russ Wrightstone

dropped a pop fly in foul territory off the bat of Heathcote. The floodgates opened, as Heathcote walked to load the bases and the next eight batters also reached. Hack Miller and Bob O'Farrell both homered, and the Cubs got six hits and three walks. The Phillies made two errors, and all 10 runs were unearned. After two innings of play, Chicago led, 11-3. Philadelphia responded with two runs in the third and another in the fourth. The score was now 11-6.

A few other records were tied in this hitfest. Chicago right fielder Marty Callaghan tied a record for most times facing a pitcher in one inning. In the top of the fourth, he led off with a single to right. The Cubs sent 19 batters to the plate, and the second time up, Callaghan stroked a second single to center, driving in two runs. He made the last out of the inning, striking out. As if this weren't enough, the Cubs pushed 14 runs across the plate (12 earned) in the fourth inning. This tied a record set on July 6, 1920, when the New York Yankees scored 14 runs in the fifth inning of a 17-0 shutout against the Washington Senators. Kaiser Wilhelm, the Philadelphia manager, finally pulled Ring when Heathcote singled with the bases loaded and only one out, driving in the second and third runs of the inning. Lefty Weinert came in and proceeded to pitch batting practice to the Cubs, who collected two singles, four doubles, a walk, a hit batsman, and a home run (Miller's second of the game) off him in the inning. Suddenly it was 25-6 and the game was not even official yet. Weinert was battered but stayed in to pitch 4⅔ innings and finish the game for Philadelphia.

Chicago added another run in the sixth on a double by Heathcote and an RBI single by Charlie Hollocher. In the eighth and ninth the Phillies made the game appear closer than it was. They scored eight runs in the eighth and six in the ninth, almost making an impossible comeback.

Chicago used five pitchers. Starter Kaufmann pitched only four innings but was credited with the win. George Stueland pitched three innings, allowing three runs. Uel Eubanks started the eighth but lasted only two-thirds of an inning. Ed Morris relieved him with two outs, the bases loaded, and five Philadelphia runs already in. Frank Withrow greeted Morris with a base-clearing double. If the save was an official statistic in those days (it was not), Tiny Osborne would have earned one after relieving the ineffective Morris in the ninth inning. Osborne allowed two earned runs on three hits and two walks, but struck out the side, including Bevo LeBourveau to end the game.

Philadelphia left 16 runners on base. (Chicago left 9.) The Cubs had eight doubles and three home runs. Philadelphia had an amazing 20 singles as part of its 26-hit attack. Wrightstone led the Phillies with a 4-for-7 afternoon, scoring three runs and driving in four. For Chicago, Heathcote was perfect, 5-for-5 plus two walks. He scored five of the Cubs' runs and collected four RBIs. Hollocher, who followed Heathcote in the batting order, knocked in six runs with his 3-for-5 performance. Hack Miller added two singles to his two home runs; he scored three times and drove in six runs.

Despite allowing 16 runs in 3⅓ innings, Ring's ERA rose only slightly, from 4.22 to 4.44. He had faced 28 Chicago batters and allowed 12 hits and 5 walks, but the Philadelphia errors meant that 10 of the 16 runs off him were unearned. He and Weinert had "endured a terrific mauling."[5] In all, 21 of the 49 runs were unearned, as Philadelphia committed four errors and Chicago had five.

The game lasted 3 hours and 1 minute. Frank Schreiber of the *Chicago Tribune* wrote that "cries from various parts of the park were imploring for

In one of the wildest games in Wrigley Field history, shortstop Charlie Hollocher knocked in six runs. He enjoyed his best season in 1922, collecting 201 hits and batting .340.

a 'touchdown,' while others besought the players to 'shoot another basket.'"[6] The previous record for runs in a game was 44, set on July 12, 1890, when the Brooklyn Ward's Wonders beat the Buffalo Bisons, 28-16.

SOURCES

In addition to the sources mentioned in the Notes, the author consulted baseball-reference.com, mlb.com, and retrosheet.org.

NOTES

1   For more information on games in which a team has scored at least 20 runs, see Michael R. Huber and Rodney X. Sturdivant, "Building a Model for Scoring 20 or More Runs in a Baseball Game," *Annals of Applied Statistics*, Volume 4, Number 2, June 2010.

2   The story of August 26, 1922, in the *New York Times* led with, "Two world's records were smashed and two other marks were equaled in a weird slugging match which the Cubs won from the Phillies today by a score of 26 to 23." The article had neither a staff byline nor a wire-service credit, so its source is unknown.

3   In the other Cubs-Phillies game, on May 17, 1979, the Phillies and Cubs combined to score 45 runs on 50 hits in a game played at Wrigley Field. For more information, read this SABR Games Project article.

4   According to retrosheet.org, the Reds forfeited the game to the Giants.

5   Frank Schreiber, "Comedy of Runs, Hits, and Errors to Cubs, 26-23," *Chicago Tribune*, August 26, 1922.

6   Ibid.

CUBS WALLOP DEFENDING WORLD CHAMPIONS ON OPENING DAY

APRIL 12, 1927
CHICAGO CUBS 10, ST. LOUIS CARDINALS 1

By Russ Lake

IN THE EARLY PART OF 1927, THE MID- west was bursting with anticipation as the baseball season segued from projections to facts delivered by daily sports accounts. By mid-April, pitching matchups, game summaries, and season standings would replace the "dreary box-scoreless winter" to provide "something in the newspapers." Even an umpire might expect applause for one day with fans feeling "mighty peart" as the new campaign stepped off.[1]

In Chicago, the ballpark just west of Lake Michigan on Addison Street had undergone another name change before its 14th season of operation took shape with the site being rechristened as Wrigley Field. Originally named Weeghman Park in 1914, its identifier was followed by North Side Ball Park, Federal League Ball Park, Whales Park, and Cubs Park.[2] Despite cloudy and cold weather conditions on April 12, an above-capacity crowd was expected to squeeze into the venue by 3 P.M. to watch right-hander Charlie Root and their Cubs take on the defending World Series champion St. Louis Cardinals.

Chicago manager Joe McCarthy directed his team through a workout the day before the opener.[3] Two months earlier, Marse Joe had said his squad should contend for the National League pennant after finishing fourth at 82-72 in 1926.[4] New Cardinals skipper Bob O'Farrell planned to start former Cub (and 1926 World Series hero) Grover Cleveland "Pete" Alexander. O'Farrell would defer to southpaw

Bill Sherdel should Alexander decide that his right arm could not answer the bell.[5]

St. Louis fans were excited for the new season, and still rejoicing about the '26 World Series triumph over Babe Ruth and the New York Yankees. A sports-section cartoon in the *St. Louis Post-Dispatch*, captioned "A.W.O.L.," portrayed an empty business desk with the wall clock chiming three bells.[6] The *St. Louis Star*, in a bordered box on its lead sports page, asked readers not to call the paper for game results, because its telephone trunk line would be unable to handle the extra congestion.[7]

McCarthy was in his second year at the Cubs' helm. Besides O'Farrell, seven new major-league managers would be tasked with improving their clubs' previous season. The Cleveland Indians, Chicago White Sox, Detroit Tigers, St. Louis Browns, and Boston Red Sox signed new mentors in the American League, while the Pittsburgh Pirates and Philadelphia Phillies did likewise in the senior circuit.[8] O'Farrell was a playing manager like his predecessor, Rogers Hornsby. Despite winning the Cardinals' first world championship in 1926, Hornsby had been astonishingly traded by owner Sam Breadon, to the New York Giants in December in a deal that was prompted by a personality and salary dispute.[9]

With Baseball Commissioner Kenesaw Mountain Landis seated nearby,[10] Cubs owner William Wrigley Jr. was all smiles standing at the box-seat rail when Chicago Mayor William Hale "Big Bill" Thompson tossed out the first ball of the season. Hats, gloves, and overcoats made up the grandstand apparel for the chilly afternoon.[11] Because of the overflow crowd, especially in the outfield, ground rules would be implemented by umpires Bill Klem, Frank Wilson, and Beans Reardon. O'Farrell had Alexander and Sherdel warm up together before the 40-year-old Aleck, after a long conference with the manager and coach Bill McKechnie, convinced them that he would be okay.[12]

After Klem shouted "Play Ball!" Root fired a pitch and Taylor Douthit lined a ground-rule double down the right-field line. Any other day Douthit might have had a triple; however, two bases was the limit when the ball went into the crowd. Billy Southworth smacked a hard grounder to shortstop Jimmy Cooney, who fired to third baseman Riggs Stephenson to nab Douthit. Root had Southworth picked off first but threw wild and Southworth advanced to second. Frankie Frisch flied out to center, but slugger Jim Bottomley walked, and Les Bell knocked home Southworth with a double. Bell drove in 100 runs in 1926 (along with six postseason RBIs), so he was picking up where he left off. Root settled down and struck out Chick Hafey to retire the side.

Alexander, a longtime Cubs pitcher, had already been booed and cheered mightily by the Chicago faithful. He retired the first two batters, Sparky Adams and Cliff Heathcote, in the bottom of the first, but a Cubs newcomer, outfielder Earl Webb, blasted a home run to right field completely out of the park to tie the score, 1-1, and the partisan crowd roared its approval.[13] Although Webb had hit very well during spring training at Catalina Island, the 29-year-old left-handed-hitting rookie might not have been in the lineup had lefty Sherdel been the St. Louis starter.[14]

The Cubs missed a scoring chance in the second inning when Stephenson was thrown out after rounding third base too far on an infield hit by Mike Gonzalez. Root opened the third with a ground-rule double and advanced a base as Adams legged out a bunt. With the bases loaded, Hack Wilson barely beat out a potential inning-ending twin killing,

allowing Root to score.[15] Stephenson's single plated Adams, and Charlie Grimm crashed a three-run homer to climax the five-run assault and provide Chicago with a 6-1 advantage.

Root fetched a bit of bulldog determination in the top of the fourth with a pair of strikeouts for his first 1-2-3 inning. The tobacco-juice-spitting 28-year-old hurler was suitably nicknamed "Chinski" for throwing high and inside to hitters. For batters wary of where the pitch was going, his curve (described by Root as a "wrinkle ball") effectively confounded hitters.[16]

Alexander held the Cubs during the fourth, and was lifted for a pinch-hitter the next inning, as Root set the Cardinals down again for nine in a row. In Alexander's four innings he gave up six earned runs on six hits, one walk and no strikeouts. Herman "Hi" Bell relieved for St. Louis, and pitched around a walk. Frisch and Bottomley opened the St. Louis sixth with singles, but Root fanned Les Bell and Hafey. A passed ball by Gonzalez moved St. Louis runners up and the Cardinals were a clutch safety away from making it close. Root would have none of that though, as he struck out O'Farrell.

Chicago attempted to add to its lead in the sixth, but second baseman Frisch pegged out Stephenson trying to steal home. Root was the benefactor of a double play in the seventh after Tommy Thevenow walked. Specs Toporcer, pinch-hitting for Hi Bell, lined to Adams, who tossed to Grimm to double up Thevenow. Southpaw Eddie Dyer entered the game for St. Louis and retired the Cubs in order.

The bottom of the eighth was a totally different story for the 27-year-old Dyer, who allowed four runs on five hits and two walks. Webb smashed his second home run of the game leading off the frame. Wilson walked and went to third on Stephenson's ground-rule double. Grimm and Gonzalez hit consecutive run-scoring singles to make the score 9-1, and Adams singled home another tally to make it a 10-1 blowout. After retiring Heathcote on a groundball to first to end the frame, Dyer trekked off a major-league diamond for the final time during a pitching career that covered six seasons. (He returned to the

St. Louis dugout as the manager in 1946-50 and won the World Series in '46.)

Root finished off an impressive complete-game victory in 1 hour and 57 minutes. Chicago scored 10 runs on 12 hits and the Cardinals one run on seven hits. Each team committed an error. Since 1907, the Cubs had opened the season against the Cardinals seven times and now sported a 5-1-1 mark in those games.

The victory started Root on the way to a major-league-leading 26 wins (against 15 losses) for the 1927 Cubs, who finished fourth with an 85-68 record. The team was in first place at the end of August, but ended the season 12-18 to drop out of the pennant race. Alexander rebounded from the Opening Day loss to finish 21-10 with a 2.52 ERA for the second-place Cardinals. At the end of the '27 season Aleck's remarkable career won-loss record stood at 348-188.

Wrigley Field seated just over 34,000, but some accounts reported this Opening Day gathering as large as 45,000 with patrons standing on the field, in the aisles, and even among the structure's rafters.[17] The Cubs led the NL in attendance in 1927 with a then-record 1,159,168 flowing through the gates.

SOURCES

In addition to the sources cited in the Notes, the author also accessed Retrosheet.org, Baseball-Reference.com, Newspapers.com, SABR.org/bioproj, and *The Sporting News* archive via Paper of Record.

NOTES

1 James M. Gould, "Gould's Gossip," *St. Louis Star and Times*, April 12, 1927: 17.

2 Scott Ferkovich, "The Friendly Confines of Wrigley Field," SABR Baseball Biography Project, sabr.org/bioproj/park/wrigley-field-chicago.

3 "Pointing the Path to a Pennant," *Chicago Tribune*, April 12, 1927: 29.

4 Bob Ray, "M'Carthy Says Cubs Stronger," *Los Angeles Times*, February 2, 1927: 40-41.

5 J. Roy Stockton, "Cards Open in Cold at Chicago," *St. Louis Post-Dispatch*, April 12, 1927: 17.

6 Quill (artist), "A.W.O.L.," *St. Louis Post-Dispatch*, April 12, 1927: 17.

7 *St. Louis Star and Times*, April 13, 1927: 16.

8 Davis J. Walsh-INSS Editor, "Trouble Over Hornsby Case Ended, Baseball Is Now All Set to Go," *St. Louis Star and Times*, April 11, 1927: 16.

9 Rob Rains, *The St. Louis Cardinals, the 100th Anniversary History* (New York: St. Martin's Press, 1992): 43-44.

10 "Looking Over His Boys," *Chicago Tribune*, April 13, 1927: 23.

11 "'Big Bill' Thompson Sees Cubs Win," *St. Louis Star and Times*, April 13, 1927: 16.

12 Ray J. Gillespie, "World Champions Lose First Game of Season," *St. Louis Star and Times*, April 13, 1927: 16.

13 Irving Vaughan, "Cubs Beat Cards, 10-1, Before 45,000," *Chicago Tribune*, April 13, 1927: 23.

14 Vaughan, "Aged Aleck to Climb Hill for World Champs," *Chicago Tribune*, April 12, 1927: 29.

15 Gillespie, "World Champions Lose."

16 Gregory H. Wolf, SABR Baseball Biography Project, sabr.org/bioproj/person/22e9a7e7.

17 Vaughan, "Cubs Beat Cards, 10-1."

EHMKE SETS WORLD SERIES STRIKEOUT RECORD

OCTOBER 8, 1929
PHILADELPHIA ATHLETICS 3, CHICAGO CUBS 1

GAME ONE OF THE WORLD SERIES

By Norm King

POOR CHARLIE ROOT. HERE'S A GUY WHO had a very respectable 17-year career, almost all with the Chicago Cubs, in which he won 201 games, lost 160 and had a respectable 3.59 ERA. Yet for all that, he is best known for giving up Babe Ruth's "Called Shot" in the 1932 World Series, when the Bambino allegedly pointed to center field, then smacked the next pitch into the stands.

Giving up a home run that achieves the status of lore or myth – depending who you ask – is bad enough. Root was also on the wrong side for two other famous games, both of which occurred in the 1929 fall classic against Connie Mack's mighty Philadelphia A's. One of these was Game Four, Root's second start of the Series, when the Cubs blew an 8-0 lead in the eighth inning and went on to lose 10-8. He also started Game One against a middling pitcher whom Mack put on the mound on a hunch ahead of two 20-game winners. That hunch proved correct, as said pitcher set a one-game World Series strikeout record (13) that lasted until October 2, 1953, when Carl Erskine of the Brooklyn Dodgers struck out 14 New York Yankees. His name was Howard Ehmke.

Both teams were loaded with power. Root, who went 19-6 with a 3.47 ERA, faced an A's club that won 104 games and finished 18 games ahead of the second-place New York Yankees. Its lineup was second in the American League in runs (901) and home runs (122), and included future Hall of Famers Mickey Cochrane, Jimmie Foxx, and Al Simmons.

While it was understandable that Cubs manager Joe McCarthy would choose Root to open the Series, Mack's decision to go with Ehmke was a head-scratcher. Or was it? While he had a good 7-2 record with a 3.29 ERA, he hadn't pitched since September 13, when he went eight innings in a 5-2 win over the Chicago White Sox. Mack also had a smorgasbord of starters to choose from, including Lefty Grove (20-6, 2.81) and George Earnshaw (24-8, 3.29). The two had each pitched three innings in an 8-4 win on October 5 over the Yankees, which in an era when pitchers started one day and relieved the next, meant that both were ready. So why Ehmke? According to the great sportswriter Damon Runyon, the scenario went something like this:

"A long-legged, knock-kneed, loose-jointed supplicant shambled into the presence of old Cornelius McGillicuddy, the master mind [sic] of Philadelphia's Athletics, this morning.

"'Mis't [sic] Connie, sir,' implored the caller, 'you lemme [sic] pitch today's game against these Cubs. You forget about Earnshaw, or any of our cock-eyed pitchers, and lemme pitch. "It's my last season in baseball, and I'll stand 'em on their ears. I'll do it, Mis't Connie, sir, as sure as eggs is eggs.'"[1]

Anybody who saw the show *Guys and Dolls* would be familiar with Runyon's ability to write fiction. The real story began during the A's mid-September series in Chicago. Both teams had huge leads in their respective leagues, so it was obvious they were going to meet in October. Since the Cubs happened to be at home against the Phillies, Ehmke scouted them at Wrigley Field prior to his start at Comiskey.

The 1929 Northsiders easily matched the A's in offensive firepower. They led the National League in runs scored (982), were second in home runs (139), and could boast their own trio of future Hall of Famers: Rogers Hornsby, Kiki Cuyler, and Hack Wilson.[2] But of the starting eight for Game One, only Charlie Grimm was a left-handed hitter; Ehmke also noticed that they were free swingers. Armed with this information, Mack decided that starting the 35-year-old submarine-style hurler just might work.

The game remained scoreless through the first six innings, but each pitcher managed to escape early jams. In the second, singles by Foxx and Jimmy Dykes left Philadelphia with two on and one out. Root got out of that jam by inducing Joe Boley to hit into a double play.

Ehmke faced a much tougher problem in the third when Norm McMillan singled and Woody English doubled to put runners on second and third with one out and Hornsby and Wilson due up. Well, let's just say that these two sluggers have had better days, as both flailed helplessly at Ehmke's offerings before striking out.

"Hornsby was as futile as a gnat's attack on an elephant, while Wilson's efforts were as weak as boarding house coffee," wrote the legendary Grantland Rice. "Rog and Hack have scuttled many a good right-handed National League star this year, but they were duck soup for this certain individual Connie Mack sprang upon them in one of the most sensational pitching selections ever worked in a World's Series starter by a manager to upset the guessers and dopesters."[3]

Foxx broke the scoreless tie in the seventh with a solo home run to left-center. In the bottom of the inning, Cuyler and Riggs Stephenson both singled and advanced to third on Grimm's sacrifice. McCarthy went to his bench for a couple of pinch-hitters, but Ehmke wiggled out of this jam, too, by getting Cliff Heathcote on a popup and striking out Gabby Hartnett.

English's double was part of a 2-for-4 day at the plate, but it was his sloppiness in the ninth that sealed his team's fate. After Cochrane singled, Simmons and Foxx both reached on errors by English to load the bases with nobody out. Bing Miller cashed in two runs to give Philadelphia a 3-0 lead, and make the Cubs' chances for victory more difficult. They were not, however, going down easily.

Ehmke had 12 K's going into the ninth, which tied the record set by Ed Walsh of the White Sox in Game Three of the 1906 Series, also against the Cubs. Things got off to a rough start for him when Wilson smacked a liner that hit Ehmke in the groin, but he recovered and made the out at first. Dykes then rushed to field a bounder by Cuyler, but threw it away, which enabled Cuyler to reach second. Stephenson cashed Cuyler in to make it 3-1. Grimm gave Chicago fans hope with a single of his own that put two runners on and brought the winning run to the plate. McCarthy sent Footsie Blair up to pinch-hit for Mike Gonzalez, but Blair forced Grimm at second. Now there were two out.

It's doubtful that Chick Tolson, pinch-hitting for reliever Guy Bush, knew that Ehmke had tied the strikeout record, and he certainly didn't want to be yet another victim. To that end, he didn't panic after falling behind 1-and-2, and worked Ehmke to a full count before swinging at strike three, which put Ehmke's name in the record books and, more importantly, put the A's up 1-0 in the Series.

After the game, Ehmke wasn't shy about discussing his performance with reporters. "I don't like to say it, but it's a fact that when I'm anywhere near right I'm not afraid of any man who comes to the plate," he said. "That's not conceit – it's just confidence."[4]

The victory was the last of Ehmke's career, and helped Mack's charges take the world championship in five games. Lightning, however, did not strike twice. Ehmke started Game Five but was removed after allowing two runs on six hits in just 3⅔ innings. And he had no strikeouts.

SOURCE

In addition to the sources cited in the Notes, the author also accessed Retrosheet.org, Baseball-Reference.com, SABR.org, Mlb.com, the *Chicago Tribune*, and the SABR biography of Howard Ehmke by Gregory H. Wolf.

NOTES

1   Damon Runyon, "I'll Stand 'em on Their Ears," Ehmke Promised – And He DID," *Philadelphia Inquirer*, October 9, 1929: 16.

2   A fourth Hall of Famer, catcher Gabby Hartnett, was limited to only 29 plate appearances in 1929 due to injury. He was hitless in three at-bats as a pinch-hitter during the World Series.

3   Grantland Rice, "A's Triumph 3-1; Ehmke Fans 13, Sets New Mark," *Philadelphia Inquirer*, October 9, 1929: 16.

4   Roscoe McGowen, "Athletics Joyful, but Remain Calm," *New York Times*, October 9, 1929: 25.

THE DOUBLE-X AND BUCKETFOOT AL SHOW ON THE NORTH SIDE

OCTOBER 9, 1929
PHILADELPHIA ATHLETICS 9, CHICAGO CUBS 3

GAME TWO OF THE WORLD SERIES

By J.G. Preston

IN GAME ONE OF THE 1929 WORLD Series, the Chicago Cubs set a Series record by striking out 13 times. Twenty-four hours later, they did it again, but this time they had a better excuse. In Game One the Cubs fell victim to Howard Ehmke, who recorded almost as many strikeouts in that game as he had during the entire regular season. In Game Two the whiffs were recorded by the pitchers who finished one-two in the American League in strikeouts in 1929.

Philadelphia A's owner-manager Connie Mack had shocked the baseball world by choosing the 35-year-old Ehmke, who had pitched only 54⅔ innings all season, to start Game One instead of George Earnshaw, who led the AL with 24 wins and ranked second in the league in strikeouts, or Lefty Grove, a 20-game winner who led the league in ERA and strikeouts. After Ehmke's record performance in beating the Cubs in the opener, Mack was coy about his choice to pitch Game Two. In his syndicated newspaper column, Mack refused to reveal his pitcher,[1] while the *Chicago Tribune* had a full-page headline that blared in big capital letters, "Earnshaw or Quinn to Pitch for A's Today."[2] Mack was said to be considering 46-year-old Jack Quinn because of the success Burleigh Grimes had against the Cubs that year, going 5-1 with a 2.29 ERA; Quinn, like Grimes, had been "grandfathered in" and allowed to continue throwing the spitball after the pitch was banned

in the major leagues in 1920.[3] But Mack settled on Earnshaw, while Cubs manager Joe McCarthy went with his ace, Pat Malone, who had led the National League in wins and strikeouts.

Game Two was played on "a day that was no sort of day for any sort of ball game," according to the *Tribune*'s Westbrook Pegler. "The wind bustled in off the lake [Lake Michigan], cold and aggressive, and the flags on the masts around the eaves of the ballpark stood out like boards all afternoon."[4] The visiting A's didn't seem to appreciate the conditions. "Al Simmons wanted to know whether or not there was a rule against wearing overcoats in the outfield," John Kieran reported in the *New York Times*. "Jimmy Dykes suggested he take out some wood with him and make a fire."[5]

Ehmke's still-fresh strikeout record was in peril from the beginning, and at first it looked as if Malone would be the one to break it. He got all three first-inning outs on strikeouts and added another in the second when he fanned Earnshaw to end the inning with Dykes on third base. Then in the third inning Malone retired the first two batters to face him before Mickey Cochrane singled and Simmons walked, bringing Jimmie Foxx to the plate. Foxx had broken up a scoreless tie in Game One with a seventh-inning homer, and history was about to repeat.

Malone's first pitch was a ball, the second was a strike. Then came a fastball, high and inside. "It would have been called a ball," William E. Brandt wrote in the *New York Times*, "if Foxx had not exercised again his propensity for overhead swinging at pitches most batters never try to hit."[6] Foxx connected and sent the ball into the temporary bleachers in left field for a three-run homer.

Afterward Malone told the *Tribune*'s Irving Vaughan that Foxx homered on what was intended to be a brushback pitch. "Malone shot it at his head with the idea of giving him a scare," Vaughan wrote. "Pat managed to get it close to his target, but Foxx, instead of flopping to the ground, waved his stick and the ball went away."[7]

The Cubs mounted a threat in the bottom of the third, even though none of the first five batters hit a fair ball. Norm McMillan walked to lead off; Woody English and Rogers Hornsby both struck out (giving Earnshaw six to that point); then Hack Wilson and Kiki Cuyler both walked to load the bases. "A deafening roar rent the air at this moment," wrote John Drebinger in the *New York Times*, "for the great crowd was certain Chicago's big moment had arrived."[8]

The wildness continued, and the noise increased, when the first three pitches to Riggs Stephenson were balls, all missing the plate by quite a bit.[9] After the next pitch Stephenson tossed his bat and started for first, only to hear home-plate umpire Bill Dinneen call it a strike.[10] A called strike two followed, then Stephenson hit a soft fly to Simmons in left to end the inning with the Cubs still scoreless.

The A's added to their lead in the fourth inning. Dykes led off with a single and was sacrificed to second by Joe Boley. Earnshaw then hit a groundball to shortstop English, whose two errors in Game One led to two unearned A's runs, and the ball rolled off English's glove and up his arm for another error to put runners on first and third. Max Bishop followed with a walk to load the bases. With the infield in, Mule Haas bounced a grounder to English, who looked to start an inning-ending double play. But second baseman Hornsby, expecting a play at home,

didn't cover second. English ran to the bag himself to force out Bishop, but the delay caused his throw to first to be too late to retire Haas, and Dykes scored.[11] Cochrane then walked and Simmons singled to center, scoring Earnshaw and Haas to make it 6-0 and knock Malone out of the box.

Earnshaw started to struggle in the bottom of the fifth. After English popped out to lead off, Hornsby and Wilson singled. Cuyler struck out for the second out, Earnshaw's seventh of the day. But then Stephenson singled home Hornsby, Charlie Grimm drove in Wilson with a single and Zack Taylor singled off Earnshaw's glove to score Stephenson. That cut the A's lead to 6-3 and brought the tying run to the plate.

McCarthy called on left-handed-swinging Cliff Heathcote to bat for pitcher Sheriff Blake, and Mack countered by bringing in Grove to relieve Earnshaw in order to regain the platoon advantage. McCarthy then replaced Heathcote with right-handed hitter Gabby Hartnett, the star catcher, who was limited to pinch-hitting in 1929 because of a sore arm.

Grove struck out Hartnett on "a fast ball that could scarcely be seen," according to Drebinger,[12] and from then on the A's were firmly in control. Dykes singled in a run in the seventh and Simmons hit a two-run homer in the eighth to make the final score 9-3. Grove held the Cubs to three singles and a walk in his 4⅓ innings, striking out six. "Grove has a ball that is swifter than a stock market collapse and he had the Cubs swinging at it after it had landed in the catcher's mitt," wrote H.I. Phillips in the *Philadelphia Inquirer*.[13] The Cubs' 13 strikeouts remained a World Series record for a nine-inning game for another 24 years.[14]

Despite the fact that he was lifted before finishing the fifth inning – and despite the fact that Grove had a more impressive pitching line – Earnshaw was designated the winning pitcher by the official scorer, the last time in postseason play a win has been credited to a starting pitcher who failed to go five innings.[15]

The World Series did not return to Wrigley Field in 1929. The Cubs won Game Three in Philadelphia, but the A's came back from an 8-0 deficit to win Game Four and then rallied after being behind 2-0 with one out in the bottom of the ninth to take Game Five and the Series.

SOURCES

Game stories in the *Chicago Tribune* and *Philadelphia Inquirer* were accessed via Newspapers.com. The author also used BaseballReference.com, Retrosheet.org, and SABR.org.

NOTES

1   Connie Mack, "Always Had Faith in Howard Ehmke, Says Connie Mack," *Philadelphia Inquirer*, October 9, 1929: 18.

2   *Chicago Tribune*, October 9, 1929: 23.

3   Mack's theory was proved wrong when Quinn started Game Four of the Series and allowed six runs in five-plus innings. The next year he became the oldest pitcher to appear in a postseason game when he pitched in relief for the A's in Game Three against the Cardinals.

4   Westbrook Pegler, "Foes Continue to Humiliate Cub 'Sluggers,'" *Chicago Tribune*, October 10, 1929: 24.

5   John Kieran, "Sports of the Times," *New York Times*, October 10, 1929: 29.

6   William E. Brandt, "Superior Batting Decided 2nd Game," *New York Times*, October 10, 1929: 25.

7   Irving Vaughan, "Defeat Fails to Shake Courage of Cubs," *Chicago Tribune*, October 10, 1929: 23.

8   John Drebinger, "Athletics Defeat Cubs, 9-3, and Win Second Straight Game in World's Series," *New York Times*, October 10, 1929: 24.

9   S.O. Grauley, "What Happened to Every Pitch as Mackmen Again Bagged Windy City Bruins – And How," *Philadelphia Inquirer*, October 10, 1929: 23.

10   Irving Vaughan, "Defeat Fails To Shake Courage Of Cubs," *Chicago Daily Tribune*, October 10, 1929: 24.

11   William E. Brandt, "Superior Batting Decided 2d Game," *The New York Times*, October 10, 1929: 25.

12   John Drebinger, "Athletics Defeat Cubs, 9-3, and Win Second Straight Game in World's Series," *The New York Times*, October 10, 1929: 24.

13   H.I. Phillips, "Chicago Pineapple Tossers Get Change Of Venue After Mack's Reformers Clean Up," *Philadelphia Inquirer*, October 10, 1929: 20. This game was played nearly three weeks before Black Tuesday, October 29, the date normally associated with the stock-market crash, but the decline had already begun. The Dow Jones Industrial Average dropped 15 percent from its then-record high close of 381.17 on September 3, 1929, through October 4, and while it had bounced back a bit by the date of this game, the closing price of 198.69 on November 13 would be 48 percent below its peak. See measuringworth.com/DJA/.

14   The St. Louis Browns struck out 13 times in Game Two of the 1944 World Series against the Cardinals in an 11-inning game, but only 10 strikeouts came in the first nine innings. The Yankees struck out 14 times against Brooklyn's Carl Erskine in Game Three of the 1953 Series to break the Cubs' record.

15   "Earnshaw Is Credited With Win, Not Grove," *Philadelphia Inquirer*, October 10, 1929: 22. The only other starting pitcher to be credited with a World Series win despite not pitching five innings was Hugh McQuillan of the Giants, who got the win even though he worked only 3⅔ innings against the Senators in Game Three of the 1924 Series. There were 10 occasions during the 1929 regular season when the official scorer used his discretion to award the win to a starter who did not complete five innings, and Earnshaw was one of those pitchers. baseball-reference.com/tiny/rkl3Q.

HACK WILSON HITS FOR THE CYCLE AS CUBS POUND PHILLIES

JUNE 23, 1930
CHICAGO CUBS 21, PHILADELPHIA PHILLIES 8

By Mike Huber

IN A MONDAY-AFTERNOON GAME AT Wrigley Field, the "Cubs buried Philadelphia under an avalanche of twenty-four hits," defeating the Phillies, 21-8.[1] Every Chicago batter had at least one hit, reached base at least twice, and scored at least one run.[2] Cubs center fielder Hack Wilson led the barrage with five hits, including the cycle. The game was chock full of excitement, featuring not only the cycle but also a rundown, a double steal, and lots (and lots) of singles.

The two teams were headed in opposite directions. Chicago, the defending National League champion, again knocked at the first-place door of the league for much of the season. The Cubs came to this contest 11 games above .500 (36-25) and had just won five of their last six. They were in the midst of a 15-game homestand. This game began a three-game series with the not-so-successful Phillies. The Phillies, departing St. Louis in the midst of a 12-game road trip, had lost three of four to the Cardinals, and were 23-31, positioned 12 games behind the league-leading Brooklyn Robins.

Chicago's Guy Bush faced Claude Willoughby on the mound. Despite his 6.62 earned-run average, Bush had won five in a row after losing his first two decisions. Willoughby came into the game with a 1-4 record and an ERA of over 9 runs per game. In 1929, he led the National League in both runs and walks allowed. Though his free passes were down in

1930, he was still allowing far too many runs for the Phillies to stay competitive.

The Cubs "revealed their intentions right at the start,"[3] getting to Willoughby in the first inning. Footsie Blair reached on an error by Phillies second baseman Bernie Friberg, and he scored after a walk to Woody English and a single by Kiki Cuyler. Center fielder Denny Sothern misplayed Cuyler's ball, allowing the runners to advance. Wilson then smashed his 22nd home run of the season, a three-run shot into the right-field seats.

In the top of the second, Philadelphia's bats tried to make up for their "wabbly fielding."[4] Pinkey Whitney doubled but was thrown out at third when Friberg grounded to short. Tommy Thevenow singled and Spud Davis launched a three-run home run, putting the Phillies back in the game. The next four half-innings went by without much incident.

With Chicago still leading 4-3 in the fourth, "a double by [Gabby] Hartnett inaugurated the five run riot."[5] Then Clyde Beck, Bush, Blair, Cuyler, Wilson, and Riggs Stephenson all reached on singles, and the Cubs added five more runs to their tally. Charlie Grimm grounded into a double play, or Chicago might have made more trouble for the Phillies. An inning later, Willoughby walked Beck with one out and then surrendered a triple to right to pitcher Bush. That led to a mound visit by Philadelphia skipper Burt Shotton and a ticket to the showers for the Phillies hurler. By Speece came on in relief.

In the Phillies sixth, Lefty O'Doul and Chuck Klein led off with back-to-back singles. Whitney walked, but O'Doul rounded third base too far, and was tagged out in a rundown (shortstop to catcher to third to pitcher). Both Klein and Whitney moved up on the play, and Klein scored on a sacrifice fly to center by Thevenow. Davis then "belted another circuit smash which was good for half of a four run rally."[6] The Phillies had clawed their way back, but Chicago still led, 10-7.

The Cubs continued the hit parade. In the sixth, Cuyler reached on an error and Wilson followed with a triple. Stephenson singled; so did Grimm. An out later, Beck walked to load the bases, but Bush struck out. With two outs, Blair singled, driving in two runs and sending Beck to third. Then, with English batting, Beck and Blair pulled off a double steal; Beck stole home and Blair took second. English was then called out on strikes, but nine Cubs batters had been in the batter's box, and five of them had scored. In the seventh, Chicago again batted around and again scored five runs. The first six batters reached on five singles and a double (Wilson singled for his fourth hit of the game). Bush drove in his third run with a groundout. After Blair flied out, English struck out to end the inning and his participation in the game. Twice he had ended the inning by being called out on strikes, and the second time, he argued the call, so home-plate umpire Lou Jorda ejected the Cubs third baseman. In the sixth and seventh innings, Speece did not fare much better than Willoughby, the starter. He had allowed 10 runs, nine earned. Then Speece yielded another run in the eighth, when "Wilson and Stephenson had to have their bit of fun."[7] Wilson doubled and scored on Stephenson's single, giving the Cubs their 21st run.

Although Bush didn't cruise in the complete-game victory, "he was enabled to loaf along with the big margin presented him by his team-mates."[8] He picked up his sixth win of the season. In nine games against Philadelphia, Bush started four and won all four with complete-game victories. Manager Joe McCarthy also was not afraid to use Bush as a

reliever (he started only 25 of 46 games in which he appeared in 1930). At the plate, the right-hander had two singles and a triple with three RBIs. His batting average was a phenomenal .423 (11-for-26).[9]

According to the *Chicago Tribune*, "Winning was merely incidental,"[10] as the Cubs mustered 24 hits, sending 51 batters to the plate. There were only six extra-base hits (three by Wilson), meaning that Chicago had banged 18 singles. Stephenson had four of those singles, increasing his batting average to .394. Philadelphia had 12 hits (seven singles). Still, the game was completed in 2 hours and 7 minutes.[11]

For Philadelphia, O'Doul, Klein, and Davis accounted for seven of the Phillies' 12 hits. Davis smashed two round-trippers and drove in five runs. O'Doul's 3-for-4 performance raised his batting average to .402.

The 21 runs scored were the highest total for the Cubs in the 1930 season. In a five-game stretch from June 1 to June 6, they scored at least 10 runs in each contest, but the most before this game was *only* 18 runs (against Boston). Chicago scored 19 runs twice, later in the season, on July 24 versus Philadelphia and on September 6 against Pittsburgh (both were away games). Only four teams scored at least 20 runs in a game in 1930, but they all scored them against Philadelphia opponents.[12]

Wilson had hit for the cycle, the first Cubs player to ever do so and the second of three major leaguers to hit for the cycle in 1930.[13] Further, he added five RBIs to his record-setting season total of 191.

SOURCES

In addition to the sources mentioned in the Notes, the author consulted baseball-reference.com, mlb.com, retrosheet.org, and:

Schott, Thomas E. "Hack Wilson," sabr.org/bioproj/person/e2c5ebeb.

NOTES

1 "Cubs' 24 Safeties Overcome Phillies," *New York Times*, June 24, 1930: 35.

2 Cubs infielder Les Bell entered the game in the top of the eighth inning as a defensive replacement for Woody English at third base, but Bell did not have a plate appearance.

3   Irving Vaughan, "Cubs Roll Up 24 Hits; Overwhelm Phillies 21 to 8," *Chicago Tribune*, June 24, 1930: 19.

4   Ibid.

5   Ibid.

6   Ibid.

7   Ibid.

8   "Cubs' 24 Safeties Overcome Phillies."

9   This was the highest Bush's average would get to all season. He finished 1930 batting .282, and three of his seven RBIs came in this game.

10   Vaughan.

11   From box score in *Chicago Tribune*, June 24, 1930: 19.

12   The other three teams were the Cleveland Indians (25-7 on May 11 versus the Philadelphia Athletics), the New York Yankees (20-13 on May 22 in the second game of a doubleheader versus the Athletics), and the Brooklyn Dodgers (22-8 on September 6 versus the Phillies).

13   In the nineteenth century, Jimmy Ryan had accomplished the rare feat twice for the National League Chicago club, on July 28, 1888 (for the Chicago White Stockings), and on July 1, 1891 (for the Chicago Colts). In 1930, the other two batters to hit for the cycle were New York Giants' Freddie Lindstrom (May 8) and St Louis Cardinals' Chick Hafey (August 21).

COMEBACK CUBS PREVAIL AS WILSON SETS RBI MARK

SEPTEMBER 28, 1930
CHICAGO CUBS 13, CINCINNATI REDS 11

By Tom Pardo

IT IS OFTEN SAID IN SPORTS THAT records are meant to be broken. Yet it is also true there are some achievements in baseball that may never be topped, such as Joe DiMaggio's 56-game hitting streak, Johnny Vander Meer's back-to-back no-hitters, or Cy Young's 511 victories. Joining this elite company is certainly Hack Wilson's 191 RBIs generated in one season. Wilson attained baseball immortality when he drove in two runs on the final day of the 1930 season as the Chicago Cubs overcame a nine-run deficit to defeat the Cincinnati Reds, 13-11.

Hack Wilson was the epitome of a Prohibition-era ballplayer in Chicago, that "toddlin' town." Nicknamed after a professional wrestler, George Hackenschmidt, Wilson thrived on the adoration of Cubs fans who waited patiently after games for a glimpse of their hero or possibly an autograph. Although he had a penchant for drinking and his escapades in Chicago's speakeasies were legendary, Wilson was an affable sort, willing to strike up a conversation with anyone, stranger or friend.[1]

On the diamond, Hack Wilson looked like an "ambulatory beer barrel."[2] He stood just 5-feet-6 and weighed 200 pounds – a human fireplug. Further accentuating his unique physique were an 18-inch neck, 16-inch biceps, a massive chest, and thunder thighs tapering to very tiny feet.[3] Understandably, Wilson had a very powerful swing, rotating hard from his heels to achieve maximum torque. The ball often launched off the bat like a cannonball. As

Sparky Adams, infielder for several National League clubs, recalled years later, "Hack could hit a ball with his eyes shut, and he could hit it a long way. I have a mark on my shin yet."[4]

Wilson joined the Cubs from the New York Giants through the Rule 5 draft in the 1925 offseason. From 1926 to 1930, he proved to be an integral part of

In a five-year span (1926-1930), Hall of Famer Hack Wilson led the NL in home runs four times, culminating with his epic season in 1930: 56 round-trippers, a big-league-record 191 runs batted in, and a .356 batting average. (Photo by Mark Rucker/ Transcendental Graphics, Getty Images)

the Cubs' offensive juggernaut that included Gabby Hartnett, Charlie Grimm, Riggs Stephenson, Woody English, Kiki Cuyler, and Rogers Hornsby. In 1930, when the baseball was reportedly "juiced" and more runs were scored per game since 1895, the defending NL champions sported a .309 team average. The starting outfield of Cuyler, Stephenson, and Wilson averaged an unbelievable .358! Yet even in the midst of such offensive power, Hack Wilson achieved a career year that remains to this day one of the best in the history of professional baseball.[5]

For much of the 1930 season, the Cubs were locked in a tight pennant race with the Cardinals and Giants, and at times with the Brooklyn Robins and Pittsburgh Pirates. Most baseball scribes of the day believe the Cubs' quest to repeat as NL champions came to an end on Labor Day when the lowly Reds took both ends of a doubleheader. These key losses, combined with a surging Cardinals finish and winning only half of the games played against the hapless Reds during the season, sealed the Cubs' fate.[6]

With nothing to play for, the Cubs came home from a 14-game road trip to conclude the 1930 season with a four-game series against those pesky Reds. Playing perhaps with a vengeful heart, the Cubs won the first three games, supported by Wilson's three home runs and seven RBIs.

The season finale was played in a manner fitting for two teams that were extremely eager to get the offseason quickly underway. In fact, there was more chatter in the "Friendly Confines" among the 22,000 attendees concerning the coming crosstown series against the White Sox later that week than the poor excuse of a contest about to be played.[7]

Taking the mound for the Cubs was veteran right-hander Guy Bush. Opposing the North Siders was right-hander Si Johnson, who was completing his first full season in the big leagues.

Both hurlers sailed through the first inning unscathed. However, in the second, the Reds erupted for nine runs on nine hits and two walks, sending Bush to an early shower. Interestingly, the Reds' rally was a classic demonstration of "small ball," as

shortstop Leo Durocher had the only extra-base hit – a triple – in the inning.

The Cubs began the long climb back into the game by scoring three on just one hit in the home half of the third. Third baseman Les Bell opened the frame with a walk and went to third on relief pitcher Jess Petty's base hit. Second baseman Footsie Blair drew another pass, loading the bases. Shortstop Wally English continued the free passes, scoring Bell. Right fielder Kiki Cuyler forced Petty at the plate for the first out. Wilson then drew another walk, scoring Blair for the center fielder's 190th RBI. Cuyler scored the third run when left fielder Dan Taylor forced Wilson at second.

In the fifth, the Cubs added two more runs as a result of an error by Reds second baseman Pat Crawford, a base hit by English and a double by Cuyler.

The Cubs closed the gap to 9-8 in the sixth, forcing Johnson out of the game. Relieving the youngster was right-hander Benny Frey, who was the only Reds hurler to have success against the Cubs that season.[8] With one out, Bell walked and advanced to third again on Petty's second single of the contest. Blair smashed a triple to right-center, scoring both Bell and Petty. Blair crossed the plate shortly thereafter with the Cubs' eighth tally on a passed ball.

With the crowd buzzing excitedly about the Cubs' gradual comeback, Jess Petty, who surrendered only one Reds' tally over the course of 5⅔ innings, was relieved by left-hander Bud Teachout in the eighth inning. Teachout was not as sharp as his predecessor, as the Reds padded their lead by scoring two insurance runs via a single by right fielder Curt Walker, a walk to third baseman Tony Cuccinello and a triple by first baseman Joe Stripp.

Now down by three, 11-8, heading into the bottom of the eighth, the Cubs executed their best late-inning rally of the season. The drama began when Frey walked English and then served up a double to Cuyler, the right fielder's second of the game and 50th of the season, advancing English to third. Wilson collected his 191st RBI on an infield single that scored English and moved Cuyler to third.[9] Frey gave up his second pass of the inning, to Taylor, loading the bases for Hartnett. The scrappy Cubs catcher drove in Cuyler to reduce the Reds' lead to one when Durocher bobbled a surefire double-play grounder. Wilson crossed the plate with the tying run when Frey uncorked a wild pitch. After first baseman High Pockets Kelly popped out to Crawford, Bell sealed the Cubs' victory by driving a single to left, scoring Taylor and Hartnett.

This final game of the 1930 season was a true laugher technically speaking, but one that Cubs fans would long remember. Si Johnson was effective in spots for the Reds, as witnessed by his seven strikeouts. Johnson's six walks, however, proved his undoing. Four of the batters he walked eventually scored, more than the margin of victory. Benny Frey also lacked control as his four walks and wild pitch set the table for disaster. For the Cubs, the combination of a tenacious offense and Jess Petty's strong long-inning relief work was simply too much for a talent-deficient Reds squad.

The North Siders finished the season with 90 wins, only two games behind the league champion Cardinals. The Reds completed their woeful campaign with 95 losses, the most for a 154-game schedule by a Reds team since 1914.

For Hack Wilson, though, this matinee contest was the capstone of an unforgettable season:

- Wilson's 191 RBIs set a new major-league record that will most likely not be surpassed.[10]
- Wilson's 56 home runs stood as the NL record for 68 years until fellow Cubs outfielder Sammy Sosa hit 66 and Mark McGwire of the St. Louis Cardinals hit 70 in 1998.[11]
- Wilson got only 97 of his 191 RBIs by home runs. A quarter of his total (48 RBIs) was generated from singles.
- Wilson drove in an average of three of every 10 Cubs runners on base.[12]
- Wilson produced RBIs in three of every five games played (92 of 155 games).

- Wilson's RBI output of 53 in August is perhaps the most productive month of any hitter in major-league history.
- In addition to his RBI and home-run exploits, Wilson hit .356 with an astonishing slugging average of .723. He scored 146 times and accumulated 423 total bases.

In 1952, veteran baseball writer James Crusinberry reflected on the legendary Cubs outfielder: "Hack Wilson was as great a hero in Chicago as Babe Ruth was in New York. From 1926 through 1930, Wilson's feats on the ball field for the Chicago Cubs were tremendous and his popularity with Chicago's fans was greater than that of any Windy City player before or since his time."[13]

SOURCES

In addition to the sources cited in the Notes, the author consulted the following:

Baseball-Reference.com.

"Bruins Outlast Reds to Annex Last Game, 13-11," Associated Press, September 28, 1930.

"Cubs Rally to Beat Reds," *Chicago Evening American*, September 29, 1930: 13.

Burns, Edward. "Cubs Overcome Reds' 9 Run Lead; Win 13-11," *Chicago Tribune*, September 29, 1930: 13.

Lieb, Frederick G. "Baseball Is Still the National Sport," *Baseball Research Journal*, v.1, 1972, sabr.org/research/baseball-still-national-sport, accessed July 17, 2017.

"Hack Wilson Signs, Given Boost in Pay," *Sporting News*, February 5, 1931: 1.

Simons, Herbert. "The One Record They'll Never Break," *Baseball Digest*, July 1963: 5-7.

"Howleyites Blow Big Lead and Hand Game to Chicago," *Cincinnati Times-Star*, September 29, 1930: 16.

"Notes on the Cubs," *Chicago Evening American*, September 29, 1930: 16.

Retrosheet.org.

"Right to Form," *Cincinnati Enquirer*, September 29, 1930: 11-12.

Swope, Tom. "Reds Finish With Worst Record in City's History," *Cincinnati Post*, September 29, 1930: 12.

NOTES

1   Thomas E. Schott, "Hack Wilson," SABR Baseball Biography Project, sabr.org/bioproj/person/e2c5ebeb, date unknown, accessed July 7, 2017; James Crusinberry, "Baseball's Forgotten Men," *Baseball Magazine*, April 1952: 30.

2   Harold Rosenthal, "Hack Wilson – What The 190-RBI Man Was Like," *Baseball Digest*, August 1963: 13.

3   Clifton Blue Parker, *Fouled Away: The Baseball Tragedy of Hack Wilson* (Jefferson, North Carolina: McFarland & Company, Inc.), 5.

4   Parker, 97.

5   The aggregate 1930 National League average was .303. Six of the eight NL clubs batted .303 or higher, the highest being, ironically, the last-place Philadelphia Phillies at .315. Jerome Holtzman, "On Baseball: Lively Ball Put Wilson in Record Book," *Chicago Tribune*, September 6, 1999, Sports Section: 3.

6   Parker, 113.

7   In 1930, the Cubs fell just 20,000 shy of their 1929 attendance record of 1,485,000. "Cubs Fall 20,000 Short of 1929 Attendance Mark," *Chicago Tribune*, September 29, 1930: 23.

8   Going into the game, Frey had a 5-3 record versus the Cubs in 1930. Frey pitched seven innings of more in all but one of his victories. retrosheet.org/boxsetc/1930/Kfreyb101002r930.htm, date unknown, accessed July 7, 2017.

9   Wilson hit a high bouncer to Reds first baseman Joe Stripp who lost the ball in the sun momentarily before knocking it down as Wilson's foot touched the base. There was some debate about whether Stripp committed an error on the play, but the official scorer ruled the play a hit. Wayne K. Otto, "Cubs Rally to Win From Reds, 13-11," *Chicago Herald and Examiner*, September 29, 1930: 21.

10 Wilson was credited with only 190 RBIs at the time he achieved his record in 1930. For almost 69 years, the 190 total remained intact until June 23, 1999, when Major League Baseball awarded Wilson an additional RBI, bringing his 1930 total to 191. Thanks to excellent game-by-game research by James Braswell and Cliff Kachline, National Baseball Hall of Fame historian and co-founder of the Society for American Baseball Research, the "lost" RBI was discovered in the second game of a doubleheader played by the Cubs against the Reds on July 28, 1930. An RBI was credited erroneously to first baseman Charlie Grimm instead of Wilson. "Around the Horn: Credit Grimm Reapers for Hack Wilson 191st RBI," *Seattle Times*, June 27, 1999; "69 Years Later, Hack Wilson Gets Another RBI," Associated Press, June 23, 1999.

11 Mark McGwire hit 58 home runs in 1997, but he split that season playing for the Oakland Athletics (34 home runs) and St. Louis Cardinals (24 home runs).

12 Herbert Simons, "Hack Drove in Three of Every Ten Runners," *Baseball Digest*, October-November 1963: 67-71.

13 Crusinberry.

THE BABE CALLS HIS SHOT... OR DOES HE?

OCTOBER 1, 1932
NEW YORK YANKEES 7, CHICAGO CUBS 5

GAME THREE OF THE WORLD SERIES

By Gary Sarnoff

"KEEP UP THE PEPPER, BOYS!"[1] CHICAGO manager Charlie Grimm told his team in the clubhouse after the Chicago Cubs' 7-5 loss to the New York Yankees in Game Three of the 1932 World Series to put the Cubs at a three-games-to-none disadvantage.

"You can't take it away from that pair; they can hit," said Cubs losing pitcher Charlie Root, who had served up two home runs apiece to Babe Ruth and Lou Gehrig in the game. "If I had to do it all over again I'd pitch the same way."[2]

"It was a change of pace ball, low and outside," Root said of the second home run he had yielded to Ruth. "If it had been a fastball I wouldn't have been surprised. But he picked it out and sent on the line to center field. That convinced me of the power he has in his swings."[3]

"We'll be going home tomorrow," Babe Ruth bellowed in the joyous New York clubhouse, referring to his expectation of his team winning the next day to wrap up the 1932 World Series.[4]

"Well I picked a couple of 'em out today anyhow," Ruth continued, "and I seldom get more fun out of doing it. They've got some pretty good bench jockeys on that Cubs bench. But I think I had the last laugh."[5]

Before the game Ruth stepped into the batter's box for his turn during batting practice on a warm Indian summer day, with the temperature reaching an unseasonable 78 degrees. As one might expect, Ruth put on a good show by hammering a half-dozen baseballs over the fences, "and he knew he had the trick for the day," wrote sportswriter Westbrook Pegler, who also told his readers, "I'm telling you that before the game began the Babe knew he was going to hit one or more homeruns."[6]

After slamming the last practice pitch into the far distance, "(H)e waddled toward the Cubs dugout, his large abdomen jiggling in spite of his rubber corsets and yelled, 'You mugs are not going to see Yankee Stadium any more this year. The World Series is going to be over Sunday afternoon, four straight.'"[7]

He then turned to a group of autograph seekers along the third-base barrier to inform them: "Did you hear what I told them? I told them over there? I told them that they ain't going back to New York. We lick 'em here, today and tomorrow."[8]

"The Babe is on fire," Lou Gehrig said as he laughed. "He ought to hit one today; maybe a couple."[9] Then the Yankees first baseman, having a poor turn in his batting practice session, focused on himself. "I'm not catching them right, but I know what's the trouble. I'm catching them on the end of the club. I ought to catch them about four inches down to make 'em ride."[10]

Cubs starting pitcher Charlie Root drew the assignment to tame the Yankees in Game Three. A 15-game winner in 1932, he was currently hot, with four wins during the last month of the season. He seemed to start off right by getting New York's first batter, Earle Combs, to ground one to the shortstop. However, Cubs shortstop Billy Jurges threw the ball away, allowing Combs to take second. Then Root walked the next batter, bringing up Ruth for his first at-bat with runners on first and second.

A salvo of boos greeted Ruth as he paced his way to the plate. Several lemons, thrown from the stands, landed on the field and rolled by Ruth's feet. He stepped up to the plate and readied himself as he looked out at the Cubs pitcher. Root made his pitch and, "With a step forward, a lurch of his massive shoulders and sweep of his celebrated bat, Ruth drove the ball high into temporary bleachers that had been erected beyond the right field fence. Upward and onward the ball flew, a white streak outlined against the bright blue sky."[11]

The top of the first concluded with a 3-0 Yankees lead. When the Yankees took the field in the bottom of the inning, Ruth was greeted by booing from the left-field bleachers. A fan threw a lemon that hit Ruth on the leg. "With graphic gestures, old Mr. Ruth called on them for fair play."[12]

The Cubs scored one in their half of the first inning against New York's starting pitcher, George Pipgras. In the top of the second, Ruth came to the plate with a runner on first and two outs. He got hold of a Root pitch and backed Cubs right fielder Kiki Cuyler up against the screen fence in right. Cuyler made the catch to retire Ruth.

In the top of the third, the score still 3-1, Gehrig came up for his second at-bat. Hoping to fool the Yankees first baseman, Root threw a change-of-pace pitch. Gehrig connected and sent the ball for a long ride into the right-field bleachers. "It wasn't as far as Ruth's, and it came with nobody on the bases, but it was just as effective in throwing fear into the hearts of the Cubs."[13]

The Cubs, who were not going to go down without a fight, rallied for three runs to tie the game, 4-4, after four innings. In the top of the fifth Ruth led off. "As Ruth came to the plate, swinging three bats over his shoulder, a concerted shout of derision broke in the stands. There was a bellowing of boos, hisses, and jeers. There were cries of encouragement for the pitcher, and from the Cubs dugout came a storm of abuse directed at the Babe."[14]

"Ruth, grinning in the face of the hostile greeting, laughed back at the Cubs and took his place, supremely confident."[15]

In the Cubs dugout pitchers Guy Bush and Bob Smith, both seated at the top of the dugout steps, were the loudest among the Cubs.

Root's first pitch sailed by Ruth for a called strike. He responded by holding up one finger as he looked into the Cubs dugout to indicate strike one. "Wait, mugg; I'm going to hit one out of the yard," he shouted.[16] Guy Bush responded by inching up the steps and yelling more insults. Then after two balls, Ruth let another one go by for strike two. Ruth held up two fingers and told the Cubs, "That's only two strikes, boys. I still have one coming."[17] Bush again responded while scooting closer to the point where he was now sitting on the grass at the edge before the Cubs dugout.

"Then, with a warning gesture of his hand to Bush, he sent the signal for the customers to see, as if to say, 'Now this is the one, look.'"[18]

With a count of two balls and two strikes, Root threw his change-of-pace pitch. Ruth swung and "there was a resounding report like the explosion of a gun. The ball soared on a line to center field. Johnny Moore (Cubs center fielder) raced back then stopped and stared."[19]

The ball sailed over the center-field fence, passed a flagpole, and dropped into the street. Ruth rounded the bases, and after he passed second base, he slowed down to deliver a message to Bush and the Cubs in the Chicago dugout. "The Yankees spilled out of the dugout and danced with glee. They moved forward to shake Ruth's hand and pat him on the back."[20]

As the Yankees continued to talk about Ruth's home run, Gehrig hit a high curveball and sent it for a ride into the right-field bleachers for his second homer of the game. The score was now 6-4 in favor of the Yankees.

In the bottom of the ninth, with the Yankees nursing a two-run lead, a runner on first and Rollie Hemsley at the plate for the Cubs, Guy Bush, who was warming up in the left-field bullpen, shouted advice for the Yankees left fielder. "Say Babe, don't you know that Hemsley is a left-field hitter? You better come over close to the foul line."[21]

"Well, if that's true, I will," responded Ruth, who then walked to his right until he was 12 feet from the left-field foul line. "Is this the right spot?" asked Ruth.[22]

Bush assured him that it was.

Hemsley struck out, the next batter grounded out, and then Cubs third baseman Woody English grounded out to end the game. "Well, I'll see you tomorrow, Joe," Ruth told Bush, and then jogged toward the infield.[23]

An angry look then came across Bush's features: not because Ruth called him by the wrong name. He tried his best, but he was unable to get Ruth's goat that day.

SOURCES

In addition to the sources cited in the Notes, the author also accessed Retrosheet.org, Baseball-Reference.com, SABR.org, and *The Sporting News* archive via Paper of Record.

NOTES

1   Irving Vaughan, "Root Sees Ruth, Gehrig Ruin Perfect Pitches," *Chicago Tribune*, October 2, 1932: A1.

2   Ibid.

3   Ibid.

4   *Chicago Herald American*, October 2, 1932.

5   Ibid.

6   Westbook Pegler, "Gehrig Hit 'Em; Foxx Or Hoover Might Have – But Not Like Babe," *Chicago Tribune*, October 2, 1932: 1A.

7   Ibid.

8   Ibid.

9   Ibid.

10 Ibid.

11 *New York Herald-Tribune*, October 2, 1932.

12 Vaughan.

13 *New York Herald-Tribune*, October 2, 1932.

14 Ibid.

15 Ibid.

16 Pegler.

17 Ibid.

18 Ibid.

19 *New York Herald-Tribune*, October 2, 1932.

20 Ibid.

21 Vaughan

22 Ibid.

23 Ibid.

THE YANKEES CRUSH THE CUBS TO TAKE TITLE

OCTOBER 2, 1932
NEW YORK YANKEES 13, CHICAGO CUBS 6

GAME FOUR OF THE WORLD SERIES

By Mark S. Sternman

WINNING THEIR FOURTH TITLE, THE NEW York Yankees crushed the Chicago Cubs 13-6 to sweep the 1932 World Series.

Guy Bush started for Chicago and opposed Johnny Allen of New York. Both exited early.

After averaging eight runs over the first three games of the Series, the Yankees got off to another good start offensively, thanks to a batting order whose first six hitters eventually went on to Cooperstown. Earle Combs and Joe Sewell both singled. After Bush plunked Babe Ruth to load the bases with none out, Lou Gehrig drove in a run on a "great catch"[1] of his fly ball by center fielder Frank Demaree that gave New York a 1-0 lead. Bush then walked Tony Lazzeri, and player-manager Charlie Grimm hurried Lon Warneke into the game to relieve Bush, who "failed because of an injury he had concealed for two weeks."[2] Warneke induced consecutive groundouts to minimize the damage.

Allen started better than Bush but finished worse. Yielding a single to Woody English, he faced Riggs Stephenson with two out and English on first. Stephenson singled and Demaree hit a three-run homer to put the Cubs up 3-1. Grimm reached on Frankie Crosetti's error, which preceded consecutive singles by Gabby Hartnett and Billy Jurges. The Jurges hit extended the Chicago lead to 4-1 and knocked Allen out of the game. Wilcy Moore, reacquired by the Yankees from the Red Sox on

August 1, relieved and retired Warneke to end the action-packed first frame.

After that, no batter reached for either team until Gehrig doubled with two outs in the top of the third. Lazzeri followed with a two-run blast to pull New York to within 4-3. Bill Dickey and Ben Chapman both singled, but Warneke got Crosetti to preserve the lead.

Moore, with his "tremendous sidearm sinkerball,"[3] kept getting the Cubs to beat the ball into the dirt, getting two outs that way in the second and all three in the third. The Yankees threatened in the fourth as the weak-hitting Moore, with a lifetime New York batting average of .087, singled to start the inning and Combs walked. Grimm lifted Warneke, who departed "rubbing his right elbow, which he seemed to have strained beyond its endurance in a vain attempt to check this Yankee avalanche."[4] On came Jakie May; he retired Sewell, Ruth, and Gehrig to keep Chicago in front.

Moore had his second 1-2-3 frame in the fourth, and the Yankees put on two baserunners again in the fifth via a Lazzeri single and a walk to Chapman. Crosetti, who had struggled both offensively and defensively, hit into a 4-6-3 double play to end the threat.

For the third time in four innings, Moore set down the Cubs in order in the bottom of the fifth, "one of the finest defensive innings ever played.

Crosetti started it by tearing almost to the bullpen and careening off the wall as he clutched English's foul. … [Kiki] Cuyler bounded one over Moore's head. Crosetti dashed in, picked up the ball while on the dead run, and threw to first ahead of the runner. Then Lazzeri made a dive to his right to get … Stephenson's liner."[5]

In the top of the sixth, Moore fanned, Combs walked, and Sewell doubled him to third. With first base open, May struck out Ruth. The legendary reporter Grantland Rice lauded "portly Jakie May [for fanning] the great Ruth twice in succession and this for the 50,000 Cubs rooters was the only jewel left in the toad's head of defeat."[6]

Chicago could have walked Gehrig to face Lazzeri. Perhaps because Lazzeri had homered in his prior appearance, or perhaps because the southpaw May would rather face the lefty Gehrig than the righty Lazzeri, May pitched to Gehrig. Lou's single plated both runs. Lazzeri struck out to end the frame, but New York had seesawed back in front, 5-4.

Porous defense allowed Chicago to tie the game. With one out, Grimm had an infield single and advanced to second on Gehrig's error. Grimm scored on Crosetti's throwing error, his second miscue of the game and fourth of the Series, which put Hartnett at second. Moore escaped additional damage by fanning Jurges and getting May, who had no RBIs on the season in only nine plate appearances, on a grounder to leave the go-ahead run in scoring position. Grimm passively let May hit, an unfortunate oversight given the need to manage aggressively against the high-scoring Yankees.

May would not survive the seventh, which started poorly for the Cubs on a leadoff single by Dickey and Crosetti's one-out double. With Moore due, Joe McCarthy, who had managed Chicago in its last World Series appearance, in 1929, did what Grimm had failed to do, pinch-hit for his hurler. Pitcher Red Ruffing (.306 BA in 1932) was the batter. Grimm sought to set up a double play and ordered an intentional walk for Ruffing. This move backfired for the Cubs in a sequence that essentially sealed Chicago's fate.

A single by Combs on a ball that "dropped on the outer edge of the foul line"[7] put New York up 6-5. Sewell's single extended the lead to 8-5. Then Ruth singled to put the Yankees ahead 9-5. May hit Gehrig to reload the bases, and Grimm yanked him in favor of Bud Tinning, who retired Lazzeri and Dickey.

Herb Pennock came on for New York. During the season, he had started 21 of his 22 games and had had no regular-season saves since 1929. In Game Three of this Series, however, Pennock had pitched the ninth inning when McCarthy made him the first Yankee reliever of the Series. With a runner on first and no outs, Pennock set down the final three batters of the game to protect the New York win.

In Game Four, Pennock again set down the first three batters in the seventh but ran into difficulty in the bottom of the eighth. Stephenson singled, and Demaree walked. With one out, Hartnett reached on the fourth New York infield error of the day, this one by Sewell, to load the bases and bring the tying run to the plate. But Pennock pitched stoutly, getting Jurges to fly to right and fanning pinch-hitter Rollie Hemsley. The Yankees had a four-run lead and one inning to go to win the World Series.

The New York bats boosted the margin against veteran spitballer Burleigh Grimes. Combs, who had smacked a career-high nine homers in 1932, turned the trick again to put the Yankees up 10-5 with what would turn out to be his only Series round-tripper in the 72nd and last plate appearance of his postseason career. Gehrig walked with two outs and scored on Lazzeri's second homer of the game. Dickey singled, advanced to second on center fielder Demaree's muff, and scored on Chapman's double. Pennock carried a comfortable 13-5 lead as he toed the rubber needing but three outs to secure another New York championship.

Billy Herman got the Cubs off to a good start with a single. He took second and third on defensive indifference, and scored Woody English's grounder. Pennock whiffed Cuyler and got Stephenson to fly to Chapman. New York had won its fourth World Series, the last three of which (1927, 1928, and 1932) had lasted the minimum four games.

The undermanned Chicagoans could not keep up with the big bats from the Bronx, forcing a hometown scribe to concede, "Other world series decided in the minimum of four games have, obviously, been eminently decisive, but it is doubtful that any world title was so consistently devoid of class as the Cubs proved to be in the struggle with the Yankees."[8] Few would have thought that the Cubs would return to the World Series before the Yankees.

SOURCES

In addition to the sources cited in the Notes, the author also accessed Retrosheet.org, Baseball-Reference.com, SABR.org, and *The Sporting News* archive via Paper of Record.

NOTES

1   Woody English, "'Better Team Won,' Says Cub Captain," *Boston Globe*, October 3, 1932: 13.

2   Irving Vaughan, "Injuries Bring Downfall of Bush, Warneke," *Chicago Tribune*, October 3, 1932: 23.

3   Fred Glueckstein, "Wilcy Moore," SABR BioProject, sabr.org/bioproj/person/3a388917 (accessed July 6, 2017).

4   John Drebinger, "Yankees Defeat Cubs, 13-6, Before 51,000; Win World's Series in Four Straight Games," *New York Times*, October 3, 1932: 21.

5   Arch Ward, "Get Refunds Tomorrow on Fifth Game," *Chicago Tribune*, October 3, 1932: 23.

6   Grantland Rice, "Yankees Win World Series Again, Crushing Cubs, 13-6," *Boston Globe*, October 3, 1932: 1.

7   Joe Sewell, "Cubs Outclassed, Says Sewell after Triumph," *Boston Globe*, October 3, 1932: 13.

8   Edward Burns, "Yanks Win World Title; Four Straight," *Chicago Tribune*, October 3, 1932: 23.

BABE HERMAN'S THREE HOMERS OVERWHELM PHILLIES

JULY 20, 1933
CHICAGO CUBS 10, PHILADELPHIA PHILLIES 1

By Tom Pardo

HIS PARENTS NAMED HIM FLOYD AND his fans knew him as Babe. In certain baseball writing circles, he was the "other Babe." Born in Buffalo, New York, and raised in Los Angeles, this Babe – Babe Herman – was a conundrum to those who followed his career. He suffered from mental lapses on the field, especially on defense. But could Babe Herman hit! He sported a lifetime .324 batting average and .532 slugging average, more than making up for the suspect aspects of his game. On July 20, 1933, he proved for a day that he was the full measure of the "Great Bambino" when he socked three home runs and drove in eight runs in a 10-1 drubbing of the Philadelphia Phillies by the Chicago Cubs at Wrigley Field.

Babe Herman seemed destined for baseball greatness. Hall of Famer Al Lopez said of the tall outfielder with a warm smile, "Babe swung a bat with more ease and grace than any man I ever saw."[1]

He began his major-league career playing six outstanding seasons with Brooklyn before being dealt to Cincinnati over a contract dispute in 1932. In that season with the beleaguered Reds, Herman led the team in batting (.326), home runs (16), and RBIs (87). Herman was sent to the Cubs in the offseason because the Reds were plagued with financial troubles and needed the cash – $75,000 – offered for the star outfielder.[2]

The Herman acquisition was considered the missing piece in the Cubs' quest to repeat as National League champions. Unfortunately for Cubs fans,

the new face in the dugout was struggling with a leg injury during the early part of the 1933 season. Herman's batting average had dipped to .288 by the Philadelphia series, respectable for most ballplayers but clearly not up to expectations for a player of Herman's capability. Nevertheless, the star-studded cast of future Hall of Famers Gabby Hartnett, Billy Herman, and Kiki Cuyler led by player-manager Charlie Grimm had just completed an eight-game winning streak during an extended homestand and was locked in a tight pennant race with the New York Giants and the Pittsburgh Pirates by late July.

Coming into Wrigley Field for a four-game series against the Cubs was a Philadelphia club deeply burdened by too many losses and few bright lights. During the interwar years and beyond, the Phillies resided in the NL cellar 16 times and emerged from the second division only once, in 1932, when they finished in fourth place. But by late July of the 1933 season, the Phillies were two games shy of last place, thanks to an even weaker Cincinnati Reds squad. Hopes for a momentary rebound ran high in the Phillies clubhouse, however, as they had won two of three the last time both teams met at Wrigley Field, in late May.

The July 20 contest between the Cubs and the Phillies was a ladies day affair, attracting a crowd of 27,000 under sunny skies and a slight breeze blowing out toward right field. On the mound for the Cubs was right-hander Bud Tinning, who had just enjoyed a seven-game winning streak in June and early July.

Tinning seemed to pitch his best against the Phillies, beating them three times in 1932 and nine times overall in his brief major-league career.[3] Facing the Cubs was the workhorse of the Philadelphia staff, Ed Holley, who entered the game with an 8-6 record.

The only major change in the Cubs' lineup for this game was noteworthy. Grimm inserted Babe Herman in right field for Riggs Stephenson, who was suffering from a cold. During the previous series against the Boston Braves, Herman had been benched because of his hitting woes.[4]

Grimm's decision proved to be the right tonic for the Cubs right fielder as Herman began to climb out of his rut with a single to right in his first at-bat. That hit and Phillies' singles by right fielder Chuck Klein and left fielder Wes Schulmerich, were the only offense generated through the first 2½ innings.

The Cubs began their hitting barrage in their half of the third when third baseman Mark Koenig scored on a single to center by second baseman Billy Herman. Left fielder Kiki Cuyler got to first on a force play on Herman at second. Babe Herman advanced to the plate and proceeded to deposit the ball into the center-field bleachers for a two-run homer, his eighth round-tripper of the season.

The Phils continued to scatter hits off Tinning in the fourth and fifth innings, but failed to manufacture any runs. In the Cubs' fifth, Babe did it again. With one out, Cuyler slammed a triple off the wall in right field. As in the third, Herman took advantage of a Holley mistake and sent a towering shot into the right-field bleachers to put the home team ahead 5-0.

As the crowd buzzed over the renewed hitting exploits of their Babe, the Phillies' bats woke up and ended Tinning's hope for a shutout in the sixth. With one out, shortstop Dick Bartell beat out a well-placed bunt. Klein singled to right, advancing Bartell to second. After first baseman Don Hurst flied out to Frank Demaree in center, Schulmerich singled to center, scoring Bartell for the only Phillies run of the game.

Right-hander Clarence Pickrel relieved Holley in the bottom of the sixth and retired the Cubs in order. In the seventh, right-handed reliever Ad Liska came in for Pickrel and was treated rather rudely by the explosive Cubs' bats. With one out, Billy Herman hit a line drive over second baseman Jack Warner's head into right field. Cuyler doubled to left, moving Herman to third. Babe Herman came to the plate for the fourth time and grounded out to Warner, his only hitless appearance that afternoon. Demaree walked to load the bases. With the crowd sensing a huge rally, Hartnett spoiled the party by hitting a high foul fly near the Phillies' bullpen and first baseman Don Hurst made a nifty catch to end the inning.

After Tinning worked out of a bases-loaded jam in the Phillies' eighth by getting catcher Spud Davis to ground into a double play, the Cubs took full advantage of Liska. With two outs, Tinning helped his cause with a single to left. Koenig also singled to left, and when Schulmerich bobbled the ball, Tinning advanced to third. Billy Herman drew a walk to fill the bases. Cuyler continued his excellent day at the plate by driving in Tinning with an infield single to deep short. The bases remained loaded when up to the plate strode the day's hero. Liska threw an underhanded slow pitch practically over Herman's head. Babe somehow managed to make solid contact and sent the ball into the right-field bleachers for a grand slam, his 10th home run of the year and his third round-tripper of the day.

After the Phillies' Warner singled and third baseman Jim McLeod walked to open the ninth, Tinning ended the contest by striking out pinch-hitter Harry McCurdy and getting center fielder Chick Fullis to ground into a double play. With the crowd cheering mightily for their Babe, the Cubs headed into the clubhouse with a 10-1 victory.

For Babe Herman, this was the best day of his career in terms of hitting home runs (3) and driving in runs (8) in a single game. While he did not set any club or league records, it was the biggest hitting display by a Cub since Rogers Hornsby hit three homers in a 10-6 victory over the Pittsburgh Pirates on April 24, 1931. A tip of the cap should also be made to Bud Tinning, who yielded only one tally and 11 Phillies hits, and Kiki Cuyler, who came within a home run of hitting for the cycle. As for the Cubs, the win moved them to within 2½ games of the league-leading Giants. They would go on to sweep the Phillies in this four-game series.

As Cubs fans headed for the exits, it was Chicago's very own Babe who was the undisputed king of the diamond on this day. A disgruntled baseball scribe for the *Philadelphia Evening Ledger* cried in his beer when he commented, "From the Philly viewpoint, the opener was not so much a baseball episode as a terrifying experience with a bench-crazy athlete gone berserk to the great distress of pitchers Ed Holley and Ad Liska, and, of course, the rest of the Phillies. …"[5]

Playing for his third team in three seasons, Babe Herman was the offensive powerhouse for the 1933 Cubs, tying for the team lead with 16 home runs while pacing the club in RBIs (93) and slugging (.502). (Photo by William Greene/Sports Studio Photos/ Getty Images)

SOURCES

In addition to the sources cited in the Notes, the author consulted the following:

"Macks Win in 10th as Cubs Crush Phillies," *Philadelphia Inquirer*, July 21, 1933: 15.

"Chicubs Trounce Phillies, 10-1," *Philadelphia Public Ledger*, July 21, 1933: 12.

NOTES

1   Wayne K. Otto, "Babe Herman Hits 3 Homers; Cubs Whip Phils, 10-1," Chicago Herald and Examiner, July 21, 1933: 20-21.

2   Greg Erion, "Babe Herman," SABR Baseball Biography Project (sabr.org/bioproj/person/48d34e71), undated, accessed April 22, 2017; Jim Gallagher, "Babe Herman's 3 Homers Drive Eight Cubs Over Plate," Chicago American, July 20, 1933: 1.

3   John W. Keys, "Babe Herman Hit Two Home Runs as Cubs Get Big Lead Over Phillies," Chicago Daily News, July 20, 1933: 19.

4   Edward Burns, "Babe Herman Hits 3 Homers; Cubs Win, 10-1," Chicago Tribune, July 21, 1933: 23; "Cubs Jolt Phils, 10-1," Philadelphia Record, July 21, 1933: 18; "Herman Off Bench Hits 3 Home Runs," Philadelphia Evening Bulletin, July 21, 1933: 16; "Herman Shakes Off Slump; His 3 Homers Defeat Phils," Philadelphia Evening Ledger, July 21, 1933, Sports Section: 1-2.

5   "Herman Shakes Off Slump."

GALAN'S SLAM AND SIX RBI'S FLATTEN PHILS TO START 21-GAME WINNING STREAK

SEPTEMBER 4, 1935
CHICAGO CUBS 8, PHILADELPHIA PHILLIES 2

By Greg Erion

ON THE MORNING OF SEPTEMBER 4, 1935, longtime *Chicago Tribune* sportswriter Irving Vaughan wrote an article examining the National League pennant race, specifically, how the Cubs' prospects looked going into the final weeks of the season.[1] From his perspective, the odds did not appear promising for the Wrigley Field squad.

Chicago was in third place, 2½ games behind the St. Louis Cardinals and a half-game behind the New York Giants. St. Louis had wrested the lead from New York at the end of August in the midst of winning 15 of their last 20 contests. Despite the seeming closeness in standings, Vaughan felt Chicago had a daunting challenge ahead.

While observing that Chicago would play 18 of its remaining 23 games at home, usually an advantage, he noted that the five road games were all in St. Louis. Meanwhile the Cardinals' remaining 28 games were all at home. St. Louis, which had gone 24-8 since August 1 with players like Dizzy Dean, Frankie Frisch, and Joe Medwick, hadn't shown any signs of slowing its pace in its quest for a second straight pennant. All this and nothing mentioned of the Giants. Ahead of the Cubs, world champions in 1933 and a close second to the Cardinals in 1934, their roster included the likes of future Hall of Famers Carl Hubbell, Travis Jackson, Mel Ott, and Bill Terry.

The last sentence of Vaughan's article shared that Larry French would start against the Phillies in the first of a four-game series that day. French had come to the Cubs in a winter deal with the Pittsburgh Pirates after a disappointing 12-18 performance in 1934. The 27-year-old left-hander had started slow with Chicago, losing his first three decisions, but had come on strong, winning 10 of his last 15 decisions and entering the game with a 12-10 record. By September 4, French had shown he was fitting in well with fellow Cubs starters Lon Warneke, Bill Lee, and Charlie Root.

Opposing French was Philadelphia's Orville Jorgens. Jorgens, also 27, was in his rookie year for the sixth-place Philadelphians. He started the game with a 9-11 record. The Phils were slumping, having lost seven of their previous 10 games. They had reason to be optimistic, however, as they had split the season's series with the Cubs thus far.

Before an estimated crowd of 5,000 at Wrigley Field, the Phils immediately went on the offense in the top of the first as leadoff batter Lou Chiozza singled and moved to third on an errant throw from Chicago's right fielder Chuck Klein. Ethan Allen drove Chiozza home with a sacrifice fly to left. The score remained 1-0 until the bottom of the fourth, when the Cubs struck back.

After giving up a leadoff single to Gabby Hartnett, Jorgens induced two successive force plays, the second of which left Phil Cavarretta at first. Jorgens then walked Stan Hack. Billy Jurges singled, driving Cavarretta in to tie the game. Jorgens next committed the unpardonable sin of walking French, his pitching counterpart, to load the bases, bringing leadoff batter Augie Galan to the plate.

Galan was one of the Cubs' major success stories in 1935. After he was brought up in mid-1934 as a second baseman, it soon became apparent he was not going to dislodge Billy Herman from the job. Converted to an outfielder in spring training, Galan found his niche, performing solidly on defense and offense. Going into the game against Philadelphia, Galan was second in the league in runs (107) and steals (17) while batting a solid .309. He also excelled in walks, ranking second in the league in bases on balls.

Galan's ability to garner walks was evidenced when Jorgens issued a base on balls to him, forcing Hack home and giving the Cubs a 2-1 lead. The score remained unchanged until the sixth, when Galan came to bat again. He hit his eighth home run of the year, giving the Cubs a 3-1 lead.

In the bottom of the eighth inning John "Pretzel" Pezzullo relieved Jorgens and promptly ran into trouble. Cavarretta singled, Hack was safe on a fielder's choice, and Jurges was hit by a pitch. Pezzullo was replaced by Jim Bivin. Bivin was in the first – and last – year of his major-league career. He entered the game with a 2-6 record (both wins against Chicago) and a 5.89 ERA.[2] On Bivin's first pitch, French singled Cavarretta in to make the game 4-1.

On Bivin's next pitch, with the bases loaded, Galan planted it in the right-field seats for a grand slam, making the score 8-1.[3]

Philadelphia scored a meaningless run in the ninth. Chicago won 8-2, giving French his 13th victory for his eight-hit, four-walk, complete-game effort.

The loss started Philadelphia on a five-game losing streak, dropping the Phillies to seventh place, where they ended the season. That finish was the third of what would become 13 consecutive years in which the Phillies finished either seventh or eighth.

Only three major-league games were played this day. While Chicago won, so did New York and St. Louis. The Cardinals remained two games ahead of New York and 2½ games ahead of Chicago. Vaughan had noted, "The Cubs, who are counting on success in their long home stand to put them in first place," had merely kept place.[4]

Prior to the game Vaughan had calculated that if St. Louis merely played .500 ball the rest of the season, Chicago would have to post a 15-8 record to win the pennant. Counting their victory on September 4, St. Louis played much better than break-even ball, going 17-9 through the rest of September. Of their five home games against Chicago at the end of the season, St. Louis won two.

What was totally beyond Vaughan's or anyone else's vision was that including their victory on September 4 against Philadelphia, Chicago won 21 straight games, including the first three of the season-ending five-game series in St. Louis. The Cubs ended the year 100-54, the best record in major-league baseball, four games ahead of the Cardinals and 8½ ahead of New York. In modern times (since 1900) Chicago's 21-game winning streak is second only to the 1916 New York Giants' 26 consecutive wins. Unlike Chicago, however, New York did not win the pennant.[5]

French and Galan continued to do well through the end of the season. French's victory on September 4 was the first of five he contributed to the streak, ending the season with a 17-10 record. Galan continued to hit well, eventually batting .314, while leading the league in runs scored (133) and steals (22). He also set a major-league record by not hitting into a double play the entire season.[6]

SOURCES

In addition to the sources cited in the Notes, the author also accessed Retrosheet.org, Baseball-Reference.com, SABR.org, and *The Sporting News* archive via Paper of Record.

NOTES

1   Irving Vaughan, "Cubs Set Out Today on Trail of Cardinals," *Chicago Tribune*, September 4, 1935: 17.

2   Bivin's major-league career ended with a 2-9 record. He became a footnote in major-league baseball when earlier in the year, on May 30, while pitching against the Boston Braves; he induced Babe Ruth to ground out. It proved to be Ruth's last major-league at-bat. Mathew Clifford, *Jim Bivin*, sabr.org/bioproj/person/1b48bc9a.

3   Irving Vaughan, "Augie's Second Smash Clears Bases in Eighth," *Chicago Tribune*, September 5, 1935: 23.

4   Ibid.

5   "MLB Record for Consecutive Wins by a Team, mlb.mlb.com/mlb/history/rare_feats/index.jsp?feature=winning_streaks. New York finished fourth, seven games behind the Brooklyn Robins. Retrosheet, retrosheet.org/boxesetc/1916/Y_1916.htm.

6   Detroit's Dick McAuliffe equaled the record in 1968; Houston's Craig Biggio in 1997. Oddly, while Galan never hit into a double play in 1935, he hit into a triple play on April 21 in a game against Cincinnati.

CUBS TAKE OVER FIRST

SEPTEMBER 14, 1935
CHICAGO CUBS 18, BROOKLYN DODGERS 14

By Greg Erion

ON SEPTEMBER 4, 1935, CHICAGO TRIBUNE sportswriter Irving Vaughan wrote an article analyzing the National League pennant race. He specifically reviewed how the Cubs were faring in a three-way race involving themselves, the New York Giants, and the St. Louis Cardinals. He observed that if the front-running Cardinals played just .500 ball the rest of the season, third-place Chicago would have to win 15 of the remaining 23 contests to win the pennant.[1]

Based on this, the Cubs' flag hopes should have faded considerably by the morning of September 14, as St. Louis had gone on to post an 8-3 record. What Vaughan had no way of knowing was that the Cubs would reel off 10 straight wins at the same time. Feasting on second-division clubs, they had taken four straight from the seventh-place Philadelphia Phillies, another four from the cellar-dwelling Boston Braves and the first two of a four-game set against the fifth-place Brooklyn Dodgers.

As 13,328 fans moved through the turnstiles at Wrigley Field on the afternoon of the 14th, many undoubtedly were still trying to take into account what had taken place the day before.[2] Larry French, who began the Cubs' streak on September 4 with his 13th win, had just beat the Dodgers for his 15th victory, scattering eight hits to gain a 4-1 decision. About 300 miles southwest that afternoon, Cardinals ace Dizzy Dean came on to pitch the ninth inning in a 10-10 game against the Giants. Dean, the league's leading pitcher with 26 wins, gave up three runs. giving the Giants a 13-10 victory.

The outcome of these two games put the Cubs just .004 percentage points behind the Cardinals, essentially in a tie for first. So now, as the third game of the series with Brooklyn was about to begin, Chicago had an opportunity to forge into the lead if they could win and New York could oblige with another defeat of St. Louis.

Starting for the Cubs was the oldest member of their staff, 36-year-old Charlie Root. Root had already earned two wins as part of the Cubs' burgeoning win streak, including a six-hit shutout on September 10 against the Braves, boosting his record to 13-8 for the year. Facing him on the mound was Brooklyn's Johnny Babich with a 5-12 record. Accompanying that rather dismal set of numbers was Babich's even more ominous 6.62 ERA, worst in the National League.[3] He had lost his last four decisions. None of this augured well for the Dodgers. Babich's appearance in the game mirrored the season he had so far experienced. It would be brief and ineffective.

After Root shut the Dodgers down in the top of the first inning, the Cubs immediately went to work on Babich. A walk, error, triple off the bat of center fielder Freddie Lindstrom, and single by catcher Gabby Hartnett combined to send Babich to an early shower after recording just one out. His successor, rookie Bobby Reis, the second of seven pitchers sent out to hurl that afternoon by Brooklyn manager Casey Stengel fared just as poorly, giving up five runs in an inning and a third of pitching.

By the end of the second, Reis had departed the mound, giving way to Tom Baker. Baker in turn was pummeled by a Cubs relentless offense that saw another eight runs cross the plate in the bottom of the sixth. Then Root who had thrown no-hit ball through the first four innings, was seemingly bitten by the hitting bug. He gave up a pair of runs in the fifth and sixth but held what looked to be a commanding 16-4 lead. Root was then touched for five runs in the top of the seventh, three runs coming in on a home run by light-hitting outfielder Buster Mills; his first – and only – homer on the year. The 11-year veteran Root departed the game in the bottom of the inning for a pinch-hitter as Chicago scored its final two runs.

Root was replaced by Roy Henshaw, who in the spirit of things that afternoon, gave up five runs to the suddenly resurgent Brooklyns in the top of the ninth before little-used Cubs righty Fabian Kowalik was called in. Kowalik promptly struck out Johnny McCarthy to end the 18-14 slugfest.

The game's balance sheet was a pitcher's nightmare. Every batter in Chicago's starting lineup managed at least two hits except right fielder Frank Demaree and shortstop Billy Jurges, who had one each. Six doubles and two triples came off the Cubs' bats. Those doubles included Billy Herman's major-league-leading 50th and 51st. Even Root, who gained his 14th victory, got into the act with two singles and an RBI. Ten walks also aided their scoring spree. The Dodgers were not offensive slouches either, rapping out 15 hits, including two homers: Mills's three-run shot and a solo blast by second baseman Jim Bucher.

The Cubs' streak reflected a team simply overwhelming its competition. The 11 straight wins were fueled by a team batting average of .317 and a team ERA of 2.38, outscoring their opponents by 79-29. It was a micro reflection on the entire season, in which the Cubs would have the highest team batting average (.288), score the most runs (847), and sport the lowest ERA 3.26). But these numbers were for the future. There was still a pennant race going on.

The Cubs' 18-14 win was but half of the equation that day. In St. Louis, the Giants and Cardinals battled 4-4 into the 11th inning. Successive doubles

by pitcher Slick Castelman and Jo-Jo Moore plated a fifth New York run the Cardinals were unable to answer, giving New York a second straight win.[4] The Cardinals' loss gave the Cubs a one-game lead, something unthinkable just a week and a half earlier.

Over the course of the year, New York had taken the lead in late April and relinquished it to St. Louis at the end of August. Would the Cubs now be able to maintain their newly acquired hold on first? They had run off an 11-game winning streak in late July – could they now top that streak?

More to the point was the nature of their future schedule. There was one more game against Brooklyn. Observers could rightfully point out that Chicago had taken advantage of second-division teams. How would they fare against more meaningful competition? Vaughan pointed out that after the Dodgers left, the Giants were coming into town. They were in third, just 3½ games behind Chicago, and had just taken "apart the world champion Cardinal machine for the second consecutive day."[5] After New York the fourth-place Pirates were scheduled to come to Wrigley Field.

All the while looming in the background was the fact that the Cubs would be facing the Cardinals the last five games of the season at Sportsman's Park. Chicago had done well but the roughest part of the schedule for September remained ahead.

SOURCES

In addition to the sources listed in the Notes, the author also consulted Baseball-Reference.com, Retrosheet.org, and *The Sporting News*.

NOTES

1   Irving Vaughan, "Cubs Set Out Today on Trail of Cardinals," *Chicago Tribune*, September 4, 1935: 17.

2   Ibid. Retrosheet shows an attendance of 10,000, Vaughan's article of the 14th gives the 13,328 figure.

3   Technically the leader in highest ERA at that point on the year in the National League was Philadelphia's Jim Bivin at 6.14 based on individuals qualifying to be ranked in ERA. Babich, whose ERA was nearly half a run per game higher than Bivin's, had not quite pitched enough innings to qualify for this dubious distinction.

4   "Cards Beaten, Lose Lead to Cubs," *Washington Post*,
    September 15, 1935: 13.

5   Irving Vaughan, "Gain Full Game Hold on Lead as Cards
    Lose," *Chicago Tribune*, September 14, 1935: B3.

CUBS STYMIED BY EJECTIONS, ERRORS, AND THE SCHOOLBOY

OCTOBER 4, 1935
DETROIT TIGERS 6, CHICAGO CUBS 5 (11 INNINGS)

GAME THREE OF THE WORLD SERIES

By Doug Feldmann

AFTER SPLITTING THE FIRST TWO contests of the 1935 World Series in Detroit, the Tigers and Cubs trekked westward to Wrigley Field for Game Three. With no travel day scheduled, the players struggled to catch up on their rest, with a few of them dozing off as their trains caromed around the southern shore of Lake Michigan and into Union Station at Canal and Jackson – from which the Tigers found their way to the Knickerbocker Hotel while the Cubs dispersed to their residences.

When the tired teams reached Wrigley late the next morning, they found the weather to have warmed slightly to a moderate 57 degrees. The Tigers, outlasted by Dizzy Dean and the St. Louis Cardinals in the fall classic a year earlier, were on a mission to redeem themselves. But they would have to forge ahead without the services of their fearsome slugger, 1935 American League MVP Hank Greenberg. Suffering a wrist injury in Game Two, Greenberg begged Mickey Cochrane to let him play despite the wrist remaining badly swollen – but the player-manager would not relent. Instead, Cochrane opted to move regular third baseman Marv Owen across to Greenberg's position of first base while Flea Clifton took over at third.

In attendance at Game Three were Chicago Mayor Ed Kelly and US Postmaster General James Farley. The two dignitaries sat next to each other in the first row while receiving a pregame visit from

Cubs catcher Gabby Hartnett. As they turned to acknowledge the crowd, Kelly and Farley were surprised to see empty seats in the upper reaches of the ballpark. "The actual attendance fell short of expectations," noted one writer by the conclusion of the afternoon, "as ticket poachers once again struggled to release their wares. Evidence of this was provided by a fan, Michael Hammerman, who according to the *Chicago Tribune* had purchased two box seats for 25 cents just before the Cubs took the field."[1]

In advance of the first pitch by Bill Lee, Cubs owner Phil Wrigley himself strutted out to center field and raised the National League championship banner to the top of the flagpole. Confident that his club would repeat as champion in the senior circuit again in 1936, Wrigley told the fans that "the team would clinch in plenty of time to process World Series tickets by mail only for the following year."[2]

The home did not disappoint as play got underway. "The Cubs, apparently comforted by the sight of their own Wrigley Field, jumped off to a flying start," wrote Irving Vaughan in the *Tribune*. "They fairly frolicked on their way with diving catches, leaping catches, machine-like plays and timely hitting."[3] Their offensive assault was sparked by Frank Demaree, who blasted a home run to lead off the Chicago second inning against Detroit pitcher Elden Auker, the side-armer who was rumored to have learned his submarine style by throwing in tornado shelters back home in Kansas. Stan Hack followed with a single to center, and after stealing second, he reached third on an error by Clifton before scoring on a Lee groundout. When Augie Galan singled home Bill Jurges in the fifth inning, the lead grew to 3-0.

The Cubs were flashing their leather as well – including a great play by Demaree on Cochrane in the Tigers fifth, "a short fly to right and apparently headed for open territory just inside the foul line," as Vaughan described it. "Demaree, playing deep, charged in, skidded feet first along the ground as he neared the ball, turned over and came up with the ball in his hands."[4] Not to be outdone was the gritty leader Hartnett. "Twice he galloped over to the stands, once as far as the Tiger dugout, to snatch foul balls off the necks of spectators."[5] On one such occasion in nabbing a foul pop off the bat of Auker, Hartnett had inadvertently pinned home-plate umpire Dolly Stark against the wall along the box seats.

Looking to bury the Tigers to make sure his club took control of the Series, Cubs manager Charlie Grimm kept his foot on the gas in the sixth. Among his troops was a teenage rookie first baseman, Phil Cavarretta, fresh out of Lane Tech High School, which stood just a few blocks away from Wrigley Field on Addison Street.

But when Cavarretta bolted in an attempted steal of second, he was called out by umpire George Moriarty. Charging over to the scene from the third-base coaching box, Grimm was quickly ejected for arguing. "He kept on talking after being banished," Vaughan noticed, "but the Cubs refused to forget the incident."[6] Earlier in the Tigers' half of the sixth, another umpire, Ernest Quigley, had given the heave-ho to Tigers third-base coach Del Baker after Pete Fox was picked off third by Hartnett.

Although officially exiled from the game, Grimm continued to manage from the tunnel leading to the locker room, feeding instructions to coach Red Corriden while staying out of view.

Through the seventh, Lee held a firm grip on the game for Chicago, despite the Tigers creeping closer at 3-1. "But there was a crash in the eighth," Vaughan continued, "and the battle started in earnest. Down in the crash went Lee. For seven innings he had been well nigh invincible."[7] A four-run outburst in that frame suddenly put Auker in the lead at 5-3, as Lon Warneke entered in relief for the Cubs. "It wasn't the same Warneke," Vaughan wrote in comparison to the four-hit shutout the pitcher had authored in Game One in Detroit. "The Tigers kept on hitting just as if Lee still were in there."[8]

Corriden – or perhaps it was Grimm – gambled by pinch-hitting Chuck Klein for Jurges in the ninth; for if the Cubs did not win the game with three runs, there were no infielders remaining to play shortstop in the 10th, as Woody English (and outfielder Tuck Stainback) had also been ejected by Moriarty for hollering from the bench in the eighth.

But the roll of the dice paid off, as Klein followed a single by Hack with one of his own. Backup catcher Ken O'Dea (batting for Warneke) plated Hack with yet another, with Galan subsequently adding a fly ball to tie the game, 5-5, sending it into extra innings. The runs had come at the expense of Lynwood "Schoolboy" Rowe, the Tigers ace who had relieved Auker in the top of the eighth.

Adjusting the defensive pieces as best he could, Corriden moved Hack from third to short, Freddie Lindstrom from center to third, and Demaree from right to center, and kept Klein in the game in right.

The makeshift alignment did the job for one inning, but came apart in the 11th. Billy Rogell led off and dribbled a single up the middle and past Hack, a ball Jurges likely would have reached. A couple of batters later, Lindstrom bobbled a slow grounder. With two out, Jo-Jo White drove a single to center that scored Owen with an unearned run (Owen had forced Rogell with an unsuccessful bunt).

The Schoolboy, meanwhile, had settled down after permitting Chicago to send the contest into the extra frames. "Rowe avenged his defeat in the opening game by throttling the Cubs on one hit in the last two," Vaughan wrote of the final chances for Grimm's men ... [the conclusion of] eleven wild, thrilling, spectacular, even boisterous, umpire baiting innings."⁹

Hitting stars in the game included Rogell and Goose Goslin for the Tigers with three safeties apiece, while the Cubs – led by two each off the bats of Hack, Lindstrom, and Galan – carried their frustration into the locker room. "No matter where you may travel, into high society or low, you will never hear such picturesque cuss words as flew from the mouths of the raging Chicago Cub team today," wrote Doc Holst of the *Detroit Free Press,* who held his ear to the door, "when they dashed into their clubhouse stinging with defeat."¹⁰

Across the hall, Cochrane gloated to W.W. Edgar of the *Detroit Free Press* in between swigs of a bottle of soda. "They threw everything they had at us and it wasn't enough," he said of the Cubs. "I wonder how Grimm feels now after he has seen his pitching staff battered up. Who's left to throw tomorrow? He used Lee, Warneke, and [Larry] French, three of his best bets today, and wound up on the wrong end."¹¹

But then Cochrane wiped his brow and relented a bit. "It was the toughest World Series game I've ever played in," he admitted.¹²

SOURCES

In addition to the sources listed in the Notes, the author also consulted Baseball-Reference.com, Retrosheet.org, and *The Sporting News.*

NOTES

1   Doug Feldmann, *September Streak: The 1935 Chicago Cubs Chase the Pennant* (Jefferson, North Carolina: McFarland, 2002), 192-193.

2   Ibid.

3   Irving Vaughan, "Cubs Lose, 6-5; Use Carleton Today," *Chicago Tribune,* October 5, 1935: 1.

4   Vaughan: 22.

5   Ibid.

6   Ibid.

7   Vaughan: 1.

8   Ibid.

9   Ibid.

10 Doc Holst, "'T'isn't Right!' Bemoan Cubs," *Detroit Free Press,* October 5, 1935: 14.

11 W.W. Edgar, "Mickey Feels Cubs Are Lost," *Detroit Free Press,* October 5, 1935: 15.

12 Feldmann, 196.

DEFENSE DOOMS CUBS

OCTOBER 5, 1935
DETROIT TIGERS 2, CHICAGO CUBS 1

GAME FOUR OF THE WORLD SERIES

By Doug Feldmann

WITH THE DETROIT TIGERS SEIZING A two-games-to-one lead in the 1935 World Series on the Chicago Cubs after a wild extra-inning affair in Game Three, managers Charlie Grimm and Mickey Cochrane were compelled to shuffle their lineups. "The two managers, reckless in their manipulation of talent in the turbulent concluding innings, forced themselves into a new setup for the fourth of the series today," wrote Irving Vaughan of the *Chicago Tribune* in previewing the day's contest.[1]

The fourth game pitted two veteran pitchers who had yet to prove themselves capable of World Series success. Grimm handed the ball to Tex Carleton, a winner 11 times during the regular season but who had appeared only once during the Cubs' incredible 21-game winning streak in September. Carleton had also faced the Tigers in Game Four of the 1934 fall classic while a member of the St. Louis Cardinals, but he was pulled in the third inning by Cardinals skipper Frankie Frisch while permitting three runs as part of a 10-4 thrashing by Detroit. The following afternoon, Carleton relieved Dizzy Dean as the Cardinals lost again in Game Five.

Cochrane, meanwhile, was turning to General Crowder. Crowder himself had appeared twice in the 1934 Series – including a loss in Game One against Dean, when Cochrane infamously had let word leak that he did not want to waste his own number-one starter, Schoolboy Rowe, against the St. Louis ace. Crowder had been on the losing end of the 1933 World Series as well while pitching for the Washington Senators, dropping Game Two to Hal Schumacher.

During batting practice, Rowe – victorious in relief the previous day in Game Three – had been greeted with angry booing from those in Wrigley's outfield stands. The jeers from the ancestors of the future "Bleacher Bums" turned into cheers, however, when Rowe launched a total of nine baseballs into the seats as souvenirs.

As part of Cochrane's makeshift order, he was forced to do without his slugging first baseman, Hank Greenberg, for the second straight day as Marv Owen once again moved over from third base while Flea Clifton took Owen's spot at the hot corner.

Would this be the day that either Carleton or Crowder would finally shine in postseason play?

Both men were determined to make it so. But while each would pitch well, Crowder made an additional statement with his bat while the normally surehanded Chicago defense abandoned Carleton.

The Cubs starter escaped trouble early, enduring a flurry of Detroit baserunners but permitting only a lone run. This included a particularly perilous second inning in which shortstop Bill Jurges made a leaping snag of a Clifton liner with the bases loaded, "going into the air like a man springs," wrote Charles Ward of the *Detroit Free Press* – spearing a ball and turning it into an inning-ending double play by throwing to Billy Herman at second to catch Pete Fox off the bag.[2] Gabby Hartnett followed in the bottom half by leading off the Cubs' turn with a home run, staking Carleton to 1-0 lead. The advantage was short-lived, however, as in the Tigers third, star second baseman Charlie Gehringer doubled home Crowder (who had led off with a single) to tie the game.

The two pitchers of past World Series misfortune were not about to let another opportunity slip away. Each shut down the opponents' bats time after time; but the difference in the game came from misplays by the Chicago gloves in the Tigers' sixth. "The assembled multitude saw Augie Galan let a fly ball trickle through his hands after he had set himself to make the catch," wrote Vaughan. Clifton, hustling all the way, made it into second, and scored on the next play with Crowder batting. "A moment later they saw Bill Jurges stage a sandlot error on the easiest sort of roller … who reached down nonchalantly for the ball, but it wasn't there."[3] An unnerved Carleton then balked Crowder to second, but was able to end the malaise with no further damage.

The Cubs appeared to be staging a rally in the bottom half, but Crowder got revenge for Hartnett's homer as he fanned the Cubs catcher with the tying run on third and one out, followed by Frank Demaree popping out to Gehringer to end the inning.

Going the distance, Crowder had permitted only three Cubs hits until the ninth, when Demaree and Phil Cavarretta each hit the first pitch for singles after Hartnett opened the inning by hitting a screaming liner to Bill Rogell at short. But Rogell took care of the final two outs as well, turning a double play on a tapper off the bat of Stan Hack by flipping to Gehringer, who fired on to Owen to end the game. "(Crowder) made it easy for his fielders, also for himself, by refusing to let the Cubs get hold of anything with their bats," an impressed Vaughan continued. "Except for the five hits, only one ball was driven to an outfielder."[4] The effort was nearly wasted by Cochrane's men, however, as the Tigers left 13 runners on base with Carleton and reliever Charlie Root (who entered in the eighth) able to keep any further runners from crossing the plate.

Like Vaughan, the Detroit writer Ward had been equally moved by Crowder's performance: "He grinned wearily and trudged off the field with his tired, slow-footed gait, happy in the thought that he had proved that he could do what everybody had said he couldn't do – pitch winning ball in a World Series."[5]

Cochrane, the veteran of so many October battles, claimed to have never seen a finer effort. "This was a game we had to win, and the General knew it," the manager said. "In my opinion, it was one of the smartest games I've ever seen a pitcher work."[6] But the greatest source of inspiration for Crowder had come from his wife, who was bedridden back at their home in Winston-Salem, North Carolina, for the past several months with a serious but undisclosed illness. "I've just prayed that boy would win one game – one game in the World Series," a grateful Mrs. Crowder said. "For three years, that's all I've been living for."[7]

As for the Cubs, the spirit of their amazing streak to end the regular season seemed to be burning out. "A crowd of 49,350 draped itself around the Wrigley Field arena to see the Cubs finally lose the glamour with which they adorned themselves in their spectacular September pennant drive," Vaughan wrote in conclusion.[8]

With no offdays scheduled during the Series, the Tigers would attempt to wrap up the 1935 crown the following afternoon in Game Five at Wrigley.

SOURCES

In addition to the sources cited in the Notes, the author also accessed Retrosheet.org, Baseball-Reference.com, SABR.org, and *The Sporting News* archive via Paper of Record.

NOTES

1   Irving Vaughan, "Cubs Lose, 6-5; Use Carleton Today," *Chicago Tribune*, October 5, 1935.

2   Charles Ward, "Crowder Gives Tigers 2-Game Lead," *Detroit Free Press*, October 6, 1935.

3   Vaughan.

4   Ibid.

5   Ward.

6   Grantland Rice, "Spring Promise," *New York Herald Tribune*, October 6, 1935.

7   Doug Feldmann, *September Streak: The 1935 Chicago Cubs Chase the Pennant* (Jefferson, North Caolina: McFarland, 2002), 199.

8   Vaughan.

CUBS STAVE OFF ELIMINATION ON KLEIN'S HOMER

OCTOBER 6, 1935
CHICAGO CUBS 3, DETROIT TIGERS 1

GAME FIVE OF THE WORLD SERIES

By Greg Erion

AFTER GAME ONE OF THE 1935 WORLD Series, Detroit's playing manager, Mickey Cochrane, shared, "You'll go a long time until you see better pitching than that Warneke tossed at us this afternoon."[1] Cochrane knew of what he spoke firsthand, having gone 0-for-4 including three taps back to Lon Warneke. Warneke's performance was outstanding; he shut out the Tigers' formidable lineup, 3-0, on four hits. Detroit had averaged six runs per game during the year on the strength of a .290 team batting average with a lineup including four future Hall of Famers.[2] And Warneke had silenced them.

Now, four days later, Warneke was scheduled to pitch again. Despite his dominance of Detroit in Game One, the pressure was decidedly on Warneke to repeat his performance. After winning the opening contest, Chicago proceeded to lose the next three games and was on the verge of elimination. It did not help their chances that center fielder Freddie Lindstrom broke his middle finger the previous day attempting to field a Charlie Gehringer line drive. Lindstrom had been a solid performer in Chicago's run toward the pennant in September and was lost for the remaining games of the Series. Nor did it help that hanging over the Cubs was that going back to 1918 they had lost seven straight World Series games at Wrigley Field.

Despite Detroit's commanding lead, Cochrane did not assume winning the championship was inevitable – events of the previous season had shown that. One win away from taking the World Series in 1934 against the St. Louis Cardinals, Detroit lost the last two games allowing the Cardinals to claim the title. Also hanging over the team was a further cloud: The Tigers had never won a fall classic despite appearing in four previous Series.

Warneke faced Schoolboy Rowe again. Rowe (19-13 for the season) had pitched well in the first game; however, his seven-hit venture did not match Warneke's scoreless effort. Rowe was pitching just two days after relieving in Game Three, going the last four frames of a game won by Detroit in 11 innings. Starting on such short rest did not seem a problem for the 25-year-old Rowe, who had thrown 275⅔ innings and 21 complete games during the season.

As a night of light rain and early-morning fog gave way to a cool afternoon sporting a "brilliant sun," 49,237 people trekked to Wrigley Field to see, win or lose, their last glimpse of the 1935 Cubs at home.[3] Warneke picked up where he left off in Game One, allowing a harmless single to Cochrane, who advanced to second before the Tigers went down. Warneke dispatched the Detroit sluggers on a total of just 12 pitches in the second and third.

Meanwhile Chicago was held scoreless by Rowe the first two innings. The closest they came to scoring was on back-to-back singles by Chuck Klein and Gabby Hartnett in the first. In the bottom of the third, Billy Herman led off with a triple. Klein came to bat again.

He was in the lineup only because of Lindstrom's injury. Klein had been a major frustration to the Cubs since he joined them in a trade with Philadelphia after the 1933 season. In almost 5½ years with the Phillies, Klein had averaged .359 with 35 home runs and 134 RBIs. His efforts had peaked when he won the Triple Crown in 1933.

In Klein's first two seasons with Chicago, his performance averaged.297, 21 home runs, and 77 RBIs, not bad for many but hardly what had been expected of him, making him a target of Cubs fans' derision. At the beginning of September, Klein went into a 0-for-18 slump. He was benched just as Chicago started on the 21-game winning streak that propelled it to the pennant. Clearly not part of the winning effort, Klein was castigated for his subpar play, his negligible role in the team's win on the eve of the World Series described in decidedly negative terms: "Considering the number of times his name is entered in the all-time records of the game, Chuck is a pathetic figure, if one may feel sorry for someone who may receive $5,000 for simply watching a World Series."[4]

Klein had already singled in the first off Rowe, Now, with Herman at third, Klein turned on a 1-and-1 pitch and deposited it over the screening at the right-field wall putting Chicago in the lead, 2-0.[5]

After Klein's blast, Rowe settled down, preventing further scoring in the next three innings. Warneke allowed two singles in the fourth, then retired Detroit's lineup in order in the fifth and sixth. In the sixth, fans noticed Bill Lee, then Charlie Root warming up in the Chicago bullpen. This was unusual, as Warneke seemed to be doing quite well, having allowed only three hits and no runs. In the top of the seventh Lee came on to pitch.

Warneke had pulled a tendon in his arm. Later he told reporters that he felt a "twitch" in his shoulder while pitching to Rowe in the third. In the sixth, after he threw a strike to Gehringer, Hartnett came out to the mound and signaled Manager Charlie Grimm to begin warming up a new pitcher. Warneke got Gehringer on a line drive to Klein in center but his day was done.[6]

A sense of disquiet filled the ballpark as Lee began to pitch. Warneke had thrown exceptionally well and now was out of the game. Lee, who was 20-6 during the season, had given up four runs in 7⅓ innings in Game Three – not exactly a sterling performance. Neither Warneke's departure from the game or Lee's entrance into it augured well for the team.

The crowd grew more uneasy as Lee walked Goose Goslin to lead off the seventh – the first walk of the day for Detroit. Pete Fox came to bat with a .350 average for the Series, but Lee induced him to fly out to right field. Shortstop Billy Rogell stepped up and slapped a grounder to his counterpart, Billy Jurges, who stepped on second to force Goslin and threw out Rogell at first for an inning-ending double play.

Chicago had been quiet for three innings after Klein's home run but in the bottom of the seventh the Cubs' offense came to life again. Jurges singled to lead off and was sacrificed to second by Lee. Augie Galan rapped a hard groundball through Marv Owen at first for an error. Jurges tried to score, only to be thrown out at the plate by Fox on a close play. Jurges argued the call to no avail with Umpire George Moriarty.

There had been friction with Moriarty through the Series, most visible with a mass ejection of three players (including Cubs manager Charlie Grimm) in Game Three for excessive bench jockeying.[7] Despite Jurges' ranting, peace was eventually restored. With Galan at second on Jurges' failed attempt to score, Herman ripped his second extra-base hit of the afternoon, a double to right, and the Cubs had an insurance run as Galan scored easily.

Despite the 3-1 score, the Cubs were not out of the woods; Detroit's lineup was too potent to ease up. Lee flirted with disaster in the eighth after there was one out. Flea Clifton was in the lineup only because Hank Greenberg had injured his wrist in Game Two.[8] Clifton came to the plate 0-for-10 in the Series – and Lee walked him.[9] Rowe, a good hitting pitcher singled Clifton to second.[10] With Detroit on the cusp of a rally, Lee struck out Jo-Jo White and induced Cochrane to ground out to end the frame.

After Chicago went down in order in the bottom of the eighth, Detroit made one last push to claim the World Series that day.

Gehringer, Goslin, and Fox hit successive singles to score one run. Rogell flied out and Gee Walker pinch-hit for Owen. Walker, who had hit .301 for the season and had power, represented the go-ahead run. He grounded out, moving Goslin to third and Fox, the tying run, to second. Fortunately for Lee, the hapless Clifton was up next. Clifton lofted a foul popup down the first-base line, where Phil Cavarretta made the putout, just missing crashing into the concrete wall along the playing field.[11]

It had been a narrow thing. Chicago staved off elimination – the Cubs had won at home but now faced Detroit on their turf at Navin Field. They would so without Warneke, who was done for the Series – even the possibility of relieving.[12] The Cubs were set to face Tommy Bridges, who had beaten them in Game Two of the series.

SOURCES

In addition to the sources listed in the Notes, the author also consulted Baseball-Reference.com and Retrosheet.org.

NOTES

1   Don Duren, Lon Warneke, sabr.org/bioproj/person/5a2fe3c9.

2   The Hall of Famers were Mickey Cochrane, Charlie Gehringer, Goose Goslin, and Hank Greenberg.

3   John Drebinger, "Klein Hits Homer as Cubs Win, 3 to 1," *New York Times*, October 7, 1935: 1.

4   Quoted without source in James Lincoln Ray, Chuck Klein, sabr.org/bioproj/person/8dd27865.

5   Drebinger, "Klein Hits Homer."

6   Frederick Lieb, "Goslin's Hit Spells Victory for Tigers," *The Sporting News*, October 10, 1935: 9.

7   Moriarty ejected Grimm, Woody English, and Tuck Stainback for heckling Detroit's Hank Greenberg over his Jewish ethnicity, setting a record for ejections during the World Series. Under then existing protocol, no player could be ejected from the World Series without the approval of Commissioner Kenesaw Mountain Landis. For this indiscretion, Moriarty was fined $200. Eric Enders, George Moriarty, sabr.org/bioproj/person/44c82f26.

8   Marv Owen, the regular third baseman had taken over first, and Clifton took his spot at third base.

9   Clifton would end up 0-for-16 for the Series.

10   Rowe hit .312 during the season with three home runs.

11   Lieb, "Goslin's Hit Spells Victory."

12   Warneke's injury did not prove serious. He was the Cubs' Opening Day pitcher in 1936.

A MID-SUMMER OFFENSIVE EXPLOSION

AUGUST 13, 1937
CHICAGO CUBS 22, CINCINNATI REDS 6

By Seth Moland-Kovash

THE MIDDLE OF AUGUST IS OFTEN CALLED the "dog days" of summer and of the baseball season. It can be hard to generate interest or excitement because the season has been going for more than four months but late-season pennant races have not yet gotten red-hot. The Chicago Cubs found a way by scoring a season-high 22 runs and spreading the offense around so that each starting position player got at least two hits on a Friday afternoon against the Cincinnati Reds. The morning of August 13 found the Cubs sitting at 65-37 and solidly in first place, with a comfortable 6½-game lead over their closest competitors, the 58-43 New York Giants. The Cubs were a robust offensive team that year, leading the NL in runs scored per game (5.5) thus far. At the same time nobody could have expected just this kind of offensive outburst on that day when manager Charlie Grimm's Cubs welcomed Chuck Dressen's 41-57 Reds to Wrigley Field. In eight previous meetings between the two teams, the Cubs had averaged 4.9 runs scored and 8.5 hits against Reds pitching, but on this afternoon the Cubs' bats were much more active.

The day before had seen the Cubs on the wrong end of a decisive 16-6 win by the Pittsburgh Pirates. The Cubs burned through four pitchers, including starter Tex Carleton and the 13-year veteran Charlie Root. With a depleted pitching staff coming off that kind of game in mid-August, one could be forgiven for not expecting much excitement from the home squad the next day. Apparently, the Cubs' faithful were not deterred, as 10,732 paid ticket-holders, plus "a flock of women guests," according to the Chicago Tribune, came out to witness the first game of a four-game series.[1] Every Friday at Wrigley Field in this era was Ladies Day, which meant that women were admitted to the game free. While figures for this date are not available, there were often as many as 10,000 women in attendance who were not accounted for in the official tally.

Roy Parmelee started for the Cubs and things started to look similar to the day before. The 30-year-old Parmelee was in his first and, as it would turn out, only year with the Cubs at the end of a career highlighted by three years as a regular if unspectacular starting pitcher for the New York Giants. He came into that day with a 7-6 record and an ERA of 4.78 in 130 innings. Parmelee had been used in a mixed role so far, with 16 starts and nine relief appearances. In the second inning, Parmelee gave up four runs on three singles and two doubles. The scoring was capped off by a single by Hub Walker, driving in Cubs pitcher Paul Derringer, who had doubled in two runs. At that point, Grimm called on the veteran Root, who had pitched the final inning the day before.

At 38, Charlie Root was near the end of his career, but he was still a mainstay on the mound for the Cubs. He was a regular at Wrigley Field from 1926 until 1941 and still holds the Cubs record (as of 2017) for wins at 201 though he may be most remembered as the pitcher involved in Babe Ruth's "called shot" in the 1932 World Series.

Root got out of the inning with a fly ball to center field. He then went the rest of the way in relief, pitching 7⅓ innings and giving up only four hits and two runs as the Cubs turned the offensive tables and allowed him some breathing room.

In the bottom of the second the Cubs responded with four runs, three singles, two walks, and an error by shortstop Billy Myers. The big blow was a two-out, bases loaded single by second baseman Lonny Frey, driving in two runs before Derringer was relieved by Wild Bill Hallahan.

Phil Cavarretta, the Cubs' 20-year-old first baseman, led off the bottom of the third by reaching when Reds second baseman Alex Kampouris botched his grounder. As the Chicago Tribune put it, "Kampouris made the arrangements for the nine run third inning by proving that two errors could be made on one play. He fumbled Cavarretta's grounder and then after losing the runner, threw wild to first."[2] Cavarretta ended up on second, then scored on a triple (one of only two extra-base hits by the Cubs that day) by the next batter, Frank Demaree. The power- hitting cleanup batter Demaree was in the midst of a streak of 20 straight games reaching base safely. Three consecutive Cubs singles drove Hallahan out of the game in favor of Joe Cascarella. A walk, a bases-loaded groundout by pitcher Root, three singles, a walk, another single, and another bases-loaded groundout saw the Cubs plate nine runs on eight hits. Fourteen Cubs batted in the inning, and the rout was on.

The Cubs' other big inning was the eighth; it began with the Cubs up 16-6 and Reds reliever Jake Mooty facing the top of the lineup. Stan Hack opened the inning with the Cubs' only other extra-base hit, a triple to left field. The Cubs managed just three more hits in the inning, all singles. But three walks, two errors, and a passed ball allowed six runs to score, finishing the scoring for the day as 10 men came the plate in the frame.

This 22-run outburst was the Cubs' highest scoring output for 1937, but their 21 hits were not a season high. They knocked out 23 hits in a 14-inning victory over the St. Louis Cardinals on July 5. Against the Reds, Demaree and Ken O'Dea led the Cubs with four hits each. The Cubs scoring outburst was even more remarkable for the absence of their two best sluggers. All-Stars Billy Herman had a turned ankle and Gabby Hartnett catcher Hartnett got a breather after the long day behind the plate the day before.

Though the Cubs had only two extra-base hits, they benefited from eight Reds errors and nine walks. Their hits were spread among the team; each starting position player (all of whom played the entire game) had at least two hits.

SOURCES

In addition to the sources cited in notes, the author also used Baseball-Reference.com and Retrosheet.org

NOTES

1   Irving Vaughan, "Sox Lose; Cubs Rout Reds, 22-6: A Record," *Chicago Tribune*, August 14, 1937: 11.

2   Ibid.

EPPERLY WINS STARTING DEBUT AS CUBS PULVERIZE PHILLIES

MAY 5, 1938
CHICAGO CUBS 21, PHILADELPHIA PHILLIES 2

By Matt Albertson

LONGTIME CHICAGO TRIBUNE WRITER Irving Vaughan left no doubt in his readers' minds as to who won the May 5, 1938, rubber-match contest between the Cubs and Phillies: "Albert Paul Epperly, the Iowa farm boy, was introduced yesterday in his maiden start as a big leaguer and his Cub mates turned the event into a carnival in which the humble Phillies were the unwilling stooges."[1] The Cubs entered the day 10-6, 3½ games behind the New York Giants in the National League standings, while the Phillies trailed by 9½ games with a 3-11 record.[2]

In the top of the first inning, Epperly and his Chicago teammates took the field in clean white uniforms with familiar the Cubs nickname stitched on the left breast, featuring the iconic red Cubs "C," and trimmed in blue piping on the shoulders and down the pants legs. Phillies leadoff hitter Heinie Mueller strode to the plate in the Phillies' new tributary uniforms, with the Phillies script stitched in yellow and outlined in blue; the uniforms celebrated the tricentennial of Swedish settlement in the Delaware Valley and Philadelphia's city colors.[3] Mueller popped out to third to open the frame, then Chuck Klein singled. Epperly stranded Klein on base and retired the next two batters via foul fly and strikeout.

Wayne LaMaster started the game for the Phillies and what ensued is arguably one of the most painful opening frames in Phillies history. LaMaster managed to throw only three pitches before he left the game with an arm injury. Tommy Reis replaced LaMaster while pitching to Stan Hack and walked Hack and Billy Herman to open the inning. Ripper Collins grounded out to first base while Hack and Herman advanced. Reis then intentionally walked Frank Demaree to load the bases. Joe Marty singled to left field and scored Hack and Herman. Reis was pulled while pitching to Augie Galan, and was replaced by Pete Sivess with one out and two runs in; one run was charged to LaMaster and the other to Reis. Sivess finished a walk to Galan, struck out Tony Lazzeri looking, and walked the next two batters, Gabby Hartnett and Epperly, which brought home two more runs. Sivess and the Phillies finally got out of the inning on a Stan Hack groundball. The Cubs had batted around and scored four runs on one hit and six walks as the Phillies used three pitchers in the inning.

The Phillies tacked a run onto the board in the second inning when Pinky Whitney scored on Bill Atwood's fly ball to left field. The game remained 4-1 Chicago from the bottom of the second inning to the top of the fifth inning as both Epperly and Sivess settled in and retired their opponents in order, save the bottom of the fourth when Stan Hack knocked a triple to center field. The first-inning fireworks were a distant memory until the Cubs' Ripper Collins smacked a 2-and-1 pitch into the right-field bleachers. The Cubs again got to Sivess in the sixth inning when he walked the first two batters, Hartnett and Epperly. Stan Hack scored Hartnett on a double to right field and Epperly scored on a wild pitch. The Cubs continued their attack in the seventh inning when Joe Marty opened the inning with a double to center and scored on Augie Galan's home run.

Epperly continued to wire his way through the Phillies' lineup with little issue. He stranded George Scharein on third base when he induced Philadelphia catcher Bill Atwood to ground out to end the inning. In the eighth inning, he was able to overcome two walks and Chuck Klein's double by striking out Hersh Martin and getting George Scharein to pop up to shortstop with the bases loaded.

By the bottom of the eighth inning, the Cubs held a comfortable 9-1 lead over the Phillies. Phillies manager Jimmie Wilson replaced slugging outfielder Chuck Klein in a double switch before the inning began, inserting pitcher Hal Kelleher into Klein's spot in the batting order and sent Art Rebel out to replace Klein in right field. Kelleher faced Billy Herman to open what became a disastrous inning. The Cubs sent 16 batters to the plate, scoring 12 runs on 10 hits, only two of which were for extra bases. The Cubs' lead ballooned to 20 runs after the offensive bombardment.

Epperly gave up one more Phillies run in the top of the ninth inning but pitched a brilliant six-hit complete game and earned the win in the Cubs' 21-2 drubbing. He started only three more games in his very brief career, sporting a 2-0 career record in 14 games. The Cubs compiled eight extra-base hits in the game; they hit three doubles, three triples, and two home runs and were 11-for-22 with runners in scoring position. The unlucky LaMaster, who left the game after throwing just three pitches, was charged with the defeat. "He left the game with two balls and one strike on the first batter and under scoring rules he issued the base on balls which put the first Cub run on base," the *Chicago Tribune* noted.[4] The loss dropped LaMaster to 0-3 for the season so far. His career was also brief; he went 19-27 over two seasons with the Phillies and Dodgers. The Phillies finished the year at 45-105, the first of five straight 100-loss seasons. The Cubs finished the year with an 89-63 record but were swept in the World Series by the New York Yankees.

SOURCES

In addition to the sources listed in the Notes, the author also consulted Baseball-Reference.com, Retrosheet.org, and *The Sporting News*.

NOTES

1   Irving Vaughan, "12 Run Eighth Gives Epperly Easy Victory," *Chicago Tribune*, May 6, 1938.

2   All statistics obtained from baseball-reference.com.

3   Uniform details obtained from exhibits.baseballhalloffame.org/dressed_to_the_nines/index.htm.

4   Vaughan.

HARTNETT HITS HOMER IN THE GLOAMIN'

SEPTEMBER 28, 1938
CHICAGO CUBS 6, PITTSBURGH PIRATES 5

By James Forr

PITTSBURGH MANAGER PIE TRAYNOR trudged back to the Belmont Hotel in Chicago wondering what the hell had just happened. Four weeks earlier, his Pirates led the National League by seven games. Fans in Pittsburgh were buying World Series tickets. The club had expanded the press box to accommodate all the writers who would be descending on Forbes Field from all over the country. But now the lead--and, as it turned out, the season--was gone, thanks to one swing of the bat from Gabby Hartnett.

For much of the season, the Chicago Cubs had been the least of Traynor's concerns. As late as August 20 they were nine games out, in fourth place. In September, though, the Cubs were unstoppable. Heading into a September 27-29 series against the Pirates in Wrigley Field, they had won 18 of 23 games and had charged to within 1 ½ games of the lead. A gutsy 2-1 victory by sore-armed Dizzy Dean in the series opener put Chicago right on the Bucs' heels.

A raucous crowd of 34,465 jammed Wrigley Field on Wednesday, September 28th as the teams sent two of their best pitchers to the hill for the second game of the series. Traynor went with 30-year-old rookie Bob Klinger (12-5) while the Cubs countered with 19-game winner Clay Bryant. Sloppy defense by the Pirates gave Chicago a 1-0 second-inning lead, and the game stayed that way until the sixth, when things got wild.

Johnny Rizzo homered and Lee Handley mashed a two-run single in the top of that inning to put Pittsburgh ahead, but the Cubs answered with two of their own in the bottom half to tie the game, 3-3.

Then in the seventh, the Bucs had Chicago reliever Vance Page in a tight spot when they were bitten by the first of two controversial non-calls. With men on the corners and one out, Rizzo was at the plate with a 2-and-1 count. As Page began his delivery, third-base coach Jewel Ens began screaming and pointing, certain that Page had balked. First-base umpire Dolly Stark flinched, as if he saw something, too--but he didn't call anything. Rizzo swung at the pitch and grounded into an inning-ending double play. Traynor, Ens, and several players swarmed home plate, screaming at umpire George Barr, but their protests got them nowhere. "[Stark] saw it. Why the hell didn't he call it?" Ens fumed later.[1]

The Pirates shrugged that off to score two in the top of the eighth on run-scoring singles by pinch-hitter Heinie Manush and Handley, yet they easily could have had more. With the two runs in, men again at the corners, and this time no outs, Al Todd bounced back to pitcher Bill Lee, who threw home to erase Manush. Then, curiously, Traynor allowed Klinger to bat for himself. It ended in the worst way possible--a 1-6-3 double play. The Cubs were in trouble, but still alive.

Ripper Collins singled to lead off bottom of the eighth, which prompted Traynor to lift Klinger in favor of Bill Swift. But the right-handed Swift, who had pitched a perfect eighth on Tuesday, didn't have it on this day. After Billy Jurges walked, veteran Tony Lazzeri laced a pinch-hit double to right field, scoring Collins and advancing Jurges to third. With the Cubs' faithful in a frenzy, Swift intentionally walked Stan Hack to load the bases for Billy Herman.

The all-star second baseman responded with a line-drive single to right. Jurges scored to tie the game, but Paul Waner's throw cut down pinch-runner Joe Marty, heading home with the potential go-ahead run. Traynor yanked Swift in favor of workhorse relief ace Mace Brown, who induced a rally-killing double-play ball off the bat of Frank Demaree.

By the time the Pirates went down against Charlie Root in the ninth, it was around 5:30 p.m. Sunset, according to the *Chicago Tribune*, was 5:37 p.m. The umpires met between innings and, although it was becoming very difficult to see, decided to squeeze in one more half-inning. "Just 60 seconds and it might have been different," Traynor said wistfully. "Dolly Stark told me they were going to call it."[2]

Brown quickly retired the first two hitters and then jumped out in front of Hartnett 0-and-2. "He made Hartnett look bad on a couple of curves that went down. Then he came back with one more," recalled Pittsburgh backup catcher Ray Berres. "He was really going to snap one off. And as so often happens when you try too hard, he hung it."[3]

Hartnett, the Cubs' player-manager, was looking for another curve and guessed right. "I felt it was gone the second I hit it," he recalled.[4] At the crack of the bat, Brown buried his head in his arms. He knew it too. In the semi-darkness, the fans couldn't track the ball very well, but they could see Rizzo edge back toward the wall, and then look up helplessly as the ball landed in the left field bleachers for a game-winning home run. Chicago had prevailed, 6-5. The crowd erupted, a beaming Hartnett was mobbed at home plate by teammates and fans, and the Cubs had taken over first place on what would be forever known (thanks, apparently, to Associated Press writer Earl Hilligan) as "The Homer in the Gloamin'"[5]

In the Pirate clubhouse, Brown sobbed in front of his locker. Paul Waner stayed by his side all night. "I was so afraid he was going to commit suicide."[6] Traynor wasn't in much better shape. He sat silently for the longest time before getting dressed and making that long, silent walk back to the hotel with

his confidant Ens. "I was so wrought up inside I was ready to explode. If Jewel had so much as opened his mouth, I believe I would have slugged him."[7]

Hall of Fame catcher Gabby Hartnett took over as player-manager in mid-July of 1938 and led the Cubs to an unlikely pennant. His "Homer in the Gloamin'" put the Cubs in first place after they trailed by seven games to start the month of September. (Photo by Mark Rucker/Transcendental Graphics, Getty Images)

The Pirates, though down only a half-game were emotionally spent. The Cubs, on the other hand, came into the series finale the next day feeling invincible. "We could've beaten nine Babe Ruths" crowed Herman.[8] They crushed the Bucs 10-1, which all but wrapped up the National League pennant.

Traynor, who was fired after one more season, never got over it. Long afterward, he insisted that the umpires should have called the game in the ninth. "I think [years later] he was still very bitter about that," according to a friend, Chuck Reichblum. "That was probably the biggest disappointment in his life. That was the only time I ever heard him be in any way bitter or regretful."[9] After the World Series, Traynor beat a hasty retreat the woods of Wisconsin, where he spent much of the snowy winter hunting and trying to get away from it all.

Mace Brown never seemed to get over it, either, as Paul Waner related to author Lawrence Ritter. "He can laugh about it now, practically 30 years later. Well, he can almost laugh about it anyway. When he stops laughing, he kind of shudders a little bit, you know, like it's a bad dream he can't quite get out of his mind."[10]

SOURCES

In addition to the sources cited in the Notes, the author also accessed Retrosheet.org, Baseball-Reference.com, SABR.org, and *The Sporting News* archive via Paper of Record.

NOTES

1   *Chicago Daily News*, September 29, 1938.

2   *Connellsville (PA) Daily Courier*, September 23, 1958.

3   Bob Smizik, *The Pittsburgh Pirates: An Illustrated History*, (New York: Walker, 1990), 57.

4   Jim Enright, *Chicago Cubs* (New York: Macmillan, 1975), 80-81.

5   Marc Zarefski, "'Homer in the Gloamin' Most Memorable," MLB.com, August 8, 2007 (accessed February 4, 2014).

6   Lawrence Ritter, *The Glory of Their Times* (New York: William Morrow, 1984), 344.

7   *Pittsburgh Press*, April 27, 1942.

8   Donald Honig, *Baseball When the Grass was Real* (New York: Berkley Publishing, 1974), 137.

9   Chuck Reichblum, telephone interview, September 28, 2006.

10   Ritter, 344.

RUFFING SHACKLES THE CUBS

OCTOBER 5, 1938
NEW YORK YANKEES 3, CHICAGO CUBS 1

GAME ONE OF THE WORLD SERIES

By Mark S. Sternman

AFTER A SIX-YEAR HIATUS, THE CHICAGO Cubs and the New York Yankees resumed hostilities in the 1938 World Series. The pairing pit the underdog but hard-charging National League Cubs against the two-time defending champion big boppers from the American League. Before the games began, Chicago miracle-maker/player-manager Gabby Hartnett boldly predicted, "We'll win the Series. We have the kind of pitching that will fool those Yankee sluggers and we'll do some slugging ourselves."[1]

Notwithstanding this verbal bluster and the fact that many of the boldfaced names had changed since 1932, when the Yankees swept the Cubs, the 1938 World Series began with another victory for the Bronx Bombers. On a blustery Wrigley day, New York prevailed 3-1 in the opener thanks in large part to the outstanding performances of a trio of players, pitcher Red Ruffing, catcher Bill Dickey, and shortstop Frankie Crosetti.

Unlike Game Four of the 1932 fall classic, when neither starting pitcher survived the first inning, both Bill Lee, "whose whipcord right arm virtually lifted Chicago into this world series,"[2] and Ruffing hurled strong games following strong seasons (Lee had gone 22-9, and Ruffing 21-7). Both aces faced the minimum number of batters in the opening frame. Stan Hack of the Cubs did single, but, thwarting a hit-and-run, "Ruffing calmly tossed a pitch-out to Dickey, and Hack, out to get the jump by stealing second base, was thrown out with room to spare."[3]

In what would be his last World Series, New York's Lou Gehrig began a rally in the top of the second with a one-out walk. Dickey singled Gehrig to third and advanced to second on a throw from right field by Phil Cavarretta, who started there for the injured Augie Galan. "With the infield in, George Selkirk slapped a tricky grounder at [Billy] Herman. That usually infallible second sacker booted it all over the lot, Gehrig scored, Dickey moved to third and Selkirk was safe at first."[4] Joe Gordon drove in Dickey with a single to put the Yanks up 2-0. Lee induced a 6-4-3 DP from Ruffing to keep the margin manageable.

No batter reached again until Tommy Henrich legged out an infield single in the third. Hartnett threw out Henrich trying to steal; early on, Game One showcased the defensive prowess of two of the game's most lauded backstops in Dickey and Hartnett.

Perhaps inspired by its player-manager's howitzer, the Cubs got the bats going in the bottom of the third. Ripper Collins began the inning with a base hit. With two outs and Collins having advanced to second on a groundout, Hack singled to cut the New York lead to 2-1. Hack moved to second on Henrich's throw to Dickey. In a matchup of future Hall of Famers, Ruffing confronted Herman in what would prove to be the pivotal sequence of Game One. "Herman's hard smash toward third base went as a hit. Red Rolfe knocked it down, but couldn't find it," reported the *New York Times*. "But Eagle-Eye

On the mound for the Cubs in Game One of the 1938 World Series is Bill Lee, who led the NL with 22 wins, a 2.66 ERA, and 9 shutouts. The Yankees' George Selkirk is at bat; Lou Gehrig is on third. (Photo by Mark Rucker/Transcendental Graphics, Getty Images)

Crosetti spotted the ball, retrieved it, pegged it to Bill Dickey and Bill held it low to the ground by the plate. That was where Stanley Hack put his foot in it. Instead of tying the score he had retired his side."[5]

Chicago flashed some leather of its own in the fourth to prevent New York from adding a third run. Billy Jurges threw out Joe DiMaggio. In his last complete season, "Gehrig looked bad as a base runner when he attempted to stretch his sharp single down the right field foul line into a double in the fourth," wrote the *Chicago Tribune*.[6] With no mates on base, a Dickey infield hit proved harmless.

The Cubs went out in order in the bottom of the fourth, but the Yankees had a major threat in the top of the fifth after Gordon doubled, the first extra-base hit of the game. Ruffing smartly sacrificed, but Lee bore down to fan Crosetti and to retire Rolfe on a grounder to Herman.

Again Chicago went out in order in the bottom of the fifth, and again a New York batter, Henrich this time, doubled to start the top of the next frame "on the hardest clout of the game … a double off the right field fence …"[7] This time, the Yankees eschewed the small ball and cashed in the run. Neither DiMaggio nor Gehrig got the job done, but Dickey came through with his third straight hit and second RBI to plate Henrich and put New York up 3-1. After the game, Lee lamented, "I threw only two bad balls all afternoon. They were inside balls to Dickey and he whacked them in the scoring innings."[8]

Trailing by two, the Cubs had Lee scheduled to lead off the bottom of the sixth. Hartnett could have managed aggressively and sent up a hitter for Lee, but instead Lee, who had a .198 batting average in 1938, stayed in to hit and flied out. Hack singled, but Chicago failed to score him.

New York threatened to extend its lead in the seventh. With one out, Lee hit Crosetti, who advanced to third on a Rolfe single. Henrich lined to Collins, who turned an unassisted twin killing to douse the threat.

Chicago had two hits in the bottom of the seventh, which turned into an unlucky inning. Cavarretta led off with a single, but Carl Reynolds grounded into a 6-3 double play. With just one triple in 353 appearances during the 1938 season, Hartnett surprisingly followed with a three-bagger but failed to score after Collins grounded to short on a "nice pickup"[9] by Crosetti. The Cubs had a single and a triple in the same frame but still could not tally.

With two outs in the top of the eighth, Dickey singled for his fourth hit of the day and then swiped second. Dickey had made a prophet of the renowned sportswriter Grantland Rice, who in a syndicated preview column commented, "The star of any World Series usually or often pops out from the unexpected entry. If I had to make one guess it would be Bill Dickey."[10] Selkirk flied out to leave the catcher in scoring position.

Chicago had a good start in the bottom of the eighth with a Jurges single, but pinch-hitter Ken O'Dea hit into a force out on a "treacherous bounder to Crosetti"[11] before Hack bounced into another DP.

Jack Russell relieved Lee and pitched around a two-out double by Crosetti in the top of the ninth. Facing the heart of the batting order, Ruffing got Herman and Frank Demaree on flies to the outfield. In a last-chance at-bat, Cavarretta kept hope alive with a single and, on "a ball which took a bad hop and struck Tom [Henrich] in the face,"[12] advanced to second with an error charged to the usually reliable Henrich.

Representing the tying run, Reynolds came to the plate. Over the first decade of his career with the White Sox, Browns, Red Sox, and Senators, Reynolds had frequently faced Ruffing and had at least two homers. But in 1938, the 35-year-old Reynolds had just three home runs in 530 plate appearances. On this day, Reynolds, late on the Ruffing pitch, could only pop to Gordon, a fitting coda to the opener of the fall classic that would end with Reynolds going 0-for-12 and the Cubs once again getting swept by the relentless and versatile Bronx Bombers.

NOTES

1   James P. Dawson, "World Series Spirit Grips Chicago as Throngs Arrive for First Game," *New York Times*, October 5, 1938.

2   John Drebinger, "Yanks Start Bid for Third Straight World Title at Chicago Today," *New York Times*, October 5, 1938.

3   John Drebinger, "Yanks Top Cubs, 3-1, in Series Opener as 43,642 Look On," *New York Times*, October 6, 1938: 28.

4   Gerry Moore, "Beaten Cubs Gamble on Dean," *Boston Globe*, October 6, 1938: 1.

5   John Kieran, "Action on the Western Front," *New York Times*, October 6, 1938.

6   Arch Ward, "In the Wake of the News," *Chicago Tribune*, October 6, 1938: 23.

7   "Gossip of First Game," *The Sporting News*, October 13, 1938: 6.

8   James P. Dawson, "Hartnett Says Yanks Were Lucky to Win; Counts on Dean to Even Series Today," *New York Times*, October 6, 1938.

9   Edward Burns, "Cubs Will Send Dean Against Gomez Today," *Chicago Tribune*, October 6, 1938: 24.

10 Grantland Rice, "Cubs Enter Series With the Fans Solidly Behind Them," *Boston Globe*, October 5, 1938: 21. One can quibble with Rice's characterization of Dickey as "unexpected" given that he finished second in the 1938 AL MVP balloting behind Boston's Jimmie Foxx and ahead of Detroit's Hank Greenberg, who hit 58 homers that season. Ruffing finished fourth.

11 Irving Vaughan, "Yankees' Brilliant Defense Halts Cubs," *Chicago Tribune*, October 6, 1938: 23.

12 "Timely Hits Decided Opener; Ruffing Victor Over Bill Lee," *The Sporting News*, October 13, 1938: 3.

SORE-ARMED DIZZY LOSES ON CROSETTI'S LATE HOMER

OCTOBER 6, 1938
NEW YORK YANKEES 6, CHICAGO CUBS 3

GAME TWO OF THE WORLD SERIES

By Ed Gruver

KNOWING VISITORS TO WRIGLEY FIELD realize upon entering the venerated confines that they are walking into a veritable baseball museum.

Visit Wrigley in the fall, when the ivy has faded from bright green to brown, and you can almost hear those iconic brick walls whisper a tale. A tale of what occurred on October 6, 1938, in Game Two of the World Series between the Chicago Cubs and New York Yankees.

As United Press sportswriter Henry McLemore wrote from Wrigley late that afternoon, one of the game's immortals "shuffled down baseball's 'last mile' today. … Let it be said that Dizzy Dean walked it gloriously.[1]

War clouds were gathering around the globe but on that bright, sun-streaked afternoon, sore-armed legend Jay Hanna "Dizzy" Dean dueled a dynastic Bronx Bombers squad featuring five future Cooperstown inductees: Lou Gehrig, Joe DiMaggio, Bill Dickey, Joe Gordon, and Lefty Gomez.

Dean was far removed from the flamethrower of the Gas House Gang St. Louis Cardinals. When he won 30 games in 1934, Diz was the ringleader of a roguish, rowdy band of ballplayers whose filthy uniforms and five o'clock shadows stood in stark contrast to the rest of the baseball. Dean won 120 games from 1932 to 1936. When he defeated Detroit in Game Seven of the '34 fall classic, Diz was the

"Great Dean," the self-proclaimed "best pitcher in baseball."[2]

A foot injury in the 1937 All-Star Game eventually shortened Dean's career. But he would have one final memorable campaign in the summer of '38. Shipped to the Cubs, Dean went 7-1 in the pennant drive. No longer firing his famous "fog ball," Dean was delivering pitches so slow McLemore said spectators could read NL President Ford Frick's signature on the ball.

Though Cubs fans regarded him as "Ol' Diz," Dean was just 28. His rubber-arm, however, was ready to be retired. Still, when he got the call to start Game Two of the World Series against the Yankees in Wrigley Field, the supremely confident son of the South stirred the Windy City with wild bombast.

"'I'll flatten 'em,' says Diz," was emblazoned in a banner headline on the *Chicago Tribune's* front page the morning of the game.[3]

New York won Game One in Wrigley Field, 3-1, prompting some to chastise Cubs manager Gabby Hartnett for starting Bill Lee and not Dean in the opener. Ol' Diz, they thought, was the only Cubs pitcher with the aura to handle the Bronx Bombers' mystique.

Before a packed house of more than 42,000, Dean climbed the hill at Wrigley Field on this cold Thursday afternoon to face the fearsome Yankees.

It was 53 degrees but a stiff northeast wind off Lake Michigan made it feel like 33.

"I don't like playin' none in the winter," Dean said, but he found solace in seeing a familiar face at first base, former Gas House Gang teammate Ripper Collins.[4] In the crowd he could see another Gas Houser; Pepper Martin was in Wrigley to cheer Dean.

High above the field the press box was filled with the sound of clattering typewriters and telegraph keys as 450 reporters and telegraphers relayed the news to a waiting nation. It was a scenic setting. Red, white, and blue bunting flapped in the breeze, clouds scudded against a blue-gray sky and October shadows slanted across an outfield as green as a billiard table. The infield dirt was bright red, courtesy of cinders being pulverized to a fine powder.

Dean stared in at leadoff hitter Frankie Crosetti and fired a first-pitch strike – a side-arm curve that caught the outside corner of the plate. Four years earlier he would have heaved his high hard one but his throbbing arm dictated that he duel the champs with off-speed stuff. At times Diz mustered his country hardball — the "Ol' No. 1," he called it — and blew high heat past the Bombers; mostly he pitched gritty, gutsy ball.[5]

Lefty Gomez yielded a run in the first but Dean surrendered the slim lead in the second when Joe Gordon's two-run double to left scored DiMaggio and Gehrig. "A freak double," radio announcer John Harrington said, noting that Cubs third baseman Stan Hack and shortstop Billy Jurges collided as they converged on what should have been an easy, inning-ending out.

The Cubs regained the lead with two runs off Gomez in the third. Changing speeds and pitching with guile, Dean deceived the Yankees by throwing his slow pitches with the same motion he used when muscling up on his fastball. Diz's second-inning offering to DiMaggio had such little spin, Harrington told his audience, that he could see the red stitching on the ball.

In the fourth inning Dean delivered an inside pitch to Gehrig that was so slow the Iron Horse stepped back and grinned. The two legends then engaged in gamesmanship. Diz was working fast to keep his ailing arm warm; Gehrig sought to break his rhythm by stepping out of the box four times in the at-bat. Dean grew angry and made Gehrig wait by stepping off the mound and reaching for the rosin bag. Gehrig ended the gamesmanship by lining the next pitch off Ripper Collins for a single.

Dean was suffering. His arm began stinging in the second inning and by the sixth it felt, he said later, "like a bone was stickin' out the elbow." Hurting physically, the Great Dean would not be beaten mentally.

At one point Diz stared hard into the Yankees dugout and shouted defiantly, "Why don't you great sluggers get out your press clippin's and read how great you are?"[6]

Dean's emotion-packed performance was one for the ages. This was a legendary pitcher in the twilight of his career seeking to survive a squad of ferocious sluggers on the game's greatest stage.

Seeing Diz stymie the Yankees' strongmen with side-arm curves, radio announcer Pat Flanagan called it "a spectacular ballgame."[7] Joe Williams of the *New York World-Telegram* found it astonishing watching Dean take one lordly Yankee hitter after another and make a "first-class sap of him."[8]

The Wrigley crowd knew Dean was dealing against a stacked deck. The staggering odds against him made his performance more fascinating. The big crowd hung on every pitch; when Dean left the mound at the end of the sixth, thousands rose and gave him a rousing ovation. John Harrington noted in the seventh that it was still a "beautiful, bright day" on Chicago's North Side.[9] Dean added to the atmosphere by retiring DiMaggio, Gehrig, and Dickey on just nine pitches, bringing Cubs fans to their feet again.

Diz was four outs away from a historic victory when Crosetti stepped in with two outs and a man on base in the eighth. Crosetti had been hitting the ball hard all afternoon. Pitching deliberately, Dean worked the count to 3-and-2. Cubs fans in the stands and those watching from rooftops on Waveland Avenue and waving from apartment windows on Sheffield pleaded for the inning-ending out.

Presaging a dramatic postseason homer by another light-hitting Yankees shortstop, Bucky Dent, 40 Octobers later, Crosetti cracked a chest-high offering for a two-run homer that put New York on top 4-3. At first it appeared a harmless fly to left. But the ball kept carrying until it landed in the bleachers.

"You wouldn't a-got a loud foul off a-me two years ago," Dean shouted in his Ozark drawl as Crosetti rounded the bases.[10]

Crosetti, according to Dean, yelled back, "I know, Diz."[11]

One observer believed Crosetti's homer a "bell of doom" for Dean and the Cubs. The crowd sensed it, and in their silence one might have heard the fall of snow. Suddenly, the onset of a dark, cold winter in Chicago seemed not so far off.

Ol' Diz headed back to the hill in the ninth but DiMaggio ended his day by pulling a two-run homer to left, closing the scoring at 6-3. McLemore called Dean's performance "one of the greatest exhibitions of heart and head and competitive spirit" in baseball history.[12]

In the press box Lloyd Lewis thought "an eloquent silence" fell as reporters and telegraphers stared at the spectacle below.[13] The typewriters and telegraph keys were silent as the American press stood out of respect for Dean. Lewis thought it a salute to what each writer feared was the "passing of a great man."

As he left the mound and walked that glorious last mile, Ol' Diz – holding his head high and his chin up – stopped and stood for a moment. Raucous cheers and wild applause washed over him.

The Great Dean, thought McLemore, was "drinking in his last deep draught of glory."[14]

SOURCES

In addition to the sources cited in the Notes, the author also accessed Retrosheet.org, Baseball-Reference.com, and SABR.org.

NOTES

1   Henry McLemore, "Dizzy Walks Last Mile," *Los Angeles Times,* October 7, 1938.

2   Vernona Gomez and Lawrence Goldstone, *Lefty: An American Odyssey* (New York: Ballantine Books, 2012) 178.

3   Charles Storch, "New York Yankees vs. Chicago Cubs," *Chicago Tribune,* June 6, 2003.

4   Robert Gregory, *Diz* (New York: Penguin Books, 1992), 352-357.

5   Ibid.

6   Ibid.

7   NBC broadcast, October 6, 1938.

8   Gregory, 352-357

9   NBC broadcast, October 6, 1938.

10   Gregory, 352-357

11   Ibid.

12   McLemore.

13   Gregory, 352-357.

14   McLemore.

HANK LEIBER PROVIDES FIREWORKS WITH THREE HOME RUNS

JULY 4, 1939
ST. LOUIS CARDINALS 6, CHICAGO CUBS 4
(GAME ONE OF DOUBLEHEADER)

By Russ Lake

SIXTEEN GAMES INTO THE 1939 SEASON, Cubs player-manager Gabby Hartnett had seen enough. The defending National League champions had just lost 10-3 to the New York Giants on May 7 to fall into sixth place. Hartnett announced the benching of some lineup regulars, including team captain Billy Herman. Unsatisfactory play, not hustling, and low batting marks were the targets of Hartnett's "whip-cracking" for a squad that had been hailed as a "happy family" during spring training. Herman's banishment lasted just eight innings.[1]

In the third week of June, the Northsiders seemed to straighten themselves out with a six-game win streak. Nevertheless, the Cincinnati Reds had locked in on first place as July emerged. Meanwhile the Cubs seemed stalled in either third or fourth place as the season schedule crept toward the halfway mark. The team's borderline showing did Hartnett no favors since former Chicago major-league managers Charlie Grimm (Cubs) and Lew Fonseca (White Sox) reported game action on WJJD radio.[2]

On July 2, Chicago split a Sunday doubleheader with league-leading Cincinnati that was attended by a season-record home gathering of 42,094. A passive turnout of 12,749 filtered in the next afternoon to watch the Cardinals' Johnny Mize collect four extra-base hits (double, triple, two home runs) in a 5-3 St. Louis victory. This loss dropped the Cubs to fourth place and 6½ games behind the Reds.

Independence Day arrived, and with it a holiday doubleheader at Wrigley Field. The Cubs would wrap up a three-game series with their current "dance partners" in the standings, the St. Louis Cardinals. The day's weather forecast called for slightly cloudy conditions with a chance of a thunderstorm, coupled with a southerly wind and temperatures in the upper 70.[3] A crowd of 26,409 made their way into the confines at Clark and Addison to enjoy another afternoon of baseball.

For Game One, Hartnett selected longtime American League hurler Earl Whitehill to start for Chicago, while St. Louis rookie skipper Ray Blades tabbed Bill McGee. Whitehill, a 40-year-old southpaw, sported a 4-3 record with a 3.84 ERA during his 17th major-league season and had won 218 games. The veteran, signed by the Cubs in February, possessed a tantalizing curveball, and was not above planting a fastball in the ribs of a batter who was digging in.[4] Right-hander McGee (6-4, 3.44), making his sixth start of the season, was normally employed in relief.

Both teams went down in order in the opening frame, and Whitehill etched another scoreless round in the second. Chicago center fielder Hank Leiber, who came in hitting .302, led off the bottom of the second with a long home run into the left-center-field bleachers to give the Cubs a 1-0 lead.[5] The slugging flychaser was acquired in a six-player trade with the New York Giants during the offseason.

III

Ironically, Leiber was one of the Cubs Hartnett had benched in May; he was hitting .213 with two home runs and seven RBIs from the cleanup spot. At the time Hartnett announced the players on his "splinter-gathering crew," he emphasized that Leiber had indeed been hustling.[6] Leiber's exile on the pines lasted two games, and beginning May 11, he started a 12-game hitting streak, batting .404.

Whitehill dispatched the Cardinals in the third and had not allowed a hit. McGee, on the other hand, was having location issues, walking two in the second. In the third, he gave a one-out free pass to Herman. With two away, Leiber stepped in and swatted his second homer of the game to increase the lead to 3-0.[7] The two-run blast landed near his second-inning solo wallop. It was the fourth time in his career (the first with the Cubs) that Leiber had logged a multihomer game.[8]

The advantage evaporated quickly in the top of the fourth as St. Louis sent seven men to the plate, scoring three runs while playing small ball. Jimmy Brown got the Cardinals' first safety, and scored from second base when Mize singled to center with one out. Mize took second on Leiber's throw to the plate, and scored on a single to right by Joe Medwick. Terry Moore also singled to right, sending Medwick to third. Mickey Owen flied deep enough to left fielder Augie Galan to score Medwick, and the game was tied.[9]

With two out in the top of the sixth, Medwick hammered his sixth home run to put St. Louis up, 4-3.[10] Remarkably, Leiber struck again in the bottom half, tying the game with a one-out solo smash that landed halfway up the center-field bleachers for his ninth homer of the year.[11] It was Leiber's third consecutive circuit clout. All of Leiber's blasts were propelled off the Cardinals' starter, McGee.

Whitehill, who was the oldest player in the NL,[12] returned to the mound for the seventh and held the Cardinals in check. Blades sent rookie right-hander Mort Cooper to the hill for St. Louis. McGee's line for six frames showed four runs on five hits with three walks and one strikeout. The 26-year-old Cooper,

making his 21st appearance of the season, had gone six innings in a no-decision as the starter the day before. Cooper matched zeroes with Whitehill, allowing only a walk and one hit while zipping his fastball past several of the Cubs, including the "hot-swinging" Leiber, who fanned in the eighth.

Leading off the top of the ninth, Mickey Owen worked Whitehill for a walk. Don Gutteridge sacrificed Owen to second, and Blades let Cooper bat for himself.[13] This late-game decision proved fruitful as Cooper launched a deep drive down the left-field line. Galan gave chase, bad knees and all,[14] but could only watch as the ball barely cleared the wall, thumped against the rail screen, and bounded back on the field. Galan scooped up the sphere and pegged it to shortstop Dick Bartell, who turned to see teammates angrily rushing toward third-base umpire Lee Ballanfant after he signaled that Cooper's drive was a home run. A heated argument commenced, but the "rhubarb" was short-lived when the other arbiters, George Magerkurth and Ziggy Sears, joined the dispute and confirmed Ballanfant's ruling.[15] Three days before, a new Wrigley Field ground rule had gone into effect stating that batted balls hitting the screens near each foul pole were home runs.[16] Thus, Cooper's first major-league homer gave St. Louis a two-run lead.

Cooper (3-3) completed a third scoreless frame when he retired pinch-hitter Gus Mancuso to close out the Cubs' "heart-breaking" 6-4 defeat in 2:13. Whitehill (4-4),[17] who struck out four and walked five, suffered the complete-game loss. Line-score numbers displayed six runs and eight hits for St. Louis versus four runs on six hits for Chicago, with no errors by either side. The Cubs dropped to 36-34, while the third-place Cardinals improved to 35-30. As the teams walked to their clubhouses to relax before the second game, Leiber thought about his hitting exploits, but another look at the massive scoreboard trumped his pleasure. In a first for the Cubs organization, Leiber's triplicate longball performance came during a loss instead of a stimulating victory. Leiber joined Babe Herman (1933), Rogers Hornsby (1931), Hack Wilson (1930), Cap Anson, and Ned

Williamson (both in 1884), who had previously hit three homers for the franchise in a contest.

Leiber[18] went hitless in Game Two, and ended up upstaged offensively by the third baseman of the Red Sox. In Philadelphia, Jim Tabor drove in 11 runs and tallied four home runs, with three clouts in the second game during Boston's doubleheader thrashing of the Athletics.[19] Additional baseball stories the next day (outside of Chicago) hailed the attendance record set (249,538 for the eight doubleheaders),[20] along with the poignant ceremony in New York that honored Lou Gehrig at Yankee Stadium.[21]

SOURCES

In addition to the sources cited in the Notes, the author also accessed Retrosheet.org, Baseball-Reference.com, Newspapers.com, SABR.org/bioproj, and *The Sporting News* archive via Paper of Record.

NOTES

1   Ed Burns, "Hartnett Cracks the Whip on Cubs in Shake-up," *The Sporting News*, May 11, 1939: 1-2.

2   *Chicago Tribune*, July 4, 1939: 19.

3   "Our Weather Man," *Belvidere* (Illinois) *Daily Republican*, July 3, 1939: 8.

4   Bill Johnson, SABR Baseball Biography Project, Earl Whitehill (sabr.org/bioproj/person/c510cd32).

5   Ed Burns, "Cubs, Cardinals Split," *Chicago Tribune*, July 5, 1939: 19-20.

6   Burns, "Hartnett Cracks the Whip."

7   Burns, "Cubs, Cardinals Split."

8   Photo Captions, "Leiber Hits Three Homers for Cubs in First Game," *Chicago Tribune*, July 5, 1939: 28.

9   Burns, "Cubs, Cardinals Split."

10 Ibid.

11 "Leiber Hits Three Homers."

12 Johnson, Whitehill biography.

13 Burns, "Cubs, Cardinals Split."

14 Greg King, SABR Baseball Biography Project, Augie Galan (sabr.org/bioproj/person/10f4ef3f).

15 Burns, "Cubs, Cardinals Split."

16 "Dean and French Face Reds Today in Twin Bill," *Chicago Tribune*, July 2, 1939: 16.

17 Whitehill ended the 1939 season for the Cubs at 4-7. He was released on October 18.

18 Leiber hit a career-high 24 home runs for the Cubs in 1939. An All-Star selection in 1940 and 1941, Leiber was traded back to the New York Giants for pitcher Bob Bowman on December 3, 1941.

19 "Red Sox Lace Mackmen Twice," *Allentown* (Pennsylvania) *Morning Call*, July 5, 1939: 18

20 "Holiday Ball Games Draw 249,538 for New High Attendance Mark," *St. Louis Star and Times*, July 5, 1939: 18.

21 "'Iron-Man' Gehrig Weeps as 61,808 pay Tribute to Him," *St. Louis Star and Times*, July 5, 1939: 18.

CLAUDE PASSEAU BESTS MAX LANIER IN EXTRA-INNING DUEL

MAY 5, 1943
CHICAGO CUBS 2, ST. LOUIS CARDINALS 1
(14 INNINGS)

By Russ Lake

ON MAY 5, 1943, THE *CHICAGO TRIBUNE* was chock-full of news. For a cost of 3 cents, one could absorb 48 pages from the *Trib*, self-described as the "World's Greatest Newspaper." With the United States nearing its 17th month as a combatant in World War II, the bulk of the front page centered on military reporting. On this day, the page-one headlines highlighted the death of a high-ranking US Army general in a noncombat plane crash, and a pending congressional vote to forgive 75 percent of the nation's 1942 taxes.[1]

A flip to the sports section did not elevate the mood of Chicago Cubs fans as their team was 3-8, bundled with the New York Giants at the bottom of the National League standings. After 11 games, the Cubs had been outscored 50-25, but were spared from being the worst team in the majors by their South Side brethren. The White Sox were 2-7, and had plated just 15 tallies. While the North Siders' offense struggled to produce runs with the NL's controversial "dead" baseball, the pitching staff could be described as "sick."[2]

This negative tag on the hurlers was more about ailments affecting the starting rotation than their overall performance. Chicago skipper Jimmie Wilson had a preseason "Big Four" set with Bill Lee, Paul Derringer, Claude Passeau, and Lon Warneke that unfortunately opened the campaign completely "under the weather" due to various health problems.[3] Derringer's illness became so severe that he had to be hospitalized in St. Louis. His recovery slipped to personal insult after he exited Wrigley Field as a spectator after the May 4 contest. Derringer had parked his car outside Wrigley Field, at Waveland and Clifton, but discovered that someone had smashed a window and taken two leather traveling bags worth $130.[4]

Manager Wilson was thankful that second-year hurler Hi Bithorn stepped in with an effective fastball to post two victories. The fun-loving Bithorn joked with Wrigley Field grounds crew chief Harry Hazlewood after being asked about any special treatment the Latin ace would prefer when they curried the mound for him. "There certainly is," replied Bithorn. "Just move the rubber about two feet closer to the plate."[5] With his rotation blueprint tattered, Wilson elevated rookie Ed Hanyzewski to starter status. The 22-year-old right-hander had impressed in his first three outings, but was charged in his latest start with a loss during an 11-3 thrashing by the St. Louis Cardinals.

Wilson selected the veteran right-hander Passeau to start on the 5th, while Cardinals manager Billy Southworth went with southpaw Max Lanier for the defending World Series champions. The 27-year-old Lanier had yet to earn a decision this season, but was 10-6 lifetime versus the Cubs. Passeau, at 34, was still nursing a virus that had plagued him for weeks.[6] Beginning his fifth season in Chicago, he was 0-1 starting his ninth year in the majors with a career

104-107 mark. He had also pitched for the Pittsburgh Pirates and the Philadelphia Phillies. Passeau, an All-Star the past two seasons, was 14-16 lifetime against the Cardinals.

Though mild weather with unseasonably warm temperatures settled in, only 4,213 spectators entered the ballpark. Wartime restrictions, specifically gasoline rationing,[7] had reduced baseball attendance in the Windy City. Another "stay-away" aspect was that the Cubs had lost five straight games while producing woeful offensive statistics. The team had already been shut out four times, averaged a mere two runs per game, and had not homered at all this season. The new Spalding baseball implemented by the NL had been blamed for the base-hit drought around the league. In late April, complaints were so bad that league President Ford C. Frick had allowed teams to switch back to their supply of spheres from the previous season. Analysis of the '43 ball determined that the rubber cement core had soaked into the yarn and hardened it into what players called the "clunk" ball. Frick promised that fans could soon expect some livelier play after all the teams had received their replacement baseballs, now being manufactured with a balata center.[8]

Passeau pitched around a double by Stan Musial in the first inning, while Lanier struggled with control in the bottom half; walking two and throwing a wild pitch. Shortstop Lou Klein fielded an infield hit by Heinz Becker and threw out Eddie Stanky trying to score from second to end the frame. Both hurlers survived safeties again in the second inning. Zeroes were posted until the top of the fifth when the Cardinals' Debs Garms singled to plate Lanier for a 1-0 lead. Jimmy Brown also raced for home, but right fielder Bill Nicholson fired to catcher Chico Hernandez who tagged Brown out.

The Cardinals attempted to add another run in the sixth, but Musial was tagged out by Passeau on an attempted steal of home after Musial tripled. However, before that happened, manager Wilson was ejected by third-base umpire Larry Goetz after he vehemently argued a call at second.[9] Wilson entertained his own bench personnel with gyrations

and insulting gestures toward Goetz before departing for the clubhouse. A sparse section of Chicago fans next to the dugout bellowed catcalls toward the arbiter.[10] The Cubs managed three singles in the bottom of the sixth, but a pickoff and a 6-4-3 double-play grounder kept Chicago off the scoreboard. Peanuts Lowrey singled in the bottom of the seventh and was sacrificed to second. Passeau, allowed to bat for himself with two outs, doubled for his first hit of the season to tie the game.

While the Chicago bats had gone into a "deep sleep" against Lanier for the equivalent of six innings, Passeau turned up his competitive fire and kept the score tied by dauntingly moving through a gantlet of scoring opportunities for St. Louis. In the eighth, Musial tripled high off the right-field wall with two outs, but was left stranded when Ray Sanders flied out. Pinch-runner Buster Adams was on second with one gone in the ninth when Whitey Kurowski hammered a drive that 5-foot-6 left fielder Dom Dallessandro tracked down near the wall with a one-handed leaping grab. After an intentional pass to Klein, Passeau retired the side on Lanier's infield fly.[11]

Passeau remained "deep-rooted" with his fruitful mound work during the 10th when Musial again knocked a two-out triple, only to have Sanders pop to third baseman Stan Hack. In the 11th, Walker Cooper led off with a double and moved to third on a groundout. Kurowski lifted a fly ball to left that was too short for Cooper to score. Klein was intentionally passed, and Lanier flied to center. With one out in the 12th, Musial singled for his fourth safety of the day to send Garms to third. Sanders lifted a high foul ball that Hernandez corralled near the field-box railing. Hernandez whirled around after the catch and pegged toward Stanky since Musial was moving toward second base. Garms broke for home, but Stanky relayed to Passeau covering the plate for an unconventional 2-4-1 twin killing.[12]

The "good-luck" procession took the same route for Passeau in the 13th after Cooper singled and moved to second on a sacrifice. Kurowski's smash went off Hack's glove, but he was able to whirl around and make a lunging tag on Cooper at third base. Then Klein flied out. Passeau spurned the dramatics in the top of the 14th by retiring the Cardinals in order for the first time since the ninth, and just the third time in the contest.[13]

Becker opened the bottom of the 14th with a hit to left. Musial charged in while watching the runner, but the ball glanced off the young left fielder's glove for an error allowing Becker to scamper into scoring position. Lowrey failed in two bunt attempts before flying to Harry Walker in short center. Lennie Merullo, who had been hitless in five plate appearances, was intentionally walked.[14] Hernandez smacked a hard grounder at second baseman Brown that had inning-ending double play written all over it. However, prosperity remained entrenched on the Cubs' side as the ball took a wicked hop, skipped high over Brown's right shoulder, and slithered into center field while Becker romped home with the winning tally.[15]

The hard-fought 2-1 victory moved the Cubs out of the cellar, while the Cardinals remained in second place behind the Brooklyn Dodgers. Nicholson and Becker each had three hits for Chicago while Musial went 4-for-5 for St. Louis.

Line scores for the Cubs showed two runs, 12 hits, and no errors, with the Cardinals at one run, 12 hits, and one error. St. Louis left 13 runners on while Chicago stranded 11. The game took 3:31 to play, and was the longest at Wrigley Field since May 17, 1939, when a 9-9 tie versus Brooklyn lasted 4:41. Passeau walked five, but amazingly struck out none of the 56 batters he faced during the 14 innings. Lanier, who challenged 53 batsmen, fanned five and walked seven during his 13⅓ frames of duty.

SOURCES

In addition to the sources cited in the Notes, the author also accessed Retrosheet.org, Baseball-Reference.com, Newspapers. com, SABR.org/bioproj, and *The Sporting News* archive via Paper of Record.

NOTES

1   *Chicago Tribune*, May 5, 1943: 1.

2   Ed Burns, "Cubs Blowing Horn Over Bithorn," *The Sporting News*, May 13, 1943: 4.

3   Ibid.

4   Burns, "Cubs Lose to Cardinals; 5th Defeat in a Row," *Chicago Tribune*, May 5, 1943: 33.

5   Burns, "Cubs Blowing Horn Over Bithorn."

6   Burns, "Hits by Becker and Hernandez Beat Cards, 2-1," *Chicago Tribune*, May 6, 1943: 27.

7   "Gas Ration Revoked, but Speeder Laughs; Has No Book, No Car," *Chicago Tribune*, May 5, 1943: 1.

8   Associated Press, "'Corrected Baseball' Is Ready, Says Frick," *St. Louis Post-Dispatch*, May 5, 1943: 22.

9   Burns, "Hits by Becker and Hernandez Beat Cards."

10 Photo Caption, "Jimmy Wilson Gets the Dugout Gate," *Chicago Tribune*, May 6, 1943: 29.

11 Burns, "Hits by Becker and Hernandez."

12 Ibid.

13 Ibid.

14 Ibid.

15 "Bad Bounce, Error Lead to Cub Victory," *St. Louis Post-Dispatch*, May 6, 1943: 22.

THE FIRST GAME PLAYED UNDER THE LIGHTS AT WRIGLEY FIELD

JULY 1, 1943
INAUGURAL AAGBBL ALL-STAR GAME

By Merrie A. Fidler and Jim Nitz

PHILIP K. WRIGLEY, CHEWING-GUM magnate and longtime owner of the Chicago Cubs, was an innovator and experimenter, and during World War II, he was committed to supporting the war effort.[1] For instance, he assigned all his radio time to selling the war rather than gum – $2 million for two CBS programs alone. He also converted part of his gum-packing factory into an assembly line for packing K rations; and he directed his gum tappers in Central and South America to tap as many rubber trees as they could while working on gum trees.[2]

Thus, in the late fall of 1942, when the War Department notified major-league baseball owners that the 1943 season might have to be postponed because of increasing manpower needs, Wrigley approved and funded his committee's recommendation to organize a women's professional softball league to fill the possible void in major-league parks, to keep baseball alive, and to provide entertainment for war workers and service personnel.[3] He reasoned:

World War One showed to the world for the first time on a large scale what women could and did do, and World War Two is going to carry this even further. American women have taken a very definite share of the load in the country's progress, and in the fields of science, business and sports they are now also working in ever increasing numbers."[4]

Originally Wrigley named the new professional league the All-American Girls Soft Ball League (AAGSBL), but he changed that title to the All-American Girls Base Ball League (AAGBBL) in midseason 1943, because except for the 12-inch ball, the shorter field distances, and underhand pitching, the playing rules he instituted were those of baseball.[5]

Wrigley established the AAGBBL with some experimental policies:

- He established the league on a nonprofit, trusteeship basis to provide entertainment for service personnel and war-factory workers in cities near Chicago.

- He recruited the most skilled players in the United States and Canada.

- Player contracts belonged to league administration instead of individual teams to facilitate equalized competition through a player allocation board.

- He established strict, college-based rules of on- and off-field behavior.[6]

Major-league baseball survived the manpower push of 1943, and as the team owners had done in 1942, they earmarked the proceeds of the 1943 regularly-scheduled June 30 and July 18 games, as well as the July 13 All-Star Game, to go to various war-relief agencies as part of their contribution to the war effort. Most of the proceeds from these games benefited servicemen.[7]

The fact that Wrigley hosted a large Women's Army Auxiliary Corps (WAAC) rally in Wrigley Field the night after the June 30 benefit game confirms that considerable planning and coordination took place between Wrigley and Army commanders stationed in the Chicago area. Wrigley's efforts aimed to benefit servicewomen.

A league newspaper noted that an intensive WAAC recruiting push was underway to enlist 30,000 new WAACs by July 1, 1943, because each WAAC recruit freed a serviceman for combat duty. The "mammoth" WAAC program at Wrigley Field the night of July 1, 1943, contributed to this effort and included the following:[8]

- A WAAC softball game between a Camp Grant team (near Rockford, Illinois) and a Fort Sheridan team (on Lake Michigan north of Chicago).
- WAAC entertainment including military drills, calisthenics, a band performance, and a uniform display.
- Recruiting talks by members of the 6th Service command.
- At least 150 WAACs circulating in the stands to answer questions.
- An All-Star AAGBBL game with ballplayers from the four original league teams (Racine Belles, Kenosha Comets, South Bend Blue Sox, and Rockford Peaches) to cap off festivities.[9]

Scheduling the WAAC softball game at 6:00 P.M. enabled more working women to attend. Making the event free of charge coincided with the league's nonprofit status and possibly enabled young women unable to attend otherwise to participate. In addition, the 8:30 P.M. AAGBBL game provided Wrigley with an opportunity to experiment with a night game at his ballpark. Interestingly, Wrigley experimented with the first-ever twilight game at Wrigley Field on June 26, 1943, between the Cubs and Cardinals, and it may have been a test run for the upcoming WAAC rally.[10]

To help involve AAGBBL fans in the WAAC rally and AAGBBL All-Star Game, sportswriters in the league's cities advised them that the Chicago league office requested their votes to determine the All-American All-Stars. Sportswriters also advised

fans that those who submitted ballots would receive a free ticket to a local game[11]

Apparently, local AAGBBL fans turned in a considerable number of ballots. A Rockford sportswriter reported the following: "A flood of votes, mailed last night [June 29] just before the midnight deadline descended on the Register Republic sports department today and were turned over immediately to league officials who said that they had been making an attempt to summarize the local vote but had been unable to keep up with the flow of ballots."[12]

In pregame publicity, the *Rockford Morning Star* introduced the Camp Grant team with a team photo on the sports page and noted their "Nifty Uniforms." The photo revealed the surprising fact that the Camp Grant team uniforms were identical to the AAGBBL skirted uniforms![13]

In South Bend, fans learned that league officials recruited Joe Boland, the public-address announcer for their Blue Sox, to serve as the field announcer for the WAAC rally at Wrigley Field.[14]

Postgame publicity on July 2, 1943, recorded that 7,000 fans attended the WAAC rally, and that the Fort Sheridan WAACs defeated the Camp Grant team, 11-5.[15]

The AAGBBL game began with the teams' usual wartime, pregame routine of lining up in a V-for-Victory formation during the national anthem. The game itself proved to be a one-sided affair with the Wisconsin All-Stars trouncing the Indiana-Illinois All-Stars, 16-0. Apparently, it was one of those nights when one team could do no wrong, and the other team couldn't do much.[16]

Three banks of temporary lights were installed on poles situated behind home plate, first base, and third base. One sportswriter judged them suitable for softball.[17] Researcher Jay Feldman recorded players' recollections of playing under those lights:

Shirley Jameson: "The lights weren't all that great, but we were used to that – we had to play with whatever we had. Besides, just the fact that we were playing in Wrigley Field was enough. We'd have done it whether it was light or dark, because we were all on Cloud Nine."

Mildred Warwick echoed Jameson's sentiments about playing in Wrigley Field: "All of a sudden I'd landed in Wrigley Field. I was overwhelmed by the size of it, and I thought, 'Oh my goodness, I'm playing in Wrigley Field.' I was thrilled."

Pitcher Helen Nicol noted that the lighting conditions challenged the outfielders: "The shadows would come up and all of a sudden you wouldn't be able to decipher where the ball was. It was pretty hard for the outfielders to see, especially if the ball got up high."

Betsy Jochum didn't realize she was part of a historic event: "I didn't realize at the time that they didn't have lights at Wrigley Field. ... I just thought those lights were there all the time. We showed up for the game, the lights were on, and we played."[18]

AAGBBL sportswriters' recaps recognized the game's outstanding players and events:

"... the brilliant outfielding and baserunning of Shirley Jameson, Kenosha center fielder, thrilled the big crowd throughout the game.[19]

Eleanor Dapkus hit a triple with the bases loaded to drive in three Wisconsin runs.[20]

Sophie Kurys got three singles in four trips and drove in two runs besides scoring three herself. Dorothy Wind scored three runs and got one hit in two official turns at bat. Clara Schillace had two hits in three tries.[21]

Gloria Marks was hit by a line drive and forced to retire after pitching just two-thirds of an inning. Mary Nesbitt pitched the last 2⅓ innings and got in just enough work to sharpen her pitching for tonight.[22]

Helen Nicol, Kenosha hurler from Calgary, Canada, pitched no-hit ball during her three-inning effort and a teammate, Elise Harney, of Jacksonville, Illinois, was nicked for the first Illinois-Indiana hit when Josephine D'Angelo singled after two out in the seventh inning. The other hit by the losers was pitcher Olive Little's infield hit to open the ninth."[23]

Sportswriters didn't provide a WAAC box score, but they did provide the AAGBBL's:

AAGBBL 1943 ALL-STAR GAME BOX SCORE

WISCONSIN ALL-STARS (Kenosha and Racine, WI)							ILLINOIS-INDIANA ALL-STARS (Rockford, IL & South Bend, IN)						
	Team	AB	R	H	PO	A		Team	AB	R	H	PO	A
Jameson, cf	Ken	3	3	2	3	0	D'Angelo, cf	S.B.	4	0	1	1	0
Perlick, lf	Rac.	3	1	1	1	0	Warwick, 3b	Roc.	2	0	0	1	1
Kurys, 2b	Rac.	4	3	3	2	0	Florreich, 3b	S.B.	2	0	0	1	2
Harnett, 3b	Ken.	1	1	1	1	3	Davis, ss	Roc.	2	0	0	1	4
English, 3b	Rac.	3	1	0	2	4	Stefani, 2b	S.B.	3	0	0	3	3
Wind, ss	Rac.	2	3	1	2	4	Hageman, 1b	S.B.	3	0	0	12	0
Dapkus, rf	Rac.	2	1	1	1	0	Jochum, lf	S.B.	2	0	0	1	0
Schillace, rf	Rac.	3	1	2	1	0	Fritz, lf	Roc.	1	0	0	0	0
O'Hara, 1b	Ken.	3	1	1	11	0	Burnmeister, rf	Roc.	3	0	0	0	0
Westerman, c	Ken.	2	0	0	2	0	Baker, c	S.B.	2	0	0	2	1
Hickson, c	Rac.	2	0	1	1	0	Green, c	Roc.	1	0	0	2	1
Nicol, p	Ken.	1	0	0	0	0	Berger, p	S.B.	1	0	0	0	1
Harney, p	Ken.	2	0	0	0	0	Peters, p	Roc.	0	1	0	0	0
Marks, p	Rac.	0	1	0	0	1	Barr, p	Roc.	1	0	0	0	0
Nesbitt, p	Rac.	1	0	0	0	0	Little, p	S.B.	1	0	1	0	0
Totals		**34**	**16**	**13**	**27**	**12**	**Totals**		**30**	**0**	**2**	**24**	**13**
Coach:	Josh Billings – Kenosha						**Coach:**	Eddie Stumpf – Rockford					
Chaperone:	Marie Andeson – Racine						**Chaperone:**	Rose Virginia Way – S.B.					

Errors: Harnett, Warwick, Perlick, Green, Jochum; Two-base hits: Harnett; Three-base hits: Dapkus; Sacrifice Hits: Perlick, English; Stolen bases: Jameson 2, O'Hara, D'Angelo; Walked: Peters 2, Barr,, Little; Struck out: Nicol 2, Harney 1, Barr 1, Little 2; Hit by pitched ball: By Little: Kurys, Wind; Double Plays: Stefani to Florreich; Wild Pitch: Barr 2; Hits: Off Berger: 2 runs, 3 hits in 2 innings; off Peters: 3 runs, 1 hit in 2 innings; off Barr: 6 runs, 2 hits in 2⅓ innings; off Little: 3 runs, 3 hits in 2 innings; off Nicol: 0 runs, 0 hits in 3 innings; off Harney, 0 runs, 1 hit in 3 innings; off Marks: 0 runs, 0 hits in ⅓ inning; off Nesbitt: 0 runs, 1 hit in 1⅓ innings; Passed Ball: Baker; Umpires: Bill Green and Knotty Porter; Time: 1:55.

Source: *Kenosha Evening News*, July 2, 1943: 8; *Racine Journal Times*, July 2, 1943: 16; *Rockford Register Republic*, July 2, 1943: 14.

So ended the "mammoth" July 1, 1943, World War II WAAC rally, which incorporated the historic first-ever lighted night game at Wrigley Field. It provided Philip Wrigley an opportunity to benefit women service personnel and to experiment with a night game. The players were thrilled to play in a major-league park and Wrigley Field in particular. At the time, none of Wrigley's women players imagined they had just made history that would be repeated once more by their league in 1944 and not again until the Cubs played a night game at Wrigley Field in August 1988 – 44 years later.

SOURCES

The *Rockford Morning Star* and *Boise Idaho Statesman*, were accessed through genealogybank.com.

NOTES

1   Merrie A. Fidler, *The Origins and History of the All-American Girls Professional Baseball League* (Jefferson, North Carolina: McFarland and Company, 2006), Chapter 1.

2   "Chewing Gum Is War Material," *Fortune*, January 1943: 100.

3   *Kenosha Evening News*, May 27, 1943, 16; June 1, 1943: 9.

4   "Mr. Wrigley's Statement for the Press on the Girls' All-American Softball League," February 17, 1943, Arthur Meyerhoff Files, drawer 19, 1943 News Release Folder.

5   Fidler, 36.

6   Fidler, 34-36.

7   "Majors to Put on Big Show for War Benefit Wednesday," *Racine Journal Times*, June 19, 1943: 10.

8   Carl E. Lundquist, "News Views," *Rockford Morning Star*, June 15, 1943: 2; "All-American Girls' Softball League Play All-Star Contest for WAACs," *Kenosha Evening News*, June 24, 1943: 8.

9   *Chicago Tribune*, July 1, 1943: Section 2, 21; "Belles to Play Sox Tonight," *Racine Journal Times*, June 30, 1943: 10.

10 "Redbirds Lose Fourth Time to Puerto Rican," *Boise Idaho Statesman*, June 26, 1943: 7.

11 See sports pages of the *Rockford Register Republic*, the *Kenosha Evening News*, the *Racine Journal Times*, and the *South Bend Tribune* between June 23 and June 29, 1943; "Big Vote Cast for All-Stars," *Rockford Register Republic*, June 30, 1943: 15.

12 *Rockford Register Republic*, June 30, 1943: 15.

13 *Rockford Morning Star*, June 27, 1943: 35.

14 "Jim Costin Says," *South Bend Tribune*, June 24, 1943: 8.

15 "Wisconsin Girls Win, 16-0 on WAAC Program," *Chicago Tribune*, July 2, 1943: 21.

16 *Racine Journal Times*, June 30, 1943: 10; "Peaches Meet Kenosha Again," *Rockford Register Republic*, July 2, 1943: 14.

17 "Cook to Face Nicol Tonight When Peaches Tackle Kenosha," *Rockford Register Republic*, June 29, 1943: 10.

18 Jay Feldman, "The Real History of Night Ball at Wrigley Field," *Baseball Research Journal*, Society for American Baseball Research, No. 21, 1992: 93-95.

19 "Blue Sox Fight to Retain Lead," *South Bend Tribune*, July 2, 1943: Section 3, p. 1.

20 "Belles to Play Sox Tonight; Seek Lead," *Racine Journal Times*, July 2, 1943: 16.

21 Ibid.

22 Ibid.

23 "Wisconsin Team Triumphs, Comets Star," *Kenosha Evening News*, July 2, 1943: 8.

THE AAGPBL PLAYS IN THE SECOND NIGHT GAME EVER AT WRIGLEY FIELD

JULY 18, 1944
MILWAUKEE CHICKS 20, SOUTH BEND BLUE SOX 11

By Jim Nitz

THE SECOND NIGHT GAME EVER PLAYED at Wrigley Field was a Red Cross "Thank You" program exhibition between the Milwaukee Chicks and the South Bend Blue Sox of the All-American Girls Professional Baseball League. This was the first contest of a doubleheader held on Tuesday evening, July 18, 1944, serving as a break between the two halves of the AAGPBL championship season. In 1943, the first year of the league, an AAGPBL night all-star game had also been played at Wrigley Field.[1] The 1944 event matched the fully-rostered teams of the Chicks and the Blue Sox, followed by the Racine Belles against the Kenosha Comets. The second game was stopped at 11 P.M. with a 6-6 tie after 3½ innings because the teams needed to get to their trains to begin the second half of the season the next day.[2]

The AAGPBL, founded by Chicago Cubs owner Philip Wrigley, promoted this Red Cross doubleheader by offering free admission to Wrigley Field that evening to anyone showing a Red Cross worker's button, contributor's pin or card, or blood donor's button, as appreciation for their wartime work. Furthermore, uniformed servicemen and anyone they escorted were also invited to enjoy women's baseball at no charge.[3] The day of the event, free admission for all was highlighted in the newspapers, in the hope of filling all 40,000 Wrigley Field seats.[4] In addition to local radio spots and newspaper coverage, 25,000 bright red flyers were distributed throughout the Chicago area to promote the 7:30 P.M. twin bill. A special box-seat section was open only to members of the armed forces and Red Cross volunteers and contributors who arrived before 7:15.[5]

The Chicks and Blue Sox got the evening off to an exciting start, as Milwaukee, managed by future Hall of Famer Max Carey, won in a slugfest, 20-11, over South Bend, led by former big leaguer Bert Niehoff. The Chicks scored 11 runs in the sixth inning to put away the Blue Sox before a crowd estimated at 20,000 by the *Chicago Tribune.*[6] The *Racine Journal-Times* reported that 16,000 fans attended the game, which went 2 hours and 25 minutes. Sylvia Wronski, the 19-year-old Chicks number-4 starter, earned the win, besting Blue Sox starter, Kay Bennett. Seven pitchers were used in a game that was much longer and higher-scoring than usual for the AAGPBL. Milwaukee's leading hitters were shortstop Pat Keagle with four hits, including two triples, and four runs scored; outfielder Thelma Eisen (called "Pigtails" by the Racine newspaper) who drove in six runs and also hit a triple; and third baseman Doris Tetzlaff, who added four hits. The Racine paper said the sixth inning "looked like a track meet" with 15 Chicks batters facing Doris Barr. South Bend was led by catcher Lucella MacLean with three RBIs on three hits; third baseman Lois Florreich and her three hits; and outfielder Betsy Jochum's three singles and a triple.[7] The *Milwaukee Journal,* the *Kenosha Evening News,* and the *South Bend Tribune* concurred with the *Racine Journal-Times* on the 16,000 attendance figure. The *Journal* continued to be the only newspaper to refer to the Milwaukee team as the Schnitts, which means "small beer" in German or, alternatively, "little Brewers" in reference to the Milwaukee minor-league team at the time.[8]

The inadequate portable lighting at Wrigley Field was said to have contributed to the high hit, run, and error totals as outfielders had difficulty seeing fly balls. The planned 300,000 watts were reduced to only 38,500 due to problems securing and installing the necessary electrical cable. Chicks chaperone Dorothy Hunter, in a 1976 interview with groundbreaking AAGPBL researcher Merrie Fidler, recalled the temporary lights as "little bitty flood lights on the grand stand."[9] Seventy-three years after the game, Viola Thompson Griffin, left-handed Chicks pitcher, still remembered those lights being stationed around the outfield and in the grandstand and as "poor and pathetic, making it hard to see, which led to many errors."[10]

In an effort to further entertain the crowd, Victor Mature, popular film actor of that time, was on hand. The *Racine Journal-Times* had this to say about what became Mature's unwelcome appearance at Wrigley Field that night: "The appearance of "That (self-advertised) Beautiful Hunk of Man was, to put it charitably, unfortunate. Mature, a chief bo'sun mate in the coast guard who has put in 14 months of sea duty and is now recruiting with the Tars and Spars show, made an 'entrance' when the game was in progress, had the over-long contest held up while he made an inconsequential series of wise-cracks about himself, and was given a sound round of razzberries as he left. We certainly don't like to see a service man booed, but the Beautiful Hunk certainly asked for it."[11] Betsy Jochum clearly recalled this incident in a 2017 interview, stating that fans wanted to watch the ballgame rather than listen to a Hollywood star.[12] Viola Thompson Griffin enthusiastically remembered that she and her teammates "as young girls, we thought Mature was great!"[13] Mature did War Bond promotional tours and performed in morale and recruiting shows in 1944. Interestingly, he had been rejected by the Navy in 1942 due to color blindness.

The very same day, he enlisted in the Coast Guard after passing a different vision test.[14]

Ballplayer reactions to playing at Wrigley Field were fascinating. Sylvia Wronski said it was immensely satisfying but added, "I loved playing ball. Even at Wrigley Field, nothing else ran through my head but playing the game. Baseball was my only passion until I got married."[15] Jochum did not recall specific details, other than Victor Mature getting booed. However, she did have vivid memories of the 1943 AAGPBL tryouts, also held at Wrigley Field.[16] Griffin, in a 1995 oral-history interview, said that she "was very much conscious" that the AAGPBL was contributing to the war effort by playing in that Red Cross doubleheader. She also remembered the Mature incident by stating that "he was so handsome, and we wanted to watch him, and the people wanted to watch us play ball."[17] Almost three-quarters of a century after the game, Griffin said that, at the time, it was "so wonderful, amazing, and exciting to say I'm in Wrigley Field and walk out on that diamond."[18] Wronski recalled other AAGPBL war efforts during 1944 in which the Chicks played at several veterans hospitals, including Milwaukee's.[19] In addition, she was pictured in the August 10, 1944, *Milwaukee Journal*, promoting a coming Red Cross "Thank You" game at Borchert Field, home of the Chicks.[20]

As unforgettable as this exhibition appears now, no box score or pictures have been found for it. The only statistical record is a *South Bend Tribune* line score (showing the Blue Sox as visitors and the Chicks as home team) which included the runs for each of the nine innings, total runs, hits (South Bend 13, Milwaukee 16), and errors (South Bend 6, Milwaukee 5). Only the starting pitchers and catchers were included in this line score.[21] AAGPBL press coverage in 1944 was more detailed for regular-season games in the teams' hometown newspapers. However, the crowd of at least 16,000 watched the AAGPBL make history at Wrigley Field's second night game ever, under those inadequate temporary lights in July 1944.

NOTES

1 Merrie Fidler, *Origins and History of the All-American Girls Professional Baseball League* (Jefferson, North Carolina: McFarland & Company, 2005), 52.

2 "Racine Club Adds 2 Players, Ties Comets in Chicago Show," *Racine Journal-Times*, July 19, 1944.

3 "Schnitts Split a Double Bill," *Milwaukee Journal*, July 13, 1944.

4 "Wrigley Field Scene of Girls' Games Tonight," *Chicago Tribune*, July 18, 1944; "Belles to Play in Chicago," *Racine Journal-Times*, July 18, 1944.

5 Fidler, 54-55.

6 "Girls' Games for Red Cross Attract 20,000," *Chicago Tribune*, July 19, 1944.

7 "Racine Club Adds 2 Players, Ties Comets in Chicago Show," *Racine Journal-Times*, July 19, 1944; "Comets, Racine Tie 6-6 After Short Contest," *Kenosha Evening News*, July 19, 1944.

8 "Comets, Racine Tie 6-6 After Short Contest"; "16,000 Watch Schnitts Win," *Milwaukee Journal*, July 19, 1944, "Rockford, Blue Sox Meet Here Tonight," *South Bend Tribune*, July 19, 1944; Thomas J. Morgan and James R. Nitz, "Our Forgotten World Champions: The 1944 Milwaukee Chicks," *Milwaukee History*, vol. 18, no. 2 (1995): 36.

9 Fidler.

10 Viola Thompson Griffin, telephone interview with author, April 29, 2017.

11 Jim O'Brien, "Sidelines," *Racine Journal-Times*, July 19, 1944.

12 Betsy Jochum, telephone interview with author, April 13, 2017.

13 Griffin.

14 John Keyes, DVCP. "Victor Mature Shadow Box." TogetherWeServed – Connecting US Coast Guardsmen. Together We Served, 2011. Web. 14 Apr. 2017. coastguard.togetherweserved.com/uscg/servlet/tws.webapp. WebApps?cmd=ShadowBoxProfile&type=Person&ID=9597.

15 Sylvia Wronski Straka, personal interview with author, May 25, 1994.

16 Jochum.

17 Viola Thompson Griffin, oral history interview with Robert Carter, University of Wisconsin-Milwaukee Graduate Public History Class Project: The Forgotten Champs-The Milwaukee Chicks of 1944, March 8, 1995.

18 Griffin, 2017.

19 Sylvia Wronski Straka, oral history interview with Lisa Hutchinson, University of Wisconsin-Milwaukee Graduate Public History Class Project: The Forgotten Champs-The Milwaukee Chicks of 1944, March 20, 1995.

20 *Milwaukee Journal*, August 10, 1944.

21 "Rockford, Blue Sox Meet Here Tonight," *South Bend Tribune*, July 19, 1944.

THE CURSE OF THE BILLY GOAT

By Glen Sparks

WILLIAM SIANIS PLANNED TO SPEND THE afternoon at Wrigley Field with his pet goat, Murphy. Sianis, a Chicago businessman and first-class attention-getter, had purchased two box-seat tickets for $7.20 apiece.

It was Saturday, October 6, 1945. The Cubs were playing the Detroit Tigers in Game Four of the World Series. Chicago led the best-of-seven match-up two games to one. Some fans had shivered all night in 30-degree temperatures to buy bleacher tickets that morning. Scalpers were demanding as much as $200 for choice box seats.

Sianis and Murphy strolled up to the ballpark's front entrance. Murphy wore a blanket across his back. A sign attached to the blanket read "We got Detroit's goat."[1] Sianis, meanwhile, looked resplendent, dressed in a pinstriped suit, topcoat, bow tie, and a wide-brimmed white hat. He also sported an elegant goatee. Just like a billy goat. Sianis, a native of Paleopyrgos, Greece, owned the Lincoln tavern – a former speakeasy – located at 1855 S. Madison St., across the street from Chicago Stadium.

Supposedly, Sianis bought the Lincoln in 1934 "with a $200 check from someone who owed him and $5 of his own money."[2] Later that year, a baby goat fell off a truck nearby and wandered into Sianis's establishment. A friend told him to keep the animal. "This will be worth a million dollars of free publicity," he said.[3] But Sianis didn't just keep the goat. He formally adopted it. A local court paroled it "into the custody of William Sianis for life."[4] Sianis let his new pet chomp on a small patch of grass behind the Lincoln.

The goat often accompanied Sianis to local events. On this World Series day in 1945, Sianis handed the usher two tickets. The usher, though, cast a suspicious eye and called Cubs owner Philip K. Wrigley. The chewing-gum magnate nixed any idea of allowing a barnyard beast into a major-league ballpark. (Supposedly, Wrigley said, "Let Billy in, but not the goat." Sianis asked, "Why not the goat?" Wrigley: "Because the goat stinks.")[5] Well, that did it.

An indignant Sianis wheeled around and left, his goat in tow. The anger stirred inside him. Finally, he could take this embarrassment no longer. He cursed the Cubs forever. Sianis exclaimed, "You are going to lose this World Series and you are never going to go to another World Series again! You are never going to win a World Series again because you insulted my goat!"[6]

"Billy Goat" Sianis and billy goat Murphy hustled back to the Lincoln (later renamed the Billy Goat Tavern). Reporters and photographers, eager for a colorful story, followed. One photographer asked if Murphy could, please, just eat the ticket. It would make for a great photo, the newsmen agreed. No, sir, Sianis said. He'd keep that ticket for himself and settle the humiliating episode in court.

"I am going to sue for $100,000!" Billy said.

No, that wasn't enough. "I'm going to sue for $1 million!" he decided.[7]

Well, that's one version of the story. According to another, Sianis and Murphy made it into the ballpark and were shown to their seats. The two even paraded on the Wrigley Field grass briefly during a rain delay. The goat acted like a real ham. Gene Kessler of the *Chicago Daily Times* explained: "The ushers led Bill to the head of the grandstand aisle, but Mr. Goat balked, turned around and insisted on going back on the field. He got his wish when photographers asked that he return for poses, and the goat wound up proudly roaming close to the visiting dugout while cameras snapped."[8]

Now, the *Daily Times* did print a photo of Sianis doffing his cap alongside Murphy. The background, though, is grainy and doesn't show the visiting dugout or anything else. Of note, years later, Cubs shortstop Lenny Merullo did not recall seeing a goat traipsing across Wrigley Field. Nor did Chicago outfielder Andy Pafko. Anyway, Sianis and Murphy made an early exit. The goat apparently did indeed smell bad; the rain just made the animal's odor that much more pungent. Also, a goat has sharp horns, and it likes to munch on everyone else's snacks, plus purses and pants legs. Fans complained, and ushers asked Sianis and Murphy to leave. They did, prompting Billy to pronounce his forever-hex upon the Cubs.

The Cubs lost Game Four by a 4-1 score. Dizzy Trout tossed a complete game and allowed five hits. The Tigers celebrated an 8-4 victory in Game Five, but the Cubs took Game Six in 12 innings, 8-7. Detroit scored five runs in the first inning of Game Seven and won 9-3 behind Hal Newhouser. Soon after that final out, *Chicago Sun-Times* columnist Irv Kupcinet asserted, Sianis fired off a simple, but direct, wire to P.K. Wrigley: "Who smells now?"[9]

What should baseball fans make of Sianis's outcry? Did it really spell doom for the North Siders? Well, history shows that the once-mighty Cubs floundered for decades after that fall classic. Between 1876 and 1945, the Chicago franchise won 16 pennants and the World Series in 1907 and 1908. The 1946 Cubs went 82-71 and slipped to third place. Then, the problems really began. Over the next 20 years, only the 1963 club managed a winning record.

So maybe the Cubs really were cursed. But hardly anyone knew about it. The *Chicago Tribune*, for instance, did not report anything about a curse until December 26, 1967. By then, Sianis had moved the Billy Goat Tavern to 430 N. Michigan Ave. The eccentric businessman – he would formally apply to NASA for the first liquor license on the moon – claimed that he had lifted the bad-luck charm as a favor to Wrigley. The owner, though, apparently failed to notify anyone about this supposed exorcism.

In 1969, *Tribune* columnist David Condon wrote a couple of articles about a billy-goat curse. That was the year the Cubs looked like a sure thing. They were 74-43 and enjoyed a nine-game lead in the National League Eastern Division on August 13. But, Condon had warned in April, the curse was still in effect. Sianis had not lifted it; instead, he had placed "an eternal hex"[10] on the North Siders.

And wouldn't you know it, on September 9, 1969, at Shea Stadium, a black cat slinked past Cubs on-deck batter Ron Santo, hissed, and slipped into the Chicago dugout. The Cubs, already in full swoon and in first place by just 1½ games, ended the season eight games out of the top spot. The Cubs, already in a swoon and in first place by just 1½ games, ended the season eight games out of the top spot. New York's Miracle Mets won the division, the National League pennant, and, ultimately, the World Series.

Soon after that latest chapter in Cubs despair, William Sianis died, on October 22, 1970. Sam Sianis, Billy's nephew, took over the family business. Newspapers revved up talk about a curse. Fans pleaded for Sam Sianis to lift the hex. Sianis, mindful of history, refused. "The double-whammy will last forever," he promised.[11] Even so, on July 4, 1973, Sianis walked up to the front gate at Wrigley Field with a goat. The animal wore a painted sign: "All is Forgiven. Let me lead you to the pennant. Your Friend, Billy Goat."[12] Ushers turned them away.

Tsk, tsk, Condon wrote: "The Cubs had their golden opportunity to cast out the devil on July 4. … So, the hex still holds."[13] It took years for the Chicago front office to get the hint. Club officials finally invited Sam Sianis and his goat to the ballpark in 1984 and again in 1994. Sianis swore that he lifted the curse both times. Tom Trebelhorn, hired to manage the Cubs in 1994, didn't believe it. "That goat's got to go," he said as his team faltered in the early going. "There's all there is to it."[14] Three years later, one local TV show even summoned a witch to "cast a lucky spell on the Cubs."[15] Cubs general manager Andy MacPhail answered questions that year from fans at a Broadcast Advertising Club luncheon. MacPhail preached patience. One fan asked a question about the goat. Broadcaster Harry Caray spoke up: "Shoot him!"[16] The goat, not MacPhail. The crowd applauded.

Legendary newspaperman and Billy Goat Tavern regular Mike Royko wrote several columns surrounding the so-called curse. At last he grew fed up with the talk. "It's about time that we stopped blaming the failing of the Cubs on a poor, dumb creature that is a billy goat," he wrote. "It was Wrigley, not some goat, who cursed the Cubs."[17] Wrigley, Royko pointed out, did not sign a black baseball player until 1953, six years after Jackie Robinson played his first game for the Brooklyn Dodgers.

The Cubs qualified for the playoffs seven times between 1984 and 2015 and still could not make it into the World Series. Fans even suffered through the infamous Steve Bartman incident during the 2003 playoffs.[18] Finally, in 2016, the Cubs knocked off the Los Angeles Dodgers to win the National League pennant. They celebrated a World Series title 11 days later by beating the Cleveland Indians in seven games. Millions of fans attended the victory parade on November 4 in downtown Chicago.[19]

What would Billy "Goat" Sianis have thought?

NOTES

1   Gil Bogen, *The Billy Goat Curse: Losing and Superstition in Cubs Baseball Since World War 2* (Jefferson, North Carolina: McFarland, 2008).

2   Bogen.

3   Glenn Stout and Richard A. Johnson, *The Cubs* (Boston, New York: Houghton Mifflin: 2007).

4   Stout and Johnson.

5   "Let the Goat in!" billygoattavern.com, billygoattavern.com/legend/curse/.

6   Bogen.

7   Rick Kogan, *A Chicago Tavern: A Goat, A Curse, and the American Dream* (Illinois: Lake Claremont Press, 2006).

8   Gene Kessler, "World Series Highlights," *Chicago Times*, October 7, 1945.

9   Irv Kupcinet, "Kup's Column," *Chicago Times*, October 9, 1945.

10   David Condon, "In the Wake of the News," *Chicago Tribune*, April 15, 1969.

11   David Condon, "If the Cubs Blow It, Look for Goat," *Chicago Tribune*, July 6, 1973.

12   Ibid.

13   Ibid.

14   Joseph A. Reaves, "Cubs' Streak Starting to Get Manager's Goat," *Chicago Tribune*, April 30, 1994.

15   Fred Mitchell, *Chicago Tribune*. April 10, 1997.

16   Paul Sullivan, "Cubs' MacPhail Preaches Patience," *Chicago Tribune*, April 17, 1997.

17   Mike Royko, "It Was Wrigley, Not Some Goat, Who Cursed the Cubs," *Chicago Tribune*, March 21, 1997.

18   The Cubs led the best-of-seven National League Championship Series against the Florida Marlins three games to two. The Cubs were ahead 3-0 in the eighth inning of Game Six. Luis Castillo hit a foul ball down the left-field line that Cubs outfielder Moises Alou tried to catch even as the ball headed into the stands. Steve Bartman, a lifelong Cubs fan, appeared to interfere with Alou, who failed to catch the ball. The Cubs ended up losing the game 8-3 and lost the series the following day. Bartman was the subject of ridicule and went into hiding.

19   "Cubs World Series Celebration Ranks as 7th Largest Gathering in Human History," Fox32chicago.com. fox32chicago.com/news/local/215601786-story.

GOAT, TROUT LEAVE CUBS DIZZY

OCTOBER 6, 1945
DETROIT TIGERS 4, CHICAGO CUBS 1

GAME FOUR OF THE WORLD SERIES

By Scott Ferkovich

FOR DIZZY TROUT, THE 30-YEAR-OLD right-hander, no victory had meant so much.

Sure, he had posted 98 wins in his seven seasons with the Detroit Tigers, including 20 in 1943 and 27 the following year. But on October 6, 1945, in Game Four of the 1945 World Series against the Chicago Cubs, Trout shined like never before.

What made it so special, however, was beating the team that had rejected him 11 years earlier.

Back then, Trout was just a raw, gangly teenager from Indiana, fresh off a Chicago-bound freight train. With dreams of starring in the majors, he headed to the North Side of Chicago, to Wrigley Field, seeking a tryout. The garrulous Trout finagled his way into pitching batting practice. Afterward, when he appealed to the management for some meal money (after all, he had walked four miles to get to the park), all he received in return was a big, blank stare. Bent but not broken, Trout packed his grip and headed back to Indiana, to semipro ball, determined to make the Cubs rue their loss one day.

At least, that is how Trout himself told the story.

"And that ain't all," he added to anyone who would listen. "When the Indianapolis club sold me to Detroit, the Cubs were red hot after me to buy me then."[1]

Revenge is a dish best served cold, as Trout would agree. With calculated precision, he coolly mowed down the Cubs through nine innings this October afternoon, silencing the 42,923 at Wrigley Field, hundreds of whom had begun lining up along Sheffield Avenue the night before. This was the first appearance in the Series for Trout, an 18-game-winner in 1945. Tigers skipper Steve O'Neill had been holding the pitcher in reserve due to his persistent cold, sore throat, and aching back.

Trout showed no ill effects from whatever may have been ailing him. All told, Chicago managed only five measly hits in their 4-1 defeat, which evened the World Series at two victories apiece. Spotting his fastball well throughout the gloomy, damp day, Trout walked one and fanned six. He would have tossed a shutout were the Tigers not guilty of some fielding hijinks in the sixth inning. With the Cubs trailing 4-0, Don Johnson led off the frame with a triple. Peanuts Lowrey hit a grounder to Jimmy Outlaw at third. Johnson, already halfway to home plate, looked like a goner. But Outlaw, eyeing a double play, threw a strong peg to first baseman Rudy York to get Lowrey. Then, with both Outlaw and Johnson scrambling back toward the third-base bag, York's reverse throw sailed high and wide and bounced off Outlaw's outstretched glove into the box seats, and Johnson bolted home for an unearned run. His shutout gone, the unfazed Trout got two lazy fly balls to quell the mini-rally.

The Bengals did all their damage in the fourth inning off starter Ray Prim. Silent Ray, a 38-year-old journeyman, would likely not have had a job in 1945 were it not for the depleted wartime rosters. But he fashioned himself a very nice year, indeed, leading the National League in earned-run average at 2.40 and picking up 13 wins. His big appearance on the grand stage began well enough, as he retired the first 10 men to face him. But in the fourth, a one-out walk to Eddie Mayo and consecutive hits by Doc Cramer, Hank Greenberg, and Roy Cullenbine sent him to an early shower. Paul Derringer was called upon to stop the bleeding, but by the time the inning was over, Detroit had put up a four-spot.

Prim felt his stuff was as good as it had been all summer. "Detroit simply was dropping them in spots where there were no fielders," he rationalized.[2]

Trout, meanwhile, got stronger as the game progressed. He needed only five pitches to dispatch Phil Cavarretta, Andy Pafko, and Swish Nicholson in the ninth inning.

Before the contest had even begun, certain goings-on ensured that the afternoon would be destined to enter Cubs lore. There are differing versions of the story, and one is free to believe what one chooses, either completely or in part. October 6, 1945, saw the birth of the Curse of the Billy Goat. For it was on that day that one William Sianis, owner of the Billy Goat Tavern, brought his pet goat to Wrigley Field to take in the game. The goat, named Murphy, exuded a fragrance that did not mix well with the typical ballpark aromas of hot dogs, cigars, and beer, at least to the noses of the patrons surrounding him. Citing assaulted nostrils, Wrigley Field security asked Sianis

to remove his goat from the premises. (No doubt Andy Frain's female usherettes used their newfangled walkie-talkies to summon the uniformed heavies.)

Although Sianis took exception to the request to scram, he got up and left in a huff, with Murphy in tow. On his way out, Sianis, so the story goes, uttered a curse on the Cubs, declaring something to the effect that they would never win again. Nobody knows for sure if he was referring to that day's game specifically, the 1945 Series more broadly, or the rest of the history of humankind in general. Spoiler alert: The Cubs wound up losing the Series, a result that had little to do with hexes and goats and more to do with the Tigers' superior pitching. For the next seven decades, however, the Curse of the Billy Goat became, for superstitious types, an excuse for the Cubs' general bad luck and futility, until the organization finally won a World Series again in 2016, goats be damned.

SOURCES

In addition to the sources cited in the Notes, the author also consulted Baseball-Reference.com, Retrosheet.org, and SABR.org.

NOTES

1   "Trout Recalls Time the Cubs Rejected Him," *Chicago Tribune*, October 7, 1945.

2   Arch Ward, "In the Wake of the News," *Chicago Tribune*, October 7, 1945.

TIGERS GAIN SERIES EDGE BEHIND NEWHOUSER'S PRINCELY PITCHING

OCTOBER 7, 1945
DETROIT TIGERS 8, CHICAGO CUBS 4

GAME FIVE OF THE WORLD SERIES

By Scott Ferkovich

IN THE SECOND HALF OF 1945, NO pitcher in baseball had been as hot as Chicago Cubs right-hander Hank Borowy.

Acquired from the New York Yankees in late July, the strapping 29-year-old went 11-2 from that point on, leading the National League in earned-run average at 2.13. In Game One of the 1945 World Series at Briggs Stadium (what would come to be known as the last wartime fall classic), Borowy had pitched a brilliant six-hit shutout. He bested Hal Newhouser, winner of 54 games the past two seasons. Newhouser, along with Dizzy Trout and Virgil Trucks, was part of a fantastic Tigers rotation dubbed the "TNT formula" by teammate Hub Walker. With all eyes watching in October, however, the shell-shocked Newhouser could not make it through the third inning, finally exiting ignominiously with a 7-0 deficit as the Cubs captured Game One.

Chicago was the scene for Game Five, where over 43,000 Cubs rooters jammed Wrigley Field. Included in the crowd were nearly 2,500 standing-room patrons. Several scalpers were hauled away for demanding $6 for seats in the bleachers, which in any event were filled shortly after breakfast.

The sun had finally come out: With the tarp on the field before the previous two contests, neither team had been able to take batting practice. The Series was tied at two games apiece, and Borowy and

Newhouser were again set to square off. Oh, what a difference four days would make.

Through the first five innings, it was a classic pitchers' duel, with Detroit riding home-plate umpire Bill Summers for what the team viewed as some questionable ball and strike calls. The Bengals got on the scoreboard in the third inning when Doc Cramer's long fly to center scored Skeeter Webb. Newhouser gave the lead right back in the home half of the frame, however. After reaching on a double, Borowy dashed home on Stan Hack's single up the middle.

That is how things stayed, with the two pitchers exchanging goose eggs until Detroit broke open the game with four runs in the sixth (the third time in five games that the Tigers had clustered that many in a frame). Borowy never retired a batter that inning, giving up four straight hits, including an RBI double by Hank Greenberg and a single by Rudy York that plated a run and sent Borowy to the showers. The final line for the New Jersey native read five earned runs in five innings. (By a strange coincidence, while the departing Borowy trudged off the field an announcement was made over the Wrigley Field loudspeaker: "Will coroner Al Brodie call his office at once."[1]) The Cubs used five pitchers in the game (Borowy, Hy Vandenberg, Bob Chipman, Paul Derringer, and Paul Erickson), and the Tigers romped to an 8-4 win. They were now one win away from their second world championship. The first, coincidentally, had come 10 years ago to the day in 1935.

For Detroit, it was a balanced attack: Only third baseman Jimmy Outlaw and Newhouser went hitless, and only second baseman Eddie Mayo and catcher Paul Richards failed to drive in a run. Left fielder Hank Greenberg (who had returned to the team on July 1 following a four-year stint in the US Army) slashed three doubles and scored three times, while right fielder Roy Cullenbine also hit a two-bagger and drove in a pair.

For Borowy, it was his first defeat since August 24. He figured his stuff was just as good as it had been in Game One. He just wasn't fooling anybody this time. That Detroit had gotten to him was indeed surprising: Back in his Yankee days, he has been a true Tiger killer, posting an 11-3 mark in 16 starts against Detroit with a 2.76 earned-run average.

The man of the hour, however, was the pitcher known as Prince Hal, the Tigers' 24-year-old wunderkind, the pride of Wilbur Wright High School in Detroit. The two-time reigning American League Most Valuable Player pitched far better than his four earned runs would indicate. He allowed only two hits through the first six innings, and no Chicago runner was left on base during that period. Staked to a big lead, he eased up on the gas. The Cubs managed five hits in the final three innings, but "four

of them were of the blooper variety," according to Irving Vaughan of the *Chicago Tribune*.[2] Newhouser fanned nine (including Andy Pafko three times and Don Johnson twice) and walked only two.

Afterward, Cubs skipper Charlie Grimm did not sugarcoat the loss. "We got the hell kicked out of us. It was just boom, boom, boom – that's all."[3] He gave credit where it was due, insisting that Newhouser's change of pace was the best he had ever seen. Were the Cubs guilty of looking past the Tigers? *The Sporting News* noted that many of Grimm's men were slated for a hunting trip after the Series ended. Before the game, "the clubhouse looked like an arsenal," it quipped.[4]

Phil Cavarretta, the Cubs' first baseman, who had managed one of those bloop hits in the late innings, had a simple explanation for Prince Hal's success: Controlling the curveball. "He was getting them over today and he wasn't (in Game One)."[5]

NOTES

1   *The Sporting News*, October 11, 1945.

2   Irving Vaughan, "North Siders Beaten, 8-4, by Newhouser," *Chicago Tribune*, October 8, 1945.

3   Arch Ward, "In the Wake of the News," *Chicago Tribune*, October 8, 1945.

4   *The Sporting News*, October 11, 1945.

5   Ward.

"TRAGEDY AND FARCE": HACK'S HIT WINS IT IN 12TH; CUBS TIE SERIES

OCTOBER 8, 1945
CHICAGO CUBS 8, DETROIT TIGERS 7

GAME SIX OF THE WORLD SERIES

By Scott Ferkovich

TODAY, IT WOULD BE CALLED AN "instant classic."

For the 41,708 fans at Wrigley Field that October afternoon, it was one of the wildest games ever witnessed, an emotional rollercoaster of an affair that never let up until the final, madcap hit.

Game Six of the 1945 World Series between the Chicago Cubs and the Detroit Tigers not only was thrilling, it was long: The outcome remained undecided until the bottom of the 12th inning. At 3 hours and 28 minutes, it was the longest postseason contest ever to that point (the previous record was 2:54, set in 1941). There was a lack of timely hitting: The teams set a World Series high for men left on base with 24 (12 each). More players were used than in any previous World Series game – 38, shattering the old mark of 29. Wrote Arch Ward of the *Chicago Tribune:* "The traffic between both benches and home plate looked like State and Madison at the rush hour."[1]

Much was at stake. Manager Steve O'Neill's Tigers were one victory away from grabbing the franchise's first world championship in 10 years. The Cubs, meanwhile, just wanted to live to see another day.

For most of the afternoon, it looked as though they would do just that.

With cloudy skies, temperatures in the 40s, and a brisk, swirling wind, it was hardly baseball weather. On the mound for Detroit was Virgil Trucks, coming off a dominant win in Game Two. The 28-year-old right-hander was happy just to be on the mound again, having pitched only one regular-season game the past two years due to service in World War II. Back in 1943, he had won 16 games, and 14 the year before that as a rookie. Opposing Trucks was Claude Passeau, the 11-year veteran with 151 victories under his belt. Passeau had pitched his heart out in Game Three, one-hitting the Tigers.

Staked to an early 1-0 lead, Trucks cruised through the first four innings with only minimal trouble. He never got out of the fifth, however. The Cubs lit up Trucks for four hits and a walk, including Phil Cavarretta's two-run base knock that finally sent him to an early shower. The North Siders tacked on another run an inning later off former ace Tommy Bridges to make it 6-1.

Passeau, meanwhile, had been on thin ice. He escaped a bases-loaded jam in the second inning, inducing Skeeter Webb to hit into a force out, and again in the fourth, this time retiring Webb on a fly to deep center field. The turning point came in the sixth: Jimmy Outlaw hit a line drive back at Passeau, who instinctively reached out with his right (pitching) hand, only to have the ball tear the nail off his third finger. He pitched through the pain, but was not effective, and after giving up a walk and two singles in the seventh, manager Charlie Grimm finally took him out. By the time the frame was over, Detroit had whittled it down to a 5-3 game.

Chicago, however, got the two runs back in the very next inning. Bridges, the former World Series hero for Detroit, was past his prime at 38, another returning war vet who had seen little baseball action the past two seasons. He issued a single and three walks, including one with the bases loaded, before exiting. Roy Hughes's run-scoring single off Al Benton upped the lead to 7-3, giving the Cubs some breathing room.

The Tigers, however, refused to go quietly in the eighth. They scored a pair to drive reliever Hank Wyse from the mound. Enter ancient lefty Ray Prim, the National League's ERA leader in 1945. With a man at third and one out, Doc Cramer drove a fly to deep left field. Peanuts Lowry made a spectacular diving catch, but the run scored to close the gap to one.

That brought up Hank Greenberg, another hero of World Series past for Detroit (He had added to his legend by swatting a key three-run homer back in Game Two). On a full count, Greenberg launched a titanic shot through a crosswind of gale force, the ball landing on the catwalk beyond left field. The game was tied.

Both teams had their chances after that. In the bottom of the eighth, reliever Dizzy Trout walked leadoff man Stan Hack, who reached third with two down. Phil Cavarretta, however, could manage only a fly ball to Greenberg in left field to end the threat. The Tigers made a bid in the ninth, putting runners at the corners with only one out. Trout bounced to the shortstop Hughes, who fired home in time to catch Outlaw in a rundown. When Andy Pafko led off the bottom of the ninth with a double, the Cubs faithful could taste victory. He never made it home, however, and the game went into extras.

Trout was still on the mound in the 12th. He retired the leadoff man on an easy grounder, but then ran into trouble. Little-used Frank Secory, a .158

hitter in the regular season, pinch-hit for the injured Lenny Merullo. He shocked everyone by lining a sharp single to left-center. Pinch-running specialist Billy Schuster came in for him at first base.

One out later, Stan Hack made his way to the plate. Hack already had three hits and two RBIs this afternoon. His two-run bases-loaded single back in the fifth had given his team its first lead of the game. A fan favorite for 14 seasons in Chicago, he had hit a career-high .323 in 1945.

Hack looked at an outside pitch for ball one, then took two quick strikes. He followed with a sinking line drive to left field. Clearly, it was going to fall in front of Greenberg; the only question was whether he could hold Schuster at second base. Greenberg charged in on the ball … but it took a funny hop, bouncing over his shoulder and on toward the wall. Greenberg turned and made chase, but there was no stopping the speedy Schuster, who scored easily, running faster than he ever had in his life. The emotionally spent crowd erupted in euphoria. There would indeed be a Game Seven in the 1945 World Series.

The three official scorers huddled, and their verdict was "E-7." Greenberg had charged the ball unnecessarily, they surmised. He should have played it safe, keeping the ball in front of him. In a span of mere innings, Greenberg had gone from hero to goat, at least in the eyes of the scorers.

Others quickly came to Greenberg's support, claiming that the ball had hit something on the turf. (Grimm swore it must have struck a drain cover.) The bounce was too high, too sudden, they argued, and Greenberg did not stand a chance.

In the end, the scorers changed their ruling, crediting Hack with his fourth hit of the game. But it did nothing to change the outcome for the Tigers. Greenberg took it particularly hard, heading straight to the shower without speaking to anyone. Later, he insisted that the bouncing ball never touched him.

The exuberant Cubs, on the other hand, stormed into the clubhouse as if they had just won the Series. Grimm had his highest praise for winning pitcher

Hank Borowy, the Game Five starter who was working on only one day's rest. With his rubber arm, Borowy tossed four shutout frames after taking over for Prim to start the ninth.

"This game of games," as Edward Burns of the *Tribune* called it, filled with "tragedy and farce," was "unprecedented in world series history."[2] *The Sporting News* deemed it, "one of the dizziest World's Series games ever played."[3]

NOTES

1   Arch Ward, "In the Wake of the News," *Chicago Tribune*, October 9, 1945.

2   Ed Burns, "Cubs Win, Tie Series in 12-Inning Game," *Chicago Tribune*, October 9, 1945.

3   "Cubs Bounce Back on Hop Over Greenberg's Head," *The Sporting News*, October 11, 1945.

NEWHOUSER LEADS TIGERS TO TITLE

OCTOBER 10, 1945
DETROIT TIGERS 9, CHICAGO CUBS 3

GAME SEVEN OF THE WORLD SERIES

By Stephen V. Rice

THE CHICAGO CUBS DEFEATED THE Detroit Tigers in the 1907 and 1908 World Series, but lost to the Tigers in 1935. The teams met again in the 1945 World Series and were tied three games apiece heading into the deciding Game Seven on Wednesday, October 10, 1945, at Wrigley Field in Chicago.

World War II had finally ended. Slugger Hank Greenberg rejoined the Tigers in June of 1945 after four years of military service. During the war, major-league baseball was played by men too young or too old for military service, and those classified as 4-F due to some physical limitation.[1] Sportswriters disparaged the caliber of play, but in 1945 fans went to the games in record numbers. Servicemen in uniform were given free admission. Baseball boosted morale and provided a welcome distraction from events of the day. On the eve of Game Seven, the *Washington Post* conveyed the prevailing mood: "Please don't talk to us about atomic bombs, or the Russian impasse, or the strike crisis, or full employment, or such matters, until the issue of this hair-raising 1945 World Series is settled one way or the other."[2]

In Game Seven, Tigers manager Steve O'Neill sent 24-year-old left-hander Hal Newhouser to the mound. "Prince Hal" was the top pitcher in the American League in 1944 and 1945. Cubs manager Charlie Grimm countered with 29-year-old right-hander Hank Borowy, who was acquired from the New York Yankees in late July. Borowy had won his last seven games of the season. Newhouser and Borowy had already faced each other twice in this World Series; Borowy won Game One in Detroit, and Newhouser won Game Five in Chicago. Borowy also pitched four innings in Game Six, two days before Game Seven, and there was concern over whether he was sufficiently rested to start this all-or-nothing game.

The Tigers infield featured big Rudy York at first base; sparkplug Eddie Mayo at second base; slick-fielding Skeeter Webb at shortstop; and cheerful Jimmy Outlaw at third base. Greenberg played in left field, but his bad ankle restricted his range "to about the area of a victory garden."[3] Forty-year-old Doc Cramer patrolled center field and led the Tigers with eight hits so far in the Series. Right fielder Roy Cullenbine had a keen eye at the plate; he led the AL in walks during the season. The Tigers' Paul Richards had two positions: catcher and teacher. Over the past three seasons, Richards taught Newhouser the changeup and the slider, and taught him control – of his pitches and his temper.[4] Newhouser attributed his success to Richards' mentoring.

Cubs first baseman Phil Cavarretta led the major leagues in 1945 with a .355 batting average. Don Johnson at second base and Roy Hughes at shortstop took care of the middle infield. Third baseman "Smiling Stan" Hack led the Cubs with 11 hits so far in the Series. Harry "Peanuts" Lowrey was a speedy left fielder. Center fielder Andy Pafko drove in 110 runs during the season. Right fielder Bill Nicholson had an off year after leading the National League in home runs and RBIs in 1943 and 1944. Mickey Livingston was the Cubs' hustling catcher.

On this cool autumn day, Wrigley Field was packed with 41,590 fans wearing coats and hats. The ivy clinging to the outfield walls was brown at this time of year. The game's play-by-play was given by Al Helfer and Bill Slater, and was broadcast by more than 300 radio stations affiliated with the Mutual Broadcasting System. It was heard by servicemen and women overseas via the Armed Forces Radio Service. The broadcast's sponsor reminded men to "look sharp, feel sharp, be sharp – use Gillette Blue Blades with the sharpest edges ever honed."

The game began with consecutive singles by Webb, Mayo, and Cramer, and Webb scored the first run. Grimm decided that starting Borowy on short rest was a bad idea and replaced him with 38-year-old Paul Derringer. As a member of the Cincinnati Reds, Derringer beat the Tigers in Games Four and Seven of the 1940 World Series. With Cramer on first and Mayo on second, the powerful Greenberg surprised everyone with a deft sacrifice bunt that advanced the runners. Derringer walked Cullenbine intentionally to load the bases and got York to pop up for the second out. Outlaw drew a walk on four pitches to force in the Tigers' second run. Richards followed with the biggest hit of his career: a double into the left-field corner that drove in three runs and gave the Tigers a 5-0 lead. Cubs fans sat in stunned silence. Even radio announcer Helfer was speechless. Newhouser grounded out for the third out. The Cubs got one run back in the bottom of the first inning when Johnson doubled and Cavarretta singled him home.

After Cramer singled with two outs in the second inning, Derringer walked three batters in a row (Greenberg, Cullenbine, and York), and Cramer scored. The wild hurler was replaced by Hy Vandenberg, who retired Outlaw to end the threat. In the fourth inning, after a Cavarretta single, Pafko tripled over Cramer's head in center field to drive in the Cubs' second run. Pafko was stranded on third base, though, as Nicholson and Livingston each tapped the ball weakly to Newhouser. In the fifth

inning, the Tigers ace struck out Hughes and pinch-hitter Ed Sauer, and announcer Slater remarked that Newhouser "is looking mighty keen."

Paul Erickson replaced Vandenberg in the sixth inning. In the seventh, Cullenbine drew his third walk of the game and scored when Richards doubled to center field. Meanwhile, Newhouser continued his fine pitching. Early in the game, Richards called for changeups that fooled the eager Cubs batters, and when they began to look for the changeup, Richards called for fastballs.[5]

In the top of the eighth, with Claude Passeau on the mound for the Cubs, Webb walked and Mayo doubled to knock him in. Cramer's groundout advanced Mayo to third base. Lowrey then made a spectacular running catch of Greenberg's line drive, and Mayo scored from third. In the bottom of the inning, after singles by Lowrey and Cavarretta, Nicholson stroked a double to center field, scoring Lowrey. There was no further scoring in the game.

The final score was Tigers 9, Cubs 3, and the Tigers were world champions. It would be 23 years before the Tigers would return to the World Series in 1968, and a torturous 71-year wait for the Cubs to return to the World Series in 2016.

AUTHOR'S NOTE

The author dedicates this article to his father, Frank Rice. During the 1945 season, 11-year-old Frank attended Tigers games at Briggs Stadium in Detroit. It was safe for him to go to games by himself. He rode an electric streetcar six miles to the ballpark. The total cost of transportation, admission ticket, scorecard, and hot dog was less than a dollar, which he could afford from the money he earned delivering newspapers. From his bleacher seat, he had an excellent view of Doc Cramer in center field. "Cramer could throw a strike to home plate if required," he said. In the late 1960s, Frank taught baseball to three sons and managed their Little League teams. In 2017, at the age of 83, Frank rooted for the Tigers and the Cubs from his home in Illinois.

SOURCES

In addition to the sources cited in the Notes, the author also accessed Retrosheet.org, Baseball-Reference.com, SABR.org, and *The Sporting News* archive via Paper of Record.

NOTES

1   James D. Szalontai, *Teenager on First, Geezer at Bat, 4-F on Deck: Major League Baseball in 1945* (Jefferson, North Carolina: McFarland, 2009), 9-10.

2   *Washington Post*, October 9, 1945.

3   *Burlington* (North Carolina) *Daily Times News*, September 28, 1945.

4   Warren Corbett, *The Wizard of Waxahachie: Paul Richards and the End of Baseball as We Knew It* (Dallas, Texas: SMU Press, 2009), 75, 78.

5   Ibid., 87.

COBB MEETS WAGNER IN THE WINDY CITY

AUGUST 10, 1946
WEST 10, EAST 4

ESQUIRE'S ALL-AMERICAN BOYS BASEBALL GAME

By Alan Cohen

IN 1946, THE ESQUIRE'S ALL-AMERICAN
Boys' Baseball Game, in its third year, was moved from New York to Chicago and was played at Wrigley Field on August 10. The game brought together 33 boys, aged 16-18, sponsored by 32 US newspapers. The players represented 25 states, and the East All-Stars played the West All-Stars. In front of a crowd of 20,211, the West team, pounding out 10 hits and taking advantage of 14 walks, defeated the East, 10-4. The West team took the lead with three first-inning runs and didn't look back, sealing the win with a five-run rally in the sixth inning.[1] Walter Pocekay was chosen MVP after going 4-for-5 in the contest. Pocekay had been sent east by the *San Francisco Chronicle*. He played in parts of nine minor-league seasons and batted .308, but never made it to the majors.

Commissioner Happy Chandler added his name to the growing list of supporters for the game when he commented:

"I am tremendously interested in amateur baseball and want to encourage all of those who sponsor ethical competition among the younger ballplayers. There is a marked upsurge in interest in junior baseball all over the country and I think this is a very healthy sign."[2]

American League President Will Harridge selected the umpires for the game, newcomers Bill Boyer and Jack McKinley.[3]

Jerry Ahrens was a double threat. He was accompanied to the game by Harold Tuthill of the *St. Louis Post-Dispatch*. Ahrens, who had two no-hitters, was so prodigious a hitter that manager Ty Cobb batted him fourth in the lineup and sent him to the outfield once his pitching chores were complete. He pitched the first three innings, striking out two, and was the winning pitcher. He had one hit in three appearances, driving in two runs. He was signed by Detroit and pitched two minor-league seasons, posting a mark of 21-8 while batting .223. However, he would not get past Class A.

The boys stayed at Hotel Stevens, overlooking Lake Michigan. Before playing on August 10, they saw two games between the White Sox and Cleveland. In one of those games, Bob Feller pitched a one-hitter, and the boys met with him after the game. They also attended a performance of the Ringling Brothers Circus, took a 2½-hour boat ride on Lake Michigan, and attended a practice of the College All-Stars football team at Soldier Field. They also took trips to the Shedd Aquarium, the Field Museum, and Riverview Park.[4]

Present at the game were Chandler along with former heavyweight boxing champions Gene Tunney and Max Baer. Proceeds from the game went to the Chicago Servicemen's Centers and the American Commission for Living War Memorials. Before the game, there was a moment of silence in memory of Vic Picetti. Picetti had played in the 1944 Esquire's Game in New York and, on June 26, 1946, had been among the nine killed when a bus carrying members of the Spokane team (Western International League) careened off a slippery mountainside in Washington state.

Ty Cobb, who had managed the West squad in the 1945 game in New York, returned in that capacity and applauded the game, saying, "When any event makes it possible for boys from all sections of the country to meet on common ground, and where all have a common interest, it is a big step forward in making this country a better place for our coming generation to live in."[5] Assisting him were two Chicago Cubs scouts, Bill Conroy and Bill Prince. The pair had run the baseball school in Chicago that summer.

Honus Wagner, then 72 years old, managed the East squad. His coaches were Luke Appling and Mike Tresh. Wagner said, "Working with these boys will take me back to my kid days in Carnegie, Pennsylvania. We'll dig in and learn a lot of baseball while we are together. I can't say that we'll win, but I will say the West will get all the competition they are looking for when the umpire calls, 'Play Ball!'"[6]

Wagner was posed with an unusual challenge: Five of his players were first basemen and he had to do some juggling to field all nine positions. Cobb had his woes as well: Two of his pitchers stayed home and participated in local American Legion tournaments. They were replaced at the last minute.

Braven Dyer of the *Los Angeles Times*, attending the contest for the third consecutive year, wrote, "The value of this annual game cannot be estimated. In the first place, the thrill of a cross-country trip provides an educational experience which cannot be gauged in dollars and cents. Association with men such as Cobb and Wagner is a privilege seldom accorded youngsters of today. Ty is worth millions and no amount of money could make him take part in this type of promotion unless he loved kids and baseball."[7]

Players making it to the majors included Hobie Landrith, Chuck Stobbs, Harry Agganis, Pete Whisenant, John Powers, and Harold "Tookie" Gilbert.

Agganis, the top-ranking player in the Eastern Massachusetts School League, was sent to the game by Ernie Dalton of the *Boston Globe*. He was born Aristotle George Agganis, and was called Ari growing up. Although only a Lynn Classical High School sophomore at the time, he had been awarded the Fred Ostergren Memorial Trophy as the outstanding New England athlete and student of 1946. Later that year, on Christmas Day in the Orange Bowl in Miami, he led his football team to the National High School Championship, defeating Granby High School of Norfolk, Virginia, and its star quarterback, Chuck Stobbs. He represented Boston on the 1947 US All Star team in the Hearst Classic. Agganis then brought Boston University into national prominence on the gridiron. He made it to the majors with the Red Sox in 1954. The future was bright and he was en route to the most promising of careers, batting .313 in his second major-league season, when he was hospitalized with what was diagnosed as a massive pulmonary embolism. He died six weeks later, on June 27, 1955, at the age of 26.

Gilbert was sent to the game by Fred Digby of the *New Orleans Item*. He was the outstanding prospect of those playing in the game, having never hit below .600 in school and sandlot play, and batted .415 in American Legion play during the summer of 1945. Gilbert's father, Larry, played in the majors with the Boston Braves for two seasons, and was part of the 1914 Miracle Braves squad. Larry managed the New Orleans Pelicans from 1923 through 1938. Young Tookie was a fixture at the ballpark. "Harold grew right up in baseball, and his dad had him out to the New Orleans home games before he knew how to walk."[8] At the time of the Esquire game in 1946, Larry was managing at Nashville and took the day off to travel to Chicago and watch his son play. Tookie signed with the New York Giants and batted .334 with 33 homers in 154 games at Nashville in 1949. Tookie made his major-league debut on May 5, 1950. His .220 batting average in 113 games played showed that he had been called up too soon.[9] He was sent back to the minors, then returned to the Giants for an unproductive 70 games, batting only .169, in 1953. That was the end of his major-league career.

Whisenant of Paw Creek, North Carolina, was selected after starring in an all-star game in Charlotte, North Carolina, between teams from North and South Carolina. He was selected by a seven-man panel of judges headed by the coaches for the two teams, four writers including Wilton Garrison of the *Charlotte Observer*, and Claude Dietrick, head scout of the Atlanta Crackers.[10] He was the best performer for the East Squad in the Esquire game, getting three hits in five at-bats. He made it to the major leagues with the Boston Braves in 1952 and played parts of eight seasons for six teams. After his playing days, he continued in baseball and managed for two seasons in the Oakland A's organization. He was named the California League's Manager of the Year in 1982 when he led Modesto to a 94-46 record.

Stobbs was a hard-hitting, hard-throwing first baseman and pitcher from Norfolk, Virginia, starring at Granby High School. He starred in the Eastern Virginia-Western Virginia All Star game, pitching his squad to a 7-1 win and earning a trip to the game in Chicago. At Chicago, he pitched the last 2⅔ innings. He was named Virginia Player of the Year in high school in 1946, was named to the All-State basketball team, and led his high-school football team to three consecutive undefeated seasons. He signed with George "Specs" Toporcer of the Boston Red Sox[11] for a bonus estimated at $50,000, right after graduating from high school. When he made his major-league debut, on September 15, 1947, he was two months past his 18th birthday. He pitched with Washington for eight years, and accompanied the team to Minnesota in 1961. He is perhaps best known for one pitch. On April 17, 1953, at Griffith Stadium in Washington, Mickey Mantle sent one of Stobbs's offerings far and long. The tape-measure shot was said by a Yankees PR man to have gone 565 feet before coming to a rest. Stobbs won 107 games in the majors (with 130 losses), but that one pitch will never be forgotten.

Landrith was selected for the game by Lyall Smith of the *Detroit Free Press*. In 1948, he played in the Hearst game. He is best known as being the first-round draft pick of the New York Mets in the expansion draft after the 1961 season. But his career started much earlier. After attending Michigan State University for one year, Landrith signed with the Cincinnati organization prior to the 1949 season, and first appeared in the big leagues in 1950. He spent parts of 14 years in the majors, usually as a backup catcher. His first opportunity as a starter came with the 1956 Cubs, and he was also a starter with the 1959 Giants. Landrith was one of seven catchers to play for the Mets in 1962. Through 23 games with the Mets, he was batting .289 on June 6 when he became the "player to be named later" when the Mets traded him to Baltimore for Marv Throneberry. After his playing days, Landrith had a series of executive positions for Volkswagen of America, for whom he worked for 30 years.

Powers hailed from Birmingham, Alabama. He was selected for the game after starring in the Alabama All-Star game sponsored by the *Birmingham News*. In that game, his three doubles impressed the judges, one of whom was Commissioner Chandler. He was signed by the Red Sox before the 1949 season, was acquired by the Pirates organization the next year, and finally made it to the big leagues in 1955. Powers had 304 homers as a professional, all but six in the minor leagues. He slammed 298 homers in 13 minor-league seasons. Twice, with Class-B Waco in 1950 and with Double-A New Orleans in 1956, he banged out 39 round-trippers. He played in parts of six seasons in the major leagues, batting 195 with 6 home runs and 14 RBIs in 215 at-bats.

Esquire planned to take the game to a different city each year, but these hopes were dashed when the magazine, in December 1946, informed the participating newspapers that there would be no games after 1946. Nevertheless, in 1947, many of these papers got together and named an All-American team. The players went to Chicago and were treated to an excellent experience. However, baseball was not on the itinerary and hopes to rekindle the All-American Game were quickly extinguished.

SOURCES:

In addition to the sources cited in the Notes, the author used Baseball-Reference.com.

NOTES

1   United Press, "West Wins Boys Game," *Miami News*, August 11, 1946: 3-C.

2   *Ogden Standard Examiner*, June 2, 1946: 12A.

3   Bob Latshaw, "Landrith Starts Esquire Game: Detroiter Will Catch for East," *Detroit Free Press*, August 10, 1946: 10.

4   Raymond Johnson, "Gilbert Given Cleanup Spot in East Lineup," *The Tennessean* (Nashville), August 9, 1946: 34.

5   *Ogden Standard Examiner*, May 9, 1946.

6   *Pittsburgh Post-Gazette*, May 10, 1946: 17.

7   Braven Dyer, *Los Angeles Times*, August 2, 1946: 6.

8   Paul O'Boynick, "Baseball Scouts to Mecca," *Kansas City Star*, August 6, 1946: 9.

9   Frank Graham, *The New York Giants, an Informal History* (reprint edition, Carbondale, Illinois: Southern Illinois University Press), 295.

10   Eddie Allen, *Gastonia* (North Carolina) *Evening Gazette*, July 12, 1946: 8.

11   Bill Nowlin, "Chuck Stobbs," SABR BioProject.

PITCHING DOMINATES

JULY 8, 1947
AMERICAN LEAGUE 2, NATIONAL LEAGUE 1

ALL-STAR GAME

By C. Paul Rogers III

THE 1947 ALL-STAR GAME WAS PLAYED for the first time in Wrigley Field and only the second time in Chicago. Fueled by fan complaints about the All-Star selection process in 1946, major-league baseball had returned the vote to the fans for 1947 for the eight position players in each league. Not surprisingly, Joe DiMaggio, who after a relatively poor year in 1946 was hitting .338 and leading the league in runs batted in, received the most votes, with a total of 782,194. On the National League side, the fans voted in two starters from the seventh-place Philadelphia Phillies, second baseman Emil Verban and center fielder Harry Walker, who was hitting .335 and would lead the league in batting. They were the Phillies' first All-Star Game starters since Pinky May in 1936 and it was the only time since the inaugural game in 1933 that the perennial bottom feeders had two starters.[1]

Verban had almost not made it to the game. He, along with teammate Schoolboy Rowe and Phillies manager Ben Chapman, chosen as a coach, had been badly shaken up in a train accident on their way to Chicago from Philadelphia.[2] Rowe had been knocked unconscious while Verban lost the feeling in his legs for a short time, but both recovered and participated in the game.[3]

The game itself was played under sunny skies with the wind blowing in from Lake Michigan in front of a capacity crowd of 41,123. National League manager Eddie Dyer predictably selected the Reds' brilliant second-year pitcher Ewell Blackwell, who was

14-2 at the break, to start for the National League, while Joe Cronin of the American League picked Hal Newhouser of the Tigers after Spud Chandler of the Yankees, his first choice, came down with a slightly sore arm.[4] The Indians' Bob Feller might well have been the top pick to start but was replaced on the roster by Early Wynn after back issues forced him out in the second inning of his last start before the break.[5]

Commissioner Happy Chandler began the festivities by throwing out the first pitch from his box seat. Blackwell took the mound and proceeded to dominate the American League just as he had the National League all summer, striking out George Kell, retiring Buddy Lewis on an unassisted groundout to Johnny Mize at first, and then catching Ted Williams looking at a third strike. In his three innings Blackwell allowed only a single to center by Joe DiMaggio in the second while he struck out four.[6] Meanwhile Newhouser mowed down the Nationals in his three innings, allowing only a third-inning pinch-hit single by the Reds' Bert Haas.

Stylish Cardinals southpaw Harry Brecheen, who had won three games in the 1946 World Series, followed Blackwell and retired Lewis on a fly ball to Walker in center to bring Ted Williams to the plate. Williams had complained after batting practice about the hitting background in Wrigley Field, saying, "I never saw this park before and it sure is pretty, but you can't see the ball."[7] Despite the poor background Williams had knocked half a dozen balls into the

141

bleachers during batting practice and now he laced a double down the line in right.[8] He stayed there when DiMaggio hit a high hopper to Frank Gustine at third for the second out. Lou Boudreau moved Williams to third on an infield roller that eluded Gustine, but Brecheen struck out the resurgent George McQuinn swinging on a 1-and-2 pitch to escape any damage.[9]

Twenty-four-year-old Yankees rookie Frank "Spec" Shea took the mound for the American League for the bottom of the inning. Shea was the first rookie to make an American League All-Star team since Dick Wakefield of the Detroit Tigers in 1943 and he certainly deserved the honor with an 11-2 record and a 1.91 earned-run average at the break. He quickly retired the first two batters on popups to bring Mize to the plate. On the third pitch Big Jawn, as he was often called by the press, stroked a fastball smack into the stiff breeze. It landed in the fifth row of the bleachers in right-center field, 380 feet from the plate, for the first run of the game.[10] After a walk to Enos Slaughter, Shea got Gustine to ground to Joe Gordon at second for a force out to end the inning.

Gordon led off the top of the fifth with a long double into the left-field corner but was left stranded as Brecheen retired Buddy Rosar, Shea, and Kell. Marty Marion began the bottom of the inning with a single to left but Verban flied to Lewis in right and Brecheen forced Marion at second on a grounder to McQuinn for the second out. Andy Pafko, who had subbed for Harry Walker, then smacked a line drive to center that DiMaggio appeared to momentarily misjudge.[11] It fell for a single, sending Brecheen to second. Shea, however, struck out Willard Marshall swinging to end the threat.

The American League finally broke through in Brecheen's final inning to tie the score on Luke Appling's pinch-hit single, a single to right by Williams that moved Appling to third, and DiMaggio's double-play grounder to Pee Wee Reese, in for Marion at shortstop, that plated Appling. Shea then finished his three-inning stint by allowing only a harmless one-out walk to Mize in the bottom of the sixth.

Johnny Sain of the Boston Braves and Bruce Edwards of the Dodgers were the new battery for the National League in the top of the seventh. Edwards replaced Walker Cooper, who had started the All-Star Game for the fifth consecutive time, tying Bill Dickey's record. With one out in the inning, Bobby Doerr ripped a single to left field. Edwards was recovering from a hand injury that hampered his throwing, so Doerr took off on the first pitch and stole second. Sain, trying to keep Doerr close at second, hit him in the back on an attempted pickoff, enabling Bobby to advance to third. Sain recovered to strike out Rosar for the second out. Cronin next sent the lefty-swinging Stan Spence to bat for Shea and he quickly went down in the count 0-and-2 on two sweeping curves. Sain then tried to sneak a fastball by him, but the Washington outfielder lined the pitch to left-center to allow Doerr to trot in from third with what would be the winning run.[12]

Warren Spahn pitched the last two innings for the Nationals, allowing only an eighth-inning walk to DiMaggio. Meanwhile the Senators' Walt Masterson had come on to pitch the seventh inning for the American League and retired the side in order. In the eighth the National League mounted a threat when Masterson issued a one-out walk to Marshall. After he struck out pinch-hitter Phil Cavarretta for the second out, Cronin brought in southpaw relief ace Joe Page to face the lefty-swinging Mize. Mize, however, nixed the strategy by singling sharply to right field for the Nationals' fifth hit of the game, sending Marshall to third. After Phil Masi ran for Mize, Page got Enos Slaughter to ground weakly to shortstop as Boudreau charged and made a nice play for the third out.

In the ninth Pee Wee Reese worked Page for a one-out walk on a 3-and-2 count. Eddie Stanky followed with a sharp groundball to the right side, but Doerr snagged it on a nice play and threw to Boudreau to force Reese at second for the second out. That brought up Spahn, who had not yet cemented his reputation as a good hitting pitcher. Dyer was out of position players and so sent Schoolboy Rowe, an outstanding hitting pitcher, up to pinch-hit.[13] Rowe lifted a high fly ball to right field that got caught in the wind and appeared for a moment that might drop in for a hit.[14] But Tommy Henrich stayed with it and made a "glittering catch" for the final out to end the game.[15]

The narrow 2-1 win, played in a brisk 2 hours and 19 minutes, was the 10th for the American League against only four losses.[16] The game was crisply played with several good fielding plays and fine pitching, in stark contrast to the last time interleague play was held at Wrigley Field, the shoddily played 1945 World Series between the Cubs and the Tigers. American League manager Cronin summed up the game well. He said, "It was a swell game and a great victory."[17] On the other side of the ledger, National League President Ford Frick, speaking to the American League dominance, said, "This is getting painful."[18]

NOTES

1   Chuck Klein and Dick Bartell had started the 1933 game while members of the Phillies.

2   John Drebinger, "American League Tops National for 10th Victory in Fourteen All-Star Games," *New York Times*, July 9, 1947: 28.

3   Chapman was able to share first-base coaching duties with Giants manager Mel Ott. David Vincent, Lyle Spatz, and David W. Smith, *The Midsummer Classic – The Complete History of Baseball's All-Star Game* (Lincoln: University of Nebraska Press, 2001), 84.

4   Drebinger: 28.

5   Two days after the All-Star Game, however, Feller was healthy enough to throw 8⅓ innings in a 2-1 win over the Philadelphia Athletics.

6   DiMaggio did reach third with two outs on a passed ball and a wild pitch. Joe Gordon then fouled off four two-strike pitches before finally swinging and missing for the third out. Drebinger:28.

7   Arthur Daley, "Star Gazing," *New York Times*, July 9, 1947: 28.

8   After the game Dizzy Trout admitted that, sitting in the American League bullpen down the right-field line, he had made "an involuntary dive" for the ball that Williams hit, thinking it was foul. Fortunately, he missed. Dixie Walker asked Trout if it was one of his "confusion" plays and Trout replied that it was. James P. Dawson, "Heroes of Victory Hear Finish on Air," *New York Times*, July 9, 1947: 28.

9   McQuinn had hit only .225 in 1946 for the cellar-dwelling Philadelphia Athletics. When the Athletics released him after the season, most thought that, at age 37, he was washed up. But the Yankees signed him as a free agent to fill a hole at first base and McQuinn responded with a career year. He was hitting .328 at the break and the fans responded by voting him to be the starting first baseman for the All-Star Game.

10   Mize's home run was the first by a New York Giant in All-Star play.

11   Arthur Daley of the *New York Times* wrote that DiMaggio played the ball "like a tyro." Daley: 28.

12   Drebinger: 28; Daley: 28. After the game, Sain said, "I pitched to Spence backward and threw just the kind of pitch Dyer had warned me against." Vincent et al., 85.

13   Rowe would finish with a .263 lifetime batting average and 18 home runs in his 15-year career. Spahn would go on to hit .194 for his career with 35 home runs in his 21 years in the big leagues.

14   Vincent et al., 85.

15   Dawson: 28.

16   The National League used 23 players while the American League used 17, with Boudreau, Williams, DiMaggio, McQuinn, and Rosar playing the entire game. Arthur Daley noted that this was the only statistical category in which the senior circuit had the edge. Daley: 28.

17   Dawson, 28. But all major-league players benefited from the game as, for the first time, their pension fund was a beneficiary of the net receipts from the game. Those totaled $105,315. Vincent et. al., 85.

18   Donald Honig, *The All-Star Game – A Pictorial History, 1933 to Present* (St. Louis: The Sporting News, 1987), 66. It would get worse before it got better as the American League would also prevail in the next two All-Star Games, making it four straight, before the National League broke through in 1950.

CHICAGO HERALD-AMERICAN ALL-STAR GAME: A TRIPLEHEADER OF FUTURE STARS

JULY 11, 1949
SUBURBAN ALL STARS 4, CITY ALL STARS 0

By Alan Cohen

FROM 1946 THROUGH 1965, THE HEARST newspaper chain sponsored events in as many as 13 cities culminating in the annual Hearst Sandlot Classic between the *New York Journal–American* All-Stars and the United States All-Stars. Chicago sent two players to the games from 1946 through 1957, and the players were selected based on their performance in the annual *Herald-American* All-Star Game, played at either Wrigley Field or Comiskey Park.

In 1949, the folks in Chicago did things up especially big in selecting their representatives for the game in New York. On Saturday, July 9, at Wrigley Field, a tripleheader was scheduled. Some 15,000 fans were in attendance and, due to a turn in the weather, the events were shortened.

First to take the field were the baseball stars of yesteryear. There was an old-timers' baseball game, including such stars as Rogers Hornsby, Gabby Hartnett, Lefty Gomez, Red Faber, Charlie Grimm, and the recently retired Ted Lyons. Among the old-timers were four men who never had the opportunity to play in the big leagues. Jack Marshall, John Donaldson, Dave Malarcher (known as one of the game's greatest bunters), and Jim Bray had played for the Negro League Chicago American Giants.[1] The American League Old-Timers defeated their National League counterparts, 5-0, in the two-inning contest played under threatening skies and delayed 30 minutes by the first storm of the afternoon.

Next on the agenda was a Movie Star World Series softball game with William "Hopalong Cassidy" Boyd serving as umpire as the "tragedians" faced off against the "comedians." Among the stars participating were Eddie Bracken, Lloyd Bridges, Roddy McDowell, Ward Bond, well-known Chicago disc jockey Dave Garroway, comic Sid Caesar, who was in town performing at the Palmer House hotel, and singer Vic Damone. Actresses served as batgirls, including a young Marilyn Monroe and Virginia Mayo, Bracken's co-star in the recently released film *The Girl from Jones Beach.* Announcing the game would be Garry Moore. One of the performers, singer Evelyn Knight, was a ballplayer in her own right, having played on her high school's boys' baseball team.[2] A second storm halted play and the final score of the abbreviated 1½-inning encounter was Comedians 4, Tragedians 0. The big winners were three charities that shared in the game's proceeds: City of Hope Hospital in Los Angeles, the Motion Picture Relief Fund, and the Herald-American Benefit Fund.[3]

The rain that interrupted the festivities before the kids could take to the field made the field unplayable. Their game was held two days later, on Monday.

The manager of the Suburban stars in the kids' game was Max Carey. The former Pirates and Dodgers star took time off from his duties as president of the All-American Girls Professional Baseball League to work with the youngsters. During his Hall of Fame career, Carey had led the National League in stolen bases 10 times, and his 738 career thefts place him ninth on the all-time list. The city stars were managed by Johnny Rigney, who was a scout with the Chicago White Sox. During his time in the big leagues, Rigney had spent eight seasons pitching with the White Sox. His best season was 1939 when he went 15-8. The *Chicago Herald-American* sponsored the event and told its readers about an event back in 1920 when 17-year-old Lou Gehrig hit a long grand slam at Wrigley Field in an intercity high-school game. In New York, two of the Chicago participants would be competing for the 1949 Lou Gehrig award.

History was made in the Chicago game when each of the teams had catchers who were African-Americans. Milt Bohannion started for the Suburban team and Curtis Pitts came off the bench for the City squad. Umpiring the game was 19-year American League veteran Emmet "Red" Ormsby, joined by Negro League umpire Virgil Blueitt and local umpire Bob Ryan. Those involved in selecting the youngsters who would go to New York were 19 of the men who participated in Saturday's old-timers' game, and their task was not easy, as ultimately 12 players from the game would play in Organized Baseball.

Before a crowd of 6,000, the Suburban team won the contest 4-0, as the pitchers had the better of the hitters. Each team was limited to four hits. Paul Dobkowski of the City team and Bob Will of the Suburban team were picked to join the US All-Stars. They edged out Bohannion and pitcher George Maier. Dobkowski punched his ticket by going 3-for-4 with two singles and a perfect bunt. He accounted for three of his team's four hits. Will's two-run, bases-loaded single keyed a three-run seventh inning rally that secured his team the win, and he played a flawless right field, registering five putouts.[4]

After the Chicago game, two participants in the game, Bohannion and pitcher Art Klein, were signed by the Cubs. Bohannion, who had graduated from Argo High School, was sent to Janesville in the Class-D Wisconsin State League. When he joined Janesville on July 17, he became the first black player in the history of the Wisconsin State League. On that day, he played second base and had three consecutive hits in a doubleheader.[5] Early in the following season, Bohannion was introduced to Mr. Jim Crow. Janesville had spring training at Carthage, Missouri, home of the Cubs affiliate in the Kansas-Oklahoma-Missouri League. The K-O-M League had no black players and during his time in segregated Carthage, he couldn't stay with his teammates. He stayed with a black family in town.[6]

Bohannion spent two seasons at Janesville before moving on to Topeka of the Class-C Western Association in 1951. During his time at Janesville, he showed his versatility by playing every position. He completed his tour of fielding positions in his team's final regular-season game, on September 4, 1950, when he started and pitched 4⅔ innings, yielding two hits and two runs. He was not involved in the decision. After a stint in the military Bohannion returned to baseball and spent three seasons in the White Sox organization at Class-C Duluth-Superior in the Northern League. In his final season, 1958, he batted a career-high .284 in 52 games, but it was the end of the line.

Klein, from Bloom High School in Arlington Heights, pitched one season of Class-D ball at Janesville and went 2-6. He was not helped by his 43 walks in 66 innings. But one of his efforts made for a lifelong memory. In a 2-1 win over Appleton, he got by on only 75 pitches. The following season, Klein developed arm trouble and saw limited action with Springfield, Missouri, in the Class-C Western Association before he was placed on the voluntarily retired list. In 1951, he returned to action with Greensboro in the Class-B Carolina League. He was sailing along with a 3-0 record when the pain returned in his arm and surgery in July shut him down for the balance of the season. After recuperating, he was drafted into the Army Air Corps, and his professional baseball career was over.

Sometimes it takes a while for early promise to achieve big-league status. In 1949, Bobby Will of Berwyn, Illinois, represented Chicago at the Hearst

Classic in New York and was named the game's Most Valuable Player after driving in three runs with a single and a double. He was selected to represent the Windy City after excelling at J. Sterling Morton High School in Cicero, Illinois. His double in the sixth inning scored the first two runs for the US All-Stars. His bases-loaded single in the seventh inning plated two more and tied the game at 5-5. The tie was broken when the next batter, Ralph Felton, drove in two runs with a single.

There wasn't much in the way of big money in those days, and the offers received by Will were in the range of $6,000 to $8,000. Bob decided to pursue his education at Northwestern University and later at Mankato Teachers College in Minnesota. He signed with the Chicago Cubs in 1954 and was assigned to Magic Valley, Idaho, in the Pioneer League. He excelled during his first years in the minors, batting .359, .335, and .304 as he rose in the Cubs' organization. Will first made it to the majors in 1957 with the Cubs, appearing in 70 games, but spent the 1957 and 1958 seasons shuttling back and forth between Chicago and the minors. In 1959, he played the full season (162 games) at Triple-A Fort Worth, batted .336, with a career-high 203 hits, and was named the American Association's MVP. There was a sense of frustration when he said, toward the end of the 1959 season, "I hope I can make it this next year. I'd like to play a few years up there in the big time before I begin to slow up."[7]

The next three years, Will was with the Cubs for the whole season. In 1960 he batted .255and hit six of his nine major-league homers. In June 1963, he was dispatched to Triple A, and he finished up at Jacksonville in the International League in 1964.

While still playing ball, Will accepted an offer to work at a local bank, and was very successful after his playing days in many executive banking positions.

Paul Dobkowski, who accompanied Will to New York, spent 1951 with Lubbock in the West Texas-New Mexico League, batting .271. He was then drafted into the military, and resumed his minor-league career in 1954. He batted .324 with 19 homers and 95 RBIs for the Artesia Numexers in the Class-C Longhorn League. In 1957, he was with El Paso in the Class-B Southwestern League, where he clubbed 13 homers and batted .326 in 77 games. The team was dropped from the league on July 17,[8] and Dobkowski elected to return to Chicago rather than join the Corpus Christi squad in the Class-B Big State League.[9] Five seasons of strong minor-league play were not enough to get a contract with a big-league organization and Dobkowski was back in Chicago playing semipro ball in 1958.

Chicago would continue to send players to the New York games through 1957, but nothing would ever quite replicate the events in 1949. Bobby Will was the only player who performed at Wrigley in the *Herald-American* game and returned to Wrigley as a major-league player.

NOTES

1   Wendell Smith, "Former American Giants Set for Old-Timers Game," *Chicago Herald-American*, July 6, 1949: 26.

2   Tommy Kouzmanoff, "Evelyn Knight Shows Prep Stars How to Hit," *Chicago Herald-American*, July 7, 1949: 28.

3   Fred Slater, "Thousands See Stars Play for Charity Here," *Chicago Herald-American*, July 10, 1949: 5.

4   Tommy Kouzmanoff, "Dobkowski, Will Picked to Play in Hearst N.Y. Game," *Chicago Herald-American*, July 12, 1949: 21.

5   *Rhinelander* (Wisconsin) *Daily News*, July 18, 1949: 6.

6   *Janesville* (Wisconsin) *Daily Gazette*, April 21, 1950: 15.

7   Lee Grimsley, "He's Cat's Whiskers in Fort Worth – Why Can't Bob Move Up?' *The Sporting News*, August 26, 1959: 29.

8   *El Paso Herald-Post*, July 20, 1957: 8.

9   *Corpus Christi Caller-Times*, July 28, 1957: C-1.

ROY SMALLEY HITS FOR THE CYCLE AND DRIVES IN FOUR

JUNE 28, 1950
CHICAGO CUBS 15, ST. LOUIS CARDINALS 3

By Mike Huber

THE CHICAGO CUBS "SWISHED HOME RUN bats that belted big George Munger out of the box within three innings"[1] and went on to crush the St. Louis Cardinals 15-3 at Wrigley Field, behind the hitting-for-the-cycle performance of Roy Smalley. The overcast skies "and a few drops of rain"[2] before game time did not deter the crowd of 12,109 from rooting the home team on.[3]

Doyle Lade pitched for Chicago, making just his fifth start of the season and first start in three weeks. He had been predominantly a reliever for manager Frankie Frisch in 1950, and in his five-season career (all with the Cubs), he started 64 of the 126 games in which he appeared. Lade was opposed by three-time All-Star Red Munger, a solid member of the Cardinals rotation, bringing a 3.54 ERA into the game.

Chicago had been holding down fourth or fifth place in the National League since about mid-May, with even a one-week drop into sixth near the end of May. With a 29-29 record, their longest winning streak of the season was just four games (twice), and their longest losing streak was only three games (also twice), but they had dropped their previous three, having been "spanked twice by the Cardinals"[4] on June 27. That doubleheader sweep placed St. Louis in a tie for first place with the Philadelphia Phillies.[5]

St. Louis got to Lade in the opening frame, as Tommy Glaviano doubled into the left-center gap. Two batters later, Stan Musial stroked a double to left, scoring Glaviano, but Musial was tagged out trying to stretch the hit into a triple.

The Cubs responded in the bottom of the second. With one out, Hank Edwards singled into right field. Smalley followed with a blast over the left-field wall, his 12th home run of the season, and this put Chicago ahead. An inning later, Bob Ramazzotti beat out a bunt single to third. Rube Walker drew a free pass from Munger, and Phil Cavarretta sent a Munger offering over the right-field wall. The first three Cubs batters had scored, prompting Cardinals skipper Eddie Dyer to make a change. Cloyd Boyer relieved Munger and retired the Cubs in order. He pitched two scoreless frames but was taken out of the game after injuring his ankle on a baserunning play. With two outs in the top of the fifth, Boyer singled. Glaviano followed with another single, and Boyer hurt his left ankle running to second base. Erv Dusak came in to run for him, but the Cardinals could not capitalize.

Jim Hearn entered as the new St. Louis pitcher. Boyer had faced seven batters, yielding only one hit, a harmless double to Smalley in the bottom of the fourth. Hearn then finished the pitching duties for the Cards, pitching the final four innings. He retired Walker on a popout to short to start the home team's fifth, but then Cavarretta singled, Hank Sauer walked, and Andy Pafko "hit his tenth home run into the left field bleachers."[6] Edwards and Smalley each grounded to second. Chicago's first eight runs were driven in with home runs.

147

Singles by Enos Slaughter and Bill Howerton and a sacrifice fly by Red Schoendienst plated the Cardinals' second run of the game in their half of the sixth inning. Hearn became a bit unglued in the bottom half. After Bill Serena worked a leadoff walk, Lade put down a sacrifice bunt, but Hearn made a throwing error and both runners were safe. Ramazzotti then bunted (with an 8-2 lead), advancing the runners. Hearn uncorked a wild pitch and Serena scored. Walker singled in Lade, and the pitcher scored Chicago's 10th run of the game.

St. Louis loaded the bases with one out in the top of the seventh, and a groundout by Musial drove in a run, his second RBI of the day. According to the *Chicago Tribune*, "The Cubs had so much fun in their last two rounds that they netted seven hits, four of them for extra bases."[7] In the seventh, Edwards doubled, Smalley singled, and Serena doubled before Hearn retired a Chicago batter. With one out, Ramazzotti hit an RBI single, driving in Serena. Sauer "opened the eighth with a double for which he is going to write Johnny Lindell and Bill Howerton a note of thanks."[8] A routine fly ball dropped between the two outfielders. Sauer moved to third on Pafko's sacrifice bunt (Chicago's third of the game). Edwards singled and Smalley tripled, bringing the score to 15-3. Roy Smalley had hit for the cycle.

Lade limited the Cardinals' powerful lineup to nine hits; St. Louis tallied solo scores in three different innings. Lade earned his fourth victory of the season. It was his first complete game of the season. The 15 runs scored were the most for the Cubs thus far in the 1950 season. Four games later, on July 2, they tallied 16 runs in a shutout against Cincinnati.

Glaviano was the leading Cardinals batter with two doubles and a single, but he scored only one run. Musial drove in two. Munger didn't survive the third inning, and his record fell to 3-5. Hearn had faced 26 Cubs batters, and he allowed 10 runs (nine earned) on 10 hits and three walks.

Every Cubs position player had at least one hit and every player, including pitcher Lade, scored at least one run. Chicago displayed its home-run power, as Pafko and Cavaretta each hit three-run shots, and Smalley's blast was good for two runs. Smalley had been batting in the seventh spot of the batting order, probably due to his .257 average. His 4-for-5 game raised that mark 13 points.

Smalley became the third Cubs player to hit for the cycle, joining Hack Wilson (June 23, 1930), and Babe Herman (September 30, 1933).[9] There were five cycles in the 1950 season: Detroit's George Kell (June 2)' Pittsburgh's Ralph Kiner (June 25, just three days before Smalley); Smalley; the Philadelphia Athletics' Elmer Valo (August 2); and Detroit's Hoot Evers (September 7). Seven years would go by before the next player in a Cubs uniform hit for the cycle (Lee Walls on July 2, 1957).

SOURCES

In addition to the sources mentioned in the Notes, the author consulted baseball-reference.com, mlb.com, and retrosheet.org.

NOTES

1   Bob Broeg, "Cubs Say It With Homers Against Cards; Munger Kayoed in 3 Innings," *St. Louis Post-Dispatch*, June 28, 1950: 28.

2   Ibid.

3   According to the *Chicago Tribune*, there were also 12,953 "guests" in attendance, in addition to the 12,109 "cash customers." See Irving Vaughan, "Cubs Whip Cards, 15-3," *Chicago Tribune*, June 29, 1950: 47-48.

4   Vaughan.

5   According to retrosheet.org, the Phillies and Cardinals were tied for first place, as Philadelphia was 35-24-1, and St. Louis was 36-25. However, baseball-reference.com placed the Cards in second place, one-half game behind the Phillies (presumably because of the tie game). Both the *St. Louis Post-Dispatch* and *Chicago Tribune* have the two teams tied at the end of play on June 27, 1950.

6   Broeg.

7   Vaughan.

8   Ibid.

9   Jimmy Ryan hit for the cycle twice in the nineteenth century: on July 28, 1888, as part of the Chicago White Stockings, and on July 1, 1891, as a member of the Chicago Colts. Both of those teams were predecessors of the Cubs.

HANK SAUER SLAMS THREE HOME RUNS

AUGUST 28, 1950
CHICAGO CUBS 7, PHILADELPHIA PHILLIES 5
(GAME ONE OF DOUBLEHEADER)

By Richard A. Cuicchi

HANK SAUER'S MAJOR-LEAGUE CAREER didn't flourish until he was 31 years old in 1948, but then he proceeded to become one of the most prodigious home-run hitters (225) in the National League through 1954, second only to Hall of Famer Ralph Kiner (277). On August 28, 1950, the Chicago Cubs outfielder highlighted his propensity as a power hitter by slamming three home runs against the Philadelphia Phillies.

Sauer had suffered a hitting drought from July 19 through August 18, a period in which he failed to hit a home run and managed to get only six RBIs while batting just .189.[1] Then he went on a home-run binge, hitting two on both August 24 and 25, and then three days later putting on his home-run fireworks show.

A doubleheader on August 28 was required because the second game of the Cubs-Phillies doubleheader at Wrigley Field on the previous day ended in a 4-4 tie, called 11 innings because of darkness.[2]

According to the *Chicago Tribune*, the attendance was 19,756. It was a relatively meaningless game for the Cubs, who were in sixth place, 22½ games behind the league-leading Phillies. The Phillies, dubbed Whiz Kids for their young roster, had not won a pennant since 1915, and were trying to maintain their five-game lead over the Brooklyn Dodgers.

The Cubs drew left-hander Curt Simmons of the Phillies as the opposing pitcher. Simmons was 16-7, having won 8 of his last 10 decisions, and was a key component in the Phillies' run at the league championship. Forty-one-year-old knuckleballer Dutch Leonard got the Cubs' starting nod, his only start in 35 appearances for the season.

The Phillies struck first with two outs in the top of the second on a single by Granny Hamner and a double by Andy Seminick, who was thrown out at third trying to stretch his hit into a triple.

Sauer, who had played in his first All-Star Game on July 11, led off the bottom of the second with a solo home run off Simmons to even the score, 1-1.

Mike Goliat led off the Phillies' third with a walk and was forced at second base on a comebacker by Simmons. Leonard then yielded his second run when Richie Ashburn tripled.

The Phillies added a third run in the top of the fourth on a single by Del Ennis, a sacrifice by Willie Jones, and a single by Hamner.

Sauer was the Cubs' leadoff batter again in the fourth, and he belted his second home run, but the Cubs still trailed, 3-2. This was the third game in Sauer's last seven in which he had homered twice.

In the sixth, Sauer hit his third homer of the game after Phil Cavarretta singled, and the Cubs led, 4-3, for the first time.

The Cubs added three more runs off Simmons in the bottom of the seventh on Wayne Terwilliger's solo home run, his eighth of the season, and Roy Smalley's double, which drove in Cavarretta and Bob Borkowski with what turned out to be the winning runs. Milo Candini relieved Simmons and denied

An overlooked slugger, Hank Sauer (on left with Ernie Banks and Monte Irvin) cranked 30-plus home runs six times in his first seven full seasons (1948-1954) in the majors. He was the NL MVP with the Cubs in 1952 after leading the league with 37 home runs and 121 runs batted in. (Photo by Mark Rucker/Transcendental Graphics, Getty Images)

Sauer a chance at a fourth home run by intentionally walking him.

In the top of the ninth, with Hamner at second on a double, Seminick homered off Leonard for the Phillies' final two runs. Johnny Vander Meer, the back-to-back no-hit pitcher who was winding down his career, relieved Leonard and walked two batters to load the bases but retired the Phillies. Powered by Sauer's three home runs and Terwilliger's solo shot, the Phillies were 7-5 victors.

Leonard logged his fourth win of the season, yielding five runs on nine hits and two walks. Simmons suffered his eighth loss of the season, giving up seven runs on nine hits and two walks.

The Phillies won the second game of the doubleheader, 9-5.

Sauer attributed his home-run spurt to advice provided by Cavarretta. "Phil caught a hitch in my swing after our last homestand," Sauer said. "He told me I was carrying my bat too high, so I practiced

with it in a lower position on the backswing and that seemed to bring me out of the slump."[3]

Sauer's journey to a full-time job in the majors had taken several twists and turns over 12 years. He first signed with the New York Yankees as a 20-year-old first baseman in 1937. Cincinnati Reds GM Warren Giles, convinced by one of his minor-league managers that Sauer would be a good addition for the Reds, instructed the Reds-owned Birmingham club of the Southern Association to draft him in the fall of 1939.[4]

Sauer turned in two solid seasons for Birmingham and earned a trial with the Reds in 1941. However, they already had a solid first baseman in Frank McCormick. Desperate for hard-hitting outfielders, the Reds decided to convert the 6-foot-3, 198-pound Sauer into an outfielder. After a brief stint at first base with the Reds at the beginning of the 1942 season, he was sent to Syracuse to learn how to play the outfield. Despite the help provided by manager

Jewel Ens, Sauer's progress, both in the field and at bat, was slow.[5]

When Syracuse's regular first baseman injured himself in 1943, Sauer returned to first base for most of the season, and his hitting picked up. Like many ballplayers during World War II, his career was put on hold; he spent the 1944 season and most of 1945 in the US Coast Guard. Returning to the Reds for the last month of the 1945 season, he appeared in 31 games and hit five home runs. However, the Reds decided he still needed more work in the outfield to hold down a regular big-league spot.[6]

So Sauer was back in Syracuse for the 1946 and 1947 seasons. Manager Ens got him to use a heavier bat, a 40-ounce Chick Hafey model, to slow down his swing and better level on pitches.[7] In 1947 Sauer responded with 50 home runs and 141 RBIs, while hitting .336, and was named the Minor League Player of the Year by *The Sporting News*.

Sauer stayed with the Reds in 1948 and hit 35 home runs as their regular left fielder. The Reds were satisfied that his outfield play was no longer a liability.[8]

However, after a slow start (4 home runs, 16 RBIs, and .237 average in 42 games) in 1949, Sauer was traded on June 15 with Frank Baumholtz to the Chicago Cubs for Peanuts Lowrey and Harry Walker. Sauer rebounded with the Cubs, finishing the season with 31 home runs, 99 RBIs, and a .275 batting average.

Sauer's selection to the National League All-Star team in 1950 was the subject of controversy. National League manager Burt Shotton announced his intention to insert his own Brooklyn Dodgers outfielder, Duke Snider, into the starting lineup instead of Sauer, even though Sauer had received more fan votes. Commissioner A.B. "Happy" Chandler initially agreed with Shotton.

But after protests from Cubs manager Frankie Frisch, and from sportswriter Arch Ward, who felt that the fan poll would lose its significance if not followed, Chandler reversed himself and overruled Shotton. At the game, Shotton was booed by the Sauer-friendly crowd at Chicago's Comiskey Park, while Sauer contributed an RBI to the National League's 4-3 victory.[9]

Remarkably, two seasons later, in 1952, Sauer repeated his three-homer performance against the Phillies and Simmons.

SOURCES

In addition to the sources cited in the Notes, the author also consulted the following:

Baseball-Reference.com.

Burns, Ed. "The Sweet Sauer Man," *Baseball Magazine*, September 1952: 8-9, 39.

Holtzman, Jerome. "Do You Remember … When Hank Sauer Was the Mayor of Wrigley Field," *Baseball Digest*, December 2001: 64-66.

Holtzman, Jerome, and George Vass, *The Chicago Cubs Encyclopedia* (Philadelphia: Temple University Press, 1997), 195.

Pietrusza, David, Matthew Silverman, and Michael Gershman, eds., *Baseball: The Biographical Encyclopedia* (New York: Total/Sports Illustrated, 2000), 1001.

Sargent, Jim. SABR BioProject biography of Hank Sauer.

Vass, George. "Baseball's 'Late Bloomers,'" *Baseball Digest*, June 2001: 40-47.

NOTES

1   Ed Burns, "Sauer Ends Homer Famine With Big Helpings at Plate," *The Sporting News*, September 6, 1950: 4.

2   Edward Burns, "Night Halts 11 Inning Duel; Play 2 Today," *Chicago Tribune*, August 28, 1950: 3:1. Wrigley Field didn't get lights until 1988.

3   "Cavarretta's Hint Started Sauer on Homer Spree," *Chicago Tribune*, August 28, 1950: 3: 1.

4   Tom Swope, "Cincy's Sweet on Sauer," *Baseball Digest*, October 1948:17-23.

5   Ibid.

6   Ibid.

7   Edgar Munzel, "Bruin Blockbuster," *Sport Life*, October 1952: 80.

8   Swope.

9   "Stengel, Shotton Kept Busy Ducking All-Star Squawks," *The Sporting News*, July 19, 1950: 8.

HANK SAUER GETS SECOND HR "HAT TRICK"

JUNE 11, 1952
CHICAGO CUBS 3, PHILADELPHIA PHILLIES 2

By Richard A. Cuicchi

BEFORE YOGI BERRA CAME UP WITH HIS now famous quip, "It looks like déjà vu all over again," Chicago Cubs outfielder Hank Sauer could very well have originated that witticism, after he scorched Philadelphia Phillies pitcher Curt Simmons with three home runs for a second time on June 11, 1952. Sauer's three solo homers were all that was needed to single-handedly defeat Simmons and the Phillies. Sauer had previously victimized Simmons on August 28, 1950.

Since coming to the Cubs from Cincinnati in a trade in June 1949, Sauer had been hailed as the team's biggest bargain since the acquisition of Hack Wilson for the 1926 season.[1] From 1949 through 1951 Sauer posted seasons of 27, 32, and 30 home runs. In 1952 he hit 37 home runs, drove in 121 runs and received the National League Most Valuable Player Award.

By June 11 Sauer was on pace for a season approaching Wilson's historic performance in 1930 —15 home runs and 55 RBIs.[2]

Playing before a Wrigley Field crowd of 10,765, the Cubs were contending with the New York Giants for second place in the National League. Second-year right-hander Turk Lown, with a 2-2 record, was manager Phil Cavarretta's starter.

The Phillies started Phillies lefty Simmons, who had missed the entire 1951 season and spring training in 1952 while serving in the Army.[3] Simmons entered the game with a 4-1 record and a 1.90 ERA.

The Cubs drew first blood in the bottom of the second on a leadoff home run by Sauer. The Phillies tied the game in the top of the fourth on a single by Smoky Burgess, a force-out of Burgess at second on Jack Lohrke's groundball, a walk to Connie Ryan, and a run-scoring single by Tommy Brown.

The Cubs threatened in the bottom of the fifth when Roy Smalley singled off Simmons and advanced to third on a sacrifice by Lown and a single by Eddie Miksis. But Simmons struck out Dee Fondy and Bill Serena.

The Phillies countered with a threat in the top of the sixth. Singles by Jackie Mayo and Connie Ryan, who advanced to second base on the throw, followed by an intentional walk to Tommy Brown loaded the bases. With two outs, Richie Ashburn singled for what apparently meant two runs. However, in his rush to reach third base from first, Brown failed to touch second base, and second baseman Miksis touched the bag for the third out.[4]

Sauer put the Cubs back on top, 2-1, with another leadoff home run in the bottom of the sixth. When he returned to the dugout, Smalley said to him, "Remember that game in '50 when you got to Simmons for three homers? I've got a hunch you're going to do it again."[5]

Smalley's hunch couldn't have been more prophetic. Sauer bashed number three off Simmons in the bottom of the eighth inning, making the score 3-1.

The Phillies tried to come back in the top of the ninth. Pinch-hitting for Simmons, Bill Nicholson drew a leadoff walk off Lown. Ralph "Putsy" Caballero ran for Nicholson and, with one out, moved to third when Granny Hamner doubled to left. Dutch Leonard relieved Lown and struck out Johnny Wyrostek. Caballero scored the Phillies' second run when first baseman Fondy booted Burgess's groundball. An aggressive Hamner attempted to score, too, but was thrown out at the plate, right fielder Gene Hermanski to second baseman Miksis to catcher Johnny Pramesa, preserving the Cubs' 3-2 victory.

In his third victory of the season, Lown gave up nine hits and six walks in 8⅓ innings but only two runs as the Phillies left 11 runners on base. Lown struck out six. Simmons was charged with his second loss, giving up eight hits and two walks; but at the end of the day it was Sauer alone who overpowered Simmons.

After the game, Sauer attended a publicity event at umpire Jocko Conlan's batting range in Chicago, where special police had to manage a huge crowd that showed up to see their superman take some cuts. Sauer downplayed his heroic day at the plate, saying, "All I want to do is help the club." He described his three homers as being in three zones: "The first one was a high fastball. The second one I hit was a curve. And the third was a fastball inside and not as high as the first one. But don't let anyone kid you about Simmons. That fellow's a real pitcher."[6]

Years later, when asked whether Simmons had been a soft touch, Sauer made light of the two three-homer performances. "I just happened to be hot those days," he said. "I don't think it would have mattered who was pitching. Besides, I can remember one game in which Simmons struck me out three times."[7]

In addition to drawing similarities with Hack Wilson's season of 1930, Sauer's 18 home runs at that point in the season were also being mentioned in comparisons with Babe Ruth's home-run pace during his 60-homer season of 1927.[8]

The Cubs wound up in fifth place in the league at 77-77, 19½ games behind the pennant-winning Brooklyn Dodgers. The season was a 15-game improvement over 1951, when the Cubs finished in last place. It would be their only .500-or-better season between 1947 and 1962. The Phillies finished the season in fourth place, 10 games ahead of the Cubs.

Sauer edged out Phillies pitcher Robin Roberts for the MVP Award by 15 points (226 to 211) and Dodgers rookie relief pitcher Joe Black by 18 points. His selection triggered considerable controversy at the time, since he played for a second-division team, the first time it had ever happened.

Sauer's detractors argued that Roberts's and Black's performances were more valuable than Sauer's. Roberts was the only 20-game winner in the National League with 28 victories, the most since Dizzy Dean's 30 wins in 1934, and had a 2.59 ERA. Black was similarly impressive as he won 14 of his 15 games pitching in relief and recorded 15 saves for the pennant-winning Dodgers.

Sauer won the award on the merits of his home-run and RBI totals, since he was only a .270 hitter and had a reputation as a marginal outfielder. However, in an article in *Baseball Digest* in February 1953, Chester L. Smith of the *Pittsburgh Press* defended Sauer's selection. "There's a general misapprehension regarding the selection of the MVP," Smith said. "He is not presumed to be the best player in the league, but the man who did the most for his club. Sauer made a respectable team out of the Cubs, who had been consigned to the basement."[9]

In the same *Baseball Digest* article, Francis Stann was critical of Sauer's selection, saying, "[T]ake the bat out of his hands and Hank isn't much of a ball player. In September Hank was no great asset even to his second division team. He batted .213 and drove in only seven runs."[10]

Cubs manager Cavarretta defended his outfielder, saying, "I wouldn't trade Sauer for both Roberts and Black. If I did I should have my head examined. No pitcher could possibly have been as valuable to us last season as Hank was. He played in 151 games. I can't tell you how many games he won for us with his bat and I want to say right now he won some games with his fielding, too." Cavaretta said Sauer's offensive famine in September was due to his playing in pain with a lame back.[11]

SOURCES

In addition to the sources cited in the Notes, the author also consulted the following:

Baseball-Reference.com.

Holtzman, Jerome, and George Vass. *The Chicago Cubs Encyclopedia* (Philadelphia: Temple University Press, 1997), 195.

Munzel, Edgar. "Rags to Riches," in Bruce Jacobs, ed., *Baseball Stars of 1953* (New York: Lion Books, 1953), 145-150.

Pietrusza, David, Matthew Silverman, and Michael Gershman, eds. *Baseball: The Biographical Encyclopedia* (New York: Total/Sports Illustrated, 2000), 1001.

Sargent, Jim. SABR BioProject biography of Hank Sauer.

NOTES

1 Ed Burns, "The Sweet Sauer Man," *Baseball Magazine*, September 1952: 8-9, 39.

2 In 1930, Wilson hit 56 home runs, second only to Babe Ruth's single-season record of 60 in 1927. Wilson's 191 RBIs remain a single-season major-league record.

3 Edward Veit, SABR BioProject biography of Curt Simmons.

4 Irving Vaughan, "Cubs Outfielder Boosts His RBI Total for Season to 58: Hank's Eighteen Homers Match Babe Ruth Pace of 1927," *Chicago Tribune*, June 12, 1952: 1, 6.

5 Al Stump, "Sauer Can't Win," *Sport*, June 1953: 28-31.

6 Edward Prell, "Fans Swarm Over Sauer in Batting Show," *Chicago Tribune*, June 12, 1952: 1, 6.

7 Milton Richman, "Homers Are His Specialty," in Bruce Jacobs, ed., *Baseball Stars of 1955* (New York: Lion Books, Inc., 1955), 113-118.

8 Vaughan.

9 Francis Stann, "Sauer Choice!," *Washington Star* article in *Baseball Digest*, February 1953: 30-32.

10 Ibid.

11 John C. Hoffman, "Sauer Grapes!" *Baseball Digest*, February 1953: 31-34.

CUBS THUMP CARDINALS IN NL'S LONGEST NINE-INNING GAME

APRIL 17, 1954
CHICAGO CUBS 23, ST. LOUIS CARDINALS 13

By Russ Lake

NEAR THE END OF MARCH 1954, STAN Hack was suddenly named to become the new manager of the Chicago Cubs.[1] Phil Cavarretta had abruptly resigned after refusing a reorganization shuffle to guide Hack's minor-league team at Triple-A Los Angeles (PCL).[2] The Cubs had finished in the second division since 1947, and several unfavorable comments Cavarretta made to team owner Phil Wrigley regarding the club's '54 season outlook accelerated Hack to an unexpected promotion.[3] Hack was confident that he was ready to handle the position, saying, "I will give the job everything I have."[4]

On April 13, Hack had a successful regular-season debut when Chicago pasted the St. Louis Cardinals, 13-4, at Busch Stadium. Two days later, during a rainy home opener, the opposite result transpired as the Cubs were blasted, 11-5, by the Cincinnati Redlegs. The Cardinals came into Wrigley Field on Saturday, April 17, for the opener of a three-game series.[5] St. Louis's manager, Eddie Stanky, a former Cub, remained puzzled about his club's 0-2 record. Comparing his team's results to the 0-3 White Sox, Stanky recalled from exhibition play, "While we were traveling with the White Sox both Paul Richards and I thought our clubs were in pretty good shape. So what happens? Both of us get 'schneidered'!"[6]

Stanky selected seven-year veteran right-hander Gerry Staley, 18-9 in 1953, to start. The 33-year-old Staley possessed an effective sinkerball[7] and a 19-7 record against the Cubs. Hack tabbed righty Johnny

Klippstein, who had split mound duties between starting and bullpen relief as he began his fifth campaign in Chicago. Klippstein, 26, was a hard thrower, though control issues limited his ability to complete games.[8] He was 3-4 in his career against the Cardinals.

After reminding the 14,609 in attendance to have their pencils and scorecards ready, public-address announcer Pat Pieper delivered the lineups.[9] The plate umpire was Lon Warneke, who had pitched for both the Cubs and the Cardinals from 1930 to 1945. Warneke was beginning his fifth year as a full-time senior circuit arbiter. Fair and warmer weather with a high of 65 was in the forecast,[10] but the atmosphere would be unstable enough to produce gusty winds from the northwest.

Klippstein escaped a jam in the first, getting Tom Alston to fly out to deep center with the bases loaded. Just days before, Alston had become the first African-American to play for the Cardinals. Staley's first inning proved to be a harbinger of things to come when rookie Bob Talbot popped a bunt single that third baseman Ray Jablonski could not corral. Dee Fondy grounded to Red Schoendienst, but Talbot beat the ill-advised force attempt at second. After Ralph Kiner walked, two runs scored when Hank Sauer lofted a short fly to center that dropped safely due to a wind-aided misjudgment by rookie Wally Moon.[11] Jablonski booted a groundball by Randy Jackson to load the bases before Staley fanned

Ernie Banks, and Gene Baker bounced into a 5-4-3 double play.

Chicago's two-run lead was shunted aside as the Cardinals plated five in the top of the second. Sal Yvars singled, and a trio of walks by Klippstein plus a sacrifice made the score 2-1. With the bases filled again, Hack summoned Hal Jeffcoat, and Schoendienst welcomed the outfielder-turned-pitcher[12] with a two-run single to put St. Louis in front, 3-2. Stan Musial hit a pop foul that catcher Joe Garagiola caught, but when the catcher staggered afterward Schoendienst went for second. Garagiola's peg to Baker was not in time, and Moon was sent plateward by Stanky. Baker's return throw forged a "madhouse at home" as Garagiola, Jeffcoat, and Moon converged at the plate. Nudging Jeffcoat out of the way, Garagiola could not hang onto the relay and fell backward as Moon sidestepped the catcher to score.[13] Jablonski singled home Schoendienst to make the score 5-2.

The Cubs' Garagiola doubled to open the bottom half and scored after Moon misplayed Jeffcoat's wind-blown fly into a double. Moon had homered in his first major-league at bat four days before, but that seemed like a distant memory right now. Stanky, seeing how uncomfortable the rookie was tracking the baseball, switched left fielder Rip Repulski to center and center fielder Moon to left. Jeffcoat, after advancing to third on a grounder, scored on Fondy's fly ball that Moon caught without issues to reduce the Chicago deficit to 5-4.

Yvars doubled to lead off the third inning and was at third base with one away when the veteran backstop noticed that Jeffcoat was not paying attention to him. With Staley batting, the veteran catcher took off for home. Garagiola reached for Jeffcoat's high throw, and dropped his left leg to block the plate. Yvars dove head-first, pulled his right hand back from the tag, and swiped his left across the dish. Warneke signaled safe and, despite a nose-to-nose argument with Garagiola, his call stood.[14] Although Yvars banged his neck against Garagiola's shin guard,[15] the action netted his first-ever stolen base to increase the Cardinals' advantage to 6-4.

Jackson bombed a home run onto Waveland Avenue to begin the bottom of the third. The blast was followed by a walk to Banks and double by Baker. Staley was removed for right-hander Hal White, who was greeted with a two-run single by Garagiola. Jeffcoat then whacked a two-run homer into the left-field bleachers to give the Cubs a 9-6 lead. Left-hander Royce Lint came out of the bullpen and got an inning-ending double play.

Jeffcoat steadied a bit in the fourth, and the Cubs added three against Lint on two singles, another error by Jablonski, and a wild pitch. With Chicago's lead now 12-6, the Cardinals jumped on Jeffcoat for four fifth-inning tallies on a solo home run by Yvars and a three-run shot by Repulski to shrink their shortfall to 12-10. First-year right-hander Jim Brosnan took over for Jeffcoat, and gave up a double plus a walk, but escaped with no additional damage.

The Cubs went to work in their fifth to widen the spread between the two squads. In 58 minutes,[16] Chicago sent 16 batters to the plate; they parlayed six singles, a double, six walks, and two St. Louis errors into 10 additional runs. The Cardinals' collapse carnage came courtesy of right-hander Mel Wright, southpaw Al Brazle, and righty Cot Deal, each of whom pitched an ineffective third of an inning. Wright and Brazle gave up five and four earned runs, respectively. Now the center-field scoreboard displayed a "football-like" halftime representation of Cubs 22, Cardinals 10, with four innings yet to play.

Brosnan and Deal closed out the remainder of the contest in anticlimactic fashion. Deal allowed an RBI double by Clyde McCullough in the seventh to push the Cubs' spread to 23-10. Brosnan gave up Alston's first major-league home run leading off the eighth, and a pair of inconsequential St. Louis tallies in the ninth to modify the scoreboard to 23-13. Deal also pulled off what none of the other eight hurlers accomplished during the game by retiring the side in order in the bottom of the eighth. The Chicago-born Jablonski struggled mightily for St. Louis, committing three errors, striking out twice, and rapping into a game-ending around-the-horn double play.[17]

The line score showed the Cubs with 23 runs, 20 hits, and one error while St. Louis mustered 13 runs, 15 hits, and 5 errors. Each team stranded 10 runners. Pitching statistics resembled a "bad accident" with 33 of the 36 runs scored applicable to ERA numbers. Nine pitchers combined for 21 walks (12 by St. Louis), and there were just five strikeouts, all logged by the two pitchers of record, Brosnan and Staley.

After three games, the Cubs were hitting a robust .388 (47-for-121), with Jackson's batting mark at .667 (10-for-15). Neither team set a record for runs scored or allowed. On August 25, 1922, the Cubs had pummeled the Philadelphia Phillies, 26-23, at Cubs Park. The Cardinals were totally embarrassed at Sportsman's Park, 24-6, by the Pittsburgh Pirates on June 22, 1925.[18]

The chaotic winds endured at Wrigley Field were strong enough to bend both foul-line flagpoles.[19] The game took 3:43 to play, an NL nine-inning record, exceeding by five minutes the first game of a doubleheader between the Brooklyn Dodgers and New York Giants on September 6, 1952, at the Polo Grounds.[20] Chicago first sacker Fondy, who retained the ball he squeezed for the final putout, said he would consider selling the sphere to the highest bidder.[21]

Hack refused a rubdown offer from Cubs trainer Al Scheuneman, who thought the skipper might be tired with waving in all of the runs. "That would be fun every day," said Hack.[22] After all baseball results for this date were in, the Cardinals remained the only team in the majors without a victory.

SOURCES

In addition to the sources cited in the Notes, the author also accessed Retrosheet.org, Baseball-Reference.com, Newspapers.com, SABR.org/bioproj, and *The Sporting News* archive via Paper of Record.

NOTES

1   "Cubs Fire Cavarretta; Name Hack Pilot," *Chicago Tribune*, March 30, 1954: 33.

2   Edward Prell, "Cavarretta Turns Down Offer to Manage Los Angeles Club," *Chicago Tribune*, March 30, 1954: 33.

3   Lawrence Baldassaro, SABR Baseball Biography Project, Phil Cavarretta (sabr.org/bioproj/person/d7db5ae3).

4   Seymour Korman, "Hack Happy Over Return to Chicago," *Chicago Tribune*, March 30, 1954: 33.

5   "Cubs, Cards Hope to Keep 'Eggs' Rolling for Easter," *Chicago Tribune*, April 18, 1954: 56.

6   Prell, "Jeffcoat May Get 1st Cubs Start Soon," *Chicago Tribune*, April 17, 1954: 17.

7   Jim Sargent, SABR Baseball Biography Project, Gerry Staley (sabr.org/bioproj/person/ea19c639).

8   Gregory H. Wolf, SABR Baseball Biography Project, Johnny Klippstein (sabr.org /bioproj/person/f6ecad17).

9   Baseball Reference Bullpen, Pat Pieper (baseball-reference.com/bullpen/Pat_Pieper).

10   "Cloudy and Cooler Weather Forecast for Easter Parade," *Chicago Tribune*, April 17, 1954: 2.

11   Bob Broeg, "Cubs Score 2, 2, 5, 3, Then 10 and Bury Cards, 23-13," *St. Louis Post-Dispatch*, April 18, 1954: 67.

12   Andrew Sharp, SABR Baseball Biography Project, Hal Jeffcoat (sabr.org/bioproj/person/1ba121fd).

13   Photo Caption, "Moon, a Rising Star," *Chicago Tribune*, April 18, 1954: 53.

14   Photo Caption, "Sal Fools Hal as Catchers Collide," *Chicago Tribune*, April 18, 1954: 56.

15   Broeg, "Cubs, Cards Set N.L. Mark – But It Was Long Struggle," *The Sporting News*, April 28, 1954: 9.

16   Ibid.

17   Broeg, "Cubs Score 2, 2, 5, 3, Then 10."

18   Ibid.

19   "Cubs, Cards Hope."

20   Broeg, "Cubs Score 2, 2, 5"; the National League record for the longest nine-inning game is now 4 hours 30 minutes, set by Arizona and Colorado on June 24, 2016, at Coors Field in Denver. The major-league record is 4 hours 45 minutes, set by the New York Yankees and Boston Red Sox on August 18, 2006, at Boston's Fenway Park.

21   "Cubs, Cards Hope."

22   Ibid.

TOOTHPICK SAM JONES FIRST AFRICAN-AMERICAN TO TOSS NO-HITTER

MAY 12, 1955
CHICAGO CUBS 4, PITTSBURGH PIRATES 0

By Gregory H. Wolf

"THERE HAVEN'T BEEN MANY – IF ANY – finer finishing touches put on a no-hit performance," gushed sportswriter Jack Hernon after the Chicago Cubs' Toothpick Sam Jones struck out the side with the bases loaded in the ninth inning to author a no-hitter against the Pittsburgh Pirates.[1] Jones "put a bizarre finish to the greatest pitching feat in Wrigley Field since 1917," declared Windy City scribe Edward Prell, evoking comparisons to a Deadball Era game when the Cubs' Hippo Vaughn and the Cincinnati Reds' Fred Toney held their opponents hitless through nine innings.[2]

In mid-May 1955, the Cubs were in the middle of the most inept period in franchise history, despite their fourth-place position and modest 13-14 record in the standings heading into the Thursday afternoon game with the Pirates. Already 10 games behind the streaking Brooklyn Dodgers, the Cubs were en route to their ninth consecutive nonwinning season and second-division finish, an inglorious double streak that would eventually reach 16 seasons. Manager Fred Haney's Bucs, coming off three consecutive 100-loss and last-place finishes, had nowhere to go but up in 1955, yet still finished in the cellar, though they avoided the century mark in defeats (60-94).

Toeing the rubber for the North Siders was Sam Jones, whose moniker "Toothpick" derived from his penchant for chewing them and not from his 6-foot-4, 200-pound frame. The Cubs had acquired the 29-year-old right-hander from the Cleveland Indians in the offseason in a multiplayer deal for aging slugger Ralph Kiner. A former Negro League star with the Cleveland Buckeyes, Jones had a cup of coffee with the Tribe in 1951 and 1952. Plagued by shoulder bursitis the following campaign, the hard-throwing Jones revived his big-league prospects by going 15-8 and fanning 178 in 199 innings for the Indianapolis Indians, the regular-season champions of the Triple-A American Association. Jones (3-3, 5.08 ERA) was making his seventh start for the Cubs, and just the 12th in his career.

On an overcast day with temperatures in the low 70s, the smallest crowd of the season thus far (2,918) in Wrigley Field witnessed history. After Jones set down the first three Pirates hitters, the Cubs wasted no time taking their whacks at rookie Nellie King, the 6-foot-6, 185-pound stringbean hurler making his fourth career start. Following one-out singles by Gene Baker and Bob Speake, Ted Tappe belted a two-out double to drive in the first run, which proved more than enough offense.

The Cubs pounded the ball all afternoon, collecting 15 hits and drawing two walks. They tacked on another run in the second on a double by Eddie Miksis. Right-handed swingman Vern Law replaced King to start the third. He hurled the last six frames and surrendered two more runs. A one-out triple by Ernie Banks in the fifth plated Tappe for a 3-0 Cubs lead, and Tappe's solo homer in the seventh rounded out the scoring, which should have been higher. The Cubs threatened seemingly every inning, yet managed only two hits in 17 at-bats with men in scoring position and left 13 men on base; six times a batter was stranded on third.

This game was not about the Cubs' offense which scored fewer runs than any NL team in 1955 except the Pirates; rather, it was Jones's statement to the baseball world that he belonged in the big leagues.

Toothpick Sam breezed through the first eight innings. He walked four, including Dale Long three times, and no Pirate reached second base. The Cubs played flawlessly in the field and the *Chicago Tribune* noted that there were no close plays or questionable calls by the umpires.[3] Through five innings, the Pirates hit only one ball out of the infield even though Jones struggled to get his curveball over the plate. "I called mostly for fastballs, with a little slow [stuff] included," said catcher Clyde McCullough.[4] Jones found his bender in the sixth, retiring the side on outfield flies. The first out of the seventh was the trickiest of the game. Leadoff hitter Dick Groat hit a bounder through the box that Jones knocked down with his glove. Second baseman Gene Baker fielded the ball on the charge and tossed underhanded to first.[5] Prell noted that two of the Pirates' three hard-hit balls came in the eighth. Center fielder Eddie Miksis raced back "near the vines" to grab Gene Freese's deep fly ball for the first out;[6] and third baseman Randy Jackson snared Toby Atwell's laser, then tossed to first to double off Long. It was second stellar defensive play for the two-time All-Star third sacker. In the fourth Jackson made a "one handed stab on a terrific liner" by Frank Thomas, reported Prell.[7]

Jones had never thrown a no-hitter in Organized Baseball and stood just three outs away from becoming the first Cubs hurler to accomplish the feat since Jimmy Lavender against the New York Giants at the Polo Grounds in August 31, 1915. Two years later Vaughn lost his gem in the 10th, while Toney completed his for a 1-0 Reds victory. Jones's glaring weakness as a pitcher was his control. He had walked 129 with Indianapolis in 1954; 178 in 267 innings with Triple-A San Diego in the Pacific Coast League in 1952; and was en route to leading the NL in walks (185 in 241⅔ innings) for the first of

four times. Suffering from a case of the yips, Jones walked leadoff hitter Gene Freese, then uncorked a wild pitch facing pinch-hitter Preston Ward, who eventually walked as did Tom Saffell, hitless in 15 at-bats thus far in 1955.

Jones's seventh free pass drew skipper Stan Hack from the dugout. The former Cubs great, known as Smiling Stan, was not smiling, however, with the game on the line. He and McCullough offered Jones words of reassurance, giving him time to collect his wits with the heart of the Pirates order due up. "I went farther with Jones than I ordinarily would have," admitted Hack who adhered to a time-honored tradition of not removing a pitcher working on a no-no regardless of the player's struggles. "But had the fourth Pirate reached base, he would have been out of there."[8]

Jones reared back and punched out Groat. The former All-American basketball player at Duke University looked at three hard curves over the plate. Roberto Clemente, a 20-year-old rookie who entered the game batting .304, went down swinging. Frank Thomas, the Pirates cleanup hitter and most dangerous home-run threat, took Jones's 136th pitch of the game, and 30th of the inning, for strike three.[9]

McCullough, the 38-year-old backstop who began his career with the Cubs in 1940 and had never caught a no-hitter, raced to the mound to congratulate Jones. Sportswriters besieged the batterymates in the clubhouse. "I pitched harder to those boys than to any of the others," said Jones, elated at fanning the last three Pirates batters to become the first African-American and first former Negro League player to toss a no-hitter in the major leagues.[10] Chimed in McCullough, "[I]n the ninth, I called for only two fastballs. Those were to Roberto Clemente."[11] Jones basked in the glory rightfully bestowed on an author of a no-hitter, yet the soft-spoken Ohioan deflected praise heaped upon him "I was just out there throwing fastballs and curves," said Jones, finishing with six strikeouts. "Clyde deserves all the credit. He knows the batters and kept telling me how to pitch to them."[12]

Jones emerged in 1955 as one of the best, yet inconsistent, pitchers in the league. He tossed eight strong innings, fanning 10 and walking eight against the Philadelphia Phillies to win his next start. At the end of the season, Toothpick Sam's name was atop the NL leader board in strikeouts (198), strikeouts per nine innings (7.4), and fewest hits per nine innings (6.5), but also walks and losses (20) to go along with his 14 wins. No one-year wonder, Jones won 102 games, including a league-best 21 for the San Francisco Giants in 1959 (tied with the Milwaukee Braves' Lew Burdette and Warren Spahn), in a career shortened by neck cancer initially diagnosed in 1962.

SOURCES

In addition to the sources mentioned in the Notes, the author consulted baseball-reference.com, mlb.com, and retrosheet.org.

NOTES

1   Jack Hernon, "Cubs Pitcher Trims Bucs on No-Hitter, 4-0," *Pittsburgh Post-Gazette*, May 13, 1955: 13.

2   Edward Prell, "Story of Cubs No-Hitter," *Chicago Tribune*, May 13, 1955: 1.

3   Ibid.

4   Edward Prell, "Jones Tells of Fight for Baseball Life," *Chicago Tribune*, My 13, 1955: C1.

5   Prell, "Story of Cubs No-Hitter."

6   Ibid.

7   Ibid.

8   Prell, "Jones Tells of Fight for Baseball Life."

9   The pitch count for the ninth inning is from Les Biederman, "Cubs Landed Sam (No-Hit) Jones in Kiner Deal," *Pittsburgh Press*, May 13, 1955: 32; the pitch count for the game from Prell, "Story of Cubs No-Hitter."

10   Prell, "Jones Tells of Fight for Baseball Life."

11   Ibid.

12   Associated Press, "Jones of Cubs Shuts Out Pirates With No-Hit Game," *New York Times*, May 13, 1955: 28.

BANKS' THREE BASHES POWER CUBS IN COMEBACK VICTORY

AUGUST 4, 1955
CHICAGO CUBS 11, PITTSBURGH PIRATES 10

By Alan Cohen

"He's been hotter than the weather, and in the Midwest, that's torrid."

Les Biederman of the *Pittsburgh Press,* discussing Ernie Banks who during the final four games of a five-game series between the Cubs and Pirates went 11-for-19 with five home runs and 13 RBIs.[1]

ERNIE BANKS, IN HIS SECOND FULL season with the Chicago Cubs, hit three home runs into the daylight at Wrigley Field, the final one being a two-run eighth-inning blast that settled the issue, on August 4, 1955, as the Cubs defeated the Pirates 11-10 in front of an announced crowd of 3,486.

The eighth-place Pirates (40-70) and fifth-place Cubs (52-58) were aided by the outward breeze, hitting eight home runs between them in a game that saw three lead changes and went down to the final play – Banks fielding a Dick Groat grounder and initiating a double play. The Cubs claimed their third win in the five-game series against their second-division rivals in a game that saw each team get 15 hits.

The starting pitchers were veteran Howie Pollet (3-3) for the Cubs and 32-year-old rookie Lino Donoso (2-6) for the Pirates. Donoso was the first person of color to pitch for the Pirates, having made his first appearance of the season on June 18. The visiting Pirates took the early lead with a pair of runs off Pollet. After singles by Eddie O'Brien and Gene Freese to start the game, rookie Roberto Clemente

singled home O'Brien. Freese subsequently scored on a sacrifice fly off the bat of catcher Jack Shepard. The Cubs got those runs back when Banks hit his first homer of the day. It was a two-run shot off Donoso that also scored Gene Baker, who had reached on a fielder's choice.

The Bucs mounted another rally in the second inning, but came away without scoring. With one out and runners on first (Groat) and second (Johnny O'Brien), the Pirates were victimized by a play that was emblematic of their sorrowful season. Eddie O'Brien (Johnny's twin brother) singled to right field. Johnny O'Brien chose to stop at third base, but the hustling Groat went from first to third. Johnny O'Brien belatedly dashed for home and became the inning's second out. Pollet, covering home, applied the tag as O'Brien slid into home plate. Freese grounded out to end the inning.

The Cubs took the lead as Eddie Miksis led off the bottom of the second with a solo home run, and added a pair in the third inning in a rally keyed by Banks's single to right field. On the Banks single, Jim King, who had walked, was able to score when Clemente misplayed the ball. Banks advanced to third on the play. With Banks standing on third, Pirates manager Fred Haney changed pitchers, bringing in Max Surkont. Ransom Jackson greeted Surkont with a single, scoring Banks and giving the Cubs a three-run lead. In the bottom of the fourth inning, the Cubs extended their lead to 9-2 with four runs. Singles by Pollet, Dee Fondy, and King brought in one run and players were on first and second when Banks came to the plate. Ernie hit his second homer of the day, a three-run blast off Surkont, and the Cubs led by seven.

With Pollet having calmed down after yielding the two first-inning runs and surviving the second-inning threat, the Pirates faced the dim prospect of coming back from a seven-run deficit. Their comeback began with five runs in the fifth inning. With one out, Clemente tripled[2] and Frank Thomas singled him home. Dale Long homered to cut the lead to 9-5 and after Johnny O'Brien reached on an infield single that traveled but a few feet in front of home plate, Cubs manager Stan Hack removed Pollet from the game. His replacement, Dave Hillman, proved ineffective, yielding a two-run homer to Groat. Although Hillman emerged from the inning with no further damage, the Bucs were back in the game.

The much-traveled pitcher Dick Littlefield entered the game in the fifth inning for Pittsburgh and put the lid on the Cubs' attack. The Pirates were his fifth major-league team; he would go on to play for four more. He was also included in the trade between the Giants and Dodgers involving Jackie Robinson – a trade that did not happen because Robinson chose to retire. The Pirates resumed their assault in the sixth inning. Freese led off the inning with a double and, with one out, came home on Thomas's home run that tied the game and sent Hillman to the showers. Bill Tremel replaced Hillman and there was no further damage in the sixth inning.

The Pirates took the lead in the top of the eighth inning on a homer by Freese, but the lead was short-lived. In the bottom of the eighth inning, the Cubs got to Littlefield. King walked and Banks hit his third homer of the day, as he banged Littlefield's first pitch into the center-field bleachers, putting the Cubs in front to stay. After Banks's homer, Jackson singled but was eliminated when Hank Sauer hit into a double play. Littlefield, however, had trouble recording the final out and after singles by Miksis and Harry Chiti put runners on first and third, manager Fred Haney called on reliever Roy Face

to replace Littlefield and record the final out of the eighth inning.

In the ninth inning, needing a run to tie, the Pirates mounted a rally. Toby Atwell looped a double down the left field line, and Jim Davis replaced Tremel on the mound for Chicago. Atwell went to third on a wild pitch by the knuckleballer but was unable to advance further. Davis struck out Long for the first out and walked Johnny O'Brien. With runners on first and third, Groat, looking for his fourth hit of the day, grounded into the game-ending double play.

Tremel, the beneficiary of Banks's third homer, was credited with the win, his second of the season, and Davis, who recorded the last two outs, was awarded the save. The loss went to Littlefield and brought his record to 4-10.

The Pirates' record for the season fell to 40-71 and they would not escape the cellar in 1955, finishing with a record of 60-94. Nevertheless, they had the core of a contender with Clemente, Groat, and Face. In 1960, they would win the World Series, with these three playing prominent roles.

The three homers by Banks tied him for the league lead with Duke Snider of the Dodgers. Banks's seven RBIs raised his season's total to 87, and set a record for RBIs by a Cubs shortstop, breaking the record of 85 previously held by Roy Smalley. Banks, who had already set the record for homers by a National League shortstop, was gunning for the major-league mark set by Vern Stephens of Boston.

Banks wound up the 1955 season third in the National League with 44 homers, setting a record for shortstops that would last only three seasons. He hit 47 in 1958, when he won the first of his two consecutive MVP Awards. His major-league record has since been eclipsed by Alex Rodriguez (57 in 2002). Banks still hold the National League record.

The Cubs, despite the presence of Banks, would not be a serious factor in the National League pennant race for some time. In 1955, they finished in sixth place with a 72-81 record. Finally, under Leo Durocher in 1967, Ernie was on a team that finished above .500. In his last season as a regular, 1969, the Cubs were in first place as late as September 9, but finished second despite 106 RBIs by Banks. The 14-time All-Star retired after the 1971 season and was inducted into the Hall of Fame in 1977

SOURCES

In addition to the sources cited in the Notes, Retrosheet.org, and Baseball-Reference.com, the author used:

Dailey, James (Associated Press). "Skinny Ernie Banks Ties for Major Home Run Lead," *Mount Vernon* (Illinois) *Register-News*, August 5, 1955: 8.

Hernon, Jack. "Banks' Three Home Runs Blast Bucs, 11-10," *Pittsburgh Post-Gazette*, August 5, 1955: 16

Vaughn, Irving. "Banks Hits Nos. 34, 35, 36!" *Chicago Tribune*, August 5, 1955: 3-1.

NOTES

1   Les Biederman, "Banks' Homers Spoil Rally by Pirates," *Pittsburgh Press*, August 5, 1955: 20.

2   United Press, "Banks Three Homers Lift Cubs Over Pirates, 11-10," *Boston Globe*, August 5, 1955: 4. According to this article, as well as the Irving article in the *Chicago Tribune*, Clemente tripled in the fifth inning and Freese doubled in the sixth inning. Baseball-Reference shows only the box score of the game and Retrosheet inaccurately shows the Freese double in the fifth inning and the Clemente triple in the sixth.

Mr. Cub, Ernie Banks, hit three home runs in a game four times and finished with 512 round-trippers in his 19-year Hall of Fame career, all spent with the Cubs. (Photo by Focus on Sport/Getty Images)

CUBS WASTE WALLS' CYCLE

JULY 2, 1957
CINCINNATI REDLEGS 8, CHICAGO CUBS 6
(10 INNINGS)

By Mike Huber

ONLY TWO MONTHS HAD PASSED SINCE outfielder Lee Walls was traded from Pittsburgh to Chicago,[1] and he had not yet become a household name in the Windy City as July 1957 began. On July 2 Walls moved up some in Cubs fans' eyes as he tried to singlehandedly lead his Chicago teammates to a victory over the Cincinnati Redlegs in an afternoon affair at Wrigley Field. Before a crowd of 10,358, the game featured plenty of action between the second-place Reds and the next-to-last Cubs, who started the day 15½ games back in the standings. As the *Chicago Tribune* put it, "The Cubs, who often lose but never quit, fought back to take a lead, slipped back into a tie, then lost in the 10th inning, 8 to 6."[2]

Walls might have been the one player on the Cubs roster least likely to hit for the cycle. He came into the game batting .228, with five doubles, four triples, and one home run in the 53 games he had played in a Cubs uniform. In eight games with the Pirates before the trade, Walls had only four hits (three singles and a double). He was slugging a meager .323. In his first 236 major-league games, Walls had gotten more than two hits just six times and more than three only once. It is reasonable to believe that no one had expectations for such a batter to amass four hits, let alone a single, double, triple, and home run, in a game.[3] Yet on this summer afternoon, Walls became the fourth player in Chicago Cubs history to hit for the cycle.

Neither starting pitcher was sharp. Chicago's Don Kaiser didn't make it out of the second inning, and Cincinnati's Don Gross lasted just 2⅓ innings. With two outs, Walls "started his biggest day as a Cub with a wasted double in the first inning."[4] Walt Moryn followed with a walk, but Ernie Banks ended the inning with a grounder to short.

The Redlegs jumped on Kaiser in the top of the second inning, scoring five runs, which were capped by Wally Post's grand slam. Frank Robinson led off with a walk. Ed Bailey singled, and Kaiser issued an intentional pass to Roy McMillan in order to pitch to Gross. Gross hit a "hard shot near the bag"[5] at first that Dale Long could not field cleanly; Long's only play was to get Gross at first, and Cincy scored a run. Johnny Temple walked to load the bases again, and Post deposited a Kaiser offering into the left-field seats. This was Post's 11th homer and second bases-loaded shot of the season. It meant a 5-0 lead for the Redlegs, and it brought Dick Littlefield in to relieve Kaiser. Littlefield retired Gus Bell, then was lifted for a pinch-hitter in the bottom of the second.

By the bottom of the fourth, however, the Cubs had fought back and tied the game. They notched three runs in the third when Walls and Banks each sent balls over the ivy wall. Walls' second home run of the season drove in Jerry Kindall. A fan "knocked it back into left field, but [first base] Umpire Frank Dascoli ruled it a homer."[6] Banks hit his 15th round-tripper of the season, a "home run that carried 425 feet into the center-field bleachers."[7] Hersh Freeman trotted out from the Cincy bullpen, as Gross's afternoon was finished. An inning later, Long and Kindall both singled, and Walls' triple to the right-center barrier drove them both in, tying the game, 5-5. In four innings, Walls was already 3-for-3 with all of his extra-base hits accounted for.

A little bit of excitement and a lot of controversy arose in the Cubs' half of the seventh. With one out, Walls laced a single. He had just hit for the cycle in four straight at-bats. He moved to third on Moryn's single. Banks hit a "likely looking double-play"[8] ball to short but was ruled safe at first base. Redlegs manager Birdie Tebbetts and bullpen coach Tom Ferrick thought otherwise, and "this precipitated quite a rhubarb,"[9] as both Cincinnati men "were banished from protesting Umpire Frank Dascoli's 'safe' call."[10] The supposedly late relay allowed Walls to score the tiebreaking run for Chicago.

Dave Hillman had been pitching for the Cubs since the top of the third. He struck out six Cincinnati batters and had been touched for only six hits coming into the eighth inning. Ed Bailey led off and launched his 11th home run of the season into the center-field stands, tying the game once more. Walls had another chance to be the hero, as he led off the bottom of the ninth, but his fly ball to right stayed in the park. With two outs, Banks also launched a fly to center, but center fielder Bell tracked it down.

The overtime inning featured extra-base hits by Cincinnati batters, as "the Reds hauled out their artillery."[11] Jim Brosnan, the fourth Cubs hurler, had pitched the ninth, and Cubs manager Bob Scheffing kept him in for the 10th. George Crowe opened the inning with a double, his third hit of the game. Robinson struck out and Bailey walked, giving the infield a force at any base. However, Don Hoak "smacked a first-pitch double to left"[12] to drive home Pete Whisenant, who was running for Crowe. Brosnan then walked Alex Grammas, and the bases were loaded. Turk Lown relieved. Raul Sanchez hit a slow roller to second and Bobby Morgan threw home for the force out. But Lown then walked Temple, providing the Redlegs with the second run of the inning.

The Cubs went in order in the 10th, and Cincinnati won, 8-6. The Cubs had failed to capitalize on Walls' slugging effort. Walls had gone 4-for-5 with two runs scored and four runs batted in. Banks knocked in two, but the Cincinnati pitching allowed only those six runs.

Cincinnati's Post became the first batter to hit two grand slams in 1957. While his big blow brought in four runs, Bailey had a 2-for-4 game with an RBI and two runs scored. Sanchez picked up his third victory, allowing just one hit in three innings pitched. The Redlegs moved into first place in the National League with the victory, a half-game over the Milwaukee Braves.[13] Chicago's record dropped to 23-43, and the Cubs spent the rest of the season shifting between seventh and eighth place in the senior circuit.

Before Walls, the last Cub to hit for the cycle was Roy Smalley, at Wrigley Field on June 28, 1950. Walls' cycle was the first in the majors in three seasons. (Don Mueller of the New York Giants did it on July 11, 1954.) Just three weeks after Walls' performance, Mickey Mantle accomplished the rare feat for the New York Yankees (July 23, 1957).

SOURCES

In addition to the sources mentioned in the notes, the author consulted baseball-reference.com, mlb.com and retrosheet.org.

NOTES

1 On May 1, 1957, Walls was traded by Pittsburgh with Dale Long to Chicago for Dee Fondy and Gene Baker.

2 Edward Prell, "Cincinnati Wins, 8-6, in 10 After 5 Run Edge Over Cubs," *Chicago Tribune*, July 3, 1957: 34.

3 Walls finished the 1957 season at .240, but the team's batting average was only .244. He had a breakout season in 1958, batting .304, when the team batting average was .265.

4 Prell.

5 Ibid.

6 Ibid.

7 "Reds Take Cubs in 10th; Regain Lead," *Pittsburgh Post-Gazette*, July 3, 1957: 14.

8 Lou Smith, "Reds Take League Lead; Defeat Cubs in 10th, 8-6," *Cincinnati Enquirer*, July 3, 1957: 33.

9 Ibid.

10 Ibid.

11 Ibid.

12 Ibid.

13 The Redlegs defeated the Braves on July 3, to take a one-game lead over the St. Louis Cardinals. Then they lost seven in a row, dropping to fourth place, where they finished the season at 80-74. The Cubs, meanwhile, finished the season at 62-92, in seventh place.

AARON AND BANKS SHINE IN LABOR DAY SHOOTOUT

SEPTEMBER 2, 1957
MILWAUKEE BRAVES 23, CHICAGO CUBS 10
(GAME ONE OF DOUBLEHEADER)

By Nathan Bierma

THE BRAVES' MOVE FROM BOSTON TO Milwaukee in 1953, the major-leagues' first franchise relocation in 50 years, installed a rival just 90 miles north of Wrigley Field. The timing was terrible for the Cubs; their new neighbor ascended to dominance in the National League while the Cubs were stranded near the cellar. By 1957, the Braves' lowest finish since their move was third place, while the Cubs' best showing was sixth.[1]

When the teams met at Wrigley Field for a Labor Day doubleheader on September 2, 1957, Fred Haney's Braves (79-49) were perched atop the National League while Bob Scheffing's Cubs (49-77) were struggling to stay out of last place. A more competitive matchup pitted Henry Aaron against Ernie Banks in the NL home-run race. Both players had entered the league around the same time and become their franchise's first African-American stars. Both were known for their understated demeanors and explosive bats. Aaron had created some distance between the two in the season's home-run race so far, leading 38 to 30 (with Brooklyn's Duke Snider at 34), but Banks was within reach.

The doubleheader drew a holiday crowd of over 34,000, the largest in the majors that day and the biggest at Wrigley Field in weeks.[2] Lew Burdette (14-7) took the mound for the Braves in Game One, while the Cubs sent out Bob Rush (4-13). The Braves bolted out of the starting blocks. On the second pitch of the game, Red Schoendienst smacked a double, then scored when Frank Torre reached base on a throwing error.[3] Two batters in, it was 1-0.

After Aaron walked, Wes Covington singled to score Torre. That brought up Bob Hazle. Summoned from Triple-A Wichita in late July after an injury to Bill Bruton, the rookie outfielder inexplicably unleashed 34 hits for a .507 batting average after one month, earning the nickname Hurricane Hazle. Author Howard Bryant called it the "greatest five-week show in the history of baseball,"[4] and Hazle kept it going at Wrigley Field with a double that brought home Aaron. Next up was Félix Mantilla, Aaron's longtime roommate and the godfather of his daughter.[5] Mantilla singled and Covington scored.

The game "became a debacle in the opening inning," wrote the *Chicago Tribune*.[6] After four runs and just one out, Rush was done for the day. In came Bob Anderson, who gave up a two-run single to Del Crandall. The score was 6-0 after half an inning.

The Cubs got one back in the first on a solo home run by Bob Speake. But in the top of the second, Eddie Mathews drove a ball into the ivy for an RBI triple and came home on Covington's sacrifice fly to make it 8-1.[7]

Still, the Cubs, as the *Tribune* put it, "kept up their fruitless chase."[8] Dale Long led off the bottom of the second with a base hit. Banks came up and belted the ball over the left-field wall to make it 8-3.

But things disintegrated for the Cubs with two outs in the top of the third. Schoendienst singled, Torre was hit by a pitch, and Mathews walked to load the bases for Aaron. This was Aaron's dream scenario – it was why he batted cleanup, why he preferred strategic singles over swinging for the fences, and why he would ultimately finish as baseball's all-time RBI leader. Aaron shot a single into center field, bringing in two, to give the Braves double digits in runs in less than three innings. Covington followed with a three-run homer, and the Braves led by a football score of 13-3.

The Cubs were getting shelled, but they kept pounding away with their bats. In the bottom of the third, Walt "Moose" Moryn, Banks, and Cal Neeman hit RBI singles, bouncing Burdette. The bad news for Burdette was that he allowed six runs and failed to finish the third inning. The good news was that his team had furnished the comfiest of cushions: a seven-run lead. Ernie Johnson came on in relief and gave up a double to Jerry Kindall that brought in Banks. After three innings it was Braves 13, Cubs 7. By the standards of this game, it qualified as a close margin.

In the fourth inning the Braves set the table once again for Aaron, with the top three hitters in the lineup reaching base with two outs. Aaron delivered again, knocking a base hit to right field, scoring two more to make it 15-7 Braves.

Each side endured their first scoreless half inning. Then Banks came to bat in the bottom of the fifth and blasted another home run, a solo shot to the left-field seats.

In Aaron's next at-bat, only two runners were aboard this time. Aaron clobbered a double to score them both for his fifth and sixth RBIs of the game.[9] Covington immediately tied the mark by batting in Aaron to reach six RBIs himself. After six innings, the score was 18-8.

After stabilizing things on the mound for the Braves, Johnson added to the runs pouring in on offense. When Mantilla led off the seventh with a single and advanced on a wild pitch, Johnson came up and lashed a single to drive in Mantilla.

The Braves had tied a Milwaukee-era team record with their 19th run of the game. They broke it the next inning, when Aaron reached on an error and came home on a double by the red-hot Hazle, who bashed his fourth hit and third double of the day. Hazle scored on a single by Crandall, and the Braves led 21-8.

The Cubs had one last offensive gasp left: an RBI double in the bottom of the eighth by Bobby Adams and an RBI single by Chuck Tanner. Banks came up with two on and two out, but grounded out to Mathews at third. The Cubs had reached double digits too – their most prodigious output in over two months – and yet trailed by a gaping margin, 21-10.

The Braves placed one last exclamation point on the game in the top of the ninth. Torre led off with his fourth hit, a triple off new Cubs hurler Elmer Singleton. Mathews followed by launching a home run to make it 23-10.

Singleton set down the next three Braves in order, as did Johnson with the Cubs. The shootout was over.

The Braves had erupted for 23 runs, 26 hits (also a Milwaukee record), and 43 total bases.[10] Every Brave in the lineup – plus the reliever, Johnson – had at least two hits, and six players had at least three. Torre reached base seven straight times and tied a modern major-league record by scoring six runs.[11]

The Braves finished Labor Day with a far quieter three-hit shutout by Bob Trowbridge. The doubleheader sweep, paired with two losses by second-place St. Louis, expanded the Braves' pennant lead to 8½ games.

Aaron's RBI barrage announced that after a tepid August, his bat was back. Down the September stretch, Bryant wrote, Aaron "took hold of the pennant" and "wrestled it to the ground."[12]

While Braves vs. Cubs was no contest, the home-run race between Aaron and Banks tightened up. Banks's two long balls on Labor Day gave him 32 for the season, inching him closer to Aaron's 38. Banks would finish the season just one back of Aaron's 44. The following year, Banks would lap the field with 47 home runs and pluck the NL MVP crown from

Aaron, the first of an unprecedented two straight MVPs for Mr. Cub.

SOURCES

In addition to the sources cited in the Notes, the author also used Baseball Reference.com and Retrosheet.org.

NOTES

1   Cubs vice president David Holland would soon outline a sobering five-point rebuilding plan: All the Cubs needed was a second baseman, a third baseman, a center fielder, a catcher, and a left-handed pitcher. See James Enright, "Holland Posts 5-Point List of Cubs' Needs," *The Sporting News*, September 11, 1957: 47.

2   "Braves Take 2; Lead 8½ Games," *Boston Globe*, September 3, 1957: 15.

3   Irving Vaughan, "Braves Whip Cubs, 23-10, 4-0," *Chicago Tribune*, September 3, 1957: 58.

4   Howard Bryant, *The Last Hero: A Life of Henry Aaron* (New York: Anchor Books, 2010), 199.

5   Hank Aaron and Lonnie Wheeler, *I Had a Hammer: The Hank Aaron Story* (New York: HarperCollins, 1991), 124.

6   Vaughan, "Braves Whip Cubs."

7   Ibid.

8   Ibid.

9   Ibid.

10   Bob Wolf, "Braves Clear Path to Pennant With Bats Instead of Pitching," *The Sporting News*, September 11, 1957: 9.

11   Keith Sutton, "185 Runs Scored on Labor Day Only Six Shy of Majors' Mark," *The Sporting News*, September 11, 1957: 31.

12   Bryant, 202.

BANKS BLASTS THREE

SEPTEMBER 14, 1957
CHICAGO CUBS 7, PITTSBURGH 3
(GAME TWO OF DOUBLEHEADER)

By C. Paul Rogers III

THE CHICAGO CUBS WERE GOING nowhere fast heading into a mostly meaningless Saturday doubleheader on September 14, 1957, with the seventh-place Pittsburgh Pirates. The Cubs were mired in eighth place, 2½ games below the Pirates. Only 6,170 fans showed up to see if the Cubs could close the gap on the Pirates in their effort to escape the National League cellar. One of the only bright spots for the Cubs that summer had been the play of their All-Star shortstop Ernie Banks, who went into the day with 37 homers and 92 runs batted in.[1]

The Cubs promptly lost the first game, 3-1, wasting an outstanding pitching performance by rookie Dick Drott when Jim Brosnan in relief surrendered a ninth inning two-run home run to Frank Thomas to break a 1-1 tie. The Pirates had taken a 1-0 lead off Drott in the fifth inning on an unearned run when center fielder Bob Speake dropped Bill Mazeroski's routine fly ball for a two-base error. Danny Kravitz, who entered the game batting .115, then looped a single to center to drive in Mazeroski for the game's first run.[2] The Cubs demonstrated their futility by loading the bases with no outs in the sixth and then failing to score.

They did manage to tie the score in the bottom of the eighth when Bobby Adams and Ernie Banks hit back-to-back one-out singles to put runners on first and third. Former Pirate Dale Long then grounded to former Cub Gene Baker at short, but Baker's errant throw to first enabled Adams to tie the score.[3] Converted position player Eddie O'Brien, who had

started his first major-league game on the mound, retired Walt Moryn and Eddie Haas to escape further trouble. Then, after Thomas's home run in the ninth, O'Brien retired the Cubs in order in the bottom half to secure a complete-game victory. It was the first, and as it turned out, only win of O'Brien's brief major-league pitching career.[4]

The second game pitted the Cubs' Dave Hillman against the Pirates' rookie side-armer Whammy Douglas. Banks got the Cubs off to a good start in the bottom of the first, cracking a two-out solo home run onto Waveland Avenue behind the left-field bleachers for his 38th home run of the season. He made it Banks 2, Pirates 0 in the bottom of the fourth, homering into the left-field bleachers for his second home run and only the second hit off Douglas. Meanwhile, Hillman had scattered three singles over the first five innings. In the sixth, however, he allowed a one-out single to Paul Smith and then, with two outs, surrendered a single to Baker and doubles to Bob Skinner and Thomas. When the dust settled, Hillman was in the showers, relieved by Brosnan, and the Pirates had forged a 3-2 lead.

To their credit, the Cubs immediately bounced back in the bottom half against Johnny O'Brien, first-game winner Eddie's twin brother, who had come on to pitch after Douglas had been removed for pinch-hitter Dee Fondy the previous inning. O'Brien began by walking Adams and Banks to put himself into immediate hot water. Dale Long was next and stroked O'Brien's second pitch over the right-field bleachers for a three-run homer to put the Cubs back in front, 5-3. O'Brien managed to settle down and retire the side after Long's blast, allowing only a two-out single to Bobby Morgan.

Brosnan retired the Pirates in order in the top of the seventh, including inducing pinch-hitter Roberto Clemente to ground out to second to end the inning. Bob Purkey relieved for Pittsburgh and set down the Cubs in order in their half of the inning. In the eighth Brosnan struck out Smith but, after walking Bill Virdon, left the game due to a sore pitching shoulder.[5] Cubs manager Bob Scheffing brought in the usually reliable Turk Lown, who struck out Baker before allowing a single to Skinner to put the tying run on base with runners on first and second. Lown escaped trouble, however, by striking out Thomas to end the inning.

In the bottom of the inning, Banks greeted Purkey with his third home run of the game, another blast into the left-field bleachers. It was his 40th home run of the year and put him into a tie with Hank Aaron for the league lead.[6] Long then worked a walk. Moryn doubled to drive him in and run the score to 7-3 before Purkey settled down and retired the side.

Lown wrapped up the victory in the ninth by retiring Gene Freese and Mazeroski on groundouts and pinch-hitter John Powers on a pop fly to first. Jim Brosnan, with his inning and two-thirds of scoreless relief, was the winning pitcher, raising his record to 1-1 for the day since he was the losing pitcher in the opener. Ironically, first-game winning pitcher Eddie O'Brien's twin brother Johnny, who surrendered Long's three-run homer in the sixth, was the losing pitcher.[7] The doubleheader split brought the Cubs' record to an uninspiring 54-87. They would go on to win eight of their last 13 games to finish 62-92. That record was good enough to tie the Pirates for seventh place and, depending on whether you view their glass as half-full or half-empty, escape the basement.[8]

Banks ended the second game 3-for-3 with a walk, four runs scored and three batted in. His three-homer game was the second of what would be his

career total of four such games. Already a bona-fide star in his fourth full big-league campaign, he was on the cusp of his two greatest seasons. Playing the demanding shortstop position, he would win the National League's Most Valuable Player Award for fifth-place teams in both 1958 and 1959, and would be well on his way to the Hall of Fame.

SOURCES

In addition to the sources listed in the Notes, the author also consulted Baseball-Reference.com for play-by-play details of the game.

NOTES

1   Banks would finish with 43 home runs, 102 runs batted in, and a .285 batting average. Other bright spots included outfielder Walt Moryn, who slammed 19 home runs and drove in 88 runs while batting .289, and Dale Long, who batted .305 with 21 homers in 397 at-bats. Rookie pitcher Dick Drott would show great promise in winning 15 games against 11 losses with a 3.58 earned-run average.

2   Speake redeemed himself slightly by throwing Kravitz out at second trying to stretch his single.

3   The Cubs had traded Baker and Dee Fondy to the Pirates on May 1 for Dale Long and Lee Walls. The trade was particularly hard on Banks, since Baker, also an African-American, was his roommate and best friend on the team. Ernie Banks and Jim Enright, *Mr. Cub* (Chicago: Follett Publishing Company, 1971), 94.

4   It was also the only game O'Brien started in his big-league career and his only complete game. He had no further decisions in five major-league appearances spread over three seasons and finished with a 3.31 earned-run average. The Pirates had signed him and his twin brother, Johnny, out of Seattle University in 1953.

5   Irving Vaughn, "Cubs Split; Banks Hits Three Homers," *Chicago Tribune*, September 15, 1957: part 2, page 1.

6   Aaron ended the season with 44 home runs to match his uniform number and edge Banks, with 43 homers on the year, for the home-run title.

7   Johnny O'Brien was also attempting to convert to pitching from the infield. He would return to second base the following year with a 1-3 lifetime record and 5.61 ERA from the mound.

8   That is, the Cubs did not finish in eighth place; but on the other hand, no team finished below them.

MUSIAL DELIVERS IN THE PINCH FOR NUMBER 3,000

MAY 13, 1958
ST. LOUIS CARDINALS 5, CHICAGO CUBS 3

By Gregory H. Wolf

STAN MUSIAL DIDN'T EXPECT TO PLAY when his St. Louis Cardinals took on the Chicago Cubs on the North Side of the Windy City. The 37-year-old future Hall of Famer was in perfect health; he was also sitting on 2,999 hits, and with the Redbirds back in the Gateway City the next day, skipper Fred Hutchinson had every intention of letting Stan the Man join an exclusive fraternity in front of his hometown fans. Only an emergency could derail Hutchinson's plan.

In his 17th season, Musial showed no sign of slowing down. He was coming off a spectacular season in 1957, having led the NL in batting average (.351) for the seventh time and in on-base percentage (.422) for the sixth time; he also belted 29 round-trippers and knocked in 100-plus runs for the 10th time. Musial was the big leagues' hottest hitter thus far in '58. He was leading both leagues with a .483 batting average (42-for-87) and a .553 on-base percentage through 22 games, and paced the senior circuit with a .782 slugging percentage. Since he debuted as a mid-September call-up in 1941, one aspect of his hitting had remained constant: his unorthodox stance. "He stands far back from the plate," wrote the *New York Times* about the converted pitcher, "his feet close together, right shoulder pointed toward the pitcher, the bat posed motionless and out farther than any player holds it. His head is bent slightly and turned toward the pitcher."[1] You can't argue with success.

Musial played on Redbird pennant winners in his first four full seasons (1942-1944; 1946; he was in the military in 1945), but the glory years of three World Series championships must have seemed far off in '58. The Cardinals (8-14) had floundered in last place most of the season, but their current five-game winning streak pulled them into sixth, tied with the Philadelphia Phillies, seven games behind the Milwaukee Braves. Skipper Bob Scheffing's fourth-place Cubs (13-13) had dropped their last six to fall out of the top spot. The pitching matchup featured a pair of struggling right-handers. The Redbirds' Sam Jones's 1-3 record (5.28 ERA) dropped his career slate to 38-50 while the Cubs' Moe Drabowksy (1-2, 5.40 ERA) was 16-21 in parts of three seasons.

The first half of the game was a Lee Walls highlight reel. He got the Cubs rolling in the first by doubling and subsequently scoring on Ernie Banks's sacrifice. After a walk, two errors and Irv Noren's single tied the game for the Cardinals in the third, Walls smacked a deep home run, his 10th, over the "wide screen in left," according to sportswriter Edward Prell of the *Chicago Tribune*, to give the Cubs a 2-1 lead.[2] With the bases loaded and one out in the fifth, Walls's sacrifice fly drove in Bobby Thomson for another run.

The Cardinals trailed, 3-1, when Gene Green led off the top of the sixth with a double. After Hal Smith grounded out, Hutchinson motioned to Musial to grab a bat and pinch-hit for Jones. Musial wasn't sitting on the dugout bench; rather, he had been "sunning himself in a green folding chair in the Cardinals' bullpen" along the first-base line, according to the *Tribune*.[3] His afternoon leisure rudely interrupted, Musial sauntered to the plate. After fouling off three pitches to the left and taking two balls, Musial took a cut at the sixth offering and sent a liner into the left-field corner for an RBI double.

Musial's hit brought the modest crowd of 5,692 at Wrigley Field on a Tuesday afternoon to its feet for a rousing standing ovation. The following few minutes were, according to St. Louis sportswriter Bob Broeg, like a scene from "Mack Sennett's old Keystone Kops" routine.[4] Photographers, normally barred from field, poured onto the diamond to record the feat for posterity. While play was interrupted, Musial walked to the pitcher's mound, where he was met by Hutchinson and third-base umpire Frank Dascoli, who gave him the historic ball. After a few ceremonial waves to the crowd, Musial walked back to the dugout, savoring the moment, and was replaced by pinch-runner Frank Barnes.

The Cardinals tied the score, 3-3, two batters later when Don Blasingame, hitless in his last 16 at-bats, singled. After Drabowsky intentionally walked Joe Cunningham to load the bases with one out, Noren's groundout force at second plated Dick Schofield to give the Cardinals the lead. Wally Moon's double to right drove in Blasingame, but Noren was out at home on second baseman Tony Taylor's relay strike to catcher Sammy Taylor.

The final 3½ frames were anticlimactic. Jones was relieved by Billy Muffett, who tossed four scoreless innings, yielding two hits and walking one. He fanned Chuck Tanner to end the game in 2 hours and 27 minutes. The victory went to Jones, whose five-hit, three-run outing was less than stellar. Tagged with the loss, Drabowsky surrendered eight hits and five runs (four earned) in seven innings.

Immediately after the game, Cubs announcer Jack Brickhouse of WGN interviewed Musial on the field. "I was pressing a little the last few games," said Musial in his Western Pennsylvanian accent. "I

was mighty anxious to get this 3000th hit and get it over with."[5] True to his approach to hitting, Musial said he was just trying to make contact and not blast one out of the park. "I went for a base hit. It was a curveball going away, I swung and the next thing I knew I was on second with a double."[6]

Musial became the first major leaguer to reach 3,000 hits since the Boston Braves' Paul Waner in 1942 (though most of his hits were as a Pittsburgh Pirate). Cap Anson (1897), Honus Wager (1914), Nap Lajoie (1914), Ty Cobb (1921), Tris Speaker (1925), and Eddie Collins (1925) preceded them.

The celebration for Musial's accomplishment began in earnest that evening when he and his teammates boarded an Illinois Central Railroad train at Union Station and headed home to St. Louis. He was in a car with close friends from Pennsylvania and Missouri, as well as his wife, Lil. According to the *St. Loui Post-Dispatch*, Musial was presented with a cake with the number 3,000. A team of St. Louis broadcasters gave him a pair of commemorative cufflinks.[7] When the train pulled into Union Station in the Mound City later that evening, about a thousand fans enthusiastically greeted Musial.

Musial continued to pelt the pill the rest of the season, finishing with a .337 batting average (third highest in the league), though his power numbers dropped. For the first time since 1947, he failed to hit at least 20 home runs, finishing with 17, and his 62 runs batted in were a career low. Musial retired after the 1963 season with an NL record 3,630 hits.

SOURCES

In addition to the sources cited in the Notes, the author also accessed Retrosheet.org, Baseball-Reference.com, and SABR.org.

NOTES

1   "Safeties in Numbers: Stanley Frank Musial," *New York Times*, May 14, 1958: 39.

2   Edward Prell, "Musial's 3000th Is Pinch Hit," *Chicago Tribune*, May 14, 1958: C1.

3   Ibid.

4   Bob Broeg, "Musial Eyes .400 Average After Getting 3000 Hits," *St. Louis Post-Dispatch*, May 14, 1958: 4D.

5   "Musial Relaxes, Now That Pressure's Off," *Chicago Tribune*, May 14, 1958: C1.

6   Ibid.

7   The *St. Louis Post-Dispatch* did not mention the names of the broadcasters; however, at the time they were Jack Buck, Harry Caray, and Joe Garagiola. See Broeg.

WALT MORYN'S THIRD BLAST CAPS COMEBACK IN STYLE

MAY 30, 1958
CHICAGO CUBS 10, LOS ANGELES DODGERS 8
(SECOND GAME OF DOUBLEHEADER)

By Gordon Gattie

THE 1958 CHICAGO CUBS STARTED SPRING training with relatively low expectations following their 62-92 record for the 1957 campaign, which tied them with the Pittsburgh Pirates for a last-place National League finish. The Cubs' spring-training roster consisted of 33 players, seven below the major-league roster limit of 40 players. An unidentified source commented that "the Cubs just didn't have enough players worthy to be placed on the parent roster."[1] Their power sources – Ernie Banks, Walt Moryn, and Dale Long – combined for 83 home runs and 252 RBIs in 1957, but their team ERA was second-worst among NL teams, and their pitchers issued more walks than any other NL staff. Manager Bob Scheffing, returning for his second year at the helm, started the season with two rookies playing infield positions, second baseman Tony Taylor and third baseman Johnny Goryl.[2] Even with two rookies as everyday players, and five regular position players who were on different teams the previous year, the Cubs' skipper was confident his squad was better than that of 1957.[3]

The Cubs quickly silenced critics when they won their first four games of the season and finished April in second place with an 8-5 record. Chicago remained among the top teams until mid-May, when a seven-game losing streak dropped the team to fourth place. The Cubs struggled throughout the month, falling to eight games behind the league-leading San Francisco

Giants before their four-game series against Los Angeles started on May 30.

The 1958 Los Angeles Dodgers were adapting to their new environs, having left Brooklyn after the 1957 season.[4] They were without Roy Campanella, their Hall of Fame catcher, who was paralyzed in a vehicle accident during the offseason.[5] The team struggled during its final season in Brooklyn, but still maintained a strong pitching staff led by Don Drysdale and Johnny Podres. The heart of Los Angeles' batting order, Gil Hodges and Duke Snider, was complemented by younger stars like Charlie Neal and Jim Gilliam. Los Angeles was inconsistent during the first two months as the team started developing its new identity.[6] The Dodgers compiled a 5-9 record in April and entered the series in last place, 11 games out of first place. Neither the Cubs nor the Dodgers were expected to win the NL pennant; the 1957 World Series Champion Milwaukee Braves were expected to repeat their performance.[7]

The Cubs won the opening game of the doubleheader, 3-2, on a game-ending single by Sammy Taylor, who plated Moryn to finish a three-run ninth-inning rally. Los Angeles scored an unearned run in the first inning, and Hodges added a solo blast in the fourth. After Chicago was blanked for eight innings, Lee Walls homered to end Podres' shutout bid with one out in the ninth. Moryn doubled home Banks with the tying run, then Taylor delivered his walk-off single.

Left-hander Taylor Phillips started the second game for Chicago. The Cubs had acquired Phillips and Sammy Taylor by trading Eddie Haas, Don Kaiser, and Bob Rush to the Milwaukee Braves during the offseason. Rush pitched solidly in Chicago for 10 years,[8] topping 200 innings eight times and compiling a 110-140 record and 3.71 ERA in 292 starts. Phillips had served mainly in relief roles during his two seasons with Milwaukee, but Scheffing inserted him into the rotation. Scheffing commented in early March, "We'll have only three starters for sure," referring to Dick Drott, Jim Brosnan, and Phillips.[9] During spring training, Chicago pitching coach Freddie Fitzsimmons helped Phillips alter his delivery to improve his effectiveness.[10] The change helped; Phillips was 3-0 with a 2.32 ERA over 54⅓ innings approaching June. Phillips entered the game having won his past two complete-game starts; in his previous appearance, five days earlier, he blanked the Braves on six hits.

Phillips faced veteran right-hander Don Newcombe, who was in his eighth year with the Dodgers. After three 20-win seasons and four All-Star nods, Newcombe was looking to rebound after his first losing season the year before.[11] Newcombe, recognized as one of the top fastball pitchers in the NL, also commanded a curveball and changeup.[12] However, Newcombe struggled from the outset that season, losing his first start while pitching only 3⅓ innings, and was winless (0-4) heading into the game.

The Dodgers grabbed a 4-0 lead in the first inning. After leadoff hitter Gilliam flied out to center field, Gino Cimoli walked, Carl Furillo singled to center, and Hodges delivered a three-run homer to left-center on an 0-and-2 pitch. Later that inning, Joe Pignatano singled home Dick Gray. Newcombe started the game by setting down the Cubs in order. In the second inning, Furillo tripled to right field and scored on Tony Taylor's throwing error to increase Los Angeles' lead to 5-0. The Dodgers padded their lead to six runs in the third inning when Don Zimmer homered. Sammy Taylor led off Chicago's

third inning with the Cubs' first hit and scored when Walls doubled to center field.

Dave Hillman relieved Phillips in the fourth and couldn't prevent the Dodgers from scoring. Leadoff hitter Gilliam walked, advanced to second base on Cimoli's single, and scored on Gray's hit. Now the Dodgers led 7-1. In the bottom of the fourth inning, the first two Cubs batters, Banks and Moryn, delivered consecutive home runs. With one out Sammy Taylor and Tony Taylor singled. Drysdale struck out pinch-hitter Jim Bolger and got Bobby Adams on a popup to shortstop, ending the threat.

In the top of the fifth inning, Dolan Nichols relieved Hillman and prevented the Dodgers from scoring during an inning for the first time in the game. Drysdale continued to stifle Chicago bats with a three up-three down fifth. Nichols faced some trouble in the sixth inning, but Gray's fly ball to center field stranded two runners. In the bottom of the inning four straight Cubs reached with two outs: Sammy Taylor singled, Tony Taylor walked, Bobby Thomson doubled to bring home both runners, and Adams's single narrowed the Dodgers' lead to a single run, 7-6. Don Bessent relieved and got the side out.

Los Angeles got a run back in the seventh when Rube Walker's sacrifice fly plated Neal, who had tripled. Against Ed Roebuck in the bottom of the inning, Moryn and Chuck Tanner smacked back-to-back homers to knot the score. Sammy Taylor tripled to center field but was stranded when Tony Taylor grounded out. Both teams threatened during the eighth inning, getting runners to second, but neither scored.

Neal led off the Dodgers' ninth inning with a single to left field, and moved to second on Zimmer's sacrifice. But two successive pinch-hitters, Pee Wee Reese and Randy Jackson, made outs. In the bottom of the ninth, Sandy Koufax, who had pitched a six-hitter at Pittsburgh two nights earlier, came in for the Dodgers. Banks greeted Koufax with a line-drive single to shortstop. Moryn, who had already hit two solo shots and scored the winning run in the opener, delivered a two-run game-winning blast to give Chicago the doubleheader sweep. The teams had combined for 29 hits, with Ed Mayer of the Cubs obtaining his second win and Koufax taking his first loss of the season.[13]

The Cubs improved upon their previous year, but faded down the stretch, completing the season in fifth place with a 72-82 record, 20 games behind the pennant-winning Braves. Banks led the NL with 47 home runs, 129 RBIs, and a .614 slugging percentage, and won his second straight MVP award with 16 of 24 first-place votes.[14] Moryn earned his lone All-Star nod, finishing second in voting among NL left fielders – voting conducted by players, managers, and coaches that season – behind the Pirates' Bob Skinner.[15] Moryn provided another dramatic finish later that month when his 11th-inning double helped Chicago defeat Philadelphia.[16] The Dodgers finished just behind Chicago with a 71-83 record. Newcombe appeared only twice more for Los Angeles before he was traded to the Cincinnati Redlegs.[17]

SOURCES

Besides the sources cited in the Notes, the author consulted Baseball-Almanac.com, Baseball-Reference.com, Retrosheet.org, and the following:

Golenbeck, Peter. *Wrigleyville: A Magical History Tour of the Chicago Cubs* (New York: St. Martin's Griffin, 1999).

James, Bill. *The New Bill James Historical Abstract* (New York: The Free Press, 2001).

Ward, Geoffrey C., and Ken Burns, *Baseball: An Illustrated History* (New York: Alfred A. Knopf, 1994).

NOTES

1   Ed Prell, "Cubs Have Few Clippings – Just Five Make Headlines," *The Sporting News*, April 2, 1958: 16.

2   Edward Prell "Cubs to Open With Rookies at 2d and 3d," *Chicago Tribune*, April 5, 1958: 31.

3   Edward Prell, "'1958 Cubs Better than 1957' – Scheffing," *Chicago Tribune*, April 14, 1958: 51.

4   Dick Young, "It's All Over, Fellows, the Dodgers Go West," *New York Daily News*, October 9, 1957: 3.

5   Roscoe McGowen, "Campy's Career Ended by Auto Accident," *The Sporting News*, February 5, 1958: 11.

6   Joe King, "Dodgers Dead? Jackie Stirs Up Lively Debate," *The Sporting News*, May 21, 1958: 5.

7   Bob Wolf, "Braves Should Win – Maybe Coast," *The Sporting News*, March 26, 1958: 3.

8   Edward Prell, "Cubs Trade Rush to Braves! Get Pitcher Taylor Phillips," *Chicago Tribune*, December 6, 1957: 60.

9   Edward Prell, "Moe in Army, Cubs in Stew," *Chicago Tribune*, March 5, 1958: 41.

10 Edward Prell, "Taylor Made Pitch Suits Cubs," *Chicago Tribune*, March 7, 1958: 40.

11 Frank Finch, "Dodgers Launch Training Thursday," *Los Angeles Times*, February 16, 1958: 75.

12 Bill James and Rob Neyer, *The Neyer/James Guide to Pitchers: An Historical Compendium of Pitching, Pitchers, and Pitches* (New York: Fireside Books, 2004), 323.

13 Edward Prell, "Sox Win 2, Cubs Take 2 in 9th Inning Before 37,799," *Chicago Tribune*, May 31, 1958: 19.

14 Hy Hurwitz, "Banks Landslide Winner in N.L. Most Valuable Player Vote," *The Sporting News*, December 3, 1958: 21.

15 Oscar Kahan, "Players Pick All-Stars on '58 Marks, Not Reps," *The Sporting News*, July 2, 1958: 6.

16 Richard Dozer, "Sox Lose, 5-0; Cubs Beat Phils in 11th," *Chicago Tribune*, July 15, 1958: 33.

17 Frank Finch, "Dodgers Get Bilko; Newcombe Traded," *Los Angeles Times*, June 16, 1958: 63.

TRADED TO CUBS, DON CARDWELL TOSSES NO-HITTER IN FIRST APPEARANCE

MAY 15, 1960
CHICAGO CUBS 4, ST. LOUIS CARDINALS 0
(GAME TWO OF DOUBLEHEADER)

By Gregory H. Wolf

PUTTING ON HIS CHICAGO CUBS UNIFORM for the first time, recently acquired pitcher Don Cardwell just wanted to secure his spot in the rotation. He did more than that – he pitched the game of his life.

The Cubs were already in disarray a month into the 1960 season. Skipper Charlie Grimm, who had guided the club to pennants in 1932, 1935, and 1945, had been hired in the offseason to end the club's streak of 13 consecutive nonwinning seasons and second-division finishes, but his third stint with the North Siders lasted only 17 days. He was dismissed with a 6-11 record, replaced by the team's broadcaster, former big-league pilot Lou Boudreau. Heading into a Sunday doubleheader with the St. Louis Cardinals to conclude a four-game series, the Cubs (8-13) were floundering in sixth place, 7½ games behind the San Francisco Giants. The once mighty Redbirds were in the midst of their worst stretch of baseball in four decades and seemed destined to post their fifth losing season in the last six years. Mired in seventh place, the Cardinals (9-15) had dropped their last eight games and remarkably had lost all 12 games they had played on the road thus far in '60. Those inglorious streaks ended when the Cardinals Larry Jackson spun a four-hitter to win the first game of the twin bill, 6-1.

Starting the second game of the doubleheader for the Cubs was 24-year-old right-hander Don Cardwell, whom the team had acquired two days earlier in a multiplayer trade with the lowly Philadelphia Phillies. In his fourth season in the majors, the stout, 6-foot-4 North Carolinian had a record of 17-26, including 1-2 in 1960. In his last start, nine days earlier in the Los Angeles Coliseum, Cardwell held the Dodgers hitless for five innings before Duke Snider tripled to lead off the sixth. Forced to depart at the end of that frame with a strained arm, he settled for a no-decision. Making his second consecutive start for the Cardinals was right-hander Lindy McDaniel, a former swingman who had been converted into a full-time reliever in 1959.

Wrigley Field was packed with 33,543 spectators, the largest crowd in the Friendly Confines thus far in '60 and more than three times the eventual average game attendance that season. It was a beautiful, 80-degree afternoon with perfect conditions to play two, which must have made Cubs star Ernie Banks even more excited. In between games, Banks was presented his second consecutive NL MVP trophy by league President Warren Giles in a ceremony at home plate.

Catcher Del Rice had no idea what to expect from his batterymate, the hard-throwing Cardwell, still recovering from his sore arm. "Before the game I asked him what he threw," said the 16-year-veteran backstop. "[H]e said a curve, slider, fastball, and changeup. I told him I had never seen his slider, so we won't use it."[1] After dispatching leadoff hitter Joe

Cunningham on a weak infield grounder, Cardwell walked Alex Grammas. Few could have imagined that he'd be the only Cardinals baserunner of the game.

With afternoon shadows making it difficult for batters on both teams to pick up the ball, the game unfolded as a scoreless pitchers' duel. Cardwell mowed down the Cardinals in the first five frames, fanning five. McDaniel, who would emerge in the course of the season as one of the most effective relievers in the big leagues and finish third in Cy Young Award voting, hurled almost as well, yielding two innocuous singles.

On a day when the infamous wind at Wrigley Field was blowing out toward Lake Michigan, located about a mile east of the ballpark, bats were unusually quiet. The Cubs got on the board in the bottom of the fifth when Frank Thomas hit a one-out single, raced to third on Rice's single, and scored on Jerry Kindall's grounder. In the sixth, Banks connected for his seventh home run of the season, a two-run shot to left field, driving in Richie Ashburn, who had walked to start the inning, to make it 3-0. Mr. Cub was en route to leading the NL in round-trippers (41) for the second time in three seasons and would surpass the 40-home-run mark for the fifth time in six campaigns. In the seventh, the Cubs tacked on their final run on Ashburn's double, plating Kindall, who had singled and swiped second.

Cardwell had not yielded the semblance of a hit through seven, but had two scares in the eighth. Hot-hitting Daryl Spencer, batting .408 (29-for-81) in his last 19 games, led off with a sharp grounder. Second baseman Jerry Kindall darted to his right and made what sportswriter Richard Dozier of the *Chicago Tribune* called a "sensational stop."[2] He scooped up the low bounder and threw across his body to erase Spencer by a hair. Leon Wagner followed with another tricky grounder. First baseman Ed Bouchee, also acquired from the Phillies along with Cardwell, added his name to the highlight reel by fielding the ball flawlessly and scampering to first to beat the speeding Wagner. To the plate stepped

the venerable 39-year-old Stan Musial, pinch-hitting for Curt Flood. Just about a year earlier, Stan the Man spoiled a different Cubs pitcher's quest for immortality. Musial doubled with two outs in the seventh to break up Glen Hobbie's no-hitter, but this time the future Hall of Famer fanned on four pitches. "I was swinging at the sound," he quipped about Cardwell's heater. "When I got up there he was throwing bee-bees."[3]

A hush fell over Wrigley Field as Cardwell took the mound to start the ninth. Pinch-hitting for Hal Smith, Carl Sawatski led off with a deep blast to right field. Sawatski was well known for his towering home runs, and this shot "appeared to be labeled a hit," opined Dozier, but fleet George Altman sprinted to snare the ball just in front of the double green doors at the wall.[4] "That ball Sawatski hit to Altman shook me up the most," said Cardwell later. "Sawatski used to catch me at Philly last year. ... He knows pretty well what I throw."[5] The first hard-hit ball of the game drew Rice to the mound for a brief conference with Cardwell, who had not pitched more than six innings in any of his previous five starts in '60. Redbirds manager Solly Hemus was pulling out all the stops and sent another slugging pinch-hitter to the plate, George Crowe. Big George had belted 31 round-trippers as a Cincinnati Red in 1957 but this time he hit a routine fly to deep center. Just an out away from a no-hitter, Cardwell fell behind against the second consecutive batter and for just the third time in the entire game. With the count full, Cunningham hit a Texas Leaguer to shallow left. Walt Moryn sprinted and, according to Dozier, made a "miraculous one-handed shoe-top catch" to secure the last out and preserve Cardwell's unlikely no-hitter.[6] "If I'd have missed that last catch I'd have been begging for an error," quipped the former All-Star.[7]

Evoking a pennant-clinching or World Series-winning game, fans rushed onto the field in a scene described by the *Tribune* and the *St. Louis Post-Dispatch* as chaotic. Cardwell was besieged by youngsters as he frantically tried to make his way from the diamond to the clubhouse.

Cardwell retired 26 consecutive batters and needed only 93 pitches, including 15 in the final frame, to complete his no-hitter in 1 hour and 46 minutes.[8] "He was able to keep the ball down all the way," said Rice of the hurler. "He was really humming at the finish."[9] Described as "blistering fast" by Dozier and possessing a heater comparable to the Dodgers' Don Drysdale's, according to Boudreau, Cardwell struck out seven while fashioning the third of his 17 career shutouts.[10] McDaniel went the distance, yielding just seven hits to absorb the loss. He made 717 more appearances, all but five as a reliever, before tossing his next complete game, on July 10, 1973, as a New York Yankee at the age of 37.

"I threw almost exclusively fast balls in the early innings," said Cardwell. "That's always been my best pitch. Later, I began to use a few changeups and some curves when they got used to looking at that fast one."[11]

Cardwell, like all other pitchers (as of 2017) didn't match the Reds' Johnny Vander Meer's 1938 feat of consecutive no-hitters. Given some extra time off, Cardwell struggled in his next start, 10 days later, yielding five runs (four earned) and lasted just 2⅔ innings in a loss to the Reds at Crosley Field. That outing inaugurated a rough stretch for Cardwell – a 6.81 ERA in 38⅓ innings spread over eight appearances. He finished the season with a combined slate of 9-16 with the league's second-highest ERA (4.38) in 205⅓ innings.

SOURCES

In addition to the sources cited in the Notes, the author also accessed Retrosheet.org, Baseball-Reference.com, and SABR.org.

NOTES

1   Richard Dozier, "'Did It With My Fast Ball' – Cardwell," *Chicago Tribune*, May 16, 1960: C1.

2   Richard Dozier, "New Cub Pitches No-Hitter; Aided by 4 Fine Plays," *Chicago Tribune*, May 16, 1960: 1.

3   Neal Russo, "Cardwell Faces Just 28 Cards in 4-0 No-Hitter," *St. Louis Post-Dispatch*, May 16, 1960: 20.

4   Dozier, "New Cub Pitches No-Hitter; Aided by 4 Fine Plays."

5   Dozier, "'Did It With My Fast Ball' – Cardwell."

6   Dozier, "New Cub Pitches No-Hitter; Aided by 4 Fine Plays."

7   Dozier, "'Did It With My Fast Ball' – Cardwell."

8   Pitch count from Dozier, "New Cub Pitches No-Hitter; Aided by 4 Fine Plays."

9   Russo.

10 Dozier, "New Cub Pitches No-Hitter; Aided by 4 Fine Plays."

11 Dozier, "'Did It With My Fast Ball' – Cardwell."

DON ZIMMER'S GAME-WINNING HIT IN 14TH OVERCOMES DOMINANT PERFORMANCE BY SANDY KOUFAX

MAY 28, 1960
CHICAGO CUBS 4, LOS ANGELES DODGERS 3
(14 INNINGS)

By Brian M. Frank

ON APRIL 8, 1960, THE LOS ANGELES Dodgers traded infielder Don Zimmer to the Chicago Cubs for three minor leaguers and $25,000. Just four days later, on Opening Day, Zimmer hit a home run off Don Drysdale at the Los Angeles Coliseum in his first at-bat against his former team. After the home run, Zimmer began to struggle, and by the time the Dodgers and Cubs met in the Windy City in late May, he was hitting just .189 for the season. Since the Opening Day home run, he had gone hitless in 13 at-bats against the Dodgers. Zimmer seemed like an unlikely hero entering the second game of a three-game series against the Dodgers at Wrigley Field.

After taking game one of the series, the defending World Series champion Dodgers sent lefty Sandy Koufax to the mound to try to extend their five-game winning streak. Koufax had started the season slowly, winning just one of five starts, with the win being a dominant complete-game one-hitter in his previous start, against the Pirates. However, it didn't seem that it was meant to be Koufax's day as he began warming up to take the Wrigley Field mound. Dodgers manager Walter Alston later told the *Los Angeles Times*, "Sandy couldn't get loose warming up, and I was about ready to call on Ed Rakow."[1] Koufax was eventually able to get himself ready to pitch and he delivered a memorable performance.

Koufax struggled to find his control in the early going. After he walked a pair of Cubs in the first, Frank Thomas grounded a single up the middle to score George Altman and give the Cubs the lead, 1-0. The Dodgers were able to score in the third and sixth innings off rookie left-hander Dick Ellsworth. In the third, Maury Wills reached when Ernie Banks was unable to throw the speedster out from deep in the hole at short. Wills stole second and scored on Jim Gilliam's double into the left-field corner. Gilliam then swiped third and scored on a Tommy Davis single to put Los Angeles ahead, 2-1. The Dodgers added to their lead in the sixth when Davis circled the bases after hitting one into the right-field gap. The official scorer ruled the play a triple, and charged an error to center fielder Richie Ashburn on his errant throw to the cutoff man.

The Cubs were able to scratch out a run off Koufax in the sixth inning with nary a hit. After walking two batters, Koufax induced Ernie Banks to hit into what looked like an inning-ending double play, but second baseman Charlie Neal's relay to first sailed past Gil Hodges and into the visitors' dugout, scoring Ashburn and cutting the Dodgers lead to 3-2.

Ellsworth and Koufax battled through a classic pitchers' duel. Ellsworth had allowed only three runs on six hits when he was lifted in the eighth inning for a pinch-hitter, while Koufax continued to dominate

Cubs hitters as the game wore into its latter stages. He steamrolled into the ninth inning having allowed only two hits, Frank Thomas's run-scoring single in the first and a harmless second-inning single by Jerry Kindall.

Koufax started the ninth by making Ed Bouchee his 10th strikeout of the game and then getting Ernie Banks to fly out to right field. With the Cubs down to their last out, Frank Thomas, who had one of Chicago's two hits off Koufax, stepped to the plate. As the *Chicago American* described it, "His first pitch to Thomas was a strike, and then bingo! Thomas drove Sandy's second serve onto the left-field catwalk for a score-tying homer."[2] The *Los Angeles Times* bemoaned Thomas's success against Koufax, writing, "Here's a guy who had a two-hitter going until Thomas, a .130 sticker against the Dodgers this season, came through with the crusher."[3] Thomas's eighth homer of the year knotted the game, 3-3. After Earl Averill reached on an error by left fielder Tommy Davis, Koufax struck out Don Zimmer for his 11th strikeout and sent the game to extra innings.

Chicago had a bit of a rally in the 10th, when Koufax walked two batters, one of them intentionally, but Jerry Kindall was thrown out attempting to steal third for the second out, and Walt Moryn grounded out to first baseman Gil Hodges to end the inning. Despite the fact that he threw 132 pitches through nine innings, Koufax continued to dominate in the extra frames. The *Chicago Tribune* wrote that he "breezed through the 11th, 12th, and 13th without the challenge of a baserunner, he struck out four in that time – evidence that he still was strong."[4] But the Cubs bullpen matched Koufax's brilliance. Seth Morehead pitched a hitless ninth and 10th, and Don Elston came in to start the 11th and shut out the Dodgers for four innings.

Having thrown 182 pitches, Koufax finally began to show signs of tiring at the start of the 14th inning.[5] He walked Ed Bouchee to start the frame for his eighth walk of the game, causing Dodgers manager Walter Alston to make a mound visit. Alston decided to leave his young lefty in the game to face Cubs slugger Ernie Banks. Koufax walked Banks on four

pitches, to put runners at first and second with no outs. With Frank Thomas, who had two of the Cubs' three hits, including the game-tying home run in the ninth, looming on deck, Alston removed Koufax after an amazing 193 pitches. Koufax had allowed only three hits, while recording 15 strikeouts with nine walks. He received a standing ovation from the Wrigley Field faithful as he strolled to the dugout.

Koufax was replaced by right-handed reliever Ed Roebuck. The first hitter to face Roebuck, Frank Thomas, whiffed on a failed bunt attempt, allowing Dodgers catcher Johnny Roseboro to fire the ball to second base and catching Ed Bouchee too far off the bag. So Bouchee made "the only good reaction he could," according to Cubs manager Lou Boudreau, and took off for third base, sliding in just ahead of the relay.[6] Roebuck then gave Thomas an intentional pass to load the bases on three walks. With the infield and outfield playing in to try to cut off the game-winning run at the plate, Earl Averill lined out to left fielder Tommy Davis for the first out, and the runners held.

Up to the plate stepped Don Zimmer, or as the *Chicago American* called him, "a Dodger discard."[7] Zimmer, now hitless in 17 at-bats against the Dodgers since his Opening Day home run, was facing his longtime friend, pitcher Ed Roebuck. The two had been roommates while coming up through the Dodgers farm system and had also played winter ball together. They were such close friends that they were married on the same day when they played for the Elmira Pioneers. The two pals wanted to have a dual wedding ceremony at home plate, but since Roebuck was Catholic, he and his bride eventually decided to be married in a church, while the Zimmers were married at the Elmira ballpark.[8] Now they faced each other with the game hanging in the balance.

Zimmer hit the first ball he saw from his old friend and sent it slicing down the right-field line. The *Chicago Tribune* reported that the "well hit fly … was out of Frank Howard's range – a drive that would have been a double if the Cubs had needed it."[9] The Wrigley Field crowd, 13,605 strong, celebrated as Ed Bouchee crossed the plate with the winning run.

It took the Cubs fourteen innings to get their fourth hit of the game, but it was just enough. In the end, a game that had been dominated by Sandy Koufax came down to a pair of old buddies, Ed Roebuck and Don Zimmer, with the "Dodger discard" getting the best of his old pal.

SOURCES

In addition to the sources cited in the Notes, the author also accessed BaseballReference.com, Retrosheet.orgm, SABR.org, and *The Sporting News* archive via Paper of Record.

NOTES

1   Frank Finch, "The Bull Pen: Dodgers Begin 19-Game Home Stand, Face Cardinals Tonight," *Los Angeles Times*, May 30, 1969.

2   James Enright, "Cubs Whip L.A. in 14th; Tuttle Blast Beats Sox: 4-3 Margin Gained on Zimmer Hit," *Chicago American*, May 29, 1960.

3   Frank Finch, "Zimmer's Hit in 14th Beats L.A., 4-3: Koufax Fans 15, But Loses Heart-Breaker as Cubs Snap Dodgers' Five Game Streak," *Los Angeles Times*, May 29 1960.

4   Richard Dozer, "Sox Lose 4-3; Cubs Beat Dodgers in 14th: Zimmer's Single Whips Former Mates, 4 to 3," *Chicago Tribune*, May 29, 1960.

5   None of the newspaper articles from the game tell Koufax's pitch count, so all pitch count references are from Baseball-Reference.com's game logs at baseball-reference.com/boxes/CHN/CHN196005280.shtml .

6   Dozer.

7   Enright.

8   Don Zimmer with Bill Madden, *Zim: A Baseball Life*, (New York: Total/Sports Illustrated, 2001), 70-71; Don Zimmer with Bill Madden, *The Zen of Zim; Baseball's Beanballs and Bosses*, (New York: Thomas Dunne Books, 2004), 194.

9   Dozer.

SANTO'S BIG DAY

JUNE 28, 1961
CHICAGO CUBS 16, CINCINNATI REDS 5
(GAME ONE OF DOUBLEHEADER)

By Alan Cohen

"The Cubs had 25 base runners, and (the public-address) announcer grew hoarse saying, 'Next batter ...'" [1]

THE LEAGUE-LEADING CINCINNATI REDS completed a four-game series at Wrigley Field with a doubleheader on June 28, 1961, and found that the seventh place Cubs were not without life. Despite their lowly station, the Cubs (25-41) had won five of their prior nine meetings with the league leaders. In the first game of the twin bill, the Cubs had their best offensive output of the season, banging out 17 hits and winning handily, 16-5.

Slumping Ron Santo emerged from his streak of 14 at-bats without a hit and slammed two homers and a pair of singles, with seven RBIs. Prior to the game, he decided to skip batting practice, hoping that it would change his luck. In 1961 the Cubs seemed to have as many managers as the proverbial cat had lives. Owner Philip Wrigley was rotating coaches that season and on June 28, the head coach was Elvin Tappe. Tappe went along with the idea. After his success in the game, Santo said, "I not only bypassed batting practice today, but I'm going to do the same thing tomorrow, because I'll never forget those seven RBIs." [2]

Glen Hobbie (4-9) pitched for the Cubs and did not need any help from the bullpen. He was matched against Bob Purkey of the Reds. Santo's first blast came in the first inning off Purkey and gave Chicago a 3-0 lead. Al Heist, who came into the game batting a lowly .186, led off for the Cubs with a single and moved to second when Don Zimmer singled. Santo followed with a three-run homer and Purkey had yet to retire a batter. Purkey had entered the game with a 9-3 record but was done after the Cubs scored in each of their first four turns at bat.

In the second inning, Sammy Taylor tripled and scored when Hobbie grounded into a double play. The Reds, down 4-0, appeared to have something going in the third inning. Eddie Kasko reached on a two-base error by Cubs rookie left fielder Billy Williams and advanced to third on a fly ball by Don Blasingame. However, when the Reds tried a safety squeeze with Vada Pinson batting, Hobbie grabbed the bunt grounder and trapped Kasko between home and third base. The pitcher threw to third baseman Santo, who tagged out Kasko as he tried to get back to the base.

In the Cubs' third inning, the first batter again reached safely, as Santo, in his second plate appearance, singled to left field. That brought up George Altman, who came into the game with a .333 batting average. Altman scored Santo with a double that fell in right-center field between Pinson and Frank Robinson and went to the wall. The Cubs had a 5-0 lead.

The Reds' bats were not silent in the game, but Hobbie maintained order. In each of the first three innings, the Reds had baserunners but failed to score. They broke through in the fourth. Gus Bell led off with a triple and a homer by Gordie Coleman made the score 5-2.

The Cubs wasted no time extending their lead to 8-2. With two out in the bottom of the fourth, Heist walked and advanced to third on a double by Zimmer. That brought Santo to the plate. A Purkey pitch eluded the grasp of catcher Johnny Edwards and Heist scored on the passed ball. Santo then hit his second homer of the game, this time a two-run blast, and after recording the last out of the inning, Purkey was given the rest of the game off.

By the beginning of the sixth inning, the contest had been decided, as the Cubs had a seven-run outburst in the fifth inning to stretch their lead to 15-2. Jay Hook had taken over the pitching from Purkey and absorbed the beating as Reds manager Fred Hutchinson was not about to overuse his staff in a game that was out of control – especially as there was the second game of the doubleheader yet to be played. After a bases-loaded walk to Heist scored the first run of the inning, Zimmer's double produced a pair. Santo followed with a two-run single, and after an Altman double (his second of the game) put two runners in scoring position, Billy Williams completed the rally with a single that plated Santo and Altman.

But the Cubs continued to marvel in front of the Wednesday afternoon crowd of 12,785. Coleman, in a bid for another extra-base hit, sent a long fly ball to center field with one out in the top of the sixth inning. Heist leapt high in the air to grab the ball before it could land in the ivy.

In the seventh inning, the Reds scored their third run of the game as rookie catcher Edwards, in his first big-league start, led off the inning by tagging a ball inside the foul pole in right field for his first major-league homer. After a two-out double by Elio Chacon, Jerry Lynch drove in the Reds' fourth run with a single to center field.

The teams completed their scoring on solo home runs by repeat offenders. Altman hit his second homer of the game with one out in Chicago's half of the seventh inning and Coleman hit his second with one out in the Reds' eighth inning. Coleman's

blast was his 14th of the season and brought his batting average for the season to .279, a noticeable improvement since earlier in the season, when his average at one point was.234. His performance in this game brought his average for June to .323 with 6 homers and 21 RBIs in 28 games.

Hobbie's complete-game win brought his record to 5-9. He would finish the season at 7-13. Purkey (9-4) was charged with the loss, and would finish at 16-12 for the Reds in 1961. The following season was the best of his career, when he went 23-5.

The Cubs went on to win the second game of the doubleheader, 7-2, giving the Reds their first doubleheader loss of the season. The next afternoon, the Cubs made it three in a row with a 15-8 thrashing. It gave the Cubs a 3-1 series win and brought their season's record against the Reds to 8-4. Nevertheless, the Reds still led the National League by 2½ games and went on to win the pennant by four games over the second-place Dodgers. In the World Series, they lost to the Yankees in five games. The Cubs, who won the season series from the Reds, 12-10, found the rest of the league harder to handle and finished the season in seventh place with a 64-90 record. They were 86 games and 55 years away from the National League pennant.

The 21-year-old Santo, in his first full season (he had appeared in 95 games in 1960 after being called up on June 26), went on to appear in 154 of the 156 Cubs games (there were two ties). Over his first 11 full seasons with the Cubs, he played in at least 150 games each year. During his career, he was awarded five consecutive Gold Gloves (1964-1968) and was named to nine All-Star teams. He was inducted into the Hall of Fame in 2012.

Altman's 4-for-5 performance took his average to .346. In the month of June, he was spectacular, garnering player-of-the-month honors with 10 homers, 29 RBIs, and a .355 batting average. He finished the season at .303, good for 10th in the league. In 1961, Altman had a breakout year, posting career highs in doubles (28), triples (12), homers (27), and RBIs (96). He was named to the first of two consecutive All-Star teams.

Hook, who pitched the last four innings of the game for Cincinnati and yielded eight runs, would finish the season at 1-3 and spend the next season with the expansion New York Mets. He gained a degree of lasting fame when, after the Mets had lost their first nine games, he pitched them to victory on April 23 with help from two players who played with him in the game at Wrigley Field on June 28, 1961 – Elio Chacon and Gus Bell.

It was a beautiful day for baseball and the Cubs did play two but, alas, Ernie Banks was on the bench with an ailing knee. He had been out of the lineup since June 22, and did not return until June 30, missing seven games.

SOURCES

In addition to the sources cited in the Notes and Baseball-Reference.com, the author used:

Smith, Lou. "Sad Day for NL Leaders as Cubs Sweep, 16-5, 7-2," *Cincinnati Enquirer*, June 29, 1961: 39.

Tharp, Fred. "Cuff Stuff," *Mansfield* (Ohio) *News-Journal*, June 29, 1961: 28.

United Press International. "Cubs Crush Reds Twice as Altman, Santo Star," *Morning Star* (Rockford, Illinois), June 29, 1961: D-1.

NOTES

1   Edward Prell, "Cubs Win 16-5, 7-2: North Siders Humble Pace-Setting Reds – Blast 17 Hits in First Game," *Chicago Tribune*, June 29, 1961: 6-1.

2   Robert Goldensteen (Associated Press), "Practice Makes Perfect?" *Chillicothe* (Ohio) *Gazette*, June 29, 1961: 18.

One of the most beloved Cubs in franchise history, Hall of Famer Ron Santo was a nine-time All Star third baseman and won five Gold Glove awards. From 1990 through the 2010 season, Santo was a color commentator for Cubs broadcasts. (Photo by Mark Rucker/Transcendental Graphics, Getty Images)

"THE HUMAN STRIKEOUT MACHINE": KOUFAX FANS 18 IN THE WINDY CITY

APRIL 24, 1962
LOS ANGELES DODGERS 10, CHICAGO CUBS 2

By Gregory H. Wolf

"I LOST TRACK," REPLIED SANDY KOUFAX when asked if he knew how many batters he struck out. "[I] didn't know I'd tied the record until everybody came off the bench to shake my hand."[1] Koufax fanned 18 to equal Bob Feller's nine-inning record set in 1938 and match his own personal best three seasons earlier.[2] "Strikeouts are nice to have, particularly in a jam, and they are going to come to a pitcher who throws hard," noted Koufax, "but I wouldn't trade a 20-game season for all the strikeout records in the books."[3]

Skipper Walter Alston's fourth-place Dodgers (8-5) were looking for some momentum when they arrived in Chicago for a three-game set to conclude a 10-game road swing. The Cubs, who at 3-9 were tied with the Milwaukee Brewers and better only than the winless, expansion New York Mets, seemed like the perfect victim. The North Siders were in the second campaign of club owner Philip K. Wrigley's bizarre experiment with the college of coaches and its revolving "head coach," a position currently occupied by El Tappe.

By the start of the 1962 season, Koufax had long been known as one of the hardest throwers in baseball history, but he was not yet the consistently dominating pitcher who combined power with control. "[S]ometimes erratic and sometimes unbeatable," according to the *Pasadena Independent*, the 26-year-old Koufax had a pedestrian 54-53 record in parts of seven seasons, but had averaged more than a strikeout an inning.[4] The southpaw whom

sportswriter Frank Finch of the *Los Angeles Times* lauded as the "human strikeout machine" was coming off a breakout season.[5] In 1961 he won 18 games, whiffed an NL-record 269 batters, and set another standard by fanning at least 10 batters in a game 11 times to bring his career total to 31. Koufax's success could be attributed to his newfound control, his hitherto most glaring weakness. On backup catcher Norm Sherry's recommendation, Koufax began throwing more changeups, which made his heater seem even faster and his knee-buckling curve even more devastating.[6] Koufax had emerged victorious in two of his first three starts in '62, but seemed to suffer from fatigue late in games. "I never pace myself," said Koufax about his approach. "I pitch as strong as hard as I can. If I run into trouble, I know there are a few guys in the bullpen who can come in and do the job."[7]

A crowd of only 8,938 patrons made its way to the intersection of Clark and Addison to take in an afternoon of baseball on a cool yet sunny Tuesday afternoon at Wrigley Field. After one inning, it looked as though it could be a long afternoon for both clubs' hitters. Cubs right-hander Don Cardwell, who had posted a 15-14 record and by some modern metrics was the best pitcher in baseball in 1961, fanned two in a 1-2-3 inning while Koufax fanned the side.[8]

Cardwell, who had lost all three of his starts with a 7.62 ERA thus far in '62, came undone in the second. Duke Snider, the 35-year-old gray-haired former Brooklyn icon, led off with a walk, moved up on a wild pitch, and scored on Tommy Davis's single. After Johnny Roseboro stroked a double that center fielder Lou Brock lost in the sun, Willie Davis's sacrifice fly gave the Dodgers a 2-0 lead.

Koufax continued his pitching clinic the next few frames. He fanned nine of the first 10 batters he faced, and had registered 10 strikeouts by the end of the fourth. Ron Santo collected the Cubs' first safety, a fourth-inning double. "Sandy's curve was marvelous in the early innings," said All-Star batterymate Roseboro. "But as the shadows came along, we started going more with the fastball."[9]

Meanwhile the Dodgers continued to whack Cardwell. After Wally Moon reached on a wind-aided single with two outs in the third, Snider hit a liner that eluded right-fielder Bob Will's shoestring attempt, and Moon scored. The Dodgers added another run, in the fourth, on Andy Carey's line drive round-tripper to left field, his first as a Dodger after spending his first 10 seasons in the AL. Los Angeles blew the game open in the fifth when Tommy Davis, en route to leading the NL in RBIs with 153, belted a three-run home run with Jim Gilliam and Moon on base via singles for a seemingly insurmountable 7-0 lead.

Koufax hit a bump in the fifth. Billy Williams reached second when his deep fly bounced off center fielder Willie Davis's glove. The play was generously ruled a double and not an error. Koufax loaded the bases on walks to Will and Elder White, then fanned Moe Thacker and pinch-hitter Andre Rodgers. One pitch from escaping the jam, Koufax issued his third free pass of the inning, to Brock, to force Williams across the plate. "I was afraid in the fifth that I might be tiring," said Koufax after the game.[10] He was obviously laboring and admitted that he started "aiming the ball."[11]

The Dodgers made it 8-1 in the seventh when Tony Balsamo, who had relieved Cardwell to start the sixth, balked with bases loaded, forcing Wills home. Tappe protested the ruling and was ejected. Sportswriter Richard Dozer of the *Chicago Tribune* noted that Balsamo had Wills picked off at third; however, first-base umpire Stan Landes overruled

the decision with his balk call.[12] The Dodgers' scoring explosion culminated in the ninth when Snider walloped a two-run homer after Moon had singled.

After his hiccup in the fifth, Koufax was much less overpowering in the next three frames, yielding two singles, issuing a walk, and fanning three. Slugger Billy Williams, whose 25 homers in '61 catapulted him to the NL Rookie of the Year Award, led off the final inning with a solo home run for the Cubs' second run. "It was a good pitch to a left-hander's strength," joked Koufax after the game. "A high inside curve, and he hit it good. If I could take two pitches back, I'd take that one and the ball to Brock [in the fifth]."[13]

The Dodgers bullpen remained silent in the ninth. It was the Brooklyn native's game to complete. No doubt Alston also knew that his prized southpaw still had a chance to tie his own record for most strikeouts in a game. Koufax punched out Will and White to raise his strikeout total to 17 and tie Dizzy Dean (1933) and Art Mahaffey (1961) for the most strikeouts in a day game in the NL. Thacker followed with what appeared to be a routine pop fly to first baseman Tim Harkness, who had replaced Moon to start the frame. Playing first for just the ninth time in his big-league career, Harkness lost the ball in the swirling wind coming off Lake Michigan, one mile to the east, and watched the orb drop in fair territory just feet away him for a single. Koufax unexpectedly had another shot at the record. To the plate stepped rookie Moe Morhardt, who had led the Class-B Northwest League in hitting with a .339 average the previous year. Koufax struck him out looking to end the game in 2 hours and 41 minutes.

As expected, teammates euphorically congratulated Koufax, who yielded six hits and walked four to go along with his 18 strikeouts. "I was trying to make them hit it," he said. "I just wanted to get the game over."[14] Frank Finch of the *Times* reported that Koufax threw 144 pitches, including 96 for strikes.[15] Koufax seemed unconcerned by that number, claiming that the total was "not high" for a fastball pitcher, while he soaked his bulging, swollen elbow in ice after the game.[16]

Koufax's record-tying strikeout performance quieted detractors who had claimed that his 18 punchouts in a complete-game, seven-hit victory over the San Francisco Giants on August 31, 1959, were the product of the "lousy" lights and poor visibility at the LA Coliseum, where the Dodgers played their home games from 1958 through 1961.[17] Koufax himself scoffed at comparing the games, noting only that there were more than 60,000 spectators in LA cheering for the Dodgers while fewer than 9,000 fans were at Wrigley Field.

Koufax suffered a career-threatening injury, not to his elbow or shoulder, but to his index finger, in his next start, on April 28, against the Pirates. In his BioProject bio on Koufax, SABR member Marc Z. Aaron writes how Koufax was hit by a pitch on his left index finger, causing a trauma that developed into Raynaud's phenomenon, a circulatory condition.[18] Koufax played through the numbness and even tossed his first of four no-hitters, on June 30. But the pain proved too intense. Koufax ultimately landed on the DL in mid-July and missed nine weeks. He returned in late September, but pitched ineffectively as the Dodgers lost to the San Francisco Giants in a three-game playoff for the pennant. Koufax finished with a 14-7 slate, and led the NL in ERA (2.54) for the first of five consecutive seasons.

SOURCES

In addition to the sources cited in the Notes, the author also accessed Retrosheet.org, Baseball-Reference.com, SABR.org, and *The Sporting News* archive via Paper of Record.

NOTES

1   United Press International, "Trying to Make 'Em Hit – Koufax," *Los Angeles Times*, April 25, 1962: III, 3.

2   Warren Spahn also struck out 18 batters, but those came in 15 innings in a route-going loss, 3-1, to the Cubs as a member of the Boston Braves on June 14, 1952, at Braves Field.

3   Frank Finch, "Koufax Whiff Pace Fastest in History," *The Sporting News*, May 23, 1962: 6.

4   "Koufax Fans 18 For Record," *Pasadena Independent*, April 25, 1962: 16.

5   Frank Finch, "Koufax Fans 18 Cubs, Equals Record," *Los Angeles Times*, April 25, 1962: III, 1.

6   Finch, "Koufax Whiff Pace Fastest in History."

7   UPI, "Sandy Aimed It in Bad 5th Inning," *Pasadena Independent*, April 26, 1962: 54.

8   In his fifth big-league season, Cardwell posted a 15-14 record in 1961 which improved his career record to 40-54. He also logged 259⅓ innings and led the NL with 38 starts. By one contemporary metric, WAR (wins above replacement, which attempts to quantify the value of a player by measuring the number of wins the player added to his team compared with what a replacement player would add), Cardwell was the most valuable pitcher in baseball with a 6.1 WAR. Jack Kralick of the Minnesota Twins also had 6.1 WAR.

9   UPI, "Sandy Aimed It in Bad 5th Inning."

10   Ibid.

11   UPI, "Trying to Make 'Em Hit – Koufax."

12   Richard Dozer, "Koufax Fans 18 Cubs to Tie Own Mark," *Chicago Tribune*, April 25, 1962: IV, 1.

13   UPI, "Sandy Aimed It in Bad 5th Inning."

14   UPI, "Trying to Make 'Em Hit – Koufax."

15   Finch, "Koufax Fans 18 Cubs, Equals Record."

16   UPI, "Trying to Make 'Em Hit – Koufax."

17   Finch, "Koufax Whiff Pace Fastest in History."

18   Marc Z. Aaron, "Sandy Koufax," BioProject, Society for American Baseball Research. sabr.org/bioproj/person/e463317c.

HOME RUN DERBY ON A COLD DAY IN MAY

MAY 29, 1962
MILWAUKEE BRAVES 11, CHICAGO CUBS 9

By John Bauer

THOUGH THE CALENDAR HAD YET TO turn to June, the Chicago Cubs and Milwaukee Braves were already having seasons to forget. Despite Glen Hobbie's outdueling Warren Spahn in a 2-1 Cubs victory the day before on Memorial Day, Chicago was mired near the bottom of the league. The one club keeping the 15-29 Cubs out of last place was the hapless expansion New York Mets. The Braves were only marginally better at 19-25, losers of 7 of 10. For the May 29 contest in Chicago, Milwaukee sent 23-year-old Bob Hendley to the mound against the Cubs; Hendley was 2-5 with a 3.69 ERA. The Cubs countered with veteran Bob Buhl (3-2, 4.91 ERA), who had pitched for the Braves since their first season in Milwaukee in 1953 before joining Chicago in an April 30 trade.

Only 3,468 fans weathered the blustery conditions at Wrigley Field, as 25-mile-per-hour winds blew toward all fields.[1] The wind would matter as it often does at Wrigley Field, as the meager but hardy crowd would be treated to the "biggest home run carnival of the National League season so far."[2] Much of the attention would land squarely on Ernie Banks; however, the power surge he would display almost did not happen. The Cubs first baseman had been out of the lineup since Moe Drabowsky beaned him four days before in Cincinnati. Though he took batting practice, Banks was not called upon to pinch-hit in the Memorial Day game. He rejoined the lineup for this game, with the hope of adding needed pop to the Cubs. Only George Altman had homered for the Cubs in their prior eight games.[3]

After a scoreless first inning, the Braves started the fireworks in the top of the second. With Mack Jones on first base and one out, Joe Adcock came to the plate. Adcock had recently missed time with a severe cold and then a pulled muscle in his right leg.[4] Against his former teammate Buhl, Adcock launched his eighth home run of the season to give Milwaukee a 2-0 lead. The winds continued to favor the Braves when Joe Torre hit his first home run of the season, a solo shot. Milwaukee took that lead into the bottom of the frame, and cleanup hitter Banks would lead off. In his first at-bat since Drabowsky's plunking, "Banks was a strange figure at the plate, decked out in a new batting helmet rather than the liner he has worn steadfastly."[5] Banks quickly rediscovered his touch and sent Hendley's pitch to the wall in center field for a double. Unfortunately for the Cubs, his inning would end at the keystone spot as three successive outs ended the second.

Gus Bell popped up to Chicago shortstop Andre Rodgers to open the third inning. Buhl walked Roy McMillan and struck out Eddie Mathews. With two out, the Braves third appeared likely over when Aaron hit a "routine roller"[6] toward Rodgers. The play proved not to be routine. Rodgers, a former Brave "whose presence at shortstop has become a growing liability,"[7] misplayed the ball and Aaron was safe. Buhl walked Jones to load the bases with first-inning home-run hero Adcock now up. Buhl's wild pitch allowed McMillan to score and moved up Aaron and Jones. With first base now open, the Cubs gave a free pass to Adcock. Torre singled to Billy Williams in left field, plating Aaron and Jones for a 6-0 lead. Buhl's struggles continued as he surrendered a three-run blast to rookie Amado Samuel. That home run, which extended the Braves lead to 9-0, was the first of Samuel's major-league career. Hendley struck out to end the inning, but six unearned runs after Rodgers' error appeared to put the game out of reach.

Rodgers led off the Cubs third and reached when Mathews muffed his grounder. Bobby Smith struck out while pinch-hitting for Buhl, whose day ended with a clear numeric theme: three innings pitched, three earned runs, three walks, three strikeouts, and three home runs allowed. (His record would also fall to 3-3.) Lou Brock singled to left field. Both baserunners scored when Ken Hubbs doubled to right field. Williams grounded out to Samuel, bringing Banks to the plate with two outs and Hubbs on third. Banks drove Hendley's pitch out of Wrigley and onto Waveland Avenue[8] to cut the deficit to 9-4. After Altman singled to center, Braves manager Birdie Tebbetts brought in Don Nottebart from the bullpen. Nottebart ended the inning by striking out Ron Santo.

Tony Balsamo assumed pitching duties for the Cubs in the fourth, and his first batter, Bell, doubled to right field. Bell, recently acquired from the Mets, scored two outs later on a Mathews groundout to Banks. The Braves held that 10-4 lead until the bottom of the fifth. Following Hubbs' leadoff strikeout, Williams hit his 10th home run of the season off Nottebart, and extended his hitting streak to 15 games.[9] Banks equaled Williams's feat with a solo shot of his own, pulling the Cubs within 10-6. After Altman singled to center, Tebbetts made his second pitching change, calling on Lew Burdette to smother the Cubs' hopes of getting back into the game. Burdette did his part in the fifth, inducing back-to-back groundballs to Mathews from Santo and pinch-hitter Moe Thacker that ended the inning.

Burdette led off the Braves' sixth with a strikeout against Balsamo. Bell doubled for the second time against Balsamo and took third base on a wild pitch

to McMillan. Bell scored on McMillan's fly ball, and the Braves now led 11-6. Balsamo continued to struggle, loading the bases with walks to Mathews, Aaron, and Jones. Richard Dozer wrote in the *Chicago Tribune*, "It was clear [Cubs head coach] Lou Klein[10] was trying to get by with as few hurlers as possible…."[11] Klein relieved Balsamo from his pitching struggles, and Bob Anderson got the final out with a fly ball from Adcock.

The Cubs whittled away at the deficit with solo home runs during the later innings, but came up short. Banks hit a one-out blast in the seventh, his third of the game and 14th of the season. It was the third time in Banks's career that he hit three home runs in a game. The previous two times were against the Pirates at Wrigley, in 1955 and 1957.[12] Bob Will led off the eighth with a four-bagger of his own against Burdette; however, the Cubs could not build off that opening and the game was 11-8, Milwaukee, headed to the ninth. Barney Schultz allowed a two-out walk to Torre, but kept the Braves from padding their lead. Facing the heart of the Cubs' order, Burdette struck out Williams and got Banks on a grounder to Mathews. With one out remaining, Altman slugged his 11th home run of the season to make the score 11-9. Altman's effort was the Cubs' sixth homer of the afternoon, the first such power surge by Chicago since an April 1955 game in St. Louis.[13] Tebbetts sent Bob Shaw to the mound against Santo, who flied out to left fielder Howie Bedell for the game's final out.

In addition to being notable for statistical reasons, the day had historical significance as well. The Cubs announced that longtime scout John "Buck" O'Neil was signed to join the major-league coaching staff. Part of the Cubs organization since 1956, O'Neil became the first African-American coach for a major-league club. The move was prompted in part to avoid the need to obtain permission from opposing teams to allow O'Neil to remain in the dugout during games. To get around this, the club signed O'Neil to a coaching contract. While a historical marker of sorts, general manager John Holland said that O'Neil would not be part of the head-coaching rotation but "will continue the scouting duties among members of his own race."[14] Sometimes progress comes with small steps.

The Cubs had fallen behind early, chipping away but coming up short. "The only thing that may have saved the Braves here Tuesday was that the Cubs ran out of time," a Milwaukee reporter wrote.[15] Indeed, there was some disappointment that the Cubs' slugging ended up for naught. "Wrigley [F]ield yesterday was the scene of the greatest waste of power since the last time a space shot fizzled at Cape Canaveral," observed the *Tribune's* Richard Dozer.[16] At 15-30, there was a lot about the Cubs season that might have seemed wasted.

SOURCES

In addition to the sources cited in the Notes, the author consulted baseball-reference.com, retrosheet.org, and SABR.org.

NOTES

1   Bob Wolf, "Braves Lose Homer Duel to Cubs but Still Win, 11-9," *Milwaukee Journal*, May 30, 1962: 18.

2   Ibid.

3   Richard Dozer, "Hobbie Wins! Defeats Braves' Spahn in 4 Hit Mound Duel, 2-1," *Chicago Tribune*, May 29, 1962: 3-1, -2.

4   Bob Wolf, "Ailing Joe Adcock Adds Robust Bat to Anemic Attack," *The Sporting News*, June 9, 1962: 18.

5   Richard Dozer, "Cubs Hit Six Homers; Beaten, 11 to 9," *Chicago Tribune*, May 30, 1962: 4-1.

6   Ibid.

7   Ibid.

8   Ibid.

9   "Cubs Hit Six Homers": 4-2.

10   The Cubs opened the season without a single designated manager. Klein shared head-coaching duties with El Tappe and Charlie Metro.

11   Dozer, "Cubs Hit Six Homers": 4-2.

12   Dozer, "Cubs Hit Six Homers": 4-1.

13   Ibid.

14   Edgar Munzel, "Cubs Sign O'Neil as Coach, First Negro in Majors," *The Sporting News*, June 9, 1962: 20.

15   Wolf, "Braves Lose Homer Duel."

16   Dozer, "Cubs Hit Six Homers."

Statue of Ernie Banks outside of Wrigley Field. Banks clubbed 40+ home runs in five of six seasons (1955–1960) and twice led the NL in round-trippers. (Photo courtesy of Gregory H. Wolf)

THE JUNIOR CIRCUIT SHOWS ITS POWER

JULY 30, 1962
AMERICAN LEAGUE 9, NATIONAL LEAGUE 4

SECOND ALL-STAR GAME OF SEASON

By Alan Cohen

"I guess it shows they play ball in that other league too." National league manager Fred Hutchinson after the AL defeated the NL 9-4 in the second All-Star game of 1962[1]

CHICAGO'S WRIGLEY FIELD HOSTED THE best of baseball on July 30, 1962, in front of a crowd of 38,359. The All-Star Games had started back in 1933 when the players congregated on Chicago's South Side to watch the American League defeat the National League at Comiskey Park.

The National League had dominated the game in recent years, and had won the first of two 1962 encounters, 3-1, at Washington. The American League lead in the series now stood at 16-15 with one tie. The NL's starting lineup featured such stalwarts as Willie Mays, Orlando Cepeda, and Roberto Clemente. Hank Aaron and Frank Robinson started the game on the bench. Some of the luster was gone from the game because beginning in 1959 two All-Star Games were held each summer. Also, the game being played on Monday (rather than the usual Tuesday) meant that some of the players had traveled long distances overnight, and some of the pitchers had no rest and would be unavailable. By late in the game at Wrigley, there had been so many replacements and so many missing stars that "Who's on First" became a statement rather than a question. In a game punctuated by four National League errors

and three American League homers, the American League emerged with a 9-4 win.

Selected to throw out the ceremonial first pitch was Mrs. Arch Ward, widow of the *Chicago Tribune* sportswriter who came up with the idea for the All-Star game 29 years earlier.

Johnny Podres was the starting pitcher for the National League, a league that boasted future Hall of Fame pitchers Don Drysdale, Juan Marichal, Sandy Koufax, Bob Gibson, and Warren Spahn. Podres was a last-minute replacement for Drysdale, who was unavailable, having pitched for the Dodgers the day before. The American League countered with rookie Dave Stenhouse (10-4) of the Washington Senators, although the league could boast of the likes of Whitey Ford, Jim Bunning, Jim Kaat, and Camilo Pascual. Pascual had been the intended starter, but when the Twins ace reported that he had a sore elbow, manager Ralph Houk made the last-minute change. Stenhouse, who had originally been signed by Cubs scout Lenny Merullo, said, "The first I knew I was going to start was when Ralph Houk tapped my shoulder on the bus to Wrigley Field. 'You're going nine today,' he said."[2]

In the early innings, it looked as though the National League would continue its dominance, but the AL's Stenhouse was able to elude catastrophe. In the first inning, Stenhouse hit Dick Groat with a pitch and yielded a single to Mays. A wild pitch advanced the runners and a walk to Cepeda loaded the bases with one out but Stenhouse retired the next two batters.

After Podres pitched two scoreless innings, allowing a leadoff hit to Minnesota's Rich Rollins but little else, the National League broke through against Stenhouse in the bottom of the second. Following a two-out double by Podres, Pittsburgh's Groat singled and the NL led 1-0.

Art Mahaffey of Philadelphia took over on the mound for Podres in the third inning and the American League, not at a loss for sluggers in recent years, started to pound away. Although Mickey Mantle was scheduled to start and had put on quite a show in batting practice, a knee strain suffered in the game the day before made him unable to run. Manager Houk scratched him from the starting lineup. Nevertheless, the starting outfield of Leon Wagner, Roger Maris, and Rocky Colavito (Mantle's replacement) had combined for 134 homers in 1961, and between them would provide three extra-base hits.

The first show of power, however, came from an unlikely source. Mahaffey's first batter was Pete Runnels of Boston, who came on as a pinch-hitter for Stenhouse. The 1960 American League batting champion, not known for his power, homered off Mahaffey on a 3-and-2 pitch. The next inning, after a walk to Minnesota's Earl Battey, Wagner of the Angels, who had begun his career with the Giants in 1958, hit a two-run homer to extend the lead. The lead could have been greater. After the Runnels homer in the third, Billy Moran of the Angels reached on an error by Groat. Then, with two outs, Colavito smashed a drive to left field that was dropped by the Dodgers' Tommy Davis. Davis recovered in time to fire a bullet to cutoff man Ken Boyer who gunned down Moran, trying to score from first on the play.

Pitching the next three innings for the AL was another largely unheralded arm who had been added to the squad days before the game. Ray Herbert of the White Sox had had an unremarkable career to that point, but he had a sinkerball that produced outs. He also was supported by superlative defensive work.

Six of the outs he recorded were via groundballs including double plays off the bats of Cepeda and John Roseboro. He was also helped by a defensive gem by Wagner. The left fielder charged an opposite-field fly ball off the bat of George Altman and made a sliding catch for the third out of the fourth inning.

The AL added to its lead while the NL bats were dormant. Bob Gibson had replaced Mahaffey on the mound and pitched a scoreless fifth inning. In the sixth inning with two out, Tom Tresh of the Yankees doubled off Gibson to drive in pinch-runner Al Kaline with his team's fourth run, but was thrown out after rounding second base a bit too far. In the next inning when Dick "Turk" Farrell took the mound for the National League, the AL built the cushion to six runs. A one-out walk to Brooks Robinson was followed by a fly ball to short center field by second baseman Billy Moran. Aaron charged the ball, grabbed it and threw to first, doubling off Robinson, only to have umpire Ken Burkhardt rule that Aaron had trapped the ball. After Maris forced Moran at second for the inning's second out, Colavito smacked a three-run homer.

The National League would chip away at the 7-1 lead when a sledgehammer was required. In the bottom of the seventh, Hank Aguirre was in his second inning on the mound for the AL. With one out, Richie Ashburn, who was finishing up his career with the Mets, singled and advanced to third on a double by Frank Bolling. The infield was playing back and conceded a run when Groat grounded out to shortstop.

The next inning provided an opportunity for the crown to cheer its hometown heroes. With one out, Ernie Banks stepped to the plate. He had entered the game in the fifth inning, replacing Cepeda at first base. Banks tripled to deep center field and scored on a groundout by his Chicago teammate Billy Williams, but the deficit was still four runs going into the ninth inning.

Marichal had taken the mound for the NL in the eighth inning and pitched a scoreless inning before sloppy play in the ninth inning resulted in the final two runs for the AL. Yogi Berra led off for the AL as a pinch-hitter and grounded to third base. NL third baseman Eddie Mathews, after bobbling the ball, overthrew first base, allowing Berra to advance to second. Mathews was charged with two errors on the play. With Maris at the plate, Bobby Richardson, pinch-running for Berra, advanced to third on a wild pitch. A double by Maris scored Richardson, and Maris subsequently scored on a fly ball by Colavito.

In the ninth inning, Roseboro of the Dodgers came to plate as the first batter. He had entered the game in the fourth inning and was hitless in his first two at-bats. Roseboro connected and sent a Milt Pappas pitch over the right-field fence. It was the only hit and run off Pappas, who retired the next three batters to secure the win for the American League.

Herbert was awarded the win and Mahaffey absorbed the loss as the AL's 9-4 win put its record in All-Star contests at 17-15-1. The following season, the major leagues reverted to the one-game format.

SOURCES

In addition to the sources cited in the Notes and Baseball-Reference.com, the author used:

Drebinger, John. "The A.L. Breathes Again," *New York Times*, July 31, 1962: 21.

Burnes, Bob. "A.L. HR Biceps Flex Again in Star Romp," *The Sporting News*, August 11, 1962: 7.

Teague, Robert L. "American League Wins All-Star Game at Chicago, 9-4, on Three Home Runs," *New York Times*, July 31, 1962: 21.

NOTES

1   Steve Guback. "Power Display Recaptures AL Prestige," *Washington Evening Star*, July 31, 1962: A-13.

2   Steve Guback. "Stenhouse Receives the Surprise of His Life," *Washington Evening Star*, July 31, 1962: A-13.

BANKS BLASTS BOUNCE KOUFAX, BUT CUBS CRUMBLE

JUNE 9, 1963
LOS ANGELES DODGERS 11, CHICAGO CUBS 8

By John Bauer

WHEN THE CHICAGO CUBS AND LOS Angeles Dodgers met on June 9, 1963, at Wrigley Field, the game provided a matchup of early-season league leaders. After winning the first two games of a three-game series, Los Angeles occupied the top spot in the NL standings, mere percentage points ahead of the Cardinals. Despite the first-place standing, manager Walter Alston saw room for improvement, saying, "It's good to be up there, but I'm still not satisfied with the way we have played so far. We've goofed up too much and haven't hit consistently."[1] The Cubs, after a miserable 1962 season, found themselves among the early leaders, tied with the Giants just one game back. General manager John Holland claimed that he had predicted the Cubs would become a first-division team, but he added, "I'm not going to say yet that we'll win the pennant. I'd like to, but I just can't."[2] The Cubs' turnaround was attributed to improved pitching and fielding,[3] but Holland also extended praise to manager Bob Kennedy. About his skipper, Holland said, "Kennedy gives the players leadership and confidence. I don't know how he does it, but they're a different ball club with him."[4] Cubs partisans were taking notice, too. Over 35,000 packed Wrigley Field for the Sunday-afternoon tilt, giving the Cubs their largest gate since a July 4, 1960, doubleheader with San Francisco.[5]

Based on the mound matchup, a pitchers' duel seemed a likely outcome. Starters Sandy Koufax and Dick Ellsworth sported 8-3 records and their respective ERAs of 1.45 and 1.51 led the NL. Events proved otherwise. Portending the hits to come, Maury Wills led off the game with a single to center off Ellsworth. With Jim Gilliam at the plate, Wills took off for second and claimed his 14th stolen base of the season; he claimed third base, too, when catcher Dick Bertell's low throw missed its mark. Gilliam lofted a fly to left fielder Billy Williams, allowing Wills to complete his trip around the bases for the first run of the game. Ellsworth settled down, giving up only a Tommy Davis single before getting out the inning. In the Cubs first, Koufax looked like Koufax, striking out Lou Brock and Ken Hubbs to start. He walked Williams, but Ron Santo's fly ball to center fielder Ron Fairly ended the frame. Koufax provided some offense in the top of the second. With two on and one out, he singled to right field as the ball got past Brock "as he tried for the shoestring catch."[6] The hit scored Bill Skrowron, and John Roseboro also crossed the plate when Ellsworth was charged with an error for failing to cut off Brock's throw. Roseboro's run made the score 3-0.

Ernie Banks led off the bottom of the second with a line-drive home run into the left-field bleachers. Banks's effort seemed like an anomaly when Koufax struck out Nelson Mathews and Bertell after Andre Rodgers grounded out to keep the score at 3-1. In the top of the third, Tommy Davis got back that run when he lofted Ellsworth's pitch over the left-center-field wall for his fifth home run of the campaign. In turn, the Cubs cut into the Dodgers' lead in the bottom of the fourth on back-to-back doubles by Rodgers and Mathews.

Koufax took a 4-2 lead into the bottom of the fifth, but the inning proved to be good for the home team. The inning started well enough when Koufax fanned Ellsworth for his sixth strikeout of the game. Brock drove the ball into left field for a double, and he might have scored on Hubbs's single but Tommy Davis nailed Brock at the plate. With Hubbs taking second on the throw, Williams lined the ball to the right-center-field wall for a run-scoring double.[7] With the Cubs within one run, Alston emerged from the dugout to talk with Koufax. After taking the first pitch, Santo powered the next pitch high into the left-field bleachers, giving the Cubs the lead, 5-4. Koufax's day ended after Banks hit a first-pitch blast onto the left-field catwalk. With his ace now trailing 6-4, Alston called for Ed Roebuck. The Dodgers reliever found the elusive third out when Rodgers grounded to Dick Tracewski.

In the Dodgers' sixth, it was Ellsworth's turn to be chased from the game. Tommy Davis opened the inning with a liner to right field for a single. Right fielder Altman was unable to reel in Howard's fly ball, which fell for a single. Ellsworth loaded the bases with none out when he walked Skowron, but steadied himself to strike out Roseboro. Tracewski tapped the ball back to Ellsworth, who, while getting the force at home, "might have turned it into a side-retiring double play with a quicker toss."[8] Likely not wanting to lose the scoring opportunity, Alston brought in Lee Walls to hit for Roebuck. When Ellsworth's first two pitches were wide of the plate, Kennedy opted for a change of his own.[9] Don Elston assumed pitching duties in mid-batter, but could not avoid allowing the walk; Walls trotted to first base while Howard crossed the plate. The walk pulled the Dodgers within a run, and the Dodgers took back the lead when Wills rapped a pitch into left-center field for a bases-clearing double and an 8-6 Dodgers lead. After missing 11 games, Wills had been rolling since rejoining the club on June 4 in Houston; an 11-for-22 run would see his batting average rise from

.252 to .290. Elston finally got the third out when Gilliam lined out to Banks.

The Cubs failed to score in the bottom of the sixth, but that did not prevent the inning from being eventful. Larry Sherry assumed pitching duties for the Dodgers. Mathews hit a grounder back to Sherry for the first out, and Bertell followed with a single. Kennedy sent Bob Will up to hit for Elston. Will launched a fly ball toward the right-field fence. As Howard positioned himself to make the catch, a fan greeted him with a shower of peanuts to the face. The ball dropped for a single that would be the 202nd and final hit of Will's major-league career.[10] Expecting Howard to make the catch, Bertell had held up and only advanced to second. The Dodgers believed Wills passed Bertell on the basepath, leading to an argument during which umpire Shag Crawford tossed the Dodgers' Walls. After all the drama, the Cubs stranded Bertell and Will, and the game remained 8-6, Dodgers.

Los Angeles added insurance runs against Cubs pitcher Lindy McDaniel in the seventh. Fairly and Tommy Davis both singled to right field. With runners at the corners, Howard's line drive to left field scored Fairly. On the throw, Williams nailed Tommy Davis at third base for the first out. Willie Davis, who had taken Skowron's spot in the batting order in the sixth, made it four Dodgers singles in a row with a shot to center field. Davis had made it to second base (and Howard to third) when Hubbs did not take the relay for which he would be charged an error. The hit parade ended only because Roseboro was intentionally walked to load the bases. With Wally Moon batting for Tracewski, McDaniel prolonged his personal misery with a wild pitch to score Howard. McDaniel's ball-four pitch to Moon hit home plate for another wild pitch and another Dodgers run as Willie Davis scored from third. After Bertell gunned down Moon at second base on an attempted steal, Kennedy made the switch to Cal Koonce with Sherry coming to the plate. Koonce struck out Sherry for the third out.

Behind 11-6, the Cubs could not dent the Dodgers' lead in the seventh or eighth. Chicago scored twice in the ninth when, with Williams on first base, Banks blasted Sherry's first pitch over the catwalk screen in left field. It was a case of "too little, too late" as Los Angeles won, 11-8. While Banks's ninth-inning home run did not affect the result, it was his third of the game. Banks now had five home runs and nine RBIs in the last week, a run of success he credited to his wife's eye doctor. According to Banks, Dr. Morris Fridell told Banks after Mrs. Banks's recent appointment that he had been taking his eye off the ball.[11] On this day, Banks had no problem seeing the ball but he could not prevent the Dodgers from sweeping the Cubs.

SOURCES

In addition to the sources cited in the Notes, the author also consulted baseball-reference.com, retrosheet.org, and SABR.org.

NOTES

1 Frank Finch, "Wills' Hitting Sparks Dodgers, 9-5," *Los Angeles Times*, June 9, 1963: D-1.

2 "Holland Called Shot on Rise of 1963 Cubs," *Chicago Tribune*, June 9, 1963: 2-3.

3 Edward Prell, "35,743 Watch Series Sweep by L.A., 11-8," *Chicago Tribune*, June 10, 1963: 3-1.

4 "Holland Called Shot."

5 Prell.

6 Prell: 3-2.

7 Ibid.

8 Ibid.

9 Ibid.

10 Will played his last major-league game on June 12 against San Francisco. He finished the year in Salt Lake City.

11 Jerome Holtzman, "Banks' Batting Binge Gives Bruins Exactly What Doc Ordered," *The Sporting News*, June 22, 1963: 6.

187 PITCHES, 10 WALKS, AND 12 STRIKEOUTS IN 10 INNINGS: JUST A NO-HITTER FOR JIM MALONEY

AUGUST 19, 1965
CINCINNATI REDS 1, CHICAGO CUBS 0
(10 INNINGS)

By Gregory H. Wolf

LET'S PONDER THESE STATISTICS FOR A moment: 187 pitches in a 10-inning complete game, 10 walks and 12 punchouts, one hit batter, at least 13 full counts, bases filled twice, 10 stranded runners, and three outfield flies. Together they produced Cincinnati Reds speedballer Jim Maloney's no-hitter, arguably the most astounding in big-league history.[1]

"It was unbelievable," Maloney's batterymate, three-time All-Star Johnny Edwards, told the author. "He walked 10 batters and every time I looked up it seemed like there was a man in scoring position. He was so wild, I had to do everything just to block the ball. He threw 187 pitches. He was worn out after the game, and I was right there with him."[2] Queen City sportswriter Bill Ford seemed equally astonished by Maloney's perseverance against the hard-hitting Chicago Cubs: "When trouble loomed – and there was plenty – he called on his resourcefulness to wriggle free."[3] Windy City scribe Richard Dozer was flabbergasted by the big right-hander's in-game Jekyll-and-Hyde act, quipping, Maloney "put together an incongruous blend of untouchable hurling and frequent brushes with trouble."[4]

The decade of the 1960s was an era defined by hard throwers, like Sandy Koufax and Don Drysdale, Jim Bunning, and Sam McDowell. Often overlooked, Maloney's name doesn't carry the cachet of the aforementioned; however, he was a threat to no-hit

an opponent every time he took the mound. As a 23-year-old, he enjoyed a break-out season in 1963, winning 23 and leading the NL in whiffs per nine innings (9.5), the only time the legendary Koufax didn't pace the circuit over a seven-year stretch (1960-66). Already in 1965, Maloney had twice flirted with a no-no. On Opening Day, April 19, he held the Milwaukee Braves hitless for seven frames before yielding a leadoff single to Denis Menke to start the eighth, and settled for his third career one-hitter. In a tense pitchers' duel against the New York Mets on June 14 at Crosley Field, he tossed 10 no-hit innings. In the 11th, he surrendered a heartbreaking leadoff home run to Johnny Lewis and lost, 1-0, yielding just two hits while fanning a career-high 18 with just one walk.

Skipper Dick Sisler's fourth-place Reds (65-52) pulled into Wrigley Field for a twin bill on Thursday, August 19, as part of a 13-game road swing. Just 3½ games behind the Milwaukee Brewers, the Reds still harbored pennant aspirations. That was not the case for the eighth-place Cubs (56-65), losers of four straight for skipper Lou Klein, who had replaced Bob Kennedy in mid-June.

As the crowd of 11,342 settled into their seats at the Friendly Confines, 34-year-old right-hander Larry Jackson worked a scoreless first, surrendering a two-out single to Vada Pinson, en route to his fourth season of at least 200 hits in the last seven years. One of the era's most dependable workhorses, Jackson was a four-time All-Star coming off an NL-leading 24 victories in '64. Eight days earlier he had beaten the Reds at Crosley Field to record his 150th career victory (along with 129 losses) and sported an 11-14 slate thus far in '65.

With a little luck, sportswriters might have been praising Jackson's tough gamesmanship in the following day's newspapers instead of Maloney. Jackson was steady, mixing heaters and breaking balls to keep the Reds, the highest-scoring and best-hitting team in the league, off-balance. Through six innings, Jackson had yielded only four baserunners, all by singles. With one out in the seventh, Frank Robinson hit what appeared to be a home run, but the swirling wind coming off Lake Michigan, about one mile to the east, held up the ball, which according to Bill Ford, caromed "high off the leftfield fence" for a triple; the former MVP was stranded at third.[5] The Reds threatened in the ninth when Pete Rose reached on Ernie Banks' fielding error at first base followed by Pinson's single. With no outs, successive deep blasts, by Robinson and Gordy Coleman, were slowed down by the wind. Jackson retired Deron Johnson, who was leading the NL with 97 RBIs, to end the threat.

Jackson's efficiency contrasted sharply with Maloney's wildness. After Maloney retired the first six batters he faced, he began the third inning by walking two and then filled the bases with his third walk, with two outs. Then he retired Billy Williams, who entered the game with 18 hits in his last 45 at-bats. A fastball pitcher, Maloney did not normally struggle with his control like McDowell or Koufax (early in his career), averaging about 3.5 walks per nine innings over a four-year stretch (1963-66) when he recorded 200 or more strikeouts each season, but this game was different. Two more free passes followed in the next frame, but Maloney fanned Don Kessinger to end the frame. Finding his groove, Maloney struck out the side in the fifth and then set the Cubs down in order in the sixth and seventh. Maloney commenced the eighth by committing a

cardinal sin, issuing a leadoff walk to Jackson, who advanced a station on Don Landrum's sacrifice bunt. After Doug Clemens was retired on the Cubs' first popup to the outfield, Dick Sisler came to the mound for the first time all afternoon to discuss what to do with Williams at bat and Banks on deck. They decided to walk the left-handed-hitting Williams intentionally to face righty Banks, who whiffed.

Depending on one's perspective, the bottom of the ninth was probably the most exciting or most disappointing inning of the game. Maloney plunked Ron Santo to start the frame, then walked Ed Bailey. Glenn Beckert fouled off two pitches trying execute a sacrifice bunt, then struck out looking. Another walk to Jackson, with two outs, loaded the bases, but Maloney retired Landrum on a popup to short to end the frame and send the game into extra innings. "So after nine innings, I was wondering plenty," said Maloney when asked if he thought about a no-hitter or another heartbreaking loss like the one to the Mets. "Larry Jackson was pitching just as good as I was."[6]

Jackson, en route to his seventh of 10 consecutive seasons with at least 200 innings pitched, was back on the mound for the 10th. After Edwards grounded to first, the wind died down as Chico Cardenas came to the plate. The All-Star shortstop hit a liner to left field that looked as if it might be curving foul. Described as a "radar" by Richard Dozer in the *Chicago Tribune*, the ball hit just above the yellow line in foul territory, caromed off the screen, and bounced back onto the field for a home run to give the Reds the only run of the game.[7] "Cardenas homered," said Maloney, "but it couldn't be any closer to going foul instead of fair."[8]

Maloney took the mound to start the 10th, three outs away from an unlikely no-hitter, yet victory was far from assured given the hurler's troubles in the previous two frames. The stout 6-foot-2, 200-pound Californian was determined to make it interesting. He issued a leadoff walk to Clemens, who entered the season batting .243 in fewer than 400 career at-bats. With the heart of the order coming up, Maloney earned his no-no by retiring Williams on a fly to left field, then inducing Banks to hit what Bill Ford called a "hard chopper" to Cardenas, who initiated a routine 6-4-3 double play to end the game in 2 hours and 51 minutes.[9]

"I wasn't real sharp today," Maloney told Cubs TV announcer Lou Boudreau in an onfield interview after the game. "I made some good pitches when I had to. When I had to come in, they popped it up. I had a lot of walks." Visibly exhausted and out of breath, Maloney added, "Edwards told me, said in the last three innings my fastball's sinking and tailing real good."[10]

Maloney's gem was just the third extra-inning no-hitter in major-league history. George "Hooks" Wiltse of the New York Giants fired the first, on July 4, 1908, followed by Fred Toney of the Reds on May 2, 1917; both were also 10 innings. The definition of a no-hitter was altered in September 1991 when the Committee for Statistical Accuracy declared it a game of nine innings or more that ends with no hits. That decision removed 12 no-hitters that went into the 10th inning, including Maloney's 1965 masterpiece against the Mets which he lost. Following his no-no against the Cubs, newspapers widely reported that Maloney became just the fourth pitcher to author two no-hitters in a season, joining Johnny Vander Meer, Allie Reynolds (1951), and Virgil Trucks (1952).[11] As of 2018, Maloney's 10 walks are the most in a no-hitter. He hurled his second and final no-no April 30, 1969, fanning 13 and walking five Houston Astros.

In the second game of the doubleheader the Cubs atoned for their missed opportunities, overcoming a 4-0 deficit by scoring three runs in the eighth and winning the game on Landrum's two-run home run with two outs in the ninth.

SOURCES

In addition to the sources mentioned in the notes, the author consulted baseball-reference.com, mlb.com, retrosheet.org, and SABR.org.

NOTES

1   Several clips of Jim Maloney's no-hitter are available on YouTube. The following show the complete 10th inning and an interview with the pitcher after the game. youtube.com/watch?v=SoE6-JbGRDc&t=40s.

2   Author's interview with Johnny Edwards on March 7, 2017.

3   Bill Ford, "000 000 000 0," *Cincinnati Enquirer*, August 20, 1965: 39.

4   Richard Dozer, "Maloney's No-Hitter Beats Cubs, 1-0," *Chicago Tribune*, August 20, 1965: 53.

5   Ford.

6   Associated Press, "Big Jim Pulls It Out," *Atlanta Constitution*, August 20, 1965: 49.

7   Dozer.

8   "Big Jim Pulls It Out,"

9   Ford.

10   You Tube video of interview. youtube.com/watch?v=SoE6-JbGRDc&t=40s.

11   See the complete list of these "lost" extra-inning no-hitters at Nohitter.com, nonohitters.com/near-no-hitters/.

RANDY HUNDLEY HITS FOR THE CYCLE

AUGUST 11, 1966
CHICAGO CUBS 9, HOUSTON ASTROS 8
(GAME ONE OF DOUBLEHEADER)

By Joe Schuster

DURING THE PEAK YEARS OF HIS 14 major-league seasons, before two knee injuries slowed him, Randy Hundley was regarded as a super-durable defensive player whose glove and leadership made him nearly indispensible to the Chicago Cubs. In 1970, when he suffered his first knee injury, manager Leo Durocher lamented, "If there's one player I hate to see out ... it's Randy Hundley; he's one guy we can't replace."[1] Cumulatively over his four full-time seasons before that injury, Hundley ranked first among all major-league catchers for defensive WAR (he won the Gold Glove in 1967 and was an All-Star in 1969) and was the only catcher in either league who played at least 600 games at the position over that stretch.[2]

That performance was precisely what the Cubs were looking for from him when they acquired him in December 1965 in a four-player deal with the Giants – the Cubs swapping relief ace Lindy McDaniel and reserve outfielder Don Landrum for Hundley and hurler Bill Hands. Both players who came to Chicago had minimal major-league experience. Hands, a future 20-game winner, had pitched six ineffective innings in 1965, allowing 11 earned runs on 13 hits, while Hundley, to whom the Giants had given a $100,000 signing bonus before the 1960 season, had had two trials with San Francisco over the previous two years, going a combined 1-for-16 over eight games. After the deal, Durocher, who announced Hundley would be the team's number-one catcher for 1966, said, "I wanted Hundley because he can catch, throw, and run. I just hope he can hit."[3]

As it turned out, Hundley never had much more than modest success at the plate during his time in the major leagues: his lifetime average was only .236, with a career OBP of .292.

However, on August 11, 1966, in the middle of his rookie year, in front of a crowd of 11,860, he had perhaps his best day ever at the plate in a big-league uniform, hitting for the cycle in an 11-inning 9-8 Cubs victory over the Houston Astros in the opener of a doubleheader brought about by a rainout the day before.

By that point in the season, it was clear neither team was destined for success. Coming into the matchup, Houston stood eighth in the 10-team league, 15½ games behind Pittsburgh and in the midst of a string in which they had won only twice in their previous 10 games and four times in their previous 20. Meanwhile, the Cubs were even worse, as they were in last, already 28½ games out of first, though they had gone 5-5 over their most recent 10 games. Both Houston and Chicago would finish the season exactly where they stood on August 11.

For the visitors, Astros manager Grady Hatton, in his first year at the helm of a major- league club, started veteran right-hander Bob Bruce, who was 2-9 with a 5.74 ERA. Cubs skipper Durocher gave the ball to future Hall of Famer Robin Roberts, who was in his final season. Roberts had joined Chicago a month earlier as a pitcher-coach after the Astros released him after he had gone 3-5 with a 3.82 ERA and had lasted less than three innings in two of his final three starts for the team. Headlines around the country about his release focused on the fact that Roberts, who then had 284 victories (more than any other active pitcher) had his sights set on 300 career wins.[4] His performance early in his stint with the Cubs suggested that even with a new lease on a baseball career, Roberts likely would not get there. Coming into the August 11 game, his record with Chicago was 1-2 with a 3.92 ERA, and he was showing the same lack of stamina he had with the Astros. While he had totaled 28 innings in his first three starts for the Cubs (in one game he threw 11 innings with no decision), in his subsequent three starts he had managed only a combined 11 innings, including his previous outing, when he lasted only two innings because he had taken a line drive off his pitching arm in batting practice.[5]

Roberts ended up in trouble early on. Both hurlers got through the first without any damage – Roberts set down Houston in order and while Bruce allowed a one-out single to Glenn Beckert, he got out of the inning when Billy Williams grounded into a double play. But the Astros hit Roberts hard in the second.[6] The first three hitters reached base on a double, a walk, and a single before Bob Aspromonte hit his fifth career grand slam, giving Houston a 4-0 lead; it was the first of six home runs Chicago and Houston would hit in the game. The Astros nudged the score to 5-0 when Rusty Staub hit a one-out solo shot in the third.

Hundley (who had been hot at the plate, going 5-for-8 in his two previous games, with three home runs and two doubles) batted for the first time in the third and struck out (the only time Houston retired him in the game). But the Cubs scored three when Don Kessinger singled and then Roberts followed with what would turn out to be the final base hit of his career, a single to right, before Adolfo Phillips hit the third homer of the game, making the score 5-3. Roberts gave up another home run in the top of the fourth, to Lee Maye, but then the Cubs tied the score in the bottom of the fourth, two of their runs coming on Hundley's first hit of the day, a triple high off the wall in left center, that drove

in Ron Santo and Ernie Banks, who had doubled and singled, respectively. Hundley came home on a single by Don Kessinger, making it 6-6 and ending the day for Bruce, who was relieved by Turk Farrell. As it turned out, Roberts was finished for the game as well, as Durocher pinch-hit for him with Marty Keough, who walked. Although the Cubs pushed two runners into scoring position when Kessinger stole second, then third, and Keough stole second, neither scored as Farrell got Phillips on a fly to center and Beckert on a groundball to short.

For the rest of regulation, the two teams traded the lead back and forth: The Astros went up 7-6 in the fifth when Chuck Harrison tripled off of reliever Curt Simmons with Sonny Jackson on third, but the Cubs tied it again in the seventh on a home run by Williams. The Astros scored again in the top of the eighth when Morgan scored on a single by John Bateman, knocking out Simmons; his replacement, Cal Koonce, retired the side with no more scoring. The Cubs tied the score again in the bottom of the eighth on Hundley's 16th home run of the season, his third hit of the day (he had doubled in the sixth) and it was still tied 8-8 until the 11th.

After Koonce retired the side in order in the top of the inning, Hatton sent Jim Owens in to pitch for the bottom of the inning and he did not retire a batter. Hundley led off with an infield single to short, completing his cycle, and went to second on a single by Kessinger. Durocher pinch-hit Lee Thomas for Koonce and he failed to sacrifice on two successive pitches before singling to left, scoring Hundley and winning the game for Chicago, 9-8.

As it turned out, the four innings Roberts pitched were his longest outing for the rest of the season. In his next start, he lasted two-thirds of an inning, giving up three runs, and in his start after that, the final one of his career, he lasted 1⅔ innings, again surrendering three runs, before making his last two major-league appearances in relief, earning his 286th and final victory in two innings of work against Atlanta on August 29. The Cubs released him on October 4.

As for Hundley: He set a league record for most games (149) and home runs (19) by a rookie catcher and wound up tied for fourth in the voting for Rookie of the Year Award, which went to the Reds' Tommy Helms.

SOURCES

In addition to the sources cited in the Notes, the author also accessed Retrosheet.org, Baseball-Reference.com, SABR.org, and *The Sporting News* archive via Paper of Record.

NOTES

1   Robert Markus, "Cubs Face Spell Without Their Indispensible Man," *Chicago Tribune*, April 24, 1970: 66.

2   For statistics, the author used Baseball-Reference and the site's Play Index tool

3   Edward Prell, "Cubs Trade McDaniel in 4-Man Deal," *Chicago Tribune*, December 3, 1965: 71.

4   As an example, the *Quad City* (Illinois) *Times*, *Lincoln* (Nebraska) *Evening Journal* and *Oshkosh* (Wisconsin) *Northwestern* referred to Roberts's chase for 300 in their headlines about his release.

5   Edward Prell, "Cubs Win 5-2; Sox Triumph," *Chicago Tribune*, August 7, 1966: 48.

6   Unless otherwise noted, play-by-play detail comes from Retrosheet.

THE BILLY WILLIAMS SHOW

SEPTEMBER 10, 1968
CHICAGO CUBS 8, NEW YORK METS 1

By John Bauer

BILLY WILLIAMS WAS ON FIRE, THE 30-year-old hammering the ball out of the park and providing one of the few reasons to make time to see the Chicago Cubs as the 1968 season wound down. The Cubs entered the game on September 10 in fourth place, decidedly mediocre at 75-71, a half-game behind Cincinnati and a half-game ahead of Atlanta, in an NL table that depicted the Cardinals marching toward a second consecutive pennant. About the Mets, it might have been said they were showing signs of life after five last-place seasons in six since the franchise started play in 1962. The Mets sat at only 65-81, but New York had already exceeded its win total from 1967.

For the 1:30 P.M. first pitch at Wrigley Field, a "select gathering"[1] of 1,501 braved the cloudy, chilly weather for an otherwise meaningless game on a cold September afternoon. Cubs manager Leo Durocher sent Bill Hands to the mound. Despite a rough outing against Philadelphia in his previous start, Hands brought a 15-9 record and a 2.99 ERA into the contest. He also brought a track record of excellence against the Mets: In three starts against them this season, Hands had pitched three complete-game wins. Hands, however, started inauspiciously with a walk to Mets leadoff hitter Bud Harrelson. Ken Boswell's groundball to second baseman Glenn Beckert forced Harrelson at the keystone sack. Larry Stahl singled to right field, and while Boswell ended up at third, Stahl was out between first and second in a rundown. Against Cleon Jones, Hands "tried to break off a slider too hard,"[2] and ball bounced into the stands for a run-scoring wild pitch that

brought home Boswell. Jones ended the inning with a grounder to shortstop Don Kessinger, but the Mets claimed an early 1-0 lead.

Dick Selma took the mound for the Mets. After he started the season 6-0, Selma's record had declined to 9-8 though he maintained a strong 2.42 ERA. Similar to Hands's solid track record against the Mets, Selma could also claim four consecutive wins against the Cubs. Kessinger led off with a popup to Jones in left field for the first out. Beckert lined a single into right field, extending his hitting streak to 13 games,[3] before Williams came to the plate. Williams was a student of the game who "spends most of his pregame spare time poring over movies of his hitting in the previous day's games . . . ."[4] He also slugged two home runs in the Cubs' last game, on September 8 against the Phillies; against Selma, Williams slammed the ball over the 368-foot mark in right-center field for a 2-1 Cubs lead.[5] After giving up the dinger, Selma recovered to strike out Ernie Banks and Ron Santo.

After the flurry of first-inning activity, the game settled down for Hands and Selma. In the Mets third, Jerry Buchek hit a leadoff single and advanced to third without scoring. Buchek and Selma hit back-to-back two-out singles in the fifth, but Harrelson's groundball to first baseman Banks ended the threat. The score remained 2-1 into the Cubs sixth, when Beckert lined the ball into left field for a leadoff single. Again, Beckert's effort served as prelude for Williams's heroics. Williams blasted another home run, this time 375 feet[6] into the bleachers. The Cubs now led 4-1. Williams, however, was not impressed

Statue of Billy Williams outside of Wrigley Field. With his sweet swing, Williams blasted 426 home runs in his 18-year big-league career. (Photo courtesy of Gregory H. Wolf)

"SWEET-SWINGING" BILLY WILLIAMS

with his efforts. "The first two homers weren't hit that well," he said after the game, "but this is a good sign for me because I was jammed on both of them and I still stayed with the pitch."[7]

With none out, Chicago pressed the advantage. Banks reached first base on Buchek's error at third base. When Santo lined the ball into center field, Mets manager Gil Hodges swapped Selma for Ron Taylor. Nineteen-year-old Cubs rookie Jimmy McMath singled into left field, and Banks scored from third base for a 5-1 Cubs lead. Taylor settled in, gathering Hundley's comebacker before striking out Adolfo Phillips and Hands to end the inning. The Mets proved unable to respond in the seventh. Hands struck out Art Shamsky before Ed Kranepool's groundout to Beckert. Buchek's third single of the afternoon kept the inning alive, but pinch-hitter

Mike Jorgensen's fly ball to Phillips in center field ended the Mets seventh.

For the bottom half of the inning, Nolan Ryan came in to pitch for the Mets. The 21-year-old Ryan had pitched for New York only once since late July. Kessinger singled to center field to start the inning and Beckert fouled out to first baseman Kranepool. Williams then "hammered his most vicious drive"[8] off the right-field foul pole for his third home run of the game. Combined with his two home runs against Philadelphia in the Cubs' last game, Williams tied a major-league mark with five homers in two consecutive games. After the game, Durocher claimed Kessinger nudged Banks after the home run, "You'd better wake up. He's going to catch you."[9] Banks seemed to take the advice to heart and hit a home run of his own, a solo shot and his 31st of the season. That blast put Banks one behind NL home-run leader Willie McCovey and kept him two ahead of Williams. Durocher complimented Banks: "That Banks is the damnedest man I've ever seen. ... His reflexes should be getting slow at his age [Banks was 37] but his are speeding up."[10] Hickman flied out to center for the final out, but the damage had been done. The Cubs were cruising, ahead 8-1 and six outs away from a win.

The Mets offered little over the remainder of the game. In the eighth, Harrelson and Boswell flied out and Stahl grounded out. J.C. Martin hit a one-out bunt single in the ninth, but Shamsky and Kranepool ended the game with groundouts. Hands had gone the distance for the Cubs to earn his 16th win of the season and 11th complete game.

The day was about the red-hot Billy Williams. With 21 round-trippers since the All-Star break, the Cubs left fielder had extended his season home-run tally to 29, within reach of McCovey and Banks. Williams's 94 RBIs moved him just ahead of McCovey.[11] About his taking over the RBI lead, Williams said, "It's as much a surprise to me as it is to you that I'm leading the league in RBIs. ... My job is to get on base along with Kessinger and Beckert so that Banks and Santo can drive us in."[12] Williams was doing plenty to push runs across the plate for the Cubs. In the end, the Cubs slumped toward a .500 finish, but Williams helped to make the slide watchable.

SOURCES

In addition to the sources cited in the Notes, the author utilized baseball-reference.com, retrosheet.org, and SABR.org.

NOTES

1   Thomas Rogers, "Williams Equals Homer Record as Cubs Trounce Mets, 8-1," *New York Times*, September 11, 1968: 53.

2   George Langford, "Williams Hits 3 Homers," *Chicago Tribune*, September 11, 1968: 3-1.

3   "Williams Hits 3 Homers": 3-2.

4   "Williams Hits 3 Homers": 3-1.

5   Rogers.

6   Ibid.

7   "Williams Hits 3 Homers": 3-2.

8   Ibid.

9   Ibid.

10   George Langford, "Banks Making Believer Out of Leo Durocher," *Chicago Tribune*, September 11, 1968: 3-2.

11   In the end, McCovey led the NL in home runs and RBIs for the 1968 season.

12   "Williams Hits 3 Homers": 3-2.

WILLIAMS' FOUR DOUBLES
LEAD TO DRUBBING

APRIL 9, 1969
CHICAGO CUBS 11, PHILADELPHIA PHILLIES 3

By Doug Feldmann

COMING OFF A THRILLING, 7-6 OPENING Day win at Wrigley Field with pinch-hitter Willie Smith homering in the 11th inning over the brown ivy in right field (and Ernie Banks homering twice as well), the Chicago Cubs looked to keep the early momentum going in their 1969 season against the Philadelphia Phillies in the second contest on April 9. When Cubs manager Leo Durocher arrived three seasons earlier, he had promised to "back up the truck" and remove players who were underperforming; and by the end of 1968, the result was a much improved team that had climbed to third place and was now looking to dethrone the two-time defending National League champion St. Louis Cardinals.

After the third-biggest Opening Day crowd in Wrigley Field history, 40,769, only 6,297 were on hand to witness the encore. The drop, however, was likely due in large part to the inclement weather expected to hit Chicago. "The flags were pointing stiffly toward the outfield like frozen wash on a clothes line," described George Langford in the *Chicago Tribune*.[1] Added Allen Lewis of the *Philadelphia Inquirer*, "A threat of rain seemed likely to postpone the game around noon.

"Unfortunately for the Phillies, it cleared off."[2]

On the mound for the Cubs was the New Jersey-born Bill Hands, who along with Ken Holtzman had settled into the role of another solid starter behind staff ace Ferguson Jenkins. In a season dominated by pitching like no other in the modern era, Hands had led the National League in 1968 in permitting the fewest walks per nine innings (1.25), topping the otherwise-overwhelming performances during the year by Jenkins (1.9), the Cardinals' Bob Gibson (1.8), and the Los Angeles Dodgers' Don Drysdale (2.1) as Hands allowed only 36 bases on balls in 258⅔ frames of work.

As Hands trudged out to the mound to start the game, taking his usual place behind him in left field was Billy Williams. Playing in his 821st consecutive game that afternoon, Williams was on his way toward surpassing Stan Musial's National League record of 895 later in the 1969 season. The native of Whistler, Alabama – appropriate for the way line drives "whistled" off his bat – would make this particular day one of the most memorable among the many in his career.

By the time Williams stepped to the plate in his customary third spot in the batting order in the bottom of the first, Philadelphia pitcher Rick Wise had quickly disposed of the first two hitters, Don Kessinger and Glenn Beckert. Wise, who had first appeared in 25 games as an 18-year-old in the Phillies' unsuccessful pennant run of 1964, had established himself as a regular starter by 1969. A promising all-around talent as a hitter and fielder from the pitcher's position, Wise had made only one error in his career coming into the day's contest.

Off in the distance behind Wise, in the area patrolled by Williams in the top half of the first, was the Phillies' rookie outfielder Ron Stone. Playing left field on Opening Day, Stone had incurred the wrath of a swath of fans in the Wrigley Field bleachers, a group that in 1968 had become more and more notorious among opposing players. Regarding his experiences during the previous afternoon, Stone "reported that he was pelted with two eggs, a salt shaker, pins, and cups of ice thrown from the bleachers during Tuesday's opener," according to Langford.[3]

Williams greeted Wise with a sharp liner in the direction of Stone, who got a late break on the ball by first glancing up toward the stands before retrieving it from the base of the wall. Williams pulled into second with a double, where he was left stranded when Banks forced Ron Santo (who had walked batting after Billy). Williams returned in the third inning to post another two-bagger, this time finding the right-field line to drive in Kessinger and give the Cubs the first run of the game.

After the Phillies came back to tie in the top of the fourth, the Cubs surged ahead once again by a 4-2 score in the bottom half with assistance from an error by Phillies first baseman Dick Allen – part of a rough day both in the field and on the bases for the Philadelphia slugger. "Richie Allen, who was supposed to be less bored playing first base than left field, failed to catch two foul pop ups, made a wide throw to second on a bunt for an error, and tried to go from second to third on a grounder to shortstop in violation of one of baseball's cardinal rules," complained Lewis.[4] After walking as part of the Cubs' turn in the fourth, Williams drove his third double of the day toward the gap in left-center in the sixth inning.

Meanwhile, the targets of Bill Conlin – Lewis's counterpart from the *Philadelphia Daily News* – were Wise and the other ineffective hurlers used by manager Bob Skinner in the season's first two days. "The Phillies pitching staff has assumed a defensive posture, throwing the ball prayerfully and hoping nobody gets killed by the line drives," he wrote the following day.[5] Conlin's words were perhaps prompted by the Cubs' onslaught in the seventh, in which 11 men batted as Don Young "began the

parade of doubles with a two-run shot down the left field line, his third major league hit and first of the season," cheered Langford in the hometown paper.[6] For Young, the start of the 1969 schedule marked the first time he had been in the big leagues since an 11-game debut in 1965.

Among the "parade of doubles" in the big inning was the fourth of the day by Williams, which tied a major-league record and made him the first to accomplish the feat in the senior circuit since Jim Greengrass of Cincinnati 15 years earlier, in 1954. Proving that no part of the ballpark was safe when Williams was at the plate, he pulled two of the doubles and sliced a pair to the opposite field as well. "I can't even remember getting three in one game," he said afterward in reflection on his achievement.[7]

It was more than enough support for the Cubs' starting pitcher. "Hands said his right arm stiffened slightly during the long seventh," Langford added about the Cubs' extended turn at bat, as the pitcher had yielded only three hits and retired 10 of his last 11 to that juncture.[8] Nonetheless, he found enough strength to go the distance and secure an 11-3 triumph, which included escaping a bases-loaded jam in the Phillies' ninth. "I thought I had worked the stiffness out in the eighth by taking a few extra warmup pitches," Hands said while dumping his elbow in a bucket of ice in the cramped Wrigley clubhouse. "I didn't feel tired then, but I sure do now."[9]

The visiting scribe Lewis, meanwhile, scattered blame all around the Philadelphia side. "The Phillies made enough mistakes of commission and omission to last a month. Of course, the Cubs had something going for them, too, as they assaulted three of the four pitchers used by the Phillies for 16 hits."[10] Along with Williams, batting stars on the day included Banks and Beckert, who each knocked three hits, while Kessinger and Al Spangler added two apiece as every Chicago position player with the exception of catcher Randy Hundley posted at least one RBI.

Yet, despite the fierce wind blowing out toward Sheffield Avenue, there were no home runs in the game as the threat of rain had long subsided.

"Relative calm descended on Wrigley Field," Langford concluded of the afternoon weather that gradually brightened on the North Side, "a seemingly appropriate setting for a man of Billy Williams' mild temperament."[11]

It was the first time in eight years the Phillies had lost the first two games of a season, while the Cubs proceeded to storm out of the gate with 11 wins in their first 12 games in 1969 – a misleading prelude to their most infamous season of all.

Hall of Famer and 1961 NL Rookie of the Year Billy Williams played 16 of his 18 big-league seasons in Cubbie blue. In 1970 the slugging "ironman" set an NL record by playing in his 1,117th consecutive game, a record since broken by Steve Garvey in 1983. (Photo by Focus on Sport/Getty Images)

SOURCES

In addition to the sources cited in the Notes, the author also accessed Retrosheet.org, Baseball-Reference.com, SABR.org, and *The Sporting News* archive via Paper of Record.

NOTES

1   George Langford, "Cubs Rout Phils, 11-3," *Chicago Tribune*, April 10, 1969.

2   Allen Lewis, "Phils Bombed By Cubs' 16-Hit Attack," *Philadelphia Inquirer*, April 10, 1969.

3   Langford.

4   Allen Lewis, "Phils Bombed by Cubs' 16-Hit Attack," *Philadelphia Inquirer*, April 10, 1969.

5   Bill Conlin, "Will Those Fumbling Phils Change To Beanie-Meanies?" *Philadelphia Daily News*, April 10, 1969.

6   Langford.

7   Ibid.

8   Ibid.

9   Doug Feldmann, *Miracle Collapse: The 1969 Chicago* Cubs (Lincoln: University of Nebraska Press), 72.

10   Lewis.

11   Langford.

A RUDE WELCOME TO THE NATIONAL LEAGUE

MAY 13, 1969
CHICAGO CUBS 19, SAN DIEGO PADRES 0

By John Bauer

BASEBALL LOOKED DIFFERENT IN 1969 from previous years. The pitching mound was lower, the number of teams was greater, and the Chicago Cubs looked like a contender. The Cubs stormed to an early lead in the new NL East Division, a creation necessitated by the expansion that brought the Montreal Expos and San Diego Padres into the National League. Ferguson Jenkins's third shutout of the young season in the Cubs' first-ever game against the Padres, on May 12, put Chicago at 21-11, three games ahead of the Pittsburgh Pirates. At 15-19, San Diego was outperforming its expansion brethren in Montreal and was avoiding the last-place spot in the NL West. That would change by season's end, but it might have been stated that the Padres were meeting expectations so far.

Dick Selma started the game for Chicago. Selma had begun the season with the Padres, having been acquired from the Mets in the NL expansion draft. In fact, he earned the first win in Padres history with a 12-strikeout complete game on Opening Day against Houston. The Cubs traded for Selma on April 25, sending Joe Niekro, Gary Ross, and Frankie Libran to San Diego to obtain the right-hander. Jerry DaVanon opened the contest with a leadoff infield single, but catcher Randy Hundley's bullet to Don Kessinger caught the Padres leadoff man trying to steal second base. After Roberto Peña grounded out to second baseman Nate Oliver, Tony Gonzalez drew a walk from Selma. The pass came to nothing when Ollie Brown struck out to end the Padres first.

Claimed in the later rounds of the expansion draft after nine years in the Braves organization, Dick Kelley took the mound for the Padres. A winner in his previous start at Pittsburgh, Kelley sported a 2-2 record and 3.69 ERA. He walked Kessinger to start the inning, but Kelley earned outs on Oliver's popup to second baseman DaVanon and a groundball from Billy Williams that forced Kessinger at second base. The third out would not come easily. Kelley walked Ron Santo, and Ernie Banks smacked his first home run since hitting two on Opening Day. With that three-run blast, Banks became the 17th major leaguer to surpass 1,500 RBIs.[1] Kelley's control remained suspect when he surrendered his third walk of the inning, to Hundley, The base on balls proved more costly when DaVanon threw away the ball on Jim Hickman's grounder, allowing Hundley to score from first. Adolfo Phillips stared at strike three to end the inning, but the Cubs led, 4-0.

The Padres could not dent the Cubs' advantage in the top of the second. Further, their hopes of getting back into the game suffered a blow when first baseman Nate Colbert exited with a pulled back muscle.[2] Colbert, who was the Padres' best hitter, "grimaced with pain after lining his double off the centerfield wall."[3] The Cubs began to put the game out of reach in their half of the second. After Selma led off by striking out, Kessinger hit his 14th double of the season into left field. Kessinger stayed at second on Oliver's infield single. Williams brought home both runners with a broken-bat triple into the right-field corner for a 6-0 lead. Manager Preston Gomez summoned Jack Baldschun to take over for the struggling Kelley. Santo reached base on an error by his counterpart at third base, Ed Spiezio; Williams scored on the play for a 7-0 advantage. Banks added to the lead when his double into left field plated Santo. Baldschun's wild pitch with Hundley batting allowed Banks to take third base. Hundley walked but neither he nor Banks made it home as Hickman struck out and Phillips popped up to end the inning.

Selma led off the Cubs third and reached on an infield single off Leon Everitt. Kessinger followed with a single to right field, advancing Selma to third. Selma scored for a 9-0 lead on a double by Oliver that "almost carried to the left field catwalk."[4] With none out and runners on second and third, it seemed likely the Cubs would hit double digits in the third inning. Everitt buckled down, however. First, he got Williams to stare at a third-strike pitch. Then, he fielded Santo's comebacker for the second out. Finally, Banks flied out to Gonzalez in center field. In the fourth, Everitt kept the Cubs from scoring at all, allowing only a two-out single to Phillips. Meanwhile, Selma continued to roll through the Padres lineup. The only San Diego baserunners in the fourth and fifth reached on walks. In fact, Selma allowed more walks (4) than hits (3) in the game, a statistic that seemed to bother the Cubs pitcher; afterward, he commented, "When a game gets out of hand like this one, there is no excuse for walking anyone. You just throw strikes."[5]

The Cubs returned to the scoresheet in the bottom of the fifth. Kessinger walked to start the inning and advanced to second on Oliver's groundout. DaVanon snared Williams's liner for the second out, but Everitt walked Santo, bringing up Banks. (Bases on balls bedeviled Padres pitchers all game; their five pitchers gave up 12.) Before the game, the 38-year-old Banks had been concerned about his hitting and was seeking remedies for an apparent loss of power. He explained, "I've been changing my stance in the last couple of weeks, spreading out a little bit more and trying all kinds of things. But my big problem is that I was

swinging too hard."[6] In this game, he rediscovered his stroke. Banks swatted Everitt's pitch over the wall for his second home run of the game, extending the score to 12-0. His 7-RBI performance against San Diego gave him 26 for the season and tied him with four others (teammate Ron Santo, Mack Jones of the Montreal Expos, the Braves' Orlando Cepeda, and the Reds' Bobby Tolan) for the league lead.

Nate Oliver made his mark on the game in the sixth. Phillips led off the inning with a walk. Selma's bunt moved Phillips to second and Kessinger's long fly out sent him to third. Oliver was playing second base because, the day before, Glenn Beckert had taken a pitch to the jaw from Gary Ross that required 15 stitches. Oliver made the most of the opportunity and homered for a 14-0 lead. After his 4-RBI game, Oliver said, "I can't ever remember driving in four runs in one game. When you're a backup man like I am, though, you have to have games like this."[7]

Cubs manager Leo Durocher pulled several starters from the game to start the seventh. Out came Hundley, Banks, and Williams, and in came Ken Rudolph, Willie Smith, and Don Young. Padres skipper Gomez swapped pitchers, bringing in Frank Reberger for Everitt. Reberger walked leadoff man Rudolph. After Hickman's lineout, Phillips singled to left field. Reberger fanned Selma for the second out, but his walk to Kessinger loaded the bases. Rudolph scored when Reberger drilled Oliver. Another Reberger miscue, a wild pitch with Young batting, permitted Phillips to cross the plate. Young made the most of his opportunity to impress and smacked a three-run homer to make the score 19-0.

Mercifully for the Padres, the Cubs did not extend the laugher beyond the 19-0 mark. The rout tied the NL record for the most lopsided shutout, equaling the standard set by the 1906 Cubs (vs. the Giants) and the 1961 Pirates (vs. the Cardinals).[8] The Cubs fell short of the major-league standard for blanking an opponent, 21-0, achieved by the 1901 Tigers and 1939 Yankees.[9] Following shutouts thrown by Ken Holtzman and Ferguson Jenkins, this game's whitewash from Hands equaled a club record of three consecutive shutouts, a feat achieved on three prior occasions, the last time occurring in 1919.[10]

With so many players contributing, it would have been hard to single out someone for particular praise. Banks, however, received many of the postgame plaudits. *San Diego Union* writer Phil Collier described him as the "liveliest thing at Wrigley Field."[11] Durocher referred to his annual inability to dislodge Banks from the lineup: "I retired Ernie three springs in a row. I'd play the kids every spring, but I'd finally have to call on Ernie and, once he was back in the lineup, he made sure he stayed there."[12] With his swing returning, Banks seemed likely to hold his spot in the lineup. Banks said, "I've got to swing easy and just try to meet the ball. Today I did that."[13]

SOURCES

In addition to the sources cited in the Notes, the author consulted baseball-reference.com, retrosheet.org, and SABR.org.

NOTES

1   George Langford, "Break Up The Cubs! They Reign, 19-0," *Chicago Tribune*, May 14, 1969: 3-1.

2   Langford: 3-2.

3   Phil Collier, "'Young' Ernie Ages Padres," *San Diego Union*, May 14, 1969: c-1, c-2.

4   Langford: 3-1, 3-2.

5   Ibid.

6   Ibid.

7   Ibid.

8   Langford: 3-1.

9   Langford: 3-2.

10   Jerome Holtzman, "Cub Power Jolts Padres to Sandals," *The Sporting News*, May 31, 1969: 17.

11   Collier.

12   Ibid.

13   Langford: 3-2.

HOLTZMAN AUTHORS NO-HITTER WITHOUT STRIKING OUT A BATTER

AUGUST 19, 1969
CHICAGO CUBS 3, ATLANTA BRAVES 0

By Gregory H. Wolf

A NO-HITTER WITHOUT A STRIKEOUT. In the history of the major leagues there have been only three. Given the current trend of hard-throwing starting pitchers with fastball velocities averaging in the mid-90s and almost a quarter of plate appearances ending in strikeouts, there'll likely never be another. Deadball Era hurler Earl Hamilton of the St. Louis Browns was the first to accomplish the feat, in 1912, followed by the New York Yankees' Sad Sam Jones in 1923. In 1969 Ken Holtzman of the Chicago Cubs joined this very exclusive fraternity of pitchers to author a no-hitter without striking out a batter.

"When I saw my curve wasn't breaking early in the game, I thought it was going to be a long day," said the 23-year-old southpaw, known for his knee-buckling breaking balls and heaters that evoked comparisons to the recently retired Sandy Koufax.[1] "I must have thrown 90 per cent fastballs," he quipped and added, "[T]he umpire (Dick Stello) was squeezing the corners on me ... wasn't giving 'em to me. I thought, 'Uh oh, if I have to throw my fastball down the center of the plate, I'm in trouble.'"[2]

A euphoric atmosphere permeated the Wrigleyville neighborhood on the north side of Chicago as the Cubs prepared to kick off an 11-game homestand on August 19. After years of inconsequence, the Cubs, the veritable lovable losers, seemed destined for the postseason for the first time since 1945. In the inaugural season of divisional play, skipper Leo Durocher's squad (76-45) was in first

place in the NL East, holding what seemed to be an insurmountable eight-game lead over the New York Mets. The visiting Atlanta Braves (66-57), who had sat atop the NL West for most of the season, were reeling. Manager Lum Harris's team was on a 7-14 skid and had slipped into a tie for third place; however, only 1½ games separated five teams in the tightly packed division. The reorganization of baseball into four six-team divisions seemed like a stroke of genius.

Toeing the rubber for the Braves was 30-year-old right-handed knuckleballer Phil Niekro. A converted reliever, he led the majors with a 1.87 ERA as a rubber-armed swingman in 1967 and earned his first All-Star berth in 1969. He had a 47-37 career slate in parts of six seasons, including 16-10 (2.63 ERA) thus far in '69. His mound opponent, Holtzman, since debuting as a teenager in 1965 had been hailed as a wunderkind, but had not yet reached his potential. He showed signs of it in 1967, going 9-0 in 12 starts in a season cut short by his stint in the Army Medical Corps. He seemed to put it all together in '69, winning 10 of his first 11 decisions, but had since gone just 3-6 and owned a 44-37 career record.

The weather was perfect for a Tuesday afternoon of baseball in the Windy City. Temperatures were in the mid-70s and the sun was bright, while a pleasant nor'easter gusted off Lake Michigan, located a mile east of the ballpark. Wrigley Field was packed with a standing-room-only crowd of 37,514. Times had indeed changed. Just three years earlier, when the

Cubs finished in the NL cellar with a 59-103 record, they averaged an NL-low 7,851 at home games.

After Holtzman set down the Braves 1-2-3 in the first, the Cubs took their whacks at Niekro. Don Kessinger and Glenn Beckert opened the game with singles, then Ron Santo crushed a one-out home run, his 25th homer of the season and his first since August 2, to give the Cubs the lead. "I knew it was gone as soon as I hit it," said the inspirational team leader who had earned his sixth All-Star berth the previous month.[3] "I hit the knuckler and it was down low," gushed Santo. "You gotta be lucky to hit one of those. I was just trying to get my bat on it."[4] The affable third baseman's blast might have portended an offensive explosion; however, an undaunted Niekro mesmerized the Cubs with his floater, yielding just two more hits through the seventh inning. Only once did the Cubs advance as far as second again, when in the seventh Bill Heath walked with one out and Don Young singled, but both were left stranded.

The story of the game was Holtzman, who was no stranger to pitching shutouts in 1969. He tossed five of them, including three straight as part of a career-best streak of 33⅔ scoreless innings in May. No soft-tosser, Holtzman had fanned at least 10 batters in a game twice already in '69.

The good-natured St. Louis native systematically retired the Braves lineup, pounding the zone. He issued three free passes and no runner advanced beyond first. He didn't yield the semblance of a hit, while the Cubs played error-free defense and chipped in with a trio of excellent plays.

The first of those plays came in the third when Felipe Alou hit a scorching grounder to the right side of second sacker Glenn Beckert. According to sportswriter Richard Dozer in the *Chicago Tribune*, the All-Star corralled the ball, then "throwing grotesquely, off-balance, almost from behind first base," retired the speedy Alou at first.[5] "The high grass slowed it up a bit," said Beckert, "but still, it was right in the hole and I didn't know if I could get it."[6]

Another All-Star chipped in with a "sensational catch," according to scribe Wayne Minshew of the

Atlanta Constitution, in the seventh.[7] Hank Aaron connected with a fastball that he sent to deep left field, but the wind slowed the ball down. Flychaser Billy Williams followed the ball's arc and snared it on the warning track, lightly falling into the ivy adorning the brick outfield walls. "It was gone if it hadn't been for the wind," said Williams. "Just one more foot over, and it was a homer. I was in the vine anyway."[8] Holtzman thought Aaron's blast had ended his no-hitter and shutout, "I thought it was gone – even with the wind blowing in."[9]

There are two cardinal sins in no-hitters: Don't talk to the pitcher and don't change the catcher in mid-game. The Cubs broke the second rule, but not willingly. Bill Heath took a foul tip off his right hand from Bob Didier to lead off the eighth. He was replaced one batter latter by veteran Gene Oliver, who had caught only nine innings all season. Taken to the hospital, Heath was diagnosed with a broken transverse metacarpal in his index finger and never played another game in the majors. The team's primary catcher, Randy Hundley, who was en route to leading all NL catchers in games played for the fourth straight season, was shelved with a finger injury suffered a week earlier in San Diego.[10]

The change in catchers bothered Holtzman. "I was worried about what Gene [Oliver] would do when he came in."[11] After a quick discussion on the mound, the batterymates decided on the obvious: Stick with the heater.

Holtzman took the mound three outs away from becoming the first Cub to toss a no-hitter at Wrigley Field since Don Cardwell held the St. Louis Cardinals hitless on May 15, 1960. The third defensive highlight occurred with leadoff hitter Alou, who popped to shallow center, behind second base. Beckert raced back to the ball just as center fielder Don Young came sprinting. A collision seemed imminent, but at the last second Young jerked out of the way and fell to the ground as Beckert snared the ball. "The crowd was making so much noise we couldn't hear anything," explained Beckert about the confusion. "Don says he called for it, but I didn't hear him."[12] The next batter, Felix Millan, sent a chopper

Hailed as the next Sandy Koufax, Ken Holtzman went 80–81 in parts of nine seasons with the Cubs. Traded to the Oakland A's, he won 59 games in 1972–1974, helping Oakland to three straight World Series titles. He posted a 174–150 slate in 15 campaigns. (Photo by Herb Scharfman/ Sports Imagery/Getty Images)

to Santo at the hot corner; however, moments earlier, he had induced a collective gasp from the crowd when his screeching bullet down the third-base line went foul by 10 feet. To the plate stepped Hank Aaron, en route to finishing second in the NL in home runs (44) in '69. On a 3-and-2 pitch, Hammerin' Hank hit a routine grounder to Beckert, who tossed to Banks at first to end the game in exactly two hours.

While the players converged on Holtzman at the pitcher's mound, Wrigley Field burst into what Windy City sportswriter Robert Markus called an "unprecedented fit of frenzy."[13] The Bleacher Bums jumped down from the outfield stands and rushed the field, mixing with the players.

"I can't believe it," said Holtzman about his masterpiece. "I threw about 14 bad pitches and got away with them all."[14] His skipper, Durocher, was equally pleased. "When you get a guy like Holtzman who has a great curve ball but it isn't working and he still wins," quipped the Lip, "he has to be some kind of pitcher."[15]

In his next outing, Holtzman fanned 10 in a complete-game victory, 11–5, against the Houston Astros on August 23. He joined the no-hit ranks again on June 3, 1971, at Riverfront Stadium, in Cincinnati, holding the Big Red Machine hitless and whiffing six.

SOURCES

In addition to the sources cited in the Notes, the author also accessed Retrosheet.org, Baseball-Reference.com, and SABR.org.

NOTES

1   Wayne Minshew, "His o-o-o! Holtzman No-Hits Braves," *Atlanta Constitution*, August 20, 1969: 45.

2   Ibid.

3   Richard Dozer, "41,033 See Holtzman Hurl No-Hitter," *Chicago Tribune*, August 20, 1969: Sec 3, 1.

4   Minshew, "His o-o-o! Holtzman No-Hits Braves."

5   Dozer, "41,033 See Holtzman Hurl No-Hitter."

6   Ibid.

7   Minshew, "His o-o-o! Holtzman No-Hits Braves."

8   Ibid.

9   Dozer, "41,033 See Holtzman Hurl No-Hitter."

10 Richard Dozer, "Cubs Escape from San Francisco; Come Home with 75 Victories," *Chicago Tribune*, August 18, 1968: Sec 3, 1.

11 Robert Markus, "Holtzman Had No Curve, but His Fast Ball Stunned Braves," *Chicago Tribune*, August 20, 1969: Sec 3, 1.

12 Ibid.

13 Ibid.

14 Minshew, "His o-o-o! Holtzman No-Hits Braves."

15 Wayne Minshew, "Another Sandy Koufax," *Atlanta Constitution*, August 20, 1969: 1C.

ROOKIE HOOTON FIRES NO-HITTER

APRIL 16, 1972
CHICAGO CUBS 4, PHILADELPHIA PHILLIES 0

By Gregory H. Wolf

FEW PITCHERS IN CHICAGO CUBS HISTORY have burst on the scene with such an immediate explosive (albeit quickly fading) impact as Burt Hooton. Described by Windy City sportswriter Bob Logan as an "instant superstar" and compared with such icons of the sports-crazed city as Bobby Hull of the Black Hawks and Gayle Sayers of the Bears, Hooton kicked off the 1972 season by tossing a no-hitter in just his fourth big-league start.[1] "You have to compare his knuckle-curve with a Sandy Koufax curve ball," said Chicago Cubs catcher Randy Hundley ecstatically about the right-hander's signature, seemingly unhittable pitch. "It starts at your head and winds up on the ground."[2]

Longtime Cubs GM John Holland must have thought that he had won the jackpot. The Cubs drafted Hooton, an All-American at the University of Texas, in the secondary phase of the 1971 supplemental draft. Hooton was bombed in his debut, but proceeded to tear up the Triple-A Pacific Coast League, fanning 135 in 102 innings, including a league-record 19 in one game. A September call-up, Hooton punched out 15 in a three-hitter against the New York Mets, then shut them out on two hits six days later.

Hooton's success rested on a knuckle curve, an innovative pitch he helped popularize. "I grab the ball with my first two fingers and let it slide off the tips, giving it a fastball motion by breaking my wrist," he explained, noting that he developed the pitch when he couldn't master a traditional flutter ball.[3] The confounding pitch rotated in the opposite direction of his fastball and had an unexpected sharp downward break at the plate.[4]

Expectations for Hooton were high in 1972. "I saw Hooton for the first time this spring and I said that his live fastball was impressive," mused Cubs pitching coach Larry Jansen, a former two-time 20-game winner with the New York Giants. "All you hear about is his knuckle-curve, but the fastball makes it effective."[5] Coming off a distant third-place finish in the NL East in '71, 14 games behind the World Series champion Pittsburgh Pirates, the Cubs needed Hooton to join perennial 20-game winner Fergie Jenkins and dependable workhorses Milt Pappas and Bill Hands to have a shot at the divisional crown.

Mother Nature provided a rude welcome to Hooton as he took the mound against the Philadelphia Phillies on a Sunday afternoon in Chicago. The temperature hovered around 40 degrees and the wind swirled off Lake Michigan at 35 MPH, creating ideal conditions for a pitchers' duel. The field was in poor shape from a rainy night and with storms in the forecast, there was discussion about postponing the game; however, players, and especially club owner Philip K. Wrigley, were itching to finally get the season started. A day earlier, the Phillies had beaten the Cubs, 4-2, on Opening Day, which had been delayed some 13 days by the first players strike in major-league history. While some players complained of not yet being in shape because of the strike-imposed layoff, that was not the case for Hooton, who had worked out with his former team at the University of Texas. According to the *Tribune*,

218

Hooton tossed 128 pitches in the bullpen trying to warm up on the blustery day.[6]

Hooton breezed through the first four frames, but the weather played havoc with his knuckle curve. He walked three, but also profited from Don Kessinger's perfectly timed leap to snare Denny Doyle's "wicked liner" in the third.[7] "I was fully extended," said the All-Star shortstop, "but all you can do on that kind (of hit) is hope."[8]

The Cubs took their whacks at right-hander Dick Selma, who had missed much of the previous season with an arm injury. In his eighth campaign with a 37-42 career slate, the converted reliever was making his first start since 1969. After twice stranding runners on first and third, the Cubs broke through in the fourth when Ron Santo led off with a sinking liner to left field. According to sportswriter Bill Conlin of the *Philadelphia Daily News*, the ball eluded Greg Luzinski's "shoestring effort" and Santo reached second.[9] After Rick Monday walked, Kessinger dropped a soft sacrifice bunt to the left side of the plate. Catcher Tim McCarver tossed the ball away for a two-base error, enabling Santo to cross the plate. Selma intentionally walked Hundley to fill the bases, then escaped the jam by retiring the next three batters.

The Cubs were still nursing a precarious 1-0 lead to start the seventh. After second baseman Glenn Beckert stabbed Deron Johnson's bullet, Luzinski, who grew up in suburban Chicago, hit a monstrous shot to deep center field. "It probably would have bounced on Waveland Avenue," quipped Bob Logan, "but the wind brought that ball back into the park."[10] Monday caught the ball on the warning track in front of the 368-foot sign. "I can't hit a ball any harder than that," claimed Luzinski, who had belted a home run off Jenkins the day before.[11] It was the second time in three innings that Hooton was saved by the wind. In the fifth, Mike Anderson had hit a deep fly to left that "fluttered to a halt like a wounded bird," wrote Conlin.[12]

Laboring after Luzinski's blast, Hooton walked the next two batters, his sixth and seventh free passes of the game. Coach Pete Reiser, serving as

manager for the second game in a row while skipper Leo Durocher recovered from a virus, came to the mound to calm his 22-year-old rookie. Hooton whiffed Doyle looking to end the frame.

The Cubs, who had stranded 10 runners through six innings, looked as though they might add three more to that total in the seventh. Billy Williams and Joe Pepitone led off with singles against Chris Short, in his second inning of relief. After Monday drew a one-out walk, Kessinger popped out. Hundley, who played in only nine games the previous season because of a serious knee injury, slapped a single to left to drive in two and give the North Siders a 3-0 cushion The Cubs tacked on another one in the eighth when Jose Cardenal led off with a triple and scored on Beckert's single.

"I went to the knuckle-curve exclusively in the eighth and ninth innings," said Hooton. "That's when I felt the adrenaline starting to flow.[13] For the first time since the third, Hooton retired the side in order in the eighth. As the sun momentarily broke through the clouds, he took the mound in the ninth just three outs away from becoming the seventh NL rookie to author a no-hitter.[14] After dispatching Willie Montanez on a weak grounder, Hooton fell behind Deron Johnson, 3-and-0, quickly prompting Reiser to warm up relievers Phil Regan and Dan McGinn. He needn't have bothered as Hooton roared back to strike out Johnson. On his 120th pitch of the game, Hooton fooled Luzinski on a sinking knuckle curve for his seventh strikeout to complete the no-hitter in 2 hours and 33 minutes.[15]

Hooton was mobbed by his teammates on the field and subsequently feted in the clubhouse. Phillip K. Wrigley announced that he was ripping up his prized hurler's contract and giving him a $2,500 raise, and tossed in $500 to Hundley, who caught the first no-hitter in his career. According to the durable former All-Star who had led or co-led the majors in games caught four straight seasons (1966-1969), Hooton tossed about half knuckle curves and half fastballs, only one slider, and no changeups.[16] Hooton faced 32 batters, punched out seven, and yielded only six outfield flies. No-hitters were not new to the affable youngster. He had thrown four in high school, two in college, and another one against Cuba as a member of the United States team in the 1970 Amateur World Series. Squandering many opportunities to pile on runs, the Cubs collected 12 hits (three each by Santo and Williams) and drew five walks, but hit only 2-for-13 with men in scoring position while leaving 13 runners stranded.

In his next start, Hooton held the New York Mets to two runs on six hits in seven innings while fanning nine, but came up short against Tom Seaver, who tossed a four-hit shutout to win, 4-0. Big-league hitters eventually adjusted to Hooton's knuckle curve, which many sportswriters described as a gimmick or trick pitch. He finished a productive rookie campaign with an 11-14 record and robust 2.80 ERA in 218⅓ innings. He went on to win 151 games (and lose 136), including 29 shutouts, in a 15-year career, spent primarily with the Cubs and Los Angeles Dodgers, but never seriously flirted with a no-hitter again.

SOURCES

In addition to the sources cited in the Notes, the author also accessed Retrosheet.org, Baseball-Reference.com, Newspapers.com, and SABR.org/bioproj.

In just his fourth big-league start, Burt "Happy" Hooton tossed a no-hitter. He went 34-44 in parts of five seasons with the Cubs and posted a 151-136 career slate. (Photo by Focus on Sport/Getty Images)

NOTES

1   Bob Logan, "Hooton No-Hits Phils, 4-0," *Chicago Tribune*, April 17, 1972: C1.

2   Ibid.

3   "Found! A No-Hit Pitcher Who Says, 'I Was a Fluke'," *Philadelphia Inquirer*, April 17, 1972: 21.

4   Bruce Keidan, "Phillies Can't Hit Knuckle-Curve Ball," , April 17, 1972: 10.

5   Logan.

6   Ibid.

7   Ibid.

8   Ibid.

9   Bill Conlin, "Phils Aren't HOOton," *Philadelphia Daily News*, April 17, 1972: 68.

10   Logan.

11   Keidan.

12   Bill Conlin, "A Walter Mitty Fantasy Comes True," *Philadelphia Daily News*, April 17, 1972: 63.

13   Keidan.

14   Hooton joined Christy Mathewson (1901), Nick Maddox (1907), Jeff Tesreau (1912), Paul Dean (1934), Sam Jones (1955), and Don Wilson (1967)

15   See a short clip of Hooton's no-hitter on YouTube. It includes Kessinger's spectacular catch in the third, Monday's catch of Luzinski's deep fly in the seventh, and Hooton striking out Luzinski to end the game. youtube.com/watch?v=iDXveU8P-TA

16   Logan.

A STRIKE AWAY FROM A PERFECT GAME, PAPPAS SETTLES FOR NO-HITTER

SEPTEMBER 2, 1972
CHICAGO CUBS 8, SAN DIEGO PADRES 0

By Gregory H. Wolf

HE WAS A TWO-TIME ALL-STAR, WON 209 games, and tossed 43 shutouts in his 17-year career but is best remembered for a walk. Milt Pappas "came so dramatically close to perfection," opined sportswriter George Langford of the *Chicago Tribune*, that "even the rare distinction of what he did achieve – pitching a no-hit game – almost seemed anti-climactic."[1] For the rest of his life, Pappas could not escape the haunting feeling that he had been robbed and dealt an injustice.

Pappas didn't really feel like pitching against the lowly San Diego Padres (46-79), heading to their fourth consecutive last-place finish in the NL West, on a cool, autumnal-like Saturday afternoon in the Windy City. The Chicago Cubs' 33-year-old hurler awoke with a head cold and only his wife's encouragement finally persuaded him to take the mound. It had been a self-described "depressing" campaign, his 16th, for the Detroit native who began his career as an 18-year-old with the Baltimore Orioles in 1957.[2] In spring training the right-hander broke a finger, then sat idle for 3½ weeks. "My arm was not strong and my elbow started hurting me," said Pappas about starting the season, delayed 13 days because of the first players' strike in league history. "I've had 30 shots of cortisone in my elbow already this season."[3] He had turned his season around in August, winning five consecutive decisions to improve his record to 11-7 (3.18 ERA) and push his career slate to 196-152.

The friendly confines of Wrigley Field were packed with 11,144 faithful spectators, undeterred by the ominous dark skies, temperatures hovering around 60 degrees, and a vicious, swirling northeasterly wind blowing off Lake Michigan toward home plate. Skipper Whitey Lockman's Cubs were in second place (68-58) in the NL East, but sat 11 games behind the Pittsburgh Pirates and needed a collapse even more profound than their notorious one in 1969 to reach the postseason for the first time since 1945.

After Pappas began the game by setting down the Padres in order in the first, the Cubs had luck on their side facing left-hander Mike Caldwell (6-7, 3.31 ERA), in his first full big-league season. Leadoff hitter Don Kessinger reached on a two-base error by shortstop Enzo Hernandez and scored on Jose Cardenal's single. Billy Williams followed with another single. Two batters later, Jim Hickman hit what appeared to be a routine inning-ending double-play grounder, but the ball struck second-base umpire Stan Landes. It was ruled a hit and filled the bases. Carmen Fanzone's groundout plated Cardenal for the Cubs' second unearned run, which proved to be more than enough on this damp afternoon.

The Cubs added six more insurance runs. Two came in the third on Hickman's RBI single driving in Williams, and Ron Santo, who had been hit by a pitch, scored on Fanzone's twin-killing groundout. Caldwell eventually found his groove, yielding just two hits from the fourth inning through the seventh inning, but came undone in the eighth. With the bases jammed, Bill North hit a one-out single to drive in Hickman. Kessinger landed the coup de grâce with a two-out, bases-clearing double, giving the Cubs an 8-0 lead.

Despite the Cubs' offensive explosion (they had trounced the Padres, 14-3, the previous day), this game was about Pappas. Relying on his trademark hard slider, Pappas kept the Padres off balance all afternoon. Through eight innings, the lowest-scoring team in the league had only three legitimate chances for a hit. Speedy Enzo Hernandez led off the fourth with what the *Chicago Tribune* described as a "perfect bunt" surprising third sacker Ron Santo, who "had no choice but to watch the ball roll and hope it trickled foul."[4] It did after 50 feet, and on the next pitch Pappas fanned Hernandez. In the following inning, Kessinger, who had earned his fifth straight berth as shortstop on the NL All-Star squad in '72, made the defensive stop of the game when he "raced behind third and 10 feet in the wet outfield grass," according to the *Tribune*, to snare Nate Colbert's sharp grounder and throw him out by a split-second.[5] Pappas himself displayed his athleticism in the eighth, in what he considered the "the biggest scare" of the game.[6] With two outs, fleet-footed Derrel Thomas smashed a hard liner that hit Pappas's glove. The hurler quickly whirled around, fielded the ball, and threw wildly to first but beat the runner.

Pappas took the mound in the ninth just three out away from the 10th perfect game in major-league history. Eight years earlier to the day, Pappas, then with the Orioles, had flirted with a no-hitter against the Minnesota Twins. Zoilo Versalles singled with two outs in the eighth and Pappas settled for what proved to be his only career one-hitter.

The Padres' Johnny Jeter led off the final frame with a routine fly to left-center field. It was just the fourth – and final – Padres' hit to the outfield all afternoon. To the horror of the Wrigley Field crowd standing on its feet since the inning commenced, center fielder Bill North slipped and fell to the ground, but left fielder Billy Williams swooped in to make the catch. "I had lost the ball completely in the sun," said North. "I was just trying to run in the

general direction of the ball."[7] After Fred Kendall was retired on a grounder to short, pinch-hitter Larry Stahl, batting just .232, dug in. Pappas got ahead in the count, 1-and-2, then missed with two sliders, for a full count.

Cubs legendary broadcaster Jack Brickhouse made the call on WGN: "Now here comes one of the most fateful pitches of the year. Ball three, strike two, two outs, perfect game on the line, no-hitter on the line. Watch it. It's a ball. And Pappas is enraged. Ball four. There goes the perfect game. The no-hitter is still intact. Milt Pappas doing a burn."[8]

Pappas pounded his glove in disbelief and screamed at the home-plate umpire, 32-year-old Bruce Froemming. Regaining his composure, Pappas retired pinch-hitter Garry Jestadt on a popup to second to complete the no-hitter in 2 hours and 3 minutes.

The celebratory mood in the Cubs' clubhouse was tempered as Froemming's call, and not Pappas's game of his life, was the focus of attention. "This is the first time in my life I felt a letdown with a no-hitter," said Santo. "[Pappas] came so close to a perfect game."[9] Sportswriters peppered Pappas, who finished with six strikeouts, with questions about losing the perfecto. "I got away with several hanging sliders and I had three or four scares," he said, trying to deflect their queries.[10] He described his last three pitches to Stahl as "balls ... borderline balls," and also congratulated Froemming for calling a "good game."[11] But Pappas was seething, and everyone knew it. "I was just hoping that Froemming might sympathize with me since it was a perfect game," he said.[12]

Froemming, in his second season of an eventual 37-year career as a big-league umpire, rejected any sentimental view of calling balls and strikes. Pappas's perfect game "never entered my mind," he said. He claimed the hurler's final three pitches to Stahl "weren't borderline at all. They were what we call shoeshinners, well below the knees."[13]

Pappas's no-hitter was part of one of the best stretches in his career. He won his final 11 starts of the '72 campaign (posting a 1.86 ERA in 82⅓ innings) to finish with a 17-7 record, matching his career high in victories, set a season earlier, and reached two milestones. He became the first pitcher to record 200 victories without having won at least 20 in a season, and surpassed 3,000 innings pitched.[14]

Pappas retired after the 1973 season and his bitterness over Froemming's call seemed to grow over time. "I still to this day don't understand what Bruce Froemming was going through in his mind at that time," Pappas told ESPN in 2007. "Why didn't he throw up that right hand like the umpire did in the perfect game with Don Larsen?" [The New York Yankees hurler's final pitch in his perfect game against the Los Angeles Dodgers in Game Five of the 1956 World Series was well off the plate].[15] Pappas argued that the gravity and historical significance of the situation demanded a different approach from Froemming. "It's a home game in Wrigley Field. I'm pitching for the Chicago Cubs. The score is 8-0 in favor of the Cubs. What does he have to lose by not calling the last pitch a strike to call a perfect game? If it's a blatant pitch that *anybody* can see it's a ball, then he should've called it a ball. But it wasn't."[16]

SOURCES

In addition to the sources cited in the Notes, the author also accessed Retrosheet.org, Baseball-Reference.com, and SABR.org.

NOTES

1 George Langford, "Pappas Pitches No-Hitter; Perfection Bid Ends on Walk," *Chicago Tribune*, September 3, 1972: D1.

2 Ibid.

3 Ibid.

4 Ibid.

5 Ibid.

6 Ibid.

7 Ibid.

8 Clip of Pappas facing the final two Padres batters on YouTube, courtesy of ESPN. espn.com/espn/print?id=3019597

9 Langford.

10 Ibid.

11 Ibid.

12 Ibid.

13 Ibid.

14 Jack Quinn won 247 games in his 23-year big-league career. He won only 20+ games in a season only once, posting 26 victories in 1914 for the Baltimore Terrapins in the Federal League.

15 See Vin Scully's call of the final pitch on YouTube: https://www.youtube.com/watch?v=roZUjcYj95k. And also Louis Jacobson, "George Will says final pitch from Don Larson in 1956 was foot-and-a-half from strike zone," *PolitiFact*, June 11, 2011, http://www.politifact.com/truth-o-meter/statements/2010/jun/11/george-will/george-will-says-final-pitch-don-larsen-1956-was-f/

16 William Weinbaum, "Froemming draws Pappas' ire, 35 Years later," *ESPN.com*, Sept 20, 2007, http://www.espn.com/espn/print?id=3019597

MITTERWALD'S MONSTER GAME

APRIL 17, 1974
CHICAGO CUBS 18, PITTSBURGH PIRATES 9

By Chris Rainey

IN THE 1950s ANNOUNCER JACK Brickhouse dubbed Wrigley Field the "Friendly Confines." Baseball fans know there is nothing friendly about the ballpark when the winds are blowing. As longtime WGN weatherman Tom Skilling put it, "When the northeast gales off nearby Lake Michigan howl in toward home plate, the most mediocre pitchers can perform as if they were Greg Maddux. And when a southwest jet stream is screaming outbound, the slightest batters can hit mammoth tape-measure home runs."[1]

Typically, the winds blow in during April, and the jet stream that Skilling mentioned is usually experienced in the warmer months. That was not the case on April 17, 1974, when the Pittsburgh Pirates were in town for the second game of a three-game series (Pittsburgh won the first game, 8-5, in 12 innings). A 12-mile-per-hour wind blowing toward center field "nudged nine balls over the Wrigley Field fence."[2] The Pirates hit three, the Cubs' M&M Boys (Madlock, Mitterwald, Monday, and Morales) accounted for six. The big surprise was three off the bat of George Mitterwald.

Mitterwald had joined the Cubs from Minnesota on December 6, 1973, in a straight-up swap for backstop Randy Hundley. Mitterwald was coming off his best season (16 homers and a .259 average in '73.) At age 28, Mitterwald was enthusiastic about joining the Cubs: "A ballplayer's most productive years are from 28 to 32. I should be right there. I've always said that if I go to bat 500 times, I'll hit 20 home runs and drive in 80."[3]

The Cubs came into the game at 3-3. Mitterwald had a four-game hitting streak and was batting .417. The Pirates, with a 2-7 record, sent their Opening Day pitcher, lefty Jerry Reuss, to the mound. The Cubs countered with Burt Hooton in his second start of the season. The Pirates got to Hooton immediately. Rennie Stennett and Richie Hebner rapped singles to put runners on first and third. Al Oliver grounded to Hooton, who threw out Stennett at the plate. Willie Stargell followed with a blast over the wall to put Pittsburgh ahead 3-0. Hooton maintained his composure and retired the next two batters.

Vic Harris opened the first with a single, then Rick Monday walked. After a fly out, future Hall of Famer Billy Williams drove in a run with a single. Another fly out followed before Bill Madlock drew a walk to load the bases for Mitterwald. Mitterwald had been battling illness and sported a black eye from a bullpen mishap the previous day. Reuss served up a straight ball that the catcher deposited into the left-field seats for the first and only grand slam of his career. Judy Mitterwald understood the significance of the event and orchestrated a deal with the young Cubs fan who retrieved the ball. She presented the ball to her husband after the game.

Hooton had the lead, but he would struggle. Two singles, a walk, and an error added a Pirate run and Hooton had to coax outs from Oliver and Stargell to end the inning with the bases loaded. The Cubs added a cushion for him when Monday and Jerry Morales launched back-to-back homers in the bottom of the second.

Hooton, in the days before pitch counts, was allowed to go the distance because the Cubs had built up a massive lead. In the third, Mitterwald sent Reuss to the showers, and gave the Cubs a 10-4 lead, with his second blast. In the fourth he faced Steve Blass with the bases loaded and was "itching for the 'go' sign on a 3-0 pitch." Instead he was given the "take" and drove in a run with a walk.[4] Blass, a former All-Star, had fallen on hard times the previous season and lost all direction on his pitches. He hurled the final five innings of this game for the Pirates and surrendered five hits and seven walks. It proved to be his final game pitched in the majors.

In the sixth, Madlock and Mitterwald delivered back-to-back homers. Mitterwald ended his day with a double in the eighth. Manager Whitey Lockman figured three homers, 14 total bases, and eight RBIs were enough for the day and sent in a pinch-runner. Mitterwald's eight RBIs were the most by a Cub since Ron Santo in July 1970 versus the Expos. Three homers by a Cub were not that unusual; after all, Ernie Banks did it four times. Madlock pointed out the most important achievement of the game: "It's a sign of a good club when you come back after you're three or four runs behind."[5]

Hooton got into a good rhythm and tossed scoreless ball until the ninth. Then, with an 18-4 lead, he tired. The result was six hits, including home runs by Richie Hebner and pinch-hitter Richie Zisk that accounted for five runs. Few pitchers toss a complete game when they surrender 16 hits or 9 runs, but Hooton went the distance for his first victory of the season.

The Cubs beat the Pirates again the next day, 1-0. Billy Williams hit a sacrifice fly in the first to score Rick Monday. The club left on an 11-day road trip

during which it dropped 9 of the 11 games. Lockman was fired shortly after midseason and replaced by Jim Marshall as the Cubs finished 66-96 in sixth place.

The Pirates left Chicago with a 2-9 record. Two months later they were at 21-34 and mired in sixth place. They played the remainder of the season at a 67-40 pace and took first place in the division over the Cardinals. They lost in the Championship Series to the Dodgers, three games to one.

George Mitterwald was well on his way to that 20-homer and 80-RBI season he aspired to. He was batting .563 with an OPS of 1.854 after April 17. Sadly, the baseball gods had other plans for him. Over the next eight games he went 3-for-28. He continued to struggle and watched as his average reached a lowly .182 in early June. Soon after, he lost his starting position to Steve Swisher. Mitterwald's hopes of 500 at-bats were gone; what's more, he hit only one more home run at Wrigley the remainder of the season; he did add three road home runs.

SOURCES

Baseball-Reference and RetroSheet are indispensable when creating game stories like this.

NOTES

1   Tom Skilling, "The Winds of Wrigley Field," *Chicago Tribune*, August 21, 2005: 12.

2   *The Pantagraph* (Bloomington, Illinois), April 18, 1974: 21.

3   Richard Dozer, "Mitterwald Eyes a Big Year as Cub," *Chicago Tribune*, January 5, 1974: 31.

4   Richard Dozer, "Mitterwald (Home) Runs, Cubs Waltz," *Chicago Tribune*, April 18, 1974: 63.

5   Dozer, "Mitterwald (Home) Runs."

PIRATES ROMP AS RENNIE RAPS RECORD SEVEN HITS

SEPTEMBER 16, 1975
PITTSBURGH PIRATES 22, CHICAGO CUBS 0

By Frederick C. Bush

IN MID-SEPTEMBER 1975, THE PITTSBURGH Pirates, on the way to a fifth National League East division title in six years, arrived in Chicago for a two-day series against the Cubs at Wrigley Field. After the teams split a Monday doubleheader, the rubber game of the brief three-game set took place the next day. The date of that game – September 16, 1975 – ended up in the baseball record books beside Pirates second baseman Rennie Stennett's name after he recorded a perfect 7-for-7 day with the bat in Pittsburgh's 22-0 thrashing of the hometown nine.

Stennett, the Pirates' usual leadoff hitter that season, entered the game with a .278 batting average. Much had been expected from the Panamanian, who had grown up in the same neighborhood and attended the same high school as future Hall of Famer Rod Carew.[1] Though comparisons to Carew may have been unfair, Stennett had knocked out 196 hits for a .291 BA the previous season. Although he had been hobbled by an injured ankle during the past week, Stennett still had played 15 innings total in the previous day's doubleheader games, so he probably could have used a day of rest.

If there were any concerns about playing through the injury, Stennett quickly put them to rest. Amazingly, he had not eaten prior to the game, and instead "had popped two York Peppermint Pattie candies for breakfast in a joking bid to keep Willie Stargell from raiding his plate at the training table. ... It turned out to be all the fuel he would need."[2]

Stennett led off the game against Cubs starter Rick "Big Daddy" Reuschel with a double to right field and scored when the next batter, Richie Hebner, singled. The rout began early as Reuschel faced the entire Pirates lineup and managed to record only one out on a sacrifice fly by Dave Parker. In addition to the leadoff double, Reuschel surrendered another five singles and two walks and left the game trailing 6-0. (He would be charged with two additional runs.)

Chicago reliever Tom Dettore proved to be no deterrent to the Pirates' bats. Stennett stepped to the plate for the second time in the inning and lined a single to right field that drove in Frank Taveras and advanced pitcher John Candelaria, who had joined the hit parade with a single, to third. Candelaria scored on a wild pitch, and Stargell singled home Stennett for the Bucs' final run of the frame, which gave them a 9-0 lead. Stennett later revealed second-base umpire Dutch Rennert to be a baseball prophet, saying, "After I got my second hit in the first inning, he said I might get five. Every time I went out there he said I'd probably get another one."[3]

After Pittsburgh's opening barrage, the rookie southpaw Candelaria and Dettore kept things quiet through the end of the second inning. In the top of the third, Stennett registered his third hit of the day, a single to center, and then scored on Hebner's home run. The Pirates tacked on one more run in the fourth and led 12-0. In contrast to the Pirates' lumber attack, Candelaria kept the Cubs' bats silent, having allowed only a harmless single to José Cardenal in the second.

In the top of the fifth, Stennett victimized Dettore for his fourth hit with his second double of the game. After Hebner reached first on an error, Al Oliver singled, and Stennett scored his fourth run of the day. Stargell singled home Hebner, which resulted in Oscar Zamora entering the game in relief of Dettore. Zamora's presence merely resulted in some more Pittsburgh runs as the first batter he faced, Parker, drilled a three-run homer. Manny Sanguillen and Taveras were on first and second with two outs when Stennett came to bat once again; it was the second time in the game that he recorded two at-bats in a single inning. He grounded a single to right field for his fifth hit of the game, which scored Sanguillen and gave the Pirates an 18-0 margin. This time around, Stennett did not score as Hebner struck out to end the Pirates' half of the inning. Candelaria allowed two singles in the bottom of the frame but continued to keep the Cubs off the scoreboard.

Buddy Schultz took the hill for the Cubs in the sixth and fared no better than his predecessors. After another Chicago error, Parker and Richie Zisk eventually scored unearned runs for a 20-0 lead that made it appear as though it were the cities' two football teams playing rather than their baseball teams. Candelaria continued his superlative effort by setting the Cubs down in order for the fourth time in the bottom half of the sixth.

Stennett led off the seventh with a single against Schultz. Two outs later, Bob Robertson (who had replaced Stargell at first base in the fifth), Parker, and Zisk hit consecutive singles; the latter two hits knocked in Stennett and Robertson with the final runs in Pittsburgh's 22-0 triumph.

The Pirates' scoring may have been finished, but Stennett was still going strong. He faced Paul Reuschel, Rick's older brother, with two outs in the top of the eighth and bounced a ball past third baseman Champ Summers that went into right field for a triple and gave him a modern-era record of seven hits in a nine-inning game. Once the record was in hand, Pirates manager Danny Murtaugh

sent Willie Randolph into the game to run for his hobbled second baseman, who doffed his helmet to acknowledge the ovation from the 4,932 spectators. Ken Brett replaced Candelaria in the bottom of the eighth, and Ramon Hernandez pitched the ninth inning for Pittsburgh as the three Pirates hurlers combined for the shutout

After the game, the focus was on Stennett's performance since he was only the second major-leaguer to amass seven hits in a nine-inning game.[4] He also had tied another record, held by three other players, by twice getting two hits in a single inning.[5] His batting line for the day included seven hits in seven at-bats, two doubles, one triple, five runs scored, and two RBIs, and he had raised his batting average to .287; he came up a home run short of hitting for the cycle as well. Afterward, the modest Panamanian said, "I don't think about records. It's great that I got it, but I never thought about it. I thought someday I might get five hits in a game, but I never dreamt I'd get seven."[6]

The Pirates had recorded a National League season-high 24 hits and also had reached base via six walks, a hit batter, and three errors. In addition to Stennett, Parker had contributed to the onslaught with five RBIs while Hebner, Stargell, and Taveras had chipped in three RBIs apiece. The 22-0 whitewash was the largest shutout margin in baseball, supplanting 21-0 drubbings administered by the Detroit Tigers against the Cleveland Blues on September 15, 1901, and by the New York Yankees against the Philadelphia Athletics on August 13, 1939.[7] The next day's Chicago Tribune jokingly noted, "It was the biggest rout ever started and finished by brothers," and it also set a record for "most organists to play at one game."[8]

Stennett added his name to two additional records when the Pirates visited Philadelphia. The day after his 7-for-7 performance, he went 3-for-5 against the Phillies to tie the major-league record of 10 hits in two consecutive games.[9] The next night he went 2-for-4 to tie the NL record of 12 hits over three straight games. Stennett's torrid hitting and record-tying feats garnered him the NL Player of the Week Award.[10] Stennett took things in stride, saying, "These records are nice to have, but the big thing is winning."[11]

In spite of its rarity, Stennett's single-game hits record is rarely mentioned. In a 2009 interview, he said, "Well, I hear about Joe DiMaggio and others, but I never hear mine mentioned. ... Maybe somebody will have to do it again for that to happen."[12] Stennett was indeed thrust back into the limelight after San Francisco Giants shortstop Brandon Crawford on August 8, 2016, became the third major leaguer to get seven hits in a single game, prompting the former Pirate to note, "I feel good just being remembered."[13]

NOTES

1   Joseph Wancho, "Rennie Stennett," sabr.org/bioproj/person/95f220e9, accessed March 18, 2017.

2   Sean Braswell, "Paying Homage to a Forgotten Baseball Record," ozy.com/flashback/paying-homage-to-a-forgotten-baseball-record/64529, accessed March 18, 2017.

3   Richard Dozer, "Yes, Cubs Lose: 22-0," *Chicago Tribune*, September 17, 1975: 60.

4   Baltimore's Wilbert Robinson had accomplished the feat in 1892, prior to the modern era.

5   Dozer, "Yes, Cubs Lose: 22-0."

6   Bob Smizik, "Blazing Bucs Enter Inferno," *Pittsburgh Press*, September 17, 1975: 65.

7   Dozer, "Yes, Cubs Lose: 22-0." The Cleveland Indians matched this feat as they trounced the Yankees in New York by the same score on August 31, 2004.

8   Ibid. Chicago White Sox organist Nancy Faust had joined the Cubs' Frank Pellico and had played a couple of tunes.

9   Numerous players share this record. Prior to Stennett, the most recent player to accomplish the feat had been Baltimore's Don Baylor in 1973.

10   "Stennett, Bonds Receive Player of Week Awards," *The Sporting News*, October 4, 1975: 32.

11   Charley Feeney, "Rennie's Record Rapping Highlights Buc Drive," *The Sporting News*, October 4, 1975: 7.

12   Dejan Kovacevic, "On the Pirates: Stennett Reflects on Sweet Seven," post-gazette.com/sports/pirates/2009/05/31/On-the-Pirates-Stennett-reflects-on-sweet-seven/stories/200905310172?pgpageversion=pgevoke, accessed March 18, 2017.

13   Associated Press, "Brandon Crawford, Rennie Stennett Meet in Miami After Seven-Hit Game," espn.com/mlb/story/_/id/17265385/rennie-stennett-brandon-crawford-san-francisco-giants-meet-miami, accessed March 18, 2017. Crawford needed 14 innings to get his seven hits; three of his hits, including the game-winner, came in extra innings. Two nights later, on August 10, Stennett was on hand at Marlins Park to congratulate Crawford prior to the Giants' game against the Marlins.

SCHMIDT BRINGS PHILLIES BACK FROM THE DEAD WITH 4 HRS

APRIL 17, 1976
PHILADELPHIA PHILLIES 18, CHICAGO CUBS 16

By Richard Cuicchi

WHEN THE HOME TEAM GETS AHEAD BY a score of 13-2 early in a game with its ace on the mound, it wouldn't be a total surprise if its opponent packed it in for the rest of the game. But that certainly wasn't the case on April 17, 1976, when slugger Mike Schmidt, beginning in the fifth inning, helped resurrect his Philadelphia Phillies teammates with four consecutive home runs to eventually defeat the Chicago Cubs, 18-16, in 10 innings at Wrigley Field.

With the Phillies' Steve Carlton and the Cubs' Rick Reuschel as the opposing starters, few in the crowd of 28,287 expected to see a game that would get out of hand early. Each was his team's ace, and a low-scoring game with a good number of strikeouts would have normally been in order. That didn't happen, though, as both teams had near-record-setting offensive performances, with Schmidt leading the dramatic comeback for the Phillies.

The Saturday afternoon game on April 17 was the seventh of the season for the Cubs and the fifth for the Phillies. Philadelphia was a team on the rise, having finished third in the NL East Division in 1974 and second in 1975, while Chicago's last winning season had come in 1972.

The 31-year-old Carlton was starting his 12th season in the majors. He had already accumulated 148 victories and posted a Cy Young Award season with the Phillies in 1972 when he led the league in victories (27), ERA (1.97), complete games (30), innings pitched (346⅓), and strikeouts (310).

Reuschel was a double-digit winner in each of his previous four seasons.

The right-handed-batting Schmidt's reputation as an emerging slugger stemmed from the fact he had been the home-run champion of the National League in 1974 and 1975. Only 26 years old with four major-league seasons under his belt, he had rapidly established himself as one of the premier third basemen in baseball and thus was a big factor in the Phillies' rise.

After a scoreless first inning, the Phillies' Garry Maddox got the scoring started in the top of the second inning with a solo home run.

Lefty Carlton was blasted for seven runs in the bottom of the second inning, when the Cubs batted around. With one out, Steve Swisher hit a solo home run to put the first Cubs run on the board. Leadoff hitter Rick Monday's second hit of the day was a home run with Dave Rosello and Reuschel aboard. Bill Madlock's double scored Jose Cardenal who had doubled before him. Andre Thornton then walked, and Manny Trillo, batting for the second time in the inning, singled in Madlock. Phillies manager Danny Ozark replaced Carlton with right-hander Ron Schueler. Swisher greeted Schueler with his second hit of the inning, a single that scored Thornton and made the score 7-1.

In the bottom of the third inning, the Cubs picked up where they left off in the previous frame. Batting around again, they added five more runs on four singles, a walk, and two hit batsmen. Madlock,

Trillo, and Rosello had run-scoring singles, while Thornton got an RBI when he was plunked by relief pitcher Gene Garber with the bases loaded.

Each team scored a run in the fourth inning, with the Phillies' coming on Dave Cash's RBI single and the Cubs getting a second home run by Monday off the Phils' Ron Reed. At that point, it appeared Monday would be the hitting star of the day.

At the start of the fifth inning with the score 13-2, the game already seemed to be out of control for the Phillies. They could have easily been given up for dead with such a deficit and having already left six runners on base. Even a two-run home run by Schmidt in the top of the fifth didn't make much of a dent.

Neither team scored in the sixth inning, but Philadelphia found new life in the seventh on a single by Larry Bowa, followed by a run-scoring triple by Jay Johnstone. Greg Luzinski's fly ball scored Johnstone; then Schmidt smacked his second homer of the game off Reuschel to make the score 13-7.

Phillies reliever Wayne Twitchell held the Cubs scoreless in the seventh for the second consecutive inning. Mike Garman, who replaced Reuschel to start the eighth inning, wasn't as lucky, as he ran into a buzz saw by giving up five runs on four hits and a walk. Dick Allen drove in two runs with a single, and, with two runners on base, Schmidt pulled the Phillies within one run by hitting his third home run of the game.

In the top of the ninth inning, the tide finally turned for the Phillies. Catcher Bob Boone led off with a home run off Darold Knowles to tie the game at 13-13. Bowa pulled the Phillies' coffin out of the grave, putting them ahead with a triple that scored Bobby Tolan. Johnstone then laid down a bunt that scored Bowa and made the Phillies lead 15-13.

Now, all the Phillies needed for the comeback win was for Tug McGraw to retire the Cubs in the bottom of the ninth. He had held them scoreless in the eighth and registered two outs in the ninth before Swisher singled in Jerry Morales and Thornton to tie the score at 15 apiece and send the game into extra innings.

However, with Allen on base with a walk in the top of the 10th inning, Schmidt came to the team's rescue again with his fourth consecutive home run. The round-tripper came off Rick Reuschel's brother, Paul, who had just entered the game in relief of Knowles. Cash's sacrifice fly added the final Phillies run to make the score 18-15.

The game ended with the score 18-16, as the Cubs managed to put up one more run with two doubles off Tom Underwood in the bottom of the 10th.

Schmidt became only the 10th major leaguer to hit four homers in a game and the second National Leaguer to hit four in consecutive at-bats (Bobby Lowe had accomplished it in 1894).[1] Before Schmidt, Willie Mays in 1961 was the last player to hit four home runs in a game. Schmidt, who was 5-for 6 at the plate with eight RBIs, was the first Phillies player to hit four homers in a game since Chuck Klein did it in 1936. Ed Delahanty also accomplished it in 1896.

Schmidt had struck out nine times in his previous four games and thus was dropped from third to sixth in the batting order by manager Ozark. He didn't seem irritated about the move, commenting, "I don't care where I hit … third … sixth … ninth. There'll be people on base to drive in." He tried to downplay any euphoria about his historic game, saying, "I just float around most of the time anyway. I try to stay on the same level whether I strike out three times or have a big day."[2] Schmidt likely benefited from a wind blowing out at 20 mph at Wrigley Field. He acknowledged that if the wind had not been blowing, two of his homers would probably have stayed in the park and gone for doubles instead.[3] The two teams hit nine home runs on the windy day.

After the game, Cubs' hitting star Monday was angry about a situation in the sixth inning when Twitchell hit him with a pitch after he had collected his fourth consecutive hit, including two home runs. Monday was the third Cubs player to be hit in the game and had to be restrained by umpire Andy Olsen from charging Twitchell on the mound. Monday felt that he had been targeted by the Phillies hurler after his earlier success. Asked if he thought he had a good day at the plate, the disgusted Monday snapped, "As far as I was concerned, it was no day at all."[4]

The Phillies collected the most hits in a game (24) since they recorded 26 on August 25, 1922. The Cubs had their most hits (19) in almost five years.[5]

McGraw was the winning pitcher, while Knowles took the loss. Carlton had his worst outing of the season, in which he won 20 games and posted a 3.13 ERA.

The Phillies took the NL East Division crown with 101 wins. Schmidt won his third straight home-run title in 1976 and went on to hit the most career homers (548) by a third baseman.

SOURCES

In addition to the sources cited in the Notes, the author consulted the following:

Baseball-Reference.com.

Goddard, Joe. "Schmidt and the 'Big Stick,'" *Chicago Sun-Times*, April 18, 1976: 131.

Lewis, Allen. "Schmidt Hits Four Home Runs," *Philadelphia Inquirer*, April 18, 1976: D-1.

NOTES

1   Ray Kelly, "Schmidt HR Bat Works Overtime, 8 in 6 Games," *The Sporting News*, May 8, 1976: 7.

2   Richard Dozer, "Schmidt's Four Homers Rally Phillies," *Chicago Tribune*, April 18, 1976: 3-1.

3   Joe Goddard, "Phils Fly in Wrigley Wind 18-16," *Chicago Sun-Times*, April 18, 1976: 130.

4   Dozer, 3-3.

5   Goddard.

SCHMIDT'S PHILLIES OUTSLUG KINGMAN'S CUBS

MAY 17, 1979
PHILADELPHIA PHILLIES 23, CHICAGO CUBS 22

By Mike Huber

IN WHAT COULD BE BILLED AS ONE OF the wildest games in major-league history, the Philadelphia Phillies and Chicago Cubs met on a Thursday afternoon in front of 14,952 fans at Wrigley Field. The wind was blowing out at 18 mph.[1] A little more than four hours later, the Phillies emerged victorious, securing a 23-22 victory in 10 innings. The game featured 45 runs, 50 hits, 11 home runs, 127 batters, 11 pitchers, 15 walks, and 37 players. The visiting Phillies were paced by Mike Schmidt and his two home runs, including the game-winner. On the Chicago side, Dave Kingman smashed three home runs.

The Phillies had scored 13 runs against the Cubs the day before as Steve Carlton shut out Chicago, so their bats were warm. Their pitchers' arms were also warm; the Phillies' rotation and bullpen had the best earned-run average in the National League (2.91). Chicago batters had mustered only three hits against Carlton, but they exploded in this game.

Randy Lerch started for the Phillies and Dennis Lamp got the nod for the home team. Philadelphia wasted no time in jumping on Lamp and Chicago, sending 10 batters to the plate. Schmidt and Bob Boone hit three-run homers. Lamp retired only one of the seven batters he faced. (Bake McBride was gunned down at home plate on a Pete Rose comebacker to the mound.) With the score 6-0, Cubs manager Herman Franks pulled Lamp in favor of Donnie Moore. Moore struck out Rudy Meoli but

gave up a solo home run to Lerch before McBride was retired. Philadelphia had seven hits in the inning.

Larry Bowa, the Phillies' shortstop, told reporters, "Whenever Lerch pitched, we never scored any runs for him. We got those early ones and said to him, 'Okay, there's your runs.' But you could tell it wasn't going to be enough."[2] Lerch pitched to six batters in the bottom of the first, and five of them got hits. The first three Cubs batters singled, scoring one run, and then Kingman launched a three-run blast. With one out, Jerry Martin doubled to right field, and Lerch was sent to the showers by skipper Danny Ozark. Doug Bird relieved and allowed two more runs on a single and triple. The Cubs' seven hits accounted for six runs.

Thirteen Phillies faced Cubs pitching in the third inning, and eight of them scored. Willie Hernandez relieved Moore after six batters had reached and four runs had scored. Again the Phillies had seven hits in the inning, including a three-run homer by Garry Maddox off Hernandez, but they also had two walks and a hit batsman. Hernandez also pitched the fourth and fifth innings, allowing two runs in the fourth and four in the fifth. In the bottom of the fourth, Kingman connected with his second blast, a two-run homer, and Steve Ontiveros sent a solo shot over the wall. By the time the Cubs came to bat in the bottom of the fifth, Philadelphia had its largest lead of the game, 21-9. It would not hold. Bowa later commented archly, "When we got up by 12, I figured we could win if we could hold them

In 1979 Dave "King Kong" Kingman led the majors with 48 home runs with the Cubs. In parts of 16 seasons, he blasted 442 round-trippers for seven teams. (Photo by Focus on Sport/Getty Images)

under two touchdowns and could block a couple of extra points."³

Tug McGraw, the third Phillies hurler, started the bottom of the fifth. Barry Foote greeted him with a single, Ted Sizemore reached on an error by Schmidt, and pinch-hitter Steve Dillard, batting for Hernandez, walked to load the bases. McGraw walked Ivan de Jesus, forcing in a run. After Mike Vail flied out to center, Bill Buckner launched a grand slam. Kingman drew a walk, and an out later, Martin followed with a two-run homer. Foote doubled, and Ozark brought in Ron Reed to relieve McGraw. Reed got Sizemore to ground out to short to end the inning, but the Cubs had put a big dent in the Phillies' lead.

McGraw recalled, "I gave up seven runs in one-third of an inning. It took me the rest of the year to get my ERA back into [three] digits."⁴ Only four of the runs were earned.

Chicago's Bill Caudill and Ray Burris, who had both pitched the day before, combined for three innings from the top of the sixth through the top of the eighth. Chicago scored three more runs off Reed in the bottom of the sixth, as the Cubs scored two on groundouts and Kingman hit his third homer. Suddenly the Phillies' lead was down to two runs, at 21-19. Boone doubled in Greg Gross in the Phillies' seventh to make it 22-19, but Chicago engineered three more runs in the eighth on RBI singles by Buckner, Martin, and Foote off Reed, and the game was tied, 22-22.

Bruce Sutter became the Cubs' sixth pitcher in the top of the ninth inning, and he retired the Phillies, allowing only a walk to Meoli. The Phillies countered with Rawly Eastwick in the bottom of the ninth, their fifth pitcher of the game. He pitched a 1-2-3 inning and the game went into the 10th.

Sutter was perhaps the best reliever in baseball at the time. When he delivered a 3-and-2 split-fingered fastball to Schmidt with two outs in the top of the 10th, and Schmidt sent it deep into the left-field bleachers, the pitcher did not move. Afterward he commented, "I didn't even turn around to look at it. I knew exactly where it was going."[5] Of Wrigley Field, Schmidt said, "Ballplayers often will say that you never can get enough runs to win in this park, but they always say it sarcastically. After today, they can forget the sarcasm."[6] The Phillies third baseman had gone 2-for-4 and walked four times in the game. Cubs manager Franks, "with 20-20 hindsight after the game, sighed and said he wished Schmidt had walked again."[7]

Eastwick, in his second inning of relief, set the Cubs down in order in the bottom of the 10th and picked up his first win of the season. He was the only pitcher to retire the side in order; in fact, he retired all six batters he faced.

The two teams were 17-for-44 with runners in scoring position. The Phillies left 15 runners on base; the Cubs stranded only seven. The Phillies' Bowa was 5-for-8 and teammate Maddox was 4-for-4 with four RBIs. Boone was 3-for-4 with two walks and five runs driven in. All 16 starting position players got at least one hit. Had Chicago won the game, Buckner would have made headlines with his 4-for-7 performance and 7 runs batted in. Kingman was 3-for-6 with 6 RBIs.

The two home-run sluggers in the contest did not shine afield. Schmidt made two errors at third for the Phillies, and Kingman made one in left field for the Cubs. Bowa summed up the experience as follows: "It was the wildest game I ever participated in. From a personal aspect, I was thinking late in the game, 'My God, I've already got five hits, and we might end up losing.'"[8] His manager, Ozark, said, "After this one, I guess we proved the National League can get by without using a designated hitter!"[9]

The other four National League games this day produced had a total of 28 runs. The National League record for most runs overcome in winning a game was 11, set on April 17, 1976, by the Phillies against the Cubs in Chicago. Philadelphia also won that game in the 10th inning,18-16, on Mike Schmidt's fourth home run of the day, a three-run blast. On this day, the Cubs had erased a 12-run deficit, but still ended up one run short of victory.

This was the second time in history that the Cubs had allowed 23 runs to the Phillies. Fifty-seven years earlier, on August 25, 1922, the Phillies and Cubs played at Cubs Park in Chicago and combined to score 49 runs on 51 hits.[10] That game still (as of 2017) held the record for most runs in a game by two teams.

SOURCES

In addition to the sources mentioned in the notes, the author consulted baseball-reference.com and retrosheet.org.

NOTES

1   "Phils Win 50-Hit Slugfest, 23-22," *New York Times*, May 18, 1979.

2   Paul Sullivan, "22 Runs, and the Cubs Still Lost," *Chicago Tribune*, May 14, 1989.

3   Dave Nightingale, "22 Cubs Runs One Too Few to Stop Phils," *Chicago Tribune*, May 18, 1979.

4   Sullivan.

5   Dave Nightingale, "Flags Blew an Early Omen to Schmidt," *Chicago Tribune*, May 18, 1979.

6   Ibid.

7   Ibid.

8   Sullivan.

9   Nightingale, "22 Cubs Runs."

10 In that game the Cubs scored 10 runs in the second inning and 14 runs in the fourth, but allowed 14 runs in the final two innings to barely hold on for the win. The Cubs hit three home runs; the Phillies had 20 singles. There were 21 walks and nine errors. For more information, read the SABR Games Project article about it.

FOOTE AND DE JESUS SLUG THEIR WAY TO WILD WALK-OFF WIN

APRIL 22, 1980
CHICAGO CUBS 16, ST. LOUIS CARDINALS 12

By Russ Lake

ON APRIL 22, 1980, THE CHICAGO CUBS were 5-3, and one game out of first place in the National League East Division. They had swept the New York Mets in a three-game home series that drew healthy turnouts to Wrigley Field. Nonetheless, the "jury was still out" in regard to the amount of support new skipper Preston Gomez and his squad would receive from the fandom. During an offseason newspaper poll that evaluated potential Cubs manager candidates, Gomez finished in a tie for 10th (with Maury Wills).[1]

With St. Louis in town, the aged venue at Clark and Addison offered a chance to watch what had developed over the past 15 years into what Midwest baseball enthusiasts plugged as baseball's best rivalry. However, the "Lou Brock for Ernie Broglio" teaser had run its course since the former Cubs outfielder Brock had retired after the 1979 season. Cubs fans did not seem enthralled that their team included ex-Cardinals Mike Tyson, Lynn McGlothen, Doug Capilla, and Mick Kelleher. Similarly, Cardinals rooters were not enchanted having ex-Cubs Steve Swisher, Darold Knowles, and Donnie Moore playing for their team.

Won-lost numbers are traditionally tossed aside when these opponents tangle. Besides, the season was not quite two weeks old. The Cardinals, tied for fifth in the NL East, entered with a 4-6 record. Bullpen ineffectiveness, with the nonstarters pitching to an overall 6.41 ERA, generated a headache for manager Ken Boyer. In right-hander Bruce Sutter, Gomez had

an All-Star reliever who could be counted on during late-inning situations. As Boyer viewed his own relief selections, he coveted an option like Sutter.

For April, it was hot. A temperature forecast of 80 was surpassed by midmorning. A record-setting mark of 91 had locals converging en masse to the beach to brave Lake Michigan water still a bone-chilling 48 degrees.[2] The unseasonable weather likely threw a wrench into Wrigley's walk-up attendance. Still, a lively shirtsleeve gathering of 18,889 entered the ballpark with many arriving early to watch batting practice.

Right-hander Dennis Lamp took the ball for Chicago. The 27-year-old Lamp was 2-0 with a 2.57 ERA. Bob Forsch got the nod for the Cardinals, and came in 0-1, 2.25. The veteran right-hander's older brother, Ken Forsch, pitched for the Houston Astros. The siblings had each hurled no-hitters, Bob's coming in 1978 (against the Phillies), and Ken's in 1979 (Braves). Lamp, beginning his third full season, was 2-3 lifetime facing St. Louis. Forsch had enjoyed a 12-4 career versus the Cubs.

Lamp retired Garry Templeton and Ken Oberkfell before Keith Hernandez reached on an infield hit. Ted Simmons walked, and Bobby Bonds singled home Hernandez with Simmons going to third and Bonds taking second on an error by left fielder Larry Biittner. George Hendrick hit a hard grounder that third baseman Steve Ontiveros muffed, allowing Simmons to score. Chicago's Ivan De Jesus led off the bottom of the first with his second home run of the season. The drive to the left-field bleachers prompted WGN's Jack Brickhouse's trademark round-tripper call of, "Hey, hey!"[3]

Tony Scott singled to start the second and advanced to third on a stolen base and wild pitch. Lamp walked Forsch, and faced more trouble as the top of the order loomed. Tyson helped Lamp by turning a 4-3 double play against Templeton as Scott sprinted home for a 3-1 lead. The Cubs clipped Forsch in their turn when Jerry Martin doubled and scored on a single by Barry Foote to narrow the deficit to 3-2. A wild pitch followed by a walk to Carlos Lezcano had Chicago vying for a big inning. However, Forsch fanned Tyson, and then turned Lamp's bunt into a 1-5-4 twin killing.

A steady swirling wind ramped up to 22 mph, switched from due south to southwest, and made life miserable for outfielders trying to corral fly balls.[4] In the Cardinals' third, Bonds blasted a towering two-run smash to left.[5] Hendrick lined a hit to the gap in left-center but was thrown out by Lezcano trying for a triple. Kenny Reitz parked a drive to right-center that the wind helped into the bleachers for his second home run of the year, and increased the Cardinals' advantage to 6-2. Chicago delivered offensive thunder right back at St. Louis. Martin's bases-loaded single in the third sent home two, and Foote's double plated another pair to knot things at 6-6.

The ex-Cardinal Lynn McGlothen, a right-hander, came in for the Cubs to begin the fourth. Forsch doubled to lead off. Templeton singled and on Ontiveros's second error he and Forsch wound up at second and third. Forsch scored on Oberkfell's groundball, and Simmons worked a two-out walk. Bonds and Hendrick rapped run-scoring singles, so Gomez waved in left-hander Capilla, another ex-Cardinal. Reitz knocked a two-run double into the left-field corner that bumped the St. Louis lead to 11-6. In the bottom of the fourth, Forsch allowed singles to De Jesus and Bill Buckner but was bailed out by Ontiveros's double-play grounder.

Forsch socked his fourth career home run with a leadoff shot to right field to open the fifth, for a 12-6

cushion. Capilla then accomplished what his mound predecessors could not by retiring three consecutive batters. In the bottom of the inning, Tyson delivered a run-scoring sacrifice fly. Scot Thompson followed with a pinch-hit double, and raced home when De Jesus tripled to right, completed the cycle with a triple to right to make the score 12-9. Forsch, tagged for 14 hits, was lifted as Boyer went to left-hander Bob Sykes, who fanned Ontiveros.

Sykes and Chicago's Bill Caudill offered semblances of effective relief work by shutting down the bats during the sixth. Caudill did the same in the top of the seventh. Cubs catcher Foote remarked, "Caudill quieting their bats was the important thing for us."[6] Sykes, after opening the bottom half with a strikeout, allowed consecutive singles to Tyson, Steve Dillard, and De Jesus to load the bases. Boyer went to righty John Fulgham, and the 24-year-old fanned pinch-hitter Mike Vail. With Buckner up, Boyer switched to southpaw Don Hood, but Buckner smacked a two-run single to close the Cubs' deficit to one run (12-11).

In the eighth, Dick Tidrow benefited from Lezcano's diving catch in right-center of Hernandez's drive,[7] but the pitcher proceeded to fill the bases with two outs on two walks and a hit by Hendrick. Gomez brought in Sutter, who struck out Scott on a split-finger fastball. Right-hander Roy Thomas was on for St. Louis in the bottom of the eighth, and Foote knocked a one-out solo homer into the left-field bleachers that tied the score, 12-12. On WGN radio Vince Lloyd assured listeners, "It's a bell-ringer!"[8]

Sutter allowed a one-out single to Templeton in the ninth, but Foote gunned down the shortstop attempting to steal. In the bottom of the inning, right-handed closer Mark Littell came on for the Cardinals, hoping to get the game into extra innings. Littell got De Jesus a grounder, the first time in the game the shortstop was retired. But pinch-hitter Dave Kingman lined a one-out single to left. Lenny Randle ran for Kingman and swiped second. Buckner was intentionally passed, then Littell uncorked a wild pitch to put runners on second and third.

Littell struck out Biittner, looking, but walked Jerry Martin to load the bases. Foote, already the author of one homer, lofted a first-pitch slider to right center. Hendrick and Scott retreated, but could only watch the "wind-aided" sphere land in the wire basket near the 368-foot mark for a walk-off grand slam.[9]

The Wrigley Field faithful responded with a roar as Foote circled the bases. The burly catcher's career-day line revealed eight RBIs on a single, double, and two home runs. At home plate, Buckner planted a congratulatory kiss on Foote's forehead before he was mobbed by teammates.[10] The line score read 16 runs, 23 hits, and 3 errors for the Cubs, 12 runs, 16 hits, and no errors for the Cardinals. Each team employed six pitchers, with Sutter getting the win and Littell the loss.

Boyer said, "It looked like where the team that scored last would win. In 20 years, I've never seen the wind blow out like this."[11]

Gomez agreed, commenting, "The wind made things very tough out there today. From batting practice on, you could see it would be one of those days. If you could write a script, this is the way you would have done it."[12]

SOURCES

In addition to the sources cited in the Notes, the author also accessed Retrosheet.org, Baseball-Reference.com, Newspapers.com, SABR.org/bioproj, and *The Sporting News* archive via Paper of Record.

NOTES

1   Bob Verdi, "Cubs' Choice Represents Victory for Status Quo," *Chicago Tribune*, October 3, 1979: 65.

2   Photo caption, "On an August Day in April," *Chicago Tribune*, April 23, 1980: 64.

3   Phil Rosenthal, "Hey, Hey Chicago, What Do You Say?" *Chicago Tribune*, November 9, 2016: 3-1.

4   Richard Dozer, "Another Slam-Bang Cub Day," *Chicago Tribune*, April 23, 1980: 57, 59.

5   Rick Hummel, "Cardinals to Claiborne: Get a Stopper," *St. Louis Post-Dispatch*, April 23, 1980: 21.

6   Dozer.

7   Ibid.

8   Verdi, "Please Feel Pity for Vince & Lou," *Chicago Tribune*, May 22, 1981: 59.

9   Dozer.

10   Photo Caption, *Chicago Tribune*, April 23, 1980: 57.

11   Associated Press, "Cubs' Foote Kicks Cardinals on His Biggest Day in Majors," *Southern Illinoisan* (Carbondale, Illinois), April 23, 1980: 9.

12   Dozer.

THE SANDBERG GAME

JUNE 23, 1984
CHICAGO CUBS 12, ST. LOUIS CARDINALS 11 (11 INNINGS)

By Scott Ferkovich

THE CHICAGO CUBS WERE STRUGGLING.

For the first two months of the season, they were a cute story. Since mid-May, the lovable losers of recent years had spent much of their time in first place in the National League East. Starting on June 6, however, the team lost ten of 16 games. The lowlight was a four-game sweep in Philadelphia in which they were outscored, 33-13. That knocked them out of the top spot, and it looked for a while like things were reverting to form at 1060 West Addison.

As the day began on June 23, the Cubs found themselves in third place, a game and a half behind the division-leading Mets. The St. Louis Cardinals were in town, a team that was barely treading water at 34-37. The Cubs sent Steve "Rainbow" Trout to the mound, while the Cardinals countered with virtual-unknown Ralph Citarella, making his first big-league start. It was a nationally televised Saturday afternoon *Game of the Week* on NBC, with Bob Costas and Tony Kubek doing the honors. Before the contest began, Kubek observed, "The wind… blowing in from right field, so it'll kill any ball hit to the right field sector. Anything hit to left-center will be… given a little help, if it's up in the air."[1]

It looked at the outset like the Cubs' swoon was going to continue. Trout bombed early, and by the time they came to bat in their half of the sixth, they were down 9-3. Suddenly, however, their bats woke up. They scored five runs in that frame, sending Citarella to the showers, to quickly turn a yawner into a tense, exciting one-run game.

That is how the score remained until the bottom of the ninth. "This has been one entertaining ball game, folks," Costas commented, just in case any of the viewers at home didn't already know it. On the mound for St. Louis was their ace reliever (and former Cy Young Award-winner with the Cubs) Bruce Sutter, who had entered the game in the bottom of the seventh. He had faced four batters so far, and gotten four harmless groundball outs. Leading off for the North Siders was their fine young second baseman Ryne Sandberg, who already had three singles and four RBIs in the game. On a 1-1 count, Sandberg took Sutter downtown, drilling a hanging curve over the left-center-field bleachers, onto Waveland Avenue. The game was tied, to the delight of the frenetic Wrigley Field faithful. The Cubs got the winning run to third base with two out in the person of Gary Matthews, but a groundout ended the inning, sending the game into extras.

St. Louis put a quick stop to the buzz going on at the ballpark, by scoring a pair of runs in the top of the tenth. Sutter was still on the mound, and Chicago appeared to have its work cut out as the bottom half of the inning loomed. Two quick ground-ball outs did nothing but deflate any remaining air left in the Cubs' party balloon. But Bob Dernier walked, and Sutter was left to again face Sandberg. The count went to 1-1, at which point Costas began rapidly reciting to the TV crowd that "our game today was produced by Ken Edmundson, directed by Bucky Gunts, Mike Weisman is the executive producer of NBC Sports, coordinating producer of baseball Harry Coyle. One-one pitch." Sutter served. Sandberg swung. Kubek belted out a distended "Ooooooh myyy!" Costas was surely more descriptive: "And he hits it to deep left center! Look out! Do you believe it! It's gone!" Both said nothing for the next 50 seconds. Viewers across the nation watched dumbfounded as 38,079 people suddenly went certifiably insane at Wrigley Field.

In the next booth over from Costas and Kubek were Harry Caray, Lou Boudreau, and Milo Hamilton, who had spent the afternoon taking turns describing the game for Chicago's WGN radio. As Sandberg's second home run soared toward the bleachers, the three went into a collective fit of frenzy, and Caray's voice was nearly drowned out in his broadcast partners' delirious "Oh-hohs!" and "Hey-heeeeys!" "THERE'S A LONG DRIVE," Caray shouted. "WAY BACK! MIGHT BE OUTTA HERE! IT IS! IT IS! HE DID IT! HE DID IT AGAIN! THE GAME IS TIED! THE GAME IS TIED! HO-LY COW!" It was Caray at his flabbergasted finest. "EVERYONE IS GONE BANANAS! HO-LY COW! WHAT WOULD THE ODDS BE," Caray asked, his voice betraying his emotion, throwing out the question to anyone with a calculator, "IF I TOLD YOU THAT *TWICE* SANDBERG WOULD HIT HOME RUNS OFF BRUCE SUTTER?!" Cardinal manager Whitey Herzog kept Sutter in the game. "Here now is Gary Matthews," Caray noted. "C'MON, YOU GUYS!"[2]

But the guys didn't come on. Matthews grounded out, and the inning was over, much to the relief of Sutter.

St. Louis threatened but didn't score in the 11th. Finally, mercifully, Dave Rucker replaced Sutter to start the Cub half of the inning. Leon Durham led off with a walk, stole second, and advanced to third as catcher Darrell Porter's throw bounced into center field. Jeff Lahti replaced Rucker on the mound. Keith Moreland and Jody Davis were both intentionally walked to set up a force at any base. "What a ballgame!" Caray exclaimed, apparently still unable to believe what he had witnessed moments before. "Hey! Was that 23-21 game against the Phillies any more exciting?" he asked, referring to a legendary 1979 Wrigley Field game (actually 23-22). "No, nope, no way," Boudreau and Hamilton stated

Hall of Famer Ryne Sandberg was a 10-time All-Star and nine-time Gold Glove–winning second baseman. In 1984 he helped the Cubs to the postseason for the first time since 1945 and was named National League MVP, pacing the circuit with 114 runs and 19 triples, along with a career-high 200 hits. (Photo by Focus on Sport/Getty Images)

emphatically. Dave Owen, the last position player available on the Cub bench, came on to pinch-hit. A switch-hitter, he batted left-handed against the righty Lahti. The trouble was, Owen was hitting .133 from the left side. It would not matter this day. Owen drove a single into right field, Durham scored, and just like that, the rollercoaster affair had come to an end. "CUBS WIN!" Caray shouted. "CUBS WIN! CUBS WIN! HO-LY COW! LISTEN TO THE CROWD!" After letting the noise wash over him for a few seconds, Caray declared: "I NEVER SAW A GAME LIKE THIS IN MY LIFE, AND I'VE BEEN AROUND A LONG LIFE! WHAT A VICTORY! WHAT A VICTORY! LISTEN TO THE HAND THE CUBS ARE GETTING!"

Costas, on the other hand, chose a more understated description of Owen's hit. "That's it!" Moments later, before cutting to a commercial, he would confess, "Can't remember the last time I saw a better one!" Indeed, neither could many people. It was a thrilling game, an instant classic, highlighted by two unforgettable at-bats involving two future Hall of Fame players in Sutter and Sandberg.

It was a coming-out party, both for Sandberg and the Cubs, as their grand performances occurred on a national stage. Back in the days before the proliferation of cable television, NBC's *Game of the Week* was so named because it was just that. For just about everyone, it was the only baseball game they could watch during the week, other than their local team's broadcasts. The victory was a catalyst for the Cubs, who went on to win the division title that year. For Sandberg, it put his name in the public consciousness, and started him on the way to a glorious career in Cub pinstripes. "It is the kind of stuff of which Most Valuable Player seasons are made," sportswriter Dave Van Dyck proclaimed soon after the game.[3] Indeed, Sandberg was named the NL MVP in 1984. He recalled years later, "It was a one-game thing that elevated my thought of what I was as a player, more of an impact-type of a guy, a game-winning type of a player."[4] As the decades passed, the contest was elevated to the status of myth, eventually becoming known simply as "The Sandberg Game."

To many Cubs fans, the game became a cultural touchstone. "Fans come up to me all the time and they want to talk about that game," Sandberg says. "They tell me where they were. They were either driving in a car listening to the game… or they were at the game or watching it on TV. They were calling their relatives, (saying) 'you've got to turn this game on!'"[5]

Nearly lost in all the brouhaha was the fact that Willie McGee, star center fielder for the Cardinals, hit for the cycle that day, with six RBIs. For Sutter, it was the low point of perhaps his most brilliant season, as he finished with a career-high 45 saves and a 1.54 ERA. Reflecting back on his days on the diamond, Sandberg admitted, "It was nothing to [Sutter's] career. It was everything to mine."[6]

SOURCES

In addition to the sources cited in the Notes, the author also accessed Retrosheet.org, Baseball-Reference.com, SABR.org, and *The Sporting News* archive via Paper of Record.

NOTES

1   All broadcast citations from the NBC *Game of the Week* are from: John Mongani, "Ryne Sandberg vs. Willie McGee," YouTube video, 19:28. Uploaded January 11, 2014. https://www.youtube.com/watch?v=dDNTCU7gMZE

2   All broadcast citations from the WGN radio broadcast are from: John Mongani, "Harry Caray's Call of the Sandberg Game vs Cards." YouTube video, 41:28. Uploaded January 11, 2014. https://www.youtube.com/watch?v=34mz7wQKTBo

3   Dave Van Dyck. "Sandberg Gets High Praise," *The Sporting News*, July 9, 1984, 21.

4   Allen Wilson. "The Sandberg Game," *Buffalo News*, http://blogs.buffalonews.com/insidepitch/2011/06/the-sandberg-game.html.

5   Jack Etkin. "When Stars Realize They 'Had Made It,'" *Baseball Digest*, May 2006.

6   Chris Rewers. "Greatest Moments #4: The Sandberg Game," *Agony & Ivy*, http://www.agonyandivy.com/2011/03/greatest-moments-no-4-the-sandberg-game.php.

CUBS CRUSH PADRES IN THEIR FIRST POSTSEASON GAME IN 39 YEARS

OCTOBER 2, 1984
CHICAGO CUBS 13, SAN DIEGO PADRES 0

GAME ONE OF THE NLCS

By Nathan Bierma

"I KNOW IT'S HAPPENING, BUT I CAN'T believe it," said a fan in the stands in a hushed voice, trying to suspend disbelief.[1]

"Thirty-nine years and here we are at last," marveled longtime Chicago columnist Mike Royko.[2]

It was the opening game of the best-of-five National League Championship Series, and the first postseason game at Wrigley Field since Game Seven of the 1945 World Series.

"The day is perfect. The wind is blowing out. There isn't a frown within five miles. How can we not do it?" Royko recalled of his pregame optimism. Then he added: "Then I [took] a couple of stomach pills."[3]

This was the undercard of the Cubs-Padres matchup for the home fans. In one corner, optimism, buoyed by the most dominant club the Cubs had fielded since at least 1969. In the other corner, anxiety, after decades of empty autumns.

The first things the teams noticed as they took the field were the warmth and the wind. "It was a June 1 day instead of an October day," said the Cubs' Bob Dernier.[4]

"Wind out of the southwest, 17 miles an hour," Gary Matthews recited later. "Checked it first thing this morning."[5] The flags on the scoreboard flapped in confirmation: the wind was blowing straight out to center.

Ernie Banks, the Hall of Famer who played 19 seasons for the Cubs, threw out the first pitch. Wearing number 14, he took a seat in the Cubs' dugout for his long-awaited first taste of playoff action.[6]

Rick Sutcliffe started for the Cubs, of course. His midseason acquisition had signaled the Cubs' seriousness about contending, and boosted their run to the division title with a Cy Young season. Sutcliffe retired the Padres in order in the top of the first.

Dernier led off for the Cubs. He and Matthews had come over from the Phillies after their 1983 run to the World Series to give the Cubs some postseason experience. But Dernier still relied on a veteran teammate for advice on how to manage playoff nerves.

"I asked Larry Bowa when the butterflies went away," Dernier said afterward. "He said after the first pitch."[7] So Dernier swung at the second pitch. It was a fastball the *Chicago Tribune* called "eye-high," and Dernier – who hit three home runs all season – lifted it into the wind, which swept the ball out and dropped it onto Waveland Avenue.[8]

Matthews was loosening up, waiting to follow Ryne Sandberg. "I flipped my bat in the air and almost hit Ryno with it," he said.[9]

"Dernier's homer gave everyone a lift," said manager Jim Frey. "People are looking around waiting to see what kind of day it's going to be, and he hits one out. That set the tone."[10]

After Sandberg struck out, up came Matthews, who launched a home run of his own into the left-field bleachers. Three batters in, the Cubs led 2-0.

Sutcliffe struck out four Padres over two more flawless innings, then led off for the Cubs in the bottom of the third. He swung and crushed the ball onto Sheffield. The wind was granting generous home runs today, but this wasn't one of them. "The only homer that would have gone out of any park on any day was Rick Sutcliffe's," Padres starter Eric Show said afterward.[11]

The Cubs weren't finished. After a Dernier walk and a Sandberg single, Leon Durham's RBI single and Keith Moreland's sacrifice fly brought in two more runs.

The Cubs were up 5-0, but it was way too early to exhale. Especially after Sutcliffe uncharacteristically walked two batters in a row to load the bases with two outs in the fourth. The next batter, Carmelo Martinez – whom the Cubs had traded to the Padres in the offseason – smacked a drive to right field.

Moreland, seldom lauded for his defense, made his move. "I started forward thinking it was a line-drive base hit," Moreland said. "As I was running in, I saw that with the wind blowing out the ball had stayed in the air, so I just took a shot at catching it."[12]

The wind was even helping the Cubs on defense. Still, it was a risky attempt, since three runs could score if he missed. "When I got to the dugout, I started thinking about it and said, 'Dang, that was stupid,'" Moreland said.[13]

But Moreland dove, snagged the ball, and tumbled into a heap. The inning was over.

"If there was any key to the game, it had to be Moreland's catch," said Padres manager Dick Williams. "That changed the whole game around."[14]

The score stayed 5-0 until the fifth, when the Cubs' offense exploded. It was as though the team had four decades' worth of postseason runs stored up, just waiting to erupt.

After Dernier hit a leadoff double and Sandberg walked, Matthews came up and swatted his second home run of the afternoon, this time to the right-field seats. When he took a curtain call, the man former teammate Pete Rose nicknamed "Sarge" gave the fans a salute.[15] Including his NLCS performance one year ago for the Phillies, for which he was named series MVP, Matthews had homered in a record four straight LCS games. The *Tribune* crowned him "Mr. First Week of October."[16]

Cubs fans couldn't believe their eyes as the scoreboard read 8-0. And there still weren't any outs in the fifth. Durham made one on a groundout, but then Moreland singled and Ron Cey walked. Jody Davis's base hit scored Moreland and moved Cey to third. Then Bowa grounded out to second, where Davis was forced out, but Cey scored on the play. Now it was 10-0. The day had begun with joy and disbelief for Cubs fans; now they were running surpluses of both.

And it was still the fifth inning. Sutcliffe singled to center for his second hit of the day. That brought up Dernier for the second time in the inning, and he walked. With two outs and the bases loaded, it was Sandberg's turn. He slapped an infield single to bring home Bowa and make it 11-0.

Matthews came to the plate with a chance to hit his third home run of the game and second of the inning. Instead, he struck out on three pitches. It may have been the only thing that didn't work out for the Cubs all day.

But everything else did. Sutcliffe kept mowing down the Padres, holding them to two hits through six innings. In the bottom of the sixth, Cey hit a solo home run off reliever Greg Harris to give the Cubs five long balls for the game, tying a postseason record.[17] Davis followed with a double to right, and scored on a throwing error on Bowa's infield single.

The Cubs had scored 13 runs. Every Cub in the starting lineup had at least one hit and one RBI – including Sutcliffe, one of five Cubs with two hits. Throats roared and minds boggled throughout Wrigley Field. Maybe an unprecedented spectacle like this is how fate sheepishly atones for past cruelty.

Sutcliffe exited after a hitless seventh inning that the Cubs closed out with a double play. Warren Brusstar entered for what would have been mop-up duty had there been anything within sight to mop up. Brusstar allowed four hits in two innings but kept the Padres off the scoreboard.

The final score was 13-0, the kind of tally you might see at a Bears game at Soldier Field. It was the biggest blowout in postseason history.[18] For the franchise for whom so much had gone wrong this time of year since 1908, everything imaginable had conspired to go right. Even the replacement umpires, brought in after an umpire strike at risk of blowing a pennant-deciding call, were rendered entirely irrelevant.[19]

"Everything we hit went over their heads or between them," said Dernier.[20] "Everything they hit went right at somebody." Matthews summed it up: "This was a Cubs kind of day."[21]

"The party started around Wrigley Field hours before game time and lasted into the night," wrote the *Tribune*. "Fans screamed, hugged one another, danced, and even wept while the action on the field fulfilled nearly four decades of their dreams."[22]

"And all of a sudden it hit me," Royko wrote. "Those are the Cubs—the Chicago Cubs—beating the hell out of people that way. Bullies, that's what we've become. Big, bad, mean bullies. And, oh boy, does it feel great. Why didn't we think of this years ago?"[23]

"There was shock, disbelief, then ecstasy. It was all too good to be true," the *Tribune* wrote. "The Chicago Cubs are two victories away from going to the World Series; two victories away from a shot at being champions of baseball for the first time since 1908; two victories away from making the magic last forever."[24]

SOURCES

In addition to the sources cited in the Notes, the author also used Baseball-Reference.com and Retrosheet.org.

Acquired in mid-June in a trade from the Cleveland Indians, Rick Sutcliffe went 16-1 to lead the Cubs to their first postseason since the 1945 World Series, and also won the NL Cy Young Award. (Photo by Rich Pilling/MLB Photos via Getty Images)

NOTES

1   Mike Royko, "Bully, Bully! Cubs Are On Way," *Chicago Tribune*, October 3, 1984: 3.

2   Ibid.

3   Ibid.

4   Glen Stout, *The Cubs: The Complete Story of Chicago Cubs Baseball* (Boston: Houghton Mifflin, 2007), 337.

5   Bernie Lincicome, "This Is Sarge's Time of the Year," *Chicago Tribune*, October 3, 1984: 49.

6   Fred Mitchell, "Cubs Blow Them Away," *Chicago Tribune*, October 3, 1984: 49.

7   Lincicome.

8   Mitchell, "Cubs Blow Them Away."

9   Robert Markus, "Moreland's Catch Slams the Door," *Chicago Tribune*, October 3, 1984: 51.

10 Mitchell.

11 Ibid.

12 Markus, "Moreland's Catch Slams the Door."

13 Ibid.

14 Phil Hersh, "Color Padres Red and Blue," *Chicago Tribune*, October 3, 1984: 51.

15 Lincicome.

16 Ibid.

17 Mitchell.

18 Ibid.

19 Jerome Holtzman, "Amateur Umps Lucky the Game Wasn't Close," *Chicago Tribune*, October 3, 1984: 49.

20 Lincicome.

21 Ibid.

22 "There's [13–0] Joy in Cubville," *Chicago Tribune*, October 3, 1984: 1.

23 Royko.

24 "There's [13–0] Joy in Cubville."

STEVE TROUT'S SOLID PERFORMANCE PUTS CUBS ONE GAME AWAY FROM WORLD SERIES

OCTOBER 3, 1984
CHICAGO CUBS 4, SAN DIEGO PADRES 2

GAME TWO OF THE NLCS

By Gordon Gattie

THE CHICAGO CUBS AND THEIR FANS were flying high on the first Wednesday in October 1984 as "Work came to a standstill, crime came to a halt and joy was the most abundant emotion in town."[1] The Cubs crushed the San Diego Padres 13-0 in the opening game of the National League Championship Series. The Cubs had reached the postseason for the first time since 1945 by winning the NL East with a 96-65 record, finishing 6½ games ahead of the New York Mets. In Game One Rick Sutcliffe and Warren Brusstar combined on a six-hitter, receiving all needed offense from Bob Dernier's leadoff homer. Gary Matthews added a clout later in the first,[2] and delivered a second blast as the Cubs exploded for six runs in the fifth inning. Sutcliffe contributed with his own solo shot in the third inning.[3]

Six months earlier, most prognosticators picked Chicago to finish fifth or sixth in the NL East. *Baseball Digest* forecast a last-place finish, citing "some power, deep bullpen, and adequate infield" but with an overall outlook of "tagging along."[4] Even most *Chicago Tribune* writers predicted a fifth- or sixth-place ending, noting that the "spotty pitching – the Cubs were last in the league last year – will make it tough for Jim Frey's new charges to climb out of fifth place."[5] But some contrarians, like Bill James, offered more hope for Cubs fans: "If anybody offers you 100-plus odds against the Cubs' winning the National League East in 1984, take it." James offered several reasons why the Cubs would fare well: inaccurately perceived differences between Chicago and other teams, managerial style change, compressed league, reigning division champion challenges, pitching upgrades, and their ability on artificial turf.[6]

The San Diego Padres suffered their worst defeat all season during that series opener. Shortstop Garry Templeton commented, "That's the first time this has happened to us all year and it had to happen in the playoffs."[7] The 92-70 Padres were the only NL West team with a winning record, finishing 12 games ahead of both the Atlanta Braves and Houston Astros. The Padres were led by future Hall of Famer and 1984 NL batting champion Tony Gwynn, outfielder Kevin McReynolds, and 15-game-winner Eric Show. The Padres had joined the NL 15 years earlier, and the 1984 NLCS was the franchise's initial postseason appearance. That season was the first time the Padres finished higher than fourth in their division[8] and the second time they attained a winning percentage higher than .500. The relatively young team included only four Padres with playoff experience: Bobby Brown, Steve Garvey, Goose Gossage, and Graig Nettles.

Cubs manager Jim Frey named Steve Trout as his starting pitcher. The left-handed sinkerball specialist set career bests for wins (13) and ERA (3.41) that season, following the previous year's inconsistent campaign. Frey was eager to improve his pitching staff's poor performance, as they finished 1983 with an NL-worst 4.08 team ERA. Trout signed a one-year contract with Chicago in late January,[9] but was not guaranteed a rotation spot. As spring training started, Frey commented, "Our fourth starter will come from guys like Ferguson Jenkins, Rick Reuschel, Steve Trout, Don Schulze, Bill Johnson or Reggie Patterson."[10] Green's expectations of Trout improving his performance increased after the Cubs failed to land a front-line starting pitcher through mid-February.[11] Trout's season didn't start well; he allowed four earned runs in 4⅔ innings and lost an early lead in his season debut,[12] but he subsequently delivered two complete-game victories and finished April with a 3-1 record and a 2.38 ERA in 34 innings. He eventually became a stalwart in Frey's rotation. Trout credited Cubs pitching coach Billy Connors for his success during the season, referring to Connor as his "avatar."[13]

Experienced Padres skipper Dick Williams selected Mark Thurmond against Chicago. The young left-hander was in his second year after finishing ninth in the NL Rookie of the Year voting the previous season. Thurmond led the Padres' starters with a 2.97 ERA in 178⅔ innings, tied with Ed Whitson for the second most wins on the staff (14). Like Trout, Thurmond was not guaranteed a rotation spot when spring training started.[14] He struggled during the season's first half, but was 9-3 with a 2.23 ERA in the second half.

Trout quickly retired the first three Padres hitters with only six pitches, inducing two groundouts and striking out Gwynn looking. For the Cubs, leadoff hitter Dernier singled to left field, advanced to third on Ryne Sandberg's groundout, and scored on Matthews' groundout to give Chicago a first-inning lead. Keith Moreland doubled and Ron Cey walked, but Jody Davis struck out, stranding the runners. In San Diego's second inning, Carmelo

Martinez singled and advanced no further. The Cubs threatened in the bottom half, leaving runners on first and second. Trout continued his effectiveness with an infield groundout and 6-4-3 double play that erased Thurmond's single in the following frame. In the Cubs' half, Matthews grounded out to shortstop and Moreland singled to right field. Cey doubled home Moreland and advanced to third on the throw home; he later scored on Davis's sacrifice fly to increase Chicago's lead to 3-0.

Gwynn started the Padres' fourth inning with a double to left field, giving San Diego its first runner in scoring position. Garvey advanced Gwynn on an infield groundout; Gwynn scored the Padres' first run in the series on McReynolds' fly to right field. The Cubs quickly responded; with one out, Trout reached first on an infield grounder and was forced at second on Dernier's groundball. With Sandberg up, Dernier stole second base, then scored on Sandberg's double. Williams wasted no time reaching into his bullpen, replacing Thurmond with Andy Hawkins, who started the year in the starting rotation but was used more often in relief during September. Hawkins walked Matthews and retired Moreland on a fly out. Both teams went down in order during the fifth inning, and the Cubs carried their three-run lead into the sixth inning. Pinch-hitter Mario Ramirez grounded out to third base, then the speedy Alan Wiggins walked. Wiggins, who finished third in NL steals with 70, had also finished first in caught stealing with 21 failed swipes. He moved to second base on Gwynn's tough groundout to first; although Wiggins advanced, Trout credited first baseman Leon Durham's defensive play from causing further damage, "Leon's play at first base was by far the biggest play of the game," Trout commented after the game.[15] Wiggins scored on Garvey's single to left field, cutting the Cubs' lead to 4-2. Trout induced McReynolds to hit into a fielder's choice, halting the rally. In the Cubs' sixth inning, Dave Dravecky replaced Hawkins and retired the Cubs in order.

Through seven innings Trout allowed two runs on four hits and one walk. In the Padres' eighth, Templeton led off with a walk, but was erased when pinch-hitter Kurt Bevacqua hit into a double play. Wiggins utilized his speed to reach second on an infield single and Trout's throwing error. But Gwynn flied out to left field to end the inning. In the Cubs' eighth, Craig Lefferts replaced Dravecky on the mound and kept Chicago bats quiet on two fly outs and a groundout.

In the ninth, Trout got Garvey to lead off with an infield groundout, but walked McReynolds, and Frey summoned his closer, Lee Smith. In 8⅓ innings, Trout had allowed five hits and more importantly, only three walks.[16] Smith saved 33 games during the regular season, finishing 12 saves behind leader Bruce Sutter of the St. Louis Cardinals. Smith quickly ended matters, striking out Martinez on four pitches, and retiring Kennedy to end the game on a fly ball to left field.

Chicago was flying high after taking the first two games,[17] but the joy was short-lived. San Diego responded with a 7-1 victory at Jack Murphy Stadium the following evening, tied the series with a 7-5 win in Game Four, then advanced to its first World Series by winning the deciding game, 6-3. The Cubs jumped out to a 3-0 lead after two innings in Game Five, but the Padres finally solved Sutcliffe and Chicago's bullpen by scoring two sixth-inning and four seventh-inning runs to secure the lead they wouldn't relinquish.[18]

SOURCES

Besides the sources cited in the Notes, the author consulted Baseball-Almanac.com, Baseball-Reference.com, Retrosheet.org, and the following:

Carr, James. *2015 Chicago Cubs Media Guide* (Chicago: Chicago Cubs Media Relations Department, 2015).

James, Bill. *The New Bill James Historical Abstract* (New York: The Free Press, 2001).

Thorn, John, and Pete Palmer, et al. *Total Baseball: The Official Encyclopedia of Major League Baseball* (New York: Viking Press, 2004).

NOTES

1 "There's [13-0] Joy in Cubville, " *Chicago Tribune,* October 3, 1984: 1.

2 Bernie Lincicome, "This Is Sarge's Time of the Year," *Chicago Tribune,* October 3, 1984: 48.

3 Fred Mitchell, "Cubs Blow Them Away," *Chicago Tribune,* October 3, 1984: 48.

4 George Vass, How Major League Pennant Races Shape Up for 1984," *Baseball Digest,* April 1984: 31.

5 Fred Mitchell, "Expos Have the Talent," *Chicago Tribune,* April 1, 1984: 529.

6 Bill James, "Cubs Appear Ripe for 'Miracle' Season, *Chicago Tribune,* April 1, 1984: 47.

7 Dave Distel, "Call This a Daymare at Wrigley," *Los Angeles Times,* October 3, 1984: 57.

8 Phil Collier, "Padres Calm for Clincher," *The Sporting News,* October 1, 1984: 22.

9 Fred Mitchell, "Sandberg, 5 More Cubs in Fold," *Chicago Tribune,* February 1, 1984: 38.

10 Fred Mitchell, "Cubs Serve Up Mound of Worries," *Chicago Tribune,* February 19, 1984: 30.

11 Fred Mitchell, "Green: Cubs Don't *Gotta* Make a Trade," *Chicago Tribune,* February 28, 1984: 37.

12 Fred Mitchell, "Cubs Fall Short Against San Diego," *Chicago Tribune,* April 8, 1984: 32.

13 Joe Goddard, "Trout Gets Fun From Winning," *The Sporting News,* October 15, 1984: 15.

14 Steven Dolan, "Is Williams Dreaming the Impossible?" *Los Angeles Times,* February 27, 1984: 164.

15 Fred Mitchell, "Cub Speed Kills Padres," *Chicago Tribune,* October 4, 1984: 72.

16 Bernie Lincicome, "Trout's in Right Zone," *Chicago Tribune,* October 4, 1984: 72.

17 "Cubs' Victory Keeps Party Going," *Chicago Tribune,* October 4, 1984: 1.

18 Dave Nightingale, "The Cubs Find a Way to Lose It," *The Sporting News,* October 15, 1984: 2.

DAWSON HITS FOR CYCLE AS ROOKIE MADDUX EARNS FIRST WIN OF THE YEAR

APRIL 29, 1987
CHICAGO CUBS 8, SAN FRANCISCO GIANTS 4

By Mike Huber

In 1987, his first season with the Chicago Cubs, Andre Dawson got his MVP season going with a 5-for-5 performance against the San Francisco Giants, including joining the ranks of those who have hit for the cycle. After 11 seasons in Montreal, he had signed with the Cubs as a free agent in March, taking less money than the Expos offered, in order to "play in Wrigley Field on natural turf that he thought might benefit his tender knees."[1]

It was almost the end of the first month of baseball, and the NL East second-place Cubs were hosting the NL West first-place Giants in a midweek day game. Only 11,120 fans braved the April weather, as Chicago lived up to its nickname, the Windy City. "Battling a bright sun and strong wind,"[2] the Giants committed four errors and the Cubs one, and "numerous windblown hits drove both managers and fans crazy."[3] Pitching for Chicago was a right-handed rookie named Greg Maddux, making his fourth start of the season,[4] bringing a record of 0-2 and an earned run average of 6½ runs per game. For the Giants, skipper Roger Craig called on right-hander Roger Mason to toe the rubber.

The Giants struck first on doubles by Chili Davis and Candy Maldonado. Chicago answered in the bottom half when Dawson launched a two-out home run, his sixth of the season, to tie the score. The *Chicago Tribune*'s sports section showed a photo of the fans scrambling for the ball in the left-field bleachers.

In the second inning, Maddux "took a low blow,"[5] as former Cub Chris Speier drilled the pitcher just below the belt with a line drive. He stayed in the game, and after a few practice tosses to recuperate, Maddux pitched to Mason. Mason sent a one-hopper into right field. Dawson charged it and threw to first in time to nail Mason for the out. After the game, Dawson said, "I was cheating in a little bit and hoping he'd hit the ball to me."[6] The box score listed the play as a lineout, RF-1B.

Davis singled in the third for the Giants. With Jeffrey Leonard batting, Maddux had Davis picked off at first base, but the young pitcher threw the ball away, enabling Davis to go to third. Leonard then stroked a single to the right side and Davis scored an unearned run. Again the Cubs answered. Dave Martinez hit a single into right field. Maldonado fielded it but dropped the ball twice, allowing Martinez to scamper to third. Maldonado was charged two errors on the play. After Maddux grounded to short, Chico Walker singled, driving in Martinez. Walker stole second and Ryne Sandberg walked, bringing Dawson to the plate. He lined a double to right. Walker scored, but Sandberg was out at home. Keith Moreland struck out, but the Cubs had taken the lead.

The Giants scored the equalizer in the fourth on rookie Matt Williams's second home run of the season. In the bottom of the fourth, Chicago took the lead for good. Leon Durham led off with a single to right. An out later, Shawon Dunston reached on a wind-blown error when center fielder Davis misplayed his fly ball. Martinez then tripled to deep center, clearing the bases. This brought San Francisco skipper Craig to the mound to make a change. Righty Greg Minton came in from the bullpen and Mason left for the showers. Maddux reached on a fielder's choice and Walker singled, making the score now 6-3. Dawson added a two-out single to load the bases, but Minton retired Moreland on a comebacker to the mound to end the rally.

In the bottom of the fifth, Chicago added another run. Durham led off with a single, Jody Davis doubled, and Minton intentionally walked Martinez after Dunston had flied out. When Jerry Mumphrey, pinch-hitting for Maddux, reached on second baseman Speier's error, Durham scored.

With Maddux done for the day, Dickie Noles was now pitching for Chicago, but he had trouble finding the strike zone. Although he allowed no runs in the top of the sixth, he walked two and threw a ball in the dirt with Mike Aldrete batting (the Cubs' catcher Jody Davis was charged with a passed ball).

Mike LaCoss became San Francisco's third pitcher in the sixth. After Sandberg grounded out, Dawson bashed an opposite-field triple, but he was stranded when his teammates could not bring him home. According to Dawson, "The toughest at-bat was probably the triple, because the pitcher was ahead in the count, and you never know what pitch he's going to get you out with in that situation. It was a good pitcher's pitch, over the plate and on the way down."[7] With the triple, Dawson had now hit for the cycle, becoming the 10th Cub to hit for the cycle and the first since Ivan de Jesus accomplished it on April 22, 1980. Dawson told the Associated Press, "I didn't know I had never hit for the cycle, but this is a game I won't forget. It came with a new club after playing 10 years with another club."[8]

In the seventh, Noles's wildness on the mound continued as Leonard drew a walk. Maldonado advanced him to third with a single, and Harry Spilman lifted a sacrifice fly to left, Leonard scoring.

Ed Lynch came in to try to save the win for the Cubs. Chicago got a run in the seventh inning. Dunston walked, stole second, and scored on Martinez's single, his third hit of the game.

Maddux picked up his first win of the season while lasting only five innings and allowing three runs (two earned). He struck out six, walked two, and yielded seven hits. Despite the short outing, his manager, Gene Michael, had faith in him, saying, "I still feel Maddux can pitch better than he did. I think everybody does, because he has a good arm."[9] Lynch pitched 2⅔ shutout innings and earned his first save in three seasons (when he struck out Dawson to end a game on July 25, 1984), as the Cubs won for only the second time in nine home games for the season (they were 8-2 on the road). Chicago kept pace with the division-leading Cardinals by remaining only one game back. Mason took the loss for the Giants, and after getting only 10 outs in the game, this was his last appearance in the big leagues until September 1989. San Francisco's three-game winning streak was halted. Manager Craig described the weather conditions: "The winds made it look like Candlestick Park. It wasn't pretty, but it was a lot prettier for them than it was for us."[10]

This was the fourth time the Hawk had collected five hits in a game. "Whenever you get five hits in five at-bats, I guess you've done all you're capable of doing," he told the *Chicago Tribune*.[11] His batting average had shot up 119 points in his last seven games, from .167 to .286, as he went 14-for-29 (a .483 clip). His slugging percentage rose from .313 to .610 in that span, and he knocked in 12 runs. Three other players, all from the National League, hit for the cycle in 1987 (San Francisco's Maldonado on May 4, Montreal's Tim Raines on August 16, and Atlanta's Albert Hall on September 23).

Dawson, the 1977 National League Rookie of the Year, finished the 1987 campaign with a league-leading 49 home runs, 137 RBIs, and 353 total bases (11 in this game).[12] His season culminated in winning the NL's Most Valuable Player Award, playing in his fourth All-Star Game, and taking home his seventh Gold Glove Award and fourth Silver Slugger Award.

After 11 seasons with the Montreal Expos, Andre Dawson was named National League MVP in 1987, his first season with the Cubs, tying for the major-league lead with 49 home runs and pacing the majors with 137 RBIs. (Photo by Focus on Sport/Getty Images)

The Cubs did not fare so well, finishing the season with a 76-85 record.

SOURCES

In addition to the sources mentioned in the notes, the author consulted baseball-reference.com, mlb.com, and retrosheet.org.

NOTES

1   "Dawson Still Taking His Cut, Goes 5 for 5 for the Cubs," *Los Angeles Times*, April 30, 1987: 303.

2   "Dawson's Cycle Runs Over Giants," *St. Louis Post-Dispatch*, April 30, 1987: 32.

3   Fred Mitchell, "Dawson's Cycle Gets Cubs Rolling at Home," *Chicago Tribune*, April 30, 1987: 47, 54.

4   Maddux had appeared in six games in 1986, making five starts and throwing 31 innings. He had a 2-4 record and 5.52 ERA.

5   Mitchell.

6   Ibid.

7   Ibid.

8   *Los Angeles Times*.

9   Mitchell.

10 *St. Louis Post-Dispatch*.

11 Mitchell.

12 Dawson hit 27 of his 49 home runs at Wrigley Field in 1987. Of his 49 blasts, 37 came in day games.

"TIRED" DAWSON HITS THREE HOMERS

AUGUST 1, 1987
CHICAGO CUBS 5, PHILADELPHIA 3

By Rory Costello

HALL OF FAMER ANDRÉ DAWSON HAD HIS finest year in 1987 after joining the Chicago Cubs as a free agent. He became the National League's Most Valuable Player, leading the NL in homers with 49 and RBIs with 137. Both were easily career highs for him.[1]

The peak moment in this peak season came at Wrigley Field on August 1. He hit three homers and drove in all of Chicago's runs in a 5-3 win over the Philadelphia Phillies. "It was a one-man show by Dawson today," said Phillies manager Lee Elia.[2]

Dawson had 39 multi-homer games during his 21 years in the majors – eight of them in 1987. He had one other three-homer game, on September 24, 1985, when he was with the Montreal Expos. That outburst also came at Wrigley. Dawson drove in eight runs – a single-game career high – in a 17-15 Montreal victory. Yet he called his showing on August 1, 1987, "a bigger thrill, because it came before the home crowd."[3] He added, "A love affair has developed between us. I really respect these fans here." He got a standing ovation after each homer, plus curtain calls for the second and third.[4]

It was 90 degrees and very humid that Saturday afternoon – night baseball at Wrigley was a little over a year away – and 33,002 "sweltering but satisfied fans" attended. Dawson noted, "I was tired, but the heat and humidity helped. When you're tired, the bat feels heavy and it helps cut down on your swing. You can get your hands into it more."[5]

It took a brilliant play by third baseman Mike Schmidt to prevent an even bigger day for Dawson.[6] In the bottom of the first inning, Phillies starter Tom Hume loaded the bases on a single and two walks. As Bill Jauss of the *Chicago Tribune* wrote, "Hume couldn't locate the plate Saturday. He walked seven Cubs and threw 91 pitches, 43 of them called balls."[7] Dawson, the cleanup hitter, ripped the ball toward left field. Schmidt made a leaping backhanded stab and stepped on third for an unassisted double play. It was nearly a triple play, but Schmidt decided not to throw to first, where Leon Durham was scrambling back.[8] Hume walked Jerry Mumphrey, loading the bases again, but got out of the inning when Keith Moreland grounded into a 6-4 force.

The Cubs starter, rookie Les Lancaster, allowed no runs and just two singles through the first three innings. He was struck on the inside of his right (pitching) forearm by Milt Thompson's liner in the third, but stayed in the game.[9]

Dawson staked Lancaster to a 3-0 lead in the bottom of the third. Dave Martinez, who reached base in four of his five plate appearances, led off with a walk. With one out, Durham doubled, putting runners on second and third. The Hawk then connected for his first homer of the day. He "had no doubt" about the drive, which landed deep in the bleachers in left-center field.[10]

The Cubs threatened to add more as Mumphrey singled and Moreland walked, but Hume escaped again by getting Jim Sundberg to ground into a 6-4-3 double play. The veteran catcher was starting for the second straight day because first-stringer Jody Davis had gotten in manager Gene Michael's doghouse that Friday. Davis was late to batting practice after filming a commercial.[11]

The Phillies then drew within a run. With two outs, Glenn Wilson walked and Chris James homered. They could have tied it in the top of the fifth when Steve Jeltz led off with a double, but Hume's sacrifice bunt wasn't good; Lancaster threw out Jeltz at third. He then retired the next two batters.

The first batter in the bottom of the fifth was Dawson. He belted his second long ball of the day, later saying, "I was sure about that one too."[12] It landed four rows deep.[13]

That was all for Hume; in came Wally Ritchie. The lefty got Mumphrey on a fly to right but then gave up a double to Moreland. The Phillies walked Sundberg intentionally, bringing up utility infielder Paul Noce, making one of his 18 starts at shortstop that year while Shawon Dunston was on the disabled list. Ritchie caught Noce looking and got Lancaster to line out to left.

Philadelphia made it close again in the top of the sixth. Von Hayes led off with a walk and Schmidt singled. It looked as though the rally would fizzle when Lancaster got Wilson to fly out to right and struck out James. Facing catcher Lance Parrish, however, he committed his sixth balk of the year, bringing home Hayes.[14] Parrish then flied out to left.

In the top of the seventh, the Phillies threatened again. Lancaster walked Jeltz to start the inning and followed by walking pinch-hitter Ron Roenicke. But then he got Juan Samuel to ground to short, and Noce threw Jeltz out at third. Elia wasn't even tempted to flash the bunt sign, though. "You hate to take the bat out of anybody's hands in this ballpark," he said. "You have a guy up there who has 20 home runs and 67 RBI."[15]

After Thompson flied out, Michael brought in southpaw Frank DiPino to face the lefty-swinging Hayes. DiPino got Hayes to pop out to Noce and the middle reliever's work was done.

Dawson capped the scoring in the bottom of the seventh. Leading off against the third Philadelphia pitcher, righty Mike Jackson, he hit a high fly. This time he wasn't sure whether it would go out. "I thought I might have hit it too high and the wind might have held it back."[16] It also went over the deepest part of the well in left field, barely making it into the first row of bleachers (in what was then the alcohol-free Family Section).[17] Dawson became the first Cub with three homers in a game since Dave Kingman on July 29, 1979.[18]

Jackson retired the next three Cubs, and closer Lee Smith entered. He got the first two outs but then landed himself in hot water. After James singled, Parrish walked and so did ace pinch-hitter Greg Gross. Jeff Stone, batting for Jackson, worked a full count. However, Smith struck him out on a high fastball. "It was a borderline pitch," said Elia. "You can't blame him for being aggressive on it."[19]

Jeff Calhoun allowed a walk but no runs in the bottom of the eighth. Smith then finished the game; it wasn't easy. Thompson and Hayes each singled with one out. That brought up Schmidt – at 37, still a premier slugger – as the potential go-ahead run. Over his career, Schmidt had five homers in 43 at-bats against Smith. He hit a smash up the middle, but second baseman Ryne Sandberg – who won his fifth of nine straight Gold Gloves in 1987 – backhanded it and made an off-balance side-arm throw to Noce.[20] The tandem, whose careers were linked in a curious way, turned a game-ending double play.[21]

"We had the big guy on the ropes," said Elia of Smith, "but he had enough to get out of it."[22] Michael said, "He had good stuff and I had to stay with him. Who else do I have who's better?" Dawson added, "I was just praying the big guy would get the job done and get us the win. That's all I cared about."[23]

The Cubs remained in fifth place in the NL East after that game ended; they wound up finishing sixth. Dawson became major-league baseball's first MVP from a last-place team and just the third from a losing team.[24]

NOTES

1   It's worth noting that the 1987 big-league season was marked by suspicions that the ball was juiced. Among many other articles, see Art Spander, "Bugs Bunny Would Enjoy 1987 'Rabbit Ball,'" *The Sporting News*, May 25, 1987: 8; Frank Deford, "Rabbit Ball: Whodunit?," *Sports Illustrated*, July 27, 1987.

2   Toni Ginnetti, "Champagne for Andre! Dawson Does It Again With 3-Homer Game," *Chicago Sun-Times*, August 2, 1987.

3   Ibid.

4   Bill Jauss, "It's Dawson 5 and Phillies 3," *Chicago Tribune*, August 2, 1987: B1.

5   Bill Jauss, "It's Dawson 5 and Phillies 3"; "Champagne for Andre!"

6   Dan Hafner, "National League Roundup: Dawson Hits Three Home Runs as Cubs End Phillies' Five-Game Win Streak," *Los Angeles Times*, August 2, 1987.

7   Bill Jauss, "Cub Notes," *Chicago Tribune*, August 2, 1987.

8   Jauss, "It's Dawson 5 and Phillies 3."

9   Jauss, "It's Dawson 5 and Phillies 3." Precautionary X-rays were taken after the game and proved negative. (Lancaster made his next start five days later.)

10   Ginnetti, "Champagne for Andre!" "Dawson Uncorks Three Homers," *Decatur* (Illinois) *Herald and Review*, August 2, 1987.

11   Ibid.

12   Ibid.

13   "Dawson Uncorks Three Homers."

14   "Dawson's 3 HRs Lift Cubs," *Kokomo* (Indiana) *Tribune*, August 2, 1987: 23.

15   "Cubs' Dawson Dings Phils 5-3," *Wilmington* (Delaware) *Morning News*, August 2, 1987.

16   Ginnetti, "Champagne for Andre!"

17   Jauss, "It's Dawson 5 and Phillies 3," "Dawson Uncorks Three Homers."

18   Jauss, "Cub Notes."

19   "Cubs' Dawson Dings Phils 5-3."

20   Jauss, "It's Dawson 5 and Phillies 3."

21   Sandberg had signed a letter of intent to go to Washington State University as a football quarterback in 1978 when the Phillies drafted him. He was then a shortstop. Washington State then recruited Noce as a shortstop, and he played there from 1979 through 1981. Noce made it to the majors in June 1987; he got his most significant playing time after Sandberg went on the disabled list with a sprained ankle. See Dan Weaver, "For Noce, Hard Work Has Finally Paid Off," *Spokane Spokesman-Review*, July 25, 1987.

22   "Dawson's Three Homers Power Cubs; Giants win," *Greenwood* (South Carolina) *Index-Journal*, August 2, 1987.

23   Ginnetti, "Champagne for Andre!"

24   As of 2017, Alex Rodriguez (2003 Texas Rangers) was the only other MVP from a last-place team. The other MVPs from losing teams were Ernie Banks (1958 and 1959 Cubs) and Cal Ripken Jr. (1991 Baltimore Orioles).

NATURE INTERVENES:
FIRST WRIGLEY NIGHT GAME RAINED OUT

AUGUST 8, 1988
PHILADELPHIA PHILLIES VS. CHICAGO CUBS
POSTPONED

By Joe Schuster

BY THE TIME THE CUBS SCHEDULED THEIR first home night game, they were, by four decades, the last holdout against baseball under the lights. The first major-league team to host a night game, the Cincinnati Reds, had done so in 1935, with the other teams following suit until 1948 when the Detroit Tigers played their initial night home game, leaving the Cubs alone with a full home daytime schedule.[1]

Although it took them 53 years from that initial night game to play their own, the team was not initially vehement in its resistance. Cubs President Philip K. Wrigley, for example, was one of four league owners who sponsored a 1934 proposal to allow National League teams to experiment with games under the lights; the proposal passed by a vote of 5 to 3, with Pittsburgh, Brooklyn, and the New York Giants voting no.[2]

By 1939, however, the team had added a condition on when, or if, it would ever play at night at home: In a statement through a spokesman after Wrigley attended the White Sox' first home night game, he said that the Cubs' home park "would not be lighted until the Cubs were certain their fans wanted night baseball."[3]

Over the next few years, however, the team flirted with the idea. Early in the spring of 1942, for example, Wrigley told the *Chicago Tribune* that the team had acquired lights it was prepared to erect

for the coming season. He suggested that, because of World War II he anticipated that night baseball would become even more in demand as recreation for the nation's workers, adding, "The stories we were opposed to night baseball because it would destroy the beauty of the park for daytime baseball are without foundation. It's our job to give the fans what they want ... and if they want night baseball, they'll have it."[4]

By the 1960s, however, Wrigley's position against night baseball was intractable, so much so that late in 1962, the league asked him to reconsider. That year, the Cubs had the majors' smallest home attendance (barely over 600,000), meaning visiting teams' portions of the gate were "pygmy-sized" and that "by holding out against lights ... the Cubs [were] not doing their share in contributing to the league's financial structure."[5]

The Cubs refused, and in 1977, when P.K. Wrigley died, one of the first things heir William Wrigley said was that the team would continue that position under his leadership.[6]

Four years later, in 1981, however, the Wrigley family sold the Cubs to the Chicago Tribune Corporation, which favored night baseball. In response, a group of residents who lived near the ballpark – the Citizens United for Baseball in the Sunshine (CUBS) – petitioned the state and city governments, seeking legislation prohibiting night ball in Wrigley, arguing that it would ruin their neighborhood (the ballpark was the only one in the majors located in a neighborhood instead of a downtown or sparsely populated area). In 1982, the Illinois legislature passed such a measure, citing federal noise-pollution rules.[7]

In 1985, the team and Major League Baseball increased their efforts against the prohibition. Commissioner Peter Ueberroth said that if the city and state continued to block night games, Major League Baseball would "have no alternative but to resolve the situation on its own, including prohibiting the Cubs from hosting any postseason games.[8]" The next month, the team petitioned the Illinois Supreme Court to declare the 1982 law unconstitutional, but the court found against the Cubs.[9]

In response, a team spokesman said club would consider moving from the neighborhood: "The decision emphasized the need to look for alternatives to Wrigley Field. ..."[10] One possibility was a 100-acre site the Tribune Company owned in nearby Schaumberg Township.[11]

That threat, as much as anything, led the state legislature, the Chicago City Council, and Mayor Harold Washington (who had previously opposed lights in Wrigley) to reconsider, and in 1987, the state took up a bill that would allow night games at Wrigley. Said state Senator Doris Karpiel, who introduced it, "Wrigley Field is such a beautiful place, we ought to encourage the Cubs to stay there."[12]

The state voted in 1987 to allow the Cubs to install lights, and in February 1988 the city followed suit, setting the stage finally for the first Cubs night home game.

The team set the game for August 8, 1988, against the Philadelphia Phillies, proclaiming the event as "precedent-setting"; immediately rumors arose that Frank Sinatra would sing the National Anthem and President Ronald Reagan would throw out the ceremonial first pitch.[13] (Neither attended.)

The Cubs actually turned the lights on for an official team event roughly two weeks before the first game: a reception for their Cubs Care charity on July 25, where for a $100 donation fans could witness a lighting ceremony, mingle with current and former players, and watch a workout capped by a home-run derby featuring Hall of Famers Ernie Banks and Billy Williams and future Hall of Famers Ryne Sandberg and Andre Dawson. (Although the official record books don't record it, it is an interesting piece of trivia to note that Dawson hit the first homer under the lights during that contest.[14])

The festivities for the night of August 8, 1988, started when 91-year-old fan Harry Grossman, who had been attending Cubs games for 82 seasons, threw the switch that illuminated the field while the Chicago Symphony Orchestra's brass section heralded the moment with "Also Sprach Zarahustra."[15] The symphony performed the anthem and, after Banks and Williams threw out ceremonial first pitches, the game got underway at 7:01 P.M. when Cubs hurler Rick Sutcliffe (who was 9-9, with a 3.79 ERA) threw his first pitch to Philadelphia's Phil Bradley, the moment even more illuminated by "hundreds of flash bulbs ... recording photographic evidence of the new era."[16]

Fans' enthusiasm dimmed three pitches later, when Bradley, who had only five home runs for the season to that point, hit one into the left-field bleachers, "an ominous beginning that [stunned] the crowd into silence."[17]

The Cubs however, responded in the bottom of the inning. Mitch Webster led off with a single against Kevin Gross (10-8, 3.45), bringing up Sandberg. Before the first pitch to him, however, infamous "kissing bandit" Morgana, who was, the *Tribune* reported, on a four-year quest to kiss Sandberg, ran onto the field but was caught by a security guard before she reached the hitter.[18] "Perhaps inspired or relieved," Sandberg hit the first pitch into the left-field bleachers, giving the Cubs a 2-1 lead.[19]

The Cubs added a run in the third when Sandberg walked, stole second, went to third on a groundout by Mark Grace, and scored on a single by Rafael Palmeiro.

The inning, however, was punctuated by lightning and in the fourth a heavy rain began, prompting the umpires to stop the game. Two hours and 10 minutes later, they halted it completely, prompting Sutcliffe to say, "It's kind of like the good Lord letting us know he's sad" about the Cubs breaking their tradition.[20]

The Cubs would have to wait another day to officially end their string of games under the sun. However, while the rained-out game would not count, Cubs vice president of operations Don Grenesko told reporters it was the historic moment that mattered.

The *Tribune* reported, "'We had a great event,' [he said]. 'We just didn't get the game in. ... This is a bad pun – but I've never seen electricity going through that crowd as [before the first pitch]. It was a once-in-a-lifetime event.

"'[The first official night game at Wrigley] will be just a night game.

"'We did our thing, and that's it. ... Everything went perfect up until the rains came.'"[21]

SOURCES

In addition to the sources cited in the Notes, the author also accessed Retrosheet.org, Baseball-Reference.com, and SABR.org,

NOTES

1   Edward Burns, "Lights to Go On for 163 N.L. Contests," *Chicago Tribune*, February 16, 1948: 54.

2   Edward Burns, "Night Games Approved by National League," *Chicago Tribune*, December 13, 1934: 25.

3   Edward Prell, "Cub Officials See Sox Play Under Lights," *Chicago Tribune*, August 15, 1939: 15.

4   "Wrigley Says Cubs May Yet Install Lights," *Chicago Tribune*, March 21, 1942: 19.

5   Edward Prell, "Review Night Game Views, League Asks Wrigley," *Chicago Tribune*, December 1, 1962: 61.

6   Bill Jauss, "Status Is Quo: Wrigley," *Chicago Tribune*, April 29, 1977: 60.

7   Philip Lentz, "No-Lights Bill Goes to Thompson," *Chicago Tribune*, June 25, 1982: 79.

8   Charles Mount, "Ueberroth Warning Revealed by Cubs," *Chicago Tribune*, February 5, 1985: 42.

9   Daniel Egler, "Court Rules No Lights for Cubs," *Chicago Tribune*, October 4, 1985: 1.

10   Ibid.

11   Ibid.

12   Daniel Egler, "Bill Backs Wrigley Lights," *Chicago Tribune*, February 6, 1987: 50.

13   Bruce Buursma, "Fans No Longer in Dark: Cubs Turn Lights On Aug. 8," *Chicago Tribune*, June 21, 1988: 43.

14   Jerome Holtzman, "The Inevitable Arrives With Dusk," *Chicago Tribune*, July 26, 1988: 49.

15   Barbara Brotman, "View From the Bleachers Puts History in Focus," *Chicago Tribune*, August 9, 1988: 17.

16   Jerome Holtzman, "Lights, Action, and Then ...," *Chicago Tribune*, August 9, 1988: 37.

17   Ibid.

18   Ibid.

19   Ibid.

20   Alan Solomon, "Bright Lights, Big City? Depends Whom You Ask," *Chicago Tribune*, August 9, 1988. 37.

21   Ibid.

FIRST OFFICIAL NIGHT GAME
AT WRIGLEY FIELD

AUGUST 9, 1988
CHICAGO CUBS 6, NEW YORK METS 4

By Joe Schuster

AFTER RAIN WASHED OUT THE CHICAGO
Cubs' initial attempt at an inaugural game under the lights on August 8, 1988, there was an anticlimactic sense to their first official night game at home the following day. True, the game itself was historic. When umpires halted the game the day before in the fourth inning, what might have been the list of "firsts" under the lights at Wrigley – first pitch (by Rick Sutcliffe), first hit, and first home run (both by Phil Bradley, leading off for the Philadelphia Phillies) – the game of August 9 produced the list that went down into the history books. It was also the game for which the Baseball Hall of Fame and Museum requested each manager's lineup card for posterity.[1]

Despite that, there was considerably less ceremony the second time around. As the *New York Times* reported, "When the lights were turned on tonight, nearly 24 hours after a sellout crowd had screamed "Let There Be Light,' at a game that would be rained out … there was no response. … Monday's emotional evening was a part of Chicago history, even if the rained-out game between the Cubs and Phillies was not. The experience was still a novelty tonight but the feeling had switched to wonder at the newness of a different routine."[2]

For *Chicago Tribune* columnist Bob Verdi, the difference in atmosphere between the events was like the difference between the postseason and the regular season. For him, Monday's failed attempt was a "make believe World Series shindig … folderol

[that] rendered the game meaningless."[3] On the other hand, he said, "Tuesday night's surroundings were a bit more familiar and less synthetic. …"[4]

While the trappings of ceremony surrounding what became the team's first official night home game were less than at the initial attempt, the game itself carried more significance. Monday's rained-out contest featured two teams that were already out of the playoff chase. Both the Cubs and Phillies were far back in the standings of what was then the National League East. Chicago (destined to finish fourth) was already 13½ games back and Philadelphia (which would finish last with the third-worst record in the majors) was already 19 games back.

On the other hand, the game that counted replaced the Phillies as the Cubs' opponent with the New York Mets, who would win the division that year. As they came to Chicago for a three-game series, they were still in the midst of something of a race for the division, leading second-place Pittsburgh by six games.

For the game, Chicago started Mike Bielecki, who was 1-0 for the season with a 4.60 ERA. Bielecki, who had come to the Cubs in an April trade with Pittsburgh, had struggled early in the season; after earning an Opening Day victory with two innings of scoreless relief, in his next six appearances he had allowed 10 runs on 16 hits and six walks over 7⅓ innings out of the bullpen and the Cubs had sent him to the minor leagues on May 6. There, he pitched well enough to earn a spot on the National

League roster for the first Triple-A All-Star game and when the Cubs lost pitcher Bob Tewksbury in early July (shoulder surgery) and then weeks later lost reliever Les Lancaster (emergency appendectomy), the team recalled Bielecki to shore up the bullpen. He allowed only one run in 6⅓ innings in his first four appearances after the recall and got the start in the historic game because of an injury to yet another Cubs hurler, Calvin Schiraldi, who had strained a hamstring in his previous game.[5] (Initially, there was a chance that Bielecki would get the start for the Cubs' first attempt at a night game, since Sutcliffe, whose turn it was in the rotation, had a sore back that had manager Don Zimmer considering skipping his turn.[6] In the end Sutcliffe was healthy enough and pitched effectively in the four innings until the umpires called the game, allowing only a run.)

Mets manager Davey Johnson sent Sid Fernandez (6-9) to the mound to oppose Bielecki. Like the Cubs starter, Fernandez had struggled early in the season; his ERA in mid-May was 5.57 but since then he had been far more effective, having shaved more than two runs off his ERA, down to 3.25. His record likely should have been better as he had taken the loss in two consecutive July games when he allowed a combined total of four earned runs on seven hits over 14 innings, striking out 15 while walking seven; in one of those games, he'd allowed only one hit but lost 2-1, largely because of a disputed "safe" call on a stolen base and an errant throw to the plate that sailed over the head of catcher Barry Lyons.

Bielecki made what became the first official pitch in a Cubs night game at 7:06 P.M., a called strike to Mets leadoff hitter Len Dykstra.[7] Dykstra flied out to center and then Bielecki recorded the first official strikeout in a night game in Wrigley when he caught the next batter, Howard Johnson, looking. Both Bielecki and Fernandez were sharp over the first four innings; neither allowed a run over that span while Fernandez limited the Cubs to only one hit, a two-out single to Mark Grace in the first (the first official hit under the lights in Wrigley), while Bielecki surrendered four singles through four innings.[8]

The Mets broke the scoreless tie in the fifth when Wally Backman led off with a single and with one out Dykstra hit the first official night-time home run in Wrigley, a line drive into the auxiliary seats in right field.[9]

The Cubs scored a run in the bottom of the fifth – after Vance Law singled, Rafael Palmeiro drove him home with a line drive to left that got past Kevin McReynolds when he slipped on turf still wet from the previous night's downpour.[10] They tied it in the sixth on a run that Shawon Dunston manufactured: He singled, stole second, advanced to third on a Ryne Sandberg groundout that shattered his bat, and, after Mark Grace walked, scored when Andre Dawson's groundball forced Grace at second.

The Cubs broke the game open in the seventh, thanks in part to a small bit of fan interference. With one out, Palmeiro hit a single to right and then with two outs, Jody Davis pinch-hit for Frank DiPino, who had relieved Bielecki in the sixth, and hit a deep fly to the wall in center field, where Dykstra attempted to catch it but failed to when fans threw beer at him. Asked later if the dousing with beer had affected the play, Dykstra said it had, adding, "And it didn't taste too good, either."[11] (The fans were ejected and, calling the behavior "unacceptable," Cubs GM Jim Frey ordered stronger security for night games after that point.[12])

Following the beer-aided double, Mets manager Johnson sent Roger McDowell in to relieve Fernandez but he did not record an out as the Cubs added three more runs on four consecutive singles before Johnson lifted McDowell for Terry Leach, who got Vance Law to fly to center and end the inning.

The Mets tightened the score with a solo home run in the eighth by Johnson and another run in the ninth when Gary Carter led off with a double against reliever Goose Gossage and scored on a single by Dave Magadan before Gossage nailed down the Cubs' win by retiring the next three batters, getting the final out when Dykstra grounded to second, forcing Magadan. Gossage earned the save, his 12th of the season, while DiPino recorded the victory for two innings of scoreless ball when he allowed no hits and one walk, while striking out one, moving his record to 2-3. The loss went to Fernandez, whose record went to 6-10.

After the game, Sandberg echoed the general sentiment in the press about the contest: Despite its historical significance, it was more like business-as-usual than the event of the night before.

"Last night was special," he said. "Tonight it was less of a circus. It felt more natural. It was a good, exciting ballgame."[13]

SOURCES

In addition to the sources cited in the Notes, the author also accessed Retrosheet.org, Baseball-Reference.com, and SABR.org,

NOTES

1   Malcolm Moran, "2nd Night of Firsts at Wrigley," *New York Times*, August 10, 1988: A21.

2   Ibid.

3   Bob Verdi, "Maybe Cubs Can Light Up Our Lives," *Chicago Tribune*, August 10, 1988: 45.

4   Ibid.

5   Joseph Durso, "Cubs Also Light Up Their Scoreboard," *New York Times*, August 10, 1988: A19.

6   "Wrigley Has World Series Atmosphere," *Cincinnati Enquirer*, August 8, 1988: 25.

7   Verdi.

8   Unless otherwise noted, play-by-play accounts come from Retrosheet retrosheet.org/boxesetc/1988/B08090CHN1988. htm, accessed August 23, 2017.

9   Alan Solomon, "Cubs Pick a Good Time to Shine," *Chicago Tribune*, August 10, 1988: 45.

10 Ibid.

11 Ibid.

12 "Cubs," *The Sporting News*, August 22, 1988: 15.

13 Joe Goddard, "Cubs Escape the Dark Ages," *The Sporting News*, August 22, 1988: 21.

ALL-STAR RAIN IN THE WINDY CITY

JULY 10, 1990
AMERICAN LEAGUE 2, NATIONAL LEAGUE 0

ALL STAR GAME

By Tom Hawthorn

THE CROWD AT WRIGLEY FIELD WORE slickers and raincoats. Some held red, white, and blue folding umbrellas with the Chicago Cubs logo. Others sported smaller, hands-free umbrellas on their head. "What's a little rain," Greg Gumbel asked the television audience, "when there's an All-Star Game to be played?"[1]

Baseball's midsummer showcase returned to Wrigley Field in 1990 for only the third time. The previous classics had been held in 1947 (a 2-1 American League win) and 1962 (a 9-4 AL win), both of those day games, of course. President John F. Kennedy threw out the ceremonial first pitch in 1962.

The 1990 All-Star Game, played on July 10, had been awarded to the club 28 months earlier. Commissioner R. Bartlett Giamatti called Chicago's mayor shortly before the decision with the promise of the All-Star showcase if city council voted to approve night baseball.[2]

The demand for tickets was intense. About 16,000 were allocated to Cubs season-ticket holders, while another 13,000 were distributed among other teams, corporate sponsors, and Major League Baseball. The remaining 6,000 tickets were available to regular fans by lottery. The club got several hundred thousand postcards for those seats.[3] In the end, 39,071 fans squeezed into the old ballpark, built in 1914.

The expectation was for a high-scoring game in the ancient bandbox. On game day itself, however, the regulars knew home runs were unlikely. "Not on a night like this," Ryne Sandberg said.[4] He had won the home-run derby the previous night, but figured wet weather and winds gusting in from Lake Michigan were going to keep balls within the playing area of the Friendly Confines.

As public-address announcer Wayne Messmer called out introductions, the Wrigley faithful saved their biggest roar for a familiar figure. "Batting second and playing second base, making his fifth consecutive All-Star start, the National League's top vote-getter, from the Chicago Cubs, Ryne Sandberg!" The infielder, wearing his familiar number 23, doffed his cap and shook hands with manager Roger Craig of the San Francisco Giants before smacking leadoff man Lenny Dysktra on the butt, the cheer lasting 40 seconds. The crowd roared again for Andre Dawson, appearing in his seventh summer classic. It was the outfielder's 36th birthday and he marked it by completing negotiations with Cubs brass, who made him the highest-paid Cub in history.[5] It was reported Dawson would make $3.3 million for the following season with an option for 1992. He was batting .324 in 78 games at the All-Star break with 19 homers and 57 runs batted in.

The ceremonial first pitch of the 61st All-Star Game was thrown by Ernie Banks, who had played in 14 classics. Mr. Cub was accompanied to the mound by a granddaughter.

In the broadcast booth, Jack Buck called the game and Tim McCarver offered analysis for CBS

Television. Eighteen cameras were positioned around the historic ballpark, but, as it turned out, the poor weather and a slow start to the game took the spirit out of the broadcast early in the proceedings.[6]

Jack Armstrong (11-3) of the Cincinnati Reds started on the mound for the National League. He induced speedy AL leadoff man Rickey Henderson to fly out to Dawson in right. Wade Boggs got the game's first hit on a nubber with topspin that third baseman Chris Sabo couldn't corral. José Canseco struck out and the half-inning ended when Cal Ripken's bouncer to Ozzie Smith at shortstop led to Boggs being forced out at second.

Bob Welch (13-3) of the Oakland A's had a similar opening as the starting pitcher for the American League – Dykstra flied out, Sandberg grounded out to third, Will Clark singled to center and the inning ended with Kevin Mitchell striking out.

So it went. In the top of the second, Ken Griffey Jr. fouled out to left on a liner; Mark McGwire struck out; Sandy Alomar Jr., whose brother would play second base for the other side in the game, popped out in foul territory to first.

In the bottom of the inning, Dawson grounded out to Welch; Sabo grounded to short; Mike Scioscia lined out to left, completing two opening innings as dreary as the weather.

Ramon Martinez replaced Armstrong to start the third inning, enlivening the game by walking Steve Sax, who then stole second base. A groundout and a strike out were followed by an intentional walk to Boggs (the first issued since the 1985 All-Star Game), the rally snuffed when Canseco grounded into a force out at second base.

It was a good night for pitchers. Montreal's Dennis Martinez and Frank Viola of the New York Mets each kept the scoresheet clean for an inning apiece. Dave Smith of Houston was touched for a one-out single in the sixth by Boggs, who lined the ball to right. Kelly Gruber replaced Boggs and took second when Canseco walked. George Bell, pinch-hitting for Ripken, struck out. Meanwhile, Gruber and Canseco pulled off a successful double

steal, so Griffey was walked intentionally, and Smith was done. Manager Craig went to his San Francisco bullpen ace, young Jeff Brantley, 26, to face Cecil Fielder, who led the majors at the break with 28 homers, six ahead of runner-up Canseco. Fielder hit a towering fly to shallow center where a charging Dykstra caught the ball to end the bases-loaded threat. What should have been a routine catch was made more difficult by rain falling in Dykstra's face as he pursued the ball.

After Boggs was pulled from the game, he said: "Someone will have to hit the ball 800 feet tonight to hit it out of here. I think it'll take a squeeze play to get a run home."[7]

On the visitors' side, Toronto's Dave Stieb, making a record ninth All-Star appearance for the AL, pitched two hitless innings, a walk to Tony Gwynn the only blemish. (Barry Larkin ran for Gwynn, stole second, and was stranded there when Sandberg grounded out to end the third.) Bret Saberhagen followed with two more hitless innings.

After six complete innings, only four singles had been hit.

Brantley returned to pitch the seventh. Sandy Alomar hit a grounder to Shawon Dunston, who fielded the ball at the edge of the outfield grass and had to make a long throw to first. Alomar awkwardly stretched to the bag for his second infield hit of the game. On a hit-and-run, he took third as Lance Parrish singled to right. The game was halted because of rain, the delay lasting 68 minutes. When play resumed, Rob Dibble had replaced Brantley. At the plate was Julio Franco, who, on an 0-and-2 count, slashed a Dibble pitch into the gap in right center reaching the ivy. Both runners scored and Franco stopped on second with a double, the game's first and, as it would turn out, only extra-base hit.

Franco advanced when Ozzie Guillen grounded out second to first. Canseco hit a fly to Darryl Strawberry in right, who took a crow-hop before throwing the ball in the air to Scioscia, who blocked Franco from getting to the plate as he swung around to apply a two-handed tag to complete the inning-ending double play. The throw was later described as the most exciting play in a mundane game.

"I set up really well," Strawberry said after the game. "It was right down the line. All I had to do is throw it straight and make the perfect throw."[8]

As one might expect, Cubs announcer Harry Caray led the crowd in the singing of "Take Me Out to the Ball Game" during the seventh-inning stretch.

The AL bullpen mopped up in convincing fashion. Bobby Thigpen, of the South Side White Sox, who led the league in saves with 27 at the break, got three uneventful outs to shut down the NL for an inning. Chuck Finley of the Angels did the same. Dennis Eckersley got the assignment to close. He gave up a leadoff single to Dykstra, but then made short work of Roberto Alomar (fly out to center) and Matt Williams (strikeout). When Tim Wallach popped out to Fielder at first base, Saberhagen had the win, Eckersley the save, Brantley the loss, and the American League its third consecutive All-Star victory.

The night's showing left Sandberg a career 2-for-20 in All-Star Games. The trio of Cubbies (Sandberg, Dawson, Dunston) went 0-for-7 on the night. Franco was named the most valuable player for knocking in the game's only runs. The NL set a new mark by using nine pitchers.

What else? The National League roster included catcher Greg Olson, while the American Leaguers had pitcher Gregg Olson.

The shutout was the third in an All-Star Game since 1946 and the two-hitter orchestrated by six pitchers set a mark for the fewest hits allowed.

"Give our pitchers credit," said AL manager Tony La Russa. "They were terrific."[9]

SOURCES

In addition to the sources cited in the Notes, the author also accessed Retrosheet.org, Baseball-Reference.com, and SABR.org.

NOTES

1   1990 All Star Game CBS broadcast, YouTube: mail.google.com/mail/u/o/#inbox/160166eacbc423d3?projector=1.

2   James Strong, "Council Vote Gives Cubs Lights, 1990 All-Star Game," *Chicago Tribune*, February 26, 1988.

3   Joseph Tybor, "Wrigley Field All-Star Game: One Tough Ticket," (Jackson, Mississippi) *Clarion-Ledger*, July 4, 1990.

4   Andrew Bagnato, "Even Sandberg Has Soggy Night," *Chicago Tribune*, July 11, 1990.

5   Alan Solomon, "Dawson Signs: To Chicago With Love," *Chicago Tribune*, July 11, 1990.

6   Ric Kogan, "CBS Wanted a Knockout, but Got a Washout on Its First All-Star Telecast," *Chicago Tribune*, July 11, 1990.

7   Jerome Holtzman, "Franco Delivers Winning Hit in 7th," *Chicago Tribune*, July 11, 1990.

8   Ed Sherman, "Throw to Plate Earns Strawberry Rare Cheers," *Chicago Tribune*, July 11, 1990.

9   Holtzman.

A GRACEFUL CYCLE

MAY 9, 1993
SAN DIEGO PADRES 5, CHICAGO CUBS 4

By Ryan Schuring with Gregory H. Wolf

LEAVING YOUR MARK IN A GRACEFUL manner can be quite difficult. "I'll probably never do it again," said the Chicago Cubs' Mark Grace about hitting for the cycle against the San Diego Padres in the Windy City. "I don't hit many triples."[1] Grace's three-run home run in the bottom of the ninth almost capped the Cubs' unlikely comeback. "Personally, it was the greatest day of my career," said Grace, but unfortunately, the Padres won."[2]

Heading into the May 9 contest, the two National League teams were both off to a struggling start to the 1993 season. The Padres were 12-16, in fourth place in the NL West Division, six games back of the San Francisco Giants. Leading the Padres into action was skipper Jim Riggleman, who had served as the team's interim manager at the end of the 1992 season. The NL East Division Cubs, piloted by Jim Lefebvre, were sitting at the .500 mark (14-14). They were in fourth place, trailing the Philadelphia Phillies by seven games.

On the hill for the Padres was a converted reliever, right-hander Greg Harris, who owned a record of 32-35 (1-5 thus far in '93) in parts of six seasons. Toeing the rubber for the Cubs was six-year veteran Jose Guzman, a prized free-agent acquisition coming off a 16-11 campaign with the Texas Rangers. Guzman's 3-2 mark thus far in '93 pushed his career record to 69-64.

It was a warm, 76-degree Sunday afternoon on the North Side of Chicago. Wrigley Field was packed with 30,062 spectators when the players stepped between the lines to play the third contest of the three-game series. In true Wrigley fashion, the wind played a factor in the game, blowing out to left field at 14 mph. Come 1:23, the game was underway as Guzman threw the first pitch. Jeff Gardner led off with a double and scored on Gary Sheffield's one-out triple down the left-field line. Fred McGriff's single put the Padres up 2-0. After three consecutive losing seasons and fourth-place finishes, Grace was tired of losing. "We need to jump out ahead and give our starters a cushion rather than play catchup the whole time," he said after the game. "It's tough to win ballgames consistently playing catchup."[3] Grace doubled with two outs in the first and moved up a station on Ryne Sandberg's single, but the Cubs failed to score.

Still trailing, 2-0, in the bottom of the third, the Cubs started a rally with singles from Jose Vizcaino (who extended his hitting streak to 11 games) and Grace. Ryne Sandberg, en route to his 10th consecutive and final All-Star selection, singled through the shortstop and third-base hole to plate Vizcaino and halve the Padres' lead. After Sammy Sosa drew a two-out walk, Rick Wilkins threatened to break the game open with a bullet to right but it was directly into the mitt of Tony Gwynn. "It's pretty much what's taken place all year," said Wilkins, who entered the game batting an atrocious .150. "[W]hen I have a good at-bat, I seem to hit it right at somebody."[4]

The Padres answered the Cubs' scoring in the top of the fifth inning when eight-time All-Star Gwynn gave the Padres a 3-1 lead by sending a two-out grounder through the box for a single, scoring Harris, the light-hitting pitcher who had singled.

In one of the most exciting plays of the game, the Cubs' Willie Wilson, pinch-hitting for Guzman, sent a screecher down the right-field line with two outs in the sixth. Still considered among the fastest players in the game at the age of 36, Wilson tried to stretch his triple into an inside-the-park home run, but was gunned down at the plate by shortstop Kurt Stillwell's perfect toss to catcher Bob Geren, who made a lunging tag. "I thought I had it," said Wilson, who did not side and admitted, "I was out of gas."[5]

Moments later, Geren, leading off the seventh, took Cubs reliever Dan Plesac deep to left field for a solo home run to increase the Padres' lead to 4-1.

Not known for his speed, Grace ripped a two-out triple to left field off Harris in the seventh. Harris retired Sandberg on his 93rd and final pitch to end the inning.

The Padres tacked on another run in the eighth when McGriff led off with a home run to deep left field off new reliever Chuck McElroy. The "Crime Dog's" fifth round-tripper extended the Padres lead to 5-1.

After squandering a leadoff single by Derrick May in the eighth, the Cubs began the final frame needing four runs to tie the game. Facing reliever Roger Mason, beginning his second inning of relief of Harris, Wilkins started the rally with a single to right. After two quick outs by pinch-hitter Rey Sanchez and Dwight Smith, Vizcaino singled. Riggleman pulled Mason and inserted southpaw Rich Rodriguez to match up against the left-handed hitting Grace.

A long ball removed from a cycle, Grace sent a 1-and-0 pitch deep over the right-center-field fence for a home run, giving him the cycle. More importantly, Grace's fourth home run pulled the Cubs within one run of the Padres. Facing closer Gene Harris, the next Cubs batter, Sandberg, lined a two-strike pitch to shortstop Stillwell to end the game in 2 hours and 34 minutes.

Lefebvre provided some insight into the Cubs' disappointing loss, their 10th of the season by one or two runs. "We've still got to keep a team down; late in the game you can't just give up one run here, one run there."[6] Guzman was charged with the loss while Greg Harris, who yielded just one run in seven efficient innings, picked up the victory. The Cubs collected 13 hits, including six for extra bases, and drew two walks, yet managed just five runs. They hit 3-for-11 with men in scoring position and left nine men on base. "We hit the ball good in a lot of situations," said Cubs skipper Lefebvre. "We just hit the ball right at 'em."[7]

Despite the Cubs' loss, the story of the game was Mark Grace, who became the first North Sider to hit for the cycle since Andre Dawson accomplished the feat on April 29, 1987. Grace was the 11th player to hit for the cycle in franchise history since Jimmy Ryan did it first on July 28, 1888, against the Detroit Wolverines; it was the seventh time a Cub hit for the cycle at Wrigley Field.

Grace's 4-for-5 afternoon raised his average to .349. "He's off to a heckuva start," admitted Riggleman. "He's always been a good hitter, but this is the best I've ever seen him."[8] Grace deflected attention away from himself after the game and suggested that the Cubs, despite falling one game under .500, were far from dead: "This is the only team I've ever played on, period, that battles all the way down to the end."[9]

SOURCES

In addition to the sources cited in the Notes, the author also accessed Retrosheet.org, Baseball-Reference.com, and SABR.org.

NOTES

1   Associated Press, Grace Hits for Cycle as Padres Tip Cubs," *Daily Chronicle* (DeKalb, Illinois), May 10 1993: 7.

2   Ibid.

3   Alan Solomon, "Cubs Fall Short Again Against Padres," *Chicago Tribune*, May 10, 1993: A3.

4   Ibid.

5   Ibid.

6   Ibid.

7   Ibid.

8   Associated Press, "Grace Hits for Cycle as Padres Tip Cubs."

9   Solomon.

TUFFY RHODES SMACKS THREE OF 13 CAREER HOMERS IN '94 SEASON OPENER

APRIL 4, 1994
NEW YORK METS 12, CHICAGO CUBS 8

By Paul Hofmann

OPENING DAY – THE DAY WHEN EVERY team is tied for first place at the beginning of play and a day of eternal hope – the hope that this year will be the year! Opening Day in Chicago has always been special. When the Cubs play their first game at Wrigley Field it doesn't matter how good the team is or what the expectations are, it is exciting and there is electricity in the air.

Monday, April 4, was Opening Day at Wrigley Field in 1994. The game pitted a pair of teams from which relatively little was expected of during the 1994 season. Chicago fans were hoping their lovable Cubbies would build on their 84-78 fourth-place (NL East) 1993 finish. Meanwhile the Mets were looking to reverse a three-year downward spiral that culminated in a dismal 103-loss 1993 season.

A standing-room crowd of 38,413 jammed sun-drenched Wrigley Field. The game-time temperature was 53 degrees, seasonal for early April in Chicago, and true to the city's moniker (The Windy City), the wind was blowing out to left field at 22 mph. The blustery weather would be a factor in the game.

Journeyman Mike Morgan was given the honor of starting the opener for the Cubs. Morgan, who was coming off a 10-15 season with a 4.03 ERA, was making his second consecutive Opening Day start for the Cubs. He was opposed by Mets right-hander Dwight "Doc" Gooden. Gooden, 5-1 in previous Opening Day starts, was making the eighth and final such start of his career. The day, however,

would belong to the relatively unknown center fielder Karl "Tuffy" Rhodes, who was batting leadoff for the Cubs.

Rhodes was drafted in the third round of the 1986 amateur draft by the Houston Astros after a standout career at Western Hills High School in Cincinnati. Rhodes rose through the low levels of the minors at a very young age, showing precocious plate discipline but very little power.[1] In the minors he was known more for his basestealing. Before 1993 he never hit more than four home runs in a season. While he began to display some power at the Triple-A level in 1993, his acquisition by the Cubs that year drew little attention. Rhodes entered the 1994 season with only five major-league home runs over parts of four seasons, and there was nothing to suggest he would enjoy the type of day he did on this April afternoon.

Morgan delivered the first pitch at 1:22 P.M. and the Cubs' and Mets' 1994 seasons were underway. After issuing a leadoff walk to second baseman Jose Vizcaino and giving up a one-out single to Kevin McReynolds, the Cubs right-hander navigated his way out of trouble to keep the Mets off the scoreboard in the first.

The fireworks started early in the Cubs half of the first. Rhodes, playing center field and leading off, deposited a 3-and-2 offering from Gooden into the deep reaches of the corner of the bleachers in left-center. Future Hall of Famer Ryne Sandberg followed with a single to right before Mark Grace grounded into a 6-4-3 double play and Gooden retired Derrick May on a comebacker to the mound. Both hurlers retired the side in order in the second.

The top of the third was highlighted by back-to-back home runs by the Mets' Vizcaino and catcher Todd Hundley. Although the wind was blowing out to left, both were able to reach the right-field bleachers. Entering the bottom of the third, the Cubs trailed 2-1. Gooden retired Shawon Dunston and Morgan, bringing Rhodes to the plate with two outs. Rhodes launched a 3-and-1 fastball into the breeze blowing out to left and tied the game with a home run that landed deep in the left-field bleachers.

The Mets answered with a big fourth inning. Second baseman Jeff Kent led off with the team's third home run of the game, to deep left-center off Morgan. Three batters later, center fielder Ryan Thompson hit a two-run double to left, was sacrificed to third by Gooden, and scored on Vizcaino's sacrifice fly.

The Cubs answered with three of their own in the bottom of the fourth. Grace was safe at first on an infield single and scored on Derrick May's double to center. Later in the inning Dunston drove in a pair of unearned runs with a double to left-center to draw the Cubs to within 6-5.

Thirty-year-old left-hander Blaise Ilsley[2] came on in relief of Morgan, who was lifted for a pinch-hitter in the bottom of the fourth. Ilsley fared no better than his predecessor. The Mets sent up eight batters and scored three runs, capped by Gooden's two-run single to right, to extend the Mets' lead to four at 9-5.

Rhodes came to the plate for the third time in the bottom of the fifth. This time he got hold of a 1-and-0 fastball from Gooden and drilled it to deep left-center for his third no-doubt-about-it home run of the game. The blast sent the Wrigley faithful into a frenzy and left Gooden with a perplexed look on his face. Tuffy Rhodes had taken Doc Gooden deep three times and earned a standing ovation and curtain call. All this and the first game of the season was only half over!

The Cubs manufactured another run in the fifth with a Sandberg double and a pair of groundouts. After five innings their deficit stood at 9-7. The Mets extended their lead to three in the top of the sixth with when Kent drove in Hundley with a single to deep short.

The Cubs started the bottom half of the sixth with singles by Rick Wilkins and Steve Buechele. After Gooden retired Dunston (fly ball to center) and struck out Glenallen Hill, the man of the hour came to plate once again. Sensing that perhaps Rhodes simply had Gooden's number that day, Mets skipper Dallas Green made a call to the bullpen and brought in left-hander Eric Hillman to face Rhodes. Pitching to Rhodes very carefully, Hillman walked him on four pitches to load the bases before he retired Sandberg on a line drive to deep left.

The score remained 10-7 in favor of the Mets as both teams failed to score in the seventh. The Mets added a run in the top of the eighth on David Segui's sacrifice fly that scored Bobby Bonilla, and another in the top of the ninth when McReynolds drove in Vizcaino with an infield single.

Trailing by five, the Cubs were down to their last three outs when Rhodes came to the plate to face Mets left-handed closer John Franco. Rhodes singled to right and extended his perfect day at the plate. His day ended when he was forced at second and the Cubs managed only a single run. Despite the team's 12-8 setback, Rhodes' unlikely 4-for-4 performance was nothing short of trilling and for one glorious day he was on pace to hit 486 homers in a 162-game season.

After his three-homer start to 1994, Rhodes played pretty well through May, but slumped in the summer and saw his playing time dry up by July. His home-run total for the season was 8. Just over 14 months after his improbable Opening Day home-run binge, Rhodes played his final major-league game, in a brief stint with the Boston Red Sox. However, Rhodes had plenty of baseball ahead of him. After the 1995 season he signed with the Osaka Kintetsu Buffalos of Japan's Pacific League. There, Rhodes became one of the greatest foreign-born sluggers in Japanese baseball history. In 13 seasons in Japan he slugged 464 home runs, including 55 in 2001 which tied Sadaharu Oh's single-season home run record.[3] His 55th came off future major leaguer Daisuke Matsuzaka.[4]

For baseball, 1994 was a season to forget. The players strike end the season on August 10, and fans were victimized by having the postseason and World Series taken from them. The Cubs finished a distant fifth in the NL Central, 16½ games behind the Cincinnati Reds, and the Mets finished third, 18½ games behind the baseball-best Montreal Expos.

SOURCES

In addition to the sources cited in the Notes, the author also consulted SABR.org, Retrosheet.org, and Baseball-reference.com

NOTES

1   Ted Berg, "Opening Day Legend Tuffy Rhodes Was Way Better Than You Think," *USA Today*. April 6, 2015.

2   Ilsley made the Cubs roster out of spring training but was optioned to Triple-A Iowa after struggling in 10 appearances with the Cubs. In 14 professional seasons he finished with a 113-73 record.

3   Michael A. Lev, "Samurai Slugger: Former Cub Tuffy Rhodes, a home run king in Japan, accepts that he always will be viewed as hired help in that nation." *Chicago Tribune*, July 11. 2004.

4   Rhodes 55th HR ties legend. *Chicago Tribune*, September 25, 2011.

KERRY WOOD WHIFFS 20 TO TIE MLB RECORD

MAY 6, 1998
CHICAGO CUBS 2, HOUSTON ASTROS 0

By Frederick C. Bush

ONE OF THE GREAT THINGS ABOUT baseball is that fans never know when a game they attend might turn into a historic occasion. This fact was borne out in an early-season, afternoon game between the defending NL Central champion and front-running Houston Astros and the Chicago Cubs on a rainy day at Wrigley Field in 1998.

Cubs rookie Kerry Wood, a power pitcher who – like most young flamethrowers – had flashed both promise and wildness, was making his fifth start of the season against an Astros team that was "the second-most prolific scoring team in the National League.[1] In this game, however, the Astros would not only fail to add to their season run total but, for one day, they would be made to look like amateur hackers as Wood struck out 20 batters to tie the nine-inning major league record in one of the most dominant pitching performances in history.

Wood began the game by flashing his wild streak as his first pitch of the game to Craig Biggio sailed over catcher Sandy Martinez and hit home plate umpire Jerry Meals square in his facemask. It would be one of only two pitches that got away from Wood on this day, and he settled down immediately to strike out Biggio, Derek Bell, and Jeff Bagwell. Astros starter Shane Reynolds took the mound in the bottom of the first and matched Wood by striking out the Cubs in order: Brant Brown, Mickey Morandini, and Sammy Sosa all went down swinging.

In the second, Wood picked up where he had left off by striking out Jack Howell and Moises Alou to give him five consecutive strikeouts before Dave Clark ended his string by flying out to center field, one of only two balls hit against Wood that would leave the infield. Mark Grace led off the bottom of the second with a double that went under Howell's glove at third base, and he advanced to third when Clark committed an error with an errant throw from left field that got past Bagwell and went all the way to wall. Henry Rodriguez worked Reynolds for six pitches until he was able to drive in Grace with a sacrifice fly to give the Cubs a 1-0 lead. Reynolds acquitted himself more than admirably on this day, especially in the face of Wood's overwhelming performance, and – had it not been for Clark's error that set up the Cubs' first, unearned run – would have taken a 0-0 tie to the bottom of the eighth, at which point he surrendered the only other run of the game.

It looked as though Reynolds and the Astros might regain a tie in the top of the third when Ricky Gutierrez led off the frame with a single off the glove of Cubs third baseman Kevin Orie. Gutierrez's base hit would be the only hit surrendered by Wood, and the scoring call generated some controversy. Cubs broadcaster Chip Caray, who had taken over WGN television play-by-play for his legendary grandfather Harry Caray who had passed away in February of that year, said it was a clean hit and a good call. Still, there were others who asserted that "[i]n the late innings of a no-hitter, it would have been scored an error, but not in the third inning.[2]

In his fifth career start, rookie Kerry Wood tossed what some have called the greatest pitched game in baseball history when he fanned 20 with no walks in a one-hit shutout of the Houston Astros. (Photo by David Banks/Getty Images)

After Brad Ausmus struck out swinging, Reynolds laid down a perfect sacrifice bunt to advance Gutierrez to second. With Biggio at the plate, Wood balked and Gutierrez advanced to third, but Biggio's groundout ended the scoring threat. In the Cubs' half of the inning, Reynolds alternated strikeouts with two singles and a walk and escaped a bases-loaded jam by striking out Rodriguez. Amazingly, at this point in the game Reynolds led Wood in strikeouts 7-6, but it was a pace that he would be unable to maintain.

Wood, on the other hand, took over the game and actually grew stronger as it progressed. He struck out five consecutive batters from the fourth through the fifth innings and registered another seven consecutive strikeouts from the seventh to the ninth. The only other blemish on his pitching line was a two-out hit-by-pitch against Biggio in the bottom of the sixth. Wood had such great command on the day that he did not walk a single batter in his nine-inning masterpiece.

While Reynolds ceased to match Wood in strikeouts, he allowed the Cubs only one additional run. In the bottom of the eighth, Morandini led off with a single and, two batters later, advanced to third on a single by Grace. Jose Hernandez, who had replaced Rodriguez in left field in the top of the eighth, hit a grounder that forced Grace at second but allowed Morandini to score and gave the Cubs the final 2-0 margin of victory.

The Cubs' second run was superfluous as it had become obvious that the Astros were not going to score against Wood. The only question left as the game entered the ninth inning was whether or not Wood was going to break the major league record of 20 strikeouts in a nine-inning game that had been accomplished twice by Roger Clemens. Wood struck out Bill Spiers, who was pinch-hitting for Reynolds, to start the inning, which gave him a tie for the NL record of 19 strikeouts that was jointly held by Steve Carlton, Tom Seaver, and David Cone. The partisan Cubs crowd booed when Biggio grounded out because it meant that Wood could only tie Clemens' record, which he proceeded to do by striking out Bell to end the game.

In the top of the ninth inning, legendary Cubs voice Jack Brickhouse called WGN color broadcaster Steve Stone to say that this was the most competitive pitching matchup he had seen since a September 9, 1965 Cubs-Dodgers game. In that game, the Cubs' Bob Hendley had pitched a one-hitter and had given up only one unearned run. Unfortunately for Hendley, Sandy Koufax pitched a perfect game – the fourth no-hitter of his career – against the Cubs that day for a 1-0 victory.

Similarly, on this day, Reynolds had pitched eight strong innings that included allowing eight hits, two runs – only one of which was earned – and two walks while striking out 10 batters. Given the Astros's offense in 1998, that would likely have earned him the win in any other game, but his pitching line paled in comparison to that of Wood, who had allowed one hit, no runs, no walks, and had struck out 20 Astros.

Wood had struck out the side four times and had struck out two batters in three other innings; he had at least one strikeout in every inning. The Astros had begun the game by flailing away at Wood's offerings; however, as the game progressed, they could not even get their bats off their shoulders anymore as Wood struck out five consecutive batters looking – Bagwell, Howell, Alou, Clark, and Gutierrez – from the fourth through fifth innings. In addition to owning the NL record and tying the MLB record with his 20 Ks, the 20-year old Wood became only the second major leaguer to match his age in strikeouts, joining Bob Feller who accomplished the feat as a 17-year old in 1936.[3]

As is to be expected on the heels of such a dominant performance, the superlatives came from all directions afterward. Cubs manager Jim Riggleman said, "There's no one in the National League who has a better arm. That game was one for the memory banks. The best I've ever seen pitched by anybody.[4] Astros manager Larry Dierker, a former 20-game winner who also pitched a no-hitter during his playing career, agreed: "He reminded me of the first time I saw [Nolan] Ryan. ... He's going to pitch a no-hitter and maybe a few no-hitters. His stuff is the real item.[5]

As for the hero of the hour, Wood said, "It felt like a game of catch out there. It was one of those games where everything you throw was crossing the plate" and also claimed, "I was focused, though, so I had no idea how many guys I was striking out."[6]

SOURCES

In addition to the sources listed in the Notes, the author also consulted Baseball-Reference.com for play-by-play details of the game and *Chicago Cubs Legends – Kerry Wood 20 Strikeouts, May 6, 1998* DVD (WGN broadcast of the game)

NOTES

1   Murray Chass, "Baseball; How to spell fast: KKKKKKKKKKKKKKKKKKKK," *New York Times*, May 7, 1998.

2   Steve Marantz, "20 at 20," *The Sporting News*, May 18, 1998: 25-26.

3   L. Jon Wertheim, "Flame Thrower," http://www.si.com/vault/1998/05/18/243269/flame-thrower-the-cubs-kerry-wood-whos-only-20-used-a-searing-heater-and-sharp-breaking-balls-to-strike-out-20-astros-in-perhaps-the-most-dominant-pitching-performance-in-baseball-history,

4   Ibid.

5   Marantz, "20 at 20."

6   Wertheim, "Flame Thrower."

SOSA HITS 60TH HOME RUN

SEPTEMBER 12, 1998
CHICAGO CUBS 15, MILWAUKEE BREWERS 12

By Rick Schabowski

THE 39,170 SPECTATORS WHO PACKED Wrigley Field on September 12, 1998, weren't so much interested in the visiting Milwaukee Brewers (70-78 and 25 games behind the Central Division-leading Houston Astros. Their focus was on the Cubs, who with an 82-66 record were tied with the New York Mets in the National League wild-card race and needed to keep winning. They also hoped to see Sammy Sosa become the fourth player to join the 60-home-run club. They weren't disappointed; Sosa's 60th helped the Cubs to a 15-12, come-from-behind victory.

One of the highlights of the 1998 season was Sosa and Mark McGwire competing to break Roger Maris's home-run record for a single season. (That competition has since been tainted by disclosures that both players used performance-enhancing substances.) McGwire hit number 62 on September 8. Sosa came into the September 12 game only three behind with 59.

Both starting pitchers, the Brewers' Rafael Roque and the Cubs' Mike Morgan, worked three-up, three-down first innings. The Brewers got their first hit in the second inning when Jeromy Burnitz lined a one-out double to right.

The Cubs scored two runs in the bottom of the second inning, but the Brewers answered in a big way in the top of the third, scoring eight runs, three of them unearned. Catcher Bobby Hughes singled to lead off the inning and went to second base on a sacrifice by Roque. Fernando Vina reached base on an error by shortstop Jose Hernandez, and after Mark Loretta singled, the bases were loaded. David

Nilsson hit a triple to center, and the Brewers took the lead, 3-2. The Brewers' bats stayed hot. Jeff Cirillo doubled, driving in Nilsson, and after Burnitz's homer, his 35th of the season, the Brewers led 6-2. Solo homers by Geoff Jenkins and Hughes gave the Brewers an 8-2 lead.

In the top of the fifth the Brewers got to reliever Dave Stevens, scoring two runs, increasing their lead to 10-2. The Cubs cut the lead to 10-5 after six innings on a solo homer by Hernandez in the fifth and a two-run shot by Gary Gaetti in the sixth.

The Brewers increased their lead to 12-5 in the top of the seventh inning. With two outs, Bob Hamelin, pinch-hitting for Roque, doubled to right field, and Jenkins scored on an error by right fielder Sosa. Felix Heredia came on in relief of Stevens, and Vina singled, scoring pinch-runner Ronnie Belliard, who was making his major-league debut. The inning ended when Vina was out at second trying to stretch the hit.

Valerio de los Santos came into pitch for the Brewers in the bottom of the seventh. He walked leadoff batter Lance Johnson, and Mark Grace had a one-out double to left field, putting runners at second and third for Sosa. On a 3-and-2 count, de los Santos threw Sosa a changeup, and the result was a 430-foot blast, home-run number 60 for Sosa, that landed on Waveland Avenue and made the score 12-8.

After the game, Sosa talked about his 60th round-tripper. "Really, in that situation, I wasn't thinking of a home run," he said. "I thought (on Friday) I was patient, and (Saturday) I was real patient. When I'm like that, I have a better chance to make contact. That's what happened. It was a 3-and-2 changeup, and I don't want to strike out in that situation. I fought through that at-bat, and I never gave up. I knew I had number 60 and I jumped and said, 'Yes, I've got it.' But besides that, I just kept it normal. My situation right now is great, and everybody knows that, but I don't want to show up the other team. I have a lot of respect for the other team."[1]

Herb Neurauter retrieved the home-run ball after it bounced off Waveland Avenue and ricocheted into an apartment building vestibule. Neurater, who lived down the street from Wrigley Field, dove for the ball and fought off other people to retain the keepsake. He returned the ball to Sosa, requesting that he have some pictures taken with him, and four autographed balls, one of them signed with the number "60."

The inning wasn't over. Glenallen Hill stepped to the plate and hit a homer, making it a 12-9 game. Chad Fox replaced de los Santos on the mound in the eighth for the Brewers, and Tyler Houston, pinch-hitting for Scott Servais, homered, making the score 12-10.

Terry Mulholland and Rod Beck pitched a scoreless top of the ninth, and the Brewers brought in their closer, Bob Wickman, for the final three outs, but things didn't go as planned. Sosa hit a first-pitch single to left. Although the fans wanted to see number 61, Sosa was happy with his single, commenting, "I just wanted a base hit, that was the key. We were losing by two runs. We didn't need a homer."[2] Hill came through, getting a single to center. With the tying runs on base and nobody out, Gaetti bunted, advancing both runners into scoring position. After Mickey Morandini walked on a 3-and-2 pitch, Houston singled just past Brewers second baseman Fernando Vina to right field, tying the game. Cubs manager Jim Riggleman had Orlando Merced, a switch-hitter, pinch-hit for Manny Alexander. Merced was a recent acquisition by the Cubs, having spent most of the season with the Minnesota Twins before being traded to the

Boston Red Sox in late July. After being released by Boston on September 1, he had gone 1-for-4 as a pinch hitter for the Cubs. That average improved when he hit a 1-and-0 pitch into the right-field seats for a game-winning home run. After his topsy-turvy season, Merced was understandably elated that his homer overshadowed Sosa's 60th. "If you said that one or two weeks ago, I'd have said you were crazy," he said.[3]

There was a lot of emotion in the Cubs locker room after the game. Riggleman had high praise for Sosa, commenting, "Sammy just continues to do great things. He's become one of the elite players in the game. He gets on base, he runs, he plays hard. He gives a great effort every day. He excited the crowd with that three-run homer that I think really lifted our ballclub and gave us a little hope. For him to get to that mark – Maris, Ruth, McGwire and Sammy are the only ones – he continues to put himself into the elite among today's players as well as in the history of the game."[4]

The man who made history, Sosa, was elated. "Unbelievable, I have to say. I could never feel more happy than I feel today. Especially since we won. It was something unbelievable."[5]

The atmosphere was very different in the Brewers' locker room. Manager Phil Garner said, "This was a tough one to lose. That was really, really tough."[6] Brewers pitching coach Don Rowe defended the bullpen, saying, "Our guys in the bullpen are gassed. The sixth inning kills us. Our starters just aren't experienced enough to get us deep into games and we end up using two or three (relievers) every night. I'm surprised some of their arms haven't fallen off."[7] Of the pitch that Sosa hit for his 60th home run, Rowe said, "That was an experience right there. De los Santos should have bounced that pitch in the dirt to see if Sammy would chase it. He wanted to strike him out. He should have let Sosa get himself out." [8]

SOURCES

In addition to the sources cited in the Notes, the author also accessed Retrosheet.org, Baseball-Reference.com, SABR.org, and *The Sporting News* archive via Paper of Record.

NOTES

1   Terry Armour, "60 'Feels Great,' but Sosa's Far From Finished," *Chicago Tribune*, September 13, 1998: 3-3.

2   Tom Haudricourt, "No. 60 Puts Sosa in Elite Quartet," *Milwaukee Journal Sentinel*, September 13, 1998: C1.

3   Paul Sullivan, "Sosa Hits 60th Homer in Thriller," *Chicago Tribune*, September 13, 1998: 3-1.

4   Armour.

5   Ibid.

6   Drew Olson, "Bullpen Takes Road to Defeat," *Milwaukee Journal Sentinel*, September 13, 1998: C1.

7   Ibid.

8   Ibid.

ROOSEVELT BROWN'S MOMENT IN THE LIMELIGHT

OCTOBER 6, 2001
CHICAGO CUBS 13, PITTSBURGH PIRATES 2

By Tim Rask

"A CUB HITS TWO HOME RUNS AND drives in seven runs – but it isn't Sammy Sosa. A starting pitcher takes a no-hitter into the eighth inning with nine strikeouts – but it isn't Kerry Wood."[1] As *Chicago Tribune* sportswriter Bob Foltman observed, unlikely heroes do tend to emerge when September call-ups get a chance to shine in late-season major-league games.

For Chicago Cubs left fielder Roosevelt Brown, his moment in the sun came on a blustery 50-degree day in Wrigley Field on October 6, 2001.

Originally drafted in the 20th round by the Atlanta Braves in 1993, the Vicksburg, Mississippi, native was still looking to establish himself at the major-league level. After being traded to the Marlins in 1996 for Terry Pendleton, Brown was selected by the Cubs in the first round of the Triple-A phase of the Rule 5 draft.[2] In his three seasons with the Cubs organization, Brown flashed some ability, but had appeared in only 88 games at the major-league level.

Brown started the 2001 season with the big club, but after appearing in only eight games in April, he was sent down to the Triple-A Iowa Cubs on April 25 when infielder Ron Coomer was activated.

If Brown was disappointed at the prospect of spending another season in Des Moines, he certainly didn't play like it. The left fielder was a productive member of the team, and flashed his offensive potential in games like a May 9 contest against Omaha in which he went 4-for-6 and drove in five runs.[3]

Brown returned to Chicago for a second time in June to fill in for an injured Rondell White. "When Rosey went down, there was no sulking on his part," said Cubs second-year manager Don Baylor. "He worked hard every day, made the All-Star team, and is back here on his merits."[4] Brown enjoyed some success, most notably a five-hit night against the Detroit Tigers,[5] but Brown returned to Iowa again on July 21.

Although fellow Iowa Cub Corey Patterson, the top prospect in the Cubs system, according to *Baseball America*,[6] was more highly touted, Brown played an integral role in leading Iowa to a Pacific Coast League (Central) Division title. In 88 games, Brown batted .346 (the best average in the Cubs organization that season) with 22 home runs and 77 RBIs to earn a Triple-A All-Star nod from *Baseball America*.[7] In fact, it was Brown's two home runs in a September 2 tilt against Salt Lake City that clinched Iowa's first division title in five years.[8]

After New Orleans swept Iowa in the first round of the Pacific Coast League playoffs, Brown returned to Chicago for his third stint of the season on September 9.

The season was interrupted by the September 11 terrorist attacks and the Cubs were still in contention for an NL Central Division crown, so Brown did not see action immediately. Once the Cubs were eliminated from wild-card contention on October 2, bench players began to get more playing time.

On Saturday, October 6, the Cubs sat locked in third place behind the Cardinals and the Astros, who would tie for the NL Central title. The Cubs had contended for much of the 2001 season, but faded badly in August and September. The recent dismissal of pitching coach Oscar Acosta, and a controversy over Baylor's use of conditioning and motivational guru, Mack Newton, cast a pall over the end of the Cubs season.[9] Still, Chicago had improved markedly from its dismal 2000 record of 65-97 (the 2001 Cubs would finish 88-74), and chilly fall weather didn't keep an announced crowd of 35,020 from coming out to Wrigley Field to enjoy the next-to-last game of the Cubs season, against the Pittsburgh Pirates.

The Pirates, saddled with an NL-worst record of 61-99 at the start of the day, went down quietly in the first inning. Cubs right-hander Julian Tavarez, making his first start since September 1, retired the first three Pirates batters in order on only 10 pitches.

The Cubs offense jumped on Pittsburgh starter Tony McKnight in the bottom of the first as Brown powered the Cubs to a 3-0 lead. After a Corey Patterson infield single and a walk to Sammy Sosa, Brown teed off on a 3-and-1 pitch and sent it over Wrigley Field's right-field bleachers and onto Sheffield Avenue.

The Cubs scoring continued in the third when Sosa led off the inning with a home run, albeit one that did not make it to the bleachers. Pirates right fielder Rob Mackowiak lost a battle with the sun, a strong crosswind, and the right-field brick wall as he watched Sosa's drive fly over his head for an inside-the-park home run.[10] Fred McGriff followed with a conventional homer over the fence to extend the Cubs' lead to 5-0. Batting after McGriff, Brown had a chance to embellish his game stats further by making it three consecutive homers for Chicago, but the left fielder lined out to center for the first out of the inning.

The Cubs added another run in the bottom of the sixth inning when Delino DeShields singled off reliever Rich Loiselle to score Todd Hundley, giving the Cubs a comfortable 6-0 lead.

All the while, Tavarez continued to mow down the Pittsburgh batters. The Cubs hurler did not allow a baserunner until the fourth inning, and recorded nine strikeouts through seven innings without allowing a hit. The pitcher credited Rick Kranitz, the Cubs' interim pitching coach, with giving him some solid advice prior to the game. "Today when I was warming up, Kranny told me to use a lot of sinking fastballs," said Tavarez after the game. "It's cold weather. It should be a good day to pitch. I'm telling you I did what he told me to do."[11]

Despite favorable pitching conditions, the Cubs continued to pile on the Buccaneer bullpen. In the bottom of the seventh, Michael Tucker tripled off Josias Manzanillo to lead off the frame, setting up another RBI opportunity for Roosevelt Brown. Brown took advantage by lofting a sacrifice fly to left field, giving the Cubs a 7-0 lead.

The Cubs starting pitcher began to run out of gas in the top of the eighth, however. Tavarez walked three of the first four Pirate batters in the inning to load the bases, then gave up his first hit of the day, a single to Mendy Lopez that plated two runs and cut the Cubs lead to 7-2. Manager Don Baylor removed his starting pitcher, and reliever Ron Mahay coaxed a double play to end the Pirates rally.

In the bottom of the frame, Brown and the Cubs quashed any hopes for a Pirates comeback by tacking on six insurance runs. Scott Sauerbeck, the Pirates' fifth pitcher of the day, gave up consecutive singles to Bill Mueller, DeShields, and Patterson. Sammy Sosa drove in two with a long double to the right-center gap, and a subsequent single by Tucker scored Patterson. With Sosa on third and Tucker on first, Roosevelt Brown stepped to the plate once more and launched his second three-run homer of the day. The six-run frame gave the Cubs a commanding 13-2 lead. Jeff Fassero closed out the Pirates in the ninth to preserve the final score.

In postgame interviews, Cubs skipper Don Baylor said he was looking forward to Brown's future with the club. "I plan on him being on this team [next season]," Baylor said. "I don't think he has more to prove in Triple-A. I think he's a major-league hitter."[12]

Brown certainly felt he deserved a long look, noting, "I just want to show what I can do. I've been doing the same thing I've been doing here down there. It's just a matter of getting time in and seeing pitches and feeling comfortable up here the same as I've done at every level I've been at."[13]

Brown got a chance to play in 111 games with the Cubs in 2002, but after he batted only .211 in 204 at-bats, Chicago released him at the end of the season.

Brown went to Japan to play two seasons for the Orix Blue Wave, who finished in the cellar of the Japan Pacific League in 2003 and 2004. Returning to the United States in 2005, Brown played one more season for the Charlotte Knights, the Triple-A affiliate of the Chicago White Sox. He never returned to the major leagues.

SOURCES

In addition to the sources mentioned in the Notes, the author consulted baseball-reference.com, mlb.com, and retrosheet.org.

NOTES

1   Bob Foltman, "Unlikely Stars Shine," *Chicago Tribune*, October 7, 2001: 3, 6.

2   Allan Simpson, "Rule 5 Keeps Teams Busy," *Baseball America*, January 5-18, 1998: 22.

3   "Offense Carries I-Cubs to 16-3 Win," *Des Moines Register*, May 10, 2001: 3C.

4   Teddy Greenstein, "Brown Has Rosier Outlook After Promotion, Outfielder Plans to Stick Around," *Chicago Tribune*, June 27, 2001: 5.

5   Teddy Greenstein, "15 Runs, 21 Hits, 50 Wins, Coomer Homers, Brown Has 5 Hits in Rout of Tigers," *Chicago Tribune*, July 7, 2001: 3.1.

6   Jim Callis, "Cubs' Cornerstone Will Require More Patience," *Baseball America*, February 19-March 4, 2001: 22.

7   "Classification All-Star Teams," *Baseball America*, October 15-28, 2001: 16.

8   Randy Peterson, "Bring on New Orleans; Brown, Cubs Cap Furious Title Run," *Des Moines Register*: 1C, 3C.

9   Teddy Greenstein, "Acosta's Firing No Easy Answer; Coach's Temper, Rift With Baylor Led to Problems," *Chicago Tribune*, October 5, 2001: 4.1.

10   Foltman.

11   Bruce Miles, "Tavarez Loses No-Hitter in 8th," *Arlington Daily Herald*, October 7, 2001: 2, 3.

12   Foltman.

13   Miles.

THE BARTMAN GAME

OCTOBER 14, 2003
FLORIDA MARLINS 8, CHICAGO CUBS 3

GAME SIX OF THE NLCS

By Brian Wright

THE PAIN HAS NOW SUBSIDED. THE wound has now healed – perhaps even slightly for the principal character of this infamous game.

A World Series championship, something the Chicago Cubs were allergic to for 108 seasons, will cause such a development.

But the notorious nature by which many North Siders acted in this moment of baseball crisis is still etched in history. It was a night when the "Friendly Confines" turned hostile on one of its own.

Twenty-six-year-old Steve Bartman – sporting a black sweatshirt over a green turtleneck, a Cubs hat, and earphones – sat in the first row along the left-field line. Aisle 4, row 8, seat 113.[1]

He, like a majority of the 39,577 in attendance and thousands more on the nearby streets and millions of loyalists around the world, was eagerly anticipating a moment that probably nobody living had ever witnessed.

Before Bartman's unexpected entrance into Chicago lore, the Cubs had the look of a pennant winner. In taking a 3-games-to-1 NLCS lead on the Florida Marlins, they had outslugged their wild-card opponent by the combined score of 33-19. A Game Five loss at Pro Player Stadium didn't elicit many thoughts of impending doom.

What it did conjure up was the hope that the Cubs could clinch a National League title – for the first time since 1945 – on their venerable home field.

A slim 1-0 edge – courtesy of a first-inning double by Sammy Sosa that scored Kenny Lofton – was extended with single runs in the sixth and seventh.

Now backed by a three-run cushion, Cubs starter Mark Prior, who had retired the last seven Marlins hitters he faced, was working on a shutout as the Marlins' eighth inning began. He continued to keep the Florida offense off-balance as Mike Mordecai flied to Moises Alou in left field.

There were just five outs remaining.

Juan Pierre lined a double to left field. The right-handed Prior and Luis Castillo battled to a full count. Then the switch-hitting Castillo hit one to left field – destined to either be an out or a foul ball.

Alou drifted toward the limited area of foul ground and over by the wall separating the fans from the field.

The barrier was short enough, and the ball came down close enough, that Alou could elevate and attempt to make a play. As Alou yearned for the ball, so did several fans in the vicinity – just as anyone else would do in that moment.

But it was Bartman's reach that obstructed Alou – not worthy of fan interference, however, in the judgment of the left-field umpire, Mike Everitt, as the ball was outside the field of play while it descended. The ball deflected off the hands of Bartman, onto the ground and eventually into the hands of someone else standing nearby.

Alou showed visible anger over what had just happened, slamming his glove to the ground and then staring in the direction of Bartman.

This anger permeated throughout the crowd as events developed.

With the count still at 3-and-2, Prior's next pitch was wild. Castillo walked and Pierre advanced to third. The tying runs were aboard. Ivan Rodriguez, Florida's Division Series hero, brought one in with a single on a two-strike curveball.

Now leading by a score of 3-1 and with a man out, Prior could still escape if he could induce a groundball from Miguel Cabrera. The 20-year-old did exactly that. A tailor-made 6-4-3 double play if there ever was one.

But surehanded shortstop Alex Gonzalez booted it. Safe all around.

Prior, on the other hand, was anything but safe. Derek Lee took his next offering and laced it to left field. Castillo and Rodriguez crossed the plate. Tied at three.

A sacrifice fly by Jeff Conine, sandwiched between two intentional passes, gave the Marlins a lead they wouldn't let go. To make sure of that, the offense continued to add on.

By now, Prior's sterling performance was but a memory. Kyle Farnsworth had come in relief, but gave little of it. Mordecai's ivy-raiding double to left-center went between and beyond either outfielder's reach and emptied the once-loaded bases.

Pierre, the 11th (and second-to-last) batter to come up in this nightmarish half-inning for Chicago, hit a single to right that drove home the eighth run, five of which were unearned because of Gonzalez's miscue.

In a matter of minutes, the Marlins completely took the wind out of the sails of the Windy City. Cubs fans went from planning a victory party to preparing for the worst.

The same supporters who used unwelcome billy goats and traversing black cats to reason their team's near-century of misfortune now had a new scapegoat to lay the blame on, no matter how unwarranted the blame was.

Coming off 18 wins and a 2.43 ERA in his first full season in the majors, Mark Prior was cruising in Game Six of the NLCS, having held the Florida Marlins scoreless through seven innings, until the infamous Bartman incident. (Photo by Jon Soohoo/Getty Images)

As the Marlins' hits and runs accumulated in a most painful fashion, so too did the abhorrent castigation, with words and debris, by abusive patrons upon Bartman – rather than toward the well-salaried players who were failing to withstand the Marlins' onslaught. The Fox television cameras relentlessly focused on Bartman, who remained solemn despite the madness that surrounded him.

Wrigley Field security staffers, worried for his safety, escorted Bartman into the bowels of the ballpark for the remainder of Florida's 8-3 victory. They dressed him in disguise and waited until just about every depressed patron had departed the surrounding area before sending him off.[2]

"I had my eyes glued on the approaching ball the entire time and was so caught up in the moment that I did not even see Moises Alou, much less that he may have had a play," Bartman said in a statement released the next day. "I am so truly sorry from the bottom of this Cubs fan's broken heart."[3]

From then on, Bartman receded into total exile. And until recently, when the Cubs bestowed him with a 2016 World Series championship ring,[4] the most notorious fan in American sports had no known contact with the organization – despite the overtures to have him appear at Wrigley Field. He also refused hundreds of media requests which, according spokesperson and friend Frank Murtha, was to avoid the notoriety and the inevitable uproar in the aftermath.[5]

The ball that he accidentally made contact with, meanwhile, lived a far less tortured life. It was sold to Harry Caray's Restaurant and demolished before a crowd of joyous onlookers.[6]

The destruction of the ball and the condemnation of Bartman would never have happened had the Cubs recovered to win the Series' deciding contest the next night. But after Game Six's debacle, you didn't have to be a psychic to know what was coming

next. You just had to know of recent curse-addled Chicago Cubs history.

Florida won Game Seven, 9-6, and won the World Series against the New York Yankees for the franchise's second championship in its 11-year tenure. The Cubs, meanwhile, were left to wait some more. Ninety-six years and counting.

SOURCES

In addition to the sources cited in the Notes, the author also used his scoresheet from the game, Baseball Reference.com, and Retrosheet.org.

NOTES

1   Chris Kuc, "Fan in 'Bartman Seat' for Game 6 just 'happy, thrilled to be here,'" *Chicago Tribune*, October 22, 2016.

2   *Catching Hell*. Dir. Alex Gibney. ESPN Films, 2011. Film.

3   ESPN.com news services, "Fan Sorry From 'Bottom of Broken Heart,'" ESPN.com, October 16, 2003.

4   Mark Gonzales, "Seeking Closure, Cubs Give World Series Ring to Steve Bartman," *Chicago Tribune*, July 31, 2017.

5   Ben Strauss, "Steve Bartman Remains Invisible, 10 Years Later," *New York Times*, October 13, 2013.

6   Gibney.

FOR THE 95TH TIME IT'S "WAIT 'TIL NEXT YEAR" FOR THE CHICAGO CUBS

OCTOBER 15, 2003
FLORIDA MARLINS 9, CHICAGO CUBS 6

GAME SEVEN OF THE NLCS

By John DiFonzo

THE CHICAGO CUBS HAD NOT WON A World Series since 1908 and their last appearance was 1945. They upset the Atlanta Braves in the division series, their first postseason-series victory since 1908. The Cubs had a 3-games-to-1 lead in the National League Championship Series over the Florida Marlins. The Marlins were an expansion team in 1993, had won the 1997 World Series, and were back in the playoffs for their second time. The Marlins were only the fourth team out of 25 since 1985 to come back and win an LCS trailing three games to one. The Marlins won the last two games in Wrigley Field and defeated a pair of young aces, Mark Prior and Kerry Wood. They went on to win the 2003 World Series.

The Marlins seized the momentum in the Series after being down three games to one. They took Game Five behind a brilliant two-hit complete game by 23-year-old rookie Josh Beckett on 115 pitches. The Marlins took Game Six after trailing, 3-0, in the top of the eighth inning and the Cubs were five defensive outs from the going to the World Series. The Marlins stunned the Cubs by rallying for eight runs. The comeback was punctuated by a possibly catchable foul ball that was deflected by a fan, Steve Bartman. That foiled a chance for Moises Alou to make a play and was followed by a costly error by shortstop Alex Gonzalez. Before the inning was over, eight runs

scored. After the game, Cubs manager Dusty Baker was asked about the "billy goat curse" and denied any connection, "It has nothing to do with the curse."[1] The Marlins were feeling overlooked, Juan Pierre said, adding, "You feel like everybody's against you. I would say 97 percent of the world probably wants … to see the Cubs and Red Sox in it."[2]

Wood was the Game Seven starter for the Cubs. The 26-year-old right-hander was 14-11 and struck out a league-high 266 batters while walking 100 in 211 innings. Wood won five of his previous seven starts, including two in the postseason. Wood relied mainly on the fastball and slider. The Marlins countered with left-hander Mark Redman, more of a nibbler who threw the changeup and curveball. Redman had pitched well in the postseason with no-decisions in both of his starts.

The crowd at Wrigley was raucous early on, but the Marlins struck first. Pierre led off the top of the first inning with a triple to right field that was aided when Sammy Sosa slipped and fell while chasing the ball. After a one-out walk to Ivan Rodriguez, 20-year-old Marlins rookie Miguel Cabrera silenced the crowd by golfing a low 1-and-2 fastball into the left-center-field bleachers for a three-run home run. Wood said, "To me, it's a pitch he shouldn't hit."[3] Cabrera began his career as a shortstop, but after making 32 errors in 2001 for the Class-A Kane

County Cougars was converted to a third baseman. Recently he had moved to the outfield because Mike Lowell was the Marlins' everyday third baseman. Cabrera was starting his fourth game of the Series in right field and would make several solid defensive plays during the game. The home run was his third of the series, a new LCS record for a rookie.[4]

Aramis Ramirez led off the bottom of the second inning and hit a foul ball down the left-field line, close to the location of the controversial Game Six foul ball. The Fox broadcast team recalled the events of Game Six and were sympathetic to Bartman, showing on a replay that other fans had reached for the ball. Bartman had to be escorted out of the stadium because of the unruly crowd. Because of overwhelming negative fan reaction, Bartman could not go to work and the news media was camped outside his home. His phone was disconnected. A statement from Bartman shown on the broadcast closed with an apology, "I am so truly sorry from the bottom of this Cubs fan's broken heart."[5]

The Cubs battled back against Redman in the bottom of the second inning. Eric Karros singled to right field, and Gonzalez doubled to center. Damian Miller grounded out to score Karros. Pitcher Wood hit a 3-and-2 pitch for a two-run home run to tie the game at 3-3, and the crowd roared back to life. "It was the loudest I ever heard it," Wood said years later.[6] Kenny Lofton stepped out of the batter's box to allow the crowd to give Wood an extended ovation.[7]

In the bottom of the third, the Cubs struck again. After Redman hit Sosa, Alou gave the Cubs a 5-3 lead by hitting a home run over the left-field wall onto Waveland Avenue, where a huge crowd of Cubs fans had gathered. The man who caught Alou's home-run ball was removed for his own security.

Wood had trouble controlling his slider in the bottom of the fifth, and walked two batters. With one out, Rodriguez extended his postseason hitting streak to 11 with a double to left to bring the Marlins within one run, 5-4. Cabrera drove in the next run on a fielder's choice and Derrek Lee knocked in Rodriguez with a single to right to put the Marlins back in the lead, 6-5. Wrigley grew silent. "That

was the most eerie part about it," Wood said. "You could hear conversations on the field – guys were yelling and you could hear every word they were saying to each other. In a matter of two hours, it was the loudest I've ever heard it and the quietest I ever heard it."[8]

In the top of the sixth, the Marlins' Jeff Conine led off with a single and went to third on a single by Pierre with two out. Wood was through after throwing 112 pitches and was replaced by Kyle Farnsworth. "You've got to understand, about 30 minutes ago, I choked. I let my teammates down, I let the organization down and I let the city of Chicago down," Wood said after the game. "They hit the ball. They put the ball in play. I didn't have my good slider. They put together good at-bats all night. I don't know how many two-strike foul balls they hit this series. They don't give up and they don't give in."[9] Farnsworth gave up a single to Luis Castillo and the Marlins increased their lead to 7-5. It was only the third time all season that Wood gave up seven runs in a game and three of the four batters he walked scored.[10]

In the top of the seventh, the Marlins had two on and two out and Baker went to his bullpen to bring in Dave Veres to face Alex Gonzalez[11] even though Beckett was on deck. Gonzalez was 0-for-10 against Veres but had success against Farnsworth. The strategy backfired as Gonzalez hit a broken-bat double to center to extend the Marlins' lead to 9-5.

A sense of desperation was starting to take hold in Wrigley. As is traditional, during the seventh-inning stretch, the crowd was led by someone singing "Take Me Out to the Ball Game." Game Seven's honor went to Billy Corgan, lead singer of the Smashing Pumpkins. After he finished he implored the Cubs, "Let's get some runs!"

Beckett had replaced Brad Penny to start the fifth inning. He was pitching on two days' rest and the only blemish in his four innings pitched came in the Cubs' seventh, with Troy O'Leary's pinch-hit home run. It was the 23rd home run of the series, setting an NLCS record.[12] After Beckett had allowed four runs in the first inning of Game One of the series, he allowed only three runs in his last 18⅓ innings, retiring 39 of the last 43 batters he faced.

That would be all of the scoring in the game. The Cubs could manage only one baserunner in the final two innings. Ivan Rodriguez knocked in an NLCS record 10 RBIs[13] and was named the series MVP. Jack McKeon, at age 72, became the oldest manager to reach the World Series for the first time. The Marlins had never lost a postseason elimination game or series. The Cubs had won just one postseason series in the previous 95 years. Baker gave his assessment after the game: "We didn't lose the pennant, the Marlins won it."[14] Baker added, "What hurt was the fact that they got three or four two-out RBI hits and we couldn't stop them from adding on in the end."[15]

There would be no Cubs-Red Sox World Series. The following evening, the other cursed team would lose Game Seven of the ALCS in heartbreaking fashion to their archrival Yankees. One newspaper summed it up for the Cubs, "Last World Series appearance: 1945. The Billy Goat Curse. And now Bartman."[16]

SOURCES

In addition to the sources cited in the Notes, the author also used the Baseball-Reference.com, and Retrosheet.org Fox telecast available on youtube.com: (youtube.com/watch?v=2laVtbFFIGw).

NOTES

1   Paul Sullivan and John Mullin, "Baker: Tough Luck Little to Do With Curse," *Chicago Tribune*, October 15, 2003, articles.chicagotribune.com/2003-10-16/sports/0310160327_1_big-game-ordinary-game-rebound-from-tough-losses. Accessed August27, 2017.

2   John Mullin, "Being Written Off Rankles Marlins," *Chicago Tribune*, October 15, 2003, articles.chicagotribune.com/2003-10-15/sports/0310150239_1_cubs-marlins-game-florida-marlins-mike-mordecai Accessed August 27, 2017.

3   Melissa Isaacson and Bonnie DeSimone, "Wood: I Choked, Let the City Down," *Chicago Tribune*, October 16, 2003, articles.chicagotribune.com/2003-10-16/sports/0310160341_1_bottom-line-matt-clement-marlins. Accessed August 26, 2017.

4   This record stood as of the 2016 playoffs.

5   Associated Press, "Statement From Cubs Fan Steve Bartman," October 15, 2003, foxnews.com/story/2003/10/15/statement-from-cubs-fan-steve-bartman.html. Accessed August 26, 2017. The full statement read:

There are few words to describe how awful I feel and what I have experienced within these last 24 hours.

I've been a Cub fan all my life and fully understand the relationship between my actions and the outcome of the game. I had my eyes glued on the approaching ball the entire time and was so caught up in the moment that I did not even see Moises Alou, much less that he may have had a play.

Had I thought for one second that the ball was playable or had I seen Alou approaching I would have done whatever I could to get out of the way and give Alou a chance to make the catch.

To Moises Alou, the Chicago Cubs organization, Ron Santo, Ernie Banks, and Cub fans everywhere I am so truly sorry from the bottom of this Cubs fan's broken heart.

I ask that Cub fans everywhere redirect the negative energy that has been vented towards my family, my friends, and myself into the usual positive support for our beloved team on their way to being National League champs."

6   Carrie Muskat, "Decade Later Game 6 Still Hard to Forget," MLB.com, October 14, 2014, m.mlb.com/news/article/62909144//. Accessed August 26, 2017.

7   It was the first postseason home run by a pitcher since Rick Sutcliffe hit one for the Cubs in Game One of the 1984 NLCS at Wrigley Field.

8   Muskat.

9   Isaacson and DeSimone.

10   Ibid.

11   Both teams had a shortstop named Alex Gonzalez. The Cubs' Alex Gonzalez was born in Miami on April 8, 1973, and played in the major-leagues from 1994 to 2006. The Marlins' Alex Gonzalez was born in Cagua, Venezuela, on February 15, 1977, and played in the major leagues from 1998 to 2014.

12   This record was broken in the 2004 NLCS between the St. Louis Cardinals and Houston Astros, who combined to club 25 home runs in their seven-game series.

13   As of the 2016 postseason, this record still stood.

14   Rick Morrissey, "Game 6 Collapse Will Define This Team," *Chicago Tribune,* October 16, 2003, articles.chicagotribune.com/2003-10-16/sports/0310160345_1_cubs-marlins-eighth-inning-error. Accessed August 26, 2017.

15   Isaacson and DeSimone.

16   Adam Rubin, "It's a Cruel Choke: Cubs Lose Game 7, Curse Lives On, Fish Win NLCS," *New York Daily News,* October 16, 2003.,nydailynews.com/archives/sports/cruel-choke-cubs-lose-game-7-curse-lives-fish-win-nlcs-article-1.520897. Accessed August 26, 2017.

CUBS OVERCOME
EIGHT-RUN DEFICIT TO WIN

MAY 30, 2008
CHICAGO CUBS 10, COLORADO ROCKIES 9

By Paul Geisler

WHEN CUBS FANS PREVIEW THE DAY'S game, they look at the weather report for Wrigley Field, even before asking, "Who's pitching?" This afternoon they could expect warm temperatures (upper 70s) with steady winds from the southwest (10 mph gusting over 30 mph, from home plate toward the batter's eye in center field). If the light morning rain would hold up, the crowd of nearly 40,000 could look forward to a good chance of fly balls carrying over the fences.

The Chicago northsiders, riding a four-game winning streak, entered the game with the best record in the major leagues (33-21). Left-hander Ted Lilly (5-4, 5.23 ERA) started against Colorado's best pitcher of the season, right-hander Aaron Cook (7-3, 2.82 ERA). Chicago also had scored baseball's best 5.63 runs per game, compared with the Rockies' 4.15; Cubs pitchers had allowed only 4.00 runs per game, compared with 5.44 runs allowed by their opponents' staff.

Lilly faced more than strong breezes as he took the mound to start the game, after a 22-minute rain delay. Willy Taveras reached first base on a bunt single and then moved to third on a single by Jonathan Herrera. The runners held their places at first and third on a lineout to third base by Ryan Spilborghs and a fly to right field by Garrett Atkins. Three runs scored on Todd Helton's home run to center field. Back-to-back doubles by Chris Iannetta and Jeff Baker brought in another run, before Omar Quintanilla ended the inning with a lineout to

second base. The Rockies led the Cubs 4-0 after the first half-inning.

Lilly struck out Spilborghs to start the third inning, then Garrett Atkins reached second base on center fielder Jim Edmonds' error. Edmonds, newly signed after San Diego released him earlier in May, received routine boos from bleacher fans who remembered his many years with the rival St. Louis Cardinals. Helton flied out to center field, then Iannetta homered to left field, bringing in two unearned runs. Baker doubled again, then scored a third unearned run on Quintanilla's single. Lilly finished the inning with a strikeout of rival pitcher Aaron Cook, the last batter he would face. In this his worst outing of the season, Lilly had allowed eight hits and seven runs – four of them earned – in three innings.

Cubs pitcher Carlos Zambrano led off the bottom of the third inning pinch-hitting for Lilly. Despite grounding out to second base in that plate appearance, Zambrano would win the National League Silver Slugger award for pitchers that season, for the second time, with a .337 batting average and four home runs in 83 at-bats. (He would also win that award again the following season, 2009.)

Jon Lieber took the hill for Chicago in the fourth inning and allowed a home run to Spilborghs, putting the Rockies up 8-0 heading into the bottom of the fourth. The two teams traded runs in the bottom of the fourth and the top of the fifth. The Cubs loaded the bases on Derrek Lee's single, Kosuke Fukudome's walk, and Edmonds' single. Mark DeRosa's one-out fly to right field got his team on the scoreboard. The Rockies then added their ninth run with a two-out double by Baker, followed immediately by Quintanilla's single. Chicago did not score in the home side of the fifth, leaving the Rockies' lead now at 9-1 after five.

Almost seeming to concede the contest, at the start of the next inning Chicago manager Lou Piniella substituted Henry Blanco for starting catcher Geovany Soto, and Micah Hoffpauir for Derrek Lee at first base. Piniella had also omitted starters Aramis Ramirez (third base) and Ryan Theriot (second base) from the starting lineup in favor of DeRosa and Mike Fontenot.

Piniella looked more like a genius with "the Midas touch"[1] over the next two innings, as the winds shifted their favor from the Rockies to the Cubs. Colorado did not score in the sixth, then Hoffpauir led off the Chicago sixth with a double, followed by a home run from Fukudome. Edmonds added a back-to-back round-tripper, his first home run as a Cub. Booed for his error earlier, Edmonds now received a standing ovation from the Wrigley crowd. DeRosa and Ronny Cedeno grounded out and Lieber struck out to finish the inning, with the Rockies still in the lead, 9-4.

The Cubs haiku blog responded to events throughout the game. For example, one fan wrote,

Hopeless, down by eight
But Hoffpauir, Kosuke, Edmonds
Cut it down to five.[2]

After Lieber got the first two outs in the Rockies' seventh, Scott Eyre came on to pitch and struck out Quintanilla.

Hockey great Bobby Hull, guest singer that day for "Take Me Out to the Ballgame," rushed through the words, ahead of the crowd's "one, two, three strikes you're out." Then he imitated Harry Caray's inimitable style with a strong, "Let's get some runs!" Hull, apparently disappointed in his performance,

commented to Cubs broadcaster Len Kasper, "It was a terrible 'Take Me Out to the Ballgame' sing, but we'll get 'em going."[3]

Colorado starting pitcher Cook endured the sixth but faced more trouble in the seventh. After a one-out single by Fontenot, Blanco homered and Hoffpauir singled. Manny Corpas took over for Cook. Corpas began the season as the Rockies' closer, but Brian Fuentes replaced him in that role after Corpas posted four blown saves and two losses in April. Totally ineffective, Corpas proceeded to allow hits to the next three batters: Fukudome singled, Edmonds doubled, and DeRosa homered. Chicago had claimed four homers over 12 batters and a 10-9 lead in the game.

Jason Grilli replaced Corpas and produced a groundout and a strikeout to end the inning.

Manager Piniella noted, "When DeRosa's ball went out, that's the loudest this place has been this year, by far. It was almost deafening."[4]

The Chicago lead thrilled Hull, who yelled, "How about that? Now I don't' feel so bad."[5]

In the top of the eighth, Carlos Marmol struck out three hitters – Scott Podsednik, Seth Smith, and Herrera – all on called third strikes, with a total of just 10 pitches. Colorado called on Taylor Buchholz to pitch the bottom of the eighth. He allowed one hit – a single – but no runs. The Cubs still led 10-9, heading to the ninth inning.

Chicago closer Kerry Wood gained his 13th save of the season when he retired the side after a leadoff walk to Spilborghs to give the Cubs the victory. They had overcome deficits of 8-0 and 9-1, scoring nine unanswered runs with Lee, Ramirez, and Soto on the bench.

"What can I say?" commented Piniella. "That's the description of a comeback win."[6]

Eyre, who struck out the only batter he faced, got credit for his second win of the season, with no losses. Corpas, who allowed three hits and three runs to the only three batters he faced, suffered his third loss of the season with no wins, as well as his fifth blown save.

Although Jeff Baker set a Colorado record with four doubles in the game, the Rockies lost their fifth game in a row; for the Cubs. It was their fifth win in a row, their 34th of the season, continuing with the best record in baseball.

After the game, DeRosa reflected on his doubts: "Early on we were like, it's going to be rough, but the way the wind was blowing, you never know." Rockies starter Cook, who seemingly had a meltdown in the sixth and seventh innings, reflected, "You never think you'll lose a game when you're up 9-1, but you still have to go out there and play 27 outs. We just didn't finish the game today."[7]

Haiku bloggers celebrated the comeback win. Steve Nawara said,

> *I stopped in the third*
> *Went about my busy day*
> *Missed a great comeback.*

Blogger "Ed" followed next with:

> *I was luckier*
> *In the car starting at noon*
> *Heard or watched it all!*[8]

For those who were counting, the Cubs' magic number for winning the National League Central Division title was now down to 106.[9] They went on to win the next two games against the Rockies, completing a four-game sweep, on their way to capturing the division title.

SOURCES

In addition to the sources cited in the Notes, the author also accessed Retrosheet.org, Baseball-Reference.com, and SABR.org.

NOTES

1   Paul Sullivan, "Cubs Stage 8-Run Comeback to Beat Rockies," chicagotribune.com, May 30, 2008.

2   thecubsinhaiku.wordpress.com.

3   Michael Pope, "Cubs Should Thank Bobby Hull for Victory," bleacherreport.com, May 30, 2008.

4   Sullivan.

5   Pope.

6   Sullivan.

7   "Cubs Overcome 8-Run Deficit with a Four-Homer Barrage," nytimes.com, May 31, 2008.

8   thecubsinhaiku.wordpress.com.

9   cubsmagicnumber.com.

TRAILING 7-0? NO PROBLEM!

JUNE 19, 2009
CHICAGO CUBS 8, CLEVELAND INDIANS 7

By Thomas J. Brown Jr.

THE BASEBALL GODS WERE SMILING down on the Cubs (31-31) when the Cleveland Indians (29-39) came to town on June 19, 2009. For the second straight afternoon, the Cubs scored four runs in the eighth inning and one in the ninth. In the first comeback, the Cubs beat their crosstown rivals, the White Sox. Although both comebacks resulted in exciting wins for the Cubs, the second game took them an extra inning to do it.[1]

The Indians were hoping to snap a three-game losing streak when they arrived at Wrigley Field. The game marked the return of Kerry Wood and Mark DeRosa, who had been instrumental in Chicago's second consecutive NL Central title in 2008, but had been let go in the offseason and signed by Cleveland.[2] Both players got standing ovations from the crowd when they entered the game.

Cliff Lee, who had won the AL Cy Young Award the previous year with a 22-3 slate, started for the Indians. The southpaw had gotten off to a rocky start to this point in '09 but had won his last two decisions to improve to 4-6. Cubs manager Lou Piniella went with right-hander Rich Harden, who entered the game with a 4-3 record and was trying to shake off losses in his previous two starts.

It was a cloudy, overcast day with temperatures in the mid-70s. After an 86-minute rain delay, the game started with only a small breeze blowing from right to left field.

A scoreless first led to a hectic second. The Indians' Jhonny Peralta ended up on third base when he hit a fly ball to deep left-center that the usually surehanded Reed Johnson couldn't handle. After Harden walked Kelly Shoppach, Luis Valbuena, hit his second home run of the season over the center-field wall for a 3-0 Indians lead.

Harden continued to struggle and walked the first two batters in the third inning. Then Victor Martinez connected for a home run to put the Indians up 6-0.

The Indians scored another run in the fourth inning. Ben Francisco led off with a single, went to second on Lee's sacrifice, trotted to third on Jamey Carroll's fly to deep center, and scored on a single by DeRosa to right field.

The Cubs scored their first run in the fifth inning, on Johnson's leadoff home run to center field. But Lee settled down and got the side out with no more damage.

Piniella removed Harden for pinch-hitter Micah Hoffpauir in the bottom of the fifth inning. "It was ugly," said Harden of his efforts that afternoon.[3]

The Cubs continued their uphill struggle with one out on the sixth when cleanup hitter Derrek Lee blasted a solo home run to right-center field to make it 7-2. Then they came alive in the bottom of the eighth inning. Milton Bradley led off with a single to center field. Joe Smith relieved Cliff Lee and struck out Derrek Lee, but Geovany Soto doubled to center field, sending Bradley to third. Smith struck out Jake Fox but walked Johnson to load the bases. The next batter, light-hitting Andres Blanco, hit a single down the right-field line that scored Bradley and Soto and made the score 7-4.

Indians manager Eric Wedge pulled Smith for Rafael Perez. Cubs pinch-hitter Koyie Hill hit a grounder to third that Peralta bobbled. Johnson scored and Blanco moved to second. Alfonso Soriano followed with an RBI single to center field to score Blanco. Matt Herges came in and got RyanTheriot to line out to center field. But the Cubs had scored four runs and trailed the Indians by just 7-6.

One of the most dramatic moments of the game came in the ninth inning. In relief for the Indians was Wood, who faced Derrek Lee with one out. Wood threw Lee a curveball, then shook off catcher Shoppach three times before throwing a fastball. Lee deposited Wood's heater into the left-field bleachers for his second home run of the game. It was a blown save for Wood and sent the game into extra innings.

"Derrek, he played behind me all those years, it's like he knew what was coming," Wood said. "He was smiling after he hit it."[4] Lee was equally complimentary of his former teammate: "He is throwing 96, he made a good pitch. He jammed me. It got up in the wind and got out of here."[5]

Wood got Soto to line out to right field and Johnson to fly out to center field, and the game went into extra innings.

In the 10th Piniella went to his bullpen again, calling on Kevin Gregg, who added to the tension. He gave up a leadoff single to Shin-Soo Choo, who was forced at second on Peralta's grounder. First baseman Lee muffed Shoppach's foul and left fielder Soriano dropped Shoppach's line drive. Gregg struck out Valbuena but hit Francisco and the bases were loaded with two outs. But Gregg escaped the jam by getting pinch-hitter Ryan Garko to line out to center field.

Before the game, manager Wedge spoke about his bullpen concerns. After the game, he said "We very easily could have sent two or three more guys out. That's the reality."[6] This night Wedge sent former Cub Luis Vizcaino to the mound with the hope that the bullpen would come through for the Indians.

Vizcaino got the first two batters, but walked Soriano, who stole second to the cheers of the crowd of 40,155. "I don't remember the last time I was trying to steal, but I went for it and I got it," he said.[7] Then,

on a full count, Theriot hit a weak groundball that took a crazy bounce over first baseman Martinez's glove. Soriano scored the game-winning run. Vizcaino took the loss in what turned out to be his last major-league game. (The Indians released him 11 days later.)

"It worked out, the baseball gods were smiling on me," said Theriot. The win was the Cubs' third in a week to come in their final at-bat.[8]

Cliff Lee had left the game with hopes of winning his third game in a row. After watching what happened after he left, he said, "It's frustrating. Not because I didn't get a win, but because the team didn't get a win. Everybody in here should be frustrated. We have that game won and let it slip away."[9]

Wedge also vented his frustrations about the bullpen's performance. "It's been struggling on and off all year," he told sportswriters. "You have games like this and it's about as bad as it can get. You have to have people who can get people out – particularly in the seventh and eighth inning."[10]

After waiting for the rain to stop, Cubs fans were treated a memorable game. For the second straight day, Chicago put together a four-run rally in the eighth inning. While fans welcomed DeRosa and Wood back with cheers, the real ovation went to Theriot for his heroics in the 10th inning. The game may have taken 3 hours and 38 minutes to complete but the drama of that extra-innings comeback would be long remembered.

SOURCES

In addition to the sources cited in the Notes, the author also used the Baseball-Reference.com, Baseball-Almanac. com, and Retrosheet.org websites for box-score, player, team, and season pages, pitching and batting game logs, and other pertinent material.

NOTES

1   Dave van Dyck, "To Relive Is Divine: Lee Blasts Two Homers, Theriot Gets Winning Hit as Cubs Come Back Again From Big Deficit," *Chicago Tribune*, June 20, 2009.

2   Dan Labbe, "Indians Open Up Series With Cubs This Afternoon," *Cleveland Plain Dealer*, June 19, 2009.

3   Dave van Dyck, "To Relive Is Divine."

4   Ibid.

5   "Cubs' Theriot Caps Rally With Single in 10th to Dump Indians," ESPN.com, June 20, 2009.

6   Paul Hoynes, "Cleveland Indians' Bullpen Blows Five-Run Lead and Tribe Loses to Cubs in 10 Innings," *Cleveland Plain Dealer*, June 19, 2009.

7   Dave van Dyck, "To Relive Is Divine."

8   Ibid.

9   Paul Hoynes, "Cleveland Indians' Bullpen Blows Five-Run Lead."

10 Ibid.

COLE HAMELS TOSSES NO-HITTER

JULY 25, 2015
PHILADELPHIA PHILLIES 5, CHICAGO CUBS 0

By C. Paul Rogers III

IT WAS WIDELY BELIEVED THAT COLE Hamels' Saturday, July 25, 2015, start against the Chicago Cubs in Wrigley Field could be his last in a Philadelphia Phillies uniform. If so, it would end his memorable 9½-year run with the team, capped by his 2008 World Series MVP Award. The Phillies were limping along sporting the worst record in baseball and, with the trading deadline just days away, were shifting into full rebuilding mode. They were seeking top prospects to replenish their fallow farm system and the Cubs, Dodgers, Red Sox, and Rangers, among others, were known to be competing for Hamels.[1]

No one, however, in the capacity crowd of 41,683 that afternoon could reasonably have expected that their Cubbies would not record a hit that day. After all, it had been 49 full seasons since the Cubs had been no-hit at Wrigley Field, the longest span in major-league history.[2] In addition, Hamels had pitched very poorly in his last two starts. After compiling a superb 2.48 earned-run average in 11 starts from May 8 to July 5, he had been rocked for 14 runs and 20 hits over 6⅓ innings in his two previous outings. That included a start on July 10 in San Francisco in which Hamels was knocked around for 12 hits and 9 earned runs in 3⅓ innings. It was the worst start of his career by a wide margin.

Hamels' mound foe on July 25 was Jake Arrieta, who, after a strong 2014, was in the midst of a breakout season. Arrieta allowed a two-out double by Maikel Franco in the top of the first before retiring Ryan Howard on a groundout. Hamels began the bottom of half of the inning by walking Dexter

Fowler before retiring the next three batters on a fly ball, groundout, and strike out. In fact, he retired the next 17 batters in a row until he again walked Fowler, this time with two outs in the sixth. Eight of those outs were strikeouts and by then he had convinced veteran catcher Carlos Ruiz that something special was afoot.[3] Meanwhile, the Phillies had jumped ahead 3-0 in the top of the third on a two-out double by Odubel Herrera, a walk to Franco, and a three-run homer to left-center field by Howard.

Hamels showed no signs of slowing down in the seventh, striking out Anthony Rizzo, Jorge Soler, and Chris Denorfia swinging to bring his strikeout total to 11. The Phillies tallied two unneeded insurance runs in the top of the eighth against reliever James Russell on a single by Cody Asche and a pop fly by Freddy Galvis that fell out of everyone's reach behind first base for a double. Galvis completed a trip around the bases on the play when Cubs first baseman Rizzo threw wildly to second.

With the tension mounting in the bottom of the eighth, Hamels retired Starlin Castro on a fly ball to right fielder Domonic Brown. David Ross then laid into a Hamels offering and sent a fly deep to center field that Herrera, aided by the wind blowing in, was able to corral just in front of the vines for the second out. Pinch-hitter Kyle Schwarber followed and topped a ball that traveled halfway to the mound, where Hamels fielded it and threw to Howard at first for the third out of the inning.

Cubs' right-hander Neil Ramirez retired the Phillies in the top of the ninth, surrendering only a one-out double to Howard. With the crowd hanging on every pitch, Hamels began the ninth by inducing Addison Russell to ground weakly to third. Third sacker Franco made a nice play on the ball, swooping in to nip Russell at first. Hamels then caught Fowler looking at a called third strike for the second out. That brought highly touted rookie Kris Bryant to the plate. Bryant had already smacked 13 home runs and was establishing himself as a force to be reckoned with. With little wasted motion, he lofted a hanging breaking ball to deep center field, sending Herrera scampering back to the warning track. He almost scampered too far back, as it turned out. With the wind blowing in, the ball seemed to die, forcing Herrera to lunge forward with his glove outstretched. He managed to snag the ball just short of the warning track and just above the ground while ending up on his stomach to secure Hamels' no-hitter. Everyone in the park, by now all rooting for Hamels, breathed a huge sigh of relief as his teammates mobbed him in the center of the diamond.[4]

After the game, Hamels labeled his feat as "just a surreal moment," adding, "Nothing will top winning a World Series but this is probably on that top list. That's right under it." Of the final play by Herrera, Hamels said, "Thank goodness the wind was blowing in."[5]

The next day teammate Jeff Francoeur said, "The whole ninth inning everyone was so quiet in the dugout. Everyone wanted it – we might have wanted it worse than he did, to be honest with you. ... [w]e all know what he's been going through a little bit. Everybody has to deal with trade rumors and I know he just hasn't been pitching like he's wanted to, and I know it's been frustrating for him. Cole's not the kind of guy that's going to show it, but I do know that it's been eating at him. To be able to come out and do that yesterday – there were a lot of smiles from Cole yesterday."[6]

In his masterpiece, Hamels struck out 13 and allowed two walks in 129 pitches, 83 of which were strikes. The no-hitter was just the 12th in the Phillies' long history, dating back to 1885.[7] It was the first time the Cubs had been no-hit since Sandy Koufax's perfect game on September 9, 1965, in Dodger Stadium.[8]

Arietta was the losing pitcher, dropping his record to 11-6. It was his last loss of the season; afterward he reeled off 11 consecutive wins to finish 22-6 and win the National League Cy Young Award by a wide margin. The up-and-coming Cubs won 97 games in 2015 to finish third in a tough division. They qualified for the wild-card game and defeated the Pittsburgh Pirates 4-0 behind a five-hit shutout by Arrieta. The Cubs went on to beat the division-winning St. Louis Cardinals three games to one in the Division Series before being swept by the New York Mets in four games in the League Championship Series.

Meanwhile, the Phillies plummeted to a 99-loss season, finishing last in the National League East Division for the second year in a row. Hamels' no-hitter was indeed his last start for the Phillies; six days later, on the trading deadline, the Phillies shipped him and Jake Diekman to the Texas Rangers in exchange for injured southpaw pitcher Matt Harrison and five highly regarded prospects.[9] After the trade, Hamels won seven of eight decisions for the Rangers and helped propel them to the American League West Division title by a mere two games over the Houston Astros.[10]

Interestingly, the Cubs and Phillies already had an odd no-hitter connection from a previous generation. On May 13, 1960, the Phillies had traded 24-year old pitcher Don Cardwell and first baseman Ed Bouchee to the Cubs in exchange for catcher Cal Neeman and second baseman Tony Taylor. In his first start for the Cubs two days later, the journeyman Cardwell pitched a no-hitter for the Cubs in a 4-0 win over the St. Louis Cardinals. So perhaps Hamels' no-hitter against the Cubs in his final start as a Phillie was in some way payback for Cardwell's gem 35 years before in his first start after leaving the Phillies.[11]

SOURCES

In addition to the sources cited in the Notes, the author also accessed Retrosheet.org, Baseball-Reference.com, and SABR.org.

NOTES

1   Ryan Lawrence, "Will Cole Win Heart of Cubs?" *Philadelphia Daily News*, July 26, 2015: 45.

2   Jim Maloney of the Cincinnati Reds had last no-hit the Cubs at Wrigley on August 19, 1965, in a 10-inning game the Cubs lost 1-0 on a home run by Leo Cardenas off Larry Jackson.

3   Fred Mitchell, "Phillie Phantastic; Hamel's Sparkler Evokes Memories of Koufax in 1965," *Chicago Tribune*, July 26, 2015: C-3.

4   Mike Sielski, "A Philly Gem – Cole Hamels Pitches a No-Hitter in What Might Have Been the Final Game of His Stellar Phillies Career," *Philadelphia Inquirer*, July 26, 2015: 1; Jake Kaplan, "Herrera Saves Day with Key Grabs," *Philadelphia Inquirer*, July 26, 2015:D7..

5   John Kaplan, "A Parting Gift – Hamels Handcuffs Cubs with No-Hitter," *Philadelphia Inquirer*, July 26, 2015: D1.

6   Ryan Lawrence, "A Cole Day in July," *Philadelphia Daily News*, July 27, 2015: 62.

7   Hamels had participated in the 11th on September 1, 2014, in Atlanta when he pitched six hitless innings against the Braves. Three relievers, Jake Diekman, Ken Giles, and Jonathan Papelbon, followed with a hitless inning each to secure the no-hitter and a 7-0 Phillies win.

8   Mitchell, "Phillie Phantastic."

9   The prospects were outfielder Nick Williams, catcher Jorge Alfaro, and pitchers Jake Thompson, Alec Asher, and Jerad Eickhoff.

10 The Rangers then lost the Division Series to the Toronto Blue Jays three games to two. Hamels started Game Two and had a no-decision in a 14-inning Rangers win. He also started the decisive Game Five and was the losing pitcher thanks to three unearned runs.

11 The trade actually worked out well for the Phillies because Tony Taylor had a long career in Philadelphia and became one of the most popular Phillies' players in their history.

ARRIETA TOSSES THREE-HIT SHUTOUT FOR 20TH VICTORY

SEPTEMBER 22, 2015
CHICAGO CUBS 4, MILWAUKEE BREWERS 0

By Gregory H. Wolf

THE CHICAGO CUBS' 29-YEAR-OLD RIGHT-handed ace Jake Arrieta was on a roll of historic proportions. "It's just incredible what he's done in the second half. He's Bob Gibson-esque," said skipper Joe Maddon, making a bold comparison to the former St. Louis Cardinals Hall of Famer.[1] Madden was not entirely correct in his assessment – Arrieta was currently pitching *better* than Gibson did in 1968 when he posted a record-setting 1.12 ERA.

Meaningful baseball in September had returned to the Windy City. Maddon's squad (88-62) was in third place in the NL Central Division, six games behind the Cardinals and two behind the Pittsburgh Pirates, but the team had won 13 of its last 18 games to reduce its magic number to four to secure a wild-card spot and its first playoff berth since 2008. Their intradivisional opponent Milwaukee Brewers (63-87) were tied with the Colorado Rockies with the second worst-record in baseball.

After five dismal, losing seasons, the Cubs had assembled a group of young, exciting hitters and fielders; however, the unequivocal focal point of this club was the emergence of Arrieta as one of the game's best pitchers. Acquired in a midseason trade with the Baltimore Orioles in 2013, Arrieta had been considered an underachiever and disappointment, given his lackluster 20-25 slate and 5.46 ERA in three-plus seasons with the Orioles. His breakout campaign (10-5, 2.56 ERA in 25 starts) in his first full season with the Cubs suggested his potential,

but no one anticipated his utter dominance in 2015. "He's made himself into this player/pitcher," glowed Maddon. "Durability-wise, everything, it's him – the look, the stare, the way he wears his hat. His delivery is different, and I'm so glad no one tried to change [it]."[2] Critics had long pointed to Arrieta's awkward, across-the-body motion as a cause of concern, but the big, 6-foot-4, 225-pounder refused to make any significant adjustments; instead, he worked diligently to improve his most glaring weakness – the command of his fastball. "That's what makes him as productive as he is," said Maddon about Arrieta's heater. "He's got this wonderful slider and this great curveball, and he's come up with the changeup; but if the fastball isn't a strike pitch, then his other pitches become moot."[3]

Entering his start against the Brewers, Arrieta was leading the majors in victories (19, with six losses) with an eye-popping 1.96 ERA, which amazingly was well behind the Los Angeles Dodgers' Zack Greinke (1.65), himself having a season for the ages. However, it was Arrieta's recent dominance that drew comparisons to Gibson and some of the best extended stretches in big-league history. In his last 17 starts (since June 21), Arrieta was 13-1 with a 1.01 ERA; in his last nine, he was 8-0, with a 0.54 ERA, which included a no-hitter with 12 punchouts against the Dodgers in California.

On a beautiful, midweek evening with the game-time temperature hovering around 70 degrees, Wrigley Field was packed with 36,270 blue-clad fans.

Jake Arrieta had one of the best seasons in Cubs history in 2015, leading the majors with 22 victories. He posted a 1.77 ERA and fanned 236 in 229 innings to win the Cy Young Award. (Photo by Jonathan Daniel/Getty Images)

They barely had time to settle into their seats when Brewers leadoff hitter Scooter Gennett sent Arrieta's second pitch down the left-field line for a double. It turned out to be the Brewers' highlight of the game. Possessing what sportswriter Mark Gonzales of the *Chicago Tribune* called a "sweeping slider and a sharp breaking curve that rarely broke above the knees," Arrieta set down the next 14 batters before yielding a single to Hernan Perez in the fifth.

While Arrieta aimed for his 20th victory, another Cubs player was on the cusp of history, too. Kris Bryant entered the game with 25 home runs, tied with Cubs icon and Hall of Famer Billy Williams (1961) for the most round-trippers by a Cubs rookie. With two outs in the third and rookie Kyle Schwarber on first via a walk, Bryant hit a line-drive missile off Brewers rookie starter Tyler Cravy, who entered the game with an unsightly 0-7 record. According to the *Tribune*, the shot barely cleared the left-field wall, but it put Bryant in the team's record book and the Cubs on the board, 2-0.[4] The ecstatic crowd applauded as Bryant rounded the bases and stopped only after he

emerged from the dugout for a curtain call. "That was a special moment for me to get up in the steps and get that recognition," he said. "It was something I'll never forget."[5]

While Arrieta mowed down the Brewers, the Cubs tacked on two more runs. With two outs in fifth and Dexter Fowler on first, Schwarber sent reliever Kyle Lohse's offering to short right field. Second baseman Scooter Gennett attempted an over-the-shoulder catch, reported the *Tribune*, but the ball dropped, enabling the speedy Fowler to score while Schwarber slid into second with a double.[6] Schwarber led off the eighth with a single off Corey Knebel, the Brewers third hurler of the game, and then scored on Bryant's double to the deep left-center-field gap for a 4-0 lead.

Through eight innings Arrieta had thrown 108 pitches, allowed only three hits, and fanned nine. Maddon thought about a reliever, but then trusted his heart and not his head. "With everything attached to [the game], I thought it was appropriate to send him back out," the Cubs manager revealed after the game. Maddon, long regarded as one of the best skippers in baseball, understood the significance of statistics. Arrieta fanned Logan Schafer and Adam Lind on seven combined pitches, then with what proved to be his season-high 123rd pitch, dispatched Khris Davis on a weak grounder to second to end the game in 2 hours and 22 minutes.

Not only did Arrieta's victory reduce the Cubs' magic number for a playoff spot to three, it enabled him to reach several milestones. He became the Cubs' first 20-game winner since Jon Lieber won 20 in 2001; he was the first Cubs hurler under 30 to win 20 games since Greg Maddux in 1992; and he became the first Cubs flinger since Fergie Jenkins in 1971 to record 20 wins and strike out 200 batters in the same season.

Arrieta, whose low-key personality stood in stark contrast to his competitive spirit on the mound, shrugged off the personal accomplishments. "[Winning 20] means I'm putting my team in position to win games. And at the end of the day, that's our goal: to try to pitch on as much as we can."[7]

"You talk about a 20-game winner," gushed Maddon in the postgame press conference. "The things that Jake's done, you saw today, the total domination of the game, which [never] even permits the other team to come back on us even when we're not scoring a lot of runs."[8]

Arrieta won his last two starts, yielding only three hits in 13 innings to extend his streak of scoreless innings to 22. He finished the season with a major-league-best 22 victories (6 losses), yielded a major-league-low 5.90 hits per nine innings, while striking out 236 batters in 229 innings, and fashioning a 1.77 ERA, the majors' second lowest behind Greinke's 1.66. He also became the Cubs' first Cy Young Award recipient since Maddux in 1992.

SOURCES

In addition to the sources cited in the Notes, the author also accessed Retrosheet.org, Baseball-Reference.com, and SABR.org.

NOTES

1   Carrie Muskat, "Arrieta Pitches His Way Into Record Books," MLB.com, September 23, 2015.

2   Mark Gonzalez, "King of the Hill. Arrieta Dominates in 20th Victory; Cubs 4, Brewers 0," *Chicago Tribune*, September 23, 2015: 1.

3   Muskat.

4   Gonzalez.

5   Brain Sandalow, "Arrieta Wins No. 20 in Style," *Northwest Herald* (Woodstock, Illinois), September 23, 2015: 17.

6   "Cubs 4, Brewers 0," *Chicago Tribune*, September 23, 2015: 3.

7   Ibid.

8   Muskat.

UNEXPECTED HERO: LESTER AT THE BAT

JULY 31, 2016
CHICAGO CUBS 7, SEATTLE MARINERS 6

By Mike Mattsey

WHO NEEDS CASEY? CUBS FANS WILL forever more repeat the tale of "Lester at the Bat."

In its century of hosting Chicago Cubs games, Wrigley Field has seen some unorthodox tilts. In 1917, Cubs pitcher Hippo Vaughn no-hit the Cincinnati Reds for nine innings only to lose the game in the 10th. Sixty-two years later, in 1979, the North Siders bombarded the Philadelphia Phillies with 22 runs. They lost. In 1984, Ryne Sandberg homered twice off future Hall of Famer Bruce Sutter to snatch victory from St. Louis in extra innings in a game that helped lead the club to their first postseason berth in 39 years. In the thick of a pennant race in July 2016, the deciding blow was struck by a man who at one point in his career was the worst hitter in major-league history. Cubs fans who were dreaming of an end to the team's 108-year-old World Series drought saw their hopes bolstered by the wild, 7-6, extra-inning comeback against former Cy Young Award winner Felix Hernandez and the Seattle Mariners. The win gave the team a jolt after a disappointing July and propelled them to successful end to a season that will be remembered as long as games are played at the corner of Clark and Addison.

Cubs skipper Joe Maddon entered the final game of the month having overseen his charges race to baseball's best record. However, fans had seen the squad limp through an 11-14 July, bringing back memories of teams past that watched big leads melt away in the summer sun. To give his rotation a day of rest, Maddon gave a spot start that doubled as an audition to journeyman pitcher Brian Matusz in the hope that the veteran could manage to give the team a quality start before giving way to the bullpen.[1] The regular starters welcomed the day off. "We'll use that day however we need to the best of our abilities," said Jake Arrieta, adding, "We'll find a way to use that day to get some work done and get better and move forward."[2] Matusz, pitching for his third team in the last three months, failed miserably, surrendering a trio of two-run homers to Mariners hitters in his brief stint. Nelson Cruz and Robinson Cano each reached the bleachers before a third-inning bomb off the bat of slugger Dae Ho Lee chased Matusz from the game to a chorus of boos from the capacity crowd who were despondent over the 6-0 score. It was at this point that a combination of stellar relief pitching and baseball magic took over, giving the Wrigley faithful a game for the ages.

The fact that the Cubs won after trailing by six runs is noteworthy but certainly not without precedent. What makes this game destined for an eternal position in Chicago Cubs history is the bizarre set of events that led to the victory. The comeback began in relatively straightforward fashion as the Cubs scored twice off Hernandez in the fifth inning via a bases-loaded walk to Ben Zobrist followed up by Addison Russell being hit by a pitch to drive home Dexter Fowler. Hernandez's wild streak elevated his pitch count to 103 pitches through five innings and led to the Mariners' bullpen being called on to finish the game for manager Scott

Servais. It was here that things got progressively stranger as the night went on.

Seattle struck back in the sixth, loading the bases with no outs before reliever Travis Wood escaped the mess with no runs scoring. Maddon then rewarded Wood in a most unusual manner for a relief pitcher: The Cubs skipper sent him out in the seventh to play left field. According to Maddon, the move was designed to keep the versatile Wood available to pitch later in the game to bolster the beleaguered Cubs bullpen. "This stuff with Travis and [Strop]," Maddon said after the game, "that was necessary … based on the length of the bullpen."[3]

Wood's outfield abilities were put to the test with one out and one on in the seventh. Franklin Gutierrez crushed a drive to deep left field that Wood corralled as he crashed back-first into the ivy-covered bricks. Wood's fielding prowess caused a long ovation from the bleacher denizens, who began bowing to him as they used to do a generation ago to the great Andre Dawson. Wood continued in left field until there were two out in the eighth when he returned to the mound to face Leonys Martin in a lefty-lefty matchup with a runner on first. Rather than deal with Martin, Wood picked Shawn O'Malley off at first base to end the inning. The sides traced scoreless frames until the last of the ninth, where the zaniness that marked the night resumed.

Leading 6-3 to start the bottom of the ninth, the Mariners summoned Steve Cishek to close out the fray as he had done the night before. With one out, the rally began. Anthony Rizzo and Zobrist hit safely and Russell's single made it 6-4 as Rizzo scored. Jason Heyward was hit by Cishek to load the bases for rookie catcher Willson Contreras. Contreras rapped a groundball to third for what looked like a game-ending double play, but the hustling catcher beat the throw to first by an eyelash to plate the Cubs fifth run. The play was reviewed by the umpires and upheld, and the delay may have rattled Cishek. The Mariners hurler uncorked the wildest of wild pitches

to Matt Szczur, easily missing the plate by a good five feet, and Russell waltzed home to knot the game, 6-6, to the delight of the partisan crowd. Bizarre? The best was still to come.

The game remained scoreless until the bottom of the 12th, when Heyward led off with a ringing double and advanced to third on a fly out. The pitcher's spot was up, but the bench was empty, so empty that Maddon called on Jon Lester to grab a bat and win the game. The same Jon Lester who, by dint of his record-setting 0-for-66 start to his batting career, was at one point the worst-performing batter in baseball.[4] Lester hadn't been put in this position since high school by his reckoning, allowing that "guys threw a lot less hard back then."[5] The career .051 hitter was up to the challenge, and the wild game got the finish it so richly deserved.[6]

Lester worked the count to 2-and-2 against Mariners reliever Cody Martin when Maddon called for the safety squeeze. Lester got the bunt down while Heyward broke perfectly from third base and dove across the plate with the winning run, setting off an epic celebration. Lester was mobbed by his teammates, who simultaneously ripped his jersey from his body, covered him with rosin, and doused him with water bottles. In a game in which a pitcher played left field, a catcher's speed saved the game, and the tying run scored on a pitch that missed the catcher's lunge by a foot, it was the unlikeliest batter of all who drove home the winning run to capture the series two games to one.

Even in a year when the Cubs were a legitimate threat to win the World Series for the first time since 1908, a certain amount of pixie dust was needed along the way to pull off the deed. Maddon seemed to agree with this assessment. "This is the kind of thing that, if it plays out properly, when you make that DVD at the end of the year this is the game that's highlighted the most."[7] Cubs fans looked forward to finding out.

SOURCES

In addition to the sources cited in the Notes, the author also accessed Retrosheet.org, Baseball-Reference.com, and SABR.org.

NOTES

1   Paul Roumeliotis, "Brian Matusz Will Be Spot Starter in Cubs' Series Finale vs. Mariners," CSNChicago.com, csnchicago.com/chicago-cubs/brian-matusz-will-be-spot-starter-cubs-series-finale-vs-mariners, July 30, 2016.

2   Ibid.

3   MLB, SEA@CHC: "Maddon Discusses Comeback, Wild Win," YouTube.com, youtube.com/watch?v=vWc6pRhhyRM, July 31, 2016.

4   Carrie Muskat, "At Long Last, a Hit for Lester," MLB.com m.mlb.com/news/article/135106696/jon-lester-records-first-career-hit/, July 5, 2015.

5   Paul Skrbina, Jon Lester on walk-off bunt: 'I Blacked Out for a Minute,' ChicagoTribune.com, chicagotribune.com/sports/baseball/cubs/ct-jon-lester-walkoff-bunt-20160801-story.html, August 1, 2016.

6   Ibid.

7   "Maddon Discusses Comeback."

HENDRICKS' GEM GIVES CUBS FIRST PENNANT IN 71 YEARS

OCTOBER 22, 2016
CHICAGO CUBS 5, LOS ANGELES DODGERS 0

GAME SIX OF THE NLCS

By Gregory H. Wolf

"THE CUBS ARE GOING TO THE WORLD Series," gushed the North Siders radio broadcaster, Pat Hughes. "The Cubs win the pennant."[1] The long-suffering lovable losers systematically dismantled the Los Angeles Dodgers and beat the best pitcher on the planet to capture their first NL flag in 71 years.

There was an electric mood at Wrigley Field on Saturday night, October 22. That contrasted sharply with a sense of dread among Cubs fans just four days earlier in Los Angeles when the Dodgers knocked around staff ace Jake Arrieta for four runs in five innings to take a 2-1 lead in the best-of-seven NLCS. But following skipper Joe Maddon's script to win every inning, the Cubs outplayed the Dodgers in the next two games at Dodger Stadium to move to the precipice of their first trip to the World Series since the end of World War II.

All the pregame hype centered on the contest's two pitchers: Dodgers skipper Dave Roberts counted on Clayton Kershaw to prolong their season. The southpaw, a three-time Cy Young Award recipient, had been limited by back pain to just 21 starts in the regular season but posted a 12-4 slate with a 1.69 ERA. He copped the win in Game Two by tossing two-hit ball over seven innings; however, in his career he had uncharacteristically struggled in the postseason, as evidenced by his 4.79 ERA, more than two runs higher than in the regular season. Toeing

the rubber for the North Siders was soft-tossing right-hander Kyle Hendricks, who had morphed from the team's fifth starter to wunderkind, leading the majors with a 2.13 ERA to go along with a 16-8 slate in his third full season.

Two years removed from a 73-89 record and a last-place finish in the NL Central Division, the Cubs (103-58 in the regular season) were a loose, exuberant bunch, mirroring Maddon's temperament. The former Tampa Bay Rays pilot arrived in 2015 and immediately established a laid-back culture of winning. It was a youthful team, too, with five starting position players for this game 24 years old or younger. One of those players was rookie Albert Almora, who surprisingly got the nod in right field over three-time Gold Glove Award winner Jayson Heyward (and his $184 million contract), whose season-long batting slump was well documented and had gotten worse in the playoffs (he was just 1-for-16 in the NLCS). Earlier in the afternoon the team received an emotional boost when club officials announced that slugger Kyle Schwarber, out since April 7 with a knee injury, would be available for DH duty if the Cubs reached the World Series.

The hundreds of Wrigleyville bars had been humming before noon in anticipation of the game. By the 7:09 P.M. start time, the 102-year-old stadium was packed with 42,386 partisan fans in a sea of Cubbie blue. They had been stirred up by former

Cubs star Kerry Wood, of 20-strikeout fame. He threw out the ceremonial first pitch decked in a number-10 jersey in honor of Hall of Famer, Cubs icon, and longtime announcer Ron Santo, who had died in 2010.

The Dodgers came out swinging. Leadoff hitter Andrew Toles sent Hendricks' first pitch to right field for a single. NL Rookie of the Year Corey Seager grounded the next pitch to second baseman Javier Baez, who chased Toles out of the basepath, tagged him, and swiftly tossed to first for a twin killing. The flashy infielder from Puerto Rico pumped his chest as the Wrigley crowd went wild. Hendricks, a model of consistency all season, retired Justin Turner to end the inning and was just getting his groove on. Save for a Baez error in the second, Hendricks set down every hitter he faced until he yielded a one-out single to Josh Reddick in the eighth.

Psychologically, the game was decided in the bottom of the first inning. Cubs leadoff hitter Dexter Fowler pounded a 1-and-1 pitch to right field for a ground-rule double. Kris Bryant, who followed his Rookie of the Year Award in 2015 with an MVP trophy in 2016 (39-102-.292), clubbed a single to right to drive in the first run. Toles took his eyes off Anthony Rizzo's liner to left field and committed a costly blunder; and suddenly there were runners on second and third with no outs. Super sub Ben Zobrist, a longtime Maddon favorite on the Tampa Bay Rays and a World Series champion with the Kansas City Royals in 2015, knocked in Bryant on a deep sacrifice fly. Kershaw escaped without further damage but seemed taxed. He tossed 30 pitches, his most in the first inning of any game since 2011; it was also the first time he had given up two first-inning runs the entire season.

The Cubs tacked on another run in the second when Addison Russell led off with a line-drive double to left field and scored on Fowler's two-out single. Fowler was thrown out at second trying to stretch the hit. The Cubs' 3-0 lead recalled a few ghosts of games past. In Game Six of the 2003 NLCS, the Cubs were just five outs from the World Series and led the Florida Marlins, 3-0, in the top of

the eighth when spectator Steve Bartman interfered with a potential catch by outfielder Moises Alou. The Marlins then scored eight runs that inning to win the game and captured the pennant in the next contest. In 1984, the Cubs led the San Diego Padres, 3-0, in the bottom of the sixth in the deciding Game Five of the NLCS, yet lost, 6-3.

This game offered no haunting images of lovable losers. Venezuelan native Willson Contreras led off the bottom of the fourth with a screeching line-drive home run and raised his hands over his head in celebration as he rounded the bases and crossed home plate for the Cubs' fourth run. It was the eighth hit in 19 postseason at-bats for the 24-year-old rookie, who had platooned behind the plate with VMiguel Montero.

In the fifth, the Cubs added their fifth and final run when Rizzo took Kershaw yard over the right-center-field fence. Just 26 years old, Rizzo was the only Cubs starter to have played on the team's three horrendous last-place teams (2012-2014). When Theo Epstein was named team president and Jed Hoyer GM after the 2011 season, one of their first moves was the acquisition of Rizzo from the San Diego Padres, where Hoyer had served as GM. Since then Rizzo, who had also been in the Red Sox organization, had developed in to a three-time All-Star and team leader.

The rest of the game was a smile fest for the Cubs as the Dodgers could not figure out Hendricks' array of cutters, sinkers, changeups, curves, and four-seam fastballs that topped out at about 90 miles per hour. The highlight for the rest of the game might have been when Chicago Bulls legend and NBA Hall of Famer Scottie Pippen sang "Take Me Out to the Ball Game" in the seventh-inning stretch. By that time, reliever Aroldis Chapman had replaced Hendricks with one out in the eighth and secured the last five outs. The Cuban-born flamethrower had been acquired in a blockbuster deal with the New York Yankees near the trading deadline and gave the Cubs a lights-out closer. Curaçaoan Kenley Jansen, himself one of the hardest throwers in baseball who vied for the mantle of best reliever in baseball, replaced Kershaw to start the sixth and set down all nine Cubs batters he faced. With Dodgers pinch-hitter Carlos Ruiz on first via a walk, Chapman induced his countryman Yasiel Puig to ground weakly to shortstop Addison Russell, who initiated a game-ending 6-4-3 twin killing, giving the Cubs the 5-0 victory in 2 hours and 36 minutes, and more importantly sent them to the World Series.

"The Cubs are celebrating on the mound," said Hughes on WSCR 670. "Anthony Rizzo waving the to the fans. Bear hugs. High fives. Handshakes. Laughter. What a great scene."[2]

"I thought we played one of our best games all year tonight," said Maddon. "The defense, the pitching, the hitting – that was a complete game of baseball."[3] The Cubs dominated the last three games, outscoring (23-6) and outhitting (33-17) the Dodgers in a convincing team effort. Baez (7-for-22 with four doubles and five RBIs) was named series co-MVP with pitcher Jon Lester (two earned runs in 13 innings; one win). The story of this game was the Cubs starter, the David who outdueled the Dodgers Goliath. "Hendricks may not be the best pitcher on the planet," gushed Cubs beat writer Paul Sullivan, "but he might be the smartest. He was lost in Kershaw's shadow."[4]

Three days later, the Cubs were in Cleveland to face the Indians in a much-anticipated World Series matchup between two clubs, each of which owned the longest championship drought in its respective league.

SOURCES

In addition to the sources cited in the Notes, the author also accessed Retrosheet.org, Baseball-Reference.com, and SABR.org.

NOTES

1   "Capture the Flag," *Chicago Tribune*, October 23, 2016: III, 3.

2   Ibid.

3   Paul Sullivan, "Reason to Celebrate," *Chicago Tribune*, October 23, 2016: III, 4.

4   Ibid.

After he won 16 games and sported the lowest ERA in the major leagues (2.13) during the regular season, Kyle Hendricks' gem in Game Six of the NLCS catapulted the Cubs into the World Series for the first time in 71 years. (Photo by Jon Durr/ Getty Images)

CUBS FALL TO INDIANS IN FIRST WORLD SERIES GAME AT WRIGLEY FIELD SINCE 1945

OCTOBER 28, 2016
CLEVELAND INDIANS 1, CHICAGO CUBS 0

GAME THREE OF THE WORLD SERIES

By Frederick C. Bush

AFTER THE CUBS HAD SPLIT THE FIRST two games of the 2016 World Series in Cleveland, they returned home to the friendly confines of Wrigley Field for what would be the first fall classic game at the venerable stadium since October 10, 1945. On that date, Chicago's North Siders had lost the seventh game of the World Series to the Detroit Tigers, 9-3. During Game Four of that 1945 Series, the Curse of the Billy Goat had originated when a fan named William Sianis, who owned the Billy Goat Tavern, was asked to leave because his pet goat's odor was offensive to other spectators. Legend has it that Sianis vowed that the Cubs would never win another World Series because they had insulted his goat.

Since that time, the Cubs had become America's "lovable losers," as they indeed continually found ways to snatch defeat from the jaws of victory. Included among the squads that had suffered the ignominies of defeat, due more likely to their own untimely ineptitude than any curse, were the 1969 team, which had a nine-game mid-August lead in the NL East but ended up finishing second, eight games behind New York's "Miracle Mets"; the 1984 squad, which squandered a 2-0 NLCS lead against the San Diego Padres; the 2003 club, which allowed the Steve Bartman foul-ball incident to rattle them so much that they lost both that game and Game

Seven of the NLCS against the Florida Marlins; and, most recently, the 2015 team, which suffered a NLCS sweep at the hands of the New York Mets in the franchise's latest attempt to return to baseball's Promised Land.

The 2016 Cubs, however, had appeared to overcome every curse and past foible when they defeated the Los Angeles Dodgers in the NLCS to earn a shot at the team's first title in 108 years. Given the team's championship drought, the excitement for the first World Series game at Wrigley Field in 71 years was palpable for their fans, and tickets for the event "were approaching the cost of a college tuition payment."[1]

Frank Colletti was one fan who did not have to pay for a ticket, thanks to his nephew Ned Colletti Jr., an executive with the Los Angeles Dodgers who had grown up in Chicago as a Cubs fan. Ned Jr. fulfilled a promise his father and two other brothers had made to Frank on October 6, 1945, as they left him behind to attend Game Five of the World Series. Frank, who was now 82 years old, recalled, "He [Ned Sr.] said, 'We promise to take you to the next one, but the next one never came.'"[2] This time around, Frank Colletti took his place among the 41,703 fans in attendance, a group that included such notables as Cubs Hall of Famers Billy Williams and Ryne Sandberg, actor Bill Murray, and musician Billy Corgan.

After Williams threw out the ceremonial first pitch, the action began as the Cubs took the field with Kyle Hendricks – who led the NL with a 2.13 ERA in the regular season – on the mound to face the Indians. Hendricks struck out leadoff batter Carlos Santana but then surrendered back-to-back singles to Jason Kipnis and Francisco Lindor to find himself in an early jam. Hendricks extricated himself from the situation by picking off Lindor at first base and then striking out Mike Napoli.

If Hendricks was hyped up for the occasion, his mound opponent, Josh Tomlin, was even more emotional in light of the fact that his parents were at the game. Tomlin was especially thankful that his father, Jerry, was able to attend since he had become partially paralyzed in August due to a condition that had caused knotting of the blood vessels near his spinal cord. After the game, Tomlin acknowledged the importance of his father's presence, saying, "I had to find him in the stands. ... I could look at him and find that comfort there and settle back down. I used it a couple of times."[3]

It hardly seemed as though Tomlin required a calming presence at any point as he dueled with Hendricks. Tomlin allowed a single to Ben Zobrist in the second and walked Kris Bryant in the fourth, but that was the only traffic the Cubs had on the basepaths through the first four innings. Hendricks had found himself in a first-and-third, two-out situation in the top of the fourth, but he again had emerged unscathed by striking out Roberto Perez for the third out.

Although both pitchers put up zeroes for the first four frames, neither would make it through the fifth inning due to their managers' penchants for going to their bullpens early in an attempt to find the best matchup for every situation. In the top of the fifth, Hendricks allowed a leadoff single to Tyler Naquin, who then advanced to second on Tomlin's sacrifice bunt. After Hendricks walked Santana and hit Kipnis with a pitch, Cubs skipper Joe Maddon replaced him with reliever Justin Grimm. Maddon's quick hook paid dividends when Grimm induced a double-play grounder from Lindor to end Cleveland's scoring threat.

Jorge Soler led off the bottom half of the inning with a single against Tomlin and advanced to second on Javier Baez's grounder back to the Indians' pitcher, whose only play was at first base. Tomlin induced another groundout from Addison Russell that kept Soler at second. In spite of the fact that he had thrown only 58 pitches and was hurling a shutout, Indians manager Terry Francona pulled him from the game in favor of ace reliever Andrew Miller. Hendricks' and Tomlin's early exits "mark[ed] the first time in World Series history both starters were removed before the sixth in a scoreless game."[4] Francona's move worked as well as Maddon's had: Miller got pinch-hitter Miguel Montero, who was batting for Grimm, to line out to right fielder Lonnie Chisenhall for the final out of the fifth and then struck out the side in the sixth inning.

Carl Edwards Jr. took over on the hill for the Cubs in the top of the sixth and set the Indians down in order, but he ran into trouble in the next frame. Perez led off the seventh inning with a single to right field and was then replaced by pinch-runner Michael Martinez. Naquin laid down a sacrifice bunt that moved Martinez to second base, and Martinez scooted quickly to third when Edwards unleashed a wild pitch with Rajai Davis at the plate. Davis walked to put Indians runners on first and third once again, and Coco Crisp came up to pinch-hit for Miller. Crisp lined a base hit to right field that knocked in Martinez and knocked Edwards out of the game. Mike Montgomery entered the fray for the Cubs and induced a Kipnis grounder to second base that limited the damage to only one run. As it turned out, it would be the only run scored in the game.

The Cubs had a chance to tie the game against Cleveland's third pitcher, Bryan Shaw, as soon as the bottom of the seventh when Soler banged a two-out triple past Chisenhall in right field. The *Chicago Tribune* bemoaned the perception that "Soler seemed to forget he was playing in a World Series, watching the ball before jogging down the line until Chisenhall missed it, only then turning on the burners."⁵ The implication was clear: Had Soler hustled out of the box, he might have tied the game on an inside-the-park home run. For his part, Soler had thought his hit would go foul and said he did not think he could have scored anyway even if he had run hard immediately.⁶ Soler was stranded at third when Baez grounded out to the shortstop, Lindor.

Shaw held Chicago in check in the eighth, and Cody Allen took the mound in the ninth inning to close out the Indians' victory. The Cubs, however, did not intend to go quietly. Anthony Rizzo led off with a single and then gave way to pinch-runner Chris Coghlan. Zobrist struck out, and Wilson Contreras grounded out to third; however, Coghlan was able to advance to second base on Contreras's grounder. Jason Heyward reached base safely on an error by Napoli at first base on which Coghlan also advanced to third. After Heyward stole second, Wrigley was rocking at the prospect of a walk-off victory. It was not meant to be, however, as Baez struck out to end the game.

When asked about the game's ending, Rizzo said, "That's the way it is. We knew it was not going to be easy. ... We've just got to come back and do what we do."⁷ While Rizzo seemed unfazed, Cubs fans were likely worried that the Curse of the Billy Goat might rear its ugly head once more and that their team would do what it had always done since 1945.

SOURCES

In addition to the sources listed in the Notes, the author also consulted Baseball-Reference.com for play-by-play details of the game.

NOTES

1 Billy Witz, "Indians' Pitchers Roar to Life, and the Cubs' Bats Fall Silent," nytimes.com/2016/10/29/sports/baseball/cleveland-indians-beat-chicago-cubs-world-series-game-3.html, accessed April 1, 2017.

2 David Waldstein, "Cubs Fan Gets His Series Ticket, 71 Years After He Was Promised One," *New York Times*, October 31, 2016: D2.

3 Colleen Kane, "Tomlin Lights Out at Wrigley," *Chicago Tribune*, October 29, 2016: 2, 7.

4 Mark Gonzales, "Zeroing Out: Cubs Shut Out for 2nd Time in Series, Now Trail Indians 2-1," *Chicago Tribune*, October 29, 2016: 2, 3.

5 Paul Sullivan, "In End, Picture Not So Perfect," *Chicago Tribune*, October 29, 2016: 2, 5.

6 Ibid.

7 Ibid.

THERE WAS NO JOY IN WRIGLEYVILLE: INDIANS PUSH CUBS TO BRINK

OCTOBER 29, 2016
CLEVELAND INDIANS 7, CHICAGO CUBS 2

GAME FOUR OF THE WORLD SERIES

By Frederick C. Bush

AS THE CUBS OCCUPIED THEMSELVES with preparations for Game Four of the World Series against the Cleveland Indians, their fans were busy trying to convince themselves that the home team could overcome the previous night's 1-0 loss – the second Cleveland shutout of the Series – that had put Chicago into a 2-1 Series deficit. A whitewashing was not what the Cubs' faithful had envisioned for the first World Series game at Wrigley Field since 1945, but there was consolation in the fact that they had overcome an identical 2-1 deficit to defeat the Los Angeles 'Dodgers in the NLCS. Optimism was still so high among Wrigley's denizens that "'It Is Happening' had become the fans' motto, replacing the less definite 'It's Gonna Happen.'"[1] After Game Four, however, Cubs fans' collective mood would best be summarized with, "Oh, no! Look what just happened!"

Chicago was up against Cleveland ace Corey Kluber, who had pitched six dominant innings in Game One and had combined with relievers Andrew Miller and Cody Allen on a 6-0 victory. The Cubs countered with John Lackey, who had been tough as nails in winning World Series Game Seven for the Anaheim Angels as a rookie in 2002. The hope that Lackey could turn back the clock and replicate his earlier performance was buoyed when the right-hander set the Indians down in order in the top of the first by getting Rajai Davis to ground out to third and then striking out Jason Kipnis and Francisco Lindor.

In the bottom of the first, the Cubs' offense also gave hope to the Cubs fans among the 41,706 in attendance that this game would be different from the previous night's contest when the team scored its first run quickly. Dexter Fowler led off with a double to left field and, after a Kris Bryant pop fly, scored on Anthony Rizzo's line-drive single to center. Kluber bore down and held the Cubs to that lone run, which the Indians would soon recoup.

Carlos Santana saw to the fact that Chicago's lead was short-lived by knocking a 3-and-2 offering from Lackey over the wall to tie the game. Later, Lackey engaged in a bit of finger-pointing by blaming home-plate umpire Marvin Hudson's strike zone for Santana's homer, saying, "I'd like that first pitch to be a strike. That changed the at-bat quite a bit."[2] Lackey could not have known at the time that his frustrations were just beginning.

After Jose Ramirez grounded out to Rizzo at first base, Lonnie Chisenhall hit a grounder to third and reached base safely on an errant throw from Bryant. Lackey retired Roberto Perez on a comebacker that advanced Chisenhall to second and then issued an intentional walk to Tyler Naquin so that he could face Kluber. The tactic backfired when Kluber hit a swinging-bunt single to Bryant that the third sacker again airmailed to first base. Bryant's second

Versatile infielder-outfielder Ben Zobrist helped lead the Cubs to their first World Series title in 108 years. He went 10-for-28 with five runs in the seven-game Series and was named Series MVP. (Photo by Kirk Irwin/Getty Images)

throwing error of the inning allowed Chisenhall to score the go-ahead run while Naquin advanced to third base. Lackey had plenty of words on that play later as well, complaining, "I don't know how that's a hit. That's not a hit on any planet in the world. If the ball is caught [at first base], he's out. How do you call that a hit?"[3] Bryant graciously conceded that Lackey's frustration was with the situation, rather than with him, and admitted about his throw on Kluber's single that "I probably should have held it."[4] Lackey then retired Davis for the third out to keep it a 2-1 game.

That score did not hold for long, though. After Kluber set the Cubs down 1-2-3, Kipnis smashed a leadoff double in the top of the third and scored on Lindor's single to center for a 3-1 Cleveland lead. Kipnis had grown up as a Cubs fan in Northbrook, a Chicago suburb, but was now sticking a dagger in the hearts of the very fan base to which he once belonged, and he would drive the blade in further before the night was over.

Lackey settled down and retired the Tribe in order in the fourth and fifth innings, but Kluber gave no quarter either, and the score remained 3-1 in favor of Cleveland.

Mike Montgomery took the mound for Chicago in the top of the sixth and created an immediate jam for himself by walking Lindor and surrendering a single to Santana. Montgomery fielded Ramirez's grounder and forced Santana out at second, but Lindor scored on Chisenhall's fly to center field to increase the Indians' lead to 4-1. After Montgomery walked Perez to put runners on first and second, Cubs manager Joe Maddon replaced him with Justin Grimm, who struck out Brandon Guyer to quash any further scoring threat.

Though Grimm had done his job well in the sixth, he flirted with disaster in the seventh. Coco Crisp, pinch-hitting for Kluber, doubled to lead off and advanced to third when Grimm uncorked a wild pitch with Davis at the plate. Grimm's control continued to desert him; he hit Davis with a pitch. Maddon now sent Travis Wood to the hill to face Kipnis with runners at the corners and no outs. Wood fell behind in the count 3-and-1, and then served up a three-run homer that gave the Indians an imposing 7-1 lead. Kipnis would have been the hometown hero had he been playing for the Cubs; instead, he was the home team's foil on this night, a role he did not mind playing. Kipnis commented afterward, "This stage is what we all dream about. To be able to do it in my hometown with my family and friends here, I was smiling ear to ear on the inside."[5]

Kipnis's dream, however, was Chicago's nightmare. When postseason standout Miller took over for Kluber in the bottom of the seventh, Cubs fans no doubt experienced déjà vu from Game One. Miller did surrender a solo homer to Fowler to lead off the bottom of the eighth, but that was the final run scored by either side in the Indians' 7-2 victory. Cleveland's Dan Otero closed out Chicago in the ninth, and a one-out single by Addison Russell was all the Cubs could muster as an attempt at a rally. Just like that, Chicago's World Series party had been crashed by the Indians, who were attempting to break their own lengthy championship drought that dated back to 1948.

The Cubs were now in a 3-to-1 Series hole, and the Chicago media and fans were in the process of bracing themselves for the ultimate bitter defeat. One *Chicago Tribune* columnist put the situation in the bluntest of terms, writing, "Maybe the Cubs' talented group of twenty-somethings suddenly realized how big the stage was and froze or maybe they have tried too hard not to suck."[6] Though some fans may have harbored the same thoughts, they mostly shared the resignation expressed by one fan who said, "It's kinda a little depressing. Quite a downer. Now we're looking for a sweep in Cleveland. And if that doesn't happen, well, it's gonna be a long winter."[7]

The Cubs themselves seemed at a loss for answers about what was happening to them. Maddon simply pointed out that the Indians were a good team and conceded, "We're obviously having a tough time, like the other teams did."[8] Bryant, who at this point was 1-for-14 with three walks, seemed mystified, saying, "They attack you, but I don't even know if it's that."[9] At least catcher Miguel Montero appeared to have identified one problem, asserting, "We're all trying to hit a grand slam with nobody on. ... We need to be a little more patient at the plate, play a little small ball."[10]

Whatever the remedy for the Cubs' ills might be, they needed to find it soon. They now had to win three in a row from the Indians, including the last two in Cleveland, which was a feat that no team had accomplished since the Pittsburgh Pirates managed it against the Baltimore Orioles in 1979. Still, there remained a voice of reason and hope in the form of catcher David Ross, a 15-year veteran who had announced that he was retiring after the World Series. In regard to the Chicago fans' rumblings, Ross said, "If they are frustrated, well, we want to win just as bad as they do, if not more. ... But we knew it wasn't going to be easy. There's no way you thought winning the World Series would be easy."[11]

No, given a 108-year run of futility, it was obvious that winning a World Series was not easy for the Cubs. However, in 2016, there at least was still the possibility that it could happen.

SOURCES

In addition to the sources listed below, the author also consulted Baseball-Reference.com for play-by-play details of the game.

NOTES

1   David Waldstein, "Indians Defeat Sloppy Cubs to Take a 3-1 World Series Lead," nytimes.com/2016/10/30/sports/baseball/world-series-cleveland-indians-chicago-cubs.html, accessed April 11, 2017.

2   Paul Sullivan, "Something Lacking," *Chicago Tribune*, October 30, 2016: 3-6.

3   Ibid.

4   Ibid.

5   Colleen Kane, "Making Himself at Home," *Chicago Tribune*, October 30, 2016: 3-7.

6   David Haugh, "Silence Not Golden for Cubs," *Chicago Tribune*, October 30, 2016: 3-3.

7   Patrick M. O'Connell et al, "Dejected Cubs Fans Put Hope on Game 5," *Chicago Tribune*, October 30, 2016: 1-16.

8   Tyler Kepner, "A Narrow Path of Hope Remains for the Cubs," nytimes.com/2016/10/31/sports/baseball/chicago-cubs-comeback-world-series.html, accessed April 11, 2017.

9   Ibid.

10   Ibid.

11   Waldstein.

FLY THE W!
CUBS' WIN SETS WORLD SERIES
COMEBACK IN MOTION

OCTOBER 30, 2016
CHICAGO CUBS 3, CLEVELAND INDIANS 2

GAME FIVE OF THE WORLD SERIES

By Frederick C. Bush

ALTHOUGH CHICAGO WAS GLOOMY IN the immediate aftermath of the Cubs' Game Four loss that put them in a 3-to-1 World Series hole against the Cleveland Indians, the faithful quickly regrouped to cheer on the hometown nine for one last time at Wrigley Field in 2016. Cubs partisans among the 47,711 fans in attendance used everything imaginable – "'Goat Busters' costumes, blue and red body paint, signs with inspirational messages like 'Believe' and 'It's Not Over'" – in an attempt to bolster their spirits and to will the Cubs to victory.[1] Their morale may have sagged again as soon as they saw that Cubs manager Joe Maddon was fielding his best defensive lineup in spite of the team's struggles on offense against Cleveland. All Maddon had to say about his gambit was, "I love counterintuitive. I love it, man."[2] After a game that was "an exercise in patience and pleading for the crowd," Cubs fans, if they still could not love it themselves, could at least appreciate it for one night.[3]

Lefty starter Jon Lester took the hill for the Cubs in Game Five. Although he had suffered the loss in Game One against the Indians, he was a two-time World Series champion with the Boston Red Sox who was a good candidate to handle the intense pressure of this elimination game. Lester indeed was pumped and set down Rajai Davis, Jason Kipnis, and Francisco Lindor on swinging strikes in the top of the first inning. Cleveland starter Trevor Bauer made it five consecutive strikeouts to start the game when he caught both Dexter Fowler and Kris Bryant looking at called third strikes. Anthony Rizzo finally put a ball in play, but his contact resulted in a mere fly ball to left field.

After Lester induced popouts from Mike Napoli and Carlos Santana to start the second inning, Jose Ramirez belted a line-drive homer to give Cleveland a 1-0 lead. Lester retired Brandon Guyer to avoid further trouble, and then he set the Indians down in order in the third and fourth frames. Nonetheless, in light of the Cubs' offensive struggles – an Addison Russell single in the second was their only hit off Bauer through three innings – it looked as though a one-run lead might be insurmountable.

If any Chicago fans were beginning to despair, Bryant's home run to lead off the bottom of the fourth inning temporarily allayed their fears by tying the game. Now, the Cubs mounted what was, for them in this Series, a veritable offensive explosion as Rizzo doubled and advanced to third on Ben Zobrist's single to right field. Russell came to bat, hit a dribbler up the first-base line that resulted in his second hit of the night, and drove in Rizzo with the go-ahead run. Bauer struck out Jason Heyward for the first out of the inning, but the Cubs were not yet finished.

After posting a 19-5 slate during the regular season, Jon Lester won three more games for the Cubs in the 2016 postseason, including the pivotal Game Five of the World Series. (Photo by Dylan Buell/Getty Images)

Javier Baez, who had entered the night batting an anemic .118 through the first four games of the Series, "laid down a bunt that was so perfect, it rated an 11" up the first-base side to load the bases.[4] Veteran catcher David Ross, who had announced that he was retiring and had received a standing ovation in his first at-bat, now stepped to the plate with the intention of giving the crowd something more to cheer. Although Ross did not hit a storybook grand slam, his fly ball to left field brought home Zobrist for a 3-1 Cubs lead. Lester struck out to end the inning, and then he went back to the mound to try to maintain Chicago's advantage.

Santana belted a double to center field against Lester to lead off the fifth inning and advanced to third on Ramirez's grounder to short, but he was stranded there when Guyer struck out and Perez grounded out. In the bottom of the inning, Mike Clevinger relieved Bauer for Cleveland and provided the Cubs with a shot at adding an insurance run. Bryant drew a one-out walk and, after Rizzo lined out to center field for the second out, stole second

base and advanced to third on catcher Perez's errant throw to the bag. Zobrist then walked to put runners on the corners, but Russell lined out to right field to keep the score 3-1.

Lester ran into trouble in the top of the sixth, which turned out to be his last inning of the night. Davis hit a one-out single and stole second base. Lester struck out Kipnis for the second time, but Lindor smashed a line-drive single to center field that plated Davis and drew the Indians within one run of the Cubs. Lindor tried to follow in Davis's footsteps with an attempted steal of second, but Baez snared Ross's throw and applied the tag to Lindor for the third out.

Bryan Shaw entered the game as Cleveland's third pitcher in the bottom of the sixth and promptly struck out Heyward, Baez, and Miguel Montero – who was pinch-hitting for Ross – in order. Ross, who was now finished for the night, later reflected on his final homestand, saying, "I'll look up in the stands a lot just because there aren't too many times you get to be in front of 40,000 to 50,000 people and they're all cheering for a team. I'm just trying to take those pictures in my brain and hold on to those nice things."5 After the uneventful end to the sixth inning, those 40,000-plus people were about to have reason to be nervous again as they feared frightful things.

Carl Edwards was the next moundsman for the Cubs, be he did not last long. Napoli greeted him with a single to lead off the seventh inning and advanced to second when one of Edwards' pitches got past new Cubs catcher Wilson Contreras. Santana flied out to left field, which prevented Napoli from advancing to third, and Maddon lifted Edwards in favor of closer Aroldis Chapman. Sending Chapman to the hill with only one out in the seventh once again demonstrated Maddon's love for all things counterintuitive.

Chapman threw his 100-plus-mph heat past Ramirez for the second out, but then he hit Guyer with a pitch to give the Indians two baserunners. However, Chapman escaped a potential calamity when he induced a Perez grounder to Baez at second base to end Cleveland's half of the inning.

Shaw retired Contreras to lead off the Cubs' seventh, but he then was replaced by Cody Allen in another of the many managerial pitching moves – this time by Indians manager Terry Francona – that were beginning to earn this Fall Classic a reputation as "The Bullpen Series."6 Allen hit Fowler with a pitch, though this was likely not in retaliation for Guyer getting plunked since Cleveland was trailing in the game. Fowler stole second to move into scoring position and, after a Bryant strikeout, Rizzo was intentionally walked to create the possibility of a force out at third base as well. The move worked out for the Indians as Zobrist popped up to the shortstop, Lindor.

After Yan Gomes struck out to start the eighth inning, Davis singled and then did his utmost to put the Indians into a tie with the Cubs. With Kipnis batting, Davis stole second base; then, after Kipnis fouled out to left field, Davis stole third while Lindor was at the plate. Davis did not, however, try to steal home, though perhaps he regretted not making such

an attempt after Lindor struck out and left him stuck at third.

The tables turned in the bottom of the inning as Heyward duplicated Davis's feat. Following a one-out single, Heyward stole second base; after Baez struck out, he stole third while Chapman flailed at Allen's pitches. Allen struck out the side when Chapman went down swinging, but that made no difference to Maddon: He had obviously left Chapman in the game to fulfill his role as closer, though asking for an eight-out save was a risky proposition.

In the end, Maddon's counterintuitiveness and Chapman's fastballs prevailed. Napoli grounded out to short, Santana flied out to right field, and, fittingly, Ramirez struck out swinging to end the game. According to Chapman's catcher, there was never any doubt about what the outcome would be. Contreras asserted, "He's big and strong. Do you really think eight outs is a problem for him? No. It seems easy. He executed everything I called."7

Chicago fans let out a collective sigh of relief and began to party as though it were 1908. Although the Cubs were still down 3 to 2 and needed to win two games at Cleveland to claim their first championship in more than a century, hope had been restored. In the words of one Cubs fan, "We pulled it off with the Dodgers [in the NLCS]. We can pull it off against the Indians, too."8

Such faith was rewarded when the Cubs won Game Seven on November 2 to become the 2016 World Series champions.

SOURCES

In addition to the sources listed below, the author also consulted Baseball-Reference.com for play-by-play details of the game.

NOTES

1   Tony Briscoe, Patrick O'Connell, and Marwa Eltagouri, "Faith Restored, Cubs Fans Rejoice," *Chicago Tribune*, October 31, 2016: 1-9.

2   Billy Witz, "Cubs Aren't History as Chicago Denies Indians a Title in Game 5," nytimes.com/2016/10/31/sports/baseball/world-series-chicago-cubs-cleveland-indians.html, accessed April 11, 2017.

3   Ibid.

4   Teddy Greenstein, "Whiffs, Then victory Scent," *Chicago Tribune*, October 31, 2016: 3-12.

5   Chris Kuc, "Ross Revels in Wrigley Finale," *Chicago Tribune*, October 31, 2016: 3-12.

6   Tyler Kepner, "The Bullpen Series," nytimes.com/2016/11/01/sports/baseball/world-series-relievers-starters-tyler-kepner.html, accessed April 11, 2017.

7   Ibid.

8   Briscoe, O'Connell, and Eltagouri.

"RESPECT ME! RESPECT ME!" CUBS OVERCOME FOUR ERRORS TO DEFEAT NATIONALS

OCTOBER 9, 2017
CHICAGO CUBS 2, WASHINGTON NATIONALS 1

GAME THREE OF THE NLDS

By Don Zminda

IN GAME THREE OF THE 2017 NATIONAL League Division Series against the Washington Nationals, the Chicago Cubs didn't get their first hit until the seventh inning.

The Cubs recorded only four hits in the game (just one off Nats starter Max Scherzer).

Those four hits matched the total of Cubs errors in the game, including two on one play by left fielder Kyle Schwarber.

During the game, Cubs manager Joe Maddon was lustily booed by the Wrigley Field fans for replacing starting pitcher Jose Quintana with reliever Pedro Strop, who promptly gave up a run-scoring double to Ryan Zimmerman.

And the Cubs' big offensive play was a bloop to left field by Anthony Rizzo, which "felt like it took about five minutes to drop," according to Schwarber.[1]

So naturally the Cubs came away with a 2-1 win, giving them a two-games-to-one lead in the series.

"It really does say a lot about us," Cubs third baseman Kris Bryant said after the game. "We're not going to get down if things aren't going our way early."[2]

Things definitely didn't go the Cubs' way against Scherzer, who was making his first start of the 2017 postseason after tweaking his hamstring nine days earlier. Scherzer had pitched two regular-season no-hitters during the 2015 season, and he displayed the same sort of form while holding the Cubs without a hit through the first six innings. Quintana was nearly as good for the Cubs, breezing through the first 5⅔ innings with only two hits allowed. Quintana looked to be out of the sixth when Daniel Murphy hit a fly ball in Schwarber's direction with two outs and the bases empty. But the ball clanked off Schwarber's glove, and then he kicked it while trying to pick it up. Murphy wound up on third base on Schwarber's double error. "I should have caught that ball and I didn't," Schwarber said after the game.[3]

Although the error was obviously no fault of Quintana's, he had now thrown 96 pitches, and Maddon replaced him with Strop to set up a righty-righty matchup with Zimmerman. The Wrigley Field fans voiced their displeasure with the move when Maddon made it – *Chicago Tribune* writer Paul Sullivan called it "an explosive booing of Maddon unprecedented at Wrigley"[4] – and even more displeasure when Zimmerman doubled home Murphy with the first run of the game.

However, Scherzer's pitch count was mounting as well, and Ben Zobrist doubled on Max's 98th pitch of the game for the Cubs' first hit with one out in the seventh. Scherzer had set a pregame objective of 100 pitches, but said he was ready to exceed that total.

However, Nationals manager Dusty Baker had seen enough; with the lefty-swinging Schwarber due up, he replaced Scherzer with left-hander Sammy Solis. "It was very difficult," Baker said of the decision to lift Scherzer.[5] "We were kind of 50-50 on what was going to happen," Scherzer said in describing the mound conference. "I know you guys are going to second-guess that. … I wasn't going to override anybody."[6] However, the switch to Solis did not produce the desired results for Baker: Albert Almora pinch-hit for Schwarber, and singled home Zobrist to deadlock the game.

It was still 1-1 in the bottom of the eighth when the left-handed-hitting Rizzo stepped to the plate with two out and a man on second, facing righty reliever Brandon Kintzler. Once again Baker opened himself up to second-guessing: Instead of issuing an intentional walk to Rizzo and having Kintzler face right-handed-hitting Willson Contreras, he opted to bring in left-hander Oliver Perez to pitch to Rizzo. The move seemed to fire up Rizzo, who was caught screaming "Respect me! Respect me!" at Baker.[7] Perez induced Rizzo to loft a soft blooper to left field, but the ball dropped between Nats shortstop Trea Turner, left fielder Jayson Werth and center fielder Michael Taylor for the hit that gave the Cubs the lead. "The ball was kind in never-never land out there between three merging players on our team," said Baker. "He couldn't have [placed it] any better if he had thrown the ball in there."[8] Wade Davis set down the Nationals in order in the ninth to preserve the 2-1 Cubs win.

"We just hung in there," said Zobrist, who had committed one of the four Cubs errors, after the game. "There was no panic on the dugout. There was no thought that it wasn't going to happen. It was just when is it going to happen, that was the question. When you make mistakes as a team, the mantra is:

'So what? Now what?'"[9] It was the first time in the Cubs' long history that the team won a postseason game while making four or more errors.

The Cubs would lose Game Four to the Nationals at Wrigley, but then advance to the National League Championship Series with a 9-8 victory in Washington in Game Five. As for Dusty Baker, the Nationals' postseason defeat wound up costing him his job: Washington announced on October 20 that he would not be returning as manager.

SOURCES

In addition to the sources cited in the Notes, the author also accessed Baseball-Reference.com.

NOTES

1 Paul Sullivan, "Super Blooper," *Chicago Tribune*, October 10, 2017.

2 Mark Gonzales, "It's Respect-ability," *Chicago Tribune*, October 10, 2017.

3 Chris Kuc, "Left Field of Screams," *Chicago Tribune*, October 10, 2017.

4 Sullivan, "Super Blooper."

5 Jorge Castillo, "Dealt a Bad Hand, Max Scherzer Looks Like an Ace in Game 3 Loss to the Cubs," washington. post.com, Washingtonpost.Com/Sports/Nationals/ Dealt-A-Bad-Hand-Max-Scherzer-Still-Looks-Like-An-Ace-In-Game-3-Loss-To-Cubs/2017/10/09/88c30b54-Ad22-11e7-9e58-E6288544af98_Story. Html?Utm_Term=.5ecaeb00e6a0; accessed 12-23-17.

6 Paul Skrbina, "Sad Max: Gem Goes to Waste," *Chicago Tribune*, October 10, 2017.

7 Gonzales, "It's Respect-ability."

8 Rick Morrissey, "Hear Anthony Rizzo Roar? The Nationals Did," *Chicago Sun-Times*, October 10, 2017.

9 Gordon Wittenmyer, "Cubs Overcome 4 Errors, Max Scherzer No-Hit Bit to Push Nats to Brink," *Chicago Sun-Times*, October 10, 2017.

TOO SICK TO PITCH? STRASBURG HAS LAST LAUGH AGAINST CUBS

OCTOBER 11, 2017
WASHINGTON NATIONALS 5, CHICAGO CUBS 0

GAME FOUR OF THE NLDS

By Don Zminda

FOR MUCH OF THE RAIN-INDUCED TWO- day gap between Games Three and Four of the 2017 Washington Nationals-Chicago Cubs Division Series, it appeared that Stephen Strasburg would be too sick to take the mound for the Nats in Game Four. But after enduring some withering criticism during the unscheduled offday, Strasburg told Washington manager Dusty Baker that he wanted the ball. And after his dominating performance against the Chicagoans, it was the Cubs who were feeling ill: Strasburg struck out 12 and permitted only three hits while working seven shutout innings, as the Nationals forced a decisive Game Five with a 5-0 victory.

Strasburg had been the center of postseason controversy in 2012, when the Nationals kept him off their playoff roster to protect him from possible injury. He found himself in the spotlight again when Game Four, which was originally scheduled for Wednesday, October 10, was postponed because of rain in Chicago. The rainout meant that Strasburg, who had been brilliant in the Nationals' 3-0 loss to the Cubs in Game One (seven innings, three hits, 10 strikeouts, zero earned runs allowed), would be able to start Game Four on four days' rest.

However, Strasburg wasn't feeling well. "He spoke with Mike Maddux, our pitching coach, after his bullpen on Monday, and looked bad and under the weather, looked sick," reported Nationals general manager Mike Rizzo.[1] Baker blamed mold from the air-conditioning in the Nationals' hotel. "It's just this time of year for mold around Chicago – I think it's mold. I mean, I have it, too," said Baker.[2] So the Nationals announced that their Game Four starter would be Tanner Roark, not Strasburg. The result was a flood of criticism for Strasburg, particularly from former players. "If I'm his teammate and I walk into the clubhouse the next day, I can't make eye contact with this dude," said former Cub David Ross. "I mean, this is as bad as it gets as a teammate."[3] "Really can't take the ball in an elimination game because of a runny nose. Sad. Not in my foxhole!' tweeted Hall of Famer Wade Boggs.[4]

However, Strasburg woke up feeling better on the morning of Game Four, and told Maddux that he wanted to pitch. He was outstanding in his seven innings of work, despite the 59-degree temperature, drizzly rain, and howling winds. "I'm surprised I was able to hang in there," Strasburg said after the game. "I think it's just situations where you try and break the game down, keep it simple, and just know that going in, whatever I have in the tank, I'm giving it everything I have."[5] The Cubs' best chance against Strasburg came in the second inning, when Ben Zobrist doubled and Addison Russell followed with a long fly ball to left field. The wind helped keep the ball in the park, and Jayson Werth caught it on the warning track.

Despite Strasburg's brilliance, the Cubs kept the game close most of the way thanks to excellent pitching from Jake Arrieta, who pitched the first four innings, and Jon Lester, who worked into the eighth. Through seven innings, the only run of the game came in the third, and it was unearned. Trea Turner doubled against Arrieta with one out, then took third on a wild pitch. Werth struck out looking, but after Bryce Harper walked and stole second, Ryan Zimmerman hit a groundball to short, and the ball hit off the heel of Russell's glove for an error as Turner raced home.

The Nationals broke the game open in the eighth. With two out and nobody on against Lester (who had walked Zimmerman but then picked him off), Daniel Murphy singled to center. Cubs manager Joe Maddon then replaced Lester with Carl Edwards Jr., who was in the midst of a terrible postseason that saw him walk six batters in only 4⅔ innings. With Anthony Rendon up, Edwards threw a wild pitch that allowed Murphy to take second, then walked both Rendon and Matt Wieters to load the bases. After Edwards started Michael Taylor off with ball one, Maddon brought in closer Wade Davis. In 34⅓ previous postseason career innings, Davis had permitted only one home run. But Taylor was able to peek at some video of Davis while the Cubs closer was warming up, and said he "felt good once I stepped back in."[6] After throwing a strike, Davis threw a fastball that Taylor belted to right field. Despite the fact that the ball was hit into the wind, it landed in the basket nearly 400 feet away for a grand slam that made the score 5-0.

"That had to be absolutely crushed," Maddon said of Taylor's drive. "That's into a gale, high, opposite field. … That surprised all of us, obviously."[7] "I didn't think any right-handed batter could hit that ball out of the ballpark like [Taylor] did tonight," said Baker.[8]

"I was kind of numb running around the bases," said Taylor. "I didn't think it was going to get out the way the wind was blowing in."[9] Ryan Madson

and Sean Doolittle each pitched a scoreless inning to complete Washington's series-tying victory.

Despite the defeat, the Cubs were upbeat after the game. "It's two heavyweights going at it," said Jon Lester. "We're going to the last round. We're going to figure it out."[10] The Cubs did bounce back the next night, finishing off the Nationals with a wild 9-8 victory to advance to the League Championship Series against the Los Angeles Dodgers. But the Cubs' bid to advance to the World Series for the second straight year ended in defeat, as the Dodgers prevailed in five games.

SOURCES

In addition to the sources cited in the Notes, the author also accessed Baseball-Reference.com.

NOTES

1 Scott Allen, "'Very, Very Depleted' Stephen Strasburg Still Wanted to Pitch Game 4, Says Nationals GM," washingtonpost.com/news/dc-sports-bog/wp/2017/10/11/very-very-depleted-stephen-strasburg-still-wanted-to-pitch-game-4-says-nationals-gm/?tid=a_inl&utm_term=.8b7330d10d51, October 11, 2017; accessed 12-24-17.

2 Jorge Castillo, "Nationals Will Stick With Tanner Roark Over Stephen Strasburg for Postponed Game 4," washingtonpost.com/news/nationals-journal/wp/2017/10/10/nationals-cubs-nlds-game-4-delayed-due-to-rain/?tid=a_inl&utm_term=.b53caceade7d, October 10, 2017; accessed 12-24-17.

3 Dan Steinberg, "Former MLB Players Were Teeing Off on Stephen Strasburg Before Plans Changed," Washingtonpost.Com/News/Dc-Sports-Bog/Wp/2017/10/11/Former-Mlb-Players-Were-Teeing-Off-On-Stephen-Strasburg-Before-Plans-Changed/?Tid=A_Inl&Utm_Term=.834057d0cb03, October 11, 2017; accessed 12-24-17.

4 Steinberg.

5 Jorge Castillo, "Stephen Strasburg, Michael A. Taylor Put Nats on Their Backs and Force Game 5," washingtonpost.com/sports/nationals/stephen-strasburg-michael-a-taylor-put-nats-on-their-backs-and-force-game-5/2017/10/11/cde055bc-aec0-11e7-a908-a3470754bbb9_story.html?utm_term=.821757762e97&wpisrc=nl_sports&wpmm=1, October 11, 2017; accessed 12-24-17.

6 Paul Skrbina, "Taylor's Cram, Slam Prove to Be Decisive," *Chicago Tribune*, October 12, 2017.

7 Castillo, "Stephen Strasburg."

8 Ibid.

9   Skrbina.

10   "Strasburg, Nationals Beat Cubs 5-0, Force NLDS to Game
     5," espn.com/mlb/recap?gameId=371011116, October 11, 2017;
     accessed 12/26/17/.

DOMINANT DODGERS PUSH LISTLESS CUBS TO THE BRINK

OCTOBER 17, 2017
LOS ANGELES DODGERS 6, CHICAGO CUBS 1

GAME THREE THE NLCS

By Nathan Bierma

THE CUBS RETURNED TO WRIGLEY FIELD for Game Three of the 2017 National League Championship Series facing the prospect of being pushed just one loss from elimination. After managing a total of three runs and seven hits in two anemic losses in Los Angeles, the Cubs still seemed to be catching their breath from a wild 9-8 win in Game Five of the Division Series in Washington, while the Dodgers looked fresh and confident after sweeping Arizona in their opening series. Now the Cubs were on the brink of going down three games to none in the NLCS.

"We've got to win this next one, find a way, any way possible, just to grind out a win," said Anthony Rizzo. "This game is the biggest game for us."[1]

Kyle Schwarber struck the right note in the bottom of the first inning, smashing the first pitch he saw from Dodgers starter Yu Darvish into the left-field seats. The early 1-0 lead brought some joy and much relief to the anxious home crowd.

But Andre Ethier led off the second inning with a solo shot in response, a line drive off Cubs starter Kyle Hendricks. The ball struck Ethier's name on the right-field scoreboard behind the ivy,[2] landing like "a pin to the balloon of enthusiasm in the ballpark," wrote the *Chicago Tribune*.[3]

Chris Taylor soon struck dual blows for the Dodgers. In the top of the third, he launched a 444-foot home run to center that put the Dodgers up

2-1.[4] In the fifth, after Joc Pederson doubled, Taylor lashed a triple that struck the chalk of the left-field line and bounded all the way to the ivy, extending Los Angeles' lead to 3-1.

In the top of the sixth inning, the Cubs stumbled at a crucial moment. After Yasiel Puig reached on an error and Ethier singled, Cubs manager Joe Maddon brought in Carl Edwards Jr., who retired Chase Utley but walked Austin Barnes to load the bases. After Pederson hit a pop fly to right, Darvish's spot in the lineup came up. Dodgers manager Dave Roberts sent pinch-hitter Curtis Granderson to the on-deck circle, then pulled him back and let Darvish bat for himself.[5] The move seemed to concede the out and the inning. Instead, Edwards walked Darvish on four pitches, forcing in a run and giving the Dodgers a 4-1 lead. Boos rumbled at Wrigley Field.[6]

Hendricks and Edwards had been two of the most reliable hurlers for the Cubs down the stretch of the 2016 postseason; now they had combined for a feeble inning that seemed to sum up the Cubs' 2017 playoff woes.

Darvish cruised through four more Cubs batters before exiting in the seventh, having scattered six hits, thrown 59 strikes on 81 pitches, and allowed only two runners to reach scoring position after Schwarber's home run.[7]

The Dodgers put the game all but out of reach in the eighth. With Logan Forsythe and Barnes aboard and Charlie Culberson at the plate, Cubs pitcher Mike Montgomery unleashed a wild pitch that advanced the runners, followed by a passed ball that scored Forsythe. (Culberson swung at the pitch for strike three but made it safely to first base.) A pinch-hit sacrifice fly to center field by Kyle Farmer brought home Barnes to make it 6-1.

The Cubs finally found some offense in the bottom of the ninth, against Dodgers reliever Ross Stripling. Alex Avila led off with a single and Albert Almora hit a ground-rule double that lodged in the ivy in left and put runners at second and third with no one out, giving the Cubs a flicker of hope. But in came Kenley Jansen, as automatic as any reliever in baseball in 2017. Jansen got Addison Russell to pop up to first base and then struck out the next two batters to end the game.

The Dodgers had won, 6-1, taking a seemingly unshakable grip on the NLCS with a 3-0 series lead.

"Tuesday was never a must-win, it just felt that way," wrote *The Athletic*. "Now every game the Cubs have left against the Dodgers this year will be win or go home."[8]

"A defending World Series champion getting beaten in the playoffs is one thing. Getting embarrassed is quite another," wrote the *Chicago Tribune*, adding that the Game Three loss "carried the feeling of finality."[9]

Granted, last year's team of destiny overcame a 2-1 series deficit to the Dodgers, winning two games on the road to regain the NLCS lead. And even more improbably, those Cubs came back from a three-games-to-one deficit in the World Series to win its elusive championship.

But that team had persevered with an uncanny concoction of optimism, confidence, clutch plays, and benevolent breaks – the kind of alchemy it takes to win any championship, let alone end a century-long curse. This year's club, by contrast, now appeared deflated and outmatched.

"The Cubs may have thought they could turn it on again in the postseason and magically bounce back from the brink, as they did so memorably last year,"

wrote the *Tribune*. "But the mojo was missing, and no one was exactly sure where it went."[10]

With their team's elimination imminent both mathematically and psychologically, Cubs fans had to come to terms with a new kind of losing: ordinary, pedestrian losing, unlike the tortured, fateful losing they'd known for generations, when postseason droughts and disasters became larger than life and futility defined Cubs fandom. One of the gifts the 2016 Cubs gave their fans by winning the World Series and purging the demons was that future losing would never haunt them in the same way. Losing would hurt, but it wouldn't cause existential angst.

So what did losing feel like now, in 2017? Mostly, it was just emptiness – the silence of fans sitting on their hands at a muted Wrigley Field, wondering where their team's bats and pitching had disappeared to, as the Dodgers relentlessly piled up runs and pushed all the right buttons. There was some retrospective relief that last year's team had broken the curse so that this loss wasn't part of it, mixed with confusion about how to process the threat of another NLCS sweep after suffering the same fate against the Mets in 2015. Two NLCS blowouts in three seasons would have been unbearable, if not for that euphoric interlude between them.

SOURCES

In addition to the sources cited in the Notes, the author also accessed Retrosheet.org, Baseball-Reference.com, and SABR.org.

NOTES

1   Rick Morrissey, "Risky to Count Out Struggling Cubs, Their Befuddled Manager," *Chicago Sun-Times*, October 16, 2017. Accessed at chicago.suntimes.com/sports/morrissey-risky-to-count-out-struggling-cubs-their-befuddled-manager.

2   Some descriptive details are based on viewing video highlights of this game at MLB.com, accessed at mlb.com/gameday/dodgers-vs-cubs/2017/10/17/526506#game_state=final,game_tab=videos,game=526506.

3   David Haugh, "Winter Is Coming," *Chicago Tribune*, October 18, 2017: 33.

4   Paul Sullivan, "Mired in Discomfort Zone," *Chicago Tribune*, October 18, 2017: 37.

5   Rick Morrissey, "Cubs' Response to World Series Hopes? Walk Yu," *Chicago Sun-Times*, October 18, 2017. Accessed at chicago.suntimes.com/sports/morrissey-cubs-go-all-retro-in-an-embarrassing-loss-to-the-dodgers.

6   Ibid.

7   Mark Gonzales, "Pushed to the Edge," *Chicago Tribune*, October 18, 2017: 35.

8   Sahadev Sharma, "The Better Team Is Winning the NLCS and It's Not the Cubs," *The Athletic*, October 18, 2017. Accessed at theathletic.com/130795/2017/10/18/sharma-the-better-team-is-winning-the-nlcs-and-its-not-the-cubs.

9   Haugh, "Winter Is Coming."

10 Sullivan, "Mired in Discomfort zone."

CUBS SHOW CHAMPIONSHIP SWAGGER TO STAY ALIVE

OCTOBER 18, 2017
CHICAGO CUBS 3, LOS ANGELES DODGERS 2

GAME FOUR OF THE NLCS

By Nathan Bierma

THE CUBS WERE PLAYING MOSTLY FOR pride in Game Four of the 2017 NLCS, the pride of defending world champions not wanting to surrender the pennant without a fight. But they were also playing for plausibility: to nudge the idea of a series comeback back into the realm of the possible. A win would leave them down three games to one – still in a hole, but the same kind of hole they climbed out of last year in the World Series to win it all.

All series, the meekly hitting Cubs had been waiting to string some big hits together to ignite their offense and their confidence. They got two strong strokes in the second inning of Game Four. With the game still scoreless, Willson Contreras crushed a shot to left field off Dodgers starter Alex Wood that crashed off the video scoreboard. It was measured at 491 feet. Contreras paused in the batter's box and then strode out slowly in admiration of his blast, letting the statement settle in. He was, the *Chicago Tribune* said, "a man with a message. *Notice us. We are still the champions.*"[1]

Two batters later, Javier Báez slammed a deep shot of his own, 437 feet down the left-field line, out of the park and over Waveland. It was his first hit after suffering an 0-for-20 showing in the postseason. After rounding the bases, Báez stomped on home plate, as if to announce that the Cubs would not go quietly in this series.

"It felt like the real Cubs had arrived at Clark and Addison for the NLCS, finally," wrote the *Tribune*.[2]

The Dodgers got one back in the top of the third, a Cody Bellinger solo home run down the right-field line off Cubs starter Jake Arrieta. But Arrieta, in what fans knew could be his last appearance as a Cub at Wrigley Field before becoming a free agent, shut down the Dodgers after that, holding them hitless the rest of the third and then all of the fourth and fifth innings.

Báez came back up to bat with the Cubs still leading 2-1. Few players had dazzled and puzzled Cubs fans in recent years as much as Báez. He was a magician in the field and at times a titan with the bat, but he was also prone to strikeouts and slumps. Now, in the fifth inning, Báez fully regained the form that earned him NLCS co-MVP last year, and sent his second home run of the night into the left-field seats. He became just the 15th player in postseason history to hit two home runs in an elimination game. "That guy, he's fun to watch," Kyle Schwarber said of Báez after the game. "He's an electric player."[3]

The Dodgers got a leadoff single by Justin Turner but nothing more off Arrieta in the sixth inning. Arrieta exited with two outs in the seventh, having surrendered just three hits and one run while striking out nine. The crowd, knowing this could be Arrieta's farewell, rose to its feet, and Arrieta tipped his cap to the ovation.

Dynamic infielder Javier Baez blasted two home runs in Game Four of the 2017 NLCS to keep the Cubs' hopes of returning to the World Series alive. (Photo by Gregg Forwerck/Getty Images)

"Hopefully it's not a good-bye," Arrieta said afterward. "It's a thank you, obviously."[4] Arrieta added that he savored every moment of his start, knowing it could be the end of an unforgettable era that included a career resurgence, a historically dominant 2015 season, and a world championship. "I took a little bit [of] extra time in between pitches just to look around," he said. "Just to kind of relish it and take it in."[5]

Brian Duensing came and retired Bellinger and the Dodgers. In the bottom of the seventh, Báez was back, lifting a fly ball to deep center, this time no farther than the warning track, where Curtis Granderson made the catch. Further heroics denied, the Cubs' lead remained 3-1.

Cubs manager Joe Maddon turned to Wade Davis in the eighth, asking for six outs from his closer, and it quickly looked like a lot to ask. The first batter was Turner, and he hit "a towering home run hit

far enough to register on radar at O'Hare," as the *Tribune* put it.[6] The crowd clenched its teeth as the Cubs' lead was cut to 3-2. All of the game's runs had been scored on solo home runs.

Two batters later Davis struck out Granderson, only to have the umpires convene and concur that Granderson had stayed alive on a foul tip. A furious Maddon came out to complain and got ejected. The inning risked unraveling for the Cubs. But Davis struck out Granderson on the next pitch, and, after walking Yasmani Grandal, struck out Chase Utley to escape the inning with the lead.

The Cubs had Kris Bryant at bat with two runners on in the bottom of the eighth, but Bryant's bat stayed quiet for the series and he grounded out to end the inning. Davis went back out to try to give the Cubs their elusive first win of the series, and his ninth inning proved as uneventful as the eighth was unnerving. He struck out Austin Barnes, and then after walking Chris Taylor, got Bellinger to hit into a game-ending double play.

The Cubs had hung on to win 3-2, with Contreras and Báez rejuvenating the offense, setting the tone, and calming their team's nerves, at least for one night.

"The Dodgers still have every reason to believe they are headed for their first World Series since 1988," the *Tribune* wrote. "But for a desperate Cubs team facing a daunting challenge, it was a start."[7]

The Cubs' reward for extending the series would be to face Clayton Kershaw in Game Five. But after losing the first three games, they knew there would be no shortcuts back to the pennant. Still, they could look to their team president, Theo Epstein, who saw his Boston Red Sox come back from a 3-0 Championship Series deficit in 2004. So what did that team do that this year's Cubs could do too?

"You've got to find a way to get the team that's been up 3-0 on a plane back home, failing to close out a series twice in a row," Epstein said after Game Four. "If you can do that, I think the momentum completely changes, and the pressure changes."[8]

SOURCES

In addition to the sources cited in the Notes, the author also accessed Retrosheet.org, Baseball-Reference.com, and SABR.org.

NOTES

1   David Haugh, "Contreras, Baez Reclaim Some Swagger," *Chicago Tribune*, October 19, 2017: 34.

2   Ibid.

3   Lauren Comitor, "Make Sure to Update Your Clocks Because It's Finally Javy Time," *The Athletic*, October 19, 2017. Accessed at theathletic.com/131615/2017/10/19/make-sure-to-update-your-clocks-because-its-finally-javy-time.

4   Sahadev Sharma, "Jake Arrieta Tipped His Cap to the Fans, But He Isn't Ready to Leave the Cubs," *The Athletic*, October 19, 2017. Accessed at theathletic.com/131809/2017/10/19/jake-arrieta-tipped-his-cap-to-the-fans-but-he-isnt-ready-to-leave-the-cubs.

5   Ibid.

6   Haugh, "Contreras, Baez Reclaim Some Swagger."

7   Ibid.

8   Jon Greenberg, "As the Cubs Fight for Their Playoff Lives, Theo Epstein Reflects on 2004 Memories, a Leaky Bullpen and More," *The Athletic*, October 19, 2017. Accessed at theathletic.com/132704/2017/10/19/as-the-cubs-fight-for-their-playoff-lives-theo-epstein-reflects-on-2004-memories-the-cubs-bullpen-and-more.

KERSHAW SHUTS DOWN CUBS; HERNANDEZ WALLOPS 3 HOMERS

OCTOBER 19, 2017
LOS ANGELES DODGERS 11, CHICAGO CUBS 1

GAME FIVE OF THE NLCS

By Mike Huber

A YEAR AFTER RALLYING TO BEAT Cleveland for their first World Series title since 1908, the 2017 Chicago Cubs used a second-half push to win their second straight National League Central title. They advanced to the National League Championship Series for the third consecutive season and second straight time against the West Division champion Los Angeles Dodgers. The Cubs became just the second team in the last 15 seasons to capture a division title the year after winning the World Series (the other was the 2009 Phillies). However, they would not move on, as this year's Cubs fell to the Dodgers in five games.

A frenzied sellout crowd of 42,735 packed Wrigley Field to root on their Cubbies. After three innings, none of the home team's fans were making any noise. Enrique Hernandez's hat trick of home runs in Game 5 gave Los Angeles seven runs of support, quieted the crowd and put an exclamation point on the series.

Los Angeles handily won the first three games of the NLCS. After the Game 4 loss to the Cubs, Dave Roberts, LA's manager, said, "I think we're in a pretty good spot. We have our number-one pitcher going."[1] That starter was seven-time All Star and three-time Cy Young Award winner Clayton Kershaw. He had not pitched at Wrigley Field since Game 6 of the 2016 NLCS, when the Cubs got to him for five runs and clinched the pennant. Despite missing five weeks of the season, Kershaw won 18

games (tops in the majors[2]) and posted a league-best 2.31 ERA. Interestingly, Kershaw was born in 1988, the same year the Dodgers last made the trip into the fall classic. Chicago countered with Jose Quintana, who was appearing in just his fourth postseason game and making his third postseason start. His 2017 numbers with the Cubs amounted to a record of 7-3, with an earned-run average of 3.74. (For the season, he was 11-11 with a mark of 4.15.)

Chris Taylor led off the game with a walk. After Quintana struck out Justin Turner, rookie Cody Bellinger stroked a double down the right-field line, driving in Taylor, and the Dodgers had a quick 1-0 lead. On the first pitch of the second inning, Hernandez met Quintana's fastball and sent it 399 feet over the center-field fence. This was his first postseason home run (in 17 games).

In the third inning, the first four Dodgers got hits to raise the lead to 3-0. Taylor doubled and scored on Turner's single. Bellinger and Yasiel Puig both singled to load the bases. Cubs skipper Joe Maddon strolled to the mound to replace Quintana with right-hander Hector Rondon. Rondon struck out Logan Forsythe on three pitches. Hernandez came up and swung at Rondon's first offering, blasting the 87-mph slider over the right-center wall for a grand slam. The ball landed 390 from home plate into the netting above the wall. With the Cubs now facing a seven-run deficit, Hernandez's smash "drained Wrigley Field of any energy."[3]

Meanwhile, Kershaw faced one above the minimum in the first three frames, only walking Kyle Schwarber in the first. John Lackey entered the game in the top of the fouirth as the third Cubs pitcher. Taylor greeted him with a single, reaching base for the third consecutive plate appearance. Turner struck out and Bellinger singled (his third hit). Lackey tossed a wild pitch, moving both runners up a base. Puig hit a grounder to third and Kris Bryant fired home to catcher Willson Contreras, who tagged Taylor out. Next up, Forsythe swung at an 0-and-1 offering, pulling the ball down the left-field line and plating both Bellinger and Puig. It was now 9-0 in favor of the visitors. After another wild pitch, on which Forsythe scampered to third, Lackey retired the hot Hernandez on a popout to short.

Schwarber worked a full count to lead off the bottom of the fourth before striking out. Bryant then jumped on Kershaw's first pitch and blasted it down the left-field line for a home run. Contreras also singled, but Kershaw retired the side without allowing any more runs. He had faced five batters in the fourth, the most he would face in any of the six innings he pitched. The Dodgers used Kenta Maeda, Brandon Morrow, and Kenley Jansen in the seventh, eighth, and ninth innings respectively, and the trio combined for five strikeouts and no walks. Morrow allowed a weak single up the middle to Ian Happ in between his three strikeouts, for the only Chicago baserunner against the trio.

With a 9-1 lead, the Dodgers had one more scoring opportunity. With Mike Montgomery on the mound, Bellinger struck out to lead off the ninth inning. Puig singled and Forsythe flied out to deep right field. Hernandez stepped into the batter's box. This time he took two pitches (both balls) before launching his third home run of the game, to left-center. The Dodgers now led 11-1, and that would be the final score. When the final out of the game was made, Los Angeles play-by-play announcer Charley Steiner described the scene: "The Dodgers win! It's

been 29 years! The wait is over! The Dodgers are going back to the World Series!"[4]

Hernandez put himself in some rare company, becoming just the 10th batter to hit three home runs in a postseason game (and the first Dodgers player to do so[5]) and the very first batter to drive in seven runs in a League Championship Series game. He was at a loss for words after the game, telling reporters, "It's unbelievable. It's amazing. The third one, I don't even know what happened. I honestly don't know what happened."[6]

Dodgers manager Roberts praised Hernandez, saying, "For Kike to have a huge night, three homers, just providing so much energy for us and we fed off that."[7] On the radio, Steiner told his listeners, "Hernandez had the offensive night of his life and one of the great postseason offensive nights of anybody as the Dodgers win it, 11 to 1."[8]

Kershaw also had a major part to play, never allowing the Cubs to get into a rhythm. He stifled the Cubs' offense in this final game of the year at Wrigley Field, allowing only three hits, a walk, and the solo home run by Bryant. After the game, amid the celebration, Kershaw said, "Up there with getting married and having kids, it's right up there with one of the best days of my life. Winning the World Series is really all that we play this game for. All the individual stuff is great, but at the end of the day, I just want to win a World Series."[9] He added, "When you're a little kid, you want to go play in the World Series. That's all you ever dream about. I'm going to play in the World Series."[10]

The Cubs hit only .156 and averaged 1.6 runs per game (despite hitting seven home runs) in the 2017 NLCS against the Dodgers, while the Chicago pitching staff allowed 28 runs and issued 28 walks in the five-game series.

In making it to the postseason, the Dodgers had won 104 games in 2017, one better than the 2016 Cubs and 12 more than Chicago's 2017 squad. The Dodgers earned home-field advantage in the World Series, which for the first time was determined by overall record. Maddon tipped his cap to the NLCS champs, saying, "The better team won over the course of these five games. They kind of out-pitched us and everything else. So give them credit. I just want to say, 'Congratulations.' [We] know what it feels like coming off of last year – we were celebrating versus them in this exact same spot. So they've had themselves a spectacular year, and I want to wish them all well in the World Series."[11]

SOURCES

In addition to the sources mentioned in the notes, the author consulted baseball-reference.com.

NOTES

1 Dylan Hernandez, "Game 5 Should Be a Fitting Moment for Clayton Kershaw," *Los Angeles Times*, October 18, 2017, found online at latimes.com/sports/la-sp-dodgers-hernandez-20171018-story.html. Accessed October 2017.

2 Kershaw's 18 victories led the National League and tied three pitchers in the American League: Cleveland's Corey Kluber and Carlos Carrasco and Kansas City's Jason Vargas.

3 Chris Kuc, "NLCS Game 5 Turning Point: Enrique Hernandez's Third-Inning Grand Slam," *Chicago Tribune*, October 19, 2017, found online at chicagotribune.com/sports/baseball/cubs/ct-cubs-turning-point-spt-1020-20171019-story.html. Accessed October 2017.

4 Phil Rosenthal, "End of Game 5 Sounded Different in Chicago, L.A. and Across the Country," *Chicago Tribune*, October 20, 2017, found online at chicagotribune.com/sports/baseball/cubs/ct-cubs-dodgers-broadcast-rosenthal-spt-1021-20171020-story.html. Accessed October 2017.

5 Carrie Muskat and Ken Gurnick, "Hollywood & Vines: LA Wins NLCS at Wrigley!" mlb.com, October 20, 2017, found online at m.mlb.com/news/article/259108988/dodgers-rout-cubs-win-nlcs-make-world-series/. Accessed October 2017.

6 Anthony Castrovince, "Trio Grand! Hernandez Has 3-HR, 7-RBI Clincher," mlb.com, October 20, 2017, found online at m.mlb.com/news/article/259105534/enrique-hernandez-has-monster-game-5-in-nlcs/?game_pk=526508. Accessed October 2017.

7 Kuc.

8 Rosenthal.

9 Muskat and Gurnick.

10 Andy McCullough, "Dodgers Crush Cubs in Game 5 to Advance to the World Series for First Time Since 1988," *Los Angeles Times*, October 19, 2017, found online at latimes.com/sports/la-dodgers-cubs-game-5-live-updates-dodgers-crush-cubs-in-game-5-to-advance-1508470354-htmlstory.html. Accessed October 2017.

11 Muskat and Gurnick.

WRIGLEY FIELD BY THE NUMBERS

By Dan Fields

Note: The ballpark was known as Weeghman Park until 1919 and as Cubs Park from 1920 through 1926.

0

Hits allowed through nine innings by Hippo Vaughn of the Chicago Cubs and Fred Toney of the Cincinnati Reds on May 2, 1917. The game's only run was driven in by Cincinnati right fielder (and future Pro Football Hall of Famer) Jim Thorpe. Toney finished with a 10-inning no-hitter.

1ST

African-American to throw a no-hitter in the major leagues: Sam Jones of the Cubs on May 12, 1955, against the Pittsburgh Pirates.

1ST

Major-league shutout shared by two brothers, Rick Reuschel and Paul Reuschel of the Cubs, on August 21, 1975, against the Los Angeles Dodgers. Starter Rick pitched 6⅓ innings, and reliever Paul pitched 2⅔ innings.

1.91

ERA of the Cubs at home in 1919.

2

Players who hit a home run on their first major-league pitch faced: Walter Mueller of the Pirates on May 7, 1922, and Willson Contreras of the Cubs on June 19, 2016. Mueller would hit only one more homer in the majors.

2

Grand slams by the New York Mets during the sixth inning on July 16, 2006, against the Cubs. Cliff Floyd hit one off Sean Marshall, and Carlos Beltran hit the other off Roberto Novoa. The Mets scored 11 runs during the frame and won 13-7.

3

All-Star Games played at Wrigley Field: 1947, 1962 (second game), and 1990. The American League won all three games.

3

Consecutive shutouts thrown by Chicago's Ken Holtzman (May 11, 1969), Fergie Jenkins (May 12), and Dick Selma (May 13). The last game was a 19-0 romp over the San Diego Padres; Ernie Banks had seven RBIs, including the 1,500th of his career.

3

Grand slams in a June 3, 1987, game between the Cubs and the Houston Astros. The bases-loaded homers were hit by Chicago's Brian Dayett (first inning), Houston's Billy Hatcher (fourth inning), and Chicago's Keith Moreland (sixth inning). The Cubs won 22-7.

3

Home runs by Tuffy Rhodes of the Cubs in his first three plate appearances of the 1994 season (April 4), all off Dwight Gooden of the Mets. Even so, New York won the Opening Day game, 12-8, and Gooden picked up the win.

3

Home runs given up on consecutive pitches by Dave Mlicki of the Astros to Fred McGriff, Rondell White, and Todd Hundley of the Cubs, in the first inning on September 29, 2001.

4

Home runs in consecutive plate appearances by Mike Schmidt of the Philadelphia Phillies on April 17, 1976, against the Cubs. Chicago led 12-1 after three innings, but Philadelphia battled back to win 18-16 in 10 innings.

5

Errors by the Cubs in the third inning on July 14, 1964, against the Mets. Although the errors led to two unearned runs, Chicago won 4-2.

5.40

ERA of the Cubs at home in 1999.

6

World Series played at Wrigley Field. The Cubs lost to the Philadelphia Athletics in 1929, the New York Yankees in 1932, the Detroit Tigers in 1935, the Yankees in 1938, and the Tigers in 1945. They beat the Cleveland Indians in 2016. The Cubs won the National League pennant in 1918 but played their home games of that year's World Series at Comiskey Park.

7

Plate appearances with zero at-bats by Bryce Harper of the Washington Nationals in a 13-inning game on May 8, 2016, against the Cubs. He drew six walks (three intentional) and was hit by a pitch.

8

No-hitters thrown at Wrigley Field. In addition to the two noted above by Fred Toney (1917) and Sam Jones (1955), the other six were by Don Cardwell of the Cubs on May 15, 1960 (second game of doubleheader);

Jim Maloney of the Reds on August 19, 1965 (first game of doubleheader; 10 innings); Ken Holtzman of the Cubs on August 19, 1969; Burt Hooton of the Cubs on April 16, 1972; Milt Pappas of the Cubs on September 2, 1972; and Cole Hamels of the Phillies on July 25, 2015. In their no-hitters, Maloney had 10 walks, and Holtzman had zero strikeouts. Pappas came within one pitch of a perfect game against the Padres; with two outs in the ninth inning, he had a 1-and-2 count against Larry Stahl before throwing three consecutive balls.

8

Grand slams hit at Wrigley Field by Ernie Banks, including three in 1955.

8

Hits in eight at-bats by Billy Williams of the Cubs in a doubleheader against the Astros on July 11, 1972.

8

RBIs each by Chicago catchers George Mitterwald on April 17, 1974, and Barry Foote on April 22, 1980. Each ended the season with 28 RBIs.

9

Innings (each inning) in which the St. Louis Cardinals scored on September 13, 1964, and the Colorado Rockies scored on May 5, 1999. The Cubs scored in each of eight innings on September 1, 1978, against the Astros.

10

Consecutive hits by the Cubs in the fourth inning on September 7, 1929, against the Boston Braves.

10

Players who have hit for cycle at Wrigley Field: Hack Wilson of the Cubs on June 23, 1930; Roy Smalley of the Cubs on June 28, 1950; Lee Walls of the Cubs on July 2, 1957 (10-inning game); Randy Hundley of the Cubs on August 11, 1966 (first game of doubleheader; 11-inning game); Tim Foli of the Montreal Expos on April 21, 1976; Mike Phillips of the Mets on June 25, 1976; Ivan De Jesus of the Cubs on April 22, 1980; Willie McGee of the Cardinals on June 23, 1984 (11-inning game); Andre Dawson of the Cubs on April 29, 1987; and Mark Grace of the Cubs on May 9, 1993.

10

RBIs by Ron Santo of the Cubs in a doubleheader on July 6, 1970, against the Expos. In the second game, he hit two home runs (including a grand slam) and drove in eight runs.

12

Runners left on base by Glenn Beckert of the Cubs in a nine-inning game against the Mets on September 16, 1972. Nonetheless, the Cubs won 18-5.

13

Strikeouts by surprise starter Howard Ehmke of the Philadelphia Athletics in Game One of the 1929 World Series (on October 8) against the Cubs. He set a single-game World Series record that would last until 1953.

16

Home runs by Sammy Sosa at Wrigley Field in June 1998.

18

Consecutive home wins by the Cubs from September 4 through September 22, 1935.

20

Strikeouts by 20-year-old Kerry Wood of the Cubs on May 6, 1998, against the Astros. In his fifth career start, Wood tied Roger Clemens's record for most strikeouts in a nine-inning game.

21

Innings in games on July 17, 1918 (the Cubs beat the Phillies 2-1), and on August 17, 1982 (the Dodgers beat the Cubs 2-1).

22-0

Score by which the Pirates beat the Cubs on September 16, 1975. Pittsburgh's Rennie Stennett had four singles, two doubles, and a triple; he was the only player in the twentieth century to have seven hits in a nine-inning game.

26-23

Score by which the Cubs beat the Phillies on August 25, 1922. Chicago led 25-6 after four innings, and Philadelphia nearly pulled off a comeback with 14 runs in the final two innings. The two teams played another high-scoring game at Wrigley Field on May 17, 1979: The Phillies beat the Cubs 23-22 in 10 innings.

27

Consecutive games at Wrigley Field in which Mark Grudzielanek had a hit from June 26 to September 27, 2003 (second game of doubleheader). The streak does not include a game on September 17 in which he was a ninth-inning defensive replacement and did not have a plate appearance.

29 AND 10

Home runs at Wrigley Field and on road, respectively, by Moises Alou in 2004.

31-50

Home record of the Cubs in 2013 (.383 winning percentage).

41

Consecutive scoreless innings pitched at Wrigley Field by Jake Arrieta from July 25 to September 27, 2015.

52

Extra-base hits at Wrigley Field by Rogers Hornsby in 1929 and Derrek Lee in 2005.

54

Home runs by Willie Mays at Wrigley Field, the most by any player who was never on the Cubs.

56-21

Home record of the Cubs in 1935 (.727 winning percentage).

58

Minutes it took for Pete Alexander of the Cubs to shut out the Boston Braves 3-0 in a nine-inning game on September 21, 1919.

60TH

Home run of the season by Sammy Sosa on September 12, 1998; September 18, 1999; and October 2, 2001.

87-66-2

Home record of Chicago's entry in the Federal League during 1914 and 1915.

120TH

Loss of the season by the Mets on September 30, 1962. The Cubs turned a triple play in the eighth inning.

190TH AND 191ST

RBIs of the season by Hack Wilson on September 28, 1930, against the Reds.

221-89-22

Record of the Chicago Bears at Wrigley Field from 1921 to 1970. The team won four NFL championship games at Wrigley Field, in 1933, 1941, 1943, and 1963. On December 12, 1965, rookie Gale Sayers scored six touchdowns against the San Francisco 49ers.

230

Total bases at Wrigley Field by Hack Wilson in 1930.

.237

Batting average of the Cubs at home in 2015.

300TH

Career win by Tom Glavine of the Mets on August 5, 2007. He became the fifth southpaw to accomplish the feat.

.315

Batting average of the Cubs at home in 1930.

373RD

And final career win by Christy Mathewson of the Reds on September 4, 1916, against the Cubs. He gave up eight runs on 15 hits but outdueled another future Hall of Famer, Mordecai Brown, who allowed 10 runs. It was the last game for both players.

500TH

Career home run by Ernie Banks on May 12, 1970, off Pat Jarvis of the Atlanta Braves. One of the umpires for the game was Frank Secory, who also worked the game in which Banks hit his first major-league home run, on September 20, 1953, in St. Louis. (Secory was a Cubs outfielder in 1944-46.)

530

Attendance at a game between the Cubs and the Reds on September 21, 1966.

536-375-3

Record of Charlie Grimm as manager at Wrigley Field. He had a record of 508-358-3 with the Cubs (1932 to 1938, 1944 to 1949, and 1960), 5-4 with the Boston Braves (1952), and 23-13 with the Milwaukee Braves (1953 to 1956).

3,000TH

Career hit by Stan Musial of the Cardinals, on May 13, 1958. It was a double off Moe Drabowsky of the Cubs. Musial was the eighth player to accomplish the feat.

3,000TH

Career strikeout by Greg Maddux of the Cubs, on July 26, 2005. He struck out Omar Vizquel of the San Francisco Giants.

4,189TH, 4,190TH, AND 4,191ST

Career hits by Pete Rose of the Reds on September 6 and 8, 1985, all singles off Reggie Patterson of the Cubs. Ty Cobb was long believed to have 4,191 career hits but is now credited with 4,189, which would mean that Rose topped Cobb on September 8.

4,266-3,743-31

Record of the Cubs at Wrigley Field from April 20, 1916, through October 1, 2017.

47,101

Attendance at Jackie Robinson's debut at Wrigley Field on May 18, 1947. The paid attendance of 46,572 is the most for a single game in Wrigley Field history.

1,485,166

Attendance at Wrigley Field in 1929, a major-league record that was broken by the 1946 Yankees.

3,300,200

Attendance at Wrigley Field in 2008, the highest single-season total.

CAREER LEADERS AT WRIGLEY FIELD

BATTING

GAMES

1285	Ernie Banks
1116	Billy Williams
1091	Ryne Sandberg
1084	Ron Santo
995	Stan Hack

PLATE APPEARANCES

5258	Ernie Banks
4785	Billy Williams
4681	Ryne Sandberg
4533	Ron Santo
4324	Stan Hack

AT-BATS

4734	Ernie Banks
4252	Billy Williams
4197	Ryne Sandberg
3905	Ron Santo
3674	Stan Hack

RUNS

725	Ryne Sandberg
722	Ernie Banks
717	Billy Williams
644	Ron Santo
638	Sammy Sosa

HITS

1372	Ernie Banks
1314	Billy Williams
1259	Ryne Sandberg
1175	Mark Grace
1165	Ron Santo

DOUBLES

242	Mark Grace
219	Gabby Hartnett
218	Ernie Banks
217	Ryne Sandberg
202	Billy Williams

TRIPLES

48	Ryne Sandberg
46	Stan Hack
44	Phil Cavarretta
42	Ernie Banks
42	Billy Williams

HOME RUNS

293	Sammy Sosa
290	Ernie Banks
231	Billy Williams
212	Ron Santo
164	Ryne Sandberg

RBIS

909	Ernie Banks
740	Sammy Sosa
733	Billy Williams
722	Ron Santo
615	Gabby Hartnett

WALKS

574	Stan Hack
558	Ron Santo
513	Mark Grace
472	Billy Williams
418	Sammy Sosa

INTENTIONAL WALKS

106	Ernie Banks
86	Billy Williams
76	Sammy Sosa
55	Mark Grace
53	Leon Durham

STRIKEOUTS

867	Sammy Sosa
613	Ryne Sandberg
611	Ron Santo
564	Ernie Banks
414	Billy Williams

HIT BY PITCH

52	Anthony Rizzo
39	Aramis Ramirez
35	Ernie Banks
25	Kris Bryant
22	Kiki Cuyler

BATTING AVERAGE

.342	Riggs Stephenson
.341	Kiki Cuyler
.335	Frank Demaree
.329	Hack Wilson
.322	Mark Grace

ON-BASE PERCENTAGE
(MIN. 1,400 AT-BATS)

.424	Hack Wilson
.418	Riggs Stephenson
.407	Kiki Cuyler
.403	Mark Grace
.401	Stan Hack

SLUGGING PERCENTAGE
(MIN. 1,400 AT-BATS)

.600	Hack Wilson
.595	Sammy Sosa
.564	Hank Sauer
.557	Derrek Lee
.551	Andre Dawson
.551	Aramis Ramirez

OPS (MIN. 1,400 AT-BATS)

1.024	Hack Wilson
.960	Sammy Sosa
.945	Derrek Lee
.937	Hank Sauer
.929	Leon Durham

STOLEN BASES

171	Ryne Sandberg
100	Kiki Cuyler
96	Shawon Dunston
86	Stan Hack
85	Max Flack

PITCHING

ERA (MIN. 500 INNINGS)

2.18	Hippo Vaughn
2.54	Lon Warneke
2.61	Pete Alexander
2.67	Claude Hendrix
2.79	Claude Passeau

WINS

115	Charlie Root
95	Fergie Jenkins
94	Guy Bush
84	Pete Alexander
80	Bill Lee

LOSSES

70	Charlie Root
69	Bob Rush
62	Fergie Jenkins
57	Bill Lee
57	Rick Reuschel

WINNING PERCENTAGE (MIN. 40 WINS)

.697	Lon Warneke
.677	Pat Malone
.667	Pete Alexander
.667	Guy Bush
.622	Charlie Root

GAMES PITCHED

302	Charlie Root
258	Carlos Marmol
256	Lee Smith
233	Guy Bush
230	Don Elston

GAMES STARTED

182	Fergie Jenkins
180	Rick Reuschel
169	Charlie Root
157	Bill Lee
157	Greg Maddux

COMPLETE GAMES

96	Charlie Root
94	Pete Alexander
87	Bill Lee
80	Lon Warneke
78	Fergie Jenkins

SHUTOUTS

16	Pete Alexander
15	Claude Passeau
14	Charlie Root
13	Bill Lee
13	Lon Warneke

SAVES

98	Lee Smith
69	Bruce Sutter
57	Carlos Marmol
57	Randy Myers
43	Rod Beck

INNINGS PITCHED

1676	Charlie Root
1415⅔	Fergie Jenkins
1220⅓	Rick Reuschel
1219⅓	Guy Bush
1216⅓	Bill Lee

WALKS

466	Charlie Root
410	Bill Lee
388	Carlos Zambrano
387	Guy Bush
381	Bob Rush

INTENTIONAL WALKS

40	Rick Reuschel
34	Willie Hernandez
33	Fergie Jenkins
32	Bob Rush
32	Greg Maddux
32	Lee Smith

STRIKEOUTS

1070	Fergie Jenkins
813	Charlie Root
774	Carlos Zambrano
753	Kerry Wood
722	Rick Reuschel

HOME RUNS ALLOWED

176	Fergie Jenkins
98	Dick Ellsworth
93	Steve Trachsel
92	Rick Reuschel
92	Charlie Root

HIT BY PITCH

51	Carlos Zambrano
42	Charlie Root
40	Kerry Wood
34	Greg Maddux
30	Fergie Jenkins

WILD PITCHES

34	Ken Holtzman
34	Carlos Zambrano
32	Claude Hendrix
32	Rick Reuschel
29	Dick Ellsworth
29	Kerry Wood

SINGLE-SEASON LEADERS AT WRIGLEY FIELD

BATTING

Games: 84 by Billy Williams, 1967

Plate appearances: 391 by Woody English, 1930

At-bats: 344 by Juan Pierre, 2006

Runs: 86 by Rogers Hornsby, 1929

Hits: 127 by Kiki Cuyler, 1930

Doubles: 36 by Billy Herman, 1936

Triples: 13 by Ryne Sandberg, 1984

Home runs: 35 by Sammy Sosa, 1998

RBIs: 116 by Hack Wilson, 1930

Walks: 65 by Hack Wilson, 1930; Richie Ashburn, 1960

Strikeouts: 89 by Kris Bryant, 2015

Hit by pitch: 18 by Anthony Rizzo, 2015

Batting average: .408 by Rogers Hornsby, 1929

On-base percentage: .501 by Rogers Hornsby, 1929; Hack Wilson, 1930

Slugging average: .796 by Hack Wilson, 1930

OPS: 1.297 by Hack Wilson, 1930

Stolen bases: 29 by Ryne Sandberg, 1985

PITCHING

ERA: 1.11 by Pete Alexander, 1920

Wins: 18 by Pete Alexander, 1920

Losses: 12 by Hank Wyse, 1944

Games pitched: 49 by Shawn Camp, 2012

Games started: 22 by Bill Lee, 1938; Fergie Jenkins, 1967; Fergie Jenkins, 1969

Complete games: 18 by Pete Alexander, 1920

Shutouts: 6 by Hippo Vaughn, 1918

Saves: 29 by Rod Beck, 1998

Innings pitched: 202⅔ by Pete Alexander, 1920

Walks: 91 by Sam Jones, 1955

Strikeouts: 156 by Fergie Jenkins, 1967

Home runs allowed: 23 by Dick Ellsworth, 1964

Hit by pitch: 12 by Kerry Wood, 2003

Wild pitches: 11 by Jake Arrieta, 2016

SINGLE-GAME LEADERS AT WRIGLEY FIELD

* denotes extra-inning game

BATTING

Runs: 6 by Frank Torre, Milwaukee Braves, 9/2/1957 (first game of doubleheader)

Hits: 7 by Rennie Stennett, Pirates, 9/16/1975

Doubles: 4 by Billy Williams, Cubs, 4/9/1969; Matt Murton, Cubs, 8/3/2006 (second game of doubleheader); Jeff Baker, Rockies, 5/30/2008

Triples: 3 by Lance Richbourg, Boston Braves, 7/31/1929 (first game of doubleheader)

Home runs: 4 by Mike Schmidt, Phillies, 4/17/1976*

RBIs: 8 by Babe Herman, Cubs, 7/20/1933; Orlando Cepeda, Giants, 7/4/1961 (first game of doubleheader); Ed Bailey, Cubs, 7/22/1965; Ron Santo, Cubs, 7/6/1970 (second game of doubleheader); George Mitterwald, Cubs, 4/17/1974; Mike Schmidt, Phillies, 4/17/1976*; Barry Foote, Cubs, 4/22/1980; Andre Dawson, Expos, 9/24/1985

Walks: 6 by Bryce Harper, Nationals, 5/8/2016*

Intentional walks: 5 by Andre Dawson, Cubs, 5/22/1990*

Strikeouts: 6 by Don Hoak, Cubs, 5/2/1956*

Stolen bases: 5 by Billy Hamilton, Reds, 6/14/2015*

PITCHING

Innings pitched: 21 by Lefty Tyler, Cubs, 7/17/1918*

Runs allowed: 16 by Jimmy Ring, Phillies, 8/25/1922

Hits allowed: 19 by Mordecai Brown, Cubs, 9/4/1916 (second game of doubleheader); Milt Watson, Phillies, 7/17/1918*; Pete Alexander, Cubs, 6/26/1921; Huck Betts, Phillies, 9/14/1921

Walks: 11 by Gene Krapp, Buffalo Blues (Federal League), 5/24/1915*

Intentional walks: 5 by Eppa Rixey, Reds, 9/8/1928*

Strikeouts: 20 by Kerry Wood, Cubs, 5/6/1998

Home runs allowed: 6 by Larry Benton, New York Giants, 5/12/1930

Hit by pitch: 4 by John Lackey, Cubs, 7/25/2017

Wild pitches: 5 by Ken Howell, Phillies, 4/5/1989

Balks: 3 by Les Lancaster, Cubs, 7/5/1987

SOURCES

Pathy, Sam. *Wrigley Field Year by Year: A Century at the Friendly Confines – Updated Edition* (New York: Sports Publishing, 2016).

Society for American Baseball Research. *The SABR Baseball List and Record Book* (New York: Scribner, 2007).

Sugar, Bert Randolph, ed. *The Baseball Maniac's Almanac* (fourth edition) (New York: Skyhorse Publishing, 2016).

Will, George F. *A Nice Little Place on the North Side: Wrigley Field at One Hundred* (New York: Crown Archetype, 2014).

2014 Chicago Cubs Media Guide

2017 Chicago Cubs Media Guide

baseball-almanac.com

baseball-reference.com

mlb.mlb.com/chc/history/timeline.jsp

nationalpastime.com

retrosheet.org/boxesetc/C/PK_CHI11.htm

thisgreatgame.com

A HALL OF FAME
CAST OF CONTRIBUTORS

MATT ALBERTSON resides in Havertown, Pennsylvania, with his wife, Jess, with whom he attends many Phillies games throughout the year. He concentrated on public history in graduate school and continues that passion through baseball. He dedicated a Pennsylvania Historical Marker to the Jefferson Street Ballparks in Philadelphia in 2017 and in the same year joined the Athletic Base Ball Club of Philadelphia. Matt is the historical columnist for SportsTalkPhilly.com.

JOHN BAUER resides with his wife and two children in Parkville, Missouri, just outside of Kansas City. By day, he is an attorney specializing in insurance regulatory law and corporate law. By night, he spends many spring and summer evenings cheering for the San Francisco Giants and many fall and winter evenings reading history. He is a past and ongoing contributor to other SABR projects.

The first two major-league stadiums **NATHAN BIERMA** set foot in as a kid were Tiger Stadium and Wrigley Field, and they forged a lifelong love of baseball and historic ballparks. Nathan is a SABR member and SABR Games Project contributor, and curates @SABRGames and @TigersHistory on Twitter. He grew up and currently lives in Grand Rapids, Michigan, but lived in Chicago during the Cubs' fateful 2003 season. Nathan's writing has appeared in the *Chicago Tribune, Chicago Tribune Magazine, Chicago Sports Review, Detroit Free Press,* and DetroitAthletic.com. He is the author of *The Eclectic Encyclopedia of English: Language At Its Most Enigmatic, Ephemeral, and Egregious.* His

website is www.nbierma.com. Nathan roots for the Tigers and the Cubs, and won't feel conflicted about that until they meet in the World Series for a fifth time someday.

THOMAS J. BROWN JR. is a lifelong Mets fan who became a Durham Bulls fan after moving to North Carolina in the early 1980s. Tom joined SABR in 1995 when he learned about the organization during a visit to Cooperstown on his honeymoon. He has been active in the organization since his retirement after teaching high-school science for 34 years, and has written numerous biographies and game stories, mostly about the New York Mets.

FREDERICK C. "RICK" BUSH has a bevy of Cubs fans for in-laws, so he cheered the North Siders on as they claimed the 2016 World Series title; however, he was happy to gain bragging rights when his hometown Houston Astros claimed their first championship a year later. He and Bill Nowlin co-edited the 2017 SABR book *Bittersweet Goodbye: The Black Barons, the Grays, and the 1948 Negro League World Series,* and are currently co-editing another Negro Leagues book, about the 1946 Newark Eagles. Rick lives with his wife, Michelle, and their three sons, Michael, Andrew, and Daniel, in the greater Houston area, where he teaches English at Wharton County Junior College.

ALAN COHEN serves as vice president-treasurer of SABR's Connecticut Smoky Joe Wood Chapter, and is datacaster for the Hartford Yard Goats, the

Double-A affiliate of the Rockies. He visited Wrigley Field for the first time during SABR 45 in Chicago in 2015. He has written more than 40 biographies for SABR's BioProject, and has expanded his research into the Hearst Sandlot Classic (1946-1965), which launched the careers of 88 major-league players. He has four children and six grandchildren and resides in Connecticut with his wife, Frances, cat, Morty, and dog, Sam.

RORY COSTELLO has been to just one game at Wrigley Field in person, but as a lifelong Mets fan he has many vivid memories from TV. He lives in Brooklyn, New York, with his wife, Noriko, and son, Kai.

RICHARD CUICCHI joined SABR in 1983 and is an active member of the Schott-Pelican Chapter. Since his retirement as an information-technology executive, Richard authored *Family Ties: A Comprehensive Collection of Facts and Trivia about Baseball's Relatives*. He has contributed to numerous SABR BioProject and Games publications. He does freelance writing and blogging about a variety of baseball topics on his website, TheTenthInning.com. Richard lives in New Orleans with his wife, Mary.

JOHN DIFONZO grew up in Somerville, Massachusetts, where he was the sports editor for his high-school newspaper. He is a lifelong Red Sox fan and season-ticket holder since 2004, currently living in Boston's Beacon Hill with his wife, Gabriella. John is a graduate of Tufts University, holds a master of science in global financial analysis from Bentley University, and is a CFA charterholder.

GREG ERION died in December 2017 after a brief illness. He retired from the railroad industry and taught history part time at Skyline Community College in San Bruno, California. He wrote several biographies and game articles for SABR. Greg was one of the leaders of SABR's Baseball Games Project.

With his wife, Barbara, he was a resident of South San Francisco, California.

DOUG FELDMANN is a professor in the College of Education at Northern Kentucky University and a former part-time scout for the San Diego Padres, Seattle Mariners, and Cincinnati Reds. He is the author of 12 books, more information on which is available at dougfeldmannbooks.com.

SCOTT FERKOVICH was the lead editor of the SABR book *Tigers by the Tale: Great Games at Michigan and Trumbull*. He is the author of *Motor City Champs: Mickey Cochrane and the 1934-1935 Detroit Tigers*. His first game at Wrigley Field was in 1984. He also attended the first "official" night game, on August 9, 1988.

MERRIE FIDLER's passion for the All-American Girls Professional Baseball League (AAGPBL) began in a women's sport-history course at the University of Massachusetts, Amherst, in the fall of 1971 and has not wavered. The AAGPBL became the topic of her master's thesis, which was published in 2006 as *The Origins and History of the All-American Girls Professional Baseball League*. In 2007, Fidler became the secretary of the AAGPBL Players Association, a position she continues to hold. Fidler roots for the Boston Red Sox, who employed her brother in their minor-league system in the 1950s, the Chicago Cubs due to P.K. Wrigley's creation of the AAGPBL in 1943, and the San Francisco Giants, who moved to her native California in 1958.

DAN FIELDS is a senior manuscript editor at the New England Journal of Medicine. He loves baseball trivia, and he enjoys attending Boston Red Sox and Pawtucket Red Sox games with his teenage son. Dan lives in Framingham, Massachusetts, and can be reached at dfields820@gmail.com.

JAMES FORR has contributed to more than a dozen SABR books as a writer or associate editor. Along with David Proctor, he co-authored *Pie Traynor: A Baseball Biography*, which was a finalist for the 2010 CASEY Award. He is a past winner of the McFarland-SABR Baseball Research Award. James lives in Columbia, Missouri.

BRIAN FRANK is passionate about documenting the history of major- and minor-league baseball. He is the creator of the website The Herd Chronicles (herdchronicles.com), which is dedicated to preserving the history of the Buffalo Bisons. His articles can also be read on the official website of the Bisons. He is a frequent contributor to SABR publications. Brian and his wife, Jenny, enjoy traveling around the country in their camper to major- and minor-league ballparks and taking an annual trip to Europe. Brian was a history major at Canisius College, where he earned a Bachelor of Arts. He also received a Juris Doctor from the University at Buffalo School of Law.

GORDON J. GATTIE serves as a human-systems integration engineer for the US Navy. His baseball research interests involve ballparks, historical records, and statistical analysis. A SABR member since 1998, Gordon earned his Ph.D. from SUNY Buffalo, where he used baseball to investigate judgment/ decision-making performance in complex dynamic environments. Originally from Buffalo, Gordon learned early the hardships associated with rooting for Buffalo sports teams. Ever the optimist, he also cheers for the Cleveland Indians and Washington Nationals. Lisa, his lovely bride, who also enjoys baseball, continues to challenge him by supporting the Yankees. Gordon has contributed to multiple SABR publications.

PAUL GEISLER is an ordained minister of the Evangelical Lutheran Church in America. He serves as pastor of Christ Lutheran Church in Lake Jackson, Texas, where he lives with his wife and their three children. For his entire life, Paul has enjoyed all aspects of baseball – playing, watching, coaching, researching, and writing. He became a Houston Astros fan from their first year in 1962, and then a Texas Rangers fan in 1971, when the Senators moved to Texas. He attended seminary in Chicago, where he added another favorite, the Cubs of Wrigley Field.

ED GRUVER has been a contributing writer to SABR for several years. An award-winning sportswriter for 34 years, he is the author of seven sports books, including *Hairs vs. Squares: The Mustache Gang, the Big Red Machine and the Tumultuous Summer of '72*. He is a contributing writer to nine additional sports books and writes for national magazines and several online sites. A north Jersey native, he and his wife, Michelle, have two children and a grandchild.

TOM HAWTHORN is a longtime journalist and author whose most recent book is *The Year Canadians Lost Their Minds and Found Their Country: The Centennial of 1967* (Douglas and McIntyre, 2017). He has been a member of the selection committees of two sports halls of fame in his native Canada. He lives in Victoria, British Columbia.

PAUL HOFMANN, a SABR member since 2002, is the associate vice president for international affairs at Sacramento State University. Paul is a native of Detroit and a lifelong Detroit Tigers fan. He currently resides in Folsom, California.

MIKE HUBER is professor of mathematics at Muhlenberg College in Allentown, Pennsylvania. His baseball research involves modeling and simulating rare events, such as hitting for the cycle and pitching no-hitters. He has been rooting for the Baltimore Orioles for 50 years, but if he had to pick a National League team, it might be the Cubs.

A prolific contributor to SABR's BioProject and its various publications, **NORM KING** died in

2018. Through his writing and research we met many of the heroes of his youth, including Warren Cromartie, Steve Rogers, Bill Lee, and Hall of Fame Expos broadcaster Dave Van Horne. In 2016, SABR published *Au jeu/Play Ball: The 50 Greatest Games in the History of the Montreal Expos*, for which Norm served as senior editor and main writer. It was SABR's top-selling book of the year.

RUSS LAKE lives in Champaign, Illinois, and is a retired college professor. The 1964 St. Louis Cardinals remain his favorite team, and he was distressed to see Sportsman's Park (aka Busch Stadium I) being demolished not long after he had attended the last game there on May 8, 1966. His wife, Carol, deserves an MVP award for watching all of a 13-inning ballgame in Cincinnati with Russ in 1971 – during their honeymoon. In 1994 he was an editor for David Halberstam's baseball book, *October 1964*.

BOB LEMOINE is a high-school librarian and adjunct professor in New Hampshire. He has contributed to several SABR book projects since joining in 2013, including co-editing with Bill Nowlin on 2016's *Boston's First Nine: The 1871-75 Boston Red Stockings*. Having baseball history on the brain, Bob is never far from jumping into yet another project.

Though he lives in far-off New England, **LEN LEVIN** has seen several games at Wrigley Field, though none involving his beloved Red Sox. He is a retired newspaper editor living in Providence, Rhode Island, and currently edits the decisions of the Rhode Island Supreme Court.

SABR member and Massachusetts native **MIKE LYNCH** is the founder of Seamheads.com and author of five books, including *Harry Frazee, Ban Johnson and the Feud That Nearly Destroyed the American League*, which was named a finalist for the 2009 Larry Ritter Award and was nominated for a Seymour Medal. His most recent work includes a three-book series called *Baseball's Untold History* and

several articles that have appeared in SABR books and on the National Pastime Museum's website. He lives in Roslindale, Massachusetts, with the love of his life and their cats, Jiggs and Pepper.

MIKE MATTSEY lives in Sacramento with his wife, Maia, and his son, Otis. He is a longtime fan of the 2016 World Series champion Chicago Cubs and is an avid collector of prewar baseball cards and sports memorabilia related to the team. His greatest Wrigley Field moment came when he took his father and his son to Opening Day 2017 to witness the North Siders hoist the World Series banner they had captured the year before. He graduated from Indiana University and holds a Master of Arts degree from Indiana State University, where he successfully defended a paper examining the role of minor-league baseball in the Progressive Era South. He has written for SABR's BioProject and is currently working on a contribution for a SABR book on the 1946 Newark Eagles.

SETH MOLAND-KOVASH is a lifelong passionate baseball fan and amateur historian. He grew up in Minnesota and his love of the game and the Twins has carried through many years, many moves, and many Twins eras. During the day, Seth is a Lutheran pastor in suburban Chicago, where he lives with his wife, Jennifer, and their son, Carl. Carl has also inherited the love of baseball and plays whenever the fields are not covered by snow. Seth's favorite teams are the Twins and whatever team Carl is on.

JIM NITZ is a Milwaukee native who loves to do research and writing on Milwaukee-based baseball topics such as Happy Felsch, Ken Keltner, Borchert Field, and the Chicks of the AAGPBL. He is a middle-school business education teacher and high-school softball assistant coach married to Wendee. Their children, Jeff and Beth, were ballplayers in high school and college.

BILL NOWLIN, an habitué of Fenway Park since the 1950s, always enjoys his visits to Wrigley Field.

TOM PARDO is retired as the information services manager for Amoco/BP worldwide. He is the author/editor of several works concerning archives and manuscript collections and most recently served as editor of *The Federal League … vs. The National League: Guide to the Digital Archive* and as a contributor to *Cincinnati's Crosley Field: A Gem in the Queen City*, both SABR publications. His essays are dedicated to his son, Jeff, who is *the* all-time great fan of the Cubs and Wrigley Field.

J.G. PRESTON lives in Santa Fe, New Mexico, and has contributed biographies and game stories to several SABR books. He has worked as a writer and broadcaster, and he enjoys playing tabletop sports simulation games and listening to old radio broadcasts of sporting events. He writes about baseball history (although it's been a while since he's done so) at prestonjg.wordpress.com.

CHRIS RAINEY was introduced to SABR by Eugene Murdock in the '70s when Chris helped Murdock with transcriptions of his interviews with players. Chris also taught and coached in Yellow Springs, Ohio, for 35 years. He enjoys retirement now in Oxford, Ohio, with his wife, Janelle. He now researches and writes for SABR BioProject and keeps up-to-date with his collection of Indians baseball cards and photos.

TIM RASK is the "Umpire-in-Chief" of the Field of Dreams (Iowa) regional chapter of SABR. He has been a Cubs fan since 1982, and has witnessed many memorable games at Wrigley Field over the years, including 10 home openers and Game Seven of the 2003 NLCS. He researches and occasionally writes about Iowa's minor-league baseball history from his home in Iowa City.

Chicago native **ALAN REIFMAN** is professor of human development and family studies at Texas Tech University and holds a Ph.D. from the University of Michigan. Within SABR, Alan's interests include ballparks and their surrounding neighborhoods, and statistics. He has contributed to the SABR books *Dome Sweet Dome: History and Highlights from 35 Years of the Houston Astrodome* (2017) and *Detroit Tigers 1984: What a Start! What a Finish!* (2012).

STEPHEN V. RICE, Ph.D., hails from Detroit and lives in Collierville, Tennessee. During his childhood he pored over statistics in the baseball encyclopedia and wondered about the players. The numbers don't say much about the players; they don't tell us who they were or what they were like. Now he writes biographies for the SABR BioProject, to help tell their stories. In his day job, he is a software architect in the Computational Biology Department at St. Jude Children's Research Hospital in Memphis.

CARL RIECHERS retired from United Parcel Service in 2012 after 35 years of service. With more free time, he became a SABR member that same year. Born and raised in the suburbs of St. Louis, he became a big fan of the Cardinals. He and his wife, Janet, have three children and he is the proud grandpa of two.

PAUL ROGERS is co-author of several baseball books including *The Whiz Kids and the 1950 Pennant* with boyhood hero Robin Roberts and *Lucky Me: My 65 Years in Baseball* with Eddie Robinson. Most recently he co-edited *The Whiz Kids Take the Pennant – The 1950 Philadelphia Phillies* and *The Team That Time Won't Forget – the 1951 New York Giants*, SABR team projects. He is president of the Ernie Banks-Bobby Bragan DFW Chapter of SABR and a frequent contributor to the SABR BioProject, but his real job is as a law professor at Southern Methodist University, where he served as dean for nine years. He has also served as SMU's faculty athletic representative for over 30 years. Since the age of 8, he has always looked at the box scores before reading any other part of the newspaper.

GARY SARNOFF has authored two baseball books and is an active SABR member. He is currently the chairman of SABR's Ron Gabriel committee, has written several baseball players' bios and historic game accounts for SABR's BioProject and stories for SABR's annual publication *The National Pastime*. His baseball articles have been published in *Minor League News*, *Nats News,* and *Base Ball: A Journal of the Early Game*. Gary currently resides in Alexandria, Virginia.

RICK SCHABOWSKI has been a SABR member since 1995. He is a retired machinist from the Harley-Davidson Company, is currently an instructor at the Wisconsin Regional Training Partnership in the Manufacturing Program, and is a certified Manufacturing Skills Standards Council instructor. He is president of the Ken Keltner Badger State Chapter of SABR, president of the Wisconsin Oldtime Ballplayers Association, treasurer of the Milwaukee Braves Historical Association, and a member of the Hoop Historians and the Pro Football Research Association. He lives in St. Francis, Wisconsin.

RYAN SCHURING's passion for baseball began in 1998 at the age of 4 when he started playing T-ball. He was fortunate to be able to play at the collegiate level at North Central College, where he pitched for two years. His love affair with the Chicago Cubs was established during the infamous 2003 season. Today, Ryan works in commercial banking and resides in Chicagoland.

JOE SCHUSTER is the author of a novel, *The Might Have Been,* a finalist for the 2013 CASEY Award for the best book about baseball. He has also written two titles for the Gemma Open Door series of books for adult literacy programs, *One Season in the Sun,* about ballplayers who had major-league careers lasting a few weeks or less, and *Jackie Robinson,* forthcoming in Fall 2018. A regular contributor to the official publications of the St. Louis Cardinals, he has also written for a number of SABR books, including *Cincinnati's Crosley Field, 20-Game Losers, Sportsman's Park in St. Louis,* and *Sweet '60: The 1960 Pittsburgh Pirates,* among others. He lives outside St. Louis, is married, and is the father of five rabid Redbird fans.

RICHARD A. SMILEY grew up in Chicago and saw his first game at Wrigley Field in 1966. He contributed biographies of Reb Russell and Matty McIntyre to SABR's *Deadball Stars of the American League* project and authored an article in *The National Pastime* on Heinie Zimmerman's chase after Eddie Collins in the 1917 World Series. He also edited the chapter on the 1906 World Series for the recent SABR publication *The World Series in the Deadball Era: A History in the Words and Pictures of the Writers and Photographers.*

GLEN SPARKS grew up in Santa Monica, California, and is a lifelong Dodgers fan. He has contributed to the SABR BioProject and the Games project. Among the projects he is working on now is a SABR book about the great Babe Ruth. Glen and his wife, Pam, live deep in the heart of Cardinals country.

MARK S. STERNMAN made his Wrigley Field debut on August 1, 1990, when Greg Maddux hurled a five-hit shutout to lead the Cubs to a 5-0 win over the Pirates. A graduate of Dartmouth College like Kyle Hendricks, Sternman has profiled Glenn Beckert for the BioProject. He wishes he could go to more games at Wrigley and eat more food at Milt's Barbecue for the Perplexed.

GREGORY H. WOLF was born in Pittsburgh, but now resides in the Chicagoland area with his wife, Margaret, and daughter, Gabriela. A professor of

German studies and holder of the Dennis and Jean Bauman Endowed Chair in the Humanities at North Central College in Naperville, Illinois, he has edited nine books for SABR. He is currently working on projects about Comiskey Park in Chicago, Shibe Park in Philadelphia, and the 1982 Milwaukee Brewers. As of January 2017, he serves as co-director of SABR's BioProject, which you can follow on Facebook and Twitter.

BRIAN WRIGHT is the author of *Mets in 10s: Best and Worst of an Amazin' History*, which was released by Arcadia Publishing and The History Press in April 2018. Brian has been featured in *Bleacher Report*, the *Washington Examiner* and on NESN.com, SB Nation and The Cauldron. For three years, he was the lead MLB writer for *The Sports Daily*. From 2014 through 2017, he hosted his own sports history podcast, "Profiles in Sports," featuring in-depth interviews with such notables as Mario Andretti,

Jack Ham, Ken Burns, and Tony Perez. He has also contributed to SABR books on the greatest games in the history of the Mets, San Diego Padres, and in the tenure of old Comiskey Park. He currently resides in Washington, D.C.

A SABR member since 1979, **DON ZMINDA** retired in 2016 after two-plus decades with STATS LLC, where he served first as director of publications and then director of research for STATS-supported sports broadcasts. Don has also written or edited over a dozen sports books, including the annual *STATS Baseball Scoreboard* (1990-2000) and the SABR publication *Go-Go to Glory: The 1959 Chicago White* Sox. His biography of Harry Caray will be published in 2019. A Chicago native, Don lives in Los Angeles with his wife, Sharon.

SABR BOOKS ON GREAT TEAMS AND GREAT GAMES

The Society for American Baseball Research, the top baseball research organization in the world, disseminates some of the best in baseball history, analysis, and biography through our publishing programs. The SABR Digital Library focuses on a tandem program of paperback and ebook publication, making these materials widely available for both on digital devices and as traditional printed books.

THE 1986 BOSTON RED SOX:
THERE WAS MORE THAN GAME SIX
One of a two-book series on the rivals that met in the 1986 World Series, the Boston Red Sox and the New York Mets, including biographies of every player, coach, broadcaster, and other important figures in the top organizations in baseball that year.
Edited by Leslie Heaphy and Bill Nowlin
$19.95 paperback (ISBN 978-1-943816-19-4)
$9.99 ebook (ISBN 978-1-943816-18-7)
8.5"X11", 420 pages, over 200 photos

THE 1986 NEW YORK METS:
THERE WAS MORE THAN GAME SIX
The other book in the "rivalry" set from the 1986 World Series. This book re-tells the story of that year's classic World Series and this is the story of each of the players, coaches, managers, and broadcasters, their lives in baseball and the way the 1986 season fit into their lives.
Edited by Leslie Heaphy and Bill Nowlin
$19.95 paperback (ISBN 978-1-943816-13-2)
$9.99 ebook (ISBN 978-1-943816-12-5)
8.5"X11", 392 pages, over 100 photos

SCANDAL ON THE SOUTH SIDE:
THE 1919 CHICAGO WHITE SOX
The Black Sox Scandal isn't the only story worth telling about the 1919 Chicago White Sox. The team roster included three future Hall of Famers, a 20-year-old spitballer who would win 300 games in the minors, and even a batboy who later became a celebrity with the "Murderers' Row" New York Yankees. All of their stories are included in Scandal on the South Side with a timeline of the 1919 season.
Edited by Jacob Pomrenke
$19.95 paperback (ISBN 978-1-933599-95-3)
$9.99 ebook (ISBN 978-1-933599-94-6)
8.5"x11", 324 pages, 55 historic photos

WINNING ON THE NORTH SIDE
THE 1929 CHICAGO CUBS
Celebrate the 1929 Chicago Cubs, one of the most exciting teams in baseball history. Future Hall of Famers Hack Wilson, '29 NL MVP Rogers Hornsby, and Kiki Cuyler, along with Riggs Stephenson formed one of the most potent quartets in baseball history. The magical season came to an ignominious end in the World Series and helped craft the future "lovable loser" image of the team.
Edited by Gregory H. Wolf
$19.95 paperback (ISBN 978-1-933599-89-2)
$9.99 ebook (ISBN 978-1-933599-88-5)
8.5"x11", 314 pages, 59 photos

DETROIT THE UNCONQUERABLE:
THE 1935 WORLD CHAMPION TIGERS
Biographies of every player, coach, and broadcaster involved with the 1935 World Champion Detroit Tigers baseball team, written by members of the Society for American Baseball Research. Also includes a season in review and other articles about the 1935 team. Hank Greenberg, Mickey Cochrane, Charlie Gehringer, Schoolboy Rowe, and more.
Edited by Scott Ferkovich
$19.95 paperback (ISBN 9978-1-933599-78-6)
$9.99 ebook (ISBN 978-1-933599-79-3)
8.5"X11", 230 pages, 52 photos

TIGERS BY THE TALE:
GREAT GAMES AT MICHIGAN AND TRUMBULL
For over 100 years, Michigan and Trumbull was the scene of some of the most exciting baseball ever. This book portrays 50 classic games at the corner, spanning the earliest days of Bennett Park until Tiger Stadium's final closing act. From Ty Cobb to Mickey Cochrane, Hank Greenberg to Al Kaline, and Willie Horton to Alan Trammell.
Edited by Scott Ferkovich
$12.95 paperback (ISBN 978-1-943816-21-7)
$6.99 ebook (ISBN 978-1-943816-20-0)
8.5"x11", 160 pages, 22 photos

MAJOR LEAGUE BASEBALL A MILE HIGH:
THE FIRST QUARTER CENTURY OF THE COLORADO ROCKIES
A look at the first 25 years (1993–2017) of the MLB team in Denver, the Colorado Rockies. Including essays on the birth of the Rockies, biographies of 24 of the most important players, managers, and club executives, and "ballpark bios" of the two fields on the Rockies have called home: Mile High Stadium and Coors Field. In addition, 18 memorable and historic games are recapped.
Edited by Bill Nowlin and Paul T. Parker
$19.95 paperback (ISBN 978-1-943816-77-4)
$9.99 ebook (ISBN 978-1-943816-76-7)
8.5"X11", 272 pages, 32 photos

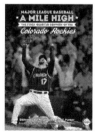

THE TEAM THAT COULDN'T HIT:
THE 1972 TEXAS RANGERS
Articles in this book cover the effort to bring a team to North Texas and the story of Tom Vandergriff, the man now known as "the father of the Rangers." Biographies of every man to play—or coach—for the 1972 team are presented, including Frank Howard, Larry Bittner, Horacio Pina and Tom Grieve, and broadcasters Don Drysdale and Bill Mercer. Owner Bob Short and Arlington Stadium itself are given full write-ups as well.
Edited by Steve West and Bill Nowlin
$29.95 paperback (ISBN 978-1-943816-93-4)
$9.99 ebook (ISBN 978-1-943816-92-7)
8.5"X11", 414 pages, 60 photos

SABR Members can purchase each book at a significant discount (often 50% off) and receive the ebook edtions free as a member benefit. Each book is available in a trade paperback edition as well as ebooks suitable for reading on a home computer or Nook, Kindle, or iPad/tablet.
To learn more about becoming a member of SABR, visit the website: sabr.org/join

NEW BOOKS FROM SABR

Part of the mission of the Society for American Baseball Research has always been to disseminate member research. In addition to the *Baseball Research Journal*, SABR publishes books that include player biographies, historical game recaps, and statistical analysis. All SABR books are available in print and ebook formats. SABR members can access the entire SABR Digital Library for free and purchase print copies at significant member discounts of 40 to 50% off cover price.

JEFF BAGWELL IN CONNECTICUT:
A CONSISTENT LAD IN THE LAND OF STEADY HABITS
This volume of articles, interviews, and essays by members of the Connecticut chapter of SABR chronicles the life and career of Connecticut's favorite baseball son, Hall-of-Famer Jeff Bagwell, with special attention on his high school and college years.
Edited by Karl Cicitto, Bill Nowlin, & Len Levin
$19.95 paperback (ISBN 978-1-943816-97-2)
$9.99 ebook (ISBN 978-1-943816-96-5)
7"x10", 246 pages, 45 photos

1995 CLEVELAND INDIANS:
THE SLEEPING GIANT AWAKENS
After almost 40 years of sub-.500 baseball, the Sleeping Giant woke in 1995, the first season the Indians spent in their new home of Jacob's Field. The biographies of all the players, coaches, and broadcasters from that year are here, sprinkled with personal perspectives, as well as game stories from key matchups during the 1995 season, information about Jacob's Field, and other essays.
Edited by Joseph Wancho
$19.95 paperback (ISBN 978-1-943816-95-8)
$9.99 ebook (ISBN 978-1-943816-94-1)
8.5"X11", 410 pages, 76 photos

TIME FOR EXPANSION BASEBALL
The LA Angels and "new" Washington Senators ushered in MLB's 1960 expansion, followed in 1961 by the Houston Colt .45s and New York Mets. By 1998, 10 additional teams had launched: the Kansas City Royals, Seattle Pilots, Toronto Blue Jays, and Tampa Bay Devil Rays in the AL, and the Montreal Expos, San Diego Padres, Colorado Rockies, Florida Marlins, and Arizona Diamondbacks in the NL. *Time for Expansion Baseball* tells each team's origin and includes biographies of key players.
Edited by Maxwell Kates and Bill Nowlin
$24.95 paperback (ISBN 978-1-933599-89-7)
$9.99 ebook (ISBN 978-1-933599-88-0)
8.5"X11", 430 pages, 150 photos

BASE BALL'S 19TH CENTURY "WINTER" MEETINGS
1857-1900
A look at the business meetings of base ball's earliest days (not all of which were in the winter). As John Thorn writes in his Foreword, "This monumental volume traces the development of the game from its birth as an organized institution to its very near suicide at the dawn of the next century."
Edited by Jeremy K. Hodges and Bill Nowlin
$29.95 paperback (ISBN 978-1-943816-91-0)
$9.99 ebook (ISBN978-1-943816-90-3)
8.5"x11", 390 pages, 50 photos

MET-ROSPECTIVES:
A COLLECTION OF THE GREATEST GAMES IN NEW YORK METS HISTORY
This book's 57 game stories—coinciding with the number of Mets years through 2018—are strictly for the eternal optimist. They include the team's very first victory in April 1962 at Forbes Field, Tom Seaver's "Imperfect Game" in July '69, the unforgettable Game Sixes in October '86, the "Grand Slam Single" in the 1999 NLCS, and concludes with the extra-innings heroics in September 2016 at Citi Field that helped ensure a wild-card berth.
edited by Brian Wright and Bill Nowlin
$14.95 paperback (ISBN 978-1-943816-87-3)
$9.99 ebook (ISBN 978-1-943816-86-6)
8.5"X11", 148 pages, 44 photos

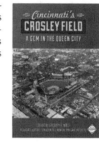

CINCINNATI'S CROSLEY FIELD:
A GEM IN THE QUEEN CITY
This book evokes memories of Crosley Field through detailed summaries of more than 85 historic and monumental games played there, and 10 insightful feature essays about the history of the ballpark. Former Reds players Johnny Edwards and Art Shamsky share their memories of the park in introductions.
Edited by Gregory H. Wolf
$19.95 paperback (ISBN 978-1-943816-75-0)
$9.99 ebook (ISBN 978-1-943816-74-3)
8.5"X11", 320 pages, 43 photos

MOMENTS OF JOY AND HEARTBREAK:
66 SIGNIFICANT EPISODES IN THE HISTORY OF THE PITTSBURGH PIRATES
In this book we relive no-hitters, World Series-winning homers, and the last tripleheader ever played in major-league baseball. Famous Pirates like Honus Wagner and Roberto Clemente—and infamous ones like Dock Ellis—make their appearances, as well as recent stars like Andrew McCutcheon.
Edited by Jorge Iber and Bill Nowlin
$19.95 paperback (ISBN 978-1-943816-73-6)
$9.99 ebook (ISBN 978-1-943816-72-9)
8.5"X11", 208 pages, 36 photos

FROM SPRING TRAINING TO SCREEN TEST:
BASEBALL PLAYERS TURNED ACTORS
SABR's book of baseball's "matinee stars," a selection of those who crossed the lines between professional sports and popular entertainment. Included are the famous (Gene Autry, Joe DiMaggio, Jim Thorpe, Bernie Williams) and the forgotten (Al Gettel, Lou Stringer, Wally Hebert, Wally Hood), essays on baseball in TV shows and Coca-Cola commercials, and Jim Bouton's casting as "Jim Barton" in the *Ball Four* TV series.
Edited by Rob Edelman and Bill Nowlin
$19.95 paperback (ISBN 978-1-943816-71-2)
$9.99 ebook (ISBN 978-1-943816-70-5)
8.5"X11", 410 pages, 89 photos

To learn more about how to receive these publications for free or at member discount as a member of SABR, visit the website: sabr.org/join